W9-BED-354

Introduction to Economics

Introduction to Economics

Stephen L. Slavin
Associate Professor of Economics
Union County College   Cranford, New Jersey

1989

IRWIN

Homewood, IL   60430
Boston, MA   02116

© RICHARD D. IRWIN, INC., 1989

All rights reserved. No part of this publication may be reproduced, stored in a retrieval system, or transmitted, in any form or by any means, electronic, mechanical, photocopying, recording, or otherwise, without the prior written permission of the publisher.

Executive editor: Gary L. Nelson
Project editor: Karen Smith
Production manager: Carma W. Fazio
Cover design: Jeanne Wolfgeher
Interior design: Harry Voight
Artist: Precision Graphics
Compositor: Better Graphics, Inc.
Typeface: 10/12 Trump
Printer: Von Hoffmann Press, Inc.

LIBRARY OF CONGRESS
Library of Congress Cataloging-in-Publication Data

Slavin, Stephen L.
    Introduction to economics / Stephen L. Slavin.
        p.   cm.
    Includes index.
    ISBN 0-256-06220-X
    1. Economics   I. Title.
HB171.5.S6276 1989
330—dc19

88-22627
CIP

Printed in the United States of America
2 3 4 5 6 7 8 9 0 VH 5 4 3 2 1 0

Foreword

"You teach economics?" asks the alumnus at the college reunion. I answer affirmatively, even proudly, but I know what the next sentence is going to be: "It was my worst subject—I *hated* it."

Indeed, he or she hated it, learned nothing, and joined the army of economic illiterates. Was this necessary? Probably not. The old grad took a course that was taught as the first step toward a Ph.D. For some students, that can be very useful. Most students, particularly vocationally oriented students, however, need a course that enables them to grasp the basic elements of economics and relate them to their world.

Professor Slavin has written a text that fulfills such a need. In the language of computer programs, the book is user friendly. The student is led gently into each topic. Each step is carefully explained in prose that is accessible. The landmines that so often destroy student interest are cleared away—how to draw a diagram, what the concept of the margin is, even how to calculate a percentage. Yes, Virginia, there *are* college students who have deep-rooted problems with simple math or even arithmetic. Such students are capable of learning complex concepts if the explanations are made clear enough.

Although the book's emphasis is on basics, the coverage is complete. The student who has mastered this book is prepared for more advanced level work. Indeed, the book's style and innovative pedagogy will enable such a student to retain more of the subject, instead of forgetting the bulk of it after the final exam.

I am happy to see this book on the market. It is an excellent teaching tool. And that is what textbooks are supposed to be all about.

Bruno Stein
Professor of Economics
New York University

Preface

Some 15 years ago, while still a graduate student, I got a part-time job helping to ghostwrite an introductory text for a major publisher. I asked my editor why so many economics texts were ghostwritten. She smiled and said, "Economists can't write." This makes me the exception that proves the rule.

Economics can be a rather intimidating subject, with its extensive vocabulary, complicated graphs, and quantitative tendencies. Is it possible to write a principles text that lowers the student's anxiety level without watering down the subject matter? To do this, one would need to be an extremely good writer, have extensive teaching experience, and have solid academic training in economics. In this case, two out of three is just not good enough.

To the Student

What have you heard about economics? That it's dull, it's hard, it's full of undecipherable equations and incomprehensible graphs? If you were to read virtually any of the introductory economics textbooks, that's exactly what you would find.

Why is this book different from all other books? For starters, this is the first economics book that is reader-friendly. While you're reading, I'll be right there with you, illustrating various points with funny anecdotes and asking you to work out numerical problems as we go along.

Are you a little shaky about the math? Your worries are over. If you can add, subtract, multiply, and divide (I'll even let you use a calculator), you can do the math in this book.

How do you feel about graphs? Do you think they look like those ultra-modernistic paintings that even the artists can't explain? You can relax. No graph in this book has more than four lines, and by the time you're through, you'll be drawing your *own* graphs.

Unlike virtually every other economics text, this one includes a built-in workbook. Regardless of whether your professor assigns the questions at the end of each chapter, I urge you to answer them because they provide an excellent review.

I can't guarantee an *A* in this course, but whether you are taking it to fulfill a college requirement or are planning to be an economics major, you will find that economics is neither dull nor all that hard.

To the Instructor

Why did I write this book? Probably my moment of decision arrived about six years ago when I mentioned to my macro class that Kemp-Roth cut the top personal income tax bracket from 70 percent to 50 percent. Then I asked, "If you were rich, by what percentage were your taxes cut?"

The class sat there in complete silence. Most of the students stared at the blackboard, waiting for me to work out the answer. I told them to work it out themselves. I waited. And I waited. Finally, someone said, "Twenty percent?"

"Close," I replied, "but no cigar."

"Fourteen percent?" someone else ventured.

"No, you're getting colder."

After waiting another two or three minutes, I saw one student with her hand up. One student knew that the answer was 28 percent—*one* student in a class of 30.

When do they teach students how to do percentage changes? In high school? In junior high or middle school? Surely not in a college economics course.

How much of *your* time do you spend going over simple arithmetic and algebra? How much time do you spend going over simple graphs? Wouldn't you rather be spending that time discussing economics?

Now you'll be able to do just that, because all the arithmetic and simple algebra that you normally spend time explaining are covered very methodically in this book. All you'll need to do is tell your students which pages to look at.

In the micro chapters, there are scores of tables and graphs for the students to plot on their own; the solutions are shown in the book. This will cut down on the amount of time you'll need to spend putting these problems on the board.

As an economics instructor these last 22 years at such fabled institutions as Brooklyn College, New York Institute of Technology, St. Francis College (Brooklyn), and Union County College, I have used a variety of texts. But each of their authors assumed a mathematical background that the majority of my students did not have. Each also assumed that his graphs and tables were comprehensible to the average student.

The biggest problem we have with just about any book we assign is that many of our students don't bother to read it before coming to class. Until now, no one has ever written a principles text in plain English. I can't promise that every one of your students will do the readings you assign, but at least they won't be able to complain anymore about not understanding the book.

Acknowledgments

It is one thing to write an unconventional, even controversial, principles text, and it is quite another to get it published. Gary Nelson saw this project through from its inception to its completion, and I want to thank him for making this book possible.

I'd also like to thank Karen Smith, the project editor; Nancy Lanum, whose editing has certainly raised the tone of the workbook and the instructor's manual; John Thoeming, who supervised the art; Elizabeth (Libby) Rubenstein, the copyeditor; and Gail Mandaville, Denise Clinton, and Ed Foley, who worked on promoting *Introduction to Economics*.

Finally, I want to thank Professor Bruno Stein (New York University) and Professor Elaine Wrong (Montclair State College) for their helpful suggestions with the manuscript. And thanks to my young niece Eleni Zimiles for so patiently posing for the picture on the back cover.

Stephen L. Slavin

Contents

Lesson
Plan
outline

Introduction to Economics

What Is Economics All About, How Do We Use This Book, and Why Is This Book Different from All Other Introductory Economics Textbooks?

You've just started reading what may be the shortest chapter with the longest title ever to appear in an introductory economics textbook. Why is this chapter so short? Mainly because I believe in economizing. What *is* economizing? Funny you should ask.

Economics deals with efficiency—getting rid of waste. That's why this chapter is so short. In fact, that's why this entire book—a textbook and workbook combined—is so short. We've eliminated most of the extraneous material, the stuff that almost no one reads and virtually no one can understand. What you'll be getting here is 99.44 percent pure introductory economics. If this book were sold in supermarkets, you'd find it with the rest of the no-frills products.

What exactly is economics? Basically, economics is a set of tools that enables us to use our resources efficiently. The end result is the highest possible standard of living.

Economics operates on two levels, the macro level and the micro level. *Macroeconomics* deals with huge aggregates like national output, employment, the money supply, bank deposits, and government spending; and how we can deal with inflation and recession. The first half of this book (through Chapter 16) is devoted to macroeconomics.

Microeconomics operates on the level of the individual business firm, as well as that of the individual consumer. How does a firm maximize its profits, and how do consumers maximize their satisfaction? These are the types of questions that are answered by microeconomic analysis, which begins with Chapter 17.

This book is very different from every other introductory text in several ways. Not only is it shorter, but it is much more readable. To paraphrase an old computer term, it is "reader friendly." There are plenty of jokes and anecdotes to illustrate points. And you will be able to do the math even if you are mathphobic.

The format of the book encourages you to read actively rather than passively. You will be asked to perform certain acts—don't read any sexual connotation into this—such as answering questions or doing calculations. Then you'll check your work against the answers.

Whenever you are asked to do any calculations (and we rarely go beyond eighth grade arithmetic), there will be a section that reviews the math. For example, just before we deal with gross national product (Chapter 5), which is expressed in trillions of dollars, there is a section showing you how to deal with large numbers. If you happen to be one of those people who doesn't know billions from trillions, then this section is for you. But if you do know your billions and trillions, you can skip this section and go directly to GNP, collect $200, and get to roll the dice again.

Actually, I won't claim that reading this book will be quite as much fun as playing Monopoly, or that you will get to collect $200 whenever you skip a section. But you do get to save some money.

This text gives you two books in one: the conventional textbook and the workbook. Go into any college bookstore and check out the prices. Almost every standard textbook-workbook package will cost you over $60, so you're already economizing. And yet, in the words of the Carpenters' popular song, "We've only just begun."

Chapter

2

Resource Utilization

Economics is defined in various ways, but scarcity is always part of the definition. We bake an economic pie each year, which is composed of all the goods and services we have produced. No matter how we slice it, there never seems to be enough. Some people feel the main problem is how we slice the pie, while others say we should concentrate on baking a larger pie.

Chapter Objectives

In this chapter you'll learn:
- The three questions of economics.
- The central fact of economics.
- The four economic resources.
- The concepts of opportunity cost, full employment, and full production.
- The law of diminishing returns.
- The law of increasing costs.
- The Malthusian theory of population.

The Three Questions of Economics

Every country in the world must answer three questions: (1) What shall we produce? (2) How shall these goods be produced? (3) For whom shall the goods be produced? We'll take up each in turn.

What shall we produce?

What Shall We Produce? In the United States, most of our production is geared toward consumer goods. Nearly 7 percent goes toward military goods. In the Soviet Union, an even higher proportion is devoted to armaments, with a proportionately smaller percentage devoted to consumer goods. Japan has concentrated on building up its plant and equipment but devotes just 1 percent of its production to military goods.

Who makes these decisions? In the United States and Japan, there is no central planning authority, but rather a hodgepodge of corporate and government officials, as well as individual consumers and taxpayers. The Russians, as you probably guessed, *do* have a central planning authority. In fact, every five years the Russian government comes up with a new plan that sets goals for their economy in numbers of cars, TVs, factories, and bushels of wheat and corn to be produced.

The shortage of consumer goods is a perennial source of jokes in the Soviet Union. One that was making the rounds a few years ago went like this:

A man walks into a store and asks the manager, "Is this the store that has no meat?"

"No," the manager replies, "This is *not* the store that has no meat."

"What store *is* this, then?"

"This is the store that has no fish. The store that has no meat is around the corner."

Shortages of consumer goods generally mean long lines, even when there is only a rumor that a shipment has arrived. In a *New York Times* article about his experiences while living in the Soviet Union, Marc Greenfield told this anecdote:[1]

> On a bus one summer day, I overheard this conversation between two women, one of them with a pair of Austrian boots:
> "Did you have to stand long?"
> "Not very. Only overnight."
> "Overnight! You call that not long?"
> "It's worse in winter, when you have to sleep in the doorways. This time it was fine. It was warm."
> "Do they fit?"
> "No; two sizes too big. But I wasn't going to stand in line for nothing."

While we're "trashing" the Russians, try this one on for size:

A man goes into a Leningrad car dealership and orders a new car. The salesman tells him that the car will be delivered to him on June 15, 1999.

"Morning or afternoon?"

"What difference could it possibly make?" asks the salesman.

"Well, on the morning of June 15, 1999, the plumber is coming to fix the toilet."

How shall these goods be produced?

How Shall These Goods Be Produced? In our country—and in most others as well—nearly everything is produced by private businesses. Not only are all the goods and services that consumers purchase produced by businesses, but so are most of what the government purchases. For example, when our astronauts landed on the moon, a long list of contractors and subcontractors was released. It read like a "who's who in American corporations."

In socialist countries, of course, the government is the main producer of goods and services. But even in the most strictly socialist country, China, there is still a substantial role for private enterprise.

For whom shall the goods be produced?

For Whom Shall the Goods Be Produced? Economics may be divided into two parts: production, which we dealt with in the first two questions, and distribution. In the first question, we asked what the economic pie should be made of, and in the second we talked about how the pie would be made. Now we are ready to divide up the pie.

Our distribution system is a modified version of one dollar, one vote. In general, the more money you have, the more you can buy. But the government also has a claim to part of the pie. Theoretically the government takes from those who can afford to give up part of their share (taxes), spends some of those tax dollars to produce various government goods and services, and gives the rest to the old, the sick, and the poor. (Nevertheless, the rich reap

---

[1] Marc Greenfield, "Life Among the Russians," *The New York Times*, Section 6, October 24, 1982, p. 96.

Henry Fairlie has come up with a capitalist credo: "From each according to his gullibility. To me according to his greed."

a major share of the subsidies to airlines, shipping companies, defense contractors, and agriculture.)

In theory, the Russians have a distributive system that is diametrically opposed to ours. The communist credo, "from each according to his ability, to each according to his need," is something the Soviet leaders claim to follow, and it does have a nice ring to it. But in actuality, their income distribution system, with its jerry-built structure of wage incentives, bonus payments, and special privileges, is probably no more equitable than our own.

This point is illustrated by a story about Leonid Breshnev. His mother visited him at the Kremlin just after he took power in the mid-1960s. He wanted to show off, so he told her how well he was living, but she didn't say anything. He showed her his magnificent quarters, but still she didn't seem very impressed. He took her for a ride out to his country estate. Still, nothing. No reaction. He couldn't understand how his aged mother, a woman of humble peasant origin, could fail to be impressed with how well her son was doing. So finally he blurted out, "Babushka![2] Tell me! What do you think?" "Leonid," the old lady replied, "What if the communists come back?"

The Central Fact of Economics: Scarcity

Scarcity and the Need to Economize

Most of us are used to economizing; we save up our scarce dollars and deny ourselves all those tempting treasures so we will have enough money for that one big ticket item—a new car, a stereo system, a trip to Europe. Since our dollars are scarce and we can't buy everything we want, we economize by making do with some lower priced items—a Cadillac instead of a Rolls Royce, chicken instead of steak, a VCR rental instead of a neighborhood movie, or a neighborhood movie instead of a first-run movie.

If there were no scarcity, we would not need to economize.

If there were no scarcity, we would not need to economize, and economists would need to find other work. Let's go back to our economic pie to see how scarcity works. Most people tend to see scarcity as not enough dollars, but as John Maynard Keynes[3] pointed out nearly 60 years ago, this is an illusion. We could print all the money we wanted and still have scarcity. As Adam Smith noted back in 1776, the wealth of nations consists of the goods and services they produce, or on another level, the resources—the land, labor, capital, and entrepreneurial ability—that actually produce these goods and services.

The Economic Problem

In the 1950s, John Kenneth Galbraith coined the term "the affluent society," which implied that we had the scarcity problem licked. Americans were the richest people in the world (we've since slipped to fourth or fifth). Presumably, we had conquered poverty. But within a few years, Michael Harrington's *The Other America*[4] challenged that contention.

---

[2] *Babushka* is an affectionate term that is roughly translated as "little grandmother." It really sounds much better in Russian, and it's okay to address an old peasant woman, not necessarily your grandmother, in this manner.

[3] Keynes, whose work we'll discuss in Chapters 8, 9, and 10, was perhaps the greatest economist of the 20th century.

[4] Michael Harrington, *The Other America* (New York: Macmillan, 1962).

E. T. and the Satisfaction of Human Wants

Remember the movie, *E. T.*? Well, suppose E. T. were to return to Earth and hand each person $50 million. What would happen when everyone rushed out to spend this money? There simply would not be enough goods and services available. Still, assuming E. T's money was good, storekeepers would accept it. But since there would not be enough goods and services to go around, they would have to raise their prices. After all, what would *you* do if a line eight miles long formed outside *your* store?

Now an extraterrestrial like E. T. would never want to cause inflation, so you can be sure he would have made some provision for more goods and services to be made available. Imagine that he and his friends set up an E. T. shopping mall in every city and town in the world and continued to charge the old prices rather than the new inflated prices. Everyone would be able to buy as much as he or she desired without having to worry about inflation.

Now we come to the greatest benefit of all. No one would ever have to take a course in economics. Why not? Because E. T. has eliminated the two conflicting forces that made economics necessary in the first place. Since we now have all the goods and services we desire, human wants are finally satisfied. Or, alternatively, the means of production are sufficient to produce what people desire. We can no longer call them the "scarce means of production."

Of course, there may well be some people who would want still more than $50 million worth of goods and services. These people would still need to economize. And they'd still need to take courses in economics.

The economic problem, however, goes far beyond ending poverty. Even then, nearly all Americans would be relatively poor when they compared what they had with what they would have liked to have had—or with what the Rockefellers, Du Ponts, Mellons, and Gettys had.

Human wants are relatively limitless. Make a list of all the things you'd like to have. Now add up their entire cost. Chances are you couldn't earn enough in a lifetime to even begin to pay for the things on your list.

The Four Economic Resources

We need four resources, often referred to as "the means of production," to produce an ouput of goods and services. Every society from a tiny island nation in the Pacific to the most complex industrial giant needs these resources: land, labor, capital, and entrepreneurial ability. Let's consider each in turn.

Land

As a resource, land has a much more general meaning than our normal understanding of the word. It includes natural resources such as timber, oil, coal, iron ore, soil, and water, as well as the ground in which these resources are found. Not only is land used for the extraction of minerals, but for farming as well. And, of course, we build factories, office buildings, shopping centers, and homes on land. The basic payment made to the owners of land is rent.

Labor

Labor is the work and time for which employees are paid. The policeman, the computer programmer, the store manager, and the assembly line worker all supply labor. About two thirds of the total resource costs—wages and salaries—is paid to labor.

Capital

Capital is mainly plant and equipment. The United States has more capital than any country in the world. This capital consists of factories, office buildings, and stores. Our shopping malls, the Empire State Building, and our automobile plants and steel mills (and all the equipment in them) are examples of capital. The return paid to the owners of capital is interest.

Entrepreneurial ability

Entrepreneurial ability is the least familiar of our four basic resources. The entrepreneur sets up a business, risks his or her own money, and reaps the profits or absorbs the losses of this enterprise. Often the entrepreneur is an innovator, such as Andrew Carnegie, John D. Rockefeller, or Henry Ford, who figures out a new way of doing business.

We may consider land, labor, and capital passive resources, which are combined by the entrepreneur to produce goods and services. A successful undertaking is rewarded by profit; an unsuccessful one is penalized by loss.

In the American economy, the entrepreneur is the central figure, and our long record of economic success is an eloquent testimonial to the abundance of our entrepreneurial talents. The owners of the nearly 20 million businesses in this country are virtually all entrepreneurs. The vast majority either work for themselves or have just one or two employees. But they have two things in common: each runs a business, and each risks his or her own money.

These resources are scarce because they are limited in quantity. There's a finite amount of land on this planet, and at any given time a limited amount of labor, capital, and entrepreneurial ability is available. Over time, of course, these three resources can be increased.

Our economic problem, then, is that we have limited resources available to satisfy relatively unlimited wants. The reason why you, and everyone else, can't have three cars, a townhouse and a country estate with servants, designer clothing, jewels, color TVs in each room, and a $50,000 sound system is that we just don't have enough resources to produce everything that everyone wants. Therefore, we have to make choices, an option we call opportunity cost.

Opportunity Cost

Opportunity cost

Because we can't have everything we want, we must make choices. The thing we give up (i.e., our second choice) is called the opportunity cost of our choice. Therefore, *the opportunity cost of any choice is the foregone value of the next best alternative.*

Suppose a little boy goes into a toy store with $10. Many different toys tempt him, but he finally narrows his choice to a Monopoly game and a magic set, each costing $10. If he decides to buy the Monopoly game, the opportunity cost is the magic set. And if he buys the magic set, the opportunity cost is the Monopoly game.

If a town hires an extra policeman instead of repaving several streets, the opportunity cost of hiring the policeman is leaving the streets unrepaved. Opportunity cost is the cost of giving up the next best alternative.

In some cases the next best alternative—the Monopoly game or the magic set—is virtually equal no matter what choice is made. In other cases, there's no contest. If someone were to offer you, at the same price, your favorite eight-course meal or a Big Mac, you'd have no trouble deciding (unless, of course, your favorite meal *is* a Big Mac).

The Young Entrepreneur

An entrepreneur is a person who sees an opportunity to make a profit and is willing and able to risk his or her funds. I went to school with such a person.

When he was 14, he was standing in line with several hundred other boys waiting for an application for a summer job. He got hungry, so he asked the guy in back of him to hold his place in line while he got a hotdog. On his way back, several boys along the line asked him where he had gotten that hotdog. Dollar signs immediately danced before his eyes.

"I went back to the store and bought as many as I could carry. They gave me a carton of them. I went up and down the line, and I charged 10 cents more than I paid." He quickly ran out. Then, using the money he had collected, he went back to that store again and again.

He made more money working that line than he made for the first two weeks on that summer job. Before he was 30, he became a vice president of Helmsley-Spear, the giant real estate company. I don't know if he's still peddling hotdogs.

Perhaps the most vivid example of opportunity cost occurred in the movie *Sophie's Choice*. When Sophie arrived at a concentration camp during World War II, a sadistic official requested that she make a choice: she could save either her little boy or her little girl. In either case, the opportunity cost was inhumanly high. Fortunately, most choices that confront us are much more mundane.

In the next section we will be dealing with the production possibilities frontier, and once again, we will have to make choices. As we shall see, the more we produce of one product, the less we can produce of another product.

Full Employment and Full Production

Everyone agrees that full employment is a good thing, even if we don't all agree on exactly what full employment means. Does it mean that every single person in the United States who is ready, willing, and able to work has a job? Is *that* full employment?

The answer is no. There will always be some people between jobs. On any given day thousands of Americans quit, get fired, or decide that they will enter the labor force by finding a job. Since it may take several weeks, or even several months, until they find the "right" job, there will always be some people unemployed.[5]

If an unemployment rate of zero does not represent full employment, then what rate does? Economists cannot agree on what constitutes full employment. Some liberals insist that an unemployment rate of 4 percent constitutes full employment, while there are conservatives who feel that an unemployment rate 5½ or 6 percent would be more realistic.

"If you took all of the economists in the country and laid them end to end, they'd never reach a conclusion."

—George Bernard Shaw

Similarly, we cannot expect to fully use all our plant and equipment. A capacity utilization rate of 85 or 90 percent would surely employ virtually all of our usable plant and equipment.[6] At any given moment there is always some factory being renovated or some machinery under repair. During wartime we might be able to more fully use our capacity, but in normal times 85 or 90 percent is the peak.

As long as all available resources are fully used—given the constraints we have just cited—we are at our production possibilities frontier. There are a few additional constraints that should also be considered because they too restrict the quantity of resources available. These are institutional constraints, the laws and customs under which we live.

There are so-called blue laws, which restrict the economic activities that may be carried out in various cities and states, mainly on Sundays. Bars and liquor stores must be closed certain hours. In some places even retail stores must be closed on Sundays.

Child labor is very carefully restricted by state and federal law. Very young children may not be employed at all, and those below a certain age may work only a limited number of hours.

Traditionally, Americans dislike working at night or on weekends, particularly on Sundays. Consequently, we must leave most of our expensive plant and equipment idle except during daylight weekday hours.

---

[5] See the second part of Chapter 9.

[6] Technically, this is the rate at which the nation's factories, mines, and utilities are operating.

We don't consider that plant and equipment unemployed, nor do we consider those whose labor is restricted by law or custom unemployed. All of this is already allowed for in our placement of the location of the production possibilities curve (shown in Figure 2–1).

Full production

By full production, we mean that our nation's resources are being allocated in the most efficient manner possible. Not only are we using our most up-to-date technology, but we are using our land, labor, capital, and entrepreneurial ability in the most productive way.

We would not want to use the intersection of Fifth Avenue and 57th Street in Manhattan for dairy farming, nor would we want our M.D.s doing clerical work. But sometimes we do just that.

Employment discrimination

Until recently, very few blacks were allowed to go to medical school (or law school or business school). Why? Because they were not white.

Remember Spiro Agnew? He was Nixon's vice president for five years until he was forced to resign because he had taken bribes while governor of Maryland. Agnew said that he would not want open-heart surgery performed on him by someone who had gotten into medical school on a racial quota. At the time that Agnew made this pronouncement, the medical schools did have racial admission quotas—virtually 100 percent white.

And until recently only a tiny minority of women employed in the offices of American business were not typists or secretaries. A woman's place, after all, if not in the home, was surely behind a typewriter (or word processor).

These are just two of the most blatant examples of employment discrimination, a phenomenon that has diminished but has not yet been wiped out. Employment discrimination automatically means that we will have less than full production because we are not efficiently allocating our labor. In a word, there are millions of Americans who really should be doctors, engineers, corporate executives, or whatever, but who have been condemned to less exalted occupations solely because they happen to not be white Protestant males.

Using the best available technology

Finally, there is the question of using the best available technology. Historically the American economy has been on the cutting edge of technological development for almost 200 years; the sewing machine, mechanical reaper, telephone, airplane, automobile, the assembly line, and the computer are all American inventions.

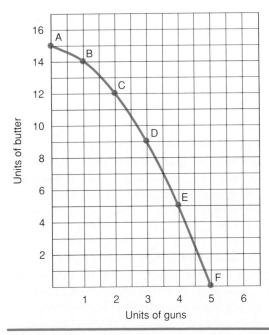

Figure 2–1

Perhaps the best case in point is the industrial robot, which illustrates both our historical innovative role and how that role has been altered. *Robotics*, a term coined by science fiction writer Isaac Asimov, was essentially an American development. But where are most industrial robots currently used? You win if your first guess was Japan.

We make and the Japanese take. Why this is so is very complex, but one thing (as President Richard Nixon used to say) should be perfectly clear. We have been losing our ability to use the best available technology, even if we invented that technology. Consequently, we are operating below our full-production level.

Full employment and underemployment

We need to tie up one more loose end, and then we'll be able to move on to the main focus of this chapter, the production possibilities frontier. We need to be very clear about distinguishing between less than full employment and underemployment of resources.

If we are using only 70 percent of our capacity of plant and equipment, as we do during some recessions, this would be a case of our economy operating at less than full employment of its resources. Anything less than, say, an 85 percent utilization rate would be considered below full employment.

More familiarly, when the unemployment rate is, say, 10 percent, there is clearly a substantial amount of labor unemployed. But how much *is* full employment? We never really answered that one.

As a working definition, and really a compromise, we'll say that an unemployment rate of 5 percent represents full employment. Why not use 4 percent, as the liberal economists suggest, or the 6 percent figure favored by the conservatives? Because a 5 percent figure represents a reasonable compromise. So we'll be working with that figure from here on in, but keep in mind that it is arbitrary.

Unemployment means that not all our resources are being used. Less than 95 percent of our labor force is working, and less than 85 percent of our plant and equipment is being used. It also means that our land and entrepreneurial ability are not all being used.

What is underemployment of resources? To be at full production, not only would we be fully employing our resources, we would also be using them in the most efficient way possible. To make all women become schoolteachers, social workers, or secretaries would grossly underuse their talents. Equally absurd—and inefficient—would be to make all white males become doctors or lawyers and all black and Hispanic males become accountants or computer programmers.

Similarly, we would not want to use that good Iowa farmland for office parks, nor would we want to locate dairy farms in the middle of our cities' central business districts. And finally, we would certainly not want to use our multimillion dollar computer mainframes to do simple word processing.

All these are examples of underemployment of resources. Unfortunately, a certain amount is built into our economy, but we need to reduce it if we are going to succeed in baking a larger economic pie.

Which brings us, at long last, to the production possibilities frontier. As we've already casually mentioned, the production possibilities frontier represents our economy at full employment and full production. However, a certain amount of underemployment of resources is also built into our model. How much? Although the exact amount is not quantifiable, it is fairly large. But to the degree that employment discrimination has declined since the early 1960s, it may be holding our output to maybe 10 or 15 percent below what it would be if there were a truly efficient allocation of resources.

The Production Possibilities Frontier

Guns and butter

Since scarcity is a fact of economic life, we need to use our resources as efficiently as possible. If we succeed, we are operating at full economic capacity. Usually there's some economic slack, but every so often we *do* manage to operate at peak efficiency. When this happens, we are on our production possibilities frontier (or production possibilities curve).

Often economics texts cast the production possibilities frontier in terms of guns and butter. A country is confronted with two choices: it can produce only military goods or only civilian goods. The more guns its produces, the less butter, and, of course, vice versa.

If we were to use all of our resources—our land, labor, capital, and entrepreneurial ability—to make guns, obviously we would not be able to make butter at all. Similarly, if we made only butter, there would be no resources to make any guns. Virtually every country makes *some* guns and *some* butter. Japan makes relatively few military goods, while the United States and the Soviet Union devote a much higher proportion of their resources to making guns.

Table 2-1 shows six production possibilities ranging from point A, where we produce 15 units of butter and no guns, to point F, where we produce 5 units of guns, but no butter. This same information is presented in Figure 2-1, a graph of the production possibilities frontier. We'll begin at point A where a country's entire resources are devoted to producing butter. If the country were to produce at full capacity (using all its resources) but wanted to make some guns, they could do it by shifting some resources away from butter. This would move them from point A to point B. Instead of producing 15 units of butter, they're making only 14.

Before we go any further on the curve, let's go over the numbers at points A and B. We're figuring out how many guns and how much butter is produced at each of these points. Starting at the origin, or zero, which is at the lower left-hand corner of the graph, let's check out point A. It's directly above the origin, so no guns are produced. Point A is at 15 on the vertical scale, so 15 units of butter are produced.

Now we'll move on to point B, which is directly above 1 unit on the guns axis. At B we produce 1 gun and 14 units of butter (shown vertically). Incidentally, to locate any point on a graph, first go across, or horizontally, then up, or vertically. Point B is 1 unit to the right, then 14 units up.

Now locate point C: 2 units across and 12 up. At C we have 2 guns and 12 butters. Next is D: 3 across and 9 up (3 guns and 9 butters). At E: 4 across and 5 up (4 guns and 5 butters). And finally F: 5 across and 0 up (5 guns and no butter).

Table 2-1
Hypothetical Production Schedule for Two-Product Economy

Point	Units of Butter	Units of Guns
A	15	0
B	14	1
C	12	2
D	9	3
E	5	4
F	0	5

The production possibilities curve is a hypothetical model of an economy that produces only two products—in this case, guns and butter (or military goods and civilian goods). The curve, formed by connecting points A, B, C, D, E, and F, represents the various possible combinations of guns and butter that could be produced if the economy were operating at capacity, or full employment.

Since we usually do not operate at full employment, we are seldom on the production possibilities frontier. So we'll move on to Figure 2–2, which shows, at point X, where we generally are. Sometimes we are in a recession, with unemployment rising beyond 8 or 9 percent, represented on the graph by point Y. A depression would be closer to the origin, perhaps shown by point Z.

What if we were at the origin? What would that represent? Think about it.

What would be the production of guns? How about the production of butter? They would both be zero. Is that possible? During the Great Depression in the 1930s we did sink to point Z, but no economy has ever sunk to the origin.

Move back to the production possibilities curve, say, at point C, where we are producing 2 units of guns and 12 units of butter. Is it possible to produce more guns? Certainly. Just move down the curve to point D. Notice, however, that we now produce fewer units of butter.

At D we have 3 units of guns and 9 units of butter. When we go from C, where we have 2 guns, to D, where we have 3, gun production goes up by 1. But at the same time, butter production declines from 12 at C to only 9 at D (a decline of 3).

If we're at point C, then, we can produce more guns, but only by sacrificing some butter production. The opportunity cost of moving from C to D (i.e., of producing 2 more guns) is giving up 3 units of butter.

Let's try another one, this time moving from C to B. Butter goes up from 12 to 14—a gain of 2. Meanwhile, guns go down from 2 to 1, a loss of 1. Going from C to B, a gain of 2 butters is obtained by sacrificing 1 gun. The opportunity cost of producing 2 more butters is 1 gun.

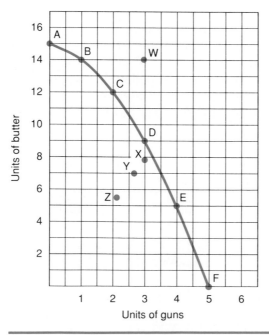

Figure 2–2

Except at point A, we can go somewhere else on the production possibility curve and increase our output of butter. Similarly, anywhere but at point F, we can go somewhere else on the curve and raise our output of guns. It is possible to increase our output of *either* guns *or* butter by moving somewhere else on the curve, but there is an opportunity cost involved. The more we produce of one (by moving along the curve), the less we produce of the other. It is not possible, then, if we are anywhere on the curve, to raise our productions of both guns *and* butter.

What if we're somewhere inside the production possibilities frontier? Would it be possible to produce more guns *and* more butter? The answer is yes. At point Z we have an output of 2 guns and 4 butters. By moving to point D we would have 3 guns and 9 butters. Or, by going to point E, output would rise to 4 guns and 5 butters.

We are able to increase our output of both guns and butter when we move from Z to D or E because we are now making use of previously unused resources. We are moving from depression conditions to those of full employment. But when we go from C to D, we stay at full employment. The only way we can produce more guns is to produce less butter, because resources will have to be diverted from butter to gun production.

Economic Growth

If the production possibilities curve represents the economy operating at full employment, then it would be impossible to produce at point W (of Figure 2–2). To go from C to W would mean producing more guns and more butter, something that would be beyond our economic capabilities, given the current state of technology and the amount of resources available.

Every economy will use the best available technology. At times, because a country cannot afford the most up-to-date equipment, it will use older machinery and tools. That country really has a capital problem rather than a technological one.

As the level of available technology improves, the production possibilities curve moves outward, as it does in Figure 2–3. A faster paper copier, a more smoothly operating assembly line, or a new generation computer system are examples of technological advances. And increasingly, industrial robots and bank money machines are replacing human beings at relatively routine jobs.

Our economic capacity is also expanded when there is an expansion of labor or capital. More (or better trained) labor and more (or improved) plant and equipment would also push the production possibilities curve outward. This is illustrated in Figure 2–3, as we go from PPC_1 to PPC_2, and from PPC_2 to PPC_3.

Back in the 1950s, when Nikita Khrushchev, then the head honcho of the Politburo, said, "We will bury you," he wasn't trying to drum up business for his funeral parlor. He meant that the Soviet Union would overtake the United States in output of goods and services. At that time the USSR was growing much faster than we were. But in the 1960s, our rate of economic growth sped up, while the Russian rate slowed down.

However, since the early 1970s, our rate of growth, which had averaged well over 3 percent a year during the last two centuries, slowed to only a little over 2 percent.

There is no question that the American economy is in trouble. Another indication is the huge trade deficits that we have been running for over a decade. What it all comes down to is that Americans are consuming too much and producing too little.

The best available technology

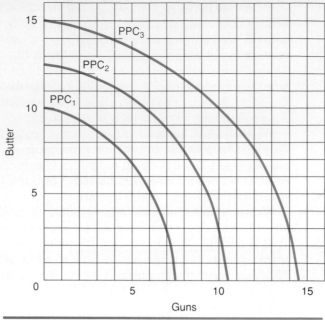

Figure 2–3

Americans are not saving enough.

Another way of putting this is that Americans are not saving enough and business firms are not investing enough. This is shown by the two alternate graphs of Figure 2–4.

Why can't we operate at point B of Figure 2–4 rather than at point A? That's a very good question. Probably the best answer is that Americans, for whatever reason, have come to believe in the adage "buy today, pay tomorrow."

Buying "on time" became popular after World War II, along with relatively easy-to-obtain home mortgages, federal income tax preferential treatment for home ownership and personal borrowing,[7] and, over the last two decades, the tremendous expansion in the use of credit cards. In addition, Americans are bombarded by well over $100 billion worth of advertising a year. The products may vary, but the message remains the same: Buy! Buy! Buy!

The more we buy, the less we save. In fact, by 1986, Americans were saving only about 2 percent of their incomes after taxes, which was just one third the rate of the 1960s. Also contributing to our shortfall of savings has been the federal government, which ran budget deficits of over $200 billion during the mid-1980s.

It all came down to this: The funds needed by business firms for investment in plant and equipment were no longer being provided in sufficient quantity by private savers, and the federal government was sopping up much of the savings that were available. Foreign investors, who had been accumulating surplus dollars from our trade deficits, were lending us back some of our own money. But this was insufficient to provide all of the investment funds needed to spur our rate of economic growth.

---

[7] Until 1987, interest paid on all consumer loans—for example, car loans, credit card loans, bank personal loans, and installment loans—was deductable from federal personal income taxes.

People who owned their own homes can deduct mortgage interest and property taxes from their federal personal income tax.

A.

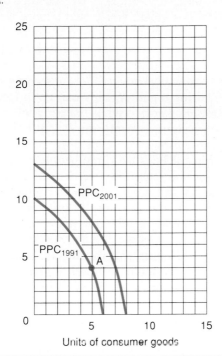

B.

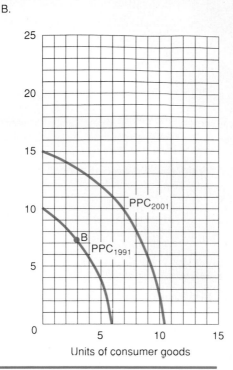

Units of consumer goods

Units of consumer goods

Figure 2–4

We noted earlier in the chapter (in the full-employment and full-production section) that our investment in new technology was lagging. The United States, which had always been on the cutting edge of technological advance, was giving up this leadership role as well. Although American inventors were no less inventive, the application of their technological discoveries required investments that we were sometimes unable to make.

Increasing Costs

You may have noticed that as we shift production from guns to butter, we have to give up increasing units of guns for each additional unit of butter. Or, shifting the other way, we would have to give up increasing units of butter for each additional unit of guns we produce.

The law of increasing costs
We will be calling this "the law of increasing costs." Stated formally, this law says that *as the output of one good expands, the opportunity cost of producing additional units of this good increases.* In other words, as more and more of a good is produced, the production of additional units of this good will entail larger and larger opportunity cost. Before we can analyze this phenomenon, however, we must first understand the law of diminishing returns and the concepts of economies of scale and diseconomies of scale.

The Law of Diminishing Returns

Next to the law of supply and demand, the law of diminishing returns is probably most often invoked. Unfortunately this very simple law is not very clearly understood by those who so blithely drop its name. The law should really be called the law of diminishing marginal output.

Using the data in Table 2–2, we see that one person working alone turns out 2 log cabins a week, while two people working together can turn out 5 per week. If you've ever attempted to move 400-pound logs, you know its easier to have someone at the other end of the log. Perhaps three people can work together even more efficiently.

Increasing returns

The first three workers give us increasing returns (or increasing marginal returns). Working together, they can get a lot more done than if each worked alone. But notice what happens when we hire a fourth worker. This person raises output, but only by 3. With the forth worker we have the onset of diminishing returns (or diminishing marginal output).

Diminishing marginal output

Why is this so? Because three people may be an ideal number to move and lift 400-pound logs. The fourth worker is certainly a help, but proportionately, he doesn't add as much as the third worker.

A fifth worker adds still less to output (2 units) and a sixth worker even less (1 unit). In other words, five people can manage building log cabins almost as well as six. As we add the seventh worker, we find that he is completely superfluous. We would say, then, that from the fourth to the seventh worker, we have *diminishing returns.*

Negative returns

The eighth worker is actually in the way, having a marginal output of minus one. Returns become negative when this eighth worker is added. A ninth worker is still more in the way. The eighth and ninth workers have negative returns.

What would be the maximum number of workers you would possibly hire? The answer is six. If the wage rate were very low, you would hire up to six. The seventh worker, however, adds nothing to output and the eighth and ninth get in the way, thereby reducing output.

The law of diminishing returns

The law of diminishing returns (or, technically, diminishing marginal returns) is defined this way: *If units of a resource are added to a fixed proportion of other resources, eventually marginal output will decline.* If we were to keep adding labor to a fixed amount of land and captial, at some point the marginal output of labor would decline. In Table 2–2 this happens with the fourth worker, since his marginal output (3) is less than the marginal output of the third worker (4).

Table 2–2
The Law of Diminishing Returns:
An Example

Number of Workers	Total Output	Marginal* Output	
1	2	2	Increasing returns
2	5	3	Increasing returns
3	9	4	Increasing returns
4	12	3	Diminishing retruns
5	14	2	Diminishing returns
6	15	1	Diminishing returns
7	15	0	Diminishing returns
8	14	−1	Diminishing and negative returns
9	11	−3	Diminishing and negative returns

*Marginal output is the additional output produced by the last worker hired. Thus, the first worker adds 2 units to output, so his marginal output is 2. The second worker hired adds 3 units to output (output has risen from 2 to 5), so his marginal output is 3. When a third worker is hired, total output jumps to 9. Marginal output has therefore risen by 4.

Economies and Diseconomies of Scale

Large-scale enterprise is expected to be more efficient than small business. And in general, we would expect large firms to be able to undersell small firms. One reason for this belief is that large firms can often get quantity discounts when they buy raw materials or inventory (A&P even uses a system of central buying and warehousing). A manufacturer would be able to give you a better price if he had to deliver 10,000 cartons of tuna fish to one warehouse rather than 100 cartons to five different stores. Also, it costs less to sell your final product in quantity than to sell it piece by piece. For this reason, a wholesaler has much lower prices than a retailer. Buying and selling in large quantities, then, is one reason for economies of scale.

Adam Smith, in *The Wealth of Nations* (1776), noted three other advantages. When a firm is large enough to provide specialized jobs for its workers, economies of scale will follow. He used a pin factory as an example.

One worker, said Smith, "could scarce, perhaps, with his utmost industry, make one pin in a day, and certainly could not make twenty." He then described how pin making has become specialized: "One man draws out the wire, another straights it, a third cuts it, a fourth points it, a fifth grinds it at the top for receiving the head."[8]

There are three distinct advantages to producing pins in this manner. First, the workers become good at their jobs—better than they would be if they went from one function to another. Second, they don't waste time going from one task to another. Third, the factory can employ specialized and expensive equipment since it will be fully used. For example, a special die to draw the wire can be purchased since it will be used continually; and a machine to cut the wire can be purchased for the same reason.

Smith estimated that 10 people working together in a factory could produce 48,000 pins a day, which would be a prime example of economies of scale.

Economies of scale enable a business firm to reduce its costs per unit of output as output expands. Often these cost reductions can be passed on to the consumer in the form of lower prices. One outgrowth of expansion is increasing specialization. People's jobs grow more and more specialized, as they did in Adam Smith's pin factory. And with the growth of specialization are sown the seeds of inefficiency, rising costs, and diseconomies of scale.

As a firm grows larger, it will create a bureaucracy. The founder of that firm hired all his employees personally. As the firm grew larger, he had his foreman do the hiring. Today, if you tried to get a job at a large company, you'd have to get through the personnel department, then meet your prospective supervisor, then your prospective supervisor's supervisor, and perhaps several other members of "the team"—or some other variation of this process.

A huge hierarchy of corporate authority is established—a hierarchy that might have once made sense, but that now may either have little relevant function or actually work at cross purposes. The American automobile industry is a good case in point. Fewer than half the employees of GM, Ford, and Chrysler actually make cars. The rest do sales, advertising, market research, litigation, accounting, personnel work, budgeting, or public relations and the like for their companies. Anything but make cars.

---

[8] Adam Smith, *The Wealth of Nations* (London: Methuen, 1950), Book I, Chapter 1, pp. 8–9.

During the blackouts and energy shortages of the mid-to-late 1970s, when Consolidated Edison (Con Ed) was having trouble generating enough electricity to keep New York going, the company ran a series of ads telling its customers to keep their lights on (don't leave your lights out when you go out of your house or a burglar will know no one is home). This was a typical case of one hand of the corporate bureaucracy working at cross purposes with the other.

Even quantity discounts enjoyed by large firms will eventually disappear as the firms use up so many resources that they bid up their prices. If a company rented office space, it could save money by renting several floors in a building. But if the firm needed a large percentage of the total downtown office space in a city, it would end up paying more per square foot.

Depicting the stages of growth of several large corporations, we would start with the initial spurt, during which economies of scale were operative and unit costs were declining. As the companies continued to mature and output continued to rise, their unit costs stayed about the same. This stage is sometimes called *proportional returns to scale*.

Proportional returns to scale

In the final stage, which several large corporations have reached—the most conspicuous being International Harvester, Continental Illinois Bank, and Bank of America—diseconomies of scale set in. The corporate dinosaurs, beset with rising unit costs, have grown so huge they may no longer be able to compete. The only question is whether their status as an endangered species will permit them to continue functioning, or if they will be permitted to die natural deaths.[9]

The Law of Increasing Costs

We will now use the law of diminishing returns and the concept of diseconomies of scale to help explain the law of increasing costs. Sometimes referred to as the law of increasing relative costs, it is applied to the problem we encountered with the production possibility curve.

We have already seen how we have had to give up the production of some guns to produce more butter and vice versa. We'll now take this a step further. To produce additional units of guns—one gun, two guns, three guns—we will have to give up increasing amounts of butter. Similarly, to produce additional units of butter, we will have to give up increasing numbers of guns.

How many units of butter would we have to give up to produce each additional gun? This is shown in Table 2–3, which is derived from Figure 2–1, or, if you want to cheat a little, from Table 2–1.

In Table 2–3, as we begin to switch from butter to guns, we move from point A to point B. We give up just one unit of butter in exchange for one unit of guns. But the move from B to C isn't as good. Here we give up 2 butters for one gun. C to D is still worse: We give up 3 butters for one gun. D to E is even worse: We give up 4 units of butter for one gun. And the worst trade-off of all is from E to F: we lose 5 butters for just one gun.

This is why we call it the law of increasing relative costs. To produce more and more of one good, we have to give up increasing amounts of another good. To produce each additional gun, we have to give up increasing amounts of butter.

---

[9] A third alternative has been grudgingly resorted to—a government bailout. Penn Central, Lockheed, and Chrysler have all received government loans to keep them afloat. In addition, the Federal Reserve and the Federal Deposit Insurance Corporation have pumped billions of dollars into failing banks to keep them going.

Table 2–3
Production Shifts from Butter to Guns

Shift from Point to Point	Change in Gun Production	Change in Butter Production
A to B	+1	−1
B to C	+1	−2
C to D	+1	−3
D to E	+1	−4
E to F	+1	−5

Three explanations for the law of increasing relative costs

There are three explanations for the law of increasing relative costs. First, there's diminishing returns. If we're increasing gun production, we will need more and more resources—more land, more labor, more capital, and more entrepreneurial ability. But one or more of these resources may be relatively limited. Perhaps we will begin to run out of capital—plant and equipment—or perhaps entrepreneurial ability will run out first.

Go back to our definition of the law of diminishing returns. If units of a resource are added to a fixed proportion of other resources, eventually marginal output will decline. Had we been talking about farming rather than producing guns, the law of diminishing returns might have set in as increasing amounts of capital were applied to the limited supply of rich farmland.

A second explanation for the law of increasing costs is diseconomies of scale. By shifting from butter to guns, the firm or firms making guns will grow so large that diseconomies of scale will eventually set in.

The third explanation, factor suitability, requires more extensive treatment here. We'll start at point A of Table 2–1, where we produce 15 units of butter and no guns. As we move to point B, gun production goes up by one, while butter production goes down by only one. In other words, the opportunity cost of producing one unit of guns is the loss of only one unit of butter.

Why is the opportunity cost so low? The answer lies mainly with factor suitability. We'll digress for a moment with the analogy of a pickup game of punchball. The best players are picked first, then the not-so-good one, and finally the worst. If a couple of players from one side have to go home, the game goes on. The other side gives them their worst player.

If we're shifting from butter to guns, the butter makers will give the gun makers their worst workers. But people who are bad at producing butter are not necessarily bad at making—or shooting—guns.

When all we did was make butter, people worked at that no matter what their other skills. Even if a person was a skilled gun maker, or a gun user, what choice did he have? Presumably, then, when given the choice to make guns, those best suited for that occupation (and also poorly suited for butter making) would switch to guns.

As resources are shifted from butter to guns, the labor, land, capital, and entrepreneurial ability best suited to guns and least suited to butter would be the first to switch. But as more resources are shifted, we would be taking resources that were more and more suited to butter making and less and less suited to gun making.

Take land, for example. The first land given over to gun making might be terrible for raising cows (and hence milk and butter), but great for making guns. Eventually, however, as nearly all land was devoted to gun making, we'd be giving over fertile farmland that might not be well suited to gun production.

Each of these three reasons—diminishing returns, diseconomies of scale, and factor suitability—helps explain the law of increasing relative costs. But now that the law is explained, we won't have to worry too much about it, because we would never devote all of our production to just one, or even a few, goods and services. Nevertheless, the law does have an applicability in certain localities and regions, or in particular economic sectors that may grow too large relative to the rest of the economy.

The Malthusian Theory of Population

Economics is called the "dismal science" largely because of the Malthusian theory. As it was originally formulated, the theory predicted that the world would, within perhaps a few generations, be beset by famine and warfare. This was inevitable because of a tendency for the world's population to double every 25 years.

The Reverend Thomas Robert Malthus wrote the first edition of the *Essay on the Principle of Population* in 1798. His two main points were that population tended to grow in a geometric progression—1, 2, 4, 8, 16, 32—and that the only ways to stop population from growing that rapidly were the "positive checks" of pestilence, famine, and war. Not a very pleasant outlook.

In his second edition, Malthus held out slightly more hope for population increase. It could be contained by the "preventive check" of "moral restraint," which meant not getting married until one could support a family (and it went without saying, no fooling around before you got married).

Malthus also noted that the food supply could not increase as rapidly as population tended to because the planet was limited in size and there was only a fixed amount of arable land. He felt that the food supply would ultimately tend to grow in an arithmetic progression—1, 2, 3, 4, 5, 6—and it would not take a mathematical genius to conclude that we would be in trouble within a few generations. The relevant figures are shown in the table below.

The Malthusian theory is a variant of the law of diminishing returns. As increasing amounts of labor are applied to a fixed amount of land, eventually marginal output will decline.

Was Malthus right? Surely not in the industrialized countries, particularly the United States, Canada, and Australia, which are major exporters of wheat and other farm products. Two things happened in these countries to ward off Malthus's dire predictions. First, because of tremendous technological advances in agriculture—tractors, harvesters, better fertilizer, and high-yield seeds—farmers were able to feed many more people.* Second, as industrialization spread and more and more people left the countryside for the cities, the birthrate fell. Demographers believe that an urbanized industrial population will have a lower birthrate because children are no longer seen as an economic asset. Not only are children no longer a cheap source of labor (as they were on farms), but they are no longer needed as a means of support in one's old age due to the growth of social insurance programs and pension funds.

However, the less developed countries are caught in a double bind. The Malthusian positive check of a high death rate has been largely removed by public health measures such as malaria control, smallpox vaccine, and more sanitary garbage disposal. But because these countries have not yet been able to industrialize and urbanize their populations, birthrates remain high. In most of Asia, Africa, and Latin America, populations are doubling every 30 to 35 years, putting hundreds of millions of people in peril of starvation. Famine is a reality in these countries, and it may well become even more widespread toward the end of this century.

Summary of the Malthusian Theory: Tendencies of Increase of Population and Food Production

Year	Food Production	Population
1800	1	1
1825	2	2
1850	3	4
1875	4	8
1900	5	16
1925	6	32

Note: Malthus did not use actual years in his predictions; these years are purely hypothetical to illustrate his theory. Also, Malthus did not predict that this would actually happen. Rather, he indicated that these were the tendencies, but that population increases could be checked by war, pestilence, famine, or moral restraint.

* Some observers have been lent encouragement by the so-called Green Revolution, which has enabled many large growers to double and triple yields by using better seeds and fertilizer. However, the prime beneficiaries have been the wealthy farmers and a few multinational agribusinesses such as Dole, Del Monte, and Ralston Purina. They have profited by producing for export such crops as sugar, soybeans, bananas, and peanuts. But they have also forced millions of small farmers off the land and actually caused the production of indigenous food staples to decline, making these countries even more dependent on food imports.

The New York region, which includes the 15 counties in and around New York City, is extremely overcrowded, particularly with respect to getting around. In a sense, then, diminishing returns have set in when it takes 90 minutes to make a 20-mile trip to work, when daytime traffic moves at less than five miles per hour in midtown Manhattan, and when the specter of rush-hour gridlock threatens to prevent any movement whatsoever. The Houston area provides another example of overdevelopment resulting in near immobility.

The law of diminishing returns (or increasing costs) explains why we don't expand certain industries or sectors too far and what would happen if we did. That there are few examples of such overexpansion is eloquent testimony to the potency of the law.

Today, only 3 percent of our labor force works in agriculture, and yet, with the same land that was available in 1900, a much smaller farm labor force produces four or five times as much. Coincidentally, during a time when our food production grew so rapidly, our population growth rate slowed to well under 1 percent a year, or a doubling time of over 100 years.

In the less developed nations of Africa, Asia, and Latin America, however, the Malthusian theory may prove more valid.[10] Hundreds of millions face starvation, with virtually no chance to substantially raise their food output. The recurrent famines in the sub-Sahara region of Africa may be mere dress rehearsals for a future crisis of much greater dimension.

Even more alarming, in the long run, the birthrates of the less developed nations show little indication of declining. And unless they decline, the emergency shipments of foodstuffs from the rest of the world are merely postponing the inevitable.

---

[10] The Malthusian theory, which predicted worldwide famine, because the world's population was expected to outstrip the food supply, is discussed in the box that concludes this chapter.

Workbook for Chapter 2

Name Lola Poles
Date Jan 11, 1990

Multiple-Choice Questions

Circle the letter that corresponds to the best answer.

1. The word that is central to the definition of economics is

a. resource **b.** wants (**c.**) scarcity **d.** capital

2. About what percentage of our production goes toward military goods?

(**a.**) under 10 percent **b.** about 20 percent **c.** about 50 percent **d.** about 75 percent

3. A central planning authority decides what goods get produced in

a. the United States **b.** Japan **c.** England (**d.**) the USSR

4. In the United States most goods and services are produced by

a. the government **b.** private individuals for themselves (**c.**) business firms

5. "From each according to his ability, to each according to his need" is the _____ credo.

(**a.**) Communist **b.** Capitalist **c.** Socialist **d.** Fascist

6. We would not need to economize if

a. the government printed more money (**b.**) there was no scarcity **c.** there was less output of goods and services **d.** everyone received a big pay increase

7. Human wants are *basic of economy*

a. relatively limited (**b.**) relatively unlimited **c.** easily satisfied **d.** about equal to our productive capacity

8. Which of the following is an economic resource?

a. gold **b.** oil (**c.**) labor **d.** rent

9. Each of the following is an example of capital except

(**a.**) land **b.** an office building **c.** a computer system **d.** a factory

10. The opportunity cost of spending four hours studying a review book the night before a final exam would be

a. the cost of the review book (**b.**) missing four hours of TV **c.** a higher grade on the exam **d.** the knowledge gained from studying

11. An economy operating its plant and equipment at full capacity implies a capacity utilization rate of

a. 40 percent **b.** 70 percent (**c.**) 85 percent **d.** 100 percent

12. The full-production level of our economy implies

(**a.**) an efficient allocation of our resources **b.** zero unemployment **c.** our plant and equipment being operated at 100 percent capacity **d.** a high unemployment rate

13. Underemployment means

a. the same thing as unemployment (**b.**) underutilization of resources **c.** a recession **d.** slow economic growth

14. The production possibilities frontier represents

a. our economy at full employment but not full production **b.** our economy at full production but not full employment (**c.**) our economy at full production and full employment

15. If we are operating inside our production possibilities frontier

a. there is definitely a recession going on **b.** there is definitely not a recession going on (**c.**) there is definitely less than full employment **d.** there is definitely inflation

16. The closer we are to the origin and the farther away we are from the production possibilities frontier

(**a.**) the more unemployment there is **b.** the less unemployment there is **c.** the more guns we are producing **d.** the more butter we are producing

17. Economic growth will occur if any of the following occur except

a. a better technology becomes available **b.** the unemployment rate declines **c.** more capital becomes available **d.** more labor becomes available

18. To attain a higher rate of economic growth, we need to devote

a. a higher proportion of our production to capital goods and a lower proportion to consumer goods
b. a higher proportion of our production to consumer goods and a lower proportion to capital goods
c. a higher proportion of our production to both consumer goods and capital goods
d. a lower proportion of our production to both consumer goods and capital goods.

19. Each of the following has contributed to our low rate of economic growth except

a. our high rate of savings **b.** our high rate of consumption **c.** our federal budget deficits **d.** our low rate of investment

20. The law of increasing costs states that as

a. output rises, cost per unit rises as well
b. the output of one good expands, the opportunity cost of producing additional units of this good increases
c. economies of scale set in, costs increase
d. output rises, diminishing returns set in

21. In general, as output rises you first attain

a. increasing returns, then diminishing returns, then negative returns **b.** diminishing returns, then negative returns, then increasing returns **c.** negative returns, then increasing returns, then diminishing returns **d.** increasing returns, then negative returns, then diminishing returns

22. The law of diminishing returns may also be called the law of

a. diminishing marginal returns **b.** diminishing positive returns **c.** negative returns **d.** increasing returns

23. As a firm grows larger,

a. economies of scale set in, then diseconomies of scale **b.** diseconomies of scale set in, then economies of scale **c.** economies of scale and diseconomies of scale set in at the same time **d.** neither economies of scale nor diseconomies of scale set in

24. Adam Smith noted each of the following economies of scale except

a. specialization **b.** employment of expensive equipment **c.** saving of time not spent going from one task to another **d.** diminishing returns

25. The law of increasing costs is explained by each of the following except

a. the law of diminishing returns **b.** diseconomies of scale **c.** factor suitability **d.** overspecialization

26. The Malthusian theory said that population tended to grow in a ＿＿＿ progression, while the food supply tended to grow in a ＿＿＿ progression.

a. geometric, arithmetic **b.** arithmetic, geometric **c.** geometric, geometric **d.** arithmetic, arithmetic

Fill-In Questions

1. The three questions of economics are:

(1) What shall we produce

(2) How shall these good be produced

(3) For whom shall the good be produced

2. The central fact of economics is (in one word)

scarcity

3. Human wants are relatively unlimited, while economic resources are relatively limited

4. List the four economic resources (1) Land; (2) Labor; (3) capital; and (4) Entrepreneurial ability

5. Opportunity cost is defined as the Second Choice (Next best alternative)

6. If you went into a store with $25 and couldn't decide whether to buy a pair of jeans or a jacket, and you finally decided to buy the jeans, what would be the opportunity cost of this purchase? _jacket_ .

7. Full employment implies an unemployment rate of about _5½ – 6_ percent.

8. List some constraints on our labor force that prevent our fully using our plant and equipment 24 hours a day, seven days a week. (1) _blue law_ ; (2) _child labor_ ; and (3) _5 day work week_

9. Employment discrimination results in the _decline_ of our labor force. _ally_

10. When we are efficiently allocating our resources and using the best available technology, we are operating on our _full production_ .

11. Most of the time our economy is operating _____ its production possibilities frontier.

12. Economic growth can be attained by:

(1) _____ _____ and

(2) _____

13. The main reason for our lagging rate of economic growth has been not enough _saving_ .

14. The law of increasing costs states that as the output of one good expands, _____

_____ .

15. The law of diminishing returns states that if units of a resource are added to a fixed proportion of other resources, _____ .

16. Large firms are able to lower their costs by taking advantage of _____ .

17. When firms get too big, _____ set in.

18. The Malthusian theory said that population tended to grow in a _____ progression, while the food supply grew in an _____ progression.

19. The Malthusian theory is a variant of the law of

_____ .

20. The Malthusian theory is most applicable today to the _____ countries.

Problems

1. If we were at point C of Figure 1, would it be possible to produce more houses *and* more cars?

2. If we were at point M of Figure 1, would it be possible to produce more houses *and* more cars?

3. If we were at point C on Figure 1, would it be possible to go to point J?

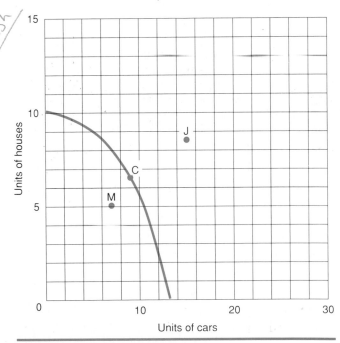

Figure 1

4. Given the information in Table 1, fill in Malthus's predictions for the years 2025, 2050, and 2075.

Table 1

Year	Food Production	Population
2000	1	1
2025		
2050		
2075		

5. Fill in the following points on Figure 2.
Point X: where our economy generally opeates
Point Y: a serious recession
Point Z: a catastrophic depression
Point W: economic growth

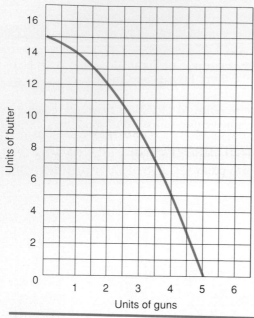

Figure 2

6. Fill in the marginal output column of Table 2.

Table 2

Number of Workers	Total Output	Marginal Output
1	1	
2	3	
3	6	
4	9	
5	11	
6	13	
7	14	
8	14	
9	13	
10	11	
11	8	

7. Diminishing returns set in with the _____ worker.

8. Negative returns set in with the _____ worker.

9. If these people would work for you for one cent an hour, how many would you hire? _____

Supply and Demand

This brief chapter provides an introduction to supply and demand. Chapter 17 provides a much more detailed discussion of demand while Chapters 18 and 19 provide a much more detailed discussion of supply.

Chapter Objectives

Four questions are covered in this chapter:
- How much will a particular good or service cost?
- How much of it will be purchased?
- What is equilibrium?
- What are some applications of supply and demand?

Demand

Definition of demand

Demand is defined as *the schedule of quantities of a good or service that people will buy at different prices.* At very high prices people don't buy too many, and at lower prices they buy more.

An example of a demand schedule appears in Table 3–1. As price falls, the quantity demanded goes up. Why? Because as price declines, people are willing and able to buy more. From the buyer's standpoint, even if he wants a good or service, he won't buy it if he can't afford it. And if he can afford it but doesn't want it, he won't buy it.

Table 3–1
Hypothetical Demand Schedule

Price	Quantity Demanded
$10	1
9	2
8	4
7	7
6	12

We have said that demand is a schedule of quantities that people are willing to buy at different prices. By "willing," we mean having the ability to pay and desiring the product. Like sex, demand requires desire—and the ability to do something about it.

Figure 3-1 is a demand curve based on the data in Table 3-1. The horizontal axis shows quantity and the vertical axis shows price. When we plot the graph, we find the quantity and then the price.

Figure 3-1

Starting with a quantity of 1 and a price of $10, we go one space to the right of the origin (0) on the horizontal axis; then we move up 10 spaces. That gives us our first point.

To find the second point on the demand curve, we go 2 spaces to the right on the quantity axis and 9 spaces up. Similarly, to find our third, fourth, and fifth points, we move to the right on the horizontal axis and then straight up. Next we connect the points.

Notice that the demand curve moves down and to the right. At high prices, people buy very little, but as price declines, they buy more. We have an inverse relationship: as price comes down, quantity purchased goes up. This is the law of demand.

Supply

Definition of supply

Supply is defined as *the schedule of quantities that people will sell at different prices.* The figures in Table 3-2 show that as the price rises, people are willing to sell more and more. There are two reasons for this. First, those already in business are willing to sell more because this will raise

Table 3-2
Hypothetical Supply Schedule

Price	Quantity Supplied
$10	14
9	12
8	9
7	5
6	1

"You can't repeal the laws of supply and demand."
—Anonymous

their profits. Second, new firms are attracted to the industry by the prospect of high profits.

This is the price mechanism in action. Suppose a bus line went out of business and the government appealed to people with cars to drive stranded commuters to work. Suppose you could even charge people. If the going rate were $1 per mile per passenger, you might well be tempted to start your own livery service. The higher the price, the more firms will appear on the scene.

To draw a supply curve in Figure 3-2, we use the same type of graph we did in Figure 3-1. Starting with the point where quantity is 14 and price is $10, we go 14 spaces to the right from the origin (0), and then straight up 10 spaces. Using the same procedure, we plot the other four points and connect them to obtain our supply curve.

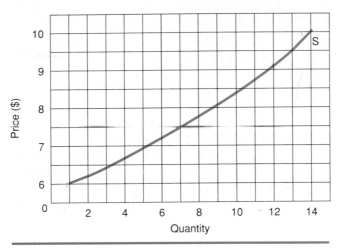

Figure 3-2

Please note that the supply curve goes up and to the right. As price rises, quantity supplied rises. This is a direct relation: price and quantity supplied move in the same direction.

Equilibrium

At equilibrium, quantity demanded and quantity supplied are equal. At a certain price all buyers who are willing to buy will be able to. And all sellers who are willing to sell will also be able to. That price is the equilibrium price.

The equilibrium point is where the demand and supply curves cross.

To find the equilibrium price and quantity, let's draw our demand and supply curves on the same graph. In Figure 3-3, we can find our equilbrium point by noting exactly where the curves cross. That tells us our equilibrium price and quantity.

Where the demand and supply curves cross is about $7.30 in price and the quantity is about 6. As a check, go back to the tables, which, if anything, are more accurate than the graph. (This is because the graph is derived from the tables.)

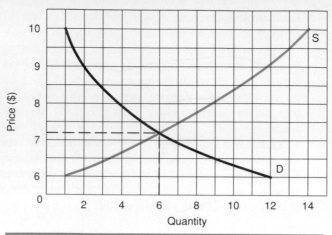

Figure 3–3

At a price of $8 in Table 3–3, the quantity demanded is 4 and the quantity supplied is 9. The difference between quantity demanded (4) and quantity supplied (9) is 5. At a price of $7, quantity demanded is 7 and quantity supplied 5. At $7, quantity demanded (7) and quantity supplied (5) are only two apart. A price of $7 is much closer to equilibrium price than $8. Remember that at equilibrium, quantity demanded equals quantity supplied. Since quantity demanded and quantity supplied are only 2 apart at $7 and 5 apart at $8, $7 is much closer to equilibrium than $8.

Table 3–3
Hypothetical Demand and Supply Schedules*

Price	Quantity Demanded	Quantity Supplied
$10	1	14
9	2	12
8	4	9
7	7	5
6	12	1

* Figures are taken from Tables 3–1 and 3–2.

Price always tends toward its equilibrium level. If it should happen to be higher, say, $9.00, it will fall to $7.30. And if it's lower than $7.30, it will rise.

Let's say the price is $9. There will be a lot of unhappy sellers who will say, "Here I go without a sale when I would have been willing to settle for a lower price." What do they do? They lower their price. And when they do—to say, $8—most of the other sellers follow suit. Why? Because otherwise they'd sell nothing. Why would any buyer pay one seller $9 when the others are selling for $8.

As the price falls to $8, a few sellers—3 to be exact—will leave the market. In Table 3–3 we see that at $9 there are 12 sellers, but at $8, there are only 9. At the same time, the number of buyers rises from 2 to 4.

We're not yet at equilibrium but we're getting closer. At $9, sellers outnumbered buyers 12 to 2. At $8 sellers outnumber buyers just 9 to 4. The price must be lowered to $7.30 for 6 buyers and 6 sellers to do business.

If price were below equilibrium, say at $6, the dissatisfied buyers would bid the price up. At $6 there would be 12 people willing to buy, but only 1 seller. Some of the buyers, 7, in fact, would be willing to pay $7. By making

"It's easy to train economists. Just teach a parrot to say 'supply and demand.'"

—Thomas Carlyle

their wishes known, these buyers would bid the price up and find 5 sellers willing to do business. We're still not quite at equilibrium. The price will be bid up slightly more to $7.30, bringing in one more seller and causing one buyer to drop out of the market. And at $7.30, there are 6 buyers and 6 sellers.

Above equilibrium price are surpluses.

An alternative way to looking at prices above and below equilibrium is to discuss them in terms of surpluses and shortages. When the price is above $7.30, there is a surplus. Quantity supplied is greater than quantity demanded and this difference is the surplus. For example, at a price of $9, the surplus is 10. How is the surplus eliminated? As we've just seen, by letting the price fall. The surplus, then, eliminates itself through the price mechanism.

Below equilibrium prices are shortages.

When the price is too low, there is a shortage. A shortage of 11 occurs when the price is $6. But the shortage disappears when the price rises automatically to its equilibrium level of $7.30.

Equilibrium price is the result of the forces of supply and demand. Together they determine equilibrium price. There will be no tendency for price to change once it has reached its equilibrium. However, if either demand or supply, or both, change, there will be a new equilibrium price.

Changes in Demand and Supply

Demand is defined as a schedule of quantities that people will purchase at different prices. A change or shift in demand occurs when there is any change in that schedule. If, at any price, people would buy more, or less, than they had been buying, there has been a change in demand. If, for example, at a price of $8, a quantity of 5 instead of 4 is now purchased, there has been a change in demand.

One of the reasons why demand changes is because there is a change in peoples' tastes. Concern about lung cancer reduces the demand for cigarettes, while concern about calories raises the demand for Tab, Diet Pepsi, Fresca, and other low-calorie soft drinks.

Figure 3-4 illustrates an increase in demand. When demand rises from D_1 to D_2, we have a new equilibrium point. Price is now $8 and quantity 9. Note that an increase in demand leads to a rise in equilibrium price and quantity.

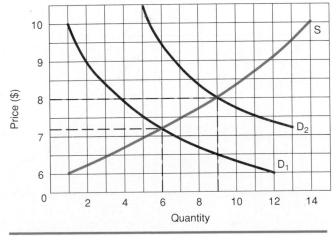

Figure 3-4

In Figure 3-5 we have a decrease in supply. Even though S_2 lies above S_1, we call this a decrease because sellers are willing to sell less at every price than they were when supply was S_1. A decrease in supply leads to a rise in price (to $8) and a decrease in the quantity sold (to 4).

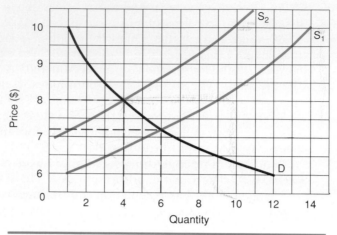

Figure 3-5

A change in supply is generally prompted by a change in the cost of production. The price of pocket calculators, color TVs, and VCRs came down quickly during the late 1970s and early 1980s for this reason. Sometimes, however, supply may be reduced by monopoly action, thereby raising price. In 1973, the OPEC nations were able to quadruple world oil prices in just a few months.

Applications of Supply and Demand

In later chapters there will be instances of price being set by supply and demand. One example would be interest rates. Interest is the price charged by the lender of money. The size of our money supply is controlled by the

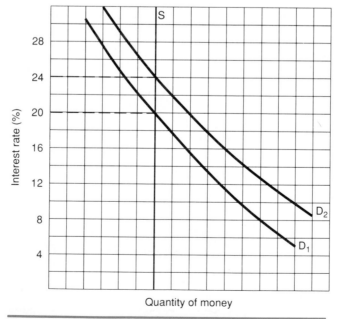

Figure 3-6

Federal Reserve. Demand reflects the credit needs of consumers, home buyers, businesses, and the federal, state, and local governments.

If the supply and demand for money were shown in Figure 3-6 as D_1 and S, how much is the interest rate? The interest rate is found on the vertical axis. First we look at where D_1 and S intersect. Then we draw a line straight across to the vertical axis. The interest rate appears to be about 20 percent.

What would happen if there was a major business expansion? Everyone would want more money—consumers, retailers, manufacturers, home buyers. If the Federal Reserve didn't increase the money supply, what would happen to the interest rate? If demand rose from D_1 to D_2, the interest rate would rise from 20 to 24 percent. This is illustrated in Figure 3-6.

In Figure 3-7 we show the effect on the interest rate of an increase in the supply of money. Starting with a money supply of S_1 and a demand for money of D, the interest rate would be 20 percent. Then the Federal Reserve raises the money supply from S_1 to S_2. This drives down the interest rate to about 14.5 percent.

When the supply curve is vertical, we call it perfectly inelastic. (The subject of elasticity will be discussed in Chapter 17.) Because the Federal Reserve is a monopolist with sole control over the money supply, when demand changes, only price will respond by changing. For example, in Figure 3-6, when demand rises from D_1 to D_2, the interest rate rises from 20 percent to 24 percent.

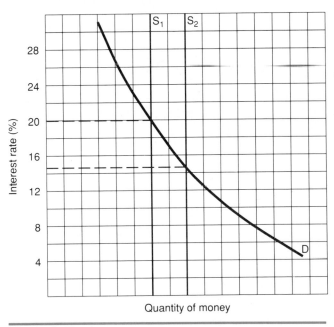

Figure 3-7

Other applications of this analysis have to do with reading graphs. Every money value is read off the vertical scale. We have already measured price and interest rates vertically. Virtually every important variable—savings, investment, consumption, GNP—will be measured vertically.

Workbook for Chapter 3

Name _____

Date _____

Fill-In Questions

1. Demand is defined as _____

_____ .

2. As price falls, the quantity demanded _____ .

3. The demand curve curves or slopes _____ .

4. Supply is defined as _____

_____ .

5. As price falls, the quantity supplied _____ .

6. The supply curve slopes or curves _____ .

7. At _____ , quantity demanded and quantity supplied are equal.

8. At the equilibrium point of a graph, the demand and supply curves _____ .

9. When quantity demanded is greater than quantity supplied, the price will _____ .

10. When quantity supplied is greater than quantity demanded, the price will _____ .

11. Price always tends toward its _____ level.

12. If demand rises and supply stays the same, price will _____ and equilibrium quantity will _____ .

13. If supply falls and demand remains the same, equilibrium price will _____ and equilibrium quantity will _____ .

14. A change in supply is generally prompted by a change in the _____ .

15. Interest rates are set by _____ and _____ .

16. What happens to interest rates when the demand for money rises? _____

17. When the supply of money falls, interest rates _____ .

Problems

1. Given the information in Table 1, draw a graph of the demand and supply curves.

2. Equilibrium price is $_____ ; equilibrium quantity is _____ . (See Figure 1.)

Table 1

Price	Quantity Demanded	Quantity Supplied
$20	1	25
19	3	24
18	6	22
17	10	18
16	16	10
15	24	2

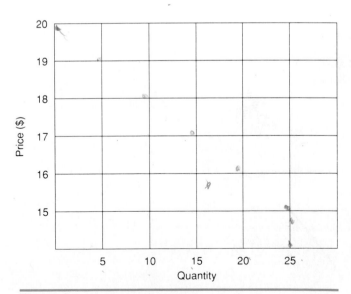

Figure 1

3. Given the information in Table 2, draw a graph of the demand and supply curves on Figure 2.

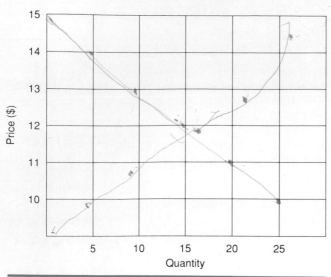

Figure 2

4. Equilibrium price is $_____; equilibrium quantity is _____.

Table 2

Price	Quantity Demanded	Quantity Supplied
$15	1	27
14	4	25
13	9	21
12	16	12
11	22	6
10	26	2

5. In Figure 3, draw a new supply curve indicating a decrease in supply. Indicate the new equilibrium price and quantity.

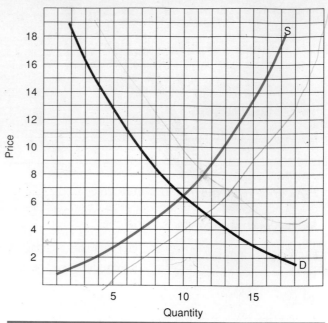

Figure 3

6. In Figure 4, draw a new demand curve indicating an increase in demand. Indicate the new equilibrium price and quantity.

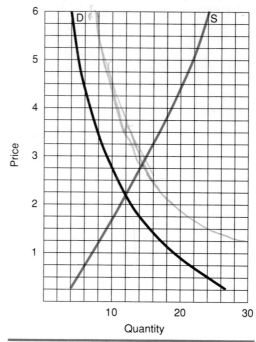

Figure 4

The Mixed Economy

Ours is a mixed economy because there is a private and a public sector. Close to 90 percent of our goods and services originate in the private sector, although the government coopts some of this production for its own use. The Soviet Union also has a mixed economy, although the public sector produces the large majority of goods and services. As we shall see, the Soviets are, to some degree, lackeys of the capitalists while Americans are, to some degree, running dogs of the Communists.

Chapter Objectives

In this chapter we'll cover:
- The concepts of the profit motive, the price mechanism, competition, and capital.
- Specialization and its consequences.
- The "isms": capitalism, fascism, communism, and socialism.

The Invisible Hand, the Price Mechanism, and Perfect Competition

Back in the 1950s there was a popular song that went:

> Love and marriage
> Love and marriage
> Go together like a horse and carriage
> Dad was told by mother
> You can't have one without the other.

Just as love and marriage go together, so do the invisible hand, the price mechanism, and perfect competition.[1] Maybe a little less catchy than the words to a popular song, it admittedly has a beat. I'd give it maybe 75—most economists kind of like to dance to it.

And like love and marriage, the invisible hand, the price mechanism, and perfect competition really do go together like a horse and carriage. In fact, you never can have one without the others.

---

[1] Perfect competition is the topic of Chapter 20. It exists only in industries in which there are many firms selling an identical product, where there are no legal, technical, or economic barriers keeping new firms from entering the industry.

The Invisible Hand

Some students go through their entire principles of economics course believing that the invisible hand is something that once grabbed them in a dark movie theater. But when Adam Smith coined the term, he was actually thinking about some kind of economic guidance system that always made everything come out all right.

In fact, he believed that if people set out to promote the public interest, they will not do nearly as much good as they would if they pursued their own selfish interests. That's right! If all people are out for themselves, everyone will work harder, produce more, and we'll all be the richer for it. And that premise underlies the free enterprise system.

Remember President Reagan? He was long a believer in supply-side economics, which placed great faith in the workings of the free enterprise system. Supply-side economics is aimed at providing people with tax-cut incentives to work, save, and invest. Instead of appealing to their sense of patriotism, supply-side economics appeals to their self-interest by letting them keep more of their earnings. One might add, parenthetically, that if all people wanted to do good, we might not have needed such strong incentives.

Perhaps the central axiom of supply-side economics is that the government's economic role has been too big. Ideally, if we reduce that role, individuals will take up the slack by performing charitable or public-spirited acts on a voluntary basis. Unfortunately, however, the response of our economy during the Reagan years was somewhat underwhelming.

In the Soviet Union, about one third of the country's food is produced on about 1 percent of the land under cultivation. That 1 percent happens to be made up of small, privately owned plots; the other 99 percent is in the form of large collective farms. Obviously the same farmers work much harder on their own land than on the land whose produce is owned by the entire society. As Adam Smith said, a person pursuing his own interest "frequently promotes that of society more effectively than when he really intends to promote it."

The invisible hand, then, is really the profit motive, or more broadly, economic self-interest, which guides us. It motivates us to do good by helping us do well.

> **The invisible hand is really the profit motive.**

The Price System

It is often said that everyone has a price. Which means that nearly all of us, for a certain sum of money, would do some pretty nasty things. The key variable here is price. Some of us would do these nasty things for $100, or $1,000, or perhaps $1 million.

Not only does every*one* have a price, but every*thing* has *its* price as well. The price of a slice of pizza or a gallon of gasoline is known to all consumers. Although they vary somewhat, gas prices never fall much below a dollar, nor would anyone pay $3 for a slice of pizza.

> **Prices send signals to producers and consumers.**

Just as prices send signals to consumers, they also signal producers or sellers. If pizza goes up to $3 a slice, I'll put an oven in my living room and open for business the next day.

The price system, which we examined in the previous chapter, is based on the law of supply and demand. When the sugar supply was curtailed about a dozen years ago, prices soared. And when people began driving less and the economy was in a recession, gasoline prices dropped in early 1982.[2]

---

[2] Not only did demand for gasoline fall in the early 1980s, but a glut of oil developed in the world market. Price declines may result, then, from declines in demand, increases in supply, or some combination of the two.

When consumers want more of a certain good or service, they drive the price up, which, in turn, signals producers to produce more. If the price rise is substantial and appears to be permanent, new firms will be attracted to the industry, thereby raising output still further.

During the 1970s, when we experienced some of the worst inflation in our history, many people called for price controls. These were very briefly and half-heartedly instituted by President Nixon, and their results in controlling inflation were decidedly mixed. Critics of controls believe that they interfere with our price mechanism and the signals that mechanism sends to producers and consumers. Others, most notably John Kenneth Galbraith, have argued that the prices of our major products are administered or set by the nation's largest corporations rather than in the marketplace. What this disagreement boils down to is whether our economic system is basically competitive, with millions of buyers and sellers interacting in the marketplace, or whether our economy is dominated by a handful of corporate giants who have subverted the price system by setting price themselves.

Competition

What is competition? Is it the rivalry between Chase and Citibank? GM and Ford? Most economists will tell you that to have real competition, you need many firms in an industry. How many? So many that no firm is large enough to have any influence over price.

When GM or Ford announces their new prices, *those* are the prices for American cars. When Bank of America, Chase, Citibank, or any of the other six or eight leading banks announces the new prime lending rate, *that* is the benchmark interest rate on which nearly every loan will be based.[3] No ifs, ands, or buts. No give and take in the marketplace. And the price mechanism? It just doesn't apply here.

Competition makes the price system work.

To allow the price mechanism to work, we need many competing firms in each industry. Would five or six U.S. auto firms be considered many? Or the 16 oil firms that refine over half the oil sold in the American market? Surely some among a handful of companies can influence price. Although there's no clear dividing line, probably most economists would consider the automobile industry at least somewhat competitive if there were 15 or 20 firms. And if there were about double the number of oil companies, that industry would also have a considerable degree of competition.

If large sectors of American industry are not very competitive, then the price system doesn't work all that well and the invisible hand becomes even more invisible. On the other hand, even without a perfectly competitive economic system, we can't just toss the price mechanism out the window. The forces of supply and demand, however distorted, are still operating. With all their price manipulation, even the largest corporations must guide themselves by the wishes of their consumers. In conclusion, then, let's just say that we have an imperfectly functioning price system in a less than competitive economy that is guided by a not too vigorous invisible hand.

---

[3] This is not to say that the nation's leading banks are free to set the prime at 50 percent, or, for that matter, at 5 percent. However, within parameters set by credit market conditions—monetary policy, credit demand, availability of funds, and inflation—the banks are free to set the prime rate.

The Circular Flow Model

In Chapter 2 we talked about the four basic resources—land, labor, capital, and entrepreneurial ability. Who owns these resources? We all do. Nearly all of us sell our labor, for which we earn wages or **salaries**. In addition, there are many people who own land or buildings for which they receive rent. A landlord may have just one tenant paying a few hundred dollars a month or he or she may own an office building whose rent is reckoned by the square foot.

We also may receive interest payments for the use of our funds. Since most of the money we put into the bank is borrowed by businesses to invest in plant and equipment, we say that interest is a return on capital.

Finally there are profits. Those who perform an entrepreneurial function, that is, own a business, receive profits for income.

The question we are asking here is: what do people do with their incomes? What happens to the tremendous accumulation of rent, wages and salaries, interest, and profit? Mostly, it is spent on consumer goods and services, which are produced by private businesses.

This is the essence of what economists call the "Circular Flow Model." Let's take this model step-by-step.

First we have some 90 million households receiving their incomes mainly from the business sector. A household may be a conventional family—a father, mother, and a couple of children, it may be a person living alone, or it may be a couple living in sin. Any combination of people under one roof— you name it—is defined as a household.

We've diagrammed the household's income stream in Figure 4–1. Businesses send money income (rent, wages and salaries, interests, and profits) to households. We've ignored the government sector (i.e., Social Security checks, welfare benefits, food stamps).

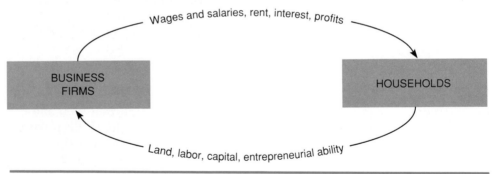

Figure 4–1
The Flow of Resources, and
Payments for Them

In Figure 4–2 we show where this money goes. It goes right back to the businesses as payment for all the goods and services that households buy. In sum, the households provide business with resources—land, labor, capital, and entrepreneurial ability—and use the income these resources earn to buy the goods and services produced by these same resources.

In effect, then, we have a circular flow of resources, income, goods and services, and payments for these goods and services. By combining Figures 4–1 and 4–2, we show this circular flow in Figure 4–3.

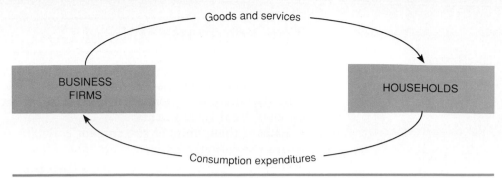

Figure 4–2
The Flow of Goods and Services, and
Payments for Them

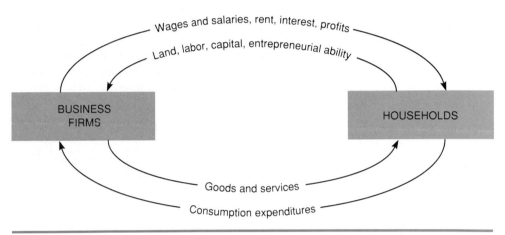

Figure 4–3
The Circular Flow

There are two circular flows.

We can distinguish two circular flows in Figure 4–3. In the inner circle we have resources (land, labor, capital, and entrepreneurial ability) flowing from households to business firms. The business firms transform these resources into goods and services, which then flow to the households.

The outer circular flow is composed of money. Households receive wages and salaries, rent, interest, and profits from business firms. This money is spent on goods and services, so it is sent back to business firms in the form of consumer expenditures.

Thus we have two circular flows: money and resources, and goods and services. These two flows respresent the economic activities of the private sector. Whenever any transaction takes place, someone pays for it which is exactly what *does* happen whenever we do business.

Although the circular flow model may appear fairly complex, it actually oversimplifies the exchanges in our economy by excluding the government. I leave it to your imagination to picture the additional flow of taxes, government purchases, and transfer payments such as unemployment and Social Security benefits. We shall now look at the government's economic role, but our analysis will be separate from our analysis of the private sector.

The Economic Role of Government

There are three levels of government.

The government under our federal system has three distinct tiers. At the top is the federal or national government, which we will generally refer to as "the government." There are also 50 state governments and tens of thousands of local governments.

Each of these units of government collects taxes, provides services, and issues regulations that have a profound effect on our economy. By taxing, spending, and regulating, the government is able to somewhat alter the outcomes of the three questions from Chapter 2—what? how? and for whom?

Some of what we produce is done in response to government demand for roads, schools, courthouses, stamp pads, and missile systems. Government regulations have prevented business firms from producing heroin, cyclamates (from the mid-1960s to the late 1970s), alcoholic beverages (from 1920 to 1933), as well as prostitutes' services (except in the state of Nevada where they are legal).

How things are produced is also influenced by child labor laws, health and safety regulations, and pollution control. And finally, the government, by taking over $800 billion away from wage earners in taxes, redistributes these funds to the old and the poor, thus strongly altering the outcome of the question for whom. In Chapter 7, we'll further consider the government's economic role.

Capital

Capital is the crucial element in every economic system. Karl Marx's classic *Das Kapital* [4] examined the role of capital in the mid-19th century industrializing economy of England. The central figure of capitalism is the capitalist, or business owner, who makes huge profits by exploiting his workers. Capitalism is denigrated by communist societies whose own economic system has been labeled "state capitalism."

Capital consists of plant and equipment.

Capital consists of plant and equipment. Marx said that whoever controlled a society's capital controlled that society. In today's economy, it takes a great deal of wealth to control much capital, so whether or not you agree with Marx's conclusions, you'd have to agree that the people who own large chunks of America's leading corporations are not exactly without influence.

Furthermore, Marx observed that one's social consciousness was determined by one's relationship to the means of production. Inevitably there would be a clash between the capitalists and the workers, leading to an overthrow of capitalism and the establishment of a communist society. Now the workers would own the means of production. In the Soviet Union, incidentally, the means of production *are* owned by the workers, but the ruling elite, the top Communist party officials, have real economic and political control.

The central economic role of capital

The role of capital in the production process is central to why our country is rich and most of the rest of the world is poor. The reason an American farmer can produce 10 or 20 times as much as a Chinese farmer is that he has much more capital with which to work—combines, tractors, harvesters, and reapers. And the reason the American factory worker is

---

[4] Karl Marx, *Das Kapital* (New York: International Publishers, 1967).

The "Isms": Capitalism, Fascism, Communism, and Socialism

Q: *What is the difference between capitalism and socialism?*

A: *Under capitalism, man exploits man. Under socialism, it's just the opposite.*

—Overheard in Warsaw*

During the 20th century perhaps no three approbriums have been hurled at more political opponents than those of Communist! Capitalist! and Fascist! Depending on where and when you lived, you might have been called any of these three. In the United States in the 1920s, it was bad to be a communist. In the 1930s and the first half of the 1940s, being a communist was acceptable in many quarters, but being a fascist was not. Although being a fascist went completely out of style in Germany and the rest of Europe by 1945, communism was "in" only in Eastern Europe. In Western Europe in the late 1940s and the 1950s, it was tolerated, but in the United States many politicians made careers by claiming to hunt down "card-carrying" communists in all walks of life. "Excuse me, m'am, may I see your card?" And heaven help you if your card was red.

All of this time, in Russia, if you were a bad guy in the 1930s and early 1940s, you were probably a fascist (except between 1939 and 1941 when the Soviet Union and Germany were nominal allies). But after 1945, the capitalists in that country became the oppressed minority, card or no card.

Enough about political freedom. Let's compare the four great economic systems.

Capitalism, as we've already seen, is characterized by private ownership of most of the means of production—that is, land, labor, capital, and entrepreneurial ability. Individuals are moved to produce by the profit motive. Production is also guided by the price system. Thus, we have millions of people competing for the consumer's dollar. The government's role in all of this is kept to a minimum; basically it ensures that everyone sticks to the rules.

Under communism, most of the roles are reversed. Instead of a guidance system of prices to direct production, there is a government planning committee that dictates what is produced, how it is produced, and for whom the goods and services are produced. The state owns and operates most of the means of production and distribution.

All the resources used must conform to the current five-year plan. Our goal is 2 million tractors, 100 million tons of steel, 15 million bushels of wheat, and so on. And so, Boris, it looks like you'll be putting in a lot of overtime.

Fascism hasn't been in vogue since Hitler's defeat in 1945, but it does provide another model of an extreme. In Nazi Germany the ownership of resources was in private hands, while the government dictated what was to be produced.

The problem with describing the facist economic model is that there really *is* no model. The means of production is left in private hands, with varying degrees of governmental interference. Generally those in power are highly nationalistic, so a high proportion of output is directed toward military goods and services.

Fascists have been virulently anticommunist, but have also been completely intolerant of any political opposition. The one-party state, suppression of economic freedom, and a militaristic orientation have been hallmarks of fascism.

The early 1940s were evidently the high watermark of fascism. Although from time to time fascist states do pop up, they appear to be a temporary phenomenon. With the possible exception of Hitler's Germany, which did put most Germans back to work after the Great Depression, albeit largely at military production, most fascist states have been economic failures that apparently collapsed of their own weight.

There are no countries today that are admittedly fascist, although Salazar's Portugal and Franco's Spain, both holdouts from the 1930s, functioned as fascist regimes until fairly recently. The military dictatorships of Africa and South America have also been likened to the fascist model, but there is nothing today to compare with Hitler's Germany or Mussolini's Italy.

Socialism has not gotten the bad press that capitalism, fascism, and communism have received, perhaps because those who dislike the socialists prefer to call them "communists." In fact, even Russian government officials refer to themselves as "socialists."

The economies of such countries as Sweden, Yugoslavia, Great Britain, and recently, France and Greece, have been described as socialist, not only by government officials in those countries, but by outside observers as well. In general, these economies have three characteristics: (1) government ownership of some of the means of production; (2) a substantial degree of government planning; and (3) a large-scale redistribution of income from the wealthy and the well-to-do to the middle class, working class, and the poor.

One of the most familiar characteristics of socialist countries is cradle-to-grave security. Medical care, education, retirement benefits, and other essential needs are guaranteed to every citizen. All you need to do is be born.

Where does the money come from to pay for all of this? It comes from taxes. Very high income taxes and inheritance taxes fall disproportionately on the upper middle class and the rich. In Israel several years ago a joke went around about a man who received an un-

(continued)

---

* Lloyd G. Reynolds, *Microeconomic Analysis and Policy*, 6th ed. (Homewood, Ill.: Richard D. Irwin, 1988), p. 435.

usually large paycheck one week. He couldn't figure out what had happened until his wife looked at his check stub and discovered he had been sent his deductions by mistake. Although only the very wealthy must give the government over half their pay in socialist countries, the story *did* have a ring of truth to it.

Rather than allow the market forces to freely function, socialist governments sometimes resort to very elaborate planning schemes. And since the government usually owns the basic industries and provides the basic services, this planning merely has one hand directing the other.

Sweden is often considered the archetypical socialist country, although perhaps 90 percent of the country's industry is privately owned. It is the government's massive intervention in the private economy that gives it its socialist tone. Not only has the government kept the un-

employment rate generally below 3 percent for several decades by offering industry and workers a series of subsidies and incentives, but the Swedish government provides one of the most elaborate cradle-to-grave programs in the world. The government doles out financial allowances for each child, and provides day-care centers, free education from nursery school through college, free medical care, and very generous unemployment and retirement benefits.

Of course taxes are very high in Sweden. Critics of the Swedish system have questioned whether the high tax rates haven't hurt work incentives. But even if they have, Sweden not only has one of the most equal income distributions in the world, but it also has one of the highest living standards. So they must be doing something right.

more productive than the Brazilian factory worker is that our factories are much better equipped. We have a tremendous stock of computers, assembly lines, warehouses, machine tools, and so on.

Take the example of the word processor. In the past, a lot of business letters had to be personally or individually typed, although they were really only form letters. Today we have a word processor that can be programmed to type out identical texts with different addressees at better than a letter a minute.

Our stock of capital enables us to turn out many more goods per hour of labor than we could produce without it. Much of the backbreaking as well as tedious labor has been eliminated by machines. Without our capital, we would have the same living standard as that of people throughout Asia, Africa, and Latin America.

Where did capital come from?

Where did capital come from? Essentially from savings. Some people would set aside part of their savings, go into business, and purchase plant and equipment. But we're really skipping a step.

Initially there was no capital, except for some crude plows and other farm tools. People worked from sunrise to sunset just to produce enough food to put on the table. But a few farmers, a little more prosperous than their neighbors, were able to spare some time to build better farm tools. Or they might have had enough food stored away to employ someone to build these tools. Either way, some productive resources were diverted from producing consumer goods to capital goods.

Factory conditions of the 19th century England that Marx described in *Das Kapital* were barbaric, but the end result was that a surplus of consumer goods was produced. The factory owner, by paying his workers meager wages, was able to use this surplus to buy more capital goods. These enabled his factory to be that much more productive, creating still greater surpluses that were used to purchase still more plant and equipment.

Under Joseph Stalin, the Russians devoted a large part of their production to capital goods, literally starving the Russian population of consumer goods. One interesting quarrel the average Russian has with the Poles today is that the Poles live better. Why then was the Solidarity party striking and making all those demands? One thing Solidarity wanted was more consumer goods. The Polish government wanted to turn out more capital goods. But the average Russian couldn't see what all the complaining was about.

Capital then is the key to every society's standard of living. In the late 1980s, as our productivity and economic growth continued to lag, economists pointed to our slow rate of capital growth as the basic problem. But are Americans any more willing than the Poles to accept a lower living standard while production is diverted from consumer goods to capital goods?

The world's developing nations face nearly insurmountable obstacles— rapidly growing populations and very little plant and equipment. The experience of the industrializing nations in the 19th century was that as people moved into the cities from the countryside and as living standards rose, the birthrate invariably declined. But for industrialization to take place, capital must be built up. There are two ways to do this: cut consumption or raise production. Unfortunately, most developing nations are already at subsistence levels, so no further cuts in consumption are possible without causing even greater misery. And production cannot easily be raised without at least some plant and equipment.

With the exception of the OPEC nations, which have been able to sell their oil in exchange for plant and equipment, the poorer nations of Africa, Asia, and Latin America have little hope of rising from extreme poverty.[5] An exchange of letters, which supposedly took place between Mao Tse-tung and Nikita Khrushchev when China and the Soviet Union were allies in the early 1960s, illustrates the futility of a third way out—foreign aid.

Mao: Send us machinery and equipment.

Khrushchev: Tighten your belts.

Mao: Send us some belts.

Specialization and Its Consequences

Specialization and Exchange

In Chapter 2, we discussed specialization as exemplified by Adam Smith's pin factory. When people specialize, they are usually far more productive than if they attempt to be jacks-of-all-trades. Doctors, lawyers, accountants, engineers, and, of course, college professors, all specialize.

If all of us become really good at something and concentrate on that one specialty, we will produce much more than if we try to do everything. A family that tries to be self-sufficient will have a relatively low standard of living because it takes a lot of time to do the hundreds of things that need to be done—all on an individual basis. Imagine not just making your own pins, but weaving your own cloth, growing all your food, and building your own means of transportation. Think how many hours it would take you to weave a yard of cloth when you could buy it in the store for a couple of dollars.

Specialization is fine only if there is a demand for your specialty. One way there would be a demand for what you make or do is if you can trade with someone who has what you want. This is called barter. Today we use money to facilitate exchange. Thus, instead of having to find someone who

---

[5] Many of these less developed countries have only one or two primary exports, usually agricultural products, with which to obtain foreign exchange. Furthermore, most are deeply in debt to banks in developed countries as well as to foreign governments and international lending organizations.

Where Capital Comes from

The following hypothetical situation will illustrate the value of capital. Suppose it takes a man 10 hours to make an optical lens, while someone working with a machine can make one in just 5 hours. Let's assume that it would take 1,000 hours to build such a machine.

Assume, however, that a person working 10 hours a day is barely able to support himself and his family. (Karl Marx observed that in most working-class families, not only did wives work, but they didn't have to worry about day-care centers for the children because factories employed six and seven-year olds.) If he could not afford to spend 100 days (1,000 hours) building the machine, he still had two choices. He could cut back on his consumption—that is, lower his family's standard of living—by working nine hours a day on the lenses and one hour a day on building the machine. Or he could work, say, an extra hour a day on the machine.

In either case, it would take 1,000 days to build the machine. If he cut back on his consumption *and* worked an extra hour a day, it would take him 500 days to build the machine.

Once he had the machine, he'd really be in business. He could double his daily output from one lens a day to two a day (remember that a person working with a machine can turn out a lens in just five hours).

Each day, if he held his consumption to the same level, he would produce two lenses, and sell one for food, rent, and other necessities. The other lens he'd save. At the end of just 100 days, he'd have saved 100 lenses. Those 100 lenses represent 1,000 hours of labor, which is exactly the same amount of labor that went into building a machine. He would probably be able to buy another machine with his 100 lenses.

Now he's really a capitalist! He'll hire someone to run the second machine and pay him a lens a day. And in another 100 days, he'll have a surplus of 200 lenses and he'll be able to buy two more machines, hire a foreman to run his shop, retire to a condominium in Miami Beach at the age of 36, and be the richest kid on the block.

---

has what you want and wants what you have, all you need to do is buy what you want and find someone to buy what you have.

Barter, unlike buying something for money, can get pretty complicated. When we use money, we can pay for something and be out of the store in a minute. But when one needs to barter, one can be there all day trying to think of something that one has that the storekeeper will accept as payment.

Without money, very little exchange; without exchange, no specialization.

The lack of money obviously inhibits trade, or exchange, and without exchange, people can't specialize. Imagine calling someone to fix your air conditioner and trying to pay this person with piano lessons, a psychotherapy session, or by correcting their overbite or fixing their transmission? It's much easier to specialize when you don't have to buy from the same person who buys from you.

Specialization and Alienation

Many factory workers have become little better than cogs in some huge industrial wheel. People whose sole function is to tighten a couple of bolts or place front right fenders on auto bodies eight hours a day for most of their lives understandably get a little bored. Some express their unhappiness by frequent absences, while some, like the workers in a Chevy Vega plant in Lordstown, Ohio, many years ago, actually sabotaged some of the cars they were assembling.

In a book simply titled *Working*, Studs Terkel used a tape recorder to interview hundreds of American workers. Here's what a spotwelder in a Chicago Ford auto assembly plant said about his work.

> I stand in one spot, about a two- or three-feet area, all night. The only time a person stops is when the line stops. We do about thirty-two jobs per car, per unit. Forty-eight units an hour, eight hours a day. Thirty-two times forty-eight times eight. Figure it out. That's how many times I push that button.[6]

---

[6] Studs Terkel, *Working* (New York: Avon Books, 1972), pp. 221–222.

One of the problems here is that the workers never see the product of their labor. Attempts have been made in Western Europe, particularly in Sweden and Japan, to involve the workers in making a larger segment of the product. Some degree of specialization is sacrificed in an effort to bolster employee morale. Although these new production modes have been successful, American factories have made only a few tentative efforts in this area.

No one seems to be asking what we can do to make jobs more interesting. Why must clerical workers do repetitive tasks instead of switching off with one another? Perhaps the classic boring job is that of elevator operator. Let's face it: being enclosed in a box riding up and down all day long is enough to drive anyone up a wall. Maybe my observations are not completely accurate, but most of these people seem ready to jump out of their skins. Couldn't they be given desk jobs for half the day and let the deskbound people ride the elevators—or be given the shaft, as they say in the trade when they're not saying the job has its ups and downs—thereby keeping everybody at least half happy and half sane?

A developed or industrial economy must necessarily have most of the features we have discussed in this chapter. Obviously a huge capital stock is required and a fairly large government sector is inevitable. Specialization is also inevitable, but worker alienation could probably be avoided, at least to a greater degree than it has been in this country.

Workbook for Chapter 4

Name _____

Date _____

Multiple-Choice Questions

Circle the letter that corresponds to the best answer.

1. We have a mixed economy because
a. we produce guns and butter **b.** we consume domestically produced goods as well as imports **c.** we consume both goods and services **d.** there is a private sector and a public sector

2. Which does not fit with the others?
a. competition **b.** government planning and regulation **c.** the invisible hand **d.** the price mechanism

3. Adam Smith believed that the best way to promote the public interest was to
a. have the government produce most goods and services **b.** let people pursue their own selfish interests **c.** wait for individuals to set out to promote the public interest **d.** get rid of the price mechanism

4. Supply-side economists believe that cutting taxes will
a. hurt the economy **b.** give people an incentive to work, save, and invest **c.** have little or no economic effect **d.** help during recessions, but be less effective than government spending increases

5. In the Soviet Union
a. the most productive plots of land are privately owned **b.** there is no private ownership of agricultural land **c.** private plots produce more food than collective farms **d.** there is more privately owned land than government-owned land

6. Adam Smith believed that people are guided by all of the following except
a. the profit motive **b.** self-interest **c.** the public good **d.** the invisible hand

7. The price system is based on
a. government regulation (i.e., the government sets most prices) **b.** the individual whim of the business person who sets it **c.** the feelings of the individual buyer **d.** supply and demand

8. Which statement is true?
a. American industry is very competitive. **b.** There is no competition in American industry. **c.** To have competition you need to have many firms in an industry. **d.** American banking is a good example of a competitive industry.

9. In the United States, resources are owned by
a. the government **b.** business firms **c.** individuals **d.** foreigners

10. Most of the money that people receive as incomes
a. goes to the government in taxes **b.** is saved **c.** is spent on consumer goods and services **d.** is unaccounted for

11. Wages, rent, interest, and profits flow from
a. business firms to households **b.** households to business firms **c.** business firms to the government **d.** the government to business firms

12. The government performs each of the following economic functions except
a. collecting taxes **b.** spending **c.** issuing regulations **d.** operating the price mechanism

13. Private ownership of most of the means of production is common to
a. capitalism and communism **b.** capitalism and fascism **c.** capitalism and socialism **d.** fascism and communism

14. The price mechanism is least important under

a. capitalism **b.** socialism **c.** fascism **d.** communism

15. The five-year plan has been the main economic plan of

a. the United States **b.** Sweden **c.** Nazi Germany **d.** the USSR

16. Fascism peaked in the

a. 1920s **b.** 1930s **c.** 1940s **d.** 1950s

17. The strongest criticism of Sweden's economic system has been that

a. it provides too many benefits **b.** its taxes are too high **c.** its taxes are too low **d.** it doesn't provide enough benefits

18. The strongest indictment of the capitalist system was written by

a. Adam Smith **b.** John Maynard Keynes **c.** Rose D. Cohen **d.** Karl Marx

19. Karl Marx said that

a. whoever controlled a society's capital controlled that society **b.** in the long run capitalism would survive **c.** the USSR's communist system was "state capitalism" **d.** capitalists and workers generally had the same economic intersts

20. The main reason the American farmer can produce more than the farmer in China is that he

a. has more land **b.** has more capital **c.** has more labor **d.** is better trained

21. Capital came from

a. gold **b.** savings **c.** high consumption **d.** the government

22. All modern economies depend on

a. alienation **b.** government ownership of the means of production **c.** free enterprise **d.** specialization

23. Alienation is one result of

a. exchange **b.** overspecialization **c.** underspecialization **d.** self-sufficiency

24. An individual can build up his/her capital by

a. working longer hours only **b.** cutting back on consumption only **c.** both cutting back on consumption and working longer hours **d.** only by borrowing

Fill-in Questions

1. The invisible hand is generally associated with (1) the _____ and (2) _____.

2. Adam Smith believed that if people set out to promote the public interest, they will not do nearly as much good as they will if they _____.

3. Supply-side economists believe that the way to provide people with incentives to work, save, and invest is to _____.

4. Supply-side economists feel that the government's economic role is _____.

5. In the Soviet Union most of the farmland is in the form of _____.

6. Under private enterprise, production is guided by _____.

7. The price system is based on the law of _____.

8. Critics feel that price controls interfere with the _____.

9. Under competition there are so many firms that no firm is large enough to _____.

10. According to the circular flow, businesses send money income to _____.

11. _____provide business firms with resources.

12. The four resources are (1) _____; (2) _____; (3) _____; and (4) _____.

13. We have two circular flows: (1) _____ and (2) _____.

14. Under our federal system there are three distinct tiers of government: (1) _____; (2) _____; and (3) _____.

15. The three powers of government— (1) to _____; (2) to _____; and (3) to _____ —have enabled it to somewhat alter the outcomes of the three questions from Chapter 2: What? How? and For whom?

16. _____ reached its peak during the first half of the 1940s in Germany and other parts of Europe.

17. Under communism, what is produced is dictated by a _____.

18. The economies of Sweden and Great Britain have been described as conforming to _____.

19. Our economic system would be an example of _____.

20. Capital consists of (1) _____ and (2) _____.

21. Technically, the means of production in the Soviet Union are owned by _____.

22. The role of _____ in the production process is central to why our country is rich and most of the rest of the world is poor.

23. Capital originally came from _____.

24. Karl Marx described working conditions in _____. How were factory owners able to accumulate savings? _____.

25. Modern economies all need to have specialization and _____.

26. Worker boredom and alienation is a consequence of _____.

Gross National Product

When was the last time someone said to you, "Mine is bigger than yours"? My *what* is bigger than your *what!* My GNP is bigger than your GNP? Well, it just so happens that our country's GNP is bigger than everyone else's. Even Japan's. Or Russia's. Gross national product, or GNP, measures a country's output over a year—which means that the United States produces more goods and services every year than any other nation in the world.

Chapter Objectives
When you have finished this chapter you will know the answers to these questions:
- What is GNP?
- How is it measured?
- What are the National Income Accounts?
- What is the difference between GNP and real GNP?
- What are the shortcomings of GNP as a measure of national economic well-being?

What Is Gross National Product?

Definition of GNP

When Ed Koch was running for Congress and later for mayor of New York, he always asked, "How'm I doin?" (Translation from New Yorkese: "How am I doing?") A nation might ask, "How big is my GNP?"

What is GNP? It is the *nation's expenditure on all the goods and services produced during the year at market prices.* For example, if we spent $8,000 per car on 7 million American cars, that $56 billion would go into GNP. We'd add in the 10 billion Big Macs at $1.80 for another $18 billion and the 1,600,000 new homes at $80,000 each for $128 billion. Then, for good measure, we'd add the 5 billion visits to doctors' offices at $40 apiece for $200 billion and the 16 billion disco admissions at $10 each for $160 billion. Add it all up and we'd get something around $4.5 trillion in 1987.

I'm throwing a lot of numbers at you—millions, billions, and trillions. The next box provides a lucid explanation of how to deal with these numbers, so if you don't know your billions from your trillions, go over "A

Word about Numbers." Or, in the immortal words of the Barbados Family Planning Association, "Better safe than sorry."[1]

How GNP is Measured

There are two basic ways of measuring GNP: the flow-of-income approach and the expenditures approach. Both are illustrated in Figure 5–1.

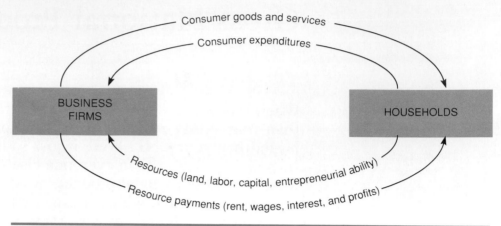

Figure 5–1

Two Ways of Measuring GNP

We're now ready to measure GNP. There are two ways of doing this: the flow-of-income approach, which shows us who gets the money that is spent; and the expenditures approach; which shows what the money buys. To make all of this more exciting, we'll use actual data from 1987. Unfortunately, these numbers will be out of date by the time you read this. Ah, well, you can't win em all.

A. Flow-of-Income Approach

Economics is said by many to be a boring subject, so one would be hard put to find more than a smattering of accountants and perhaps a handful of demented economists who would find themselves even mildly aroused by a perusal of the national income accounts. Of the two types of national income accounting that we'll take up, the flow-of-income approach is considerably more boring than the expenditure approach. Now that I've whetted your appetite, here goes.

Nearly all our goods and services are produced by business firms. The firms pay people wages to get them to turn out these goods and services. Those who own the land and buildings used are paid rent and those who supply the capital are paid interest. Add up all the goods and services produced and you have GNP. Or, alternatively, add up the incomes received by the factors of production (plus a couple of other things we'll be talking about) and you also have GNP.

The flow-of-income approach to GNP is shown in the bottom part of Figure 5–1. Households provide business firms with resources (land, labor, capital, and entrepreneurial ability) and are paid by business firms in the form of rent, wages and salaries, interest, and profits.

---

[1] That actually *is* the informal motto of the Barbados Family Planning Association. Incidentally, Barbados has one of the most successful family planning programs in the developing world, if that sort of thing interests you.

A Word About Numbers

The time has come to talk about numbers—big numbers. We need to keep our thousands, millions, billions, and trillions straight, so I've devised a little test. This will help you gauge what you know and don't know. And by the time you finish this section, believe me, you will know.

I'd like you to express some numbers in words. I'll do the first one.

(a) 1,591 <u>One thousand five-hundred and ninety-one</u>

(b) 4,338,500,000 _____

(c) 468,374 _____

(d) 2,847,600,000,000 _____

(e) 216,129,000 _____

You'll find the answers at the end of the box. But don't look yet—I have a few more problems for you. Okay, I'll do the first one—then you do the rest. This time we translate words into numbers.

(f) Seventy-six billion, three hundred million
76,300,000,000 _____

(g) Two-hundred nineteen thousand, four hundred
_____

(h) Six trillion _____

(i) Forty-five million, three hundred and eighty-eight thousand _____

Summary

(1) Thousands come after the first comma: for example, 17,000 (seventeen thousand); 391,000, (three-hundred ninety-one thousand).

(2) Millions come after the second comma: for example, 6,000,000 (six million); 410,000,000 (four-hundred ten million).

(3) Billions come after the third comma: for example, 924,500,000,000 (nine-hundred twenty-four billion, five million); 86,000,000,000 (eighty-six billion).

(4) Trillions come after the fourth comma: for example, 31,000,000,000,000 (thirty-one trillion); 570,000,000,000,000 (570 trillion).

(i) 45,388,000

(h) 6,000,000,000,000

(g) 219,400

(e) two hundred sixteen million, one hundred twenty-nine thousand

(d) two trillion, eight-hundred forty-seven billion, six hundred million

(c) four-hundred sixty-eight thousand, three hundred and seventy-four

(b) four billion, three-hundred thirty-eight million, five-hundred thousand

Answers

GNP − Depreciation = NNP

Now we come to the fun part. Many economists are unhappy with the concept of gross national product. It's simply too gross. They like net national product a lot better. What's the difference, you ask? Depreciation. *Gross national product − Depreciation = Net national product.*

GNP includes, among other things, several hundred billion dollars worth of plant and equipment spending. This is money spent on new office buildings, shopping malls, factories, stores, assembly lines, office machines, computers, and a host of other machinery and equipment.

Why are we so anxious to get rid of depreciation? Depreciation represents the machinery, equipment, and buildings (plant and equipment) that have worn out or become obsolete over the course of the year. Usually these are replaced with new plant and equipment, but this doesn't represent a net gain because we end up right back where we started. For example, if a firm has eight machines and replaces three that wore out during the year, it still has eight machines.

Similarly, when we measure a nation's GNP, one of the things we are counting is the replacement of plant and equipment, which can lead us to some dubious conclusions about a nation's economic well-being. For example, suppose that Sweden and Canada each has a GNP of 200, but depreciation in Sweden is 50, while in Canada it is only 30. The NNP of Sweden would be 150 (GNP of 200 − Depreciation of 50); Canada's NNP would be 170 (GNP of 200 − Depreciation of 30). We've worked out a more elaborate example in the next box.

Why NNP Is Better than GNP

Although GNP is the measure commonly used when people talk about national output, most economists prefer NNP. Why? Because it allows for depreciation of plant and equipment. Let's illustrate this with two hypothetical countries in the table below:

North Atlantis		South Atlantis	
GNP	500	GNP	500
− Depreciation	50	− Depreciation	100
	450		400

We see that North Atlantis and South Atlantis had identical GNP's, but that North Atlantis had depreciation of $50 billion while South Atlantis' depreciation was $100 billion.* Consequently, North Atlantis ended up with an NNP of $450 billion, while South Atlantis had an NNP of just $400 billion.

This distinction is very important. North and South Atlantis had the same GNP, but North Atlantis' NNP was $50 billion greater than that of South Atlantis. Why? Because South Atlantis had to replace $100 billion of worn-out or obsolete plant and equipment that year while North Atlantis had to replace just $50 billion of plant and equipment.

* Economists use this shorthand way of writing billions (e.g., 50 = $50 billion; 100 = $100 billion.)

In the early 1930s Babe Ruth held out for $52,000. A reporter asked him if it would be fair for a baseball player to earn more than Herbert Hoover, the President of the United States. "I had a better year than he did," the Babe replied. And so, we too may ask, who had a better year—North or South Atlantis? Based on GNP, they did equally well; based on NNP, North Atlantis did better.

South Atlantis had a lower NNP because it had to devote twice as much production to replacing worn-out and obsolete plant and equipment as did North Atlantis. When you are devoting such a large portion of your resources to replacing plant and equipment, these resources can't go toward adding to your stock of plant and equipment, or for that matter, to producing consumer goods and services.

Suppose North Atlantis devoted that extra $50 billion to production of additional plant and equipment. It would now have $50 billion worth of additional plant and equipment. Or, if it had produced $50 billion worth of consumer goods and services, its citizens would have enjoyed a much higher standard of living.

So who *did* enjoy a better year? Virtually every economist would tell you that North Atlantis did because it had a higher NNP. Stated differently, it's not as significant to know how much a country grossed as to know how much it netted.

When we make comparisons between countries or when we compare national output for a given country from year to year, we would do well to use NNP. Three additional measures, national income, personal income, and disposable personal income, will be considered in turn.

NNP − Indirect business taxes = National income

From net national product we're going to go to national income. To do so we need to subtract indirect business taxes from net national product. *Net national product − Indirect business taxes = National income.*

What are indirect business taxes? They're taxes that businesses tack on to the prices they charge us. The three main indirect business taxes are general sales taxes, excise taxes, and business property taxes. These are all indirect taxes because they are not paid directly by private individuals, even though they do come out of our pockets by being included in the prices we pay.

Direct taxes

A direct tax is a tax with your name on it. It's a tax on a person. Your personal income tax is one example. Corporate income tax is another; corporations are legal persons. (You don't sue the stockholders of a corporation; you sue the corporation itself.)

Indirect taxes

Indirect business taxes are mainly sales and excise taxes; they are levied on things rather than people. In a sense, a direct tax must be paid—it literally has your name on it—but an indirect tax can sometimes be avoided. For example, if you buy goods in a state with no sales tax, you avoid that tax. Or if you don't buy cigarettes, gasoline, or tires, you won't have to pay those excise taxes.

Now it gets a little easier. We've got a couple of pictures to look at. Figure 5-2 shows how we get from GNP to NNP, and from NNP to national income.

Read

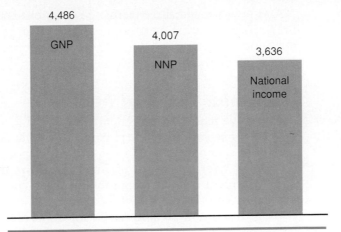

Figure 5–2
GNP, NNP, and National Income, 1987
($ billions)

Source: 1988 *Economic Report of the President,*
p. 272.

Figure 5–3 shows the four components of national income. National income is the income earned by the four basic economic resources or factors of production—land, labor, capital, and entrepreneurial ability. These incomes are: rent, wages and salaries, interest, and profits. Wages and salaries, which is by far the largest slice in Figure 5–3, is generally close to two thirds of national income.

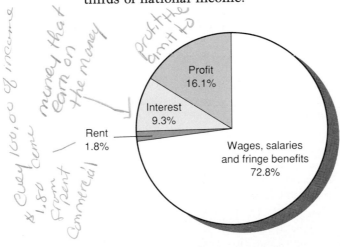

National income (total): $3,637

Figure 5–3
Distribution of National Income, 1987
($ billions)

Source: 1988 *Economic Report of the President,*
pp. 274–75.

Personal Income

To go from national income to personal income, we have to subtract two items and add three others. First we subtract corporate profits because these belong to the corporations rather than to private individuals. The other item subtracted is contributions made by employers and employees for social insurance (nearly all of which is, of course, Social Security).

And now we add three items: government transfer payments (mainly Social Security checks), net interest paid by the government and consumers, and dividends. After we make these two subtractions and three additions, we are left with personal income.

Disposable Personal Income

Once you've paid all your federal, state, and local taxes out of your personal income, what you have left is your disposable personal income. That's yours—to spend or save. For the nation, disposable personal income is usually a little over two thirds of GNP. It follows that since Americans spend over 90 percent of their disposable personal incomes, consumption is a little less than two thirds of GNP.

We're ready now to summarize all of the items included in the flow-of-income approach to GNP. This is done in Table 5–2, which brings us from 1987 GNP all the way down to disposable personal income. From a GNP of $4.5 trillion, we get a disposable personal income of $3.2 trillion.

Table 5–2
The National Income Accounts, 1987
($ billions)

Gross national product	4,486.2
Less: Depreciation	479.4
Equals: Net national product	4,006.8
Less: Indirect business taxes	367.6
Business transfer payments	23.2
Statistical discrepency	−6.8
Plus: Subsidies less current surplus of government enterprises	13.1
Equals: National income	3,635.9
Less: Corporate profits	305.3
Net interest	336.7
Contributions for social insurance	394.4
Plus: Government transfer payments to persons	519.8
Personal interest income	515.8
Personal dividend income	87.5
Business transfer payments	23.2
Equals: Personal income	3,745.8
Less: Personal taxes	564.7
Equals: Disposable personal income	3,181.1

Source: 1988 *Economic Report of the President,*
pp. 272–273, 278.

B. The Expenditures Approach

This approach will be used in the next few chapters. People buy consumer goods from business firms and pay for them. Notice that we also have a circular flow of expenditures and income by connecting the top and bottom loops of Figure 5–1. People receive incomes from business firms for their land, labor, and capital. This money flows right back to the firms in exchange for consumer goods and services. Hence the money keeps flowing around and around as more goods are produced and paid for.

We've excluded business investment expenditures and government expenditures until now. If we included them with consumer expenditures, they would add up to GNP: *Consumer expenditures + Investment expenditures + Government expenditures = GNP.*

GNP then represents spending by three major groups, the largest of which is consumers, who spend two out of every three dollars of GNP. Consumption spending is designated by the letter C.

The big three spenders of
GNP

Business firms spend hundreds of billions of dollars on plant, equipment, and inventory. We call this sector "Investment" and use the letter I to represent it.

And finally if we add up all the spending on goods and services by the federal, state, and local governments, we have government expenditures, which is represented by the letter G.

C, I, and G are the big three with respect to spending in our economy. They are so important that the next three chapters of this book are devoted to them: Chapters 6, 7, and 8 deal with the government, business, and consumption sectors, respectively.

Let's return once more to our GNP equation. We need to add net exports, which we'll designate by X_n:

GNP equation

$$GNP = C + I + G + X_n$$

There is one more variable that goes into GNP: net exports. *Net exports = Exports − Imports.* If we subtracted all the money we spend on foreign goods and services from what foreigners spend on our goods and services, we'd get net exports. This number then represents the difference between what we sell to foreigners and what they sell to us.

Until recently most economists more or less ignored the last item in the GNP equation, net exports. This figure, while positive, was usually less than 1 percent of GNP. More significantly, from the end of World War II to the early 1980s, net exports was a positive figure in every year until 1971.

In 1971 we ran a trade deficit of $2 billion. By 1987, our net exports totaled −$159 billion, with large deficits predicted for the next few years. The strong dollar, weak foreign demand, and a buying binge by American consumers all contributed to our huge negative balance of trade.[2]

Two Things Not Counted in GNP

From time to time we will go back to the definition of GNP: *the nation's expenditure on all the goods and services produced during the year at market prices.* Only "final" goods and services are counted. These include those goods and services purchased by their ultimate consumers. They are represented by the variables in our equation:

$$GNP = C + I + G + X_n$$

Substituting 1987 data for these variables, we get:

$$4,486.2 = 2,966.0 + 716.4 + 923.8 - 119.9 \quad [3]$$

Two Things to Avoid When Compiling GNP

There are two common mistakes made when GNP is compiled. First we'll talk about multiple counting, that is, counting a particular good at each state of production. Then we'll look at the exclusion of transfer payments. In a word, we count each good or service only once and we don't count transfer payments as part of GNP.

---

[2] Chapter 29 is devoted to the topic of foreign trade. I deal there with the whys and wherefores of our negative balance of trade at much greater length.

[3] If you add $C + I + G + X_n$, you'll get 4,486.3. Why are we $.1 billion (or $100 million) off? Because of how C, I, G, and X_n were rounded. This is a minor point, but if you're a perfectionist, you probably wanted an explanation of why these figures did not add up exactly.

A. Multiple Counting

We need to avoid multiple counting when we compile GNP. Only expenditures on final products—what consumers, businesses, and government units buy for their own use—belong in GNP. This is easily illustrated by the journey made by wheat from the farm until it appears as bread in the supermarket.

The farmer gets about 2 cents for the wheat that goes into a loaf of bread. This wheat is ground into flour at a mill and is now worth, say, 4 cents. When it is placed in 100-pound packages, it is worth 5 cents, and when it is shipped to a bakery, it is worth 10 cents. Baked bread is worth 20 cents, packaged baked bread is worth 23 cents, and bread delivered to the supermarket is worth 35 cents. The supermarket sells it for 55 cents.

How much of this goes into GNP? Do we add up the 2 cents, 4 cents, 5 cents, 10 cents, 20 cents, 23 cents, 35 cents, and 55 cents? No! That would be multiple counting. We count only what is spent on a final good, 55 cents, which is paid by the consumer. Of this entire process, only 55 cents goes into GNP.

GNP, then, counts only what we spend on final goods and services—not those of an intermediate nature. We are not interested in the money spent on wheat or flour, but only that which the buyer of the final product, bread, spends at the supermarket. If we counted intermediate goods, we would greatly inflate GNP by counting the same goods and services over and over again.

An alternate way of measuring GNP would be the value-added approach. The farmer grows 2 cents worth of wheat, to which the flour mill adds 2 cents by grinding the wheat into flour and 1 cent by packaging it. The shipper adds 5 cents by getting that flour to the bakery. The baker adds 10 cents by baking the flour into bread and 3 cents more by packaging it. The person who delivers the bread to the supermarket adds another 12 cents to the value of the bread and finally, the supermarket, by providing a convenient location for the sale of the bread, adds 20 cents. If you sum up the value added by each stage—2 cents + 2 cents + 1 cent + 5 cents + 10 cents + 3 cents + 12 cents + 20 cents—you should get 55 cents. If you didn't, you better get a new battery for your calculator. Or, if you did it in your head, perhaps your own battery is beginning to run down.

Just as we don't include intermediate goods in GNP, we don't count used goods either. If you buy a used car, a 10-year old house, or virtually anything from a flea market, your purchase does not go into GNP. Remember, we count only final goods and services that were purchased in the current year.

B. Treatment of Transfer Payments

Transfer payments don't go directly into GNP.

At first glance, transfer payments appear to belong in GNP. When the government issues a social security or unemployment insurance check, isn't this a form of government spending? Shouldn't it be part of G, like defense spending or the salaries paid to government employees?

GNP includes only payments for goods and services produced this year. A person receiving a social security check is not being reimbursed for producing a good or service this year. But a government clerk or a defense contractor *is* providing a good or service this year, and would therefore be included under government purchases, designated by the letter "G."

Because Social Security, public assistance, Medicare, Medicaid, and other government transfer payments—which now comprise over half the federal budget—are not payments for currently produced goods and services, they are not included in GNP. However, those who receive these payments will spend nearly all of that money, so, ultimately, they will go toward GNP in the form of consumer spending. Note that consumer spending does involve the purchase of goods and services produced in the current year.

Financial transactions don't go into GNP.

Something else not counted in GNP is financial transactions. The purchase of corporate stocks and bonds does not add anything to GNP. Isn't that an investment? It certainly is from an individual's point of view, but in strictly economic terms the purchase of corporate stocks and bonds, government securities, real estate, and other financial assets does not constitute investment because it does not represent the purchase of new plant and equipment. But aren't these funds used to buy new plant and equipment? Perhaps. If so, at that time we'll count that purchase as investment and therefore as part of GNP.

GNP versus Real GNP

Suppose you have a birthday party every year and have the same three guests, and every year you send out to the same pizza store for a large pie with everything. Pretty wild, eh? In 1980 the pie cost you $4.00; in 1981, $4.50; in 1982, $5.25; and in 1983, $6.00. Since the pie is exactly the same size each year, the only thing that got bigger was its price. It's the same way with real GNP (the pie) and GNP (the price of the pie).

To make year-to-year GNP comparisons we have to get rid of inflation.

If we wanted to compare our national economic pie, or total production (real GNP), from one year to the next, we would have to get rid of inflation. For example, the pizza pie that cost us $4 in 1980 cost us $6 in 1983. But we were getting exactly the same amount of pizza.

If our economy produced the same amount of output in 1983 as it did in 1980, then real GNP did not change. Prices may have gone up 50 percent (from $4 to $6), but we're still producing exactly the same amount of pizza.

To understand the concept of real GNP, you're going to need to calculate percentage changes. Here's one virtually all my students (and quite of few of my fellow economists) get wrong. If a number is tripled, by what percentage has it increased? Go ahead and try to figure it out.

Solution: Pick any number. An easy one is 100. Triple it. You have 300. Now find the percentage change.

Have you figured it out? Did you get 200 percent? If you did, then you might be able to skip the box that shows how to calculate percentage changes. If you're at all shaky on how to do this, this box will be so helpful it will probably change your life.

GNP is the basic measure of how much we produced in a given year. However, comparisons of GNP from one year to the next could be misleading. For example, say that GNP goes from 3 trillion in 1982 to 3.3 trillion in 1983. At first, it appears that we have done extremely well since GNP leapt by 10 percent. But before we get too excited, we should remember that GNP is a measure of all the goods and services produced during a given year *at market prices*. For all we know, perhaps the entire 10 percent increase in GNP was due to inflation. This would obviously be the case if prices *did* rise by 10 percent in 1983.

The GNP deflator

We need to be able to correct GNP for price increases so we can measure how much actual production really rose. To do this we use the GNP deflator, which is calculated quarterly by the Department of Commerce. The GNP deflator is really a price index, like the consumer price index, and it is used to measure price changes in the items that go into GNP (i.e., consumer goods and services, investment goods, and government goods and services).

Let's go back to the problem we posed earlier: GNP rises from $3 trillion in 1982 to $3.3 trillion in 1983. We need to deflate 1983's GNP to find out how much production rose. In other words, if GNP was $3 trillion in 1982,

Calculating Percentage Changes

When we go from 100 to 120, that's an increase of 20 percent. From 150 to 200 is an increase of 33⅓ percent. When we go from 50 to 25, that's a percentage decline of 50 percent. How do we know? We use this formula:

$$\% \text{ change} = \frac{\text{Change}}{\text{Original number}}$$

Using the first example, from 100 to 120 is a change of 20, and since our original number is 100, we have 20/100. Any number divided by 100 may be read as a percentage—in this case, 20 percent.

There's another way of figuring this out—and we'll need this method most of the time since 100 will rarely be the original number—is to divide the bottom number into the top. Remember, whenever you have a fraction, you may divide the bottom number into the top:

$$\frac{\text{Change}}{\text{Original number}} = \frac{20}{100} \qquad 100\overline{)20.00} \; .20 = 20\%$$

.20 is 20 percent. Any decimal may be read as a percent if you move the decimal point two places to the right.

Now let's do the other two. First, the percentage change when we go from 150 to 200. Work it out yourself in the space provided here and then go on to the last one—when we go from 50 to 25.

$$\frac{\text{Change}}{\text{Original number}} = \frac{50}{150} = \frac{5}{15} = \frac{1}{3} = 33\frac{1}{3}\%$$

And finally:

$$\frac{\text{Change}}{\text{Original number}} = \frac{25}{50} = \frac{1}{2} = 50\%$$

or:

$$50\overline{)25.00} \; .50 = 50\%$$

how much was GNP one year later in 1982 dollars? To find this out we use this formula:

$$\begin{array}{c} \text{Real GNP} \\ \text{(current year)} \end{array} = \begin{array}{c} \text{GNP} \\ \text{(current year)} \end{array} \times \frac{\text{GNP deflator (base year)}}{\text{GNP deflator (current year)}}$$

This is a general formula that we'll adapt to our specific years. We're comparing 1983 (our current year) to 1982 (the base year). Therefore, our formula will now read:

$$\text{Real GNP}_{83} = \text{GNP}_{83} \times \frac{\text{GNP deflator}_{82}}{\text{GNP deflator}_{83}}$$

To solve this equation, we need to substitute actual numbers for the three variables on the right side of the equation. We already know that GNP was 3.3 trillion in 1983. By convention, this number is written as 3,300. The GNP deflator for 1982, the base year, is 100, again by convention. The base year of virtually every index is 100.

We still need to know the GNP deflator for 1983. Since the Commerce Department publishes this figure, let's assume that it is 110. In other words, prices rose by 10 percent in 1983. Now we'll see if our formula works because our answer should be obvious. We're looking for the real GNP in 1983 and we see that GNP rose by 10 percent and prices also rose by 10 percent. Real GNP in 1983 should be equal to that of 1982. The formula is as follows:

$$\text{Real GNP}_{83} = \text{GNP}_{83} \times \frac{\text{GNP deflator}_{82}}{\text{GNP deflator}_{83}}$$

$$= \frac{3300}{1} \times \frac{100}{110}$$

$$= \frac{\overline{3300}\,30}{1} \times \frac{100}{\overline{110}\,1}$$

$$= 3000$$

Before we move on to a set of problems just like this one, we'll go over a few of the mechanics of our solution. We put the 3300 over 1 because this makes it easier to do cross division followed by multiplication. Incidentally, you are allowed to put any number over 1 because this means you are dividing that number by 1. For example, 5 is equal to 5/1. It means that one goes into five, five times.

Another thing wc did was reduce the fractions by division. One hundred ten went into 3,300 30 times. You don't have to reduce fractions, but usually you'll find that smaller numbers are easier to work with.

Here are two more problems: (1) GNP rises from 2.5 trillion in 1980 to 3.0 trillion in 1984. The GNP deflator in 1984 is 125. Find the real GNP in 1984. Find the percentage increase in real GNP between 1980 and 1984. (2) GNP rises from 3 trillion in 1982 to 5 trillion in 1988. The GNP deflator in 1988 is 150. Find the real GNP in 1988. Find the percentage increase in real GNP between 1982 and 1988.

Solutions:

$$(1)\ \text{Real GNP}_{84} = \text{GNP}_{84} \times \frac{\text{GNP deflator}_{80}}{\text{GNP deflator}_{84}}$$

$$= \frac{3000}{1} \times \frac{100}{125}$$

$$= \frac{24}{1} \times \frac{100}{1}$$

$$= 2400$$

Percentage change in real GNP from 1980 to 1984:

$$\frac{\text{Change}}{\text{Original number}} = \frac{-100}{2500} = -4\%$$

$$(2)\ \text{Real GNP}_{88} = \text{GNP}_{88} \times \frac{\text{GNP deflator}_{82}}{\text{GNP deflator}_{88}}$$

$$= \frac{5000}{1} \times \frac{100}{150}$$

$$= \frac{33.33}{1} \times \frac{100}{1}$$

$$= 3333$$

Percentage change in real GNP from 1982 to 1988:

$$\frac{\text{Change}}{\text{Original number}} = \frac{333}{3000} = 11.1\%$$

Real GNP in the current year enables us to compare the economy's output, or production, with that of the base year. In the first-solved problem we found the percentage change in real GNP between 1980 and 1984 to be -4 percent. Output in 1984 was 4 percent lower than in 1980. The second-solved problem shows that output was 11.1 percent higher in 1988 than in 1982.

Shortcomings of GNP as a Measure of National Economic Well-Being

(1) Production That Is Excluded

A. Household Production Household production consists mainly of the work done by housewives—care of children, cleaning, shopping, and cooking. Were a housekeeper hired to do these tasks, this would be counted in GNP. Were two housewives to work for each other as housekeepers (why I don't know), their work would be counted in GNP. So why not count housewives' work in their own homes? Because no money changes hands. No payments are recorded.

Food grown in backyard plots, home repairs, clothes made at home, or any do-it-yourself goods and services that people do for themselves, their families, or their friends are not counted in GNP. But when you buy these goods and services from other people they are counted (assuming they are reported by the sellers as income).

B. Illegal Production Illegal goods and services are not counted in GNP. The big three—dope, prostitution, and gambling—are ignored even though people spend hundreds of billions on these goods and services. Of course, if you place a bet at a racetrack or an off-track betting parlor, it is legal and counts in GNP. But a bet placed with a bookie is illegal. If you play the state lottery, your bet is counted toward GNP, but not if you play the numbers.

Prostitution was legal in France before World War II. Although the same services continued to be provided after the war on an illegal basis, anyone scanning France's GNP figures right after the war might think that country had been hit by a depression.

California is our leading agricultural state. Do you know its number-one crop? Lettuce? Grapes? Citrus fruit? Sorry, it's none of the above. California's number-one crop is grass—that's right, grass, as in marijuana.

C. The Underground Economy In every large city, on country roads, in flea markets, and even in suburban malls, there are people selling everything from watches to watermelons, and from corn to collectibles. And the chances are, the proceeds of these sales are not reported to the government. Not only are no taxes paid, but the sales are not reflected in GNP.

Some of the items sold were stolen, but most are simply goods produced without the government's knowledge. Together with illegal goods and services, these markets form a vast underground economy. How vast? Maybe 10 or 15 percent of GNP. Who knows? How much of *your* income is spent in the underground economy? Or, perhaps we should be asking, how much of *your* income *comes* from the underground economy?

Also, technically part of our underground economy is not just the street peddlers, cabdrivers, and lowlife entrepreneurs who underreport their incomes. Oh no. The underground economy gets a very nice class of people—doctors, dentists, lawyers, and even, heaven forbid, accountants. In fact, there is a whole branch of accounting dedicated to the underground economy. It's called "creative accounting." Often it involves keeping three separate sets of books—one for your creditors, showing an inflated profit, one for the government, and one for yourself, so you know how you're doing. The next time you're having your teeth realigned, just ask your dentist, "Would you prefer a check or cash?" Then, to make absolutely certain, ask if there's a discount for paying cash.

Let's just step back for a minute and look once again at our definition of GNP: *the nation's expenditure on all the goods and services produced during the year at market prices.*

What exactly *is* production? What we produce? For once economists are in agreement and quite clear as well about what something means. *Production is any good or service that people are willing to pay for.* And that means anything!

You go to a concert and fall asleep. How much was your ticket? $10? That was $10 worth of production.

You went to a brilliant lecture on the future of the universe. It was free. The speaker wasn't paid. No production.

You grow tomatoes in your backyard for your family's consumption. No production.

You take a course in philosophy. The professor walks into the room and lies down on the floor in the front of the class. This happens all term. How much tuition did you pay to take this course? That's how much production took place.

The problem we have then is an inconsistency between the definition of GNP and the way it is compiled by the U.S. Department of Commerce. There's a lot of stuff going on out there that they miss. Why? Are they understaffed? (one of the all-time favorite words of bureaucrats). Perhaps. The government not only refuses to count the underground economy—legal *or* illegal—but it will not even admit its existence. The bottom line is that it does not go into GNP, even as an estimate. As a result, we are grossly (no pun intended) undercounting GNP.

Production

(2) *Treatment of Leisure Time*

GNP does not take into account leisure time. We have no way of telling if the people of a country enjoy a 30-hour week or have to work 60 hours a week. Recent immigrant groups, whether the Vietnamese and Koreans in the 1970s and 1980s, the Cubans in the 1960s, the eastern and southern Europeans from the 1880s to the 1920s, or the Irish in the 1840s, have been resented for putting in longer hours than native-born Americans. For these immigrants, long hours were necessary for survival, not only in America, but in their native lands. The rice farmer in Egypt, the factory worker in Hong Kong, and the manual laborer in India do not have seven-hour workdays, paid sick leave, long vacations, 10 paid holidays, and a couple of days off for Christmas shopping.

The average workweek in the United States as in the rest of the industrial world has gradually declined. Until after World War II, most workers still put in 5½ or 6 days a week. In 1900 the 10-hour day was common, and when you wanted to take a vacation, if your boss liked you, he reached into his pocket and gave you $5 spending money.

All of this is to show that we have made marvelous gains in leisure time, but these gains are not reflected in GNP. Nor, for that matter, are differences in the respective workweeks of various countries whose GNPs might be compared. For example, the Japanese have nearly caught up with us in per capital real GNP, but they work longer hours.[4]

(3) *Human Costs and Benefits*

Another problem with comparing our GNP with that of other countries, or with our own GNP in previous years, is that the physical, mental, and psychological costs of producing that GNP and any human benefits associated with producing it are ignored.

First the costs. The strain of commuting long distances along congested routes, the tediousness, the dangers, the low status, and other unpleasantness associated with certain jobs are some of the costs. Other jobs cause anxiety because the worker is always worrying about getting ahead or just getting along. Advertising account executives, air traffic controllers, and bomb squad members are all under the gun, so to speak, during most of their working hours. Economists call the psychological strain associated with work *psychic cost*. These psychic costs detract from one's enjoyment of a job, while *psychic income* adds to that enjoyment.

Psychic cost

Psychic income

There are also physical strains and benefits associated with work. As we've already noted, the average workweek is much shorter than it was 80 years ago. Further, the amount of physical labor performed on the average job has declined as well. Not only have we shifted nearly completely from human power to mechanical power, but the nature of work has also changed from farming and manufacturing to service jobs, most of which require no physical labor.

This is not to say that there are no longer any jobs requiring physical labor or being performed under unpleasant circumstances. Just ask the people who work in asbestos, textile, or automobile factories (see the section on work and alienation in Chapter 4). Or talk to coal miners, migrant farm workers, and police foot patrolmen.

Some people, on the other hand, really enjoy their jobs. Take actors. They are willing to hold all kinds of stopgap jobs—waitress, hotel clerk, theater

---

[4] Per capita real GNP is real GNP/population; it will be discussed shortly.

doorman, cook, office temporary—waiting for that big chance. For most, of course, it never comes. In New York, where there are no more than 2,000 people who earn their entire livelihood from acting, there are tens of thousands of aspiring actors. Why are they willing to buck such outrageous odds? Because they really love acting. The *psychic income* from working in the theater—the roar of the grease paint, the smell of the crowd, the adulation, the applause—is the compensation they really seek.

Another case of someone who really enjoyed his job was reported by Dr. Reubin in his bestselling *Everything You Wanted to Know about Sex but Were Afraid to Ask*. It seems there was a foot fetishist who worked in a womens' shoe store. Only my strong sense of propriety prevents me from disclosing the shameful details of this man's work. Suffice it to say that he reported that he was so happy at his job that he would have worked for nothing.

Finally, let's consider the physical benefits from work. Literally. My friend Marty, the gym teacher, is always in great shape. What do you expect? But I really want to talk about Mr. Spalter, a little bald-headed man who taught gym (how can you *teach* gym?) at Brooklyn's James Madison High School in the 1950s. The guy had to be at least 80. Anyway, Mr. Spalter could go up a 30-foot rope in less than 15 seconds—and do it in perfect form, with his legs exactly perpendicular to his body. The physical benefits of being a gym teacher, farmer, or a health club employee are obvious.

The GNP we produce today is produced by an entirely different type of labor force doing very different work from that of 50 or 100 years ago. And our labor force works very differently from that of developing countries. This makes GNP comparisons that much less valid.

(4) What Goes into GNP?

Other problems with GNP as a measure of national economic well-being have to do with what goes into GNP (see the box titled "Measure of Economic Welfare"). When a large part of our production goes toward national defense, police protection, pollution control devices, cleanups of oil spills, repair and replacement of poorly made cars and appliances, a large GNP is not a very good indicator of how we're doing. And if a large part of our labor force staffs the myriad bureaucracies of state, local, and federal government, as well as that of the corporate world, we're not all that well off. GNP tells us how much we produce. We need to ask: how much of what?

In general, the problem with using GNP as a measure of national economic well-being is that GNP is just a single number, and no one number can possibly provide us with all the information we need. Try these examples.

My daughter is doing very well on her diet. She's down to 120. Of course she's only 3 feet 6 inches.

How's the weather? It's great—the temperature is 50. Oh yes—there's a hurricane.

My son got all A's in his college courses this semester. Unfortunately, he's taking them in jail where he is serving 10 consecutive life sentences for mass murder. Oh well, like I always say, nobody's perfect.

Per Capita Real GNP

GNP may be used to compare living standards among various countries, or between time periods within one country. Such comparisons would usually

Measure of Economic Welfare

Two economists, James Tobin (who won a Nobel Prize in economics and served on President Kennedy's Council of Economic Advisors) and William Nordhaus (who served on President Carter's Council of Economic Advisors) have developed an alternative way of measuring national output. In some respects, they say, GNP is too big because it includes certain things that either add nothing to our standard of living, or actually detract from it. However, GNP does *not* include certain things that should be counted.

Some of the "economic bads" are congestion, pollution, and littering. These unfortunate by-products of our industrial society should be subtracted from our GNP, according to Tobin and Nordhaus, because they detract from our standard of living. An example they did not use, but that illustrates the point, is a cartoon of a slave galley. You might recall that in the movie *Ben Hur*, which you probably never saw or heard of, the rowing speed is controlled by a drummer (like the cockswain's count controls the rowing speed in crew races). Anyway, in the cartoon, this slave is passing the hat among his fellow rowers. One of them asks what the collection is for. "It's going toward a new drum."

Think about it. A lot of what we produce—perhaps hundreds of billions of dollars worth—goes toward dealing with bad things like pollution. Think of how much we need to spend not only on cleaning up our rivers and streams, but on air pollution control devices, garbage disposal, as well as time lost and aggravation due to congestion. What Tobin and Nordhaus do is arrive at a figure of a few hundred billion dollars and subtract it from GNP.

They also subtract the "regrettable necessities" of defense spending, police protection, and private security measures. Defense and police you already know, but did you know that there are over two million people who work in private security—private detectives, store detectives, hotel detectives, security guards (also known as "phony cops"), night watchmen, and private housing police. In fact, call up any medium- or large-sized company and ask for "security." Most places have their own security departments.

So we subtract these "regrettable necessities" from GNP along with the "economic bads." But we have to add to GNP all the goods and services it should have counted and didn't. We have to add household production as well as the production of illegal goods and services, not to mention unreported production. Sometimes illegal production and unreported (but otherwise legal) production are lumped together as the "underground economy." Actually, that's a rather misleading label because nearly all of it takes place above ground, right on the street. And if you know where to find it, you have what is called "street smarts." Sounds a lot better than underground smarts, unless you happen to be a groundhog or a gopher.

To put this all together, the Measure of Economic Welfare is: GNP − The economic bads
− The regrettable necessities
+ Household, unreported, and illegal production.

Do you think the Measure of Economic Welfare is larger or smaller than GNP? It's larger. In other words, the additions are larger than the subtractions.

Per capita Real GNP $= \dfrac{\text{Real GNP}}{\text{Population}}$

be on a per capita basis. Per capita GNP = GNP/population. In the United States per capita GNP in 1987 was:

$$\frac{\text{GNP}}{\text{Population}} = \frac{\$4,486.2 \text{ billion}}{243,827 \text{ thousand}} = \$18,399$$

That means that in 1987 we produced $18,399 worth of goods and services for every man, woman, and child in this country.

To compare 1987 per capita GNP with that of other years we would have to correct for inflation. In other words, we really need to revise our formula:

$$\text{Per capita real GNP} = \frac{\text{Real GNP}}{\text{Population}}$$

Per capita real GNP comparisons over time

How does our per capita real GNP compare with earlier years? Just take a look at Table 5-3. Obviously our per capita real GNP has gone up dramatically since the early years of the century. Between 1900 and 1987, it has more than quadrupled. But in recent years, especially during the early 1970s to early 1980s, the gains have been less impressive. In fact, between 1978 and 1982 there was virtually no change.

Table 5–3
Per Capita Real GNP; Selected Years, 1929–87
(in 1987 dollars)

Year	Per Capita Real GNP
1929	$ 6,318
1939	5,955
1949	8,041
1959	9,891
1969	13,079
1979	15,785
1987	18,399

Sources: 1985 *Economic Report of the President*, pp. 232, 234, 265; 1988 *Economic Report of the President*, p. 248; *Statistical Abstract of the United States*, 1988, p. 15.

International per capita real GNP comparisons

How valid are per capita real GNP comparisons over time? Over the shortrun, say up to 10 years, they are quite valid. But comparisons over 20, 30, or 40 years become more and more like comparing apples and oranges; or, more to the point, like comparing video games and pocket calculators with nine-inch Dumont TVs and those big old office adding machines that were powered by a lever that you pulled every time you entered a number. Still more to the point, compare Ford Mustangs with Model-T Fords. Over long periods of time, not only do different goods and services go into GNP, but the quality of those goods and services change as well.

International comparisons of per capita real GNP must be made with even more caution. The per capita real GNP of America is perhaps 100 times the size of India's. Do we produce 100 times as much per capita? Probably not. The typical Indian, a farmer living in a rural village, is not subject to the psychological stresses, commuting problems, pollution, or crime as the average American. Furthermore, the average Indian family produces most of its own food, clothing, and shelter—items that are not counted in GNP. Therefore, we are seriously underestimating India's real GNP, or in the terminology of Tobin and Nordhaus, its Measure of Economic Welfare.

Perhaps the American real GNP is not 100 times that of India, but just 25 times as high. Per capita real GNP is not an accurate measure of international differences in production levels, but it does provide a rough measure of these differences. Comparisons of countries at similar stages of economic development are much more accurate, however, than comparisons of countries at different stages.

Workbook for Chapter 5

Name _____

Date _____

Multiple-Choice Questions

Circle the letter that corresponds to the best answer.

1. Nearly all of our output is produced by
a. the government   **b.** private buisness
firms   **c.** individual consumers

2. GNP may be found by
a. adding together money spent on goods and services and incomes received by the factors of production
b. subtracting incomes received by the factors of production from the money spent on goods and services   **c.** subtracting the money spent on goods and services from the incomes received by the factors of production   **d.** adding the money spent on goods and services

3. Which equation is correct?
a. GNP − Depreciation = NNP   **b.** NNP − Depreciation = GNP   **c.** GNP + NNP = Depreciation

4. Each of the following is an indirect business tax except
a. sales tax   **b.** excise tax   **c.** business property tax   **d.** corporate income tax

5. If Mexico had a GNP of 700 and depreciation of 100, while Italy had a GNP of 740 and a depreciation of 180, most economists would say that
a. Italy had a better year   **b.** Mexico had a better year   **c.** There is no way of determining which country had a better year

6. Which statement is true?
a. Both direct and indirect taxes are on things rather than on people.   **b.** Both direct and indirect taxes are on people rather than on things.   **c.** A direct tax is on people.   **d.** An indirect tax is on people.

7. In declining order of size, which of these is the proper ranking?
a. GNP, NNP, national income   **b.** NNP, GNP, national income   **c.** National income, GNP, NNP   **d.** National income, NNP, GNP   **e.** GNP, national income, NNP   **f.** NNP, national income, GNP

8. Wages, salaries, and fringe benefits constitute about _____ of national income.
a. 25 percent   **b.** 50 percent   **c.** 75 percent   **d.** 95 percent

9. The largest sector of GNP is
a. investment   **b.** government spending   **c.** net exports   **d.** consumer spending

10. Which is not counted in GNP?
a. a social security check sent to a retiree
b. government spending on highway building   **c.** money spent on an airline ticket
d. money spent by a company to build a new office park

11. Which one of these goes into the investment sector of GNP?
a. the purchase of a new factory   **b.** the purchase of 100 shares of Mobil Oil stock   **c.** the purchase of a 10-year-old office building   **d.** the purchase of a U.S. savings bond

12. When there is inflation
a. real GNP increases faster than GNP   **b.** GNP increases faster than real GNP   **c.** GNP and real GNP increase at the same rate   **d.** there is no way of telling whether GNP or real GNP increases faster

13. If GNP rose from $6 trillion to $9 trillion and prices rose by 50 percent over this period **a.** real GNP fell by 100 percent **b.** real GNP fell by 50 percent **c.** real GNP stayed the same **d.** real GNP rose by 50 percent **e.** real GNP rose by 100 percent

14. Which of the following is counted in GNP? **a.** household production **b.** illegal production **c.** leisure time **d.** government spending

15. Which statement is true? **a.** There is an inconsistency between the definition of GNP and the way it is compiled by the U.S. Department of Commerce. **b.** GNP is an accurate measure of production in the United States. **c.** U.S. GNP figures include estimates for production in the underground economy. **d.** Our GNP would grow faster if we had less inflation.

16. Suppose that the GNP of Argentina were 10 times that of Uruguay. Which statement would be most accurate? **a.** There is no way of comparing the output of Argentina and Uruguay. **b.** Argentina's output is greater than that of Uruguay. **c.** Argentina's output is probably around 10 times that of Uruguay. **d.** Argentina's output is 10 times that of Uruguay.

17. Which statement is true? **a.** GNP tells us how much we produce as well as what we produce. **b.** GNP tells us neither how much we produce nor what we produce. **c.** GNP tells us what we produce. **d.** GNP tells us how much we produce.

18. The Measure of Economic Welfare formulated by Tobin and Nordhaus starts with GNP and then **a.** subtracts the economic bads and the regrettable necessities and adds household, unreported, and illegal production **b.** subtracts the economic bads, the regrettable necessities, and household, unreported, and illegal production **c.** adds the economic bads and the regrettable necessities and subtracts the household, unreported, and illegal production

d. adds the economic bads and subtracts the regrettable necessities and household, unreported, and illegal production

19. Per capita real GNP is found by **a.** dividing population by real GNP **b.** dividing real GNP by population **c.** adding population to real GNP **d.** multiplying real GNP by population

20. Which statement is true? **a.** Over longer and longer periods of time, comparisons of real per capita GNP become increasingly valid. **b.** Over the short run, say up to 10 years, comparisons of per capita real GNP are quite valid. **c.** International comparisons of per capita real GNP may be made with less caution than comparisons over time within a given country. **d.** None of these statement is true.

21. Since 1929 our per capita real GNP has **a.** declined **b.** stayed about the same **c.** doubled **d.** tripled

Fill-in Questions

1. The nation's expenditure on all the goods and services produced during the year at market prices is

————.

2. Nearly all our goods and services are produced by————.

3. GNP – ———— = NNP.

4. NNP – ———————— = national income.

5. A tax with your name on it is a ———— tax.

6. A sales tax is a (n) ————————tax.

7. The four basic economic resources are (1) ————, (2) ————,(3) ————, and (4) ————.

8. Using the expenditures approach, GNP consists of four things: (1) ————, (2) ————, (3) ————, and (4) ————.

9. Net Exports = _____ minus _____.

10. GNP includes only payments for _____.

11. _____ measures total production in one year.

12. Goods and services produced without the government's knowledge are part of the _____ economy.

13. Economists call any good or service that people are willing to pay for _____.

14. Economists call the psychological strain associated with work _____.

15. The Measure of Economic Welfare developed by Tobin and Nordhaus begins with GNP and subtracts _____and _____and adds _____.

16. Per capita real GNP is found by dividing _____ by _____.

17. Over time, per capita real GNP comparisons become _____ valid.

Problems

1. Given the following information, calculate NNP and national income: GNP = $5 trillion, indirect business taxes = $300 billion and depreciation = $500 billion.

2. If national income is $3 trillion, depreciation is $400 billion, and indirect business taxes are $300 billion, how much are NNP and GNP?

3. If wages, salaries, and fringe benefits are $4 trillion, profit is $500 billion, interest is $300 billion, rent is $100 billion, and depreciation is $600 billion, how much is national income?

4. If wages, salaries, and fringe benefits are $3 billion, profit is $400 billion, interest is $200 billion, rent is $100 billion, depreciation is $400 billion, and indirect business taxes are $300 billion, how much is national income, NNP, and GNP?

5. If consumption spending is $3 trillion, investment is $800 billion, government spending is $1 trillion, imports are $1.2 trillion, and exports are $900 billion, how much is GNP?

6. If consumption is $3.8 trillion, investment is $1.1 trillion, government spending is $1.1 trillion, imports are $1.6 trillion, and exports are $1.4 trillion, how much is GNP?

7. GNP rises from 4 trillion in 1986 to 5 trillion in 1989. The GNP deflator in 1989 is 120. Find real GNP in 1989. Find the percentage increase in real GNP between 1986 and 1989.

8. GNP rises from 5 trillion in 1990 to 7 trillion in 1994. The GNP deflator in 1994 is 140. Find real GNP in 1994. Find the percentage increase in real GNP between 1990 and 1994.

9. Find the Tobin and Nordhaus Measure of Economic Welfare if GNP is 5 trillion, the economic bads are 500 billion, the regrettable necessities are 400 billion, and the sum of household, unreported, and illegal production is 1 trillion.

10. Find per capita real GNP when population is 100 million and real GNP is $2 trillion.

6

The Government Sector

In this, and in the following two chapters, we shall consider, in turn, the three main sectors of GNP: the government, business, and consumer sectors.

Chapter Objectives
We'll be looking at these topics:
- Government spending.
- Types of taxes.
- Sources of government revenue.
- The economic role of the government.

The Growing Economic Role of Government

Most of growth due to depression and World War II

The role of government has grown tremendously over the last six decades. Actually, most of that growth took place between 1933 and 1945, during the administration of Franklin Delano Roosevelt. The two major crises of that period—the Great Depression and World War II—dwarfed anything our nation has faced since. In fact, we would have to go back to the Civil War to find an event as cataclysmic as either the depression or what people over 50 still refer to as "the war."

Since 1945, the roles of government on the federal, state, and local levels expanded, but the seeds of that expansion were sown during the Roosevelt administration. Americans seem determined to *never again* experience the traumatic events that overtook us during the 1930s and 1940s. *Never again* will we leave ourselves vulnerable to a depression or military attack by another nation.

The three economic roles of government

The government exerts three basic economic influences. It spends about $1,200 billion, levies over $1 trillion in taxes, and it regulates our economy. Essentially, on the federal level, as well as on the state and local levels, the government raises the money it needs for its expenditures through taxes. And the rest it borrows.

Although state and local governments spend close to $600 billion a year, the federal government spends almost twice as much; we will be concentrating on its economic role. In a nutshell, the federal government spends hundreds of billions of dollars to provide goods and services and it redistributes still more, taxing certain groups and handing the money over

The Chronology of Budget Preparation

Preparation of the budget begins about three years before the beginning of the fiscal year. We'll be looking at the timetable for the preparation of the budget for fiscal year 1990, which began on October 1, 1989.

During early 1988, after months of internal studies, each department presented its budget for the fiscal year 1990 to the Office of Management and Budget (OMB). That agency has the job of coordinating all budget requests to ensure that they are consistent with the president's economic program. The OMB then put together a tentative budget for the president.

The president was concerned not just with individual spending programs—foreign aid, the MX missile, food stamps, Social Security—but with the bottom line, or total spending. The president and the director of the OMB then established spending ceilings for each department and the federal agencies, who were then asked to prepare a second round of expenditure plans over the summer.

During the fall of 1988, the OMB reviewed these revised programs and in late fall the budget was presented to the president for final approval. The final budget message was then drafted for submission to Congress in January 1989.

Over the next eight months the ball was in Congress' court. Both houses of Congress have budget committees that prepare "concurrent resolutions" to be reported to their respective houses by April 15. These resolutions contain two key figures: overall expenditures and overall revenue. By May 15 Congress must pass a single concurrent resolution.

Between May 15 and October 1, Congress passed various appropriations bills—agricultural subsidies, veteran's benefits, aid to mass transit, public assistance—while trying to stay within the limits set by the concurrent resolution. Finally, a second budget resolution had to be passed by October 1, the first day of the fiscal year.

As a footnote to these proceedings, at the start of fiscal year 1988 (October 1, 1988), Congress had not yet passed even 1 of the 13 regular appropriation bills. To keep the government afloat, a stopgap bill was passed.

to other groups. We will postpone our discussion of the federal government's regulatory role until later chapters.[1]

Much of the data presented in this chapter will be out of date before this book even gets to the printer. It would be extremely helpful for you to consult newspapers, news magazines, and government periodicals for more up-to-date figures.

Government Spending

Federal Government Spending

The federal government will spend over $1.1 trillion in fiscal year 1990 (which began October 1, 1989). Nearly half of all spending is for transfer payments for individuals (see Figure 6-1). These include Social Security, Medicare, Medicaid, food stamps, and public assistance. Social Security benefits account for nearly half the money spent in this budget category.

Rise in social spending

There are several explanations for the huge rise in social spending. Much of it reflects the continued expenditures on the Great Society programs of the 1960s, particularly Medicare, Medicaid, and food stamps. A second reason for the increase is that the economy, which sustained relatively full employment through the 1960s, has not been growing rapidly enough during the last 20 years to provide jobs for several million people who have wanted to work. Consequently, spending on public assistance, unemployment insurance benefits, and food stamps has shot up since the early 1970s. Finally, in

---

[1] See the end of Chapter 12, all of 13, the last half of Chapter 24, and the first half of Chapter 28.

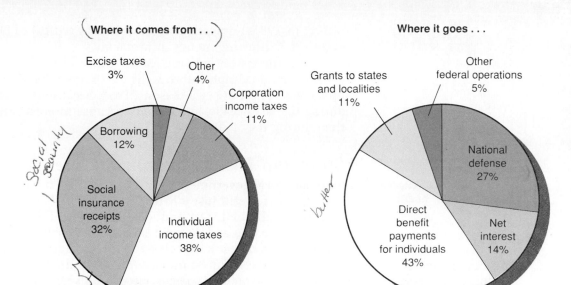

Where it comes from . . .

Excise taxes 3%
Other 4%
Corporation income taxes 11%
Borrowing 12%
Social insurance receipts 32%
Individual income taxes 38%

Social Security

Where it goes . . .

Grants to states and localities 11%
Other federal operations 5%
National defense 27%
Direct benefit payments for individuals 43%
Net interest 14%

Figure 6–1
The Federal Government Dollar—
Fiscal Year 1989 Estimate

Source: Office of Management and Budget, *The United States Budget in Brief,* fiscal year 1988 (Washington, D.C., 1987), inner cover.

1955 there were relatively few people collecting full Social Security benefits, since that program was then only 20 years old. Today, however, the number of retired people on the rolls is more than twice that of 1955, and during the last 35 years benefits have gone up substantially.

Rise in defense spending

The next big-ticket item is defense expenditures, which are budgeted in 1990 at over $300 billion. This comes to over $1,200 for each person in the United States. President Reagan had long been an advocate of a strong national defense; he sharply increased expenditures in this area from just $158

Why the Fiscal Year Starts on October 1

The federal government, as you might expect, often has to do things a little differently. While nearly all business firms issue annual reports based on the normal calendar year—January 1 to December 31—the federal government's financial, or fiscal, year begins on October 1 and runs through September 30 of the following year.

Do they start on October 1 just to be different, or is there a reason for this unorthodox starting time? There actually *is* a reason. A new Congress is elected every second November, and takes office the following January. This gives them eight months to work on the next year's federal budget. Of course, if the new budget did not go into effect until January 1, they'd have eleven months. Since Congress tends to leave its most important business for last, it would be trying to wrap up business while worrying about getting home for Christ-

mas. So they *do* have a reason for starting on October 1—maybe not a great reason, but a reason nevertheless.

By the way, what has probably been lost in my cogent explanation of why the fiscal year starts on October 1 is what a fiscal year actually is. It is a 12-month period over which the government projects a certain amount of spending and a certain level of tax receipts. The government might budget expenditures of $1.2 trillion and tax receipts of $1.1 trillion, leaving a deficit of how much?

The deficit would come to $100 billion (or $.1 trillion). If this math still bothers you, you would do well to reread the first section of Chapter 5. We'll have a lot more to say about budget deficits, government spending, and tax receipts in Chapter 11, which deals specifically fiscal policy.

billion in 1981. Ironically, Mr. Reagan was critical of Democratic social programs "for throwing money at problems."

One of the fastest growing federal expenditures is interest on the national debt, which quadrupled during the 1980s. Why have these payments gone up so fast? There are two reasons. First, because the national debt tripled during the last decade, and second, because interest rates have been higher than during the 1970s.

State and Local Government Spending

Big state and local expenditures: education, health, and welfare

State and local government spending has been rising rapidly since World War II, but it is still just a little more than half the level of federal spending. Well over half of all state and local government expenditures goes toward education, health, and welfare. One of the problems faced by these governments is that they are expected to provide more and more services with limited tax bases. For example, some 20 million teenagers are currently attending high school or college. Fifty or 60 years ago most people were working by the time they were 14, but now they are still in school. Supporting public education has traditionally been the role of the state and local governments, although in recent years Washington has provided supplementary funds covering about 6 percent of the costs of educating children through high school.

Another expenditure that has gone up enormously is police protection. Although this is another traditional function of local government, rising crime and perhaps the deterioration of neighborhoods have made it necessary to hire many more police. Until the 1950s, neighborhoods largely policed themselves informally, mainly because people spent a great deal of time on the street, most urban areas were more densely populated, and people tended to know one another. All this has changed and now the police are being called on to perform functions that neighborhoods used to handle.

Government Spending versus Transfer Payments

Of the $1,200 billion federal budget, over half was earmarked for transfer payments such as Social Security payments, public assistance, and grants to state and local government (aid to education, mass transit, highway building and maintenance).

This apportionment is summarized in Figure 6–1. The federal government also spent over $500 billion on final purchases of goods and services, the largest of which was defense spending. In addition, the state and local governments spend over $500 billion so that total government purchases in 1989 were nearly $1,100 billion. We have designated government spending on goods and services (as distinguished from transfer payments) by the letter "G", which we'll be using when we analyze macroeconomic policy, beginning in Chapter 11.

Distinction between government spending and transfer payments

It is important to distinguish between government spending and transfer payments. Only spending—government spending, business spending, or consumer spending—goes into GNP. Remember, GNP is total spending on goods and services. Transfer payments cannot be counted because they do not represent that kind of spending. However, once people (or government units) spend that money—whether public assistance checks, Social Security checks, or highway funds—it goes into GNP.

In general, then, we look toward the government to provide us with services that we either used to perform for ourselves or we considered unnecessary a few generations ago. The question is, where does the money come from?

Taxes

Taxes are so pervasive that over half the chapter will be devoted to them. Before we even begin to consider how much taxes are, we'll need to understand something about tax rates and the types of taxes that exist. Once that's done, we'll see just how onerous the American tax system really is.

The Average Tax Rate and the Marginal Tax Rate

If someone asked you what your tax rate was or which tax bracket you were in, would you have a ready answer? Generations of attorneys have taught us that the best answer to any question (and especially to those to which you don't know the right answer) is another question. So the answer to the question, "What's your tax rate?" is: Which tax rate are you referring to? My average tax rate or my marginal tax rate?

But what if your questioner replies, "Tell me your average tax rate."? What do you do then? You tell her. And if she happens to ask you your marginal tax rate, you tell her that as well.

We all pay tax at two different rates: the average rate and the marginal rate. The average rate is the overall rate you pay on your entire income while the marginal rate is the rate you pay on your last few hundreds (or thousands) of dollars earned. Your marginal rate is often referred to as your tax bracket. In nearly all cases, we're referring to the average and marginal rates that you're paying in personal income tax, but we'll apply the average tax rate to the Social Security tax as well.

The Average Tax Rate We kind of left you hanging there, didn't we? How do you answer the question, "Tell me your average tax rate?"

Let's try a simple problem:

The average tax rate is calculated by dividing taxes paid by taxable income:

$$\text{ATR} = \frac{\text{Taxes Paid}}{\text{Taxable Income}} \qquad\qquad \text{Average tax rate} = \frac{\text{Taxes paid}}{\text{Taxable income}}$$

Suppose a person paid $3,000 on a taxable income of $20,000. How much is the average tax rate?

$$\text{Average tax rate} = \frac{\text{Taxes paid}}{\text{Taxable income}} = \frac{\$3,000}{\$20,000} = .15, \text{ or } 15\%$$

If you got 15 percent, go on to the marginal tax rate in the next section. If not, let's go over all the steps in finding the average tax rate. How do we get from $3,000/$20,000 to .15? First, reduce the fraction to 3/20. Whatever you do to the top of the fraction, you do to the bottom. Get rid of the three zeros on top and get rid of three zeros on the bottom. (While you're at it, you can get rid of the dollar signs as well.)

The next step is to divide 3 by 20. Remember, whenever you have a fraction, you may divide the bottom number into the top number. If you divide the top into the bottom, you will not only violate a basic law of arithmetic, but you will also get the wrong answer. $20\overline{)3}$ is the same as $20\overline{)3.00}$. We are allowed to put a decimal point after any number. And—we are allowed to put zeros after it, because it doesn't change its value. Those are some more laws of arithmetic.

$$
20\overline{)3.00} = 20\overline{)3.00} \atop \begin{array}{r} .15 \\ \hline -20x \\ \hline 100 \\ -100 \\ \hline \end{array}
$$

The average tax rate is .15 or 15 percent. Our final law of arithmetic is that whenever you want to convert a decimal into a percentage, move the decimal point two places to the right and write a percentage sign after the number. Another example would be: .235 = 23.5%. Or, .71 = 71%, or .406 = 40.6%. If a baseball player is hitting .406, he is getting a hit 40.6 percent of the times he bats. And if your average tax rate comes to .406, it means you are paying 40.6 percent of your taxable income to the Internal Revenue Service.

Let's try one more. Suppose you pay \$12,000 on a taxable income of \$50,000. How much is your average tax rate? To solve this problem: (1) write the formula, (2) substitute numbers into the formula, and (3) solve.

$$
\text{Average tax rate} = \frac{\text{Taxes paid}}{\text{Taxable income}} = \frac{\$12,000}{\$50,000} = \frac{12}{50} = \frac{6}{25}
$$

$$
25\overline{)6.00} \atop \begin{array}{r} .24 = 24\% \\ \hline -50X \\ \hline 100 \\ -100 \\ \hline \end{array}
$$

The Marginal Tax Rate The average tax rate tells you the overall rate you pay on your entire income, while the marginal tax rate tells you the rate you pay on the last few hundred dollars you earned. Suppose you made \$100 overtime and the government took \$70. Would you work overtime? The chances are you wouldn't, and that supposition forms a cornerstone of supply-side economics. The supply-siders basic belief is that our high marginal tax rates rob people of the incentive to work as hard and as long as they would have been willing to had their tax burden been lower.

The marginal tax rate is calculated by dividing additional taxes paid by additional taxable income:

$$\text{Marginal tax rate} = \frac{\text{Additional taxes paid}}{\text{Additional taxable income}}$$

Suppose you had to pay an additional $420 on an additional taxable income of $1,000. How much is the marginal tax rate?

$$\text{Marginal tax rate} = \frac{\text{Additional taxes paid}}{\text{Additional taxable income}}$$

$$= \frac{\$420}{\$1,000} = \frac{42}{100} = .42 = 42\%$$

Did you get it right? If so, you might as well skip the rest of this section. If not, we'll go over the problem step by step.

How did we get from $42/100$ to .42? When you divide a number by 100, you are moving its decimal two places to the right. $42/100$ means we have to divide 42 by 100. If we did that we would still get .42:

$$
\begin{array}{r}
42.00 = 42\% \\
100\overline{)42.00} \\
-400X \\
\hline
200 \\
-200 \\
\hline
\end{array}
$$

Now we'll get a little fancier. Suppose your taxable income rose from $20,000 to $22,000 and the taxes you paid rose from $4,500 to $5,200. How much is your marginal tax rate?

$$\text{MTR} = \frac{\text{Additional taxes paid}}{\text{Additional taxable income}}$$

$$\text{Marginal tax rate} = \frac{\text{Additional taxes paid}}{\text{Additional taxable income}}$$

$$= \frac{\$700}{\$2,000} = \frac{7}{20} = .35 = 35\%$$

$$\begin{array}{r} .35 = 35\% \\ 20\overline{)7.00} \\ -60X \\ \hline 100 \\ -100 \\ \hline \end{array}$$

Types of Taxes

There are two basic divisions of taxes. First we'll be looking at the difference between direct and indirect taxes. Then we'll take up progressive, proportional, and regressive taxes.

Direct Taxes A direct tax is a tax with your name written on it. The personal income and Social Security taxes are examples. They are taxes on particular persons. If you earn a certain amount of money, you must pay these taxes.

The corporate income tax is also a direct tax. You might not think so, but a corporation is considered a legal person. For example, in court, you would sue a corporation rather than its owners or officers. Thus, if a corporation makes a profit, it must pay a corporate income tax, and it is a direct tax.

Indirect Taxes These are not taxes on people, but on things. Some of us may have trouble making this distinction, especially given our relationships with family, friends, and co-workers, but in economics we *do* make a sharp distinction between people and things. Taxes on things include sales and excise taxes. A state sales tax on most retail purchases and the excise taxes on tires, gasoline, movie tickets, cigarettes, and liquor are examples.

Now we shall take up, in turn, progressive, proportional, and regressive taxes. The key variable we use to differentiate among them is where the tax burden falls.

A progressive tax falls mainly on the rich.

Progressive Taxes A progressive tax places a greater burden on those best able to pay and little or no burden on the poor. The best example is, of course, the federal personal income tax. For the vast majority of American taxpayers today, the more they earn, the higher percentage they pay. In terms of the average tax rate, then, people in higher income brackets pay a substantially higher average tax rate than those in lower brackets.

But the federal income tax had been substantially more progressive before the passage of the Economic Recovery Tax Act of 1981 and the Tax Reform Act of 1986. At the upper end of the income scale, we went from a maximum marginal tax rate of 70 percent before 1981 to just 50 percent that year, and to just 28 percent in 1988.[2] Also, the number of tax brackets was reduced from 14 in 1986 to just 2 in 1988. By lumping all taxpayers into

---

[2] Technically, it can be argued that there is a third bracket of 33 percent, because there is a 5 percent surcharge on taxable income between $71,900 and $149,250 for joint returns and between $43,150 and $89,650 for single returns.

only two brackets, we further cut down on the progressiveness of the personal income tax.[3]

It is important to distinguish between progressiveness in name and progressiveness in effect. For example, the New Jersey State Personal Income Tax calls for a 2 percent rate on all income below $20,000, a 2.5 percent rate on income between $20,000 and $50,000, and a 3.5 percent rate on all income above $50,000. Nominally then, it is a progressive tax.

But in effect it is hardly progressive because it is a much greater burden on the family with an income of $10,000 to pay $200 tax (2 percent of $10,000) than it is on the $100,000 family to pay $2,900 (2 percent on the first $20,000 = $400, plus 2.5 percent on the next $30,000 = $750, plus 3.5 percent on the next $50,000 = $1,750; $400 + $750 + $1,750 = $2,900).

Proportional Taxes Proportional taxes place an equal burden on the rich, the middle class, and the poor. Sometimes a flat tax rate is advanced as a "fair" or proportional tax, but it is neither. For example, a flat income tax rate of, say, 15 percent, with no deductions, would place a much greater burden on the poor and the working class than on the rich. It would be much harder for a family with an income of $10,000 to pay $1,500 in income tax (15 percent of $10,000) than it would be for a family with an income of $100,000 to pay $15,000 (15 percent of $100,000).

A regressive tax falls mainly on the poor.

Regressive Taxes A regressive tax falls more heavily on the poor than on the rich. The examples we have already covered illustrate this. Another example is the Social Security tax. In 1989 the rate was 7.51 percent on all wages and salaries up to $53,400.[4] The maximum you would have had to pay was $4,010.34. Where did this figure come from?

That's right: we multiply $53,400 by 7.51 percent, or 0.0751.

In Table 6–1 we have worked out the Social Security taxes paid by people with various incomes. Only earned income is subject to this tax; rental in-

Table 6–1
The Incidence of the Social Security Tax at Various Income Levels in 1989

Level of Earned Income	Taxes Paid	Average Tax Rate
$ 10,000	$ 751	7.51%
53,400	4,010.34	7.51
100,000	4,010.34	4.01
1,000,000	4,010.34	0.40

---

[3] For example, suppose that two families, both in the 15 percent bracket, earned $12,000 and $20,000, respectively, and that each was entitled to $10,000 of deductions. The poorer family would pay $300 (15 percent of $2,000) and the more well-to-do family would pay $1,500 (15 percent of $10,000).

Under the pre-1987 system, these families would have been subject to rates of, say, 11 percent on any income between $10,000 and $12,000; 13 percent on income between $12,000 and $14,000; 15 percent on income between $14,000 and $16,000; 17 percent on income between $16,000 and $18,000; and, finally, 19 percent on income between $18,000 and $20,000.

The poorer family would pay $220 (11 percent of $2000). The more well-to-do family would pay $1,500 ($220 on the first $2,000, and then $260, $300, $340, and $380, on successive income increments of $2,000).

To sum up, under current tax law, the poorer family pays $300 and the more well-to-do family pays $1,500. Under the old system, they paid $220 and $1,500, respectively. Clearly, the older system was more progressive.

[4] In 1990 the Social Security tax rate rises to 7.65 percent and the maximum taxable base rises to $57,000.

How to Save on Your Income Tax

The personal income tax would be even more progressive in effect were it not for two methods of beating Internal Revenue out of some of its tax proceeds. One method is tax evasions, which is illegal. The other, tax avoidance is not only legal, but has been purposely put into the Internal Revenue Code by Congress. It is popularly known as "loopholes."

The favorite way of evading taxes is to not report income. Most people will tell you about cab drivers, waiters and waitresses, barbers and beauticians, and domestics. They often don't report all their income from tips. People who work "off the books" and those engaged in illegal activities are also cited most often. But we usually miss the big boys—the businesspeople, doctors, dentists, and others who work for themselves.

Often you can tell when a businessperson isn't reporting income. He will tell you that there's no sales tax if you pay cash. Now isn't that nice of him?

Another way of evading income tax is to take phony deductions. Even President Nixon was not above cheating on his taxes. He had made a gift of his vice presidential papers to a museum and valued them at about $500,000. So far so good. The only trouble was that a year before he made this gift, a law had been passed that made such gifts nondeductible. No problem. Nixon simply predated his gift to reflect the earlier date. The president could have pleaded ignorance of the law. The only problem was that Nixon himself had signed the bill into law.

Tax avoidance, unlike evasion, is quite legal. In fact, the Internal Revenue Code is set up to help rich people avoid a large chunk of their tax liability. Perhaps the most blatant example is the tax treatment of interest on state and municipal bonds. Unlike interest you might earn on savings accounts or corporate bonds, you pay no federal income tax on the interest earned from state and municipal bonds. The reason for this is to make it easier for states and local governments to borrow by making their securities more attractive to investors.

Now guess who the *big* investors are in state and municipal bonds? The rich. They hold most of these bonds. Why? Because they're tax exempt.

Imagine that you have $100 million lying around the house. If you were to buy some of these bonds, you might earn 7 percent interest, or $7 million a year. Normally you would have to pay one third of this income to the federal government, but since the interest on these bonds is tax free, you don't have to pay one penny. When the rich invest in these securities, we call that tax avoidance. And what's so nice about it is that it's perfectly legal.

come, interest, dividends, and profits are not taxed. It might appear at first glance that the Social Security tax is proportional, but as we examine Table 6–1 we should observe that it is not only regressive in effect, but nominally as well.

Take a yearly income of $100,000, for example. (I would gladly!) This person pays the maximum of $4,010.34 (i.e., 7.51 percent of the first $53,400). Now, what percentage of $100,000 is taxed? It comes to just over 4 percent. Not bad. Everyone with an income below $53,400 paid 7.51 percent. What happens then is that as income rises above $53,400, you pay the same tax—$4,010.34—while the proportion of your income that goes to the Social Security tax falls steadily. In fact, the person making $1 million a year also pays $4,010.34, which comes to only 0.4 percent of that income.

Sources of Federal Revenue

The largest source of federal revenue is the personal income tax.

The Personal Income Tax As we can see from Figure 6–1, the federal government has three main sources of tax revenue, the largest of which is the personal income tax. This tax was only a minor source of federal revenue until World War II. It now accounts for slightly more than two out of every five tax dollars collected by the Internal Revenue Service.

The personal income tax would be an even greater source of revenue were it not for the two landmark tax laws passed in the 1980s. First, the Economic Recovery Tax Act of 1981, better known as the Kemp-Roth tax cut,[5] lowered the average citizen's tax bill by 23 percent over a three-year period.

---

[5] Kemp was Representative Jack Kemp from upstate New York. He had been a star quarterback for the Buffalo Bills and was a 1988 Republican presidential contender. William Roth was a Republican senator from Delaware.

The maximum rate was cut from 70 percent to 50 percent, and most analysts agreed, the wealthiest third of the population got most of the benefits.

Then came the Tax Reform Act of 1986, which cut personal income taxes still further. The maximum rate was lowered to 33 percent, and most taxpayers ended up in the two lower brackets—15 percent and 28 percent. This meant that the nation's wealthiest people had marginal tax rates of 33 percent, the upper middle class was taxed at 28 percent, and the working class and lower middle class were taxed at 15 percent. At the same time, millions of poorer families were taken off the income tax rolls entirely.

The Payroll Tax What's the payroll tax? Remember the Social Security tax that you pay? What you pay is matched by your employer. In 1989, when you paid 7.51 percent of your wages, your employer also paid 7.51 percent of your wages.

The payroll tax is the federal government's fastest growing source of revenue and now stands second in importance to the personal income tax. But the Social Security Trust Fund may be running out of money because in the coming years, medical and retirement payments may be going up even faster than tax collections.

We have seen that the Social Security tax is extremely regressive. This regressiveness lessened somewhat in recent years as the earnings ceiling was raised. Each time the ceiling was raised, people in the higher income brackets paid a higher percentage of their earnings in Social Security tax.

Because the proportion of older people in our population has been rising and benefits have been steadily increased to keep up with the cost of living, there is a good chance that the Social Security Trust Fund will soon run out of money. In 1950 there were four people in the labor force for every retired person. Today that ratio is 3:1, and by the year 2010, it will be 2:1. Obviously, we are headed for a showdown, whether in the short run or in another generation or two.

There have been proposals to raise the payroll tax still more, but that will be difficult to do politically. Raising the retirement age, which is presently 65 for most Social Security categories, has also been proposed. Still others suggest that any shortfalls in the Social Security Trust Fund be covered by general federal government revenues.

The Corporate Income Tax Until the late 1970s this was the second largest source of federal revenue, but it is now a distant third. Under the Tax Reform Act of 1986 the maximum rate was lowered from 46 percent to just 34 percent,[6] but corporations have ended up paying more tax because several deductions were reduced.

The corporate income tax is a tax on a corporation's profits. Those who believe that profits provide our economy with its main incentive to produce goods and services are uneasy that they are so heavily taxed.

Excise Taxes An excise tax is a sales tax, but it is aimed at specific goods and services. The federal government taxes such things as tires, cigarettes, liquor, gasoline, and phone calls. Most excise taxes are levied by the federal government, although state and local governments often levy taxes on the same items. Cigarettes and gasoline, for example, are subject to a federal excise tax as well as excise taxes in many states. In fact, the differential in state excise taxes encourages many people to "smuggle" cigarettes from North Carolina into New York.

---

[6] All corporations earning profits of at least $335,000 pay an average tax rate of 34 percent.

How to Do Your Income Tax

One of the justifiable criticisms leveled against economics texts is that they don't teach readers anything practical, anything they can apply to their everyday lives. All right, then, here's something practical. Here's how to do your income tax.

Under the Tax Reform Act of 1986, tax returns were supposed to be simplified. They were—as long as you switched from the long form to the short form. But only a couple of million taxpayers did so.

We're going to work out a married couple's taxes for them, step-by-step. Let's give them an income of $60,000. Let's also give them two children.

This family is entitled to four exemptions at $2,000 each.*

That leaves them with a taxable income of $52,000 ($60,000 − $8,000).

They have a major decision to make. Do they fill out the long form or just do the short form?

The short form is easy. Just use the tax table below to figure it out, after taking the standard deduction of $5,000.

Go ahead and try it. Work it out in this space.

That's how much they pay using the short form. I'll bet they could save money by using the long form. The long form is used by taxpayers who itemize their deductions. There are five categories of deductions: (1) medical, (2) interest, (3) state and local taxes, (4) charity, and (5) miscellaneous.

The medical can be used by only a small minority of taxpayers, because their medical expenses must total more than 7.5 percent of their income. Interest on consumer purchases will be completely phased out by 1992, but mortgage interest on first and second homes is a biggie (the poor folks who own third, fourth, and fifth homes will not be able to deduct their mortgage interest). State and local income tax (but not sales) tax is fully deductible. Property tax is fully deductible. Charitable contributions are fully deductible. And miscellaneous expenses, usually connected with business expenses, are deductible.

Whether or not you do the long form depends on one thing. Will your itemized deductions exceed the standard deduction? This couple is entitled to a standard deduction of $5,000. If they own their own home, the chances are that their mortgage interest and real estate taxes alone might total around $5,000. If they live in a high-income tax state like New York or California, they may be paying several thousand dollars in state (and local) income tax. Do they give to charity? It's deductible.

Let's say that their itemized deductions come to $10,000. How much tax do they pay? Work it out in this space.

Individual Income Tax Rate Schedule for Joint and Single Returns—Taxable Income (Dollars)

Joint Return	Single Return	Marginal Tax Rate*
0–$29,750	0–$17,850	15%
Over 29,750	Over 17,850	28

* "[There is a] . . . five percent surcharge on taxable income between $71,900 and $149,250 for joint returns and between $43,150 and $89,650 for single returns. Taxpayers within these ranges will be subject to a marginal tax rate of 33 percent, but their average tax rate will not exceed 28 percent. Taxpayers with taxable income above these ranges will be subject to the 28 percent rate on all taxable income."

Source: Joseph C. Wakefield, "The Tax Reform Act of 1986," *Survey of Current Business* 67, no. 3, March 1987, pp. 20–21.

Here's the solution: $52,000 − $5,000 (standard deduction) = $47,000 taxable income.

The family pays 15 percent of its first $29,750 in income = $4,462.50 plus 28 percent of its next $17,250 of income = $4,830. $4,462.50 + $4,830 = $9,292.50.

Here's the solution. The family would subtract $10,000 from the $52,000 to get a taxable income of $42,000. We figure out its taxes the same way: $4,462.50 on its first $29,750 in income, plus 28 percent of its next $12,250 ($3,430) = $7,892.50.

How much did these people save by filling out the long form?

(continued)

* Beginning in 1990, personal exemptions will be raised to allow for inflation. So will the standard deduction and the income tax brackets.

They saved $9,292.50 − $7,892.50 = $1400.

Are you ready for another one? We'll make it easy. How much would a single taxpayer have to pay on an income of $20,000 if she took the standard deduction? The standard deduction on a single return is $3,000.

Finally, we'll throw you a curve ball. How much does a childless couple filing jointly pay if they have an income of $1,204,000 and deductions of $200,000? If you reread the footnote to the table in the previous box very carefully, you'll find the answer by doing some simple multiplication.

Solution: $20,000 − $3,000 = $17,000 taxable income. $17,000 × .15 = $2,550.

Here's the solution: $1,204,000 − $4,000 (two exemptions at $2,000 each) = $1,200,000. $1,200,000 − $200,000 in deductions (they obviously take the long form and itemize) = a taxable income of $1,000,000. This is taxed at a rate of 28 percent = $280,000.

Excise taxes, which account for about 8 percent of federal revenue, have another purpose besides serving as a source of revenue. They tend to reduce consumption of certain products that the federal government looks on with a jaundiced eye. Not only does the surgeon general warn us about cigarettes, but he looks on approvingly as the government taxes them.

Excise taxes are usually regressive.

Excise taxes are generally regressive because they tend to fall more heavily on the poor and working class. The tax on a pack of cigarettes is the same whether you're rich or poor, but it's easier for the rich person to handle 20 or 30 cents a day than a poor person. The same is true of liquor and gasoline. In fact, a tax on most consumer goods is regressive because the poor tend to spend a higher proportion of their incomes on consumption than the rich (who save 20 to 25 percent of their incomes).

Sources of State and Local Revenue

The sales tax is regressive.

The Sales Tax Over half the taxes collected by the states comes from the sales tax. This is a highly regressive tax. Although most food items are exempt, the poor consume a higher proportion of their incomes than the rich, who are able to save. In other words, a higher proportion of the income of the poor is subject to this tax.

The rich also avoid or evade a large proportion of the sales tax by buying their big-ticket items—stereos, TVs, cars, and so on—in states that have low or no sales tax. And the rich evade the sales tax by buying for cash (an option not feasible for the poor) from merchants who don't declare their cash incomes.

The Property Tax Over 80 percent of all local tax revenue is derived from the property tax. There is some disagreement about whether this is a regressive tax, but it *is* a deduction that you may take on your federal income tax. For example, if you paid $3,000 in property tax, you are entitled to a $3,000 deduction on your federal income tax return.

The State and Local Fiscal Dilemma

Since World War II the state and local governments have been expected to provide an increasing amount of service, most notably health, welfare, edu-

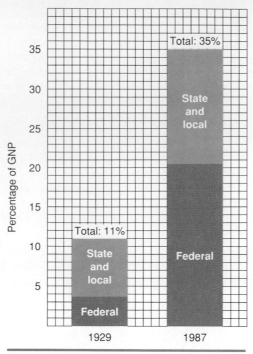

Figure 6–2
Government Tax Receipts as
Percentage of GNP, 1929 and 1987

Source: 1987 *Economic Report of the President*, pp. 256, 341.

cation, and police protection. In 1945 state and local taxes were about 5 percent of GNP, now they are just under 12 percent. During the 1960s and 1970s the federal government accommodated the fiscal needs of states and cities through increasing grants-in-aid and general revenue sharing. This increase was not only stemmed by the Reagan administration, but strongly reversed.

At a time when they can no longer look to Washington for increased aid, some of the states and cities are finding that they have gone to the well once too often with respect to raising their own taxes. Back in 1978 Proposition 13 was passed in California, limiting the growth of property taxes. Other states, most notably Massachusetts, soon followed suit.

Furthermore, under our federal system, neighboring states and local governments are in direct competition with one another for tax dollars. If one government's tax rates—particularly the sales and property taxes—rise too far above the levels of its neighbors, its citizens will vote with their feet. They will shop or even move to the areas that have lower tax rates. Were there a uniform national sales or property tax, it could be more easily raised when necessary. As long as the neighboring government units are in direct competition, it will be very hard to raise the necessary tax revenues.

Comparison of Taxes in the United States and Other Countries

Contrary to popular opinion, Americans are not very heavily taxed in comparison with the citizens of other industrial countries. As we see in Figure 6-3, taxes are about 32 percent of our GNP while in Sweden they are 51 percent and in the Netherlands 46 percent. Keep in mind that these taxes

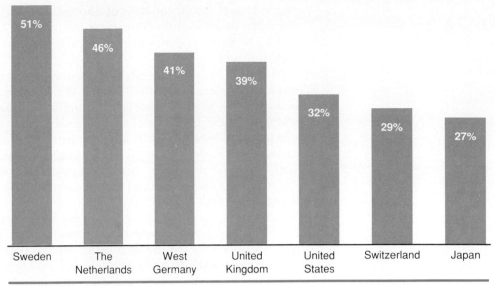

Figure 6–3
Taxes as a Percentage of GNP in
Selected Industrial Countries, 1981

Source: *OECD National Accounts of OECD Countries,*
1964–1981, vol. 2.

include federal, state, and local taxes, and that about half of that total is redistributed in the form of transfer payments such as Social Security, public assistance, food stamps, and unemployment insurance payments.

Two Principles of Taxation: Ability-to-Pay versus Benefits Received

There are two questions that economists, politicians, moralists, and other people concerned with the fairness of taxation ask over and over: (1) Should the amount of taxes that people pay be based on their ability to pay? or (2) Should they be based on the benefits that they receive? Not surprisingly, the ability-to-pay and the benefits-received principles were quickly discovered.

If taxes were based solely on ability to pay, rich people would pay much higher proportions of their incomes to the Internal Revenue Service than middle-class people, who, in turn, would be paying a much higher proportion of their incomes than poor people. Is this fair? Yes—if we are concerned only with peoples' incomes.

But what if some people received more benefits from the proceeds of these tax dollars than other people. If my house caught fire, I would receive the benefits of the fire department's services, whereas all my neighbors would not (unless, of course, the fire department, by putting out the fire in my house, prevented it from spreading to my neighbors' houses). Even more to the point, the family receiving food stamps or welfare payments is receiving greater benefits from the government than those who receive nothing.

Quite clearly, then, some people receive more benefits from the government than others. If we were to apply the benefits-received principle strictly, we would obtain some rather absurd results. We would take away in tax payments the food stamps or welfare payments that a poor family received. Would *this* make sense? And if you had the misfortune of having a fire in your house, it might pay not to call the fire department; your insurance would probably cover most of your losses, while the fire department might charge you thousands of dollars for their services. And if your neighbors also opted to collect on *their* insurance policies as the fire spread, we'd end up with very few houses in your town—all because of the benefits-received principle.

Still another problem with the benefits-received principle is that we are not always clear about the value of the benefits we are receiving. Take, for instance, the so-called nuclear umbrella that the Department of Defense was kind enough to install several miles above our country. Even though our military leaders tell us that the Russians can easily get several thousand missiles through this umbrella, we are still paying $1,200 per capita every year for this protection. Talk about protection money!

Police protection is another case in point. How do we *know* when we are being protected? Does a masked man on a white horse perform some heroic act and then, just to make sure we get the message, leave behind a silver bullet? When a police patrol car drives by, this action may well avert a mugging, but does the potential muggee realize that he has just been saved?

So what we're left with are two undeniably noble principles that are not easily applied. The federal personal income tax is an attempt to apply the ability-to-pay principle, since it is fairly progressive. Local sewer taxes are based on water usage; they are therefore an application of the benefits-received principle. Another such application is the federal and state tax on gasoline, which is geared to the number of miles we drive on public roads. And, of course, all the tolls we pay are also based on the benefits-received principle.

We cannot, however, devise a tax that is based on both principles since they are apparently mutually exclusive. Until we have a society in which everyone earns the same income and receives the same government benefits, we will have to compromise by basing some taxes on our ability to pay and others on the benefits we receive.

The Economic Role of Government

We've talked a lot in this chapter about taxes and government spending. In a word, the government giveth and the government taketh away.

One thing that should be readily apparent is that the federal government, and to a lesser degree, state and local governments, have a tremendous impact on our economy. Our analysis, however, will now be confined to the federal government. Although there is a great deal of overlap, we are going to consider, sequentially, three specific economic functions of government: redistribution of income, stabilization, and economic regulation.

(1) Redistribution of Income

Does the government take from the rich and give to the poor—or is it the other way around?

The government is sometimes seen as a modern-day Robin Hood, redistributing money from rich taxpayers to poor welfare recipients, or from huge corporations to unemployment benefit recipients. Food stamps, Medicaid, and disability payments are all programs aimed mainly at the needy, while the bill is footed by the relatively well-to-do taxpayer.

Some would dissent from this view by purporting that there is also welfare for the rich, whether in the form of subsidies to corporate farmers and shipbuilders, tax breaks for defense contractors, oil companies, and other large corporations, or huge government contracts for missile systems.

While one may well question whether the government takes from the rich and gives to the poor or vice versa, as former President Richard Nixon was fond of saying, "Let me make one thing perfectly clear": the government does redistribute hundreds of billions of dollars every year. We now have a federal budget of some $1,200 billion. In effect, then, the government taxes and borrows about $1,200 billion a year, spends nearly half of it, and gives the rest of it away in the form of transfer payments.

What is the economic impact of all this churning? The largest expenditure, defense, provides contractors and subcontractors with hundreds of billions of dollars for producing all those guns, tanks, planes, and missiles. The next largest expenditure, Social Security, obviously redistributes money from those currently working to those who have retired. But perhaps the most important economic impact of all this spending is the stabilization function, which we shall consider next.

(2) Stabilization

Two basic goals of the federal government have been stable prices and low unemployment. Stated somewhat differently, the goals may be seen as a fairly high rate of economic growth (which would hold the rate of unemployment to a minimum) with no inflation.

How the government might go about attaining these goals is the subject of Chapters 10 through 16. But at this time we can already gauge some of the economic impact of the federal budget and how that budget might affect the stability of our economy.

The $1,200 billion that the federal government now dispenses annually puts a floor under our economy's purchasing power. During the early stages of the Great Depression, the federal government was only a minor economic player. The total federal budget was under 5 percent of GNP. Now it's over 25 percent.

Thus, no matter how bad things might get, at least the government will provide a floor under total spending. However there is considerable evidence that the huge federal budget may be contributing to inflation as well as to certain other economic problems.[7]

(3) Economic Regulation

Another important function of government is to provide the economic rules of the game, and somewhat more broadly, the social and political context in which the economy operates. Some of these rules are easily understood: the fostering of competition among business firms, environmental protection laws, and a court system to adjudicate disputes and punish offenders. Beyond these, the government helps provide the social and political framework in which individuals and business firms are able to smoothly function.

In Chapter 4 we talked about the role of competition and the price mechanism in our economic system. A competitive system will function only as long as there is competition. If there are only a handful of firms in several industries, we no longer have competition. It is the government's job to make sure this doesn't happen.

"That government is best which governs least."
—Thomas Jefferson

Within our political and social framework, the government must also allow individuals and business firms to operate with the maximum degree of freedom. There are those who consider the current level of government regulation blatant interference with their economic freedom.

Does that freedom imply the right to pollute the environment or to monopolize an industry by driving competitors out of business? Perhaps Justice

---

[7] Higher interest rates, the mounting public debt, and the foreign trade deficit are the problems to which I refer. Each will be discussed in subsequent chapters.

Oliver Wendell Holmes put it best when he noted that a person's freedom to swing his fist extended only as far as his neighbor's nose. Unfortunately, in the economic environment, there is little unanimity about how far economic freedom may be extended without interfering with society as a whole or the economic rights of specific individuals or business firms.

Adam Smith's do's and don'ts

Adam Smith, in his monumental *The Wealth of Nations*, published in 1776, summed up the do's and don'ts of economic endeavor: "Every man, as long as he does not violate the laws of justice, is left perfectly free to pursue his own interest his own way, and to bring both his industry and capital into competition with those of any other man, or order of men."[8]

Smith went on to define the economic role of government:

> According to the system of natural liberty, the sovereign has only three duties to attend to; three duties of great importance, indeed, but plain and intelligible to common understandings: first, the duty of protecting the society from the violence and invasion of other independent societies; secondly, the duty of protecting, as far as possible, every member of the society from the injustice or oppression of every other member of it, or the duty of establishing an exact administration of justice; and, thirdly, the duty of erecting and maintaining certain public works and certain public institutions, which it can never be for the interest of any individual, or small number of individuals, to erect and maintain; because the profit could never repay the expence to any individual or small number of individuals, though it may frequently do much more than repay it to a great society.[9]

(4) Conclusion

Until the early 1930s, just before the advent of President Roosevelt's New Deal, the federal government more or less followed the role prescribed by Adam Smith. Although Smith never would have approved high protective tariffs, land subsidies to railroads, and possibly not even the antitrust legislation and trust-busting of the 1890–1915 period, until the 1930s the basic economic policy of the government could well have been described as laissez-faire.[10]

Big government, like rock 'n roll, is here to stay.

In 1980 Ronald Reagan campaigned for the presidency by promising to "get the government off the backs of the American people." While he did attain a certain measure of success in cutting back some government spending programs and in fostering a less rigorous approach to government regulation, it remains obvious that big government is here to stay. An open question, though, is just how big big government will be.

This concludes our analysis of the government sector. Remember that we designate government spending by the letter G. We will turn now to the business sector, where we will concentrate on investment, which is designated by the letter I. And in the succeeding chapter, consumption, or C, will be discussed. Each of these letters will then be put together in the equation $Y = C + I + G$. I know you can hardly wait.

---

[8] Adam Smith, *The Wealth of Nations* (London: Methuen, 1950), Book 4, Ch. 9, p. 208.

[9] Smith, *Wealth of Nations*, pp. 208–9.

[10] This is a French expression that means "to leave alone" or "hands off." In this context, a laissez-faire policy means that the government keeps its hands off business, allowing it to operate without interference.

Workbook for Chapter 6

Name
Date

Multiple-Choice Questions

Circle the letter that corresponds to the best answer.

1. The role of government grew most rapidly during the period

a. 1920–1933   **b.** 1933–1945   **c.** 1945–1960

d. 1960– 1975

2. The seeds of the expansion of the economic role of the federal government were sown during the administration of

a. Franklin Roosevelt   **b.** Dwight Eisenhower

c. Richard Nixon   **d.** Ronald Reagan

3. The federal government spends about $_____ a year.

a. $1,200 million   **b.** $1,200 billion   **c.** $1,200 trillion   **d.** $1,200 quadrillion

4. The key agency in the preparation of the president's budget is

a. the Treasury   **b.** the OMB   **c.** the Comptroller of the Currency   **d.** the Department of Defense

5. The federal government's fiscal year begins on

a. January 1   **b.** July 1   **c.** October 1

d. November 1

6. Transfer payments to individuals comprise about _____ percent of the federal budget

a. 20   **b.** 40   **c.** 60   **d.** 80

7. Which federal spending program grew the fastest in the 1980s?

a. defense   **b.** interest on the national debt   **c.** aid to mass transit   **d.** aid to education

8. Compared to federal spending, state and local spending is

a. twice as large   **b.** about the same   **c.** half as large   **d.** one quarter as large

9. The largest federal government purchase on final goods and services is

a. Social Security   **b.** defense   **c.** interest on the national debt   **d.** foreign aid

10. If one person earns $10,000 and the other person earns $100,000 a year, they will pay Social Security tax

a. at the same average tax rate   **b.** but the poorer person will pay at a higher average tax rate   **c.** but the richer person will pay at a higher average tax rate   **d.** but it is impossible to tell what their average tax rates are

11. The least regressive tax listed here is the

a. Social Security tax   **b.** federal personal income tax   **c.** federal excise tax   **d.** state sales tax

12. Each of the following is a direct tax except _____ tax.

a. Social Security   **b.** federal personal income

c. corporate income   **d.** federal excise

13. Which is true?

a. The rich are hurt by regressive taxes.   **b.** The poor are hurt by progressive taxes.   **c.** The federal personal income tax is a regressive tax.   **d.** None of these statements is true.

14. A tax with an average tax rate of 20 percent for the rich and 2 percent for the middle class is

a. progressive   **b.** regressive   **c.** proportional

d. none of these

15. In 1989 a person earning $200,000 will pay Social Security tax on

a. none of her income   **b.** all of her income

c. nearly all of her income   **d.** less than half of her income

16. You can cut down legally on how much income tax you pay by means of

a. tax avoidance   **b.** tax evasion   **c.** both tax evasion and tax avoidance   **d.** neither tax evasion nor tax avoidance

17. A person making $5 million in interest on municipal bonds will be taxed on this income at an average tax rate of

a. 33 percent   **b.** 28 percent   **c.** 15 percent

d. 0 percent

18. The most important source of federal tax revenue is the

a. personal income tax   **b.** corporate income tax

c. federal excise tax   **d.** payroll tax

19. Until 1981 the maximum marginal tax rate on the federal income tax was

a. 70 percent   **b.** 50 percent   **c.** 40 percent

d. 33 percent

20. Today for every retired person there is (are) _____ person(s) in the labor force.

a. one   **b.** two   **c.** three   **d.** four

21. The maximum corporate income tax rate is _____ percent.

a. 50   **b.** 46   **c.** 40   **d.** 34

22. Each of the following is subject to a federal excise tax except

a. phone calls   **b.** gasoline   **c.** cigarette

d. paper products

23. Taxes (including federal, state, and local) are about _____ of our GNP.

a. 10 percent   **b.** 25 percent   **c.** 33 percent

d. 45 percent

24. The most important source of state tax revenue is the _____ tax.

a. property   **b.** income   **c.** excise   **d.** sales

25. The most important source of local tax revenue is the _____ tax.

a. property   **b.** income   **c.** excise   **d.** sales

26. Compared with the citizens of other industrial countries, Americans are

a. much more heavily taxed   **b.** somewhat more heavily taxed   **c.** taxed at about the same rate

d. not as heavily taxed

27. As a redistributor of income the federal government plays

a. no role   **b.** a very minor role   **c.** a major role

d. a completely dominating role

28. Adam Smith endorsed each of the following roles of government except

a. providing for defense   **b.** establishing system of justice   **c.** erecting a limited number of public works   **d.** guaranteeing a job to every person ready, willing, and able to work

Fill-In Questions

1. The economic role of the federal government began to get very large in the year _____.

2. The federal government has three basic economic influences: (1) _____; (2) _____; and (3) _____.

3. Fiscal year 1993 begins on _____ (fill in month, day, and year).

4. The federal government department that plays the central role in the preparation of the president's budget is _____.

5. In 1990 we will spend about $_____ on defense.

6. Compared to 1980, interest on the federal debt by 1990 has _____.

7. In 1990 the federal government will spend about $_____.

8. Total government purchases (including federal, state, and local) come to $_____.

9. The largest federal government transfer payment

is _____ .

10. The average tax rate is found by dividing _____

by _____ .

11. Progressive taxes place the greatest burden on the

_____ .

12. Examples of regressive taxes include _____

and _____ .

13. In 1989 the Social Security tax rate was _____
percent.

14. The most important source of federal tax revenue

is the _____ tax.

15. The Economic Recovery Act of 1981 was better

known as the _____ .

16. The maximum marginal tax rate today is _____
percent.

17. Most Americans are taxed at marginal rates of

_____ percent and _____ percent.

18. If you earned $10,000 in 1989, how much would
the federal government collect in payroll tax?

$_____

19. There is currently a federal excise tax on

(1) _____ , (2) _____ , (3) _____ ,

(4) _____ , and (5) _____ .

20. The state and local governments have been faced
with a dilemma since World War II. They have been

expected to _____ , but they have had difficulty

_____ .

21. The ability-to-pay principle of taxation states that

_____ .

22. The benefits-received principle of taxation states

that _____ .

23. The federal government has three economic roles:

(1) _____ , (2) _____ , and (3) _____ .

24. If Adam Smith were alive today, he would say

that our government is too _____ .

Problems

1. If the federal government spends $2 trillion, of
which $800 billion are transfer payments, and it re-
ceives tax revenues of $1.8 trillion, how much is the
deficit?

2. Using the data from the previous problem, how
much is G?

3. If a person earned $80,000 in 1989, how much So-
cial Security tax did he/she pay?

4. If a person earned $10,000 in 1989, how much So-
cial Security tax did he/she pay?

5. If you earned $20,000 and paid $1,000 in federal
income tax, how much was your average tax rate?

6. If you had a marginal tax rate of 28 percent and
earned an extra $10,000, how much tax would you
pay?

7. If you earned an extra $1,000 and paid $150 in
taxes on that income, how much would your marginal tax rate be?

8. How much income tax would be paid by a family
of five filing jointly if their income was $40,000 and
they took the standard deduction?

9. How much income tax would be paid by a single
person if his income was $35,000 and he had $5,000
in deductions?

The Business-Investment Sector

Unlike China, the Soviet Union, and dozens of other communist and socialist nations, in the United States most investment is carried out by private business firms rather than by the government. That investment consists of the production of new plant and equipment, residential housing, and additions to our inventories.

Chapter Objectives

In this chapter you'll learn about:
- The three types of business firms.
- How investment is carried out.
- The difference between gross and net investment.
- How capital is accumulated.
- The determinants of the level of investment.

Proprietorships, Partnerships, and Corporations

Most businesses are small.

There are roughly 20 million business firms in the United States. About 7 out of 10 are proprietorships, 1 out of 10 is a partnership, and 2 out of 10 are corporations. Proprietorships are owned by a single person and they are almost always small businesses. Partnerships, which are also usually very small, are owned by two or more people. There are only a few very large businesses in our country, and virtually all of these are corporations. Most corporations, like most businesses, are very small.

The Proprietorship

The typical proprietorship would be a grocery, a barbershop, a candy store, restaurant, family farm, or filling station. Chances are, nearly all of the places in the neighborhood where you shop are proprietorships.

The Partnership

Two or more people can own a partnership. Although the typical partnership has two people, some law and accounting firms have hundreds of partners. Two key advantages of forming a partnership are raising more capital and dividing the work and responsibility of running the business.

A typical division of labor between partners would be production and sales, or, in the parlance of business, inside and outside. The advantages of forming a partnership must be weighed against two basic disadvantages. The first is that the partnership must be dissolved when any of its members die or want to leave the business. A second disadvantage is that of unlimited liability.

Both proprietors and partners are liable for all debts incurred by their businesses. For example, if the firm is sued for negligence, the owners are personally liable to pay the amount awarded if the firm cannot do so. If one partner absconds with funds, the other partners may lose their homes and cars even though they were innocent victims. The way out of ever having to face this dilemma is to incorporate.

The Corporation

The main advantage to incorporating is limited liability.

The key advantage of the corporation is limited liability. That is, each owner's liability is limited to the amount of money he has invested in the business. If there's a negligence suit or someone absconds with funds, the most you can lose is your investment. No one can touch your house, car, or any other personal property.

As we mentioned in the last chapter, a corporation is a legal person. As such, it can sue and be sued. What is significant about this attribute is that the people who own the corporation—the stockholders—cannot be sued no matter how grievous the transgressions of the corporation.

A second advantage of a corporation is its perpetual life. While a partnership must be dissolved when one of the partners leaves the business, a corporation can continue indefinitely: the stock owned by the principal who wants to pull out is purchased by someone else. In the case of very large, publicly held corporations, such transactions take place routinely at the major stock exchanges.

Still another advantage of incorporating is that the company can sell stock to the public to raise more money. Because the owners have limited liability and the firm itself has perpetual life, the corporation is in a better position than the proprietorship or partnership to go to the public to raise funds.

Most corporations are small firms.

Of course, only a tiny fraction of all corporations ever go public. Nearly all are relatively small businesses that are completely owned by just a few individuals. However, virtually all large companies in the United States are corporations.

Perhaps all of this can be cleared up by a syllogism:[1] (1) nearly all large companies are corporations; (2) nearly all corporations are small companies. Therefore, a small minority of corporations constitutes nearly all the large companies. In other words, of nearly 4 million corporations, about 2,000 are large companies, and these 2,000 large corporations constitute nearly all the nation's large companies.

Although accounting for only 20 percent of the nation's business firms, corporations collect over 90 percent of all business receipts. While most cor-

---

[1] What is a syllogism? It is a form of reasoning consisting of two statements and a conclusion drawn from them.

porations are tiny enterprises that incorporated to limit the liability of the owners, there are perhaps 2,000 really large corporations. These companies do most of the nation's business.

Only a very small percentage of corporations actually sells stock, but it should be obvious that the limited liability of the stockholders would be a great advantage in raising capital. We have already emphasized that there are only a few really large businesses in the United States out of the nearly 20 million in existence. Each large firm is a corporation and virtually each one is publicly held (that is, it sells stock to the public).

Two disadvantages to incorporating

There are two disadvantages to incorporating. First, you have to have papers drawn up and pay a fee for a charter. The expense of doing this varies, but two of the most popular states in which to incorporate, Delaware and New Jersey, appear to make things the easiest. A second disadvantage is that you will have to pay federal, and possibly state, corporate income tax. Although the rates are very low for small corporations, those with profits of over $75,000 must pay 34 percent of anything above that amount to the Internal Revenue Service. (How much tax would a company with profits of $100 million have to pay to the federal government?[2])

Stocks and Bonds

The stockholders are the owners of a corporation. Bondholders lend money to a company and are therefore creditors rather than owners. This distinction becomes important when we consider the order in which people are paid off when the corporation is doing well and when it goes bankrupt.

Two types of stock

There are two types of corporate stock—common and preferred. The advantage of owning preferred is that you will be paid a stipulated dividend, say 8 percent of the face value of your stock, provided there are any profits out of which to pay dividends. After you are paid, if there are still some profits left, the common stockholders will be paid.

Why bother to own common stock? Mainly because only common stockholders may vote on issues of concern to the corporation as well as on who gets to run the corporation. Both preferred and common stockholders own the corporation, or hold equity in the company, but only common stockholders vote.

Bondholders are creditors— not owners.

Bondholders are creditors rather than owners of the corporation. Like the preferred stockholders, they must be paid a stipulated percentage of the face value of their bonds, say 10 percent, in the form of interest, and they must be paid whether or not the company makes a profit. In fact, the interest they are paid is considered one of the costs of doing business. And should a company go bankrupt, the bondholders, as creditors, would have to be paid off before the owners of preferred and common stock saw any money.

One might ask how much money would be needed to gain control of a large corporation. Let's consider a corporation that's capitalized for $500 million—$300 million in bonds, $120 million in preferred stock, and $80 million in common stock. Theoretically, you would need slightly over $40 million or 50 percent plus one share of the common stock.

But most large corporations are rather widely held, that is, there are many stockholders with only a few holding even 1 percent. Furthermore, many stockholders either don't bother to vote their shares or they give proxies to others who will. Usually then, if you hold about 5 percent of the common stock of a company, that will be sufficient for control. And so, in this case, by holding $4,000,000 worth of common stock (5 percent of $80 million), you should be able to control this $500 million corporation.

---

2 Almost $34 million ($33,974,500, to be exact).

Investment

Investment is really the thing that makes our economy go. When we have prosperity, investment is high and rising. And when we're in a recession, it is low and falling. Let's define investment and then see how it varies.

You are investing if you are adding to your firm's plant, equipment, or inventory.

Investment, in a word, is any new plant, equipment, additional inventory, or residential housing.[3] Plant includes factories, office buildings, department and retail stores, and shopping malls. Examples of equipment are assembly lines, machine tools, display cases, cash registers, computer systems, typewriters, and office furniture—as long as it's purchased by businesses. For example, if you buy a car for your personal use, it's a consumption expenditure. But if Shell Oil buys a car for its executives to ride around in (on company business), then it's an investment. The key question we must ask is whether you are adding to the company's plant, equipment, or inventory. If not—then it's not investment.

What if you were to purchase 100 shares of New York Telephone stock? Would that be investment? Does that add (directly) to New York Telephone's plant, equipment, or inventory? It doesn't? Then it is not investment. It's merely a finanacial transaction. When New York Telephone uses those funds to buy plant, equipment, or inventory—*then* it's investment.

How to calculate inventory investment

Inventory investment is a little tricky. We include only the net change from January 1 to December 31 of a given year. For example, how much was inventory investment for General Motors in 1983 (using the figures in Table 7–1)?

Table 7–1
Hypothetical Inventory Levels of General Motors

Date	Level of Inventory
January 1, 1983	$120 million
July 1, 1983	145 million
December 31, 1983	130 million

How much was GM's inventory investment in 1983? $25 million? Nope. $395 million? Nope. The answer is $10 million. All you have to do is look at the level of inventory on January 1 and on December 31 and calculate the difference.

Let's try another one. Using Table 7–2's data, calculate the inventory investment in 1989 for Shell Oil.

Your answer should be −$10 million. Between the first of the year and the last day of the year, the level of Shell's inventory went down by $10 million. In other words, inventory investment was negative.

That we can have negative inventory investment is very significant. Since investment is one sector of GNP, if inventories decline, this will be a drag on GNP. And that's what happens during recessions.

---

[3] Economists are not in complete agreement (what else is new?) about whether new residential housing is a category of investment or consumption. Since the quasi-official position of the profession is that it belongs in the investment category, we'll go along with that position and classify residential housing as investment.

Residential construction does not properly belong in a chapter on business investment, but I am prepared, just this once, to dispense with propriety, because I don't know where else to put it.

Table 7–2
Hypothetical Inventory Levels of
Shell Oil

Date	Level of Inventory
January 1, 1989	$230 million
May 15, 1989	215 million
September 1, 1989	240 million
December 31, 1989	220 million

A glance at Figure 7-1 shows just how unstable inventory investment has been over the last 35 years. In fact, it's rather unlikely that you've ever been on a roller coaster that had as many steep ups and downs as inventory investment, especially around the time of recessions. Nearly all the steep drops are associated with recessions and the years of negative investment (when inventories were being depleted) all occurred during recession years—1954, 1958, 1975, 1980, and 1982.

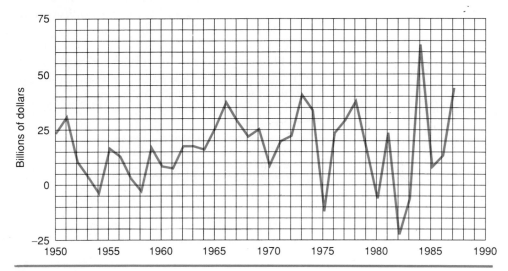

Figure 7–1
Inventory Investment, 1950–1987
(in billions of 1972 dollars)

Source: *1988 Economic Report of the President,*
p. 267.

Residential building involves replacing our aging housing stock as well as adding to it. During the 25 years following World War II we had a tremendous spurt in residential building, as a majority of the American population moved to the suburbs. Today there is continued building, particularly in the outlying areas of the suburbs (sometimes called the "exurbs") 50–100 miles from the nearest city, but the postwar housing boom has been over for just about two decades.

Residential home building fluctuates considerably from year to year. Mortgage interest rates play a dominant role. For example, during the period 1979 to 1982, when mortgage rates reached 15 and 16 percent in most parts of the country, new housing starts plunged by nearly 40 percent. Another factor that causes steep declines in home construction is periodic overbuilding. Once the surplus of new homes on the market is worked off, residential construciton will go into another boom period.

Investment is very unstable.

What this all comes down to is that investment is the most volatile sector in our economy. Fluctuations in GNP are largely fluctuations in investment. More often than not, our recessions are touched off by declines in investment and our recoveries are brought about by rising investment.

Gross Investment versus Net Investment

Gross Investment − Depreciation = Net investment.

Most of us are painfully familiar with the distinction between gross income (or what your boss tells you you are earning) and net income (or what you actually take home after taxes and other deductions). Gross and net investment are parallel concepts. In fact, gross investment − depreciation = net investment.

Gross investment is the nation's entire expenditure on plant, equipment, and inventory. It happens that inventory investment is already a net figure, so we need to take a closer look at depreciation in plant and equipment.

Let's say you started the year with 10 machines and bought another 6 during the year. Your gross investment would be 6. If 4 machines (of your original 10) wore out or became obsolete during the year, your depreciation would be 4. Therefore, your gross investment (6) − your depreciation (4) = net investment (2). In other words, you added 2 machines during the year, raising your total from 10 to 12.

Now we're ready to work out a hypothetical problem. Given all the information in Table 7–3, calculate the nation's gross investment and net investment.

Table 7–3
Hypothetical Inventory Levels
and Investment and Depreciation
Schedules of Nation

Date	Level of Inventory
January 1, 1990	$60 billion
July 1, 1990	55 billion
December 31, 1990	70 billion

Expenditures on new plant and equipment:
$120 billion
Depreciation on plant and equipment:
$30 billion

Solution to Table 7–3:

Inventory investment	$ 10 billion
Plus: Expenditures on new plant and equipment ...	120 billion
Gross investment	130 billion
Minus: depreciation	30 billion
Net investment	$100 billion

Gross investment is designated by the letter I. In fact, GNP is the sum of C + I + G (consumption, investment, and government expenditures). In subsequent chapters we will be referring to investment by using the letter I.

Building Capital

At the end of Chapter 4 we stressed that capital (plant, equipment, and inventory) is built up by producing more, consuming less, or some combination thereof. Suppose you want to open a factory with one machine. You have various alternatives.

You might be able to go out and borrow the money to buy the machine. But the person you borrowed from had saved this money by not consuming all of his or her income. And someone else, who built the machine, spent many hours working on it.

Investment involves sacrifice.

Investment, or the building up of capital, takes a great deal of sacrifice. If you decide to save the money yourself, you may have to work overtime, take on a second job, or cut back on your lifestyle.

Finally, if you decide to build the machine yourself, think of all the hours this might take you. All those hours you could have been working at a paid job, or maybe just lying around watching TV. So no matter how you go about building up capital, there's a great deal of sacrifice involved.

To invest, we must work more and consume less.

Essentially, then, to build up our plant, equipment, and inventory, we need to work more and consume less. On this all economists are agreed. Interesting. But Karl Marx parted company with the classical economists of the 19th century when he wrote his landmark *Das Kapital*. Capital, according to Marx, was created by labor, but expropriated by the capitalist, the factory owner. He wrote: "The owner of the money has paid the value of a day's labour power; his, therefore, is the use of it for a day; a day's labour belongs to him. . . . On the one hand the daily sustenance of labour-power costs only half a day's labour, while on the other hand the very same labour-power can work during a whole day, that consequently the value which its use during one day creates, is double what he pays for that use."[4]

In other words, if it costs three shillings to keep a person alive for 24 hours and this person produces three shillings worth of cloth in six hours, pay him three shillings for 12 hours' work. And if he objects, just have him look out the window at the factory gate where hundreds of people stand waiting for a chance to have his job.

They are, incidentally, the *reserve army* of the unemployed, a term I originally thought referred to the Army Reserve unit to which I once belonged. Every other Wednesday night or Sunday, we'd put on these uniforms and sit around playing cards, reading, or listening to the football game. But Karl Marx's reserve army was evidently much more anxious to do some work.

Investment in plant and equipment is not as unstable as that in inventory, but it should be clear from Figure 7-2 that plant and equipment spending also has its ups and downs. Unlike inventory investment, even in a bad year there will still be a substantial amount of investment in new plant and equipment, mainly because old and obsolete factories, office buildings, and machinery must be replaced. This is the depreciation part of investment.

A second reason for investment, even in bad years, is that most of it has been planned years ahead and will be carried out on schedule regardless of

---

[4] Karl Marx, *Das Kapital* (New York: International Publishers, 1967), Vol. 1, pp. 193–94.

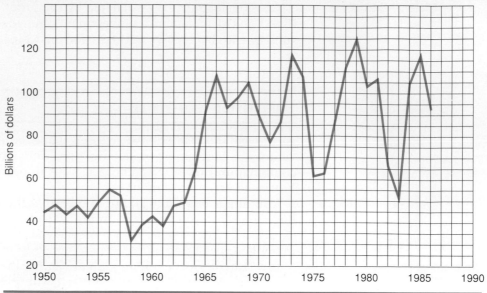

Figure 7–2
Investment in Plant and Equipment,
1950–1987
(in 1982 dollars)

Source: *1988 Economic Report of the President*,
p. 267.

what phase the business cycle is in. Since this plant and equipment is being built to meet the needs of the years ahead, little would be gained by postponing building for the duration of a recession.

A final reason for carrying out capital investment during a recession is that interest rates tend to come down at that time. Since the cost of borrowing money is a major part of construction costs, it would be advantagous to carry out construction projects during times of recession. Other resources too would tend to be available at lower costs.

Each of these factors places a floor under investment spending during recession years. Nevertheless, as we can see by the dips in Figure 7–2 during recession years—1958, 1975, and 1982—there have been major declines in spending on new plant and equipment.

The three reasons we cited for the stability of investment during business downturns were overwhelmed by the general economic collapse of the Great Depression. Why replace worn-out and obsolete plant and equipment when your plant is half idle? Why carry out long-term investment plans when your firm may not survive the next few weeks? And why bother to borrow at low interest rates when your expected rate of profit is negative?

Investment in plant and equipment plummeted from $37.5 billion in 1929 to $10.4 billion in 1933 (in 1972 dollars).[5] While there are those who believe another depression could happen at any time, we shall see in subsequent chapters that we have several safeguards built into our economy to

---

[5] In 1929 plant and equipment spending was $10.6 billion; it sank to $2.4 billion in 1933. During that period the prices of newly constructed plant and equipment fell by over 20 percent, so the decline in investment wasn't quite as bad as it appeared. To show this we would need to correct for price changes (in this case, price declines, or deflation). We do that by using 1972 dollars. We did the same thing in Chapter 5 when we used the GNP deflator, and we will do the same thing in the next chapter with the consumer price index.

prevent a collapse of such proportions. Nevertheless, investment remains the loose cannon on our economic deck, a destabilizing element that tends to push our economy to its highs and lows.

The Determinants of the Level of Investment

The level of investment is determined by many factors. We'll confine ourselves to four.[6]

(1) The Sales Outlook

You won't invest if your sales outlook is bad.

If you can't sell your goods or services, there's no point in investing, so the ultimate determinant of the level of investment is the business firm's sales outlook. If business is good and sales are expected to be good for the next few months, then business firms will be willing to take on more inventory. And if sales look good for the next few years, additional plant and equipment will probably be purchased.

(2) Capacity Utilization Rate

This is the percentage of plant and equipment that is actually being used at any given time. Since it would be virtually impossible to use every single factory, office, and piece of machinery day in and day out, we will always have *some* idle plant and equipment.

Generally, manufacturing firms use about 80 to 85 percent of their capacity. When business really gets good, the capacity utilization rate approaches 90 percent; during severe recessions, like those of 1974–75 and 1981–82, this rate dips below 70 percent (see Figure 7–3).

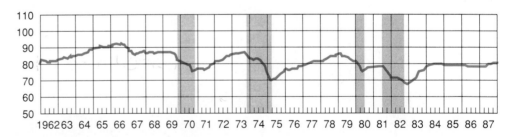

**Figure 7–3
Capacity Utilization Rate in Manufacturing, 1962–1988**

Source: U.S. Department of Commerce, *Business Conditions Digest*, March 1988, p. 20.

You won't invest if you have a lot of unused capacity.

For our purposes, we can count on the capacity utilization rate as an important influence on the level of investment in plant and equipment. At high rates, there is considerable incentive to build more plant and equipment because sales are pressing against factory capacity. During really bad

---

[6] Additional factors are corporate income tax rates, depreciation allowances, the level of technology, and the cost of constructing new plant and equipment.

recessions, when demand is slack, one third of our factories and equipment may be idle. Why build more?

We must temper this analysis by taking note of two additional factors. First, it is likely that we are understating the capacity utilization rate by counting much obsolete or unusable capacity.[7] For example, steel mill and auto plant closings in the early 1980s indicated that some of the plant and equipment in those industries had been counted for several years when their use was economically unfeasible. Second, manufacturing has been a shrinking part of our economy for at least four decades. It now accounts for less than one out of every five jobs in our economy.

(3) The Interest Rate

This is the cost of borrowing money. There are actually many different interest rates, depending on a firm's creditworthiness and the size of the loan.

You won't invest if interest rates are too high.

Suppose you want to borrow $1,000 and the bank will charge you 12 percent interest. How much interest will you have to pay if you borrow the $1,000 for one year?

Go ahead. Work it out.

What did you get? I hope you got $120. If you didn't, here's how to do it:

$$\text{Interest rate} = \frac{\text{Interest paid}}{\text{Amount borrowed}}$$

$$.12 = \frac{x}{\$1,000}$$

Now, multiply both sides by $1,000:

$$\$120 = x$$

In general, the lower the interest rate, the more business firms will borrow. But to know how much they will borrow—or whether they will borrow at all in any particular instance—we need to compare the interest rate with the expected rate of profit on our investment.

(4) The Expected Rate of Profit

Economists are not happy unless they give virtually the same concept at least three different names. Therefore, the expected rate of profit is some-

---

[7] Suppose our capacity utilization rate was 80 percent, but 10 percent of our plant and equipment was obsolete or unusable. Then our true capacity utilization would be 89 percent (80/90).

times called the marginal efficiency of capital or the marginal efficiency of investment. We'll define it this way:

$$\text{Expected rate of profit} = \frac{\text{Expected profits}}{\text{Money invested}}$$

Now, of course, we have to work out a problem. Here's an easy one: How much is the expected profit rate on a $10,000 investment if you expect to make a profit of $1,650? You know how things work around here. Do it yourself, then check your result against mine. I'm always right. But you can't be unless you try.

$$\text{Expected rate of profit} = \frac{\text{Expected profits}}{\text{Money invested}}$$

$$= \frac{\$1,650}{\$10,000}$$

$$= 16.5 \text{ percent}$$

The relationship between the interest rate and the expected profit rate was underscored by John Maynard Keynes in his landmark *The General Theory of Employment, Interest, and Money*. Keynes said that every profit opportunity would be exploited as long as the expected profit rate (which he called the "marginal efficiency of capital") exceeded the interest rate: "The rate of investment will be pushed to . . . where the marginal efficiency of capital in general is equal to the market rate of interest."[8]

You won't invest unless the expected profit rate is high enough.

Suppose your business firm is interested in borrowing $100,000 at the going interest rate of 15 percent to buy inventory. If your expected profit rate is 18 percent, would it pay to borrow? In other words, after you paid off the interest, how much money would you have left? ($18,000 − $15,000 in interest = $3,000.) You would stand to make $3,000 profit. Of course you would borrow the money.

Now we're ready for a very easy three-part problem. Suppose you could borrow money at 20 percent interest and someone offered to buy 100 pounds of a certain substance from you at $1,300 a pound. It costs you only $1,000 a pound to grow this substance. The only problem is that the money you borrow will be tied up for a year until you are able to pay it back. Answer yes or no to each of these three questions:

a. Would you accept the deal as it stands?

---

[8] John Maynard Keynes, *The General Theory of Employment, Interest, and Money* (New York: Harcourt Brace Jovanovich 1958), pp. 136–37.

b. Would the deal be acceptable if the interest rate were 10 percent?

c. Would the deal be acceptable if the interest rate were 30 percent?

You stand to make a profit of 30 percent using borrowed money. From those profits, you need to pay interest on your loan. If you borrowed money at *(a)* 20 percent interest, you would still have money left over (net profit) after you paid the interest, so it would pay to accept the deal. If you borrowed money at *(b)* 10 percent interest, it would be even more profitable than at 20 percent interest. But if you accepted the deal at *(c)* 30 percent interest, after you paid the interest from your 30 percent profit, there would be no money left over from your sales.

The Summing up of Investment

We're finally ready to include the last part of investment—residential construction spending. To show the relative size of the components of investment, we have put together the data shown in Table 7-4.

Table 7–4
Gross Private Domestic Investment, Selected Years
(in billions of current dollars)

Year	Plant and Equipment	Residential Construction	Inventory Change	Total
1949	24.4	13.9	−3.1	35.3
1959	45.9	26.6	5.7	78.1
1969	101.3	38.2	9.8	149.3
1979	290.2	118.6	14.3	423.0
1987	442.9	228.4	45.4	716.7

Source: *1985 Economic Report of the President*,
p. 232; *Economic Indicators*, February, 1988, p. 9.
(Prepared for the Joint Economic Committee by the
President's Council of Economic Advisors.)

The figures here are current rather than in 1972 dollars to make the 1987 data comparable with the data from the other two chapters dealing with GNP components. We've now covered two of the three main components of GNP: G (in the last chapter), and I (in the present chapter). Guess which component comes next?

Workbook for Chapter 7

Name _____

Date _____

Multiple-Choice Questions

Circle the letter that corresponds to the best answer.

1. In the United States investment is done ___d___
a. entirely by the government   b. mostly by the government   c. about half by the government and half by private enterprise   d. mainly by private enterprise

2. Which of these is not investment?   _b_
a. additional inventory   b. the building of a county courthouse   c. the building of a shopping mall
d. the building of an automobile assembly line

3. There are about __c__ million business firms in the United States.
a. 2 million   b. 12 million   c. 20 million
d. 32 million

4. A business firm with one owner is
a. a proprietorship   b. a partnership   c. a corporation   d. none of these

5. A partnership
a. must have exactly two owners   b. must have more than two owners   c. must have more than one owner   d. may have more than one owner

6. A key advantage of a partnership over a proprietorship is
a. limited liability   b. division of responsibility
c. perpetual life of business firm   d. none of these

7. A __c__ is a legal person.
a. proprietorship   b. partnership   c. corporation
d. business firm.

8. Most corporations are
a. publicly held   b. very large   c. very small
d. none of these

9. Corporations collect about _____ percent of all business receipts.
a. 10   b. 30   c. 60   d. 90

10. A key disadvantage of incorporating is that
a. you will have to pay corporation income tax
b. you will have to charge sales tax   c. you will have to sell stock   d. you will have to reorganize the corporation whenever an officer resigns or dies

11. Corporations are controlled by the   _operating business_
a. employees   b. bondholders   c. common stockholders   d. preferred stockholders ← _make money_
get first share of money, don't vote

12. The last to be paid off, whether the corporation does well or goes bankrupt, are the
a. employees   b. bondholders   c. common stockholders   d. preferred stockholders

13. Ownership of a corporation is based on
a. whether you work for the company   b. whether you buy from the company   c. whether you hold the bonds of the company   d. whether you hold stock in the company

14. A corporation's capitalization is based on all of the following except
a. preferred stock   b. common stock   c. bonds
d. sales

15. Which is not investment?   _purchase shares of another compr._
a. the purchase of 100 shares of IBM   b. the construction of a new factory   c. the purchase of a new delivery truck   d. the purchase of inventory

16. Inventory investment is
a. always positive   b. always negative   c. can be either positive or negative   d. can be neither positive nor negative

17. Inventory investment is
a. very stable   b. fairly stable   c. fairly unstable
d. very unstable

18. During severe recessions inventory investment is
a. negative   b. stable   c. fairly high   d. very high

19. Gross investment
a. plus depreciation equals net investment
b. minus depreciation equals net investment
c. plus net investment equals depreciation
d. equals net investment minus depreciation

20. Each of the following might be used to acquire capital except
a. working more   b. consuming less   c. borrowing
d. consuming more

21. Karl Marx said that capital is produced by
a. the worker   b. the capitalist   c. the government   d. money

22. Which is the least stable?
a. investment in plant and equipment   b. investment in residential housing   c. investment in inventory   d. overall investment

23. Business firms invest in plant and equipment during recession years for each of these reasons except
a. interest rates are lower   b. it has been planned years ahead   c. it replaces worn-out plant and equipment   d. it is needed because capacity may be fully utilized

24. During bad recessions investment in plant and equipment will
a. be negative   b. fall by 50 percent   c. fall somewhat   d. rise

25. Each of the following is business investment except
a. inventory investment   b. investment in new plant   c. investment in new equipment   d. investment in new residential housing

26. Investment will be high when the capacity utilization rate is _____ and the interest rate is _____.
a. high, high   b. low, low   c. high, low
d. low, high

27. Our capacity utilization rate is usually between
a. 10 and 30   b. 30 and 50   c. 50 and 70   d. 70 and 90

28. Firms will most likely borrow money for investment when
a. interest rates are low   b. interest rates are high
c. the interest rate is higher than the expected profit rate   d. the expected profit rate is higher than the interest rate

Fill-In Questions

1. Of the big three spending sectors of GNP, the least stable is _____.

2. There are about _____ business firms in the United States.

3. A business firm that is owned by one person is called a _____.

4. A partnership is owned by _____ people.

5. The key advantage of incorporating is _____.

6. Nearly all large companies are corporations and nearly all corporations are small companies. Therefore, _____.

7. Most of the business in this country is done by about _____ corporations.

8. The two main disadvantages of incorporating are (1) _____ and (2) _____.

9. A corporation is owned by its _____.

10. A corporation is controlled by its _____.

11. The creditors of a corporation are mainly its _____.

12. Theoretically, you would need an investment of about $_____ to control a corporation that had $100 million in preferred stock, $50 million in common stock, and $350 million in bonds.

13. The least stable form of investment is _____ investment.

14. Gross investment − _____ = Net investment.

15. According to Karl Marx, capital was created by the _____ and expropriated by the _____.

16. In Marx's terms, the people who wait outside the factory gates for work are the _____.

17. The four main determinants of the level of investment are (1) _____, (2) _____, (3) _____, and (4) _____.

18. During severe recessions our capacity utilization rate dips below _____ percent.

19. The expected profit rate is found by dividing _____ by _____.

20. An investment will be undertaken if the expected profit rate is higher than the _____.

21. Total investment is found by adding (1) _____, (2) _____, and (3) _____.

Problems

1. If a corporation has $100 million in preferred stock, $150 million in common stock, and $250 million in bonds, (*a*) how much is its capitalization? (*b*) theoretically, how much would it take to control it? (*c*) practically speaking, it may take only about how much to control it?

2. If a corporation has gross investment of $150 million and depreciation of $40 million, how much is its net investment?

3. Given the information in Table 1, find inventory investment in 1990.

Table 1

Date	Level of Inventory
January 1, 1990	$500 million
July 1, 1990	530 million
December 31, 1990	485 million

4. Given the information in Table 2, how much was total gross investment in 1991?

Table 2

Item	Amount ($ millions)
Expenditures on new plant and equipment	$100
Depreciation	15
Inventory investment	10
Residential housing investment	30

The Consumption Sector

In this chapter we will complete our examination of the three sectors of GNP: C (consumption), I (investment), and G (government spending). We will also introduce graphing techniques as a tool for macroeconomic analysis, which will be covered in Chapters 10 and 11.

Chapter Objectives
In this chapter we will introduce 10 economic concepts:
- The average propensity to consume.
- The average propensity to save.
- The marginal propensity to consume.
- The marginal propensity to save.
- The multiplier.
- The consumption function.
- The saving function.
- The determinants of consumption.
- The permanent income hypothesis.
- The paradox of thrift.

Consumption

In the United States the average individual spends over 90 percent of his/her disposable income. The total of everyone's expenditures is consumption, designated by the letter C. The largest sector of GNP, C is generally a little less than two thirds.

Consumers spend about half their money on services such as medical care, eating out, life insurance, and legal fees. The rest is spent on durable goods such as television sets and furniture, or on nondurable goods such as food and gasoline. All consumption falls into the two categories of goods or services.

Although consumption is not a steady percentage of disposable income, it is almost always between 90 and 95 percent. John Maynard Keynes noted that consumption is a stable component of income. His theory is called the consumption function, which states that *as income rises, consumption rises, but not as quickly.* For example, if a country's disposable income rises

The consumption function

by 300 (from 2,000 to 2,300), its C will rise, but by less than 300. If C were 1,800, it might rise by 250 to 2,050.[1]

Saving

Saving is simply not spending. Since the average family spends over 90 percent of its disposable income, it saves something less than 10 percent, one of the lowest savings rates among industrialized nations. Average Japanese and West German families, for example, usually save over 20 percent of their disposable incomes.

The Average Propensity to Consume (APC)

The average propensity to consume is the percentage of disposable income spent. Using the data in Table 8-1, let's calculate the APC.

Table 8-1

Disposable income	Consumption
$40,000	$30,000

To find the percentage of disposable income spent, we need to divide consumption by disposable income.

$$\text{APC} = \frac{\text{Consumption}}{\text{Disposable income}}$$

$$\text{APC} = \frac{\text{Consumption}}{\text{Disposable income}} = \frac{\$30{,}000}{40{,}000} = \frac{3}{4} = .75$$

Let's review how this is done. We use the three-step method of solving this problem. First, write the formula. Then, substitute the numbers into the formula. Finally, solve the formula.

You know that $^{\$30{,}000}/_{\$40{,}000}$ can easily be reduced to ¾. To change the fraction (¾) into decimal form, divide 3 by 4. (Remember to always divide the bottom number into the top number.)

$$\frac{\$30{,}000}{\$40{,}000} = \frac{3}{4}$$

$$4\overline{)3.00} \quad .75$$

The Average Propensity to Save (APS)

The APS is the mirror image of the APC. It is the percentage of disposable income saved. Using the data in Table 8-1, calculate the APS.

---

[1] No more Mr. nice guy. From here on we'll refer to billions of dollars in this shorthand way. The number 2,050 represents $2,050 billion (or $2.05 trillion).

Remember (from Chapter 5) that 2,000 represents $2,000 billion, or $2 trillion. This is a convention all economists use when writing about billions and trillions of dollars.

Use the same three-step method we used to calculate the APC: (1) write down the formula, (2) plug in your numbers, and (3) solve. Do it right here.

Now we'll check your work. The formula is:

$$APS = \frac{Saving}{Disposable\ income}$$

$$APS = \frac{Saving}{Disposable\ income}$$

Now we'll substitute into the formula. You already know from Table 8-1 that disposable income is $40,000. How much is saving? It's not in Table 8-1, but since consumption is $30,000, we can find saving by subtracting consumption from disposable income: $40,000 − $30,000 = $10,000. Now we can complete the problem.

$$APS = \frac{Saving}{Disposable\ income} = \frac{\$10,000}{\$40,000} = \frac{1}{4} = .25^2$$

Notice that the APC and the APS add up to one. Let's work out another one, using the data in Table 8-2.

Table 8–2

Disposable income	Saving
$20,000	$1,500

Use the space below to calculate the APC and the APS.

---

[2] To convert ¼ into a decimal, we must divide the bottom number, 4, into the top number, 1.

Solutions:

$$\text{APC} = \frac{C}{\text{Disposable income}} = \frac{\$18{,}500}{20{,}000} = \frac{185}{200} = \frac{37}{40}$$

$$\text{APS} = \frac{\text{Saving}}{\text{Disposable income}} = \frac{\$1{,}500}{20{,}000} = \frac{15}{200} = \frac{3}{40}$$

$$
\begin{array}{cc}
.925 & .075 \\
40\overline{)37.000} & 40\overline{)3.000} \\
-360\text{XX} & \underline{280\text{X}} \\
\overline{100} & 200 \\
\underline{-80} & \underline{-200} \\
200 & \\
\underline{-200} & \\
\end{array}
$$

APC + APS = 1

Notice that once again APC (.925) and APS (.075) add up to one. This is your check to ensure that you haven't made a mistake in your calculations.

Now that we've done all this work, what does it mean to say that a person has an APC of .925 and an APS of .075? Think about it for a moment. Go back to the formulas for the APC and the APS. Think of the APC and the APS as percentages. Obviously then, the APC is the percentage of a person's income that he or she spends. And the APS? That is the percentage of that person's income that is saved. In other words, 92.5 percent is spent and 7.5 percent is saved.

Just two more questions: (1) How much is the APC for the United States? Just give an approximation. (2) How much is our APS? In recent years the APC has been about .95 and the APS .05. In other words, Americans spend about 95 percent of their disposable incomes and save the remaining 5 percent.

The Marginal Propensity to Consume (MPC)

When income changes, so does consumption. When income rises, consumption also rises, but by less than income. That is the consumption function, introduced at the beginning of the chapter.

The formula for calculating the MPC is:

MPC = $\dfrac{\text{Change in C}}{\text{Change in income}}$

$$\frac{\text{Change in C}}{\text{Change in income}}$$

Table 8–3

Disposable income	C
$30,000	$23,000
40,000	31,000

Using the data in Table 8-3, calculate the MPC in the space below.

Solution:

$$\text{MPC} = \frac{\text{Change in C}}{\text{Change in income}} = \frac{\$8,000}{10,000} = \frac{8}{10} = .8$$

Marginal Propensity to Save (MPS)

When income changes, not only does consumption change, but so does saving. When income rises, both consumption and saving will rise. Similarly, when income falls, both consumption and saving fall.

The formula for calculating the MPS is:

$$\frac{\text{Change in Saving}}{\text{Change in Income}}$$

Using Table 8–3 again, calculate the MPS. (Note: Remember how to find saving when you have disposable income and consumption.)[3]

$$\text{MPS} = \frac{\text{Change in Saving}}{\text{Change in Income}}$$

Solution:

$$\text{MPS} = \frac{\text{Change in saving}}{\text{Change in income}} = \frac{\$2,000}{10,000} = \frac{2}{10} = .2$$

Graphing the Consumption Function

Through the ages, generations of economics students have been traumatized by graphs. The consumption function, savings, and later, investment, aggregate demand, and equilibrium GNP, have been undecipherable quantities. Estimating these variables on a graph is like being called on to read an exotic foreign language—without being permitted to use a dictionary.

Our first step will be to learn how to read a graph. The key to reading economic variables from a graph is knowing where to look for them, so before we even look at graphs, let's just talk about them for a while. There is a vertical line on the left side of every graph called the vertical scale, and there is a horizontal line on the bottom of every graph called the horizontal scale. You may take a peek at Figure 8–1 to see what I'm talking about.

---

[3] From Table 8–3: Disposable Income − Consumption = Saving

$30,000	−	$23,000	=	$7,000
40,000	−	31,000	=	9,000

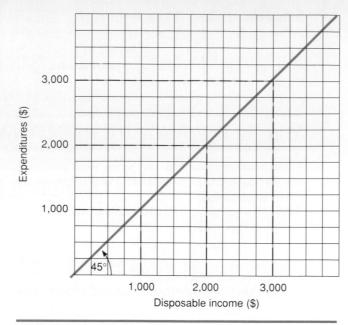

Figure 8–1

Every graph you will ever see in an economics text will have these two dimensions—the horizontal and the vertical. The vertical scale is always measured in dollars. In Figure 8-1 we have an expenditures scale with the numbers 1,000, 2,000, and 3,000, which represent expenditures of $1 trillion, $2 trillion, and $3 trillion, respectively. Notice that the distances between each of these numbers is equal. If you were to take a ruler to measure the distances between 0 and 1,000, 1,000 and 2,000, and between 2,000 and 3,000, they would be exactly the same. This is a very important point because in a few pages you'll need to estimate distances between these numbers.

The horizontal axis in Figure 8-1 measures disposable income, also in units of 1,000, 2,000, and 3,000. In the graphs you'll encounter in future chapters, the horizontal scale will sometimes be based on units of time or units of output, but here we are measuring disposable income, which is measured in terms of dollars.

Nearly every variable is read from the vertical scale. The only exception we will encounter is disposable income, which is read from the horizontal scale.

Expenditures are measured on the vertical scale and disposable income along the horizontal scale.

The graph in Figure 8-1 shows expenditures along the vertical scale and disposable income along the horizontal scale. Figure 8-1 has only one line— a 45-degree line. This line has one purpose—to equate the horizontal scale with the vertical scale, that is expenditures with disposable income.

Notice the dotted line rising from a disposable income of 1,000. It meets the 45-degree line and then moves horizontally to the vertical scale. For a disposable income of 2,000, there is another dotted line rising to the 45-degree line and then moving straight across to the vertical scale. The same pattern occurs at a disposable income of 3,000.

Let's take that first point on the 45-degree line, just above 1,000 on the disposable income scale and directly across from the expenditures (vertical) scale. That point is exactly 1,000 units from both the vertical and horizontal scales. Point 2 is 2,000 units from each scale. Thus, we see that points on the vertical scale are equal to their corresponding points on the horizontal scale.

Now we're ready to graph the consumption function. First we'll review it: *as income rises, consumption rises, but not as quickly*. How should it look on a graph? Suppose disposable income rises by 1,000. By how much should C rise? According to our definition of the consumption function, it should rise by less than 1,000.

If the consumption function stated that C rises as quickly as income, can you guess what a graph of the consumption function would look like? That's a hard one. It would look like the 45-degree line. Each point would be the same number of units from the two scales.

Figure 8-2 illustrates that consumption does not rise as quickly as the 45-degree line. Since C does not rise as quickly as disposable income, the points that compose the line are not as high as they were in the 45-degree line in Figure 8-1.

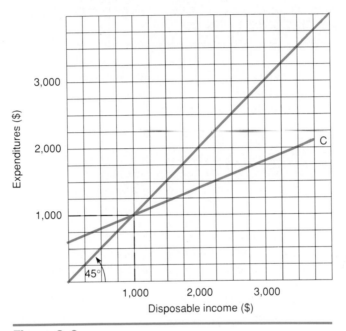

Figure 8-2

Okay, now we're ready to read the graph in Figure 8-2. How much is consumption when disposable income is 1,000? How much is it? Don't wait for me to tell you. Find a disposable income of 1,000 on the horizontal axis and work your way vertically (that means straight up) to the consumption line (C line). Then move across to the vertical axis. Now how much is C? You're not sure. Okay, get a ruler or some other straight edge. Don't worry. I'll wait for you right here. Now let's go back to that disposable income of 1,000. Using the ruler, draw a line straight up to the C line. Now draw another line, this one perfectly horizontal (that means straight across), to the vertical axis. Now read the number. It is 1,000. Voilà!

We know that I really did that one. Those lines were already on the graph. There are no guidelines for the next one. Find the level of C when disposable income is 2,000. Are you ready? Go ahead then. But just remember: up from a disposable income of 2,000 to the C line and then straight across. Oops! I'm giving it away. Go ahead: you do it and I'll let you know if you're right or not.

Read Only if You Still Don't Understand Why C is 1,000

If you're still trying to figure out why C is 1,000, we'll use the analogy of football. Suppose your team is about to receive a kickoff. One of your players catches the ball on the goal line and runs it out to your own 10-yard line. How far was his return yardage? Obviously 10 yards. How do you know it was exactly 10 yards? Because you saw him start at the goal line and get tackled at the 10. In fact, they even have markers on the sideline.

If we were to ask how much C is when disposable income is 1,000, we go vertically (or downfield) from the horizontal axis to the 1,000 mark, which we find on the vertical axis. How far did we go? We went 1,000. We have a scale on the vertical axis that enables us to measure how far we've gone—just like in football.

Now suppose a team has a first down, say on the 25 yard line. On the next play they move the ball to about the 35. Is it another first down? What will the referees do? They'll measure. How? That's right, they'll bring out the chains.

You may do the same thing to measure C or any other variable that is measured against the vertical axis. Not only is there a scale on the vertical axis (or yard markers), but you may use a ruler (chains) to make your measurements.

What did you get? To me it looks like about 1,400. Anything close to 1,400 would be fine. Incidentally, how much is the marginal propensity to consume? Figure it out in the space below using the three-step method.

Solution:

$$\text{MPC} = \frac{\text{Change in C}}{\substack{\text{Change in} \\ \text{disposable} \\ \text{income}}} = \frac{400}{1,000} = \frac{4}{10} = .4$$

Let's try another problem. How much is C when disposable income is 3,000?

What did you come up with? Your answer should be around 1,800. While we're at it, how much is the average propensity to consume? Again, use the three-step method: formula, substitute, and solve.

Solution:

$$APC = \frac{Consumption}{Disposable\ income} = \frac{1800}{3000} = \frac{18}{30} = \frac{3}{5} = .6$$

At low income levels, C is greater than disposable income.

Remember that C is measured vertically. Notice that as disposable income (which is measured horizontally) increases, C moves higher and higher. But it doesn't rise as quickly as disposable income.

At very low levels of disposable income, notice that the C line is higher than the 45-degree line. When that happens, consumption is greater than disposable income. How is that possible? Believe me, it happens—especially during depressions. Besides, didn't your consumption ever exceed your income? What's that? Your consumption always exceeds your income? Well, then, you might not have any money in the bank, but you should intuitively grasp the notion that a nation can spend more than its disposable income.

Some nations have gone into debt for tens of billions of dollars. Until just a few years ago, Mexico, Brazil, and Argentina headed the list of big debtors. However, the new champion is the United States whose external debt is now about $1 trillion.

The Saving Function

The saving function

The saving function is virtually the same as the consumption function. *As income rises, saving rises, but not as quickly.*

Now we're ready to find saving on the graph. First, how much is saving when disposable income is 1,000? Go ahead and figure it out. I know there's

---

Autonomous Consumption versus Induced Consumption

You may have noticed in Figure 8–2 that when disposable income is zero, C is about 500. We call this autonomous consumption because people will spend a certain minimum amount on the necessities of life—food, clothing, and shelter. Whether one has to dig into one's savings, go on welfare, or else beg, borrow, or steal, one will spend that minimum amount. And on a national level, we will all spend a minimum amount—what we are calling autonomous consumption—even if national disposable income is zero.*

If the autonomous level of consumption were 500, then it would continue to be 500 no matter what the level of disposable income. Since we know from the consumption function that consumption rises as disposable income rises, an increase in consumption is induced. At any given level of disposable income there is a corresponding level of consumption. Part of that consumption is autonomous and part is induced. Since autonomous consumption stays the same—no matter how much disposable income may vary—we can easily figure out how much consumption is induced. Just subtract autonomous consumption from total consumption.

Let's start with a disposable income of zero in Figure

8–2. Autonomous consumption *is* total consumption because a disposable income of zero cannot induce any consumption.

Let's go to a disposable income of 1,000. How much are autonomous consumption and induced consumption? Autonomous consumption would continue to be 500. Since total consumption is 1,000, induced consumption is 500.

We'll try one more. How much is autonomous consumption and how much is induced consumption when disposable income is 3,000? Autonomous consumption continues to be 500. If total consumption is estimated at 1,800, then induced consumption is 1,300 (1,800 – 500).

* Of course, national disposable income would never actually fall to zero because people are always spending that minimum amount, so other people are receiving most of that amount in income. For example, if people spent $20 each on food, clothing, and shelter each week, this money would end up in the pockets of those who supplied these goods and services. They, in turn, would spend most of this money on their own necessities. This analysis anticipates our discussion of the multiplier, which we will come to near the end of this chapter.

no listing of saving on the graph, but you can still figure out how much saving is from the information you already have—especially the level of C when disposable income is 1,000, which you already figured.

Your answer should be zero. If disposable income is 1,000 and C is 1,000, saving must be zero. Note that saving is the vertical distance between the C line and the 45-degree line.

Next problem. How much is saving when disposable income is 2,000? After you do that, find saving when disposable income is 3,000.

The answers to both questions are worked out in the graph in Figure 8-3. All you need to do is take the vertical distance between the C line and the 45-degree line.

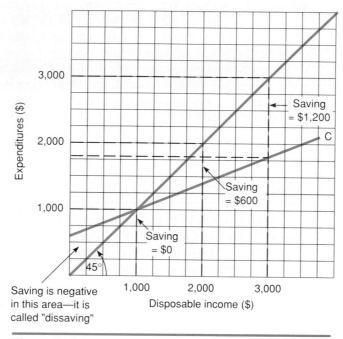

Figure 8-3

If you are having any trouble measuring these vertical distances, remember that all vertical distances are measured on the vertical axis. Horizontal dotted lines have been drawn in Figure 8-3 to locate points on the vertical axis.

Let's try another graph to make sure we're clear on how to measure consumption and saving at various levels of disposable income. In Figure 8-4, please find the levels of consumption and saving when disposable income is (a) 1,500, (b) 3,000, and (c) 4,500. To check your work, see Figure 8-5.

What the Consumer Buys

The consumer buys durables, nondurables, and services.

Consumption is traditionally divided into three categories: durables, nondurables, and services. Durables are things that last a while, say, at least a year or two. Nondurables, such as food, gasoline, and childrens' clothing, don't last very long. (In fact, a case could be made that the clothing worn by fashion-conscious adults doesn't last either, although the reason it doesn't last is because fashions change rather than that it wears out.)

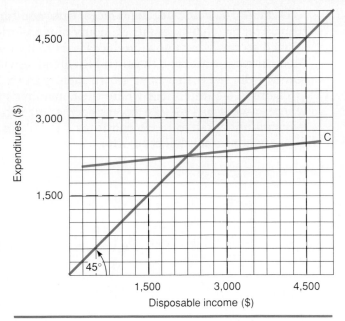

Figure 8–4

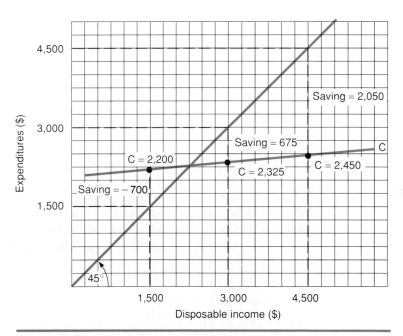

Figure 8–5

Please note that C is the vertical distance between the horizontal axis and the C line. Saving is the vertical distance between the C line and the 45-degree line. C and saving always add up to disposable income.

When disposable income is 1,500, C is 2,200, so saving must be − 700.

When disposable income is 3,000, C is 2,325 and saving is 675.

When disposable income is 4,500, C is 2,450 and saving is 2,050.

These are only approximations. Your answers may vary slightly as long as your saving and consumption add up to disposable income.

Durable goods include appliances, cars, and furniture. They last—hopefully. The big change in our economy since World War II has been in the service sector, which now produces over half of what the consumers buy. Medical care, education, legal and financial services, and entertainment are some of the fields that have grown rapidly in the last four decades.

Figure 8-6 summarizes where the consumer's dollar went in 1955 and where it went in 1987. There has been a huge shift, mainly from expenditures on nondurables to expenditures on services. Today over 50 cents out of every consumer dollar pays for a service.

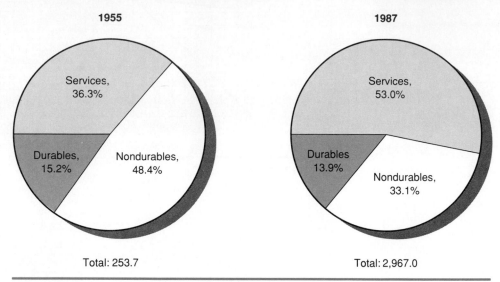

Figure 8–6
Consumer Spending, 1955 and 1987
($ billions)

Source: *1985 Economic Report of the President*, p. 232; *Economic Indicators*, February 1988, p. 4 (prepared by the Joint Economic Committee by the Council of Economic Advisors).

The Determinants of Consumption

Why do people spend money? There are some who hate to spend a penny and others who spend every penny they lay their hands on. The aphorism, if you don't have it, you can't spend it, is especially relevant to any discussion of the determinants of consumption. The six basic determinants are listed below. (As we shall see, however, the level of spending is determined largely by how much money people have.)

1. Disposable income.
2. Credit availability.
3. Stock of liquid assets in the hands of consumers.
4. Stock of durable goods in the hands of consumers.
5. Keeping up with the Joneses.
6. Consumer expectations.

The most important determinant of consumption is the level of disposable income.

Disposable Income

Many factors influence how much money people spend; by far the most important is one's disposable income. As illustrated with the consumption function, as income rises, consumption rises, but not as quickly.

At very low income levels people not only don't save, they actually dissave. Suppose, for example, you lose your job. Do you simply stop spending money? If you did, you'd sure lose a lot of weight. How do you get by? If you collect unemployment benefits, then that's your disposable income. But the chances are you would spend more each week than your unemployment checks, especially if you support a family. Rent, car payments, other installment payments, utilities, and food bills still have to be paid, as well as the cost of looking for another job.

To manage all this you might borrow—if you can get credit—and you will go into your savings. So at very low levels of income, you tend to spend more than your disposable income.

At the other end of the economic spectrum are the rich, who usually manage to save some of their disposable income. Every so often we'll read about a professional athlete or entertainer who has gone bankrupt, but these are the rare exceptions among the rich. The Rockefellers, the Du Ponts, the Mellons, and the Fords all spend a lot of money. Still they somehow manage to save several million dollars a year.

The main point here is that rich people spend a lot more money than poor people. Why? Because they *have* more money. What is the most important determinant of consumption? Disposable income.

Credit Availability

You can't borrow if you don't have credit. The most popular ways of borrowing are credit cards, especially VISA and MasterCard. Bank loans, home mortgages, and auto loans are other ways of borrowing. When credit is eased, people tend to borrow more.

For example, suppose a furniture store, which had been asking its customers to put down 50 percent of their purchases in cash and pay out the balance in six months, now offered new terms: nothing down and two years to pay.

This is not to say that everyone stretches his or her credit to the limit, although some people do. However, credit availability has some influence on the level of consumption.

Credit availability varies inversely with the level of consumer debt. That is, the more you owe, the less likely you are to have more credit available. If your credit card limit is $1,500 and you already owe $1,400, you have only $100 of credit available. Furthermore, people who owe a lot are somewhat reluctant to take on still more debt.

Stock of Liquid Assets in the Hands of Consumers

People own things that can quickly be turned into cash. These are called liquid assets. Prime examples include government and corporate bonds, corporate stocks, bank accounts, and money market funds.

In the United States today, people hold a stock of liquid assets of a few trillion dollars. This makes some people feel rich. Suppose, for example, you hold 1,000 shares of IBM, and the price of that stock rose $2. You would indeed be $2,000 richer (at least on paper). This might induce you to go out and spend some of that money you just made.

In addition to *feeling* rich, if your liquid assets rise, you do indeed have more money to spend. That is, you can quickly convert some of these assets into money and go out and spend it. Economists have found that there is some correlation between consumption and the amount of liquid assets held. The reasoning here is that if you don't have it, you can't spend it, and if you do have it, you will spend some of it.

Stock of Consumer Durables in the Hands of Consumers

In 1929 most Americans owned relatively new radios, toasters, vacuum cleaners, waffle irons, and other appliances since America had been electrified only a decade and half before. More than 95 percent of the cars on the road were under 10 years old. By 1930 the market for consumer durables was temporarily saturated.

When few people own items such as personal computers, VCRs, or TV video games, sales will rise. But when the market is saturated (and people own relatively late models), it will be some time before sales pick up again.

Consumer durables are now a relatively small part of total consumption—only 13.9 percent of all goods and services sold to consumers in 1987. However, they are somewhat erratic, largely because they vary inversely with the stock of consumer durables in the hands of consumers. When people hold a large stock (of consumer durables), consumer durable sales tend to be low; conversely, when that stock is low, sales tend to be high.

Keeping up with the Joneses

Most of us, at least a few times in our lives, have been guilty of showing off our expensive clothes, our jewelry, our cars, or even our Florida tans. And most of us have been tempted to keep up with our neighbors, relatives, and friends. When the Joneses buy something, we have to go out and buy one too—even if we can't afford it—because if we don't buy it, we won't be keeping up.

Over 80 years ago Thorstein Veblen coined the term *conspicuous consumption*. In a marvelous book titled *The Theory of the Leisure Class*, Veblen stated that "The only practicable means of impressing one's pecuniary ability on these unsympathetic observers of one's everyday life is an unremitting demonstration of ability to pay."[5]

Consumer Expectations

When people expect inflation, they often buy consumer durables before prices go up. On the other hand, when they expect recession, they tend to reduce their purchases of big-ticket items such as cars, furniture, and major appliances. Many people fear being laid off or having their income reduced because of recessions, so they tend to postpone major purchases until times get better.

---

[5] Reprinted in *The Portable Veblen*, ed. Max Lerner, (New York: Viking Press, 1948), pp. 127–28.

The Permanent Income Hypothesis

According to Milton Friedman, a very prominent conservative economist, the strongest influence on consumption is one's estimated average lifetime income. No one ever knows what his or her average lifetime income will actually be, but people can generally figure out if they are earning more or less than that average.

If a factory worker earning $18,000 a year expects to remain a factory worker, she can estimate her future earnings until she retires. According to Friedman, people gear their consumption to their expected earnings more than to their current income.

Suppose that someone's income temporarily contracts, say, because of a factory layoff. Would the person cut back very sharply on her consumption? No, she would not, says this theory, since she knows she will be back on the job within a few months. She has to continue paying her rent, meeting her car payments, and eating three times a day.

Earnings tend to rise until late middle age (about 55 or so), and then decline. Therefore the permanent income hypothesis would predict that most people's consumption is greater than their income until their mid or late 20s. From the late 20s to the early 60s, current disposable income is usually greater than consumption. In old age, the relationship between consumption and current disposable income is again reversed, so consumption is greater than income.

Thus, our consumption is determined by our average expected income, or permanent income. That income is a constant; consumption is a constant percentage of that income. For most Americans consumption would be about 90 to 95 percent of permanent income.

According to Friedman's hypothesis, if you suddenly win the lottery, hit a number, win a huge sum of money on a quiz show, or get some other windfall, you will not spend very much of it. You will spend *some* of it because it will raise your permanent income, but you will spend only a small part of it.

For example, suppose you receive a windfall of $100,000. If the permanent income hypothesis applies, you might spend $6,000 or $8,000 a year over the next 15 years or so. Is this how most lottery winners have handled their windfalls? Apparently there are quite a few deviations from the behavior predicted by the permanent income hypothesis.

The Determinants of Saving

Savings may be viewed as a residual of disposable income, what is left after most or nearly all of it has been spent on consumption. Some people spend virtually all of their income, while others manage to spend more than they earn year after year.

Still, most Americans manage to save at least a small part of their incomes. Some people are saving for a big-ticket item like a couch, a new bedroom set, or possibly a car or a VCR. Others are saving for a vacation or perhaps the down payment on a house. Many Americans try to put away some money each year for their childrens' education. Some people may save money every year for a rainy day or their old age while still others are simply penny-pinchers.

There are many reasons why people save.

There is obviously no single reason why people save. Whether you are saving for a rainy day or you have a specific purchase in mind, there is one basic fact that you should know. On the average, Americans save about 5 percent of their disposable income. Can you figure out from this one fact how much our APS and APC are?

APS =   APC =

If you remember what we covered near the beginning of the chapter, you would have said that the APS = .05 and APC = .95. In other words, we spend, on the average, 95 percent of our disposable income and save 5 percent.

For most of the 20th century Americans saved between 7 and 10 percent of their disposable incomes. A decline to 5 percent (and even less in recent years) may not seem like much, but it amounts to quite a bit of money when we consider that our disposable national income is over $3 trillion. Now figure out by how many dollars our savings would decline if the savings rate fell by 3 percent. Work it out here and then check the solution in the space below.

Solution: $3,000,000,000,000 × .03 = $90,000,000,000 (or $90 billion). Incidentally, this problem can be reduced to a very simple problem in arithmetic. How much is three times three. Okay. Now when you multiply a number by .03, how many zeros do you take from it? I hope you said two. Thus we have $9,000,000,000,000. When we move the commas over we get $90,000,000,000.

A $90 billion shortfall is particularly important at a time when we need all the savings we can lay our hands on to finance $200 billion deficits and the hundreds of billions of investment funds that large corporations need to build new plant and equipment.

A policy issue that will plague our country for years to come will be what we can do about an APS that is too low. Or conversely, what we can do about an APC that is too high. This issue will come up again in subsequent chapters.

The Multiplier

The multiplier is based on two concepts covered in Chapter 5: (1) GNP is the nation's expenditure on all the goods and services produced during the year at market prices. (2) GNP = C + I + G + net exports.

It is obvious that if C went up, GNP would go up. Or if I went down, so would GNP. Now we'll add a new wrinkle. When there is any change in spending, that is, in C, I, or G, it will have a multiplied effect on GNP.

When money is spent by one person, it becomes someone else's income. And what do we do with most of our income? We spend it. Once again, when this money is spent, someone else receives it as income, and, in turn, spends most of it. And so, if a dollar were initially spent, perhaps someone who received that dollar would spend 80 cents, and of that 80 cents received by the next person, perhaps 64 cents would be spent. If we added up all the spending generated by that one dollar, it would add up to four or five or six times that dollar. Hence, we get the name the multiplier.

Any change in spending (C, I, or G) will set off a chain reaction, leading to a multiplied change in GNP. How *much* of a multiplied effect? Perhaps a $10 billion increase in G will increase GNP by $50 billion. In that case, the multiplier is 5. If a decline of $5 billion in I causes GNP to fall by $40 billion, then the multiplier would be 8.

First we concentrate on calculating the multiplier, for which we'll use the formula

$$\frac{1}{1 - MPC}$$

$$\text{Multiplier} = \frac{1}{1 - MPC}$$

Then we'll see how it is used to predict changes in GNP.

The formula above is exactly the same as 1/MPS. Remember, MPC + MPS = 1 (or: 1 − MPC = MPS). Since the multiplier (like C) deals with spending, 1 − MPC is a more appropriate formula.

The MPC can be used to find the multiplier. If the MPC were .5, find the multiplier. Work this problem out in the space below. Write down the formula first, then substitute and solve.

Solution:

$$\text{Multiplier} = \frac{1}{1 - MPC} = \frac{1}{1 - .5} = \frac{1}{.5} = 2$$

Many students get lost at the third step. How do we get .5? How come 1 − .5 = .5? Look at it this way:

$$\begin{array}{r} 1.0 \\ -\ .5 \\ \hline .5 \end{array}$$

If it's still not clear, then think of 1 as a dollar and .5 (or .50) as 50 cents. How much is a dollar minus 50 cents?

Step four is just as easy. How many times does 50 cents go into a dollar? Or, you can just divide .5 into 1.0. Either way, it comes out to 2.

Let's try another problem. When the MPC is .75, how much is the multiplier?

Solution:

$$(1) \text{ Multiplier} = \frac{1}{1 - \text{MPC}} = \frac{1}{1 - .75} = \frac{1}{.25} = 4$$

After you've substituted into the formula, think of 1 as a dollar and .75 as 75 cents. From there (1/.25) we divide .25 into 1, or a quarter into a dollar.

The multiplier is really a shortcut for addition. In the case illustrated in Table 8–4, $1,000 of additional money is spent by a consumer. If the MPC is .5, that means that the person who receives this $1,000 in additional income will spend $500. The $500 spent will add to others' incomes, and—still assuming an MPC of .5—$250 will be spent. Ad infinitum (that's Latin for without limit or forever).

Table 8–4
Step-by-Step Working of the Multiplier when MPC is .5

$1,000.00
500.00
250.00
125.00
62.50
31.25
15.625
7.8125
3.90625
1.953125
.9765625
.48828125
.244140625
.1220703125
.06103515625
.030517578125
.0152587890625
1,999.9847402109375*

* In arithmetic, addition and multiplication are one and the same. Multiplication is just a shortcut. If we were to carry out even more steps in our addition, we would approach a sum of $2,000. It is surely much easier to use the multiplier of 2 (2 × $1,000 = $2,000) than to add up all these figures.

Applications of the Multiplier

The multiplier is used to calculate the effect of changes in C, I, and G on GNP.

Knowing the multiplier we can calculate the effect of changes in C, I, and G on the level of GNP. If GNP is 2,500, the multiplier is 3, and C rises by 10, what is the new level of GNP?

A second formula is needed to figure the new level of GNP:

New GNP = Initial GNP + (change in spending × multiplier)

Notice the parentheses. Their purpose is to ensure that we multiply before we add. In arithmetic you must always multiply (or divide) before you add or subtract. Always. The parentheses are there to make sure we do this.

Copy down the formula, substitute, and solve.

Solution:

(1) New GNP = Initial GNP + (change in spending × multiplier)

(2)   =   2500   + (10   ×   3)

(3)   =   2500   + (30   )

             =   2530

Here are a few variations of this type of problem. Suppose that consumer spending rose by $10 billion and the multiplier were 3. What would happen to GNP?

Solution: It would rise by $30 billion: $10 billion × 3.

Try this one: Government spending fell by $5 billion with a multiplier of 7.

Solution: −$35 billion: −$5 billion × 7. In other words, if government spending fell by $5 billion with a multiplier of 7, GNP would fall by $35 billion.

Graphing the C + I Line

Now we're ready to do some more work on the graphs—something I'm sure you've been looking forward to. So far we've had a graph with just one line—the C line, or consumption function. From this one-line graph, C and savings could be calculated. To calculate I (actually C + I), a second line is necessary. Figure 8–7 graphs a C + I line, which is drawn parallel to the C line. Actually this is the same graph (as in Figures 8–2, 8–3, 8–4, and 8–5), with the C + I line added.

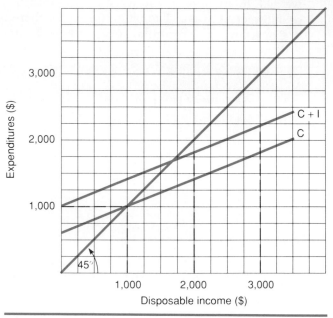

Figure 8–7

The question for you to solve has three parts: How much is I when disposable income is (a) 1,000, (b) 2,000, and (c) 3,000? Look at the graph and figure out the answers. Keep in mind that the C line and the C + I line are parallel.

The answer to the question, "How much is I when disposable income is (a) 1,000, (b) 2,000, and (c) 3,000?" is "around 400" (350, 375, 390, 405, 425, 440, or 450 are acceptable). More important, since the C line and the C + I line are parallel, the vertical distance between them remains the same. If you estimated I at 375 with a disposable income of 1,000, it remains 375 when disposable income is 2,000 or 3,000.

I'm going to give you a chance to catch your breath in the next chapter. No more graphs with the 45-degree angle. But watch out; it gets worse in Chapter 10.

The Paradox of Thrift

Since childhood we have been taught that savings is good. Benjamin Franklin once said, "A penny saved is a penny earned." Franklin, it turns out, never followed his own advice. It also turns out that if we all try to save more, we'll probably end up with a really bad recession. This outcome is explained by the paradox of thrift.

You have probably heard that the sum of the parts does not necessarily add up to the whole. Consider, for example, if you were in a room full of people and that room suddenly burst into flames. What would you do? Would you politely suggest to your companions that everyone file out of the room in an orderly fashion? Or would you bolt for the door?

What if the door opened inward (i.e., into the room)? Whoever got there first would attempt to pull open the door. But if everyone made a dash for the door, they would all arrive at just about the same time. The person trying to pull open the door wouldn't have room to do this since the door opened inward and everyone else would be pushing him against the door. Several people would get injured in the crush. Unless they backed off, no one would get out of the room.

We call this an example of the fallacy of composition. What makes perfect sense for one person to do—rush to the door and pull it open—makes no sense when everyone tries to do it at the same time.

The paradox of thrift is a variant of the fallacy of composition. If everyone tries to save more, they will all end up saving less. Let's say that every week you save an extra $10 from your paycheck. At the end of a year, you will have saved an extra $520. Right? Right! Now what if everyone tries saving an extra $10 a week. At the end of a year we should have tens of billions in extra savings. Right? Wrong!

How come? Because what makes sense for one person to do does not make sense for everyone to do. If everyone tries to save more, everyone is cutting back on consumption. Business sales fall by hundreds of millions of dollars a week. If 110 million people all cut back by $10, that comes to $1.1 billion. Over the course of a year this would add up to $57.2 billion!

This $57.2 billion decline in consumption will have a multiplied effect on GNP. If the multiplier is 4, GNP will decline by $228.8 billion; if it is 6, GNP will decline by $343.2 billion. Surely such declines are typical of depressions.

But that's just for starters. When retailers get the idea that business will be off over the next few months, they do two things: lay off employees and cut back on their inventory. The workers who lose their jobs cut back on their consumption. Meanwhile the retailers have begun canceling their orders for new inventory, prompting factories to lay off people, and cutting back on their orders for raw materials.

As the recession spreads, more and more people get laid off and each will cut back on his consumption, further aggravating the decline in retail sales.

Now we come back to saving. Millions of people have been laid off and millions more are on reduced hours. Still others no longer get overtime. Each of these people then has suffered substantially reduced income. Each is not able to save as much as before the recession. Savings declines.

And so we're back where we started. We have the paradox of thrift: *If everyone tries to save more, they all will end up saving less.*

Summary of GNP Components

We've now covered the three big components of GNP—C, I, and G. When we tack on net exports, a figure that will probably be negative for at least the rest of the decade, we have GNP for 1987. Let's go over the information we have gathered in the last four chapters, and then summarize it in Table 8–5.

Table 8–5
The Components of GNP, 1987
(in $billions)

Consumption:	
Durable goods	$ 413.8
Nondurable goods	981.6
Services	1,571.6
C	$2,967.0
Investment:	
Plant and equipment	$442.9
Residential housing	228.4
Inventory change	45.4
I	$716.7
Government purchases:	
Federal	$380.6
State and local	543.2
G	$923.8
Net exports	$−119.9
GNP	$4,486.2

Source: *Economic Report of the President*, 1988, pp. 248, 342, 343; *Economic Indicators*, February, 1988 (prepared for the Joint Economic Committee by the Council of Economic Advisors), pp. 4, 9.

First, we'll use the GNP equation from Chapter 5:

$$GNP = C + I + G + \text{Net exports}$$

Back in Chapter 5 we substituted numbers for each of the variables in the equation. The letter C comes from the present chapter, I comes from Chapter 7, and G from Chapter 6. Net exports won't be covered until Chapter 34.

$$GNP = C + I + G + n$$

$$GNP = 2,967.0 + 716.7 + 923.8 - 119.9$$

$$GNP = 4,486.2[6]$$

Table 8-5 summarizes this information in somewhat more detail. Each of the three major GNP sectors is broken down into its main components. Most of this information will be useful over the next seven chapters as we deal with economic fluctuations and the macroeconomic policies that have been designed to mitigate these fluctuations.

---

[6] Due to rounding, the sum of the components of GNP come to slightly more than 4,486.2.

Workbook for Chapter 8

Name _____

Date _____

Multiple-Choice Questions

Circle the letter that corresponds to the best answer.

1. Since 1955 Americans have been spending
a. a larger percentage of their incomes on services   **b.** a smaller percentage of their incomes on services   **c.** about the same percentage of their incomes on services

2. When the C line crosses the 45-degree line, how much is saving?
a. positive   **b.** negative   **c.** zero   **d.** There is not enough information to know

3. When disposable income is zero
a. autonomous consumption is equal to induced consumption   **b.** autonomous consumption is equal to total consumption   **c.** induced consumption is equal to total consumption

4. The minimum amount that people will spend even if disposable income is zero is called _____ consumption.
a. autonomous   **b.** induced   **c.** total

5. According to the permanent income hypothesis, if a person received a windfall, say $100,000, he would spend _____ that year.
a. some of it   **b.** most of it   **c.** nearly all of it
d. all of it

6. According to the paradox of thrift, if everyone tries to save more,
a. GNP will rise   **b.** saving will rise   **c.** savings will fall   **d.** consumption will rise

7. The largest component of GNP is
a. net exports   **b.** investment   **c.** consumption
d. government purchases

8. The largest component of C is
a. durable goods   **b.** services   **c.** nondurable goods

9. The consumption function tells us that as income rises, consumption
a. declines   **b.** remains the same   **c.** rises more slowly than income   **d.** rises more quickly than income

10. When income levels are very low, C is
a. zero   **b.** lower than income   **c.** higher than income

11. When income is equal to consumption, saving is
a. negative   **b.** zero   **c.** positive   **d.** impossible to calculate because there is insufficient information

12. Which of the following relations is *not* correct?
a. MPC + MPS = 1   **b.** APC + APS = 1
c. MPS = MPC + 1   **d.** 1 − APS = APC
e. 1 − MPC = MPS

13. Induced consumption expenditures
a. fall as income rises   **b.** are always equal to autonomous consumption expenditures   **c.** plus saving equals total consumption expenditures
d. represent consumption that is independent of income   **e.** are influenced mainly by income

14. Autonomous consumption expenditures are
a. equal to induced consumption expenditures
b. proportional to disposable income   **c.** not influenced by income   **d.** influenced primarily by the savings function

15. The average propensity to save
a. is savings divided into disposable income   **b.** is a measure of the additional saving generated by additional income   **c.** is negative at very high income levels   **d.** varies directly with income; as income rises, the APS rises

Fill-In Questions

1. Americans spend about _____ percent of their disposable incomes on services.

2. The average propensity to consume is found by dividing _____ by _____.

3. The APS + the APC = _____.

4. The consumption function states that _____ _____.

5. Dissaving takes place when _____ is larger than _____.

6. Induced consumption is induced by _____.

7. According to the saving function, as disposable income rises, _____.

8. The most important determinant of the level of consumption is _____.

9. The average propensity to consume in the United States today is about _____.

10. The paradox of thrift says that when people try to _____.

11. As the marginal propensity to consume rises, the multiplier _____.

12. 1 − MPS = _____.

13. When the C line crosses the 45-degree line, saving is equal to _____.

14. Of the three main categories of goods and services that consumers buy, the least stable over the business cycle is _____.

15. According to Milton Friedman's permanent income hypothesis, our consumption is determined by our _____.

16. A decline in our APS from .06 to .05 would lead to a decline in savings by $_____.

Problems

1. Given the information shown in Table 1, calculate the APC and the APS.

Table 1

Disposable Income	Consumption
$10,000	$8,400

2. Given the information shown in Table 2, calculate the APC and the APS.

Table 2

Disposable Income	Saving
$50,000	$7,000

3. Given the information shown in Table 3, calculate the MPC and MPS. (Assume disposable income rises from $10,000 to $11,000.)

Table 3

Disposable Income	Consumption
$10,000	$8,200
11,000	9,000

4. Given the information shown in Table 4, calculate the MPC and MPS. (Assume disposable income rises from $35,000 to $37,000.)

Table 4

Disposable Income	Saving
$35,000	$4,600
37,000	5,300

5. Using the information in Figure 1, how much is consumption and saving when disposable income is:

	C	Saving
a. 1,000	_____	_____
b. 2,000	_____	_____
c. 3,000	_____	_____

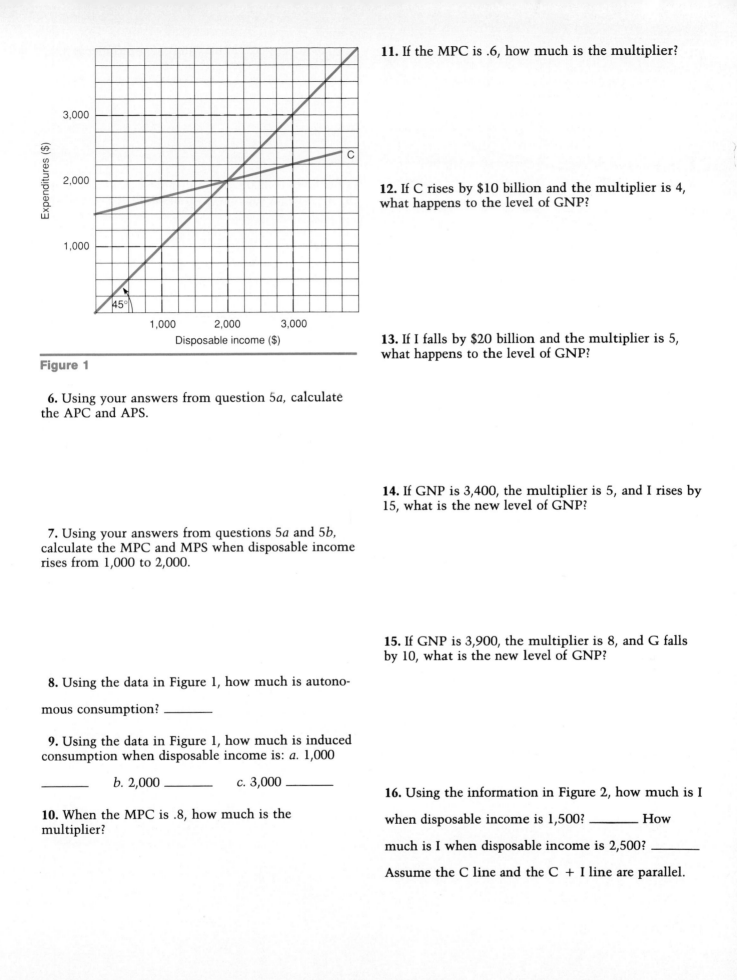

Figure 1

11. If the MPC is .6, how much is the multiplier?

6. Using your answers from question 5a, calculate the APC and APS.

12. If C rises by $10 billion and the multiplier is 4, what happens to the level of GNP?

13. If I falls by $20 billion and the multiplier is 5, what happens to the level of GNP?

14. If GNP is 3,400, the multiplier is 5, and I rises by 15, what is the new level of GNP?

7. Using your answers from questions 5a and 5b, calculate the MPC and MPS when disposable income rises from 1,000 to 2,000.

15. If GNP is 3,900, the multiplier is 8, and G falls by 10, what is the new level of GNP?

8. Using the data in Figure 1, how much is autonomous consumption? _____

9. Using the data in Figure 1, how much is induced consumption when disposable income is: a. 1,000 _____ b. 2,000 _____ c. 3,000 _____

10. When the MPC is .8, how much is the multiplier?

16. Using the information in Figure 2, how much is I when disposable income is 1,500? _____ How much is I when disposable income is 2,500? _____ Assume the C line and the C + I line are parallel.

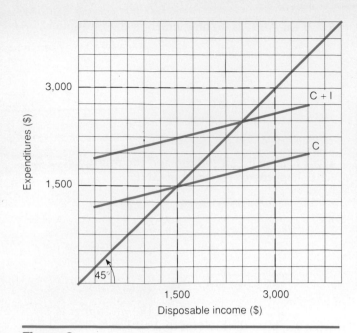

Figure 2

18. If I falls by $20 billion and the multiplier is 4, what happens to the level of GNP?

19. If GNP is 3,000, the multiplier is 6, and G rises by 20, what is the new level of GNP?

20. State the paradox of thrift.

17. When the MPC is .9, how much is the multiplier?

Recall

Economic Fluctuations, Unemployment, and Inflation

As the title indicates, we'll be covering the major problems that our economy has encountered in recent years. First, however, we'll review some of the major economic events of the past seven decades.

Chapter Objectives

In this chapter we will:

- Present a brief history of the American economy since World War I.
- Examine the business cycle.
- Consider various business cycle theories.
- Show how economic forecasting is done.
- Learn how the unemployment rate is computed.
- Look at the types of unemployment.
- Construct a consumer price index.
- Consider the theories of inflation.

Part I   A Brief History of the American Economy since World War I

"Those who cannot remember the past are condemned to fulfill it."
—George Santayana

What did the great philosopher mean by this? Perhaps he meant that those who do not learn enough history the first time around will be required to repeat History 101. But whatever he meant, it is clear that to understand our economy today, we need to know how we got there.

1920 to 1945

Soon after World War I we went into a sharp recession, but once we recovered, we enjoyed the unparalleled prosperity of the roaring twenties. This was the beginning of the era of mass consumption. The automobile, the telephone, indoor plumbing, and electrical appliances became commonplace.

The stock market was soaring and it was possible for people to quickly become millionaires.

But our economy and our financial institutions, in particular, were very vulnerable. And so, when the economic downturn finally arrived in 1929, it developed into the Great Depression.

The New Deal

Output fell by 50 percent between 1929 and 1933, the official unemployment rate hit 25 percent (and if you counted all the people who just gave up looking for jobs it was probably a lot higher), and one third of the nation's banks failed. Under President Franklin Roosevelt's New Deal, the federal government spent billions of dollars in an effort to get us out of the depression. However, it wasn't until the massive defense spending incurred by the war effort in the early 1940s that we were finally brought back to full employment.

1945 to 1970

From the beginning of the depression in 1929 until the end of World War II in 1945, we built very little new housing. The birthrate was at a historic low during this period, first, because people couldn't afford babies, and second, because most of the men were overseas. When 12 million men were demobilized in 1945 and 1946, they returned to cramped apartments that they often had to share with their parents or in-laws. So there were two things they wanted: babies and new housing.

Suburbanization

The logical place for new housing was in the suburbs. The federal government subsidized the suburbanization of America through low-cost mortgages (the Veteran's Administration and the Federal Housing Administration provided the mortgage money) and an extensive highway building program. By the late 1950s, America had become a suburbanized society.

The 25-year economic boom

Suburbanization created a demand for five basic things: (1) new housing, (2) new highways and local roads, (3) new cars, (4) new home furnishings, and (5) a new social infrastructure (schools, sewers, electrical, gas, and water mains). This demand was enough to keep our economy prosperous for the 25 years following World War II, but at the end of that period the impetus of suburbanization was almost completely spent.

The late 1940s and most of the 1950s were years when American industry faced little foreign competition, mainly because its potential competitors, particularly West Germany and Japan, were still rebuilding from the war. Oil prices were very low and our highways were filled with gas-guzzling monsters. Our 20-foot cars looked more like boats, or perhaps fish, with their long sleek bodies and outrageous tail fins. In fact, it wasn't until the Arab oil boycott of 1973 and subsequent run-up of gasoline prices that the chickens finally came home to roost.

While tens of millions of middle-class citizens were following their split-level suburban dream, a somewhat smaller number of rural poor, largely displaced by the mechanization of agriculture, took their places in the cities. Thus, by the 1960s, America was a very different place from what it had been two decades earlier.

Still another thing that provided an economic boost in the late 1960s was the Vietnam War. Although the war also brought about massive resistance and the downfall of Lyndon Johnson's presidency, it also pumped $30 billion a year into the economy by 1968 and kept the post-World War II expansion going for another few years.

1970 to the Present

A lot of the things which had been boosting our economic growth since World War II came to an end in the early 1970s. The suburbanization of the country was now completed; the Vietnam War was finally winding down (and with it, our massive spending); West Germany, Japan, and a host of other countries were now competing with us not only in the world markets, but in our own markets as well; and, finally, in 1973 when the OPEC nations quadrupled the price of oil, the era of cheap energy was over.

There were now millions of Americans, most of them black and Hispanic, trapped in urban slums. They're part of our society's socioeconomic scrapheap, a group of people who are grudgingly thrown a few crumbs to keep them alive while the rest of us secretly hope they'll somehow just go away. The problem is largely a lack of jobs. There are no longer many entry-level jobs in the cities, and those that do exist in the suburbs are largely inaccessible to the cities' poor. The growing number of white-collar office jobs springing up in the cities demand either a college degree or technical training, neither of which the urban poor possess. What we have then is a classic mismatch of available skills and available jobs.

Are recessions good for anyone? Ann Cooper, who does paintings for hotels and motels, notes that recessions are good for her business, because her clients redecorate rather than build.

The 1970s brought us a period of intermittent recession and inflation. Occasionally the two occurred simultaneously, giving us a new word for our economic vocabulary—*stagflation* (a contraction of *stagnation* and *inflation*). There were recessions in 1969–70, 1973–75, 1980, and 1981–82. During each of these periods prices rose, sometimes at double-digit rates. Americans, who had experienced a steadily increasing standard of living since World War II, were now being told that the roller coaster ride was over, or at least the up part of the ride was over.

But the pessimism of the 1970s gave way to optimism in 1980 when Ronald Reagan was elected president and pledged to "get America working again." As luck would have it, within six months after he took office, we went into the worst recession we had had since the Great Depression. The unemployment rate hit 10.8 percent in December 1982, and it became very hard to believe that everything would work out if only we would "stay the course," as the president urged.

Ronald Reagan: The government is too big.

The main trouble with our economy, Reagan stated, was that the government was too big. It had a long-standing policy, under the Democrats, of "tax, tax, tax, spend, spend, spend." Under the Reagan Revolution, we had two major personal income tax cuts, in 1981 and 1986 (See Chapter 6). But Reagan was unable to cut government spending, and we were saddled with federal budget deficits of over $200 billion by the mid-1980s. Then too, economic growth, which Reagan had predicted would pick up under the stimulus of tax cuts, actually slowed down after a short spurt in 1983 and 1984.

As our economy enters the 1990s we are faced not only with massive federal budget deficits, but with huge foreign trade deficits as well. Perhaps most symbolic of our economic difficulties was that over the last 25 years or so the quality connoted by the terms "made in America" and "made in Japan" has been reversed.

In short, our economic prospects are clouded. We still produce more goods and services than any other country in the world, but our standard of living has slipped to number four or five. We are still an economic superpower, but we are losing our lead.

"Let's look at the record."
—Alfred E. Smith[1]

Our economic record since 1945 is shown in Figure 9–1, but before we are in a position to analyze that record, we need a little background information on the business cycle.

Is There a Business Cycle?

Economists and noneconomists have long debated whether there is a business cycle. It all depends on what is meant by the term. If *business cycle* is defined as increases and decreases in business activity of fixed amplitude that occur regularly at fixed intervals, then the answer is no, there is no business cycle. In other words, business activity does have its ups and downs, but some ups are higher than other ups and some downs are lower than others. Furthermore, there is no fixed length to the cycle. For example, as shown in Figure 9–1, we went for nearly the entire decade of the 1960s without a recession, but had back-to-back recessions in 1980 and 1981.

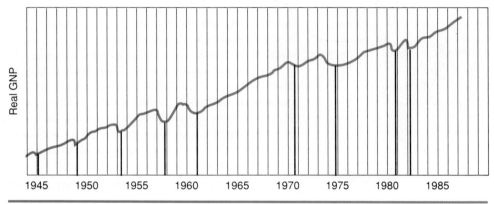

Figure 9–1

Note: Each dark vertical line indicates a recession.
Source: U.S. Dept. of Commerce, *Business Conditions Digest*, April 1982, p. 10, and March 1988, p. 19.

If we define the business cycle as alternating increases and decreases in the level of business activity, of varying amplitude and length, then there is definitely a business cycle. What goes up will eventually come down and what goes down will rise again.

Cycle Turning Points: Peaks and Troughs

Peaks

At the end of economic expansion, business activity reaches a peak (see Figure 9–2). Usually there is a certain degree of prosperity, but over the last 20 years, there was full employment only at the 1969 peak. In the month following the peak, the economy goes into a decline, known as a recession.

---

[1] Smith was governor of New York in the 1920s, and a man indiscreet enough to run for president in 1928, even though he was a Catholic.

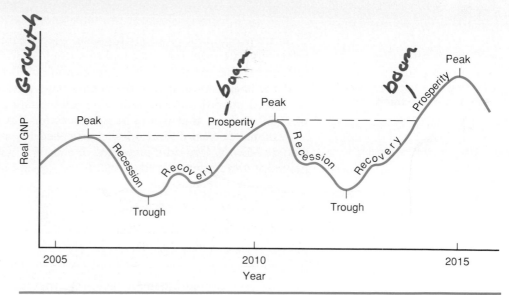

Figure 9-2

Not all economic declines turn out to be recessions. As a rule of thumb, most economists agree that a recession has occurred if real GNP declines for at least two consecutive quarters. However, in the decline that occurred in the second half of 1981, real GNP actually rose slightly in the third quarter, but it is generally accepted that the recession started in August, the second month of the third quarter.

Troughs

When the economy bottoms out, a trough occurs. From this low point, economic recovery sets in, and eventually most sectors share in the expansion.

Business cycles may be measured from peak to peak or trough to trough. As we have noted, these cycles vary greatly in amplitude and length. Note the severity of the 1973-75 and 1981-82 recessions in Figure 9-1, and the varying lengths of the cycles shown in the same graph.

The Conventional Three-Phase Business Cycle

We'll begin our analysis with the first peak in Figure 9-2. The decline that sets in after the peak is called a recession, which ends at the trough. Occasionally there is a false recovery when business activity turns upward for a few months, but then turns down again. If the next low point is the lowest since the previous peak, then *that* is the trough.

Recovery begins at the trough, but only if the expansion eventually reaches the level of the previous peak. Occasionally business activity rises without reaching the previous peak; unless it does, it does not qualify as a recovery.

Some people say that prosperity is when the prices of the things that you are selling are rising, and inflation is when the prices of things that you are buying are rising.

Once recovery has definately set in, we move upward until we pass the level of the previous peak, when we enter the third phase of the cycle, prosperity. This phase does not necessarily mean there is full employment, or even that we are approaching full employment. As long as production (real GNP) is as high as it was during the previous peak, we are in the prosperity phase.

Prosperity is the second part of the economic expansion and is accompanied by rising production, falling unemployment, and often accelerating inflation. Sooner or later we reach a peak and the process starts all over—recession, recovery, and prosperity.

This is the conventional three-phase cycle. A two-phase cycle would consist of contraction (recession) and expansion (recovery and prosperity) lumped together.

Some people talk of a fourth phase—depression. Although depressions are relatively rare—we have not had one in close to 50 years—there is always talk about the possibility that a recession could turn into a depression.

Dividing line between recession and depression

What is the dividing line between a recession and a depression? There is no agreed-upon or official definition. Obviously if the unemployment rate were 20 percent, that would be a depression. But would 10 percent qualify?

Perhaps the best definition was proposed by, among others, the late George Meany, longtime president of the AFL–CIO. He said that if his neighbor were unemployed, it would be a recession. If *he* were unemployed, it would be a depression!

Business Cycle Theories

We have stated that business cycles are inevitable; what goes up must come down and what goes down must come back up. Although there is generally agreement among economists that there are business cycles, there are many competing theories of their causes. We'll briefly consider two types of theories: endogenous (internal) and exogenous (external) theories.

Endogenous Theories

These theories place the cause of business cycles within rather than outside the economy. We'll consider first the theory of innovations, which was advanced primarily by Joseph Schumpeter.

Theory of innovations

When a businessman attempts to market a new product such as a car or a television set, at first he will encounter resistence ("Get that contraption off the road—it's frightening my horses!"). But when others perceive the profits being made by the innovator, they will imitate his new product with their own versions and production will soar. Eventually the market will be saturated—as it was by cars in 1929 and televisions in 1953—and an economic downturn will occur. The downturn continues until a new innovation takes hold and the process begins anew.

Psychological theory

A second endogenous theory is the psychological theory of alternating optimism and pessimism, which is really an example of a more general theory of the self-fulfilling prophecy. If businessmen are optimistic, they will invest in plant, equipment, and inventory. This will provide more jobs and result in more consumer spending, justifying still more investment, more jobs, and more spending. But eventually businessmen will turn pessimistic, perhaps because they figure this prosperity can't keep up. As pessimism sets in, investment, jobs, and consumer spending all decline, and a recession begins. The contraction continues until businessmen figure that things have gone down so far, there's no place to go but back up again.

Inventory cycle theory

Still another endogenous theory is that of the inventory cycle. During economic recovery, as sales begin to rise, businessmen are caught short of inventory, so they raise their orders to factories, in the process raising factory employment. As factory workers are called back to work, they begin to spend more money, causing businessmen to order still more from factories. Eventually they are able to restock their inventories, so they cut back on factory orders. This causes layoffs, declining retail sales, further cutbacks in factory orders, and a general economic decline. This decline persists until inventory levels are worked down low enough for factory orders to increase once again.

The Accelerator Principle

The accelerator principle is a variant of the overinvestment theory of the business cycle. It is somewhat analogous to the predicament of the Red Queen in *Alice in Wonderland,* who had to keep running just to stay where she was. The accelerator principle requires sales to keep increasing at the same rate to prevent investment from falling.

A Hypothetical Example of the Accelerator Principle

Year	Sales	Machines	Net I (+)	Replacement I (=)	Gross I
1991	100	200	0	10	10
1992	110	220	20	10	30
1993	120	240	20	10	30
1994	130	260	20	10	30
1995	135	270	10	10	20
1996	130	260	−10	10	0

This particular example is based on three assumptions:

1. Two dollars worth of machinery will produce $1 worth of output. This ratio of 2:1 is the capital-output ratio.
2. Each machine has a life of 20 years.
3. We'll assume that sales have been 100 and that we've had 200 machines for the past 20 years. Therefore, we need to replace 10 machines each year just to stay at 200 machines. In other words, each year we start out with 200 machines, 10 wear out, so we have to replace those 10 just to stay at 200.

Now we're ready to use the table. When sales are 100 we need 200 machines. In 1991 we start with 200 machines, which is the number we'll need that year since sales are 100 and the capital-output ratio is 2:1. We just need to replace the 10 machines that wore out. There's no Net I, but we replace 10 machines and have a Gross I total of 10 (Net I (0) + Replacement (10) = Gross I (10). This, by the way, is the same as saying that Net I plus Depreciation = Gross I.

In 1992 sales rise from 100 to 110. Since the capital-output ratio is 2:1, we need 220 machines. Net I is 20 machines and we replace 10, so our Gross I is 30.

Machine makers, who had been making 10 machines for years are suddenly deluged with orders. "Thirty machines! What should we do? Should we enlarge our plant and build more equipment to handle these orders? Will business continue to be so good?"

In 1993 sales go up to 120, which means we now need 240 machines. Again net I is 20 and replacement is 10, which adds up to a Gross I of 30.

We've now gotten to what economists call "the Red Queen Effect." We're running just to stay where we are. Sales went up by 10 and Gross I stayed at 30.

In 1994 sales again go up 10 to 130, 260 machines are needed, and Gross I stays at 30. Let's see what happens if sales go up by just 5, from 130 to 135. Now we need 270 machines, which leads to a Gross I of only 20.

An increase in sales has led to a decline in Gross I! Sales, which had been increasing by 10 in 1992, 1993, and 1994, rose by only 5 in 1995. So sales, which had been increasing at a constant rate during the previous three years, increased at a decreasing rate in 1995. This led to a decline in Gross I.

When orders for machines fall from 30 to 20, the machine maker must lay off one third of his employees. And his plant is now being used at only two thirds of capacity.

In Chapter 8 we worked out problems with the multiplier. Any change in C, I, or G had a multiplied effect on GNP. Now we have a decline of 10 in I. If the multiplier were 5, GNP would decline by 50. This means we would be in a recession.

When machine makers lay off their workers, even though they'll collect unemployment insurance, they'll still cut back on their consumption. This, in turn, will depress sales in the following year, 1996. This decline of 5, from 135 to 130, means that we need 10 less machines. Net I is actually negative, −10, canceling replacement demand of 10 so that Gross I is 0.

This is really a bad year. Gross I has fallen from 20 to 0. Sales are down by 5. The economy sinks still deeper into the recession.

What brings us out? Perhaps more machines wear out and have to be replaced. Maybe sales pick up. If, for some reason, sales eventually start to rise, then Gross I will rise and we'll be back on the ascending part of our roller coaster ride.

Let's recap. The accelerator principle states that if sales or consumption is rising at a constant rate, Gross I will stay the same; if sales increase at a decreasing rate, both Gross I and GNP will fall.

Monetary theory

Still another endogenous theory is the monetary theory. It may well explain the 1980 and 1981–82 recessions when the Federal Reserve stepped heavily on the monetary brakes, as well as our subsequent recoveries, when monetary growth was increased. Finally, there is the overinvestment theory, hypothesizing that business firms overinvest in plant and equipment during the latter phases of prosperity, and then cut back, bringing on recessions.

Exogenous Theories

Sunspot theory

Just as endogenous theories place the causes of the business cycle within the economy, exogenous theories place the causes of the business cycle outside the economy.

The very first business cycle theory, the sunspot theory, was formulated by William Stanley Jevons over a century ago. Jevons believed that storms on the sun, which were observed through telescopes as sunspots, caused periodic crop failures. Because 19th-century economies were primarily agricultural, crop failures, by definition, caused declines in production, or recessions. Subsequent better harvests led to recovery, then prosperity, until the next sunspots occurred.

War theory

Another external theory is the war theory. The production surge caused by the preparation for war and the war itself causes prosperity and the letdown after the war causes a recession. Our experience before, during, and after World War II, the Korean War, and the Vietnam War seems to validate this theory.

Perhaps no one explanation, whether exogenous or endogenous, can explain each of the cycles we have experienced. The best we can do then is to treat each cycle separately, seeking single or multiple causes as they apply.

Business Cycle Forecasting

There are two main types of business cycle forecasts: analytic and barometric. Analytic forecasts attempt to explain the entire process from start to finish. Such-and-such will happen to real GNP because such-and-such is happening in each sector. These forecasts usually involve economic models, some of which have over 1,000 equations that are solved simultaneously.

Barometric forecasts are much simpler affairs, usually consisting of tracking only a few economic variables. The reasoning usually runs as follows. If these variables decline, then the economy goes into a recession, or, similarly, if they rise, then recovery soon will set in.

Analytic Forecasts

Econometric models

Econometric or computer models of the economy are the main tool for analytic forecasting. Various universities such as MIT, the Wharton School of Business, and the University of Michigan, as well as many private economic consulting firms, have developed scores of econometric models. By constantly plugging new data into the hundreds, or even thousands, of equations used, the model is continually able to update its forecasts.

How good are these forecasts? They are usually better than simple seat-of-the-pants guessing, but the models are only as accurate as the assumptions on which they're based.

Barometric Forecasts

The index of Leading Economic Indicators

The most widely used barometric forecasting device is the Index of Leading Economic Indicators, which is compiled monthly by the Department of Commerce. This series, which is a weighted average of 11 variables, is a valuable forecasting tool, particularly when it is used with caution.

The 11 leading indicators consist of variables that "lead" general economic activity by several months. For example, orders for durable goods rise before a rise in durable goods production and sales. Similarly, new building permits must be secured before buildings can be started.

When the index turns downward, particularly for two or three months in a row, there is a good chance the economy may be heading into a recession. However, as some pundits have put it, the index has predicted 13 of the last five recessions. In other words, the index may have turned downward for two or three months a total of 13 times, but in only five instances did a recession follow.

On the other hand, if the index moves steadily upward, there is virtually no chance of a recession in the next few months. But when it begins to move downward, watch out! A downturn *may* be at hand.

Similarly, when the Index of Leading Economic Indicators moves down steadily for 11 months in a row, as it did from April 1981 through March 1982, we not only had a recession, but there was virtually no chance of an upturn until later in the year, which is exactly what happened.

Figure 9-3 presents a record of the performance of the Index of Leading Economic Indicators since World War II. You may judge for yourself how well the index predicted recessions.

Where does all of this leave us? It leaves us with the observation that economics is an inexact science that attempts to forecast certain conditions in an uncertain world.

"To err is human; to get paid for it is divine."

—William Freund,
economic consultant

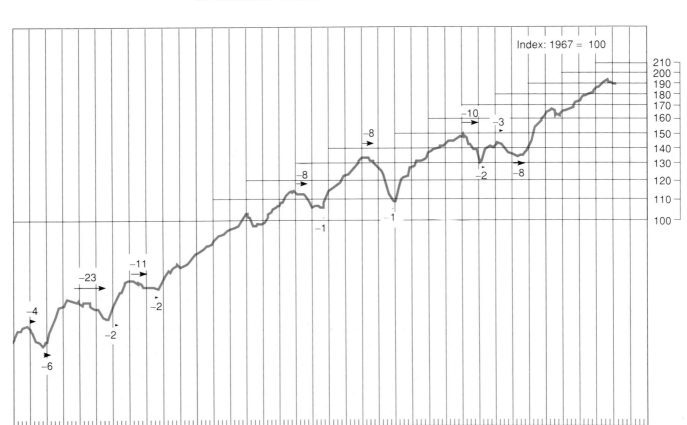

Index: 1967 = 100

Figure 9-3
The Index of Leading Indicators,
1952—1988

Note: Numbers entered on the chart indicate length of leads (−) and lags (+) in months from reference turning dates. Beginning with data for January 1984, the series changed from 11 to 12 indicators.

Source: U.S. Dept. of Commerce, *Business Conditions Digest*, March 1988, p. 10.

On Economic Forecasting

Economics' claim of being a science is based mainly on its ability to predict the future. Although economists have not often been too successful at the art of prediction, they are great at explaining why their forecasts were wrong. Even the boy who cried wolf was right that last time.

Pierre Renfret, then one of the richest economists (he owned a large consulting firm) predicted in early 1970, "There ain't gonna be no recession." Although his grammar was not impeccable, his forecast was technically correct. There wasn't going to be a recession because one had already begun—in December 1969. On the other end of the pay scale, I had written two articles for the *Journal of Commerce* in early 1979 titled "A Recession in April?" (January 24, 1979), and "Recession Likely to Get Worse" (September 18, 1979). There was only one problem. The recession I had been talking about did not actually begin until January 1980. Oh well, nobody's perfect.

The Index of Leading Economic Indicators rose five out of six months (April through October) of 1982, prompting me to proclaim the 1981–82 recession finally over in the same article titled "Pessimist Sees Economic Breakthrough," *Ocean County* (New Jersey) *Reporter*, November 24, 1982, and "Economic Recovery Has Finally Arrived," *Boston Post-Gazette*, November 12, 1982. Just so you don't get the impression every economic forecast is wrong, this one was right on the money. The recession of 1981–82 *did* end in November 1982.

Part III   Unemployment

"How can you expect somebody who's warm to understand somebody who's cold?"

—from *One Day in the Life of Ivan Denisovich,*
by Aleksandr Solzhenitsyn

The Problem

How does it feel to be out of work?

One of the most devastating experiences a person can have is be out of work for a prolonged period of time. Most of us have been unemployed once or twice, but only those who have been unable to find work after looking for six or eight months, or even longer, really know that feeling of hopelessness and self-doubt, not to mention one's depressed standard of living.

Most of the families on welfare are headed by women. Where are the men? Most of them just gave up when they found they couldn't support their families. In fact, the way most states administer the main type of welfare, Aid to Families with Dependent Children (AFDC), the family is eligible for assistance only if the father is *not* in the household. Thus, if we were to look for the major cause of the entire welfare pathology that has emerged over the last three decades, we would find that it has been the long-term joblessness of the fathers of the children on welfare.

We've talked about the official unemployment rate and about "discouraged" workers who have simply dropped out of the labor force. We've talked about fathers deserting their families to make them eligible for welfare. Where *are* these people?

Walk around the slums of our great cities. Walk through Watts, Bedford-Stuyvesant, and the Hough district of Cleveland. Walk through Roxbury in Boston or central Newark, or through most of our nation's capital. Walk through any of these places in midafternoon and you'll see block after block of teenagers and adults hanging around with nothing to do.

Wanted: a *real* job

Ask them what they want more than anything else. A bigger welfare check? More food stamps? A bigger color TV? Most of them would tell you that all they want is a decent job. Not a dead-end, minimum-wage, low-status, menial job, but a *real* job.

Are these people unemployed? No, these people have given up, dropped out, and are, for all intents and purposes, no longer living in the United States. They may reside here physically, but they are not part of our society.

The GNP Gap

The economic effects of unemployment are more quantifiable than the social effects. To measure them we shall use the GNP gap, which is the difference between what we could potentially produce and what we actually produce.

We'll try an analogy first. Do you bowl? What's your high game? Suppose your high game was 180. If you went out tonight and bowled 178, how would you feel? Good? What if you bowled 185? Great?

Living up to our potential GNP

Our potential GNP is like our high game at bowling. We know we can do it—maybe not that often, but sometimes. And there's always the chance that we can do still better. Our potential GNP then is our output when our resources are fully employed and we are using the best available technology. Remember the production possibilities frontier in Chapter 2? If we are attaining our potential GNP we are on our production possibilities frontier.

How often do we produce our potential GNP? About as often as we can bowl our high game; it happens but it's unusual. Usually our economy operates below our potential GNP.

Potential GNP and the productions possibilities curve

What's the difference then between our production possibilities curve and our potential GNP? They both represent our output when our economy is at full employment (that is, with an unemployment rate of 5 percent), but the production possibilities curve (or frontier) represents our economy at a particular moment in time while the graph of our potential GNP shows how much our economy would produce over time if it were to operate at full employment. Thus, the production possibilities frontier is a snapshot of our economy at full employment at a particular time while a graph of our potential GNP might show how much the economy would produce at full employment over a period of decades.

Figure 9–4 shows our economic record since World War II. In fact, you find that it's a reproduction of Figure 9–1, except that it has a smooth curve

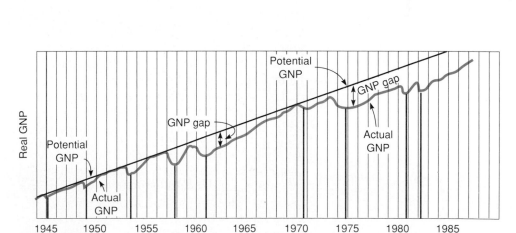

**Figure 9–4
The GNP Gap**

added to the record of our actual GNP. That's our potential GNP. Notice that potential GNP is greater than actual GNP for almost every year. There is a gap, which we call the GNP gap. It is the amount of production by which potential GNP exceeds actual GNP.

You'll also notice that in some years, most recently 1969, potential GNP exceeds actual GNP; there's no GNP gap at all. This is like having a high bowling game of 180 and going out and bowling a 185. These things *do* happen, but they happen so rarely that we can safely say we don't expect our actual GNP to exceed our potential GNP. On those rare instances when that happens, we can be pleasantly surprised, and then wait maybe another 20 years for it to happen again.

What is the significance of the GNP gap?

What then is the significance of the GNP gap? Obviously it shows by how much we are leaving our potential unfulfilled. Or, more concretely, we're saying that if we had only operated our economy at full employment we could have had another $100 billion or $150 billion worth of goods and services. While no one expects the economy to operate at its potential very often, if we run persistently large GNP gaps, say on the order of over $100 billion a year, it's clear that something is seriously wrong with our economy.

How the Unemployment Rate Is Computed

Where unemployment data comes from

The Bureau of Labor Statistics (BLS) is in charge of compiling statistics on the number of Americans who are employed and unemployed. Where do they get their data? Most people believe they get it from unemployment insurance offices, but if you stop and think about it, only about half of all unemployed Americans are currently collecting unemployment insurance benefits. The BLS gets its unemployment statistics by conducting a random survey of 60,000 households.

Essentially the bureau asks a series of questions: (1) Are you working? If the answer is no, (2) Did you work at all this month—even one day? Anyone who has answered yes to 1 or 2 is counted as employed. For those who have not been working, the BLS has one more question: (3) Did you look for work during the last month (i.e., did you go to an employment agency, send out a resumé, go on an interview, etc.)? If your answer is yes, you're counted as unemployed. If your answer is no, you're just not counted; you're not part of the labor force. If you want to work, but have just given up looking for a job, you're a "discouraged worker," but you are not in the labor force and you are not considered "unemployed."

The labor force consists of the employed and the unemployed. For example, in March 1987, 113,104,000 Americans were employed and 7,854,000 were unemployed. We can compute the unemployment rate by using this formula:

$$\text{Unemployment rate} = \frac{\text{Number of unemployed} \ \textit{reported}}{\text{Labor force}}$$

$$\text{Unemployment rate} = \frac{\text{Number of unemployed}}{\text{Labor force}}$$

How much was the unemployment rate in March 1987? Work it out right here.

Did you get 6.5 percent? The key here is to figure out how many people are in the labor force. Add the employed and unemployed and you should get 120,958,000. From there it's simple division: 120,958,000 into 7,854,000.

Thus, in March 1987, our official unemployment rate was 6.5 percent. The liberal economists (is there anyone who still calls himself a "liberal"?) would say that the true rate of unemployment is somewhat higher, perhaps 8 or 9 percent, if we included all the people who were ready, willing, and able to work, but were counted as "not in the labor force" (or as discouraged workers) by the BLS. Do you remember any scenes from the movie *Butch Cassidy and the Sundance Kid?* Paul Newman kept asking Robert Redford about the posse that had been pursuing them through the badlands: "Who *are* those guys?"

Who are the "discouraged" workers?

Let's ask that same question about all those guys—the two or three million of them—who are not working but are not officially unemployed. If we asked the BLS—Who *are* those guys?—they would tell us that they're discouraged workers. Discouraged? Why discouraged? Because they're *so* discouraged they've given up looking for work. Therefore, they don't meet the BLS criteria for being officially unemployed. If a person has not actively looked for a job during the last month—sent out a resumé, gone on a job interview, or visited an employment agency—that person is not counted as unemployed. He is not in the labor force. And as far as our unemployment rate statistics go, he is not there at all.

The liberals say the true unemployment rate is higher than the official rate.

The liberals have a couple of additional bones to pick with the BLS definition. A person who worked one day in the last month is counted as employed. Also, someone who works part time, but wants to work full time is counted as employed. The liberals ask: Doesn't this sort of measurement overstate the number of employed?

When you put it all together, they maintain, the BLS is overstating employment and understating unemployment. This gives us an unemployment rate that is perhaps a couple of points too low.

The conservatives say the true unemployment rate is lower than the official rate.

That's the liberal view. As you would expect, the conservatives say that the official unemployment rate *over*estimates the true rate of unemployment. Using the BLS definition of an unemployed person—someone who has not worked this month and who has actively sought work—the conservative focuses on those who are required to report to state employment or other government employment offices in order to remain eligible for unemployment insurance, welfare, or food stamps. Is this, asks the conservative, really an effort to look for work, or are these guys just going through the motions?

Another factor boosting the unemployment rate that the conservatives cite is the change in the composition of the labor force. The percentage of married women who work has risen from only 25 percent in the late 1940s (when the birthrate was very high) to over 50 percent today. The advent of married women seeking work raises the unemployment rate in three different ways. First, married women who are reentering the labor force after having had children will have to find jobs (unless their employers held their old positions open for 5, 10, or 20 years). Second, because their husbands are employed, they can shop around a bit for a job. And third, their husbands, if unemployed, can also shop around a bit if their wives are working.

And so, in each case, the rise in labor force participation by married women has tended to raise the unemployment rate over the last four decades. It has also been pushed up as the baby-boom generation (those born from the late 1940s to the mid-1960s) came of age. Young adults tend to have a relatively high unemployment rate because, like the housewives returning to the labor force, they need time to find that first job. Next, they tend to go from job to job until, like Goldilocks, they find a position that is "just right." And finally, because many young adults still live at home or receive help from their parents, they experience less pressure to take the first job that comes along.

The bottom line, according to the conservatives, is that perhaps a couple of million of the "officially" unemployed are not really looking for work. The liberal bottom line is that there are at least a couple of million people out there who want to work but aren't being counted.

Are the conservatives or the liberals right? Guess what? I'm going to let *you* decide.

Figure 9–5 is a record of the official unemployment rate from 1948 through 1987. You'll notice a marked upward trend since the late 1960s, which apparently lends credence to the conservative interpretation—but the results are not yet all in. This trend could be reversed, especially now that the baby boomers have all come of age and the federal government may be playing a more activist economic role in the post-Reagan years.

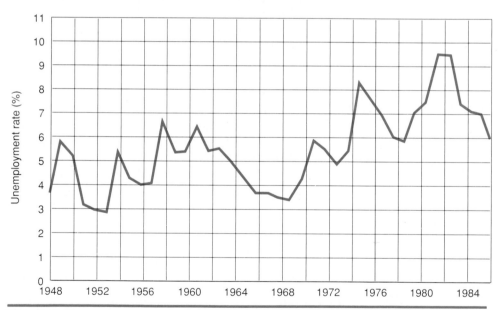

Figure 9–5

Source: 1988 *Economic Report of the President,* p. 284.

When It's a Recession for Whites, for Blacks It's a Depression

In Part II of this chapter, we jokingly referred to the difference between recessions and depressions. For blacks, however, unemployment is no joking matter. Historically, the unemployment rate for blacks has been double that of whites. And for black teenagers, during the 1981–82 recession, their "official" unemployment rate topped 50 percent. One can only guess at their true unemployment rate if all the "discouraged" black teenagers who dropped out of the labor force were counted.

A survey in the early 1980s by the Center for the Study of Social Policy turned up this interesting fact. Black college graduates earn about the same income as white high school graduates. So much for the notion of equality of opportunity.

Of course, there have been major strides toward equality of economic opportunity since the mid-1960s, but they have left in their wake a huge black (and Hispanic) underclass. If you are black or Hispanic, your chances of being poor are three times as great as if you are white, and your chances of being unemployed are twice as great.

There are apparently two things that can be done to ease the economic burden of minority groups. One is to make greater efforts to end employment discrimination. The other is to avoid recessions and keep the unemployment rate as low as possible.

Types of Unemployment

Frictional Unemployment

Our economy is far from a well-tuned, efficient, smoothly functioning machine. When a job opening occurs somewhere, it is rarely filled instanteously, even when there is someone ready, willing, and able to fill it. In a word, our economy has a certain degree of friction.

The frictionally unemployed are people who are between jobs, or who are just entering or reentering the labor market. Because our system of filling jobs—newspaper help-wanted ads, employment agencies, corporate recruiters, executive headhunters, help-wanted signs, and word-of-mouth—is

A Computerized Job Bank

Imagine that we have a computerized network listing every job opening in the country and every person seeking employment. Every job opening and every job seeker will be matched instantly. What effect will this have on frictional unemployment? It will practically wipe it out in one fell swoop.

Why don't we set up such a system? Believe it or not, we have. Virtually every state employment office* has a computer bank of job openings. There are just two problems.

First, only a small minority of employers list their jobs with their state employment services. One reason they don't is that they're reluctant to hire peope who are collecting unemployment insurance because they are sometimes perceived as being lazy or having low motivation. "Hi! I was referred to you by the Missouri State Employment Service." Also, employers in general will

look askance at anyone who is out of work. "*Why* are you unemployed?" You'll always stand a better chance of finding a job if you already *have* a job, or at least if people think you do.

A second reason why the state employment services don't have a perfect match between job openings and jobseekers is that not everybody out of work registers at their state employment office. If they're collecting unemployment insurance benefits, they *have* to. If they're not, they may. But in certain lines of work—executive positions, many professional jobs, and, in general, higher paying positions—job applicants rarely register at their state employment service.

* There are the employment agency counterparts to the state unemployment insurance offices where unemployed people sign for their unemployment checks.

imperfect, it is usually a matter of weeks or months until most positions are filled.

About 2 to 3 percent of our labor force is always frictionally unemployed.

At any given time about 2 or 3 percent of the labor force is frictionally unemployed. Students who are looking for their first full-time jobs, housewives reentering the labor market after 5, 10, or 20 years, and servicemen and women, who have recently been discharged by the armed forces, are frictionally unemployed until they find jobs. In addition, there are those who leave their jobs voluntarily, perhaps so they can spend all their time looking for better jobs. Maybe they're looking in another part of the country. Add to these the people who get fired, quit, or are just plumb unhappy and decide to make a fresh start somewhere else. These people too are between jobs or frictionally unemployed.

Structural Unemployment

A person who is out of work for a relatively long period of time, say a couple of years, is structurally unemployed. The economy does not have any use for this person. The steelworker in Youngstown, Ohio, and the coal miner from Kentucky are no longer needed because of the closing of the local steel mills and coal mines. And the clerical workers, typists, and inventory control clerks who staffed a corporate office have skills made obsolete by a computer system. Add to these the people whose companies have gone out of business or whose jobs have been exported to low-wage countries and you've got another 2 to 3 percent of the labor force structurally unemployed.

About 2 to 3 percent of our labor force is always structurally unemployed.

Ours is a dynamic economy and the opportunities for retraining and subsequent employment *do* exist. But the prospects for a 50- or 60-year old worker embarking on a second career are not too auspicious. To compound the problem, most of the structurally unemployed reside in the "Rustbelt" of the East and Midwest, while most of the new career opportunities are in the Sunbelt.[2]

What if someone were "between jobs" for six months, or a year, or even two years? When someone is out of work for a long period of time, he or she is classified as "structurally unemployed." But where do we draw the line between frictional and structural unemployment? The answer is that we don't. There *is* no clear-cut dividing line.

Cyclical Unemployment

As you well know, our economy certainly has its ups and downs, a set of fluctuations known as business cycles. During a recession, the unemployment rate rises to 8, 9, or even 10 percent. During really bad times, like the Great Depression, the "official" unemployment rate hit 25 percent, which definitely understated the true unemployment picture.

Fluctuations in our unemployment rate are due to cyclical unemployment.

If we allow for a certain amount of frictional and structural unemployment, anything above the sum of these two would be cyclical unemployment. Let's say that the sum of frictional and structural unemployment is 5 percent. If the actual rate of unemployment is 7.7 percent, then the cyclical rate is 2.7 percent.

---

[2] With the fluctuations in the worldwide price of oil, the employment picture in Texas, Louisiana, and Oklahoma has become uncertain, at best. In the meanwhile, there has been a veritable explosion of high-tech jobs in Massachusetts, New Jersey, and a few other eastern states.

Are You Eligible to Collect Unemployment Benefits?

There are a lot of people out there who are eligible to collect who don't know they're eligible. The eligibility requirements are a yes answer to these three questions:

1. Did you work for at least parts of 20 of the last 52 weeks (or 15 of the last 52 weeks and 40 of the last 104)?

2. Did you lose your last job through no fault of your own?

3. Are you ready, willing, and able to work?

The second question is open to interpretation. What if you were fired from your last job? Why? Did you provoke your own dismissal? Then you can't collect. What if you and your boss had an argument? Then you may be eligible.

What if you got fired because your boss didn't like you, or because you couldn't get the hang of the job, or because there was just no work for you to do? Then you could collect. But what if you got fired because you were always late, often absent, or refused to do any work? Obviously you provoked your own dismissal and are not eligible for unemployment benefits.

But the answer to the second question is not always a clear-cut yes or no. As a one-time employee of the New York State Employment Service, I am offering you this advice: If you lose your job and you think you *may* be eligible, it pays to apply for unemployment benefits. There are a lot of people collecting right now who may have had even more dubious claims than you have. Just go down to your state unemployment insurance office and find out if you're eligible for a $200-a-week, 26-week (possibly tax-free), paid vacation.

If we take a 5 percent unemployment rate as our working definition of full employment, anything above 5 percent would be cyclical unemployment. You may wonder whether 5 percent is a reasonable level for full employment. Surely we can never expect our unemployment rate to reach zero, since we'll always have some frictionally and structurally unemployed people. Our unemployment rate once did get down to 1.2 percent in 1944, but as they said then, "There's a war going on." With 12 million men in the armed forces and the economy going full-steam ahead, jobs went begging. Employers were desperate for help and anyone who could walk and spell his name had no trouble finding a job.

There are liberal economists who insist that we could realistically get the unemployment rate down to 4 percent, while there are conservative economists who consider a 6 percent rate the lowest that is attainable. We'll split the difference and call 5 percent full employment.

Part IV   Inflation

"Inflation is not all that bad. After all, it enables us to live in a more expensive neighborhood without having to move."

—Anonymous

What exactly *is* inflation? It is a rise in the price level. Generally we consider inflation a sustained rise in the price level over a period of years. In our own lifetimes we have known little *but* inflation.

Our inflation has been persistent since World War II, particularly in the 1970s when, for much of the decade, it was at double-digit proportions. And yet, when compared to an inflation rate of over 100 percent in several South American countries in the 1980s,[3] ours has been relatively mild.

---

[3] In 1987, Brazil had an annual rate of inflation of 1,000 percent.

Ask the man on the street what inflation is and he'll tell you that everything costs more. To be more precise, the Department of Commerce compiles an average of all items that consumers buy—the prices of cars, appliances, haircuts, TVs, VCRs, steaks, medical services, Big Macs—and figures out how much it costs the average family to live. Let's say that in January 1986 it cost the Jones family $20,000 to maintain a certain standard of living. If it cost the Joneses $22,000 to buy the same items in January 1989, we would say that the cost of living went up 10 percent.

No one would complain if the cost of living rose 2 or 3 percent a year, but during the 10-year period from 1972 the consumer price index rose from 125.3 to 289.1. By what percentage did the cost of living rise? Figure it out right here.

It went up by 130.7 percent.[4] In other words, it cost the typical American family more than twice as much to live in 1982 than it did 10 years earlier.

Deflation is a decline in the price level, but once again, not for just a month or two, but for a period of years. The last deflation we had was from 1929 to 1933, when prices fell 50 percent. Significantly, that deflation was accompanied by the Great Depression.

Some people think a mild deflation might be a good thing, but it would be disastrous for the economy. Business profits would become losses and people would be thrown out of work. If a retailer contracted to buy inventory at $100 a unit and hoped to sell it at $120, he might end up getting only $110. After paying all his expenses—rent, salaries, telephone, electric, advertising, and so on—he might end up with a loss of $2 or $3 per unit.

Until the inflationary recessions of the 1970s, business downturns were called deflations, since they were invariably accompanied by price declines. As much as businessmen dislike inflation, particularly that of double-digit proportions, they hate deflation even more.

The Post-World War II History of Inflation

During each war in our history, prices rose sharply. Each war was accompanied by a combination of money supply increases and large budget deficits.

In 1945, as World War II ended, a tremendous pent-up demand for consumer goods was unleashed. Consumer prices rose sharply. Too many dollars were chasing too few goods. Just as the inflation was being brought

---

[4] Fear not! Help is on the way in the next section, when we'll be working out more percentage changes. If you can't wait, you may glance back at the third section of Chapter 5, when we first introduced percentage change problems.

under control, the Korean War broke out. This brought on another wave of consumer spending and price increases.

President Eisenhower took office in 1953, pledging to end the war in Korea and the inflation at home. It took him only a month to end the war, but it wasn't until 1960, three recessions later, that inflation was controlled.

Until 1965, consumer prices rose at an annual rate of only 1 percent (see Figure 9–6). Then the Vietnam War, accompanied by huge federal budget deficits, rekindled another inflationary fire.

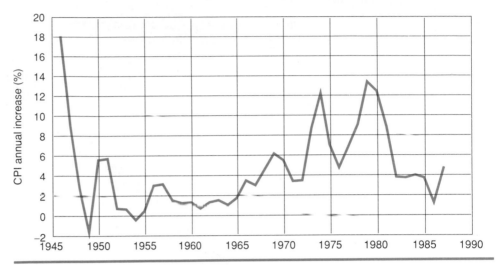

Figure 9–6

Source: 1988 *Economic Report of the President,* p. 317.

Inflation seems inevitable.

By this time most Americans had become conditioned to rising prices; they seemed inevitable. When prices have been rising for some time, it is reasonable to assume that they will keep rising. So what did we do? We ran out to buy still more goods and services before prices rose still further. And when businessmen saw that demand for their products was high, they were encouraged to raise *their* prices.

What was taking place was a self-fulfilling prophecy. We thought something would happen. In other words, so long as people *believe* that inflation is inevitable, it is indeed inevitable!

Early in President Nixon's first term, he recognized this self-fulfilling prophecy, so, he reasoned, all he needed to do was convince people that prices would not be rising in the near future. Then they wouldn't stock up on goods, and prices wouldn't rise.

Nixon's premise was correct. So too was his conclusion. If people believed that prices would be stable, they wouldn't buy too much and drive up those prices, *but* no one believed Nixon when he told the country that prices would be leveling off.

Since then a lot has happened to affect the rate of inflation. Nixon's wage and price freeze didn't really take, perhaps because it was tried only half-heartedly. When OPEC quadrupled oil prices in the fall of 1973, inflation accelerated (see Figure 9–6). The deep recession that followed did damp down the inflation, but in the late 1970s, it returned with renewed vigor. It was not until the back-to-back recessions of 1980 and 1981–82 that the rate of inflation was finally brought down to acceptable levels.

But in 1987 the rate of inflation, fueled by a rapid increase in the money supply and huge federal budget deficits, once again started back up. As we enter the 1990s, we are faced with a Hobson's Choice of another round of inflation or another round of tight money, lower budget deficits, and possibly another couple of recessions to bring down the inflation rate.

The Construction of the Consumer Price Index

The most important measure of inflation is the consumer price index. Now we'll see how the Department of Commerce goes about constructing this index.

First a base year is picked, usually one ending with a 7. In 1987, we were still using 1967 as our base year. What the consumer price index did was measure the change in the cost of living from the base year, 1967, to the current year, 1987.[5]

The base year is always 100.

The index in the base year is set at 100. If the index in the current year is 350, by what percentage did prices rise?

Did you say 250 percent? If not, here's an easy way to figure out percentage changes from the base year. Subtract 100 from the current CPI and you've automatically got the percentage change. In this case: 350 − 100 = 250.

If the index is currently 425, by what percentage did the index rise since the base year? It rose 325 percent (425 − 100).

In the case of deflation, the index will fall below 100. For example, if the index is 85 in the current year, by what percentage did prices *fall* since the base year? 85 − 100 = −15. So prices fell 15 percent since the base year.

Let's see how the index is constructed. The Department of Commerce compiles a market basket of thousands of goods and services that the typical family buys in 1967. Assuming that they buy that same market basket of goods and services in 1977, the Department of Commerce figures out how much that family would have had to spend. It then comes up with an index number for 1977. In fact, it does this every month.

We're going to construct a consumer price index for 1987 and then for 1992. But to make things a little easier, we're going to include only six goods and services.

These six items are shown in Table 9-1. In A, we have a month's expenditures for 1987, the base year. To find them, we multiply quantity purchased times price. Then, adding up the money spent on each item, we find how much was spent during a month in 1987.

Now we'll compare that amount with the amount spent for a month in 1992, which is shown in Table 9-1B. What happened then was that the family spent $848 for these six items in 1987 and $994 for these same items in 1992. Obviously their cost of living went up, But by how much?

---

[5] In 1988, the Commerce Department designated a base period, 1982–84, evidently because it was thought that it would provide a better measure of subsequent inflation than would a single year.

Table 9–1
Cost of Living for One Month, 1987 and 1992

A. 1987

Item	Quantity	Price	Quantity × Price
Loaf of bread	10	.70	7.00
Quart of milk	15	.60	9.00
Pair of jeans	2	23.00	46.00
New car	0.02	7800.00	156.00
Mortgage payment	1	590.00	590.00
Movie admission	8	5.00	40.00
Total			848.00

B. 1992

Item	Quantity	Price	Quantity × Price
Loaf of bread	10	.90	9.00
Quart of milk	15	.80	12.00
Pair of jeans	2	31.00	62.00
New car	0.02	9000.00	180.00
Mortgage payment	1	675.00	675.00
Movie admission	8	7.00	56.00
Total			994.00

To find the CPI in the current year, divide the cost of living in the current year by the cost of living in the base year and multiply by 100.

To find out, we'll construct a consumer price index. To do this, just divide the cost of living in the base year, 1987, into the cost of living in the current year, 1992. After you've done that, multiply your answer by 100 to convert it into an index number. Do your work right here and then check it with the results below.

$$994/848 = 1.172. \quad 1.172 \times 100 = 117.2.$$

That's our consumer price index for 1992. You'll notice that we've carried it to one decimal place, which is exactly how the Department of Commerce does it, and how you'll find it listed in the newspaper.

One last question. By what percentage did prices rise between 1987 and 1992? The envelope please. Prices rose by 17.2 percent.

Let's try another one using the same format but different years. Suppose that 1977 is the base year and you want to find the cost of living index in 1993. Use the information in Table 9–2.

Table 9–2
Cost of Living for One Month, 1977 and 1993

A. 1977

Item	Quantity	Price	Quantity × Price
Gallon of gas	30	.60	
Mortgage payment	1	175.00	
17-inch TV	0.03	400.00	
Doctor visit	3	20.00	
1-lb. steak	10	1.50	
Pair of shoes	0.5	20.00	

B. 1993

Item	Quantity	Price	Quantity × Price
Gallon of gas	30	1.20	
Mortgage payment	1	300.00	
17-inch TV	0.03	100.00	
Doctor visit	3	40.00	
1-lb. steak	10	3.50	
Pair of shoes	0.5	30.00	

After you've found the CPI for 1993, figure out by what percentage prices rose between 1977 and 1993.

First we take the cost of living in the current year, $509, and divide it by the cost of living in the base year, $290. This gives us 1.755, which we multiply by 100. Thus the CPI in 1993 will be 175.5, and prices rose 75.5 percent since the base year, 1977.

Anticipated and Unanticipated Inflation

Why farmers like inflation

Traditionally creditors have been hurt by inflation and debtors have been helped. Throughout our history, the farmers have been debtors. During times of deflation or stable prices, the farmers' cries of anguish are heard loud and clear all the way to Washington, but during times of inflation, there is scarcely a peep out of them.

It is easy to see why. Suppose a farmer borrows $100, which he agrees to repay in one year along with 4 percent interest ($4). In one year he pays back $104. But what if, during the year, prices doubled? The money he paid back would be worth much less than the money he borrowed.

Let's say that when the farmer borrowed the money, wheat was selling at $2 a bushel. He would have been able to buy 50 bushels of wheat ($100/$2). But farmers don't buy wheat; they sell it. So one year later, this farmer harvests his wheat and pays back the loan. If the price level doubles, assume that the price of wheat doubles. How much wheat would the farmer need to sell at $4 a bushel to pay off his $104 loan payment? He would need to sell only 26 bushels ($104/$4).

Obviously this farmer, who is a debtor, benefits magnificently from unanticipated inflation because he has borrowed money worth some 50 bushels of wheat and pays back his loan—with interest—in money worth only 26 bushels of wheat. Debtors, in general, gain from unanticipated inflation because they repay their loans in inflated dollars.

Just as obviously, those hurt by unanticipated inflation are people who lend out the money—the creditors. We generally think of creditors as banks, but banks are really financial middlemen. The ultimate creditors, or lenders, are the people who put their money in banks, life insurance, or any other financial instrument paying a fixed rate of interest. And the biggest debtor and gainer from unanticipated inflation has been the U.S. government. The national debt, which is now approaching $3 trillion, would be a lot easier to pay off if there were a great deal of inflation.

Another group helped by unanticipated inflation is businessmen. Just as businesses suffer losses on their inventory during periods of deflation, so too, during inflations do they obtain inventory price windfalls. Between the time inventory is ordered and the time it is actually sold, prices have crept upward, swelling profits.

Who is hurt by inflation? Those who are hurt by unanticipated inflation are people who live on fixed incomes, particularly retired people who depend on pensions (except Social Security), those who hold long-term bonds, whether corporate or U.S. government bonds. And finally, people whose wages are fixed under long-term contracts and landlords who have granted long-term leases at fixed rent are hurt by unanticipated inflation.

In other words, under unanticipated inflation, some people gain and others lose. In fact, the gains and losses are exactly equal.

When inflation is fully anticipated, there are no winners or losers. The interest rate takes into account the expected rate of inflation. Normally, without anticipated inflation, the interest rate would be around 5 percent. In 1980, and again in 1981, when the rate of inflation ran at close to 15 percent, the prime rate of interest (paid by top credit-rated corporations) soared over 20 percent.

For inflation to be fully anticipated and built into interest rates, people need to live with it for several years. Although we have had relatively high inflation for most of the last dozen years, it was only in 1979 that the prime rate finally broke the 12 percent barrier. Today, however, unanticipated inflation is a thing of the past.

Creditors have learned to charge enough interest to take into account, or anticipate, the rate of inflation over the course of the loan. This would be tacked onto the regular interest rate that the lender would have charged had there been no inflation expected.

Real rate of interest We'll work out a few examples. If the real rate of interest, the rate that would be charged without inflation, were 5 percent, and there was an expected rate of inflation of 3 percent, then obviously the creditors would charge 8 percent.

If the real rate of interest were 4 percent and the expected inflation rate were 6 percent, how much would the nominal rate (the rate actually charged) be? Good—I know you said 10 percent. So the real rate of interest plus the expected rate of inflation equals the nominal rate of interest.

If the nominal interest rate accurately reflects the inflation rate, then the inflation has been fully anticipated and no one wins or loses. This is a good thing for our economy because it means that no one is hurt and no one is forced out of business because of inflation.

But if the rate of inflation keeps growing—even if it is correctly anticipated—our economy will be in big trouble. In a hyperinflation there are ultimately only losers.

People on fixed incomes, especially those who are retired, have also traditionally been hurt by inflation. But in recent years Social Security benefits have been indexed for inflation, that is, they have gone up by the same percentage as the consumer price index.

Many wage earners too are now protected against inflation by cost-of-living adjustment clauses (called COLA agreements) in their contracts.[6] One way or another then, most sectors of our society have learned to protect themselves from at least the short-term ravages of inflation.

Theories of the Causes of Inflation

Demand-Pull Inflation

Excessive demand causes demand-pull inflation.

When there is excessive demand for goods and services we have demand-pull inflation. What is excessive? When people are willing and able to buy more output than our economy can produce. Something's gotta give. And what gives are prices.

Demand-pull inflation is often summed up as "too many dollars chasing too few goods." The problem is that we can't produce any more goods because our economy is already operating at full capacity.

To help explain what happens when there's excess demand, we'll select another term from the economist's tool kit—the *aggregate supply curve*. In Figure 9–7 we have a horizontal curve that begins to slope upward to the right and eventually becomes completely vertical. Notice that it becomes vertical at full employment.

At very low levels of output—depression levels—it would be easy to increase output without raising prices. After all, with high unemployment and idle plant and equipment, it would be easy to put those resources back to work without raising costs very much. For example, if a person who has been out of work for several months is offered a job at the going wage rate, she will jump at the chance to get back to work.

As output expands, most of the idle resources will be put back into production. Firms that need more plant and equipment will have to buy them. Employers will have to raise wages to induce new employees to work for them. In effect then, business will have to bid for resources, and in doing so, they will bid up the prices of land, labor, and capital.

As their costs go up, business firms will be forced to raise their prices. We are now in range 2 of the aggregate supply curve. We're moving closer and closer to full employment. It becomes increasingly difficult to get good help. New workers have to be lured away from other employers. There's only one way to do this—pay them more.

---

[6] In recent years, employers have become increasingly reluctant to grant COLAs. Between March 1985 and March 1987, the percent of workers in major unions covered by this protection declined from 56.7 percent to just 38 percent. See Louis Uchitelle, "As Output Gains, Wages Lag, *New York Times*, June 4, 1987, Section D, page 7.

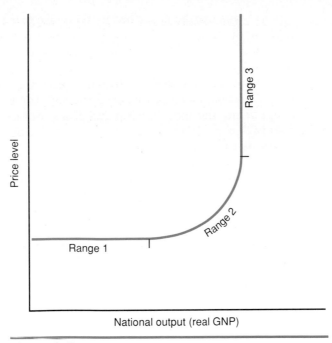

Figure 9-7

This pushes costs up still further until finally we've reached the full-employment level of output. Any further spending on goods and services will simply bid up prices without any corresponding increase in output. Welcome to range 3.

Our economy rarely operates in either range 1 or range 3. Both depressions and runaway inflations are relatively rare occurances, but they *do* happen. The twin goals of macroeconomic policy are to avoid these two extremes, or anything approaching them. But runaway inflations in particular are sometimes unavoidable. This happens when macroeconomic policy must subordinate itself to military necessity. During World War II, for example, the federal government bought up half our output for military use. The only problem was that private citizens had plenty of money to spend and not enough output to spend it on. So we had a bidding war between civilians and the government for our limited resources. It was a classic case of too much money chasing too few goods.

Cost-Push Inflation

The wage-price spiral

There are three variants of this type of inflation. Most prominent is the wage-price spiral. Because wages constitute nearly two thirds of the cost of doing business, whenever workers receive a significant wage increase, this increase is invariably passed along to consumers in the form of higher prices. Higher prices raise everyone's cost of living, engendering further wage increases.

Imagine a 3 percent rise in the cost of living. Labor unions will negotiate for a 3 percent catch-up increase and a 3 percent increase on top of that for an anticipated cost-of-living increase *next* year. That's 6 percent. If every labor union gets a 6 percent increase, undoubtedly prices will rise, not 3 percent, but—you guess it—6 percent! In the next round of labor negotiations, the unions might want not just a 6 percent catch-up, but 12 percent, to take care of next year as well.[7]

---

[7] Labor unions are a major topic of Chapter 27.

All of this can be described as the wage-price spiral. Regardless of who is to blame for its origin, once it gets started it spawns larger and larger wage and price increases. Round and round it goes, and where it stops nobody knows.

This variant of cost-push inflation may well explain a great deal of the inflation that we have experienced through the early 1970s. However, in recent years, the membership and power of our labor unions have been sharply declining, so the wage-price spiral would serve today, at best, as only a partial explanation for inflation.

Profit-push inflation

The second variant of cost-push inflation is profit-push inflation. Because many industries are dominated by just a handful of huge firms, for example, cigarettes, detergents, breakfast cereals, cars, and oil, these firms have the power to administer prices in those industries rather than accept the dictates of the market forces of supply and demand. To the degree that they are able to protect their profit margins by raising prices, these firms will respond to any rise in costs by passing them on to their customers.

Supply-side cost shocks

Finally we have supply-side cost shocks, most prominently the oil price shocks of 1973–74 and 1979. When the OPEC nations quadrupled the price of oil in the fall of 1973, they touched off not just a major recession, but also a severe inflation. When the price of oil rises, the cost of making a lot of other things rises as well, for example, electricity, fertilizer, gasoline, heating oil, and long distance freight carriage. And as we've seen again and again, cost increases are quickly translated into price increases.

Inflation as a Psychological Process

How inflation takes on a life of its own

Have you noticed that once inflation gets underway, it soon doesn't matter what the initial cause was because the process takes on a life of its own? To come to grips with inflation, we must get at its roots. We have discussed the psychology of inflation. If people believe that prices will rise, they will act in a way that keeps them rising. The only way to curb inflation is to counter inflationary psychology.

Various things can set off an inflationary spiral—wars, huge federal budget deficits, large increases in the money supply, sudden increases in the price of oil—but once the spiral begins, inflation psychology takes over.

Once prices have been jolted upward, the original cause no longer matters; other forces are soon activated. Labor unions seek catch-up wage increases. Businesspeople raise their prices to keep up with costs—primarily wage increases. Consumers with money in their pockets spend it before prices rise further.

To stop inflation then we need to convince workers, businesspeople, and consumers that prices will stop rising. If we can do that, prices *will* stop rising.

Breaking the back of the inflationary psychology

Once we attain a period of price stability, the psychology of inflation will be destroyed. We will enjoy that stability as long as we can avoid triggering another round of inflation. In the early 1960s, we attained such a period of stability, but then came the Vietnam War and its attendant federal budget deficits. Again in the mid-1980s we had a very low rate of inflation, but continuing deficits and rapid monetary growth may have rekindled the inflationary fires.

To break the back of the inflationary psychology is to bring down the rate of inflation for a sufficiently long period of time so that people actually expect price stability to continue. That has happened in the recent past only after inflation has been wrung out of the economy by successive recessions. To date, this has been the only cure we've come up with, but obviously it's a cure with some unpleasant side effects, particularly for those who lose their jobs during these recessions. After we examine creeping and hyperinflation, we'll turn to the problem of unemployment.

Creeping and Hyperinflation

Creeping inflation in one country would be hyperinflation in another.

Because *inflation* is a relative term, what may be considered creeping inflation in one country would be hyperinflation in another. Even what might have once been called creeping inflation in one particular country 10 years ago might now be considered hyperinflation.

For example, when the United States suffered from double-digit inflation in the mid-1970s and again in the late 1970s and early 1980s, a rate of 6 or 7 percent would have been welcomed as creeping inflation. But by the mid-1980s, anything above 4 percent would have been considered by some as hyperinflation.

Let's take an annual rate of increase in the consumer price index of 1 or 2 percent as something that virtually everyone would agree is creeping inflation. Very few people would be alarmed by this price increase. Businesspeople would generally like it because it would swell profits and in general be good for business. And as we have seen, many wage earners and all Social Security recipients are protected from inflation by cost-of-living increases tied to the consumer price index.

But once we cross that line, which keeps shifting from creeping inflation to hyperinflation, we run into trouble. It becomes increasingly difficult to conduct normal economic affairs. Prices are raised constantly. It becomes impossible to enter into long-term contracts. No one is sure what the government might do.

Prices serve as a signal system for business firms. If prices are rising, business firms will produce more goods and services. But what if costs are rising faster?

Suppose Bethlehem Steel agrees to supply General Motors with 50,000 tons of steel at $30 a ton. Suddenly Bethlehem's costs rise by 50 percent. Will GM be willing to accept a price increase of $15 a ton to $45 a ton if it has a signed contract calling for only $30 a ton?

Meanwhile, the government—meaning Congress, the president, and the Federal Reserve Board—may decide to act precipitously. On August 15, 1971, President Nixon suddenly announced the imposition of wage and price controls—based on a law he had been saying he would never use. In October 1979, the Federal Reserve Board suddenly stopped monetary growth, sending interest rates through the roof and touching off a sharp recession.

The German inflation

The classic hyperinflation took place in Germany after World War I. You may think that double-digit inflation (that is, 10 percent or more per year) is hyperinflation, but in Germany prices rose 10 percent an hour! The German government had to print larger and larger denominations—100 mark notes, then 1,000 mark notes, and eventually, 1 million mark notes. The smaller denominations became worthless; parents gave them to children for use as play money.

The German inflation eventually led to a complete economic breakdown, helped touch off a worldwide depression, and paved the way for a new chancellor named Adolf Hitler. No wonder the Germans begin getting nervous whenever their inflation rate begins to inch up.

Another classic example is what happened in Hungary during and after World War II. Before the war, if you went into a store with a pengo, you had some money in your pocket. In those days a pengo was a pengo. But by August 1946, you needed 828 octillion pengos—that's 828 followed by 27 zeros—to buy what one pengo bought before the war.

When inflation really gets out of hand, people begin to refuse to accept money as a means of payment. We are reduced to a state of barter, making it extremely difficult for our economy to function. If you don't have what I want or I don't have what you want, we can't do business.

One of the worries that people have when there is *any* inflation, even a creeping inflation of just 1 or 2 percent a year, is that the rate will keep increasing until we have a runaway inflation. Does this always happen? The answer is a definite no!. However, there's always the chance that things may get out of control. Like fire, a little inflation is not bad at all, but if it gets out of control, we'll be in big trouble.

Conclusion

One thing we have rarely been able to attain simultaneously is a low unemployment rate and stable prices. A British economist, A. W. Phillips, even had a curve named after him illustrating that there is a trade-off between price stability and low unemployment.

As Phillips showed, in the 1950s and 1960s we attained price stability at the cost of higher unemployment and vice versa. In the 1970s, though, we had high unemployment *and* rapidly rising prices. During the presidential campaign of 1976, Jimmy Carter castigated President Gerald Ford with his "misery index," which was the inflation rate and the unemployment rate combined.[8] Anything over 10 was unacceptable, according to Carter.

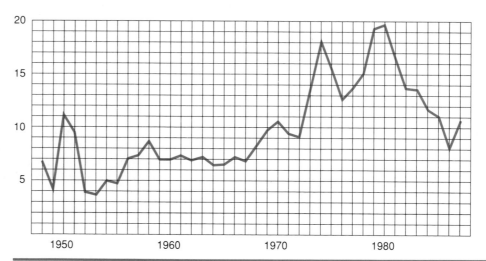

Figure 9–8
The Misery Index

Source: 1988 *Economic Report of the President,*
pp. 284, 317.

---

[8] During the 1960s, Arthur Okun, while he was President Johnson's Chairman of the Council of Economic Advisors, coined the term "economic discomfort index," which Jimmy Carter renamed the misery index.

The misery index

In 1980 Ronald Reagan resurrected the misery index for the voters, reminding them that it had gone from 10, when President Carter took office, all the way to 20.

Although the misery index has obvious political uses, it does provide us with a snapshot view of our economic performance over the last four decades. In Figure 9-8, we can gauge just how stable our economy has been during this period. When taken together with Figure 9-1, we can safely say that our economic record, particularly that of the last two decades, is not one we would want to write home about.

We certainly can try to improve on this record. We'll be examining macroeconomic policy beginning in Chapter 11 to learn how things are supposed to work and why they sometimes don't. But first, we'll try to tie things together a bit in the next chapter when we look at equilibrium GNP.

Workbook for Chapter 9

Multiple-Choice Questions

Circle the letter that corresponds to the best answer.

1. What finally got us out of the depression?
a. The New Deal   **b.** The Federal Reserve Board
c. It ended by itself   **d.** World War II

2. The world's number one economic power, in terms of total output is
a. the United States   **b.** the Soviet Union
c. China   **d.** Japan

3. The era of mass consumption began in the United States around the year
a. 1920   **b.** 1930   **c.** 1940   **d.** 1950

4. At the low point of the depression, about what fraction of the U.S. labor force was offically unemployed?
a. one tenth   **b.** one fourth   **c.** one half   **d.** two thirds

5. The most prosperous decade of those listed was the
a. 1920s   **b.** 1930s   **c.** 1970s   **d.** 1980s

6. Between 1929 and 1933 output
a. rose by 25 percent   **b.** stayed about the same
c. fell by 25 percent   **d.** fell by 50 percent

7. A business cycle forecasting method that tries to explain the entire economic process is
a. endogenous   **b.** exogenous   **c.** barometric
d. analytic

8. Very little new housing was built from
a. 1915–1930   **b.** 1930–1945   **c.** 1945–1960
d. 1960–1975

9. What gave our economy much of its impetus between 1945 and 1960 was
a. suburbanization   **b.** defense spending   **c.** a government jobs program   **d.** cheap imports from Japan

10. Gasoline prices remained very low until
a. 1945   **b.** 1960   **c.** 1973   **d.** 1981

11. In which decade listed did our economy perform the worst?
a. 1920s   **b.** 1940s   **c.** 1950s   **d.** 1970s

12. The main problem that the urban poor have today is
a. laziness   **b.** lack of jobs   **c.** too much government help   **d.** none of these

13. The worst recession we had since the depression occurred in the
a. 1950s   **b.** 1960s   **c.** 1970s   **d.** 1980s

14. The main trouble with our economy, said Ronald Reagan when he was running for president, was that
a. the government was not spending enough
b. we were spending too much on defense
c. the government was too small   **d.** the government was too big

15. The last time we had full employment was in
a. 1929   **b.** 1945   **c.** 1957   **d.** 1969

16. We have business cycles of
a. the same length and amplitude   **b.** the same length but different amplitudes   **c.** the same amplitude but different lenghts   **d.** different lengths and amplitudes

17. During business cycles
a. troughs are followed by recessions   **b.** troughs are followed by peaks   **c.** peaks are followed by troughs   **d.** peaks are followed by recessions

18. The second part of the expansion phase of the cycle is
a. recovery   **b.** prosperity   **c.** recession
d. depression

19. An example of an exogenous business cycle theory would be

a. overinvestment   **b.** inventory   **c.** money

d. war

20. The accelerator principle is a variant of the _____ theory.

a. monetary   **b.** innovations   **c.** psychological

d. overinvestment

21. The GNP gap is found by

a. subtracting actual GNP from potential GNP

b. subtracting potential GNP from actual GNP

c. adding potential GNP and actual GNP

d. none of the above

22. Among the following cases, the person who would be considered unemployed is someone who

a. worked three days in the last month, but is now out of work   **b.** is ready, willing, and able to work, but gave up looking for work three months ago

c. reported to the state employment office last week, but is not very enthusiastic about finding a job

23. A person who has not worked in six months and has given up looking for work is officially classified as

a. employed   **b.** unemployed   **c.** discouraged

d. in the labor force

24. Our actual GNP is _____ equal to our potential GNP.

a. never   **b.** sometimes   **c.** usually   **d.** always

25. When the unemployment rate rises, the GNP gap

a. will rise   **b.** will fall   **c.** will remain the same

d. none of the above are correct

26. The unemployment rate is computed by the

a. nation's unemployment insurance offices

b. Bureau of Labor Statistics   **c.** Department of Commerce   **d.** Office of Management and Budget

27. If the number of unemployed stays the same and the number of people in the labor force rises

a. the unemployment rate will rise   **b.** the unemployment rate will fall   **c.** the unemployment rate will stay the same   **d.** there is not enough information to determine what will happen to the unemployment rate

28. Which statement is true?

a. Both liberals and the conservatives feel that the official unemployment rate is too high.   **b.** Both liberals and conservatives feel that the official unemployment rate is too low.   **c.** The liberals believe that the official unemployment rate is too high and the conservatives feel it is too low.   **d.** The conservatives feel that the official unemployment rate is too high and the liberals feel that it is too low.

29. Greater participation by young people in the labor force tends to **a.** push the unemployment rate up

b. push the unemployment rate down   **c.** has no effect on the unemployment rate   **d.** has an unknown effect on the unemployment rate

30. Which statement is false?

a. over the last two decades there has been an upward drift in the unemployment rate.   **b.** The unemployment rate for blacks is about twice that for whites.   **c.** The official unemployment rate includes "discouraged" workers.   **d.** None of the above is false.

In questions 31–36, use one of these three choices:
a. frictional unemployment   **b.** structural unemployment   **c.** cyclical unemployment

31. An auto worker who is still out of work two years after his plant closed is an example of _____.

32. A housewife returning to the labor market after an absence of 10 years and looking for work is an example of _____.

33. A blue-collar worker who is laid off until business picks up again is an example of _____.

34. People who are "between jobs" are examples of _____.

35. A person whose skills have become obsolete and is in her mid-50s would be an example of _____.

36. When the unemployment rate goes above 5 percent, anything above that 5 percent level is _____.

37. An example of deflation since the base year would be a CPI in the current year of
a. 90   **b.** 100   **c.** 110   **d.** 200

38. Inflation generally occurs
a. during wartime   **b.** before wars   **c.** during recessions   **d.** during peacetime

39. The period of greatest price stability was
a. 1950–56   **b.** 1958–64   **c.** 1968–76
d. 1976–82

40. Traditionally, those hurt by inflation have been
a. creditors and people on fixed incomes   **b.** debtors and people on fixed incomes   **c.** debtors and creditors

41. Farmers have generally been _____ by inflation.
a. hurt   **b.** helped   **c.** neither helped nor hurt

42. Creditors generally do better when inflation is
a. anticipated   **b.** unanticipated   **c.** neither anticipated nor unanticipated

43. Businesspeople generally like a little _____ but dislike a little _____
a. inflation, deflation   **b.** deflation, inflation

44. Inflationary recessions first occurred in the
a. 1950s   **b.** 1960s   **c.** 1970s   **d.** 1980s

45. Inflation is
a. a rise in the price of every good and service   **b.** a rise of exactly the same percentage in the price of every good or service   **c.** a general rise in the price level   **d.** a general rise in prices of at least 10 percent a year

46. Our economy is usually operating in range _____ of the aggregate supply curve.
a. 1   **b.** 2   **c.** 3   **d.** 4

47. Oil price shocks are a cause of a _____ inflation.
a. demand-pull   **b.** cost-push   **c.** psychological

Fill-In Questions

1. The worst recession since World War II began in

_____.

2. Stagflation is a contraction of _____ and

_____.

3. The least prosperous decade since World War I

was the _____.

4. The era of mass consumption began in the _____.

5. When 12 million men were demobilized in 1945

they wanted two things: (1) _____ and (2) _____.

6. We faced very little foreign competition in the

decades of the _____ and the _____.

7. In the two decades after World War II, millions of

_____ people moved from the _____ to the

_____ while millions of _____ people moved to

the _____.

8. In _____ the OPEC nations quadrupled the price of oil.

9. In the 1970s our economy suffered from _____

and _____.

10. In late 1982 our unemployment rate hit _____ percent.

11. Business cycles are rises and declines in the level

of economic activity that have no fixed _____ or

_____.

12. The three phases of the business cycle are

(1) _____, (2) _____, and (3) _____.

13. The prosperity phase of a three-phase cycle sets

in after the _____ phase.

14. The low point of a business cycle is the _____;

the high point is the _____.

15. Those theories that place the cause of business cycles within the economy rather than outside are

known as _____ theories.

16. According to the inventory theory of the business

cycle, a recession is set off when retailers _____.

17. The monetary theory of the business cycle hypothesizes that recessions are set off when _____ and recoveries begin when the monetary authorities _____.

18. The acceleration principle requires sales to keep increasing at the _____ to prevent investment from _____.

19. Two exogenous theories of the business cycle are the (1) _____ theory; and the (2) _____ theory.

20. Economic forecasts that attempt to explain the entire economic process are _____ forecasts, while those that track only a few economic variables are _____ forecasts.

21. Econometric models are examples of _____ forecasts while the index of leading economic indicators is an example of the _____ forecast.

22. Economic forecasts are _____ right.

22. To be eligible for unemployment insurance benefits, you need to be able to answer yes to these three questions:

(1) _____

(2) _____

(3) _____

23. Liberals say that the unemployment rate is actually _____ than the BLS says it is; conservatives say it is really _____.

24. Between the mid-1970s and the mid-1980s our unemployment rate has rarely dipped below _____ percent.

25. The unemployment rate for blacks is about _____ the white unemployment rate.

26. Most families living on welfare are headed by _____.

27. The most effective solution to poverty is _____.

28. The GNP gap is computed by subtracting _____ from _____.

29. When the unemployment rate declines, the GNP gap _____.

30. When we are on our production possibilities frontier, _____ GNP gap.

31. The unemployment rate is computed by the _____. This agency conducts a _____.

32. People who are out of work, not looking for work, but want to work are called _____.

33. Conservatives say that our unemployment rate is inflated by three groups: (1) _____, (2) _____, and (3) _____.

34. We could wipe out most of frictional unemployment with a _____.

35. A person who has been out of work for several years is _____ unemployed.

36. To be eligible for unemployment insurance you need to have worked at least _____ or _____.

37. During a very severe recession when over 11 percent of the labor force is out of work, most of the unemployment is _____ unemployment.

38. In 1973, the OPEC nations _____ the price of oil.

39. According to A. W. Phillips, there is a trade-off between _____ and _____.

40. The misery index is the sum of the _____ and the _____.

41. During President Eisenhower's two terms, inflation was brought under control by three _____.

42. Farmers generally favor _____ and hate _____.

43. If the consumer price index rises from 150 to 180, the cost of living rose by _____ percent.

44. Deflation is _____.

45. Deflation would be disasterous to _____.

46. In the 1940s, 1950s, and 1960s, inflation was generally associated with _____.

47. Too many dollars chasing too few goods is a description of _____ inflation.

48. The three variants of cost-push inflation are:

(1) _____, (2) _____, and (3) _____.

49. Once inflation is underway, an _____ takes over.

50. To stop inflation, we need to convince people that _____.

51. The two periods when we suffered from double-digit inflation were from _____ to _____ and from _____ to _____.

52. When there are too many dollars chasing too few goods, something's gotta give. That something is

_____.

53. During very bad recessions, if demand rises, aggregate supply will rise in the form of higher _____.

54. When we are at full employment, if demand rises, aggregate supply will rise in the form of higher _____.

Problems

1. If the unemployment rate is 7 percent, how much is cyclical unemployment?

2. Given the following information, compute the unemployment rate: 8 million unemployed; 117 million employed.

3. Given the following information, how many people are in the labor force: 3 million people are collecting unemployment insurance; 7 million people are officially unemployed; 2 million people are discouraged workers; and 110 million people are employed.

4. How much would the nominal interest rate be if the real rate of interest were 6 percent and the expected rate of inflation were 7 percent?

5. How much would the real rate of interest be if the nominal interest rate were 12 percent and the expected rate of inflation were 4 percent?

6. If the CPI is currently 178.9, by what percentage did prices rise since the base year?

7. If the CPI rose from 200 in 1991 to 240 in 1997, by what percentage did prices increase?

8. If the rate of inflation is 5 percent, the prime rate of interest is 6 percent, and the unemployment rate is 7 percent, how much is the misery index?

9. If actual GNP is 4,400 and potential GNP is 4,600, state the GNP gap in dollars.

10. Given the information in Table 1, find the CPI in 1997, and state the percentage increase in prices since 1987, the base year.

Table 1
Cost of Living for One Month, 1987 and 1997

A. 1987

Item	Quantity	Price	Price × Quantity
New car payment	1	200.00	
Mortgage payment	1	390.00	
VCR movie rental	15	2.00	
Doctor visit	2	35.00	
Gallon of gas	40	1.00	
Big Mac	10	2.50	

B. 1997

Item	Quantity	Price	Price × Quantity
New car payment	1	300.00	
Mortgage payment	1	510.00	
VCR movie rental	15	1.00	
Doctor visit	2	50.00	
Gallon of gas	40	1.50	
Big Mac	10	3.50	

Equilibrium GNP: Aggregate Demand Equals Aggregate Supply

Equilibrium means being in a state of rest. We shall finally attain such a state toward the end of this chapter. But we will cheat a little; we will hold the price level constant.

Since price level variation (or more specifically price level increases) is a fact of economic life, the attainment of equilibrium with price level variation is worked out in the appendix to the chapter. Since it involves a more technical analysis, it may be skipped by the less adventurous reader.

Chapter Objectives

In this chapter we shall take up:
- The classical system.
- The Keynesian critique of the classical system.
- The Keynesian system.
- Equilibrium and disequilibrium.
- Equilibrium at varying price levels.

The Classical Economic System

Say's Law

The centerpiece of classical economics is Say's Law. Named for Jean Baptiste Say, a late 18th-century (that means the late 1700s) French economist, the law stated, *"Supply creates its own demand."* Think about it. Somehow, what we produce—supply—all gets sold.

People who produce things are paid. What do they do with this money? They spend it. On what? On what *other* people produce.

Say's law can be illustrated by means of the production figures in Table 10–1.

Until the Great Depression, classical economics was the dominant school of economic thought. Adam Smith, credited by many as the founder of classical economics, believed that the government should intervene in economic affairs as little as possible. Indeed, laissez-faire economics was

Table 10-1

Joe	10 bushels of tomatoes
Sally	5 Mao jackets
Mike	20 loaves of bread
Bill	10 pounds of butter
Alice	5 pairs of wooden shoes

practiced down through the years until the time of Herbert Hoover, who kept predicting that prosperity was just around the corner. Finally it was John Maynard Keynes who proclaimed the end of the classical era when he advocated massive government intervention to bring an end to the Great Depression.

Let's look at Table 10-1. Everyone eats tomatoes, bread and butter, and wears Mao jackets and wooden shoes. Joe sells eight bushels of tomatoes, keeping two for his own use. Sally wears one of her Mao jackets and sells the other four. And so forth.

What do they do with the proceeds from their sales? They use them to buy what they need from each of the others. Joe, for example, buys a Mao jacket from Sally, four loaves of bread from Mike, two pounds of butter from Bill (they all like to put a lot of butter on their bread), and a pair of wooden shoes from Alice.

"Why does anybody work?" asked Say.

"Why does anybody work?" asked Say. Because that person wants money with which to buy things. Why do *you* work?

As long as everyone spends everything that he or she earns, we're okay. But we begin having problems when people start saving part of their incomes.

Basically, producers need to sell everything they produce. If some people save, then not everything produced will be sold. In a world with large companies instead of self-employed producers, when demand for production falls some workers must be laid off. In fact, as unemployment mounts, demand falls still farther, necessitating further cutbacks in production and employment.

The villain of the piece is clearly saving. If only people would spend their entire incomes, we'd never have unemployment. But people do save, and saving is crucial to economic growth. Without saving we could not have investment—the production of plant, equipment, and inventory.[1]

Think of production as consisting of two products: consumer goods and investment goods (for now, we're ignoring government goods). Therefore, people will buy consumer goods; the money spent on such goods is designated by the letter C. Money spent by businesses on investment goods is designated by the letter I.

If we think of GNP as total spending, then GNP would be C + I. Once this money is spent, other people receive it as income. And what do they do with their income? They spend some of it and save the rest.

If we think of GNP as income received, that money will either be spent on consumer goods, C, or saved, which we'll designate by the letter S. If we put all this together, we have two equations:

$$GNP = C + I$$

$$GNP = C + S$$

GNP = C + I
GNP = C + S

---

[1] In this chapter we're ignoring investment in residential housing and considering only business investment.

These two equations can be simplified to one short one. First, because things equal to the same thing are equal to each other:

$$C + I = C + S$$

This step is justified because both C + I and C + S are equal to GNP. Therefore, they are equal to each other.

Next, we can subtract the same thing from both sides of an equation. In this case we are subtracting C:

$$C + I = C + S$$
$$I = S$$

C + I = C + S
    I = S

Going back to Say's Law, we can see that it really does hold up, at least in accordance with classical analysis. Supply certainly does create its own demand. The economy produces a supply of consumer goods and investment goods. The people who produce these goods spend part of their incomes on consumer goods and save the rest. Their savings are borrowed by investors who spend this money on investment goods. The bottom line is that everything the economy produces is purchased.

This is a perfect economic system. Everything produced is sold. Everyone who wants to work can find a job. There will never be any serious economic downturns, so there is no need for the government to intervene to set things right.

The Keynesian Critique of the Classical System

John Maynard Keynes, who was a prominent classically trained economist, spent the first half of the 1930s writing a monumental critique of the classical system. If supply creates its own demand, he asked, why are we having a worldwide depression? What Keynes set out to do was to figure out what went wrong and how to fix it.

Keynes asked: What if savings and investment were not equal?

Keynes posed this problem for the classical economists: What if savings and investment were not equal? For instance, if saving were greater than investment, there would be unemployment. Not everything being produced would be purchased.

There's nothing to worry about, according to the classical economists. And they proved this by means of the two curves in Figure 10-1. If saving were greater than investment, the interest rate would fall. Why? Because some savers would be willing to lend at lower interest rates and some investors would be induced to borrow at lower interest rates.[2]

Keynes: Saving and investing are done by different people for different reasons.

Keynes disputed this view. Saving and investing are done by different people for different reasons. Most saving is done by individuals for big-ticket items such as cars, stereo systems, and major appliances, as well as for homes or retirement. Investing is done by business firms basically because they are trying to make a profit. They will borrow to invest only when there is a reasonably good profit outlook. Why sink a lot of money into plant and equipment when your factory and machines are half idle? Even when inter-

---

[2] This analysis is based on the material covered near the end of Chapter 3. You might want to review it if you had any difficulty with the last paragraph.

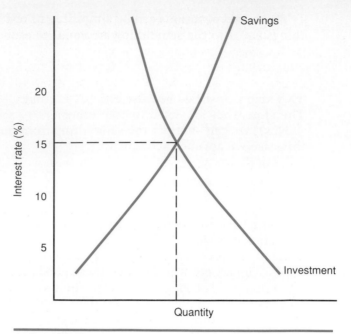

Figure 10–1

est rates are low, business firms won't invest unless it is profitable for them to do so. This point was discussed at length in the last section of Chapter 7.

The classical economists had a fallback position. Even if lower interest rates did not eliminate the surplus of saving relative to investment, price flexibility would bring about equilibrium between saving and investing. Business firms, unable to sell their entire output, would simply lower prices. And then people would buy everything produced.

One might ask if business firms could make a profit if prices were reduced. Yes, answered the classical economists, if resource prices—particulary wages—were also reduced. Although initially output and employment might decline, once prices and wages fell, production and employment would move back up again. At lower prices people would buy more, and at lower wages employers would hire more labor.

Keynes questioned whether wages and prices were flexible downward, even during a severe recession. In the worst recession since the Great Depression, the downturn of 1981–82, there were very few instances of price or wage declines even in the face of declining output and widespread unemployment. Studies of the behavior of highly concentrated industries indicate that prices are seldom lowered while similar studies of large labor unions indicate that wage cuts (even as the only alternative to massive layoffs) are seldom accepted. Even if wages *were* lowered, added Keynes, this would lower workers' incomes, consequently lowering their spending on consumer goods.

The classicals believed that recessions were temporary because the economy is self-correcting.

Let's summarize the classical position. Recessions are temporary because the economy is self-correcting. Declining investment will be pushed up again by falling interest rates while, if consumption falls, it will be raised by falling prices and wages. And since recessions are self-correcting, the role of government is to stand back and do nothing.

Keynes' position was that recessions were not necessarily temporary, because the self-correcting mechanisms of falling interest rates and falling prices and wages might be insufficient to push investment and consumption back up again. Therefore, it would be necessary for the government to intervene since the private economy did not automatically move toward full employment.

Who was right? And what should the government do when we go into a recession? At this juncture, most people would probably agree that Keynes was closer to reality than the classicals, and that government economic intervention may sometimes be necessary. Still, we have another five chapters to go before we can be more definite. After all, if you take all the economists in the world and lay them out in a line—they still will not reach a conclusion.

Equilibrium

Aggregate demand

The focal point of this chapter is equilibrium, where aggregate demand = aggregate supply. *Aggregate demand is the sum of all expenditures for goods and services.* In this chapter we'll restrict our discussion to consumption and investment expenditures, so aggregate demand = C + I.

Aggregate supply

Aggregate supply is the nation's total output of goods and services. Again, we're restricting our discussion to consumer and investment goods (we'll add government expenditures in the next chapter).

The concept of equilibrium is essential to understanding both the classical and Keynesian systems. Basically, equilibrium means state of rest. For instance, most people have an equilibrum body weight, a weight their bodies usually tend toward. When you're sick, your weight dips below equilibrium, and, upon recovering, you gain back those few pounds. (During Thanksgiving and Christmas, you tend to put on a few pounds, which you lose within the next few weeks.)

Similarly, our economy is always tending toward some level of GNP, which we call equilibrium GNP. If we are above that level, GNP will decline; if we are below equilibrium, GNP will rise.

At equilibrium, aggregate supply = aggregate demand.

At equilibrium GNP a couple of things come together. First, aggregate supply = aggregate demand. That occurs in Figure 10–2, where the C + I (aggregate demand) line crosses the 45-degree (aggregate supply) line.

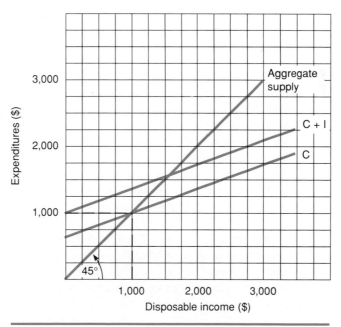

Figure 10–2

Figure 10-2 is identical to Figure 8-4 of Chapter 8. The lines are exactly the same, but now we call the 45-degree line the aggregate supply line. For every level of disposable income (read off the horizontal scale), there is a corresponding level of aggregate supply (read off the 45-degree line) and also a corresponding level of aggregate demand (read off the vertical scale). At equilibrium GNP, they are all equal.

Also, saving and investment are equal. Saving is the vertical distance between the C line and the 45-degree line. The vertical distance between the C line and the C + I line is I. Therefore, the vertical distance between the C line and the 45-degree line must be equal to (actually identical to) the vertical distance between the C line and the C + I line.

Can you figure out the equilibrium level of GNP in Figure 10-2? At that point, disposable income, aggregate demand (C + I), and aggregate supply (the 45-degree line) are all equal. Also equal are I and S.

Remember, disposable income is read off the horizontal scale, aggregate supply *is* the 45-degree line, and C, I, and aggregate demand (C + I) are read off the vertical scale. Try to find the value of (1) equilibrium GNP, (2) C, and (3) I. The answers appear in Figure 10-3.

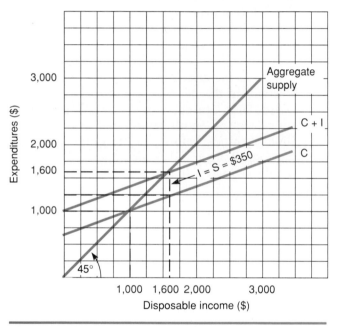

Figure 10-3

Equilibrium GNP is about 1,600 (or anything between 1,525 and 1,675). I = S at about 400.

At any disposable income of less than 1,600, I is greater than S. There would be a tendency for GNP to rise. Similarly, at disposable incomes of more than 1,600, S is greater than I, and there would be a tendency for GNP to fall.

There is only one level of GNP that is, like the porridge in the story "Goldilocks and the Three Bears," not too high, not too low, but just right. That, of course, is the equilibrium level. Everything at that level is just right: I = S, and aggregate demand = aggregate supply = disposable income.

The Keynesian System: A Brief Survey[3]

Both the Keynesian and the classical systems are based on equilibrium.

Full-employment GNP

"The chances are, we are either above or below full-employment GNP."
—Keynes

Keynes turned Say's Law upside down.

The key difference between Keynes and the classicals

The Keynesian system, like the classical system, is based on the concept of equilibrium. The classical economists assumed that the economy was always gravitating toward a full-employment equilibrium. Although there might be some temporary unemployment, the economy would automatically move back toward full employment.

Full-employment GNP is the level of spending necessary to generate enough production and jobs to provide work for everyone who is ready, willing, and able to work. The classical economists maintained that full-employment GNP was the normal economic state of affairs; any deviation from the norm was temporary. Keynes came along during the Great Depression and asked how long temporary was and how much of a deviation from the norm would we have before we swung back again toward full employment.

There are really three possibilities, said Keynes. We can have full-employment equilibrium GNP as the classicals maintain, less than full-employment equilibrium GNP, or more than full-employment equilibrium GNP. Much below full-employment GNP is a recession and much above it is an inflation.

"Why should the economy always be at full-employment GNP?" asked Keynes. Chances are, we are either above it or below it. Because he was writing during the Great Depression, he was obviously more concerned about being below full-employment GNP.

The Keynesian system is quite simple. He is concerned with one main variable—the level of aggregate demand. Once we know that, we know how much the economy will produce and how many people will be employed. The level of aggregate demand—the demand for goods and services—determines the level of aggregate supply. In fact, the Keynesian system is based on the converse of Say's Law: Demand creates its own supply (instead of supply creates its own demand).

Aggregate demand consists of two things—C + I. Later we'll be adding G. Keynes noted that C was relatively stable, but that I fluctuated considerably.

C is a function of disposable income, rising as income rises, but not as quickly. At very low levels of disposable income people will consume more than their incomes, and at higher levels they will save part of their incomes. In a word, no matter what your income level, you still have to eat.

The level of I in the Keynesian model is determined by two variables: the interest rate and the expected rate of profit.[4] Business firms will borrow to invest in plant, equipment, and inventory as long as the interest rate is lower than the expected profit rate. However, during recessions, when the expected profit rate plummets, I falls precipitously. Even at low interest rates, business firms are not that anxious to invest.

This is really the key difference between Keynes and the classicals. The classicals thought the economy would automatically bounce back toward full-employment. But what if, asked Keynes, the economy became stuck at

---

[3] The full Keynesian system will be presented in Chapter 14. It can't be done here because there are some elements of Keynesian analysis that are introduced in the next four chapters.

[4] See the last section of Chapter 7.

less than full-employment? What if profit prospects, and consequently investment, remained at very low levels?

Since aggregate demand—C + I—is insufficient to provide jobs for everyone who wants to work, it is necessary for the government to provide the spending that will push the economy toward full employment. Just spend money; it doesn't matter on what. This point was made quite vividly by Keynes:

> If the Treasury were to fill old bottles with banknotes, bury them at suitable depths in disused coalmines which are then filled up to the surface with town rubbish, and leave it to private enterprise on well-tried principles of *laissez-faire* to dig the notes up again. . . , there need be no more unemployment. . . . It would, indeed, be more sensible to build houses and the like; but if there are political and practical difficulties in the way of this, the above would be better than nothing.[5]

Disequilibrium and Equilibrium

At the beginning of this chapter we said that equilibrium and disequilibrium under constant prices would eventually be discussed. That moment has finally arrived. There are two things to keep in mind: (1) an economy in disequilibrium will automatically move toward equilibrium; and (2) equilibrium is a state of rest (i.e., there is no tendency toward change).

In both the Keynesian and classical economic systems, the economy is always tending toward equilibrium, when aggregate demand and aggregate supply are equal. Let's look at this process from two perspectives—first when aggregate demand is larger than aggregate supply, and second when aggregate supply is larger than aggregate demand.

(1) Aggregate Demand Exceeds Aggregate Supply

When aggregate demand exceeds aggregate supply, inventories decline.

When aggregate demand exceeds aggregate supply, this sets off a chain reaction that continues until the economy is back in equilibrium. The first thing that happens is that inventories start declining. What do business firms do? They order more inventory.

Suppose you own an appliance store. You had been ordering 50 blenders a month because that's about how many you were selling. But during the last month your blender sales doubled, so you decided to order 100 blenders instead of your usual 50. What does this do to the production of blenders, assuming that the other appliance stores double their orders as well?

The first thing that happens when aggregate demand is greater than aggregate supply is that inventories are depleted. Consequently, orders to manufacturers rise, and of course, production rises. Manufacturers will hire more labor and eventually, as plant utilization approaches capacity, more plant and equipment is ordered.

As more people find employment, they will consume more, raising aggregate demand. Business firms may also begin raising their prices. Retailers may perceive that their customers are willing to pay more. Eventually, the manufacturers may have trouble increasing output much farther because of shortages in labor, raw materials, plant and equipment, or the funds to finance expansion. These shortages will occur at some point—and

---

[5] John Maynard Keynes, *The General Theory of Employment, Interest, and Money* (New York: Harcourt Brace Jovanovich, 1958), p. 129.

consequently prices will have to rise—because what is happening in the appliance industry is probably happening in the rest of the economy. As the economy approaches full capacity (and full employment), prices will have begun to rise.

We started with aggregate demand exceeding aggregate supply, but this disparity told manufacturers to increase aggregate supply. First output was increased; eventually so were prices. Since GNP (which is identical to aggregate supply) is defined as the nation's output of goods and services at market prices, it appears that there are two ways to raise aggregate supply—by increasing output and prices. By doing this, we raise aggregate supply relative to aggregate demand and quickly restore equilibrium.

(2) *Aggregate Supply Exceeds Aggregate Demand*

When aggregate supply is greater than aggregate demand, the economy is in disequilibrium. Aggregate supply must fall. Because aggregate supply is greater than aggregate demand, production exceeds sales, and inventories are rising. When business firms realize this, what do they do? They cut back on orders to manufacturers. After all, if you found you were accumulating more and more stock on your shelves, wouldn't you cut back on your orders? Remember, not only does it cost money to carry large inventories—shelf space as well as money is tied up—but there is always the risk that you may not be able to sell your stock.

When manufacturers receive fewer orders, they cut back output and consequently lay off some workers, further depressing aggregate demand as these workers cut back on their consumption. Retailers, facing declining sales as well as smaller inventories, may reduce prices, although even during recent recessions price reductions have not been too common. Eventually, inventories are sufficiently depleted. In the meanwhile, aggregate supply has fallen back into equilibrium with aggregate demand.

(3) *Summary: How Equilibrium Is Attained*

We can make an interesting observation about the entire process. When the economy is in disequilibrium, it automatically moves back again into equilibrium. It is always aggregate supply that adjusts. When aggregate demand is greater than aggregate supply, the latter rises, and when aggregate supply exceeds aggregate demand, it is aggregate supply that declines.

Please keep in mind that aggregate demand (C + I) must equal the level of production (aggregate supply) for the economy to be in equilibrium. When the two are not equal, aggregate supply must adjust to bring the economy back into equilibrium.

Disequilibrium and Equilibrium: A Problem

Now we're going to get a little fancy. First we're going to present a table that illustrates some of the things we've just been talking about. We'll see how the level of output (aggregate supply) adjusts to eliminate a disequilibrium. Then we'll draw a graph based on the table.

Let's use as our starting point the first row in Table 10-2, where aggregate demand is 1,200 and aggregate supply is 1,000. The economy is in disequilibrium, inventories are falling (since sales are greater than production), and consequently, the level of output will rise.

Now we move down to the next row. Here aggregate demand (or sales) is 1,350, still larger than aggregate supply (output). Inventories continue to fall while output rises. This process continues until we reach equilibrium, when aggregate demand equals aggregate supply at 1,800.

When aggregate supply exceeds aggregate demand, inventories rise.

When the economy is in disequilibrium, it automatically moves back again into equilibrium.

Table 10–2
Hypothetical Aggregate Demand
and Aggregate Supply Schedules

Aggregate Supply (Output)	Aggregate Demand (C + I)	Inventories Are	Level of Output Will
1,000	1,200	rising	rise
1,200	1,350	rising	rise
1,400	1,500	rising	rise
1,600	1,650	rising	rise
1,800	1,800	constant	remain the same
2,000	1,950	falling	fall
2,200	2,100	falling	fall
2,400	2,250	falling	fall

Let's go the other way, starting at the bottom of the table, when aggregate supply (2,400) is greater than aggregate demand (2,250). Inventories and output will fall as we move to lower outputs (2,200) and lower aggregate demand (2,100). This process continues until we reach equilibrium at 1,800. Thus if GNP is above equilibrium it will fall to that level, and if it is below equilibrium it will rise to that level.

The equilibrium level is always determined by the point at which aggregate demand and aggregate supply are equal. This is also illustrated in Figure 10-4, which is a graph of Table 10-2.

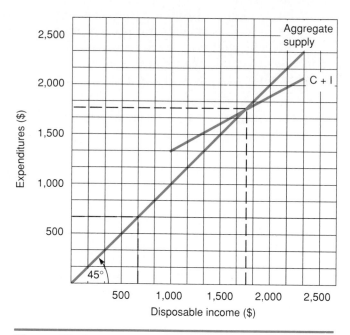

Figure 10–4

In the appendix that follows this chapter we will consider equilibrium GNP at varying price levels. This involves a rather technical analysis and should be undertaken only by those who have completely mastered the material in this chapter.

Full-Employment GNP

We have implicitly accepted the Keynesian dictum that three possible equilibriums exist: below full employment, at full employment, and above full employment. But exactly what *is* full-employment GNP?

GNP is defined as the total amount of goods and services produced by a nation during a given year at market prices. In other words, if we were to add up all the money spent on production, we'd have GNP. This implies that output is determined by the demand for goods and services. Why produce anything if no one will buy it? This idea is at the heart of Keynesian economics.

Aggregate demand then determines the level of production or output. How much we produce depends on how much individual consumers, businesses, and the government sector are willing to buy. The more they buy, the higher output will be.

To produce anything we need labor; the more we produce, the more labor we need. Therefore, the level of employment is determined by the level of output. To sum up, aggregate demand (C + I + G) determines the level of output, which in turn determines the level of employment. To attain a certain level of employment, we need a certain level of employment, and a certain level of aggregate demand and output.

Let's consider full employment. An economy has full employment when almost everyone who is ready, willing, and able to work is working. But we can't really expect every single person who wants to work to actually have a job at that exact time. For reasons explained in the last chapter, nearly all economists consider an economy at full employment when the unemployment rate is somewhere between 4 and 6 percent.

What is full employment GNP?

Now we're ready to look at full-employment GNP. In order to provide enough jobs to have full employment, we need individual consumers, businesses, and all government units to spend enough dollars to provide jobs for everyone. This amount of spending is called full-employment GNP.

We can figure out just how much spending this would take through trial and error. Let's say the unemployment rate were 9 percent. Obviously, GNP is well below the full-employment level. So let's raise G by $30 billion and cut taxes by $30 billion, sit back, and see what happens. Let's say that GNP rises, but we still have an unemployment rate of 7 percent. If we considered a rate of 5 percent as full employment, then by raising G another $30 billion and cutting taxes by $30 billion, we'd probably come pretty close to full employment. It's as simple as that!

To return to the three Keynesian possibilities, we may have an equilibrium level of GNP that is too high—above full-employment GNP—and equilibrium that is too low—below full employment GNP—and one that is just right. You guessed it—one that is at full-employment GNP.

When equilibrium GNP is too high, we have an inflationary gap while one that is too low reflects a recessionary gap. Raising and lowering taxes and government spending is the essence of fiscal policy. In the next chapter we shall apply that policy to eliminate inflationary and recessionary gaps.

Workbook for Chapter 10

Name _____

Date _____

Multiple-Choice Questions

Circle the letter that corresponds to the best answer.

1. Until the Great Depression, the dominant school of economic thought was

a. classical economics   **b.** Keynesian economics
c. supply-side economics   **d.** monetarism

2. The classical economists believed in

a. strong government intervention   **b.** laissez-faire   **c.** a rapid growth in the money supply
d. none of these

3. Say's Law states that

a. we can have an inflation or a recession, but never both at the same time   **b.** the normal state of economic affairs is recession   **c.** demand creates its own supply   **d.** supply creates its own demand

4. People work, according to Jean Baptiste Say, so that they can

a. spend   **b.** save   **c.** stay busy   **d.** none of these

5. According to the classical economists

a. people will always spend all their money   **b.** any money that is saved will be invested   **c.** saving will always be greater than investment   **d.** saving will always be smaller than investment

6. Keynes believed that

a. recessions were temporary   **b.** once a recession began, it would always turn into a depression
c. the real problem that modern economies faced was inflation   **d.** none of these is true

7. In the classical range of the aggregate supply curve, if aggregate demand rises

a. output will rise and prices will rise   **b.** output will rise and prices will fall   **c.** output will fall and prices will rise   **d.** output will fall and prices will fall   **e.** output will stay constant and prices will rise   **f.** output will rise and prices will remain constant

8. According to the classical economists, if the amount of money people are planning to invest is greater than the amount that people want to save

a. interest rates will rise and saving will rise

b. interest rates will fall and saving will fall

c. interest rates will fall and saving will rise

d. interest rates will rise and saving will fall

9. Each of the following supports the classical theory of employment except

a. Say's Law   **b.** wage-price flexibility   **c.** the interest mechanism   **d.** government spending programs

10. Our economy is definitely at equilibrium in each case except when

a. saving equals investment   **b.** aggregate demand equals aggregate supply   **c.** the amount people are willing to spend equals the amount that producers are producing   **d.** equilibrium GNP equals full-employment GNP

11. That we are always tending toward full employment is a belief of

a. Keynes   **b.** the classicals   **c.** the supply-siders
d. the monetarists

12. Keynes said that

a. the expected profit rate was more important than the interest rate   **b.** the interest rate was more important than the expected profit rate   **c.** both the expected profit rate and the interest rate were equally important   **d.** neither the expected profit rate nor the interest rate was important

13. John Maynard Keynes is most closely associated with the

a. American Revolution   b. French Revolution

c. the depression   d. inflation

14. In the Keynesian range of the aggregate supply curve, if aggregate demand rises

a. output will rise and prices will rise   b. output will fall and prices will fall   c. output will rise and prices will fall   d. output will fall and prices will rise   e. output will remain constant and prices will rise   f. output will rise and prices will remain constant

15. At equilibrium, aggregate demand will equal each of the following except

a. C + I   b. C + S   c. full-employment GNP

d. aggregate supply

16. Which best describes the classical theory of employment?

a. We will always have a great deal of unemployment   b. We will usually have a great deal of unemployment   c. We will occasionally have some unemployment, but our economy will automatically move back toward full employment   d. We never have any unemployment

17. Our economy always tends toward

a. equilibrium GNP   b. full-employment GNP

c. recessions   d. inflations

18. When saving is greater than investment, we are

a. at equilibrium GNP   b. at full-employment GNP   c. below equilibrium GNP   d. above equilibrium GNP

19. Keynes considered full-employment GNP to be

a. the normal state of economic affairs   b. a rare occurrence   c. an impossibility   d. none of these

20. Keynes was concerned mainly with

a. aggregate supply   b. aggregate demand   c. the interest rate   d. inflation

21. When aggregate demand is greater than aggregate supply

a. inventories get depleted and output rises

b. inventories get depleted and output falls

c. inventories rise and output rises

d. inventories rise and output falls

22. When the economy is in disequilibrium

a. production automatically rises   b. production automatically falls   c. it automatically moves back again into equilibrium   d. it stays in disequilibrium permanently

Fill-In Questions

1. Laissez-faire was advocated by the _____ school of economics.

2. Say's Law states that _____.

3. According to Say's Law, people work so that they can _____.

4. According to Say's Law, people spend _____.

5. The classical economists believed that savings would equal _____.

6. If supply creates its own demand, asked Keynes, why are we having a _____?

7. If saving were greater than investment, said the classical economists, they would be set equal by the _____.

8. The classical economists believed that wages and prices were flexible _____.

9. The classical economists believed that recessions were _____.

10. During recessions, said the classical economists, the government should _____.

11. Aggregate supply is _____.

12. Aggregate demand is _____.

13. At equilibrium GNP _____ will be equal to _____ and _____ will be equal to _____.

14. Our economy always tends toward _____ GNP.

15. When investment is greater than savings we are _____ equilibrium GNP.

16. Full-employment GNP and equilibrium GNP are _____ equal.

17. Keynes was most concerned with one main variable, _____.

18. According to John Maynard Keynes, the level of aggregate supply is determined by the _____.

19. When we are below the full-employment level of GNP, Keynes suggested that the _____.

20. When aggregate supply is greater than aggregate demand, the economy is in _____.

21. When aggregate demand is greater than aggregate supply, inventories will _____ and output will _____.

22. When individuals, busines firms, and the government are spending just enough money to provide jobs for everyone, we are at _____ GNP.

Problems

1. If GNP = C + I and if GNP = C + S, then _____ = _____.

2. If aggregate demand is 3,000 and aggregate supply is 2,500, if C is 2,500, how much is I?

3. Given the information in Figure 1, and assuming an interest rate of 15 percent: (a) Will the economy be at equilibrium? (b) Will savings equal investment? (c) What will happen, according to the classical economists?

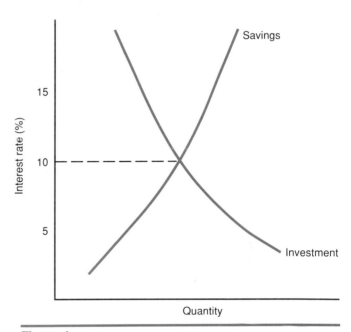

Figure 1

Appendix

Equilibrium at Varying Price Levels

Until now we have concentrated on real aggregate demand and real aggregate supply. In effect then, we have assumed a world without inflation. But as everyone knows, prices do not stay constant, even if that would simplify our economic model.

First we'll introduce the aggregate demand curve. As we shall see, this curve differs radically from Figures 10-1, 10-2, and 10-3 shown earlier in this chapter. We shall also see a very different aggregate supply curve from the one shown in those same graphs.

The Aggregate Demand Curve

The aggregate demand curve shows that as the price level declines, the quantity of goods and services demanded rises.

The aggregate demand curve of Figure 10-6, which we will show you later, depicts an inverse relationship between the price level and the quantity of goods and services demanded: as the price level declines, the quantity of goods and services demanded rises. Conversely, as the price level rises, the quantity of goods and services demanded declines. This relationship is illustrated by an aggregate demand curve that slopes downward to the right.

This curve is very different from the C + I curves of Figures 10-1, 10-2, and 10-3. Why? Because in these graphs, the price level was held constant. The C + I curves showed that as disposable income rose, there was a corresponding increase in the quantity demanded of goods and services, assuming no change in the price level.

Is it reasonable to assume constant prices? Instinctively, we would reject this assumption because in our lifetimes we have known nothing but inflation. Furthermore, in the next section, we shall see that as the economy approaches full employment, a certain amount of inflation is inevitable.

Why does the aggregate demand curve slope downward to the right?

Why does the aggregate demand curve slope downward to the right? There are three reasons: the wealth effect, the interest rate effect, and the foreign purchases effect. Let's take up each in turn.

(1) The Wealth Effect

When the price level goes up, your purchasing power goes down. The money you have in the bank, your stocks and bonds, and all your other liquid assets go down in terms of what they can buy. You *feel* poorer, so you'll tend to spend less. Therefore, if the price level goes up, the entire consumption schedule shifts downward, as illustrated in Figure 10-5, from C_2 to C_1.

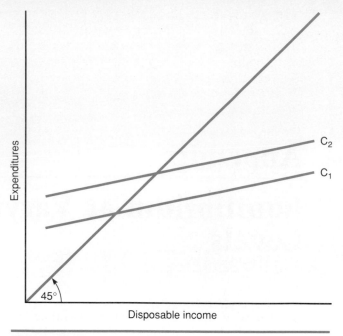

Figure 10–5

Conversely, when the price level declines—a rare occurrence since the 1930s—your purchasing power rises, so you feel richer and tend to spend more. This effect is seen in the upward shift of the consumption schedule in Figure 10-5, from C_1 to C_2.

(2) The Interest Rate Effect

A rising price level pushes up interest rates, which in turn lower the consumption of certain goods and services. Let's look more closely at this two-step sequence.

First, during times of inflation, interest rates rise, since lenders need to protect themselves against the declining purchasing power of the dollar. If you lent someone $100 for one year and there was a 10 percent rate of inflation, you would need to be paid back $110 just to be able to buy what your original $100 would have purchased.

Second, certain goods and services are more sensitive to interest rate changes than others. Can you name some especially sensitive ones? Try auto purchases and home mortgages. Clearly then, when interest rates rise, the consumption of certain goods and services falls, and when interest rates fall, they rise. In general then, when the price level rises, interest rates rise, and the consumption schedule declines.

(3) The Foreign Purchases Effect

When the price level in the United States, relative to the price levels in other countries, rises, what effect does this have on U.S. imports and exports? Since American goods become more expensive relative to foreign goods, our imports rise (foreign goods are cheaper) and our exports decline (American goods are more expensive).

In sum, when our price level increases, this tends to increase our imports and lower our exports. Thus, our net exports (exports minus imports) component of GNP declines. Conversely, when the price level declines, net exports (and GNP) rises.

To sum up these three effects, when the price level rises, the output of goods and services demanded goes down. And when the price level declines, the quantity of goods and services (or real GNP) goes up. In other words, aggregate demand and the price level are inversely related. This relationship is illustrated by the aggregate demand curve in Figure 10-6. The curve slopes downward to the right.

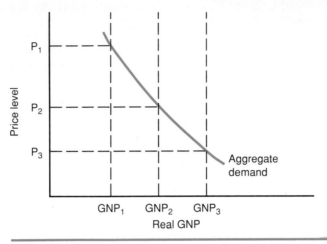

Figure 10-6

This curve may also be derived graphically as we've done in Figure 10-7. We have already demonstrated in Figure 10-4 that an increase in the price level will lead to a downward shift in the consumption schedule. By extension, an increase in the price level will lead to a downward shift in the entire aggregate demand schedule (via the wealth, interest rate, and foreign purchases effects).

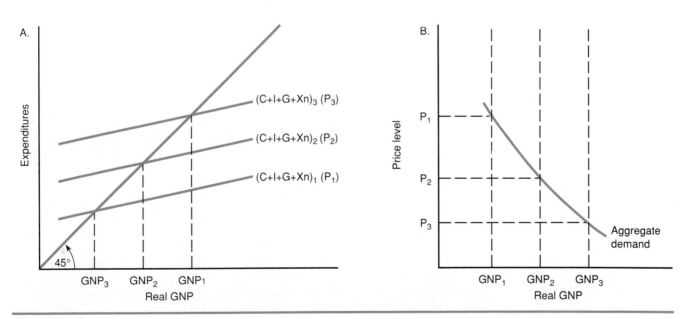

Figure 10-7

Aggregate Supply

All the way back in Chapter 2, we talked about the production possibilities curve, which showed the output of the economy when all the economy's resources were employed and the latest available technology was used.

We shall now introduce the term *aggregate supply*, which is the output of all the goods and services that will be produced by our economy at different price levels. As it happens, the aggregate supply curve slopes upward to the right, as we have shown in Figure 10-8. At higher prices, business firms are willing to supply increasing amounts of goods and services.

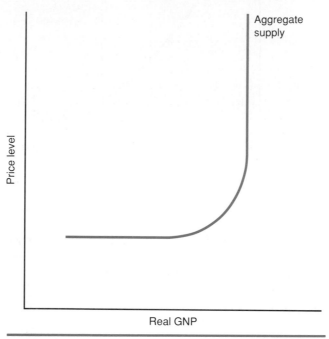

Figure 10–8

The aggregate supply curve and the production possibilities curve

The difference between the aggregate supply curve and the production possibilities curve is that the last represents one point on the first. That is, the production possibilities curve represents aggregate supply when the output of goods and services is at a maximum, but the aggregate supply curve represents the entire range of outputs of the economy. At the extreme left, we have a terrible depression where output is only about one half of potential. Things were not quite that bad during the Great Depression when output fell about one third from its 1929 peak.

As we move to the right along the curve, we have increasing output. Why? Because business owners find it more profitable to sell at higher prices than lower prices. For example, if you can provide home nursing care at $8 per hour and still make a small profit, what will you do if the going price of this service rises to $9 per hour? You will probably hire more workers and expand your output, but as you expand you will eventually encounter increasing costs, particularly increasing labor costs. Since other home nursing care providers will also be hiring available workers, pretty soon the entire pool of workers will be exhausted.

Would it be possible for you to hire still more workers? How would you get them to work for you? That's right—pay them more. Entice them away from rival firms. Of course, your rivals would be doing the same thing. Thus, costs would be rising along with prices. When this happens, profits get squeezed back down.

If we examine the slope of the aggregate supply curve as we move along it from left to right, you'll notice that it slopes upward. Why? There are two reasons. First, as we've just noted, as we approach full employment, labor costs (and the costs of other resources as well) are bid up. In other words, aggregate supply can be increased only if we can increase prices.

A second reason why the aggregate supply curve slopes upward is that when we reach full employment, we won't be able to increase the output of goods and services at all. We would run smack into the production possibilities curve. You can bid prices up all you want, but output cannot expand as long as we have a given amount of resources and are using the best available technology.

Of course, over time, real aggregate supply can be increased beyond this point, but at any given time there is a maximum output our economy can produce. When the aggregate supply curve becomes completely vertical, we've reached that point.

Figure 10-9 is just slightly more elaborate than Figure 10-8. Here we have the three ranges: Keynesian, intermediate, and classical. The Keynesian range gets its name from the time during which John Maynard Keynes was writing—the Great Depression. People were so anxious to find work that they were happy to take a job—virtually any job—at the going wage rate. Thus, business firms could easily expand output without encountering rising costs.

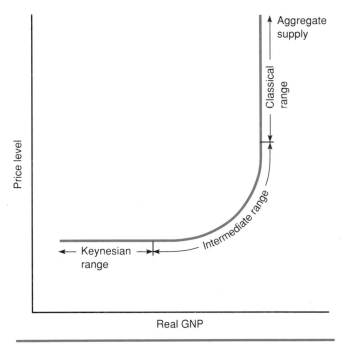

Figure 10–9

Would they raise prices? Not for quite a while. After suffering through a few years of extremely low sales, they would be grateful for more business, albeit at the same price.

As the economy expanded, bottlenecks would begin to develop, shortages of resources would occur here and there, and costs would begin to rise in some sectors and eventually spread throughout the economy. And then, too, business firms would begin raising their prices as well.

Eventually we would reach the maximum output level, at which point the only give in the economy would be in the form of higher prices. This would be the classical range of the aggregate supply curve. Remember that the classical economists believed that full employment is our normal state of economic affairs.

Equilibrium: Aggregate Demand Equals Aggregate Supply

All that is left to do is to place our aggregate demand and aggregate supply curve together on one graph and watch what happens. In Figure 10-10, the curves cross at point E. The price level is 100 and real GNP (or output) is $4 trillion.

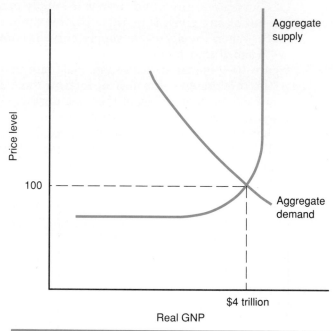

Figure 10–10

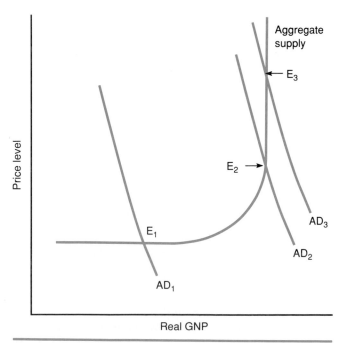

Figure 10–11

Is this a full-employment equilibrium? Maybe it is and maybe it isn't. Let's do one last bit of analysis. We'll redraw Figure 10-10, indicating the three ranges of aggregate supply. This is done in Figure 10-11.

Here we've drawn three aggregate demand curves—AD_1, which crosses the aggregate supply curve in the Keynesian range, AD_2, which crosses on the borderline between the intermediate and classical ranges, and AD_3, which crosses in the classical range.

Can you identify the state of economic affairs represented by each of the three equilibriums? E_1 is a bad recession; E_2 is full-employment GNP; and E_3 is equilibrium above full employment (or inflation). We shall have a lot more to say about E_1 and E_3 near the beginning of the next chapter when we talk about the recessionary and inflationary gaps.

Workbook for Appendix to Chapter 10

Name _____

Date _____

Multiple-Choice Questions

Circle the letter that corresponds to the best answer.

1. As the price level rises
a. the quantity of goods and services demanded falls   b. the quantity of goods and services demanded rises   c. the quantity of goods and services demanded stays the same   d. none of the above is correct

2. The aggregate demand curve slopes
a. upward to the right   b. downward to the right   c. at a right angle to the price axis   d. at a right angle to the output axis

3. The slope of the aggregate demand curve is explained by each of the following except
a. the wealth effect   b. the interest rate effect   c. the foreign purchases effect   d. the profit effect

4. Beyond the Keynesian range, the aggregate supply curve slopes
a. upward to the right   b. downward to the right
c. at a right angle to the price axis   d. at a right angle to the output axis

5. As the price level rises, the quantity of output
a. increases   b. decreases   c. stays the same
d. none of the above is correct

6. We are at full employment in the _____ range of the aggregate supply curve.
a. classical   b. Keynesian   c. intermediate
d. monetary

7. The aggregate supply curve begins to slope upward on the border between the _____ and _____ ranges.

a. classical and Keynesian   b. Keynesian and intermediate   c. intermediate and classical   d. classical and monetary

Fill-In Questions

1. The three reasons why the aggregate demand curve slopes downward are (1) _____, (2) _____, and (3) _____.

2. The extreme left of the aggregate supply curve represents _____ while the extreme right represents _____.

3. The wealth effect states that _____
_____.

4. The two reasons why the aggregate supply curve moves upward to the right are: (1) _____
_____, and (2) _____
_____.

5. The interest rate effect states that _____
_____.

6. We are at full employment at the border between the _____ and the _____ range of the aggregate supply curve.

7. The foreign purchases effect states that _____
_____.

Problems

1. Using the information in Figure A–1, how much is equilibrium GNP when aggregate demand is *((a)* AD$_1$, *(b)* AD$_2$, and *(c)* AD$_3$?

2. Which of these three equilibrium GNPs represents full-employment GNP?

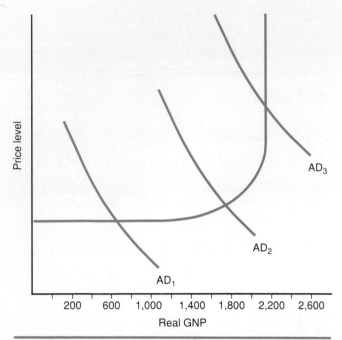

Figure A–1

Fiscal Policy and the National Debt

Fiscal policy is the manipulation of the federal budget to attain price stability, relatively full employment, and a satisfactory rate of economic growth. To attain these goals, the government must manipulate its spending and taxes.

Chapter Objectives
In this chapter you will learn about:
- The deflationary gap.
- The inflationary gap.
- Budget deficits and surpluses.
- Automatic stabilizers.
- Discretionary fiscal policy.
- Full-employment budget.
- The crowding-out and crowding-in effects.
- The public debt.

Putting Fiscal Policy into Perspective

You don't have to be a great economist to see that we haven't been too successful at attaining our fiscal policy goals, particularly since the mid-1960s. It's important that the aggregate supply of goods and services equals the aggregate demand for goods and services at just that level of spending that will bring about full employment at stable prices.[1]

In terms of equilibrium GNP, sometimes we are spending too much while at other times, we are spending too little. When equilibrium GNP is too big, we have an inflationary gap and when it's too small, a deflationary gap. Remember the story "Goldilocks and the Three Bears"? Remember the porridge that was too warm and the porridge that was too cold? Like Goldilocks, our policy objective is to find a level of GNP that is just right. We will deal with inflationary and deflationary gaps and GNPs that are just right in the next few pages.

---

[1] That's a very long sentence whose meaning will become increasingly apparent as you read this chapter.

Economics is filled with adages, some of which make perfect sense—you can't repeal the law of supply and demand—and some of which don't make much sense at all. This chapter is based on two of the second type. First, we'll consider the following dictum: The federal budget must be balanced every year. In fact, during the last decade, a constitutional convention to consider an amendment that would make an annually balanced budget the law of the land was nearly approved by the required three quarters of the state legislatures.

The second part of this chapter will be devoted to a discussion of the public or national debt. The adage in question is: The public debt is a burden on future generations. In fact, there's another adage that virtually contradicts the first one: We owe it to ourselves. As we shall see, neither holds true, but as we shall also see, neither is completely wrong.

The Deflationary Gap

This gap occurs when equilibrium GNP is less than full-employment GNP. Equilibrium GNP is the level of spending that the economy is at or is tending toward. Full-employment GNP is the level of spending needed to provide enough jobs to reduce the unemployment rate to 5 percent.[2] When too little is being spent to provide enough jobs, we have a deflationary gap, which is shown in Figure 11–1. Another way of expressing this state of economic affairs is to say that we are inside our production possibilities frontier (or curve), as we discussed in Chapter 2.

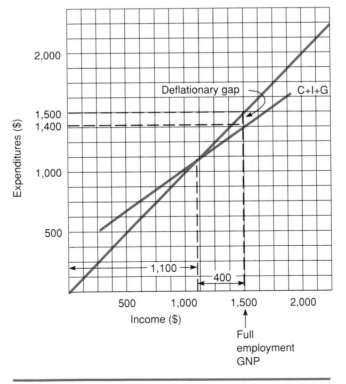

Figure 11–1

---

[2] In Chapter 9, we defined full employment as an unemployment rate of 5 percent.

What do we do to close this gap? We need to raise spending—consumption (C) or investment (I) or government expenditures (G)—or perhaps some combination of these. John Maynard Keynes tells us to raise G. Or we may want to lower taxes. If we lowered business taxes we might raise I; if we lowered personal income taxes, C would increase.

How much would we have to raise spending to eliminate the deflationary gap? In Figure 11–1, we see that the gap is $100 billion. Anything less than $100 billion would reduce, but not eliminate, the gap. Notice that equilibrium GNP is $400 billion less than full-employment GNP. Guess how much the multiplier must be? If we raise G by $100 billion and it raises equilibrium GNP by $400 billion, the multiplier must be 4.

Notice how the points in Figure 11–1 line up. Equilibrium GNP is to the left of full-employment GNP. The deflationary gap is directly above the full-employment GNP. It is the vertical distance between the 45-degree line and the C + I + G line.

The Inflationary Gap

The inflationary gap is shown in Figure 11–2. The key difference between this graph and that of the deflationary gap is the position of equilibrium GNP. When there is an inflationary gap, equilibrium GNP is to the right of full-employment GNP. It is to the left when there's a deflationary gap. In other words, equilibrium GNP is greater than full-employment GNP when there's an inflationary gap. When there's a deflationary gap, full-employment GNP is greater than equilibrium GNP.

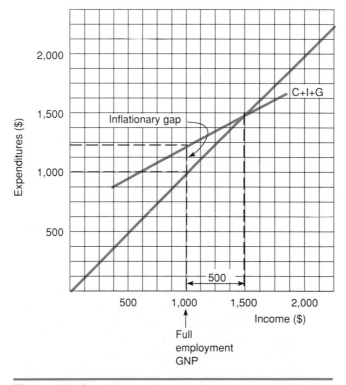

Figure 11–2

In both graphs the gap is the vertical distance betwen the C + I line and the aggregate supply line, and in both graphs the gap is directly above full-employment GNP.

Deflationary gap: Equilibrium GNP is too small.

Inflationary gap: Equilibrium GNP is too large.

In a word, when there's a deflationary gap, equilibrium GNP is too small; when there's an inflationary gap, it's too big. What Keynes would suggest to eliminate an inflationary gap is to cut G and raise taxes. Both actions are aimed at reducing spending, and therefore equilibrium GNP.

In Figure 11-2 the inflationary gap is $200 billion. If we cut spending by $200 billion, it would have a multiplied effect on GNP. Equilibrium GNP would decline by $500 billion to the full-employment level. How much is the multiplier? If equilibrium GNP falls by $500 billion in response to a spending cut of $200 billion, the multiplier is 2.5.

To summarize, if spending is too high, equilibrium GNP is above the full-employment level. To eliminate the inflationary gap, we cut G and/or raise taxes. If equilibrium GNP is less than full-employment GNP, we eliminate the deflationary gap by raising G and/or cutting taxes.

Fiscal Policy is the mina what demand, or required

How fiscal policy differs from monetary policy.

Fiscal and monetary policy have the same goals—high employment and stable prices. Students often get the two policies mixed up. Although both fiscal and monetary policy have the same ends, their means are very different.

Monetary policy regulates the rate of growth of our money supply.[3] Fiscal policy manipulates the federal budget. Any budget has two parts—income and expenditures. Fiscal policy then is the manipulation of tax revenue (or income) and government expenditures to attain price stability and high employment.

Deficits, Surpluses, and the Balanced Budget

To understand how fiscal policy works, we need to understand these three basic concepts. First, the deficit. When government spending, G, is greater than tax revenue, we have a federal budget deficit. The government is paying out more than it's taking in. How does it make up the difference? It borrows. Deficits have been a lot more popular than surpluses. In fact, we've run budget deficits every year since 1970.

Deficits: Government is paying out more than it's taking in.

This is not to say that deficits are always bad. Indeed, during recessions, they are just what the economic doctor ordered. But as you are well aware, we have certainly not had recessions every year since 1970!

Budget surpluses are the exact opposite of deficits. They are prescribed to fight inflation. When the budget is in a surplus position, tax revenue is greater than government spending. The last surplus we did have, in 1969, was rather suspect. President Lyndon Johnson had pushed a 10 percent personal income tax surcharge through Congress (this raised everyone's income taxes by 10 percent). He also pushed certain 1969 government expenditures into the 1970 budget. President Jimmy Carter promised a surplus for fiscal year 1981 (we actually had a deficit of 78.9 billion), and President Ronald Reagan promised a surplus in 1984 (when the deficit came to 185.3 billion).

We haven't had a budget surplus since 1969.

Finally we have a balanced budget when government expenditures are equal to tax revenue. We've never really had an exactly balanced budget; there were many years in the 19th and early 20th centuries when we had

---

[3] Monetary policy will be discussed in the latter part of Chapter 13.

small surpluses or deficits. Perhaps if the deficit or surplus were less than $10 billion, we'd call that a balanced budget. Remember that we're dealing with a budget that calls for over $1.2 trillion in spending, so if tax revenue and expenditures could be within $10 billion of each other, that would be close enough to call the budget balanced.

The Automatic Stabilizers

Something is called an automatic stabilizer because it is built into our economy and works automatically. Congress does not need to pass any laws and no new bureaucracies have to be created. All the machinery is in place and ready to go.

Each of these stabilizers protects the economy from the extremes of the business cycle—from recession and inflation. They are not, by themselves, expected to prevent booms and busts, but only to moderate them. To do still more, we need discretionary economic policy, which we'll discuss in the next section.

The automatic stabilizers protect us from the extremes of the business cycle.

Personal Income and Social Security Taxes During recessions the government collects less personal income tax and Social Security tax than it otherwise would. Some workers who had been getting overtime before the recession are lucky to be hanging onto their jobs even without overtime. Some workers are less lucky and have been laid off. That's the bad news. The good news is that they don't have to pay any personal income tax or Social Security tax since they have no income.

During prosperous times our incomes rise and during times of inflation our incomes tend to rise still faster. As our incomes rise, we have to pay more taxes. These taxes tend to hold down our spending, relieving inflationary pressures.

During recession, as incomes fall, federal personal income and Social Security tax receipts fall even faster. This moderates economic declines by leaving more money in taxpayers' pockets.

In Table 11-1, we have set up a hypothetical person earning $20,000 a year. Suppose she lost her job for six months during a recession. How would this affect her taxes and her take-home pay? Table 11-1 shows her situation before and after.

Table 11-1

Income before Taxes	Taxes Paid	After-Tax Income
$20,000	$3,300	$16,700
0	0	0

Don't worry too much about her. First of all, she lost her job for only six months, so she really had an income of $10,000 for the entire year. Second of all, she has some savings to help tide her over. And finally, we're going to see to it that she collects unemployment insurance benefits.

Personal Savings As the economy moves into a recession, savings decline. Many Americans lose their jobs and others get less overtime. As incomes fall, savings must fall as well. Looked at from another perspective, consumption rises as a percentage of income.

Just as the loss of income is cushioned by a falloff of saving, the reverse happens when the economy picks up again. Like higher taxes, during times of rapid economic expansion, increased savings tend to damp down inflationary pressures.

To return to the woman who lost her job during a recession, let's see what happened to her savings. This is shown in Table 11-2.

Table 11-2

After-Tax Income	Savings	Spending Money
$16,700	$2,000	$14,700
0	−4,000	4,000

That second savings figure in Table 11-2 may give you pause. Why would savings be negative $4,000? What would you do if you had money in the bank and needed it for food, car payments, rent, gasoline, and various and sundry other expenses? Wouldn't you draw on your savings? "What savings?" Maybe you didn't have the foresight to put something away for a rainy day, but this woman has been banking $2,000 a year because she knew that she might face a period of prolonged unemployment.

Credit Availability Because most Americans now hold bank credit cards, mainly MasterCard and VISA, we may think of these as automatic stabilizers that work in the same way that personal savings does. During good times we should be paying off the credit card debts that we run up during bad times.

Although many of us are quite good at running up credit card debt during good times as well as bad, our credit cards, as well as other lines of credit, may be thought of as automatic stabilizers during recessions because they give us one more source of funds with which to keep buying things. You may have lost your job and have no money in the bank, but your credit card is just as good as money.

Unemployment Compensation Here's a great example of closing the barn door after the horses ran off. We came up with a great unemployment insurance program back in 1935, which happened to be the sixth year of the Great Depression.

When you lose your job, you can sign up for unemployment benefits if you qualify. To qualify you need to have worked at an insured job for 20 weeks during the last year, or 40 weeks during the last two years. Also, you must have lost your job through no fault of your own. If you were laid off or your company moved out of town, you will be able to collect almost automatically.

During recessions, as the unemployment rate climbs, hundreds of thousands and then millions of people register for unemployment benefits. Benefit schedules and maximum payments vary from state to state. Most people who collect get about half their salaries, although those earning over $15,000 a year get considerably less.

A man whose gross income is $200 a week and $160 in take-home pay receives about $110 in unemployment benefits. For this person, the loss of his job means an income decline of just $50. Without unemployment insurance it would have been a lot worse. Chances are, by dipping into his savings and borrowing a little here and there, he can more or less maintain his standard of living until he finds another job.

But *will* he find another job? There's a recession going on. Actually, the tens of billions of dollars of unemployment benefits being paid out establish a floor under purchasing power. People who are, hopefully, only temporarily out of work will continue spending money. This helps retail sales from falling very much, and, even without further government help, the economy has bought some time to work its way out of the recession. As the economy recovers and moves into the prosperity phase of the cycle, jobs are found more easily and unemployment benefit claims drop substantially.

Sometimes during recessions Congress will extend the benefit period beyond 26 weeks to 39 or even 52 weeks in certain cases. This action is part of discretionary policy, since it does not happen automatically. You cannot automatically collect beyond 26 weeks unless Congress acts. During the recession of 1969–70, for example, a friend who had been "cut off" after 26 weeks unexpectedly heard from her local unemployment insurance office. "It was a miracle!" she told me. "They called me in and said I could collect for another 13 weeks!"

The maximum paid varies from state to state. In 1962, when the author collected for the full 26 weeks from New York, the maximum was just $50.

Let's return once again to the woman who lost her job. She had been earning $20,000 a year, or just under $400 a week. She would be eligible for about $200 a week, depending on where she lived. This would come to about $10,000 annually.

If we added the $4,000 of savings that she used to live on to the $10,000 of unemployment benefits, it would come to $14,000 on an annual basis. If we go back to Table 11-2, we see that before she lost her job she spent only $14,700 (after taxes and saving). So the standard of living during the recession hardly declined at all.

But we need to acknowledge several facts. First, she did seriously deplete her savings in order to maintain her standard of living. Second, this was a temporary occurrence. She could not have gone on drawing down her savings and she could not have collected unemployment benefits for more than 26, or possibly, 39 weeks.

Further, because her income was not all that high, it didn't have too far to fall. The person earning $40,000 or $100,000 would not begin to be compensated by a weekly unemployment check of $200.

Nonetheless, clearly most people can protect themselves from relatively short-term losses of income. Because this is so, their continued spending helps provide a floor under consumer spending during recessions, which, in turn, helps keep recessions from turning into depressions.

The Corporate Profits Tax Perhaps the most countercyclical of all the automatic stabilizers is the corporate profit (or income) tax. Corporations must pay 34 percent of their net income above $75,000 to the federal government. During economic downturns corporate profits fall much more quickly than wages, consumption, or real GNP, and, of course, during expansions, corporate profits rise much more rapidly. During the 1981–82 recession, corporate after-tax profits fell from an annual rate of $169.2 billion in the first quarter of 1981 to $118.8 just one year later.

Part of this decline is cushioned by the huge falloff of federal tax collections from the corporate sector. This leaves more money to be used for investment or distribution to shareholders in the form of dividends. And when corporate profits shoot up during economic booms, the federal government damps down economic expansion by taxing away 34 percent of the profits of the larger corporations.

Other Transfer Payments Some people think that when a recession hits, the government automatically raises Social Security benefits. This might make sense, but it doesn't happen. To do so would require that special legislation be passed.

There are three important payments that do rise automatically because of laws on the books. Each is aimed at helping the poor. They are welfare (or public assistance) payments, Medicaid payments, and food stamps.

Whenever a recession hits, millions of people become eligible for welfare, or if they are already getting welfare payments, they become entitled to larger payments. Someone earning the minimum wage ($3.35 an hour in 1987) might bring home only a little over $100 a week, which, in most states, would not be considered enough to support a family of five. This family would be eligible for welfare payments to supplement this person's earnings. During a recession, if this person loses her job and she collects unemployment benefits, these benefits will come to only a little more than half her pay, so her family will get larger welfare payments.

At the same time, this family will get more food stamps as well, since both public assistance and food stamps are based solely on family income. Furthermore, people who join the ranks of those on public assistance become eligible for Medicaid benefits.

These programs are important for two reasons. Not only do they alleviate human suffering during bad economic times, but they also help provide a floor under spending, which helps to keep economic downturns from getting still worse.

The automatic stabilizers smooth out the business cycle, keeping the ups and downs within a moderate range. Since the Great Depression, we have had neither another depression nor a runaway inflation. But the stabilizers, by themselves, cannot altogether eliminate economic fluctuations.

The automatic stabilizers may be likened to running our economy on automatic pilot—not very well suited for takeoffs and landings, but fine for the smooth part of the flight. However, when the going gets rough, the economy must resort to manual controls. Discretionary policy is our manual control system.

Discretionary Fiscal Policy — *recommend, not required*

Additional guidance or standard
Making the Automatic Stabilizers More Effective

One problem with unemployment benefits is that they run out in six months while a recession can drag on for over a year. Extending the benefit period is an example of discretionary fiscal policy because benefits are not extended automatically. An increase in the benefit ceiling or a widening of eligibility standards would be other ways of making this stabilizer more effective.

Altering federal personal and corporate income tax schedules to make them more progressive would be other examples. Of course, the most recent adjustments in personal income taxes, the Kemp-Roth Act and the Tax Reform Act of 1986, have had the opposite effect, making the tax structure less progressive and therefore less countercyclical.

Public Works

The main fiscal policy to end the depression was public works.

During the Great Depression, the Roosevelt administration set up several so-called alphabet agencies to provide jobs for the long-term unemployed. Among them, the WPA and the CCC put millions of people to work doing everything from raking leaves to constructing government buildings.

One of the problems in getting these public works projects off the ground was a lack of plans. Not only did we lack ready-to-go blueprints, but we did not even have a list of the needed projects. If we are ever again to institute a public works program, we need to be much better prepared than we were in the early 1930s. If not, by the time we get started, the recession will be over.

Although criticized as "make-work projects," these public works projects gave jobs to millions of the unemployed. These workers spent virtually their entire salaries, thereby creating the demand for goods and services in the private sector, creating still more jobs. Unfortunately, in 1937, there was a complete turnaround in both fiscal and monetary policy, plunging the economy into a deep recession from which we did not fully recover until our massive arms buildup just before our involvement in World War II.

Public works is probably not the answer to recessions unless they last so long and go so deep that these projects can be carried out. If public works are so necessary, one might ask, why wait for a recession to carry them out?

Transfer Payments

Just as we could increase the amount of money given for unemployment compensation, we could add to the welfare, social security, and veteran's pensions during recessions. Like public works, this would channel money into the hands of consumers, who, by spending this money, would create jobs in the private sector.

Increased transfer payments have the added advantage of working very quickly. No plans or blueprints are needed. Just program the computer and put the checks in the mail.

Changes in Tax Rates

The first two discretionary policy measures dealt exclusively with recessions. What do we do to fight inflation? We can raise taxes.

This was done in 1968 when Congress, under President Lyndon Johnson, passed a 10 percent income tax surcharge. If your income was $15,000 and your federal income tax was listed in the tax table as $2,300, you had to pay a $230 surcharge, which raised your taxes to $2,530.

In the case of a recession, a tax cut would be the ticket. The recession of 1981–82 was somewhat mitigated by the Kemp-Roth tax cut, which called for a 5 percent cut in personal income taxes in 1981 and a 10 percent cut in July 1982. However salutary its effects, Kemp-Roth was seen by its framers as a long-run economic stimulant rather than an antirecessionary measure.

Corporate income taxes too could be raised during inflations and lowered when recessions occurred. The investment tax credit, first adapted by the Kennedy administration, is another way of using taxes to manipulate spending.

A key advantage of using tax rate changes as a countercyclical policy tool is that they provide a quick fix. We have to make sure, however, that temporary tax cuts carried out during recessions do not become permanent cuts.

Changes in Government Spending

When we talked about increasing government transfer payments and embarking on public works projects to counter business downturns, we were calling for increased government spending. Looking back at the depression, what finally pulled us out was the massive armament spending at the beginning of World War II. To generalize then, we can beat any recession by having the government spend enough money.

But too much spending—whether C, or I, or G—will lead to inflation. To help solve that problem, we must cut government spending. Some critics of President Reagan have asked how he expected to end inflation by cutting social programs if, at the same time, he raised defense spending even more.

In sum, discretionary fiscal policy dictates that we increase government spending and cut taxes to mitigate business downturns, and we lower government spending and raise taxes to damp down inflation. In brief, we fight recessions with budget deficits and inflation with budget surpluses.

The Proposed Balanced Budget Amendment

To come back to the old adage that we must balance our budget each year—something we really tried to do even into the early 1930s—the economic wisdom today tells us that we should have deficits in lean years and surpluses in fat years. But perhaps over the course of the business cycle, we should balance the budget.

Of course, it hasn't worked out that way. During the last 20 years we managed only one surplus. Our national debt has risen year after year as we ran budget deficits in fat years as well as in lean years.

Those advocating a balanced budget amendment to the Constitution use our history of deficits and our mounting national debt to make their case. If our political leaders are unwilling or unable to exercise restraint, they will be required by law to do so.

Do we want to put ourselves in an economic straitjacket?

Most economists oppose such an amendment because it would put us in an economic straitjacket. No longer would we be able to fight recessions with deficits. Even our automatic stabilizers would be taken from us (since they are sure to cause deficits in recession years), leaving us vulnerable not just to recessions, but to depressions as well.

The irony and even hypocrisy of this recently proposed amendment lay with its principal supporter, President Reagan. It is indeed remarkable that the man who presided over the eight largest deficits in our entire history was advocating a balanced budget amendment. "Stop me," he seemed to be pleading, "before I spend again!"

Macawber's Equation

Do you remember Mr. Macawber from *David Copperfield*? This poor man was almost always just one step ahead of his creditors. Here is the advice he offered David, who was visiting him in debtor's prison:

> He solemnly conjured me, I remember, to take warning by his fate; and to observe that if a man had twenty pounds a-year for his income, and spent nineteen pounds nineteen shillings and sixpence, he would be happy, but that if he spent twenty pounds one he would be miserable.*

Should we apply Macawber's equation to the federal budget? Will our continuing budget deficits and mounting public debt lead to national misery? There are plenty of people out there who would agree with Mr. Macawber that our government must not spend one penny more than it receives in taxes.

* Charles Dickens, *David Copperfield* (Harmondsworth, Middlesex, England: Penguin Books), page 221.

The Politics of Fiscal Policy

In a sense there really *is* no fiscal policy, but rather a series of political compromises within Congress and between the president and Congress. The reason for this lies within our political system, especially the way we pass laws.

To become a law, a bill that is introduced in either house of Congress must get through the appropriate committee (most bills never get that far) and then receive a majority vote from the members of that house. It must get through the other house of Congress in the same manner. Then a House-Senate conference committee, after compromising on the differences between the two different versions of the bill, sends back the compromise bill to both houses to be voted on once again. After receiving a majority vote in both houses, the bill goes to the president for his signature.

If the president does not like certain aspects of the bill, he can threaten to veto it, hoping that Congress will bend to his wishes. If he gets what he wants, he now signs the bill and it becomes law. If not, he vetos it. Overriding a veto takes a two thirds vote in both houses—not an easy task.

Adding to the political difficulties, between 1968 and 1988, only during President Carter's four-year term were the president and the majority in both houses of Congress in the same political party. This necessitated still more compromise. For example, many Democrats in Congress wanted to scrap the third year of the Kemp-Roth tax cut scheduled to take effect July 1, 1983, while the president had considered asking Congress to make it effective January 1, 1983. Neither side got its way: the tax cut went into effect as scheduled, July 1, 1983. President Reagan wanted to cut social programs and raise military spending—priorities that many congressional Democrats wanted to reverse. Again, compromises had to be reached.

Although the president and the budget committees of the House and Senate come up with budgets for the coming fiscal year, the resulting fiscal policy is necessarily the product of political compromise. Interestingly, Republican and Democratic party leaders point the finger at each other when things don't improve with the economy. The suspicion here is that both sides are right.

The Full-Employment Budget

How big should our deficits be during recessions?

One question we have sidestepped is the size of deficits or surpluses. Besides saying that if the deficit or surplus is less than $10 billion the budget is virtually in balance and that President Reagan's $200 billion plus deficits have been huge indeed, we have not distinguished among the various sizes of deficits during the past few decades. To do that, we will use the concept of the full-employment budget.

To better understand this concept, we'll start with an economy that is at full employment with a balanced budget. The unemployment rate is 5 percent and federal expenditures are equal to tax revenues. What would happen if the unemployment rate rose just one percentage point to 6 percent? Economists have calculated that federal tax revenues would fall and government spending would rise by a total of approximately $30 billion. The government would be taking in less in taxes because about 1,200,000 workers lost their jobs and corporate profits probably declined somewhat. Also, government expenditures for transfer payments, particularly unemployment benefits, food stamps, welfare, and Medicaid, would rise. Together then, the decline in tax revenue and the rise in government expenditures would total some $30 billion. In other words, we'd have a budget deficit of $30 billion.

Now we'll take it a step further by raising the unemployment rate to 7 percent, forcing up the deficit another $30 billion to a grand total of $60 billion.

Assuming no changes in the tax structure and no new government spending programs, let's figure out how much of a deficit the government would have been running had the economy been at full employment. Think about it. Tax revenue would have been higher since about 2.4 million more people would have been working. Government expenditures would have been much lower because close to 2 million fewer people would have been collecting unemployment benefits; food stamp and welfare payments also would have been much lower. In fact, the deficit would have been zero.

When the deficit is zero, the budget is balanced. Had our economy been at full employment then, we would have had a balanced budget. In other words, with a 7 percent unemployment rate and a $60 billion deficit, we would still say that we had a full-employment balanced budget.

A deficit of $60 billion when the unemployment rate is 7 percent would provide the same economic stimulus that a balanced budget would provide when there is full employment. But earlier we said that when there is a recession, it is necessary to have a budget deficit to stimulate the economy. Would a full-employment balanced budget be adequate to reduce the unemployment rate (i.e., is our actual $60 billion deficit high enough)?

Economists are not in agreement here. (What else is new?) Some feel the actual deficit should run higher and others say the $60 billion is more than adequate to push the economy back toward full employment. Furthermore, a growing number of economists consider a 5 percent unemployment rate a far too optimistic goal and say that 5½ or even 6 percent would be our lowest attainable rate. Were that so, we would base the full-employment budget on a higher unemployment rate.

The Crowding-Out and Crowding-In Effects

The great debate:

Monetarists: Deficits cause crowding-out.

Keynesians: Deficits cause crowding-in.

Welcome to the first debate we are going to be sponsoring between the monetarists and the Keynesians over the next few chapters. In this debate the monetarists will argue in favor of the crowding-out effect while the Keynesians will take the side of the crowding-in effect.

The monetarists maintain that Keynesian deficits designed to raise aggregate demand will have little, if any, effect. First, budget deficits drive up interest rates, thus discouraging investment. Second, the more money the government borrows to finance the deficit, the less that will be available to private borrowers.

If the proper fiscal policy during recessions is a large budget deficit, one would wonder where the Treasury would get all this money. Presumably it will go out and borrow it. But from whom?

If it borrows funds from individuals who would have otherwise made this money available for business investment, won't these business borrowers be "crowded out" of the financial markets by the government? And won't interest rates be driven up in the process, further discouraging investment? Won't increased government spending financed by borrowing be replacing private investment spending?

The answer is yes to all three questions. Yes—but—to what degree?

During recessions business firms cut back on their investing, so the government would be tapping a relatively idle source of funds, and during recessions, interest rates tend to fall.

Even during relatively prosperous times, such as the mid-1980s, there is enough money to go around if the Federal Reserve is accommodating by allowing the money supply to grow at a fairly rapid clip and if foreign investors are willing to make a few hundred billion dollars available each year to major corporations as well as to the U.S. Treasury.

Nevertheless, the crowding-out effect cannot be dismissed out of hand, particularly during times of tight money, such as the late 1970s and early 1980s. That any borrower as big as the U.S. government crowds other borrowers out of financial markets is a fact. And as the late Israeli Defense Minister Moishe Dayan once put it, "You can't argue with a fact."

Let's take a closer look at the Keynesian position. When there is substantial economic slack, one would not expect increased government borrowing to have very much impact in financial markets. Not only would there be little effect on interest rates, but the Treasury would be sopping up funds that would otherwise go unclaimed. When orthodox Keynesian fiscal policy is followed, it is precisely during times of economic slack that large budget deficits are incurred.

One might also mention a possible "crowding-in" effect caused by deficit financing. This results from the stimulative effect that the deficit has on aggregate demand. If the deficit is caused by a massive personal income tax cut, consumption will rise, pulling up aggregate demand and inducing more investment. Similarly, increased government spending will raise aggregate demand, also inducing more investment. In other words, any rise in aggregate demand will induce a rise in investment.

This leaves us with one last question: which is larger, the crowding-in or the crowding-out effect? But it doesn't really matter. The point is that as long as there is a sizable crowding-in effect, every dollar the government borrows will not crowd out a dollar of private borrowing. Thus, all we really need to demonstrate is that there is a substantial crowding-in effect.

It would appear that if we accept one fact—that the total amount of loanable funds is not fixed—there probably will be a substantial crowding-in effect. If there is indeed a fixed pool of saving, then it follows that every dollar the government borrows is one dollar less available to private savers. But *is* this total pool of saving fixed? If aggregate demand, stimulated by massive budget deficits *does* rise, won't people save more money (as well as spend more)?

Therefore, as more saving becomes available, not every dollar borrowed by the government will actually be taken from private borrowers. Furthermore, as aggregate demand rises, more investment will be stimulated. If the crowding-in effect dominates the crowding-out effect, not only will government borrowing rise, but so will private borrowing and investing. All we need to show is that total borrowing—government and private—rises.

What do *you* think? Are the monetarists right in saying that government borrowing crowds out private borrowing? Or are the orthodox Keynesians correct in saying that the crowding-in effect may dominate the crowding-out effect? The betting here is that the truth lies somewhere between these two extremes.

The Public Debt

The public or national debt is the amount of currently outstanding federal securities that the Treasury has issued. Although about 10 percent is held by various federal agencies, most notably the Federal Reserve, it would be reasonable to say that the public debt is what the federal government owes to the holders of Treasury bills, notes, and bonds.

In 1981, the public debt went over the $1 trillion mark. Do you remember how much money $1 trillion is? Write it out with all the zeros right here.

Written out it looks like this: $1,000,000,000,000.[4] In 1986 the national debt broke the $2 trillion mark. That means that it took the federal government just five years to accumulate as much debt as it had taken to accumulate between 1776 and 1981. And at the rate we're going, we should reach $3 trillion sometime in 1992.

Exactly what *is* the national debt? It is the cumulative total of all the federal budget deficits less any surpluses. Most of it was run up during recessions and wars. It is owed to the holders of Treasury bills, notes, certificates, and bonds. For example, if you own any of these, you are holding part of the national debt.

Who holds the national debt? About half is held by private American citizens. Foreigners hold about 20 percent. The rest is held by banks, other business firms, and U.S. government agencies. Those who say we owe it to ourselves are substantially correct. As a taxpayer, you owe part of that debt. And if you happen to own any U.S. government securities, you are also owed part of the debt, so you would literally owe it to yourself.

Is the national debt a burden that will have to be borne by future generations? As long as we owe it to ourselves—no. If we did owe it mainly to foreigners, it is possible that if they wanted to be paid off, it would be a great burden. But that is certainly not the case at this point.

Back in 1960, foreigners held about 3 percent of the national debt. They have increased their holdings so substantially in recent years almost entirely because Americans love to spend and hate to save and because the federal government has been running megadeficits during the last decade.

By the mid-1980s, the United States was running annual trade deficits of over $150 billion and budget deficits of over $200 billion. Because our saving rate was so low, there wasn't enough domestic saving available to finance the federal budget deficits, but since foreigners, particularly the Japanese, were awash with dollars, they simply recycled them by lending them to the U.S. government.

And so, foreigners have been holding an increasing percentage of the public debt. While still nothing to be alarmed about, if the present trend continues—huge budget deficits, huge trade deficits, and a low domestic savings rate—sometime in the late 1990s the foreign share of the national debt could be approaching 50 percent. At that point we would hardly be able to say, "We owe it to ourselves."

The national debt rose substantially during wars. We paid for these wars partly by taxation and partly by borrowing. It was considered one's patriotic duty during World War II to buy war bonds. Unfortunately, however, it was also a terrible investment because the buyers were locking into low interest rates—between 1 and 1½ percent for 7 to 10 years—while immediately after the war prices jumped 35 percent in three years.

In wartime a nation will invest very little in plant and equipment, since all available resources must go toward the war effort. As a result, during the first half of the 1940s, we built no new plant and equipment. Had there been no war, billions of dollars worth of plant and equipment would have been built. The generation that came of age after the war inherited less capital than it would have had no war been fought. To that degree a burden had been placed on their shoulders.

Those who would point at the huge increase in the national debt during the war as the cause of our having less plant and equipment have misplaced the blame. It was the war, not the increase in the debt, that prevented wartime construction of capital goods.

---

[4] If big numbers like these still make you nervous, you would do well to review the second section of Chapter 5.

When do we have to pay off the debt? We don't. All we have to do is to roll it over, or refinance it, as it falls due. Each year several hundred billion dollars worth of federal securities fall due. By selling new ones, the Treasury keeps us going. But there is no reason why it ever has to be paid off.

A real problem would arise if investors thought the government might go bankrupt. That's what happened to the New York City government in 1975. Suddenly the city was unable to sell its securities, which it needed to do to roll over its debt. Had the pension plans of the municipal labor unions and the federal government not helped out, the city would indeed have gone bankrupt. However, the financial position of the governments of New York and the United States are hardly comparable. The federal government has first claim to our tax dollar, which make its securities the safest possible investment.

Isn't the national debt getting too big? Too big relative to what? In Table 11–3 we compare the debt in 1945 to GNP that year. Notice how it was even larger than GNP! Today the national debt is slightly more than one half of GNP. We make that comparison because the federal government does have first claim on our tax dollar. In fact, if the government really wanted to, it could probably pay off the national debt in just a few years by raising our taxes by about one third.

Table 11–3
GNP and the Public Debt

Year	Public Debt	GNP	Public Debt as a Percentage of GNP
1945	260	214	122
1987	2,429	4,486	54

Source: *The Economic Report of the President*, 1988, pp. 256, 346.

Why not go ahead and pay off the debt—or at least reduce it? Economists predict that if this course were followed, it would have catastrophic consequences. It would bring year after year of budget surpluses and would probably send us into a deep depression. According to our earlier analysis, when the economy is experiencing high unemployment, we need to run budget deficits, not surpluses. But during prosperity, particularly when inflation becomes a problem, we need to run budget surpluses, paying off part of the debt. This is the part of countercylical policy we have ignored during most of the last two decades.

How serious a problem is the interest on the debt? The interest payments have recently passed the $150 billion mark and threaten to climb still higher as the debt itself rises. For a long time the Treasury got a free ride. It had contracted most of the debt at relatively low interest rates—less than 2 percent in the 1940s and early 1950s, and until the late 1970s, single-digit rates. But now the debt is being rolled over at current high interest rates. Interest payments are now about one seventh of the federal budget, one of the "uncontrollable" expenditures not subject to budget cuts.

In recent years there is some evidence that government borrowing has drained funds away from private investment. To the degree that this is true, the growth rate of our capital stock—our plant and equipment—has been slower than it would have otherwise been. Again, it is not the national debt as such that is causing this problem. Rather, the national debt is merely the symptom of the government's continuing habit of living beyond its means.

Workbook for Chapter 11

Multiple-Choice Questions

Circle the letter that corresponds to the best answer.

1. In the late 1970s and early 1980s the goals of fiscal policy were

a. completely attained   **b.** largely attained
c. largely unattained   **d.** completely unattained

2. When equilibrium GNP is too small, we have

a. a deflationary gap   **b.** a depression   **c.** an inflationary gap   **d.** none of these

3. There is an inflationary gap when

a. equilibrium GNP is equal to full-employment GNP   **b.** equilibrium GNP is smaller than full-employment GNP   **c.** equilibrium GNP is larger than full-employment GNP   **d.** none of these occur

4. Fiscal policy and monetary policy are

a. different means used to attain different goals   **b.** different means used to attain the same goals   **c.** the same means to attain the same goals   **d.** the same means to attain different goals

5. Budget surpluses are most appropriate during

a. depressions   **b.** recessions   **c.** inflations

6. Each of the following is an automatic stabilizer except

a. unemployment compensation   **b.** direct taxes
c. welfare payments   **d.** social security benefits

7. If you lost a $300-a-week job and were eligible for unemployment insurance, you would probably collect about

a. $240   **b.** $200   **c.** $160   **d.** $120   **e.** $80

8. When there is a recession, the biggest proportionate decline is in

a. social security tax receipts   **b.** personal income tax receipts   **c.** consumer spending   **d.** corporate after-tax profits

9. The automatic stabilizers

a. help smooth out the business cycle   **b.** make the business cycle worse   **c.** eliminate the business cycle

10. Each of the following is an example of discretionary fiscal policy except

a. public works spending   **b.** making the automatic stabilizers more effective   **c.** changes in tax rates
d. the unemployment insurance program

11. The proposed balanced budget amendment to the Constitution would have required that the federal budget be balanced

a. over the business cycle   **b.** every three years
c. every year   **d.** every nonrecession year

12. Fiscal policy is made by

a. the president only   **b.** Congress only   **c.** both the president and Congress   **d.** neither the president nor Congress

13. The requirement to override a presidential veto is

a. a majority vote in each house of Congress
b. a two-thirds vote in each house of Congress
c. a three-quarters vote in each house of Congress
d. a majority vote of both houses of Congress combined

14. If we passed a constitutional amendment requiring a balanced budget every year, this would probably

a. make our recessions into depressions   **b.** prevent recessions   **c.** create inflations   **d.** raise interest rates

15. When there is a federal budget deficit, there could be a full-employment budget surplus if there happened to be

a. inflation   **b.** full employment   **c.** an unemployment rate of over 5 percent   **d.** a declining national debt

16. When the unemployment rate goes up one point, this increases the federal budget deficit by about

a. $30 million   **b.** $60 million   **c.** $30 billion

d. $60 billion

17. The crowding-out effect cancels out at least part of the impact of

a. expansionary fiscal policy   **b.** expansionary monetary policy   **c.** restrictive fiscal policy

d. restrictive monetary policy

18. Which statement is true?

a. About one third of the national debt is rolled over (or refinanced) every year.   **b.** The national debt is doubling every 10 years.   **c.** Unless we balance the budget within the next five years, the United States stands a good chance of going bankrupt.   **d.** None of these statements is true.

19. Since 1945 the national debt has _____ as a percent of GNP.

a. risen   **b.** fallen   **c.** remained about the same

20. Which statement is true?

a. The national debt is larger than GNP.   **b.** The national debt will have to be paid off eventually.   **c.** Most of the national debt is held by foreigners.   **d.** None of these statements is true.

21. If the federal government attempts to eliminate a budget deficit during a depression, this will

a. alleviate the depression   **b.** contribute to inflation   **c.** make the depression worse   **d.** have no economic effect

22. During times of inflation we want to

a. raise taxes and run budget deficits   **b.** raise taxes and run budget surpluses   **c.** lower taxes and run budget surpluses   **d.** lower taxes and run budget deficits

23. Which statement is true?

a. The public debt is larger than our GNP.   **b.** The public debt is the sum of our deficits minus our surpluses over the years since the beginning of the country.   **c.** We have had budget deficits only during recession years and wartime.   **d.** None of these statements is true.

24. The public debt has been increasing at the rate of $1 trillion every _____ years.

a. two   **b.** five   **c.** 10   **d.** 25

25. A major advantage of the automatic stabilizers is that they

a. simultaneously stabilize the economy and tend to reduce the size of the public debt   **b.** guarantee that the federal budget will be balanced over the course of the business cycle   **c.** automatically produce surpluses during recessions and deficits during inflations   **d.** require no legislative action by Congress to be made effective

26. The most valid argument against the size of the national debt is that it

a. will ruin the nation when we have to pay it back   **b.** is owed mainly to foreigners   **c.** leaves future generations less plant and equipment than would be left had there been a smaller debt   **d.** will bankrupt the nation since there is a limit as to how much we can borrow

Fill-In Questions

1. The goals of fiscal policy are (1) _____,

(2) _____, and (3) _____.

2. The means that fiscal policy uses to attain those goals are the manipulation of _____and _____

_____.

3. We could eliminate inflationary gaps and deflationary gaps by making _____ GNP equal to _____ GNP.

4. The two ways of eliminating an inflationary gap are (1) _____ and (2) _____.

5. The two ways of eliminating a deflationary gap are (1) _____ and (2) _____.

6. When there is an inflationary gap _____ GNP is greater than _____ GNP.

7. When there is a deflationary gap _____ GNP is greater than _____ GNP.

8. Inflationary gaps call for budget _____ while deflationary gaps call for budget _____.

9. When there is a budget surplus _____ is greater than _____; when there is a budget deficit, _____ is greater than _____.

10. The last year we had a budget surplus was _____.

11. When there is a budget deficit of $10 billion, essentially we have a _____ budget.

12. Welfare spending, unemployment compensation, and direct taxes are all examples of _____.

13. If you are earning $200 a week and then collect unemployment insurance benefits, you can expect to collect about $_____ a week.

14. Perhaps the most countercyclical of all the automatic stabilizers is the _____.

15. In addition to the automatic stabilizer, we have _____ fiscal policy.

16. When we have a full-employment balanced budget this means that the budget _____.

17. The crowding-out effect states that when the Treasury borrows a lot of money to finance a budget deficit _____.

18. The public debt passed the $1 trillion mark in _____ and the $2 trillion mark in _____.

19. Foreigners hold about _____ percent of the national debt.

20. The only way to reduce the national debt would be to _____.

21. If we tried to pay off the national debt, within a few years we would definitely have a _____.

Problems

1. *a.* In Figure 1, is there an inflationary gap or a deflationary gap?   *b.* How much is it?   *c.* How much is the multiplier?

2. To remove the gap in Figure 1, what two fiscal policy measures would you recommend?

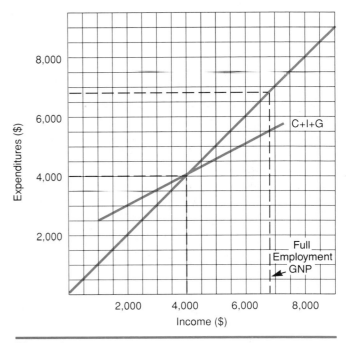

Figure 1

3. If we had a budget deficit of $60 billion and an unemployment rate of 8 percent, would we have a full-employment surplus or deficit? Of how much?

4. If the unemployment rate were 10 percent, how large should our budget deficit be?

5. We should run a balanced budget when our unemployment rate is about _____ percent.

Money and Banking

Banks create money. The rate of monetary growth itself is controlled by the Federal Reserve, which serves as our nation's central bank. In this chapter we'll look at our money supply and our banking system, and in the next, at the Federal Reserve System.

First we'll talk about the money supply in the United States and the jobs it does. Next we'll work in a little monetary theory; we'll look at the demand for money and how interest rates are set. Then we'll turn to banking, beginning with its origins in medieval times; then, moving right along, we'll look at modern banking. Now fasten your seat belt, and in the words of the late Jackie Gleason, "And away we go."

Chapter Objectives

We will discuss the following interesting topics:
- The three jobs of money.
- What money is.
- M1, M2, and M3.
- The equation of exchange.
- The quantity theory of money.
- The demand for money.
- The origins of banking.
- The FDIC.
- Branch banking and bank chartering.
- The creation and destruction of money.

The Three Jobs of Money

I don't have to tell you how important money is. About 20 years ago Abbie Hoffman and a bunch of yippies (not hippies or yuppies) created pandemonium at the New York Stock Exchange by throwing dollar bills from the visitors' gallery down to the trading floor. If money were unimportant, surely that multitude of stockbrokers would not have stopped their trading to help clean up.

Medium of Exchange

The most important job of money

This is, by far, the most important job of money: when any good or service is purchased, people use money.

Money makes it much easier to buy and to sell because it is universally acceptable. With money I can go out and buy whatever I want, provided of course, I have enough of it. Similarly, a seller will sell to anyone who comes along with enough money; he won't have to wait for a buyer who's willing to trade something he needs.

Money then provides us with a shortcut in doing business. By acting as a medium of exchange, money performs its most important function.

Standard of Value

Wanna buy a brand-name VCR? A new sports car? A Swiss watch?

"Sure," you say. "How much?"

Money performs well, then, at its second job—as a standard of value. If I told you that I got gasoline at 50 cents a gallon, you'd want to know the exact location of that gas station. But if I said that I bought a cheeseburger at a fast-food place for $8.50, you'd kind of wonder if I have both oars in the water. A job that pays $2 an hour would be nearly impossible to fill while one paying $50 an hour would be swamped with applicants.

Is money a good standard of value?

Does money work well as a standard of value? I'll bet you never heard the one about the three Jewish mothers who were comparing notes on their sons. The first one said that her son was a doctor and made $500,000 a year. The second mother had a son who was a lawyer and made $400,000 a year. They waited for the third mother to tell them what *her* son did.

"Well," she finally said, "my son is a rabbi."

"Yes," the other two said. "And?"

"And he makes $20,000 a year."

The other two mothers couldn't believe their ears. "Such a profession for a nice Jewish boy?"

Store of Value

I measure everything I do by the size of a silver dollar. If it don't (sic) come up to that standard, then I know it's no good.
—Thomas A. Edison

In economics we have a hard time doing scientific experiments because they won't allow us to use those Bunson burners. We also have a hard time explaining why we need test tubes and litmus paper, so I'll ask you to excuse my lack of equipment as I try to conduct a scientific experiment. I'll count on your help by asking you to use your imagination.

Imagine that in 1967 you put $100 under your mattress and took out that same hundred dollars in May of 1987. (I *do* hope that you've been changing the sheets regularly.) How much would that $100 be worth?

In other words, if you could buy 100 units of goods and services with your $100 in 1967, how many units could you buy with $100 in 1987? Fifty? No, less. Forty? No, less. Okay, I'll put you out of your misery. You could have bought just 29.61 units.

Did someone sneak into your bedroom in the middle of the night and steal most of your money? No, but over the years inflation obviously took its toll. During this 20-year period, inflation robbed the dollar of more than 70 percent of its purchasing power.

Is money a good store of value?

This brings us back to the third job of money. Is money a good store of value or wealth? Over the long run, and particularly since World War II, it has been a very poor store of value. However, over relatively short periods of time, say a few weeks or months, money does not lose much of its value. More significantly, during periods of price stability, money is an excellent store of value. Of course, the best time to hold money is during deflation

Double Coincidence of Wants: An Illustration

Warning: *The frank sexual nature of the following discussion may be offensive to some people. If you consider yourself a prude, read no further.*

May I ask you a personal question? Are you a swinger? What's a swinger? If you have to ask, you've answered my question.

Did you ever hear of Plato's Retreat, a swing club on the upper westside of Manhattan? Couples would go there, take off their clothes, and do all sorts of things with perfect strangers. Plato's closed years ago, but there are still hundreds of "off-premises" swing clubs all over the country. Couples go to these swing clubs to meet other couples. If two couples found they could do business, they would swap mates and go off someplace else to do whatever it was they were going to do.

What does all this have to to with the main job of money, a medium of exchange? Don't worry, we'll get to that.

Let's name our two couples Bob and Carol and Ted and Alice, which, as you probably don't remember, was the name of a movie that came out around 20 years ago. Indeed, at the end of the movie it was Bob and Alice and Ted and Carol—all in one bed, no less.

Suppose that Bob and Carol walk into an off-premises swing club and spot Ted and Alice. Bob is immediately attracted to Alice and asks Carol if she likes Ted. Ted, who happens to be, if memory serves, Elliot Gould in the movie, looks good to Carol, so they walk over to Ted and Alice.

By joining Ted and Alice, Bob and Carol are making a statement: We are attracted to you. Are you interested? Ted looks at Alice. Alice looks back at Ted. It would be rude if they excused themselves and went into a huddle, so they send each other signals, kind of the way bridge partners do when they're cheating. If they both nod their heads it means yes. Assuming that they both nod, a swap is in the offing.

Let's go over this whole transaction. Bob has to like Alice, who, in turn, has to like Bob. Carol has to like Ted, who, in turn, has to like Carol. If all four are happy, then they can do business, so to speak.

Now think of how much simpler it is to go shopping for a pound of chopped chuck steak. It's sitting there on the counter, it's clearly marked, and if you want it and feel that the price is right, you buy it. You don't have to satisfy the butcher, his wife, or your husband or wife. When there's no money and we do business by bartering, we have to have a double coincidence of wants before we can do business. As we've seen from the transaction at the swing club, that can lead to all kinds of complicated affairs.

because the longer you hold it, the more it's worth. For example, if you held money under your mattress from late 1929 to early 1933, it would have doubled in value during those years.

Money versus Barter

Without money, the only way to do business is by bartering. "How many quarter sections of beef do you want for that car?" or "Will you accept four pounds of sugar for that 18-ounce steak?"

For barter to work, we need a double coincidence of wants. I must want what you have and you must want what I have. This makes it pretty hard to do business.

Our Money Supply

What does our money supply consist of?

What does our money supply consist of? Gold? No! U.S. government bonds? No! Diamonds? No! Money consists of just a few things—coins, paper money, demand (or checking) deposits, and checklike deposits (commonly called NOW—or negotiable order of withdrawal—accounts). Coins (pennies, nickels, dimes, quarters, half dollars, and silver dollars) and paper money (dollar bills, fives, tens, twenties, fifties, hundreds, and five-hundred dollar bills) together are considered currency.

Demand deposits constitute close to three fourths of the money supply. We have to be careful, however, to distinguish between checks and demand

Where Did the Dollar Come From?

Our monetary system is based, believe it or not, on the old Spanish-milled silver dollar. You didn't think it was based on the British system, did you? You'd really have to be crazy to try to copy a system that uses pence, shillings, guineas, and pounds.

Are you any good at trivia questions? In Robert Louis Stevenson's *Treasure Island*, there was a parrot who, as parrots will do, kept repeating the same phrase over and over again. Okay now, what was the phrase? You'll have eight seconds to answer that question. What was the phrase that the parrot, who, by the way, was acquainted with Long John Silver, kept repeating over and over? Did you guess? Sorry—time's up.

The answer is "Pieces of eight. Pieces of eight." See that? You learn something every day.

By the way, how much money is two bits? It's a quarter. And four bits? That's right—50 cents. Eight bits? A dollar.

What was that parrot getting at with his "Pieces of eight. Pieces of eight"? He was talking dollars, Spanish-milled silver dollars. Those dollars were milled in such a way that eight pieces—or bits—could be torn from each dollar, like perforated slices in a metal pie. That way, if you had a dollar and wanted to spend just 25 cents, you tore off two pieces or bits. To this day there are some South American countries that have coins worth 12½ centavos.

(or checking) deposits. Jackie Gleason used to tell a story about two guys who get into an argument in a bar about who is cheaper. Suddenly, one of them pulls out a dollar bill and a book of matches, lights the bill, and lets it burn to a crisp. Not to be outdone, the other guy pulls out a five, lights it, and watches it burn to a crisp. So then the first guy does the same thing with a $10 bill. Well, the other guy doesn't want to look bad, so he reaches into his pocket, pulls out his checkbook, writes out a check for $1,000, lights it, and watches it burn to a crisp.

Checks are *not* money. Checking deposits *are*.

Incidentally, demand deposits are so named because they are payable "on demand." When you write a check, your bank must honor it, provided, of course, that you have enough money in your account to cover the check. Banks also insist that a certain number of business days go by before they will cash a specific check. It is usually 5 days for a local check and 7 to 10 days for an out-of-town check. Banks call this waiting period the time it takes for a check to clear. But any money in your checking account that has been cleared is available to depositors on demand.

M1, M2, and M3

Until a few years ago our money supply was defined as including just two things—currency and demand deposits. But the Federal Reserve was well

Are Credit Cards Money?

The answer is no! Credit cards are ID cards that enable you to buy a whole range of goods and services without having to pay until the end of the month. Who pays? The bank that issued your credit card pays the merchant: then, a few weeks later, you repay the bank.

What the bank would really like you to do is run up a large balance and pay 15 or 20 percent interest on that balance for years and years. That's the main reason they will give you a credit line of $3,000 or $4,000.

Bank credit cards such as VISA, MasterCard, and American Express have become extremely important in our economy. Not only can you travel or make major purchases without having to carry hundreds or thousands of dollars in cash, but you won't be able to rent a car, stay in some hotels, or transact certain types of business without one. But remember, they're only pieces of plastic—not money.

aware of NOW accounts (accounts that allowed negotiable orders of withdrawals) held at savings institutions other than commercial banks. After all, weren't these really checking accounts, which happened to pay interest? Then why not include them in the money supply?

Our money supply now includes not just currency and demand deposits, but also traveler's checks and what the Federal Reserve terms "other checkable deposits," which include the NOW accounts and something called "share draft accounts," which are checking accounts issued by credit unions.

M1 is shown, along with M2 and M3, in Figure 12-1. As of April 1988, our money supply totaled $768 billion. Virtually everyone considers M1 our money supply, but we're going to consider two broader measures of money, M2 and M3.

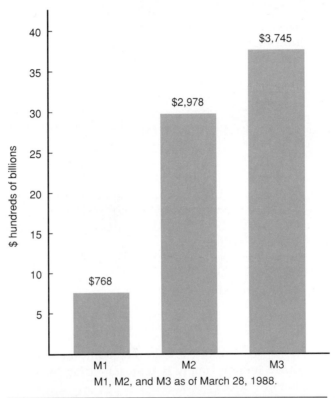

M1, M2, and M3 as of March 28, 1988.

Figure 12-1
M1, M2, M3 as of March 28, 1988

Source: *The New York Times*, April 15, 1988, p. D13.

By adding savings deposits, small-denomination time deposits, and money market mutual funds to M1, we get M2. You know what savings deposits are. Time deposits hold funds that must be left in the bank for a specified period of time—a week, a month, three months, a year, five years, or even longer.

Remember the bank ads that warn us, "There is a substantial penalty for early withdrawal"? These warnings are another way of saying that under the conditions of a time deposit, you are legally required to leave your money in the bank for a specified period of time. And so, unlike a demand deposit, time deposits are not payable until a certain date.

Technically, the money held in time and savings deposits does not have to be paid to the depositors "on demand." When you fill out a withdrawal slip to take money out of your savings account, you are completely confident that you will walk out of the bank with your money. Legally, however, your bank can require up to 30 days' written notice before giving you these funds. In practice, of course, no bank ever does this. Although nearly every bank in the country is insured by the Federal Deposit Insurance Corporation, it is quite possible that if a 30-day waiting period were enforced, many nervous depositors would rush into their banks to get their money while they could.

Money market mutual funds are issued by stockbrokers and other institutions, usually paying slightly higher interest rates than banks and offering check-writing privileges. From 1977 to 1982 there was a literal explosion in these funds, whose assets jumped from less than $4 billion to about $240 billion. Since then, however, due to legal restrictions caused by the Depository Institutions Act of 1982, these funds have grown very slowly.

We get from M2 to M3 by adding large-denomination time deposits. How large is large? The dividing line between small-denomination and large-denomination time deposits is $100,000. Any deposit of under $100,000 is small.

The Equation of Exchange

Don't get the equation of exchange mixed up with the quantity theory of money.

In this section and the next one, we will take up, in turn, the equation of exchange and the quantity theory of money. These two concepts are easily confused, perhaps because the equation of exchange is used to explain the quantity theory. I warn my students every term about how easily the unwary test taker writes down the equation of exchange when asked for the quantity theory, or vice versa. Many of my students take these warnings to heart, remaining faithful to the tradition of confusing the two concepts on the next exam.

The equation of exchange is

$$MV = PQ$$

What do each of these letters stand for? The number of dollars in the nation's money supply is represented by M—the currency, demand deposits, and checklike deposits.

The velocity of circulation or the number of times per year that each dollar in our money supply is spent is represented by V. If we were to multiply M times V, or MV, that would be our money supply multiplied by the number of times per year each dollar is spent—in other words, total spending. Total spending by a nation during a given year is GNP. Therefore, MV = GNP.

Now for the other side of the equation. The price level or the average price of all the goods and services sold during the year is represented by P. Finally, there's Q[1], which stands for the quantity of goods and services sold

---

[1] Some economists prefer to use T, total number of transactions, instead of Q. For that matter, there happen to be a large number of economists who put the cream in their coffee before the sugar, as well as a large number of economists who prefer to put the cream in their coffee after the sugar.

during the year. Multiplying P times Q, we get the total amount of money received by the sellers of all the goods and services produced by the nation that year. This is also GNP. Since things equal to the same thing are equal to each other (MV = GNP; PQ = GNP), then MV = PQ.

We'll get a better idea of how this equation works by replacing the letters with numbers. For M we can substitute $900 billion, which will probably be approximately the level of our money supply by the time you read this book.

$$MV = PQ$$
$$900 \times 9 = PQ$$
$$8,100 = PQ$$

This gives us a GNP of 8,100 or $8.1 trillion. As a form of shorthand, economists will write billions of dollars without the dollar sign. The money supply of $900 billion becomes 900 and the GNP of $8,100 billion becomes 8,100.

So far we have MV = 8,100; therefore, PQ also = 8,100. How much are P and Q? We don't know. All we *do* know is that P × Q = 8,100.

What we'll do, so we can fool around with this equation, is arbitrarily assign values to P and Q. That might not be very nice or proper, but let me assure you that people do this sort of thing every day. Let's take P. Who can possibly guess what the average price of all the goods and services sold actually is. In other words, what is the average price of all those cars, houses, hotdogs, pairs of shoes, toothbrushes, cans of beer, cavity fillings, and so on? Since there's no way of even guessing, we'll make the number $81. Why $81? Because it's going to be easy to work with. But perhaps $61.17 or $123.98 is what P actually denotes. We'll never know.

We'll do the same with Q. How many goods and services were sold during the year? 23 billion? 345 billion? Again we can't possibly know, so we'll arbitrarily assign a number. If we've already picked $81 for P, and PQ = 8,100, Q must equal 100 (meaning, in economists' shorthand, 100 billion). Therefore:

$$MV = PQ$$
$$900 \times 9 = 81 \times 100$$
$$8,100 = 8,100$$

That's the equation of exchange. It must always balance, as must all equations. If one side rises by a certain percentage, the other side must rise by the same percentage. For example, if MV rose to 9,000, PQ would also rise to 9,000.

The Quantity Theory of Money

The crude version of the quantity theory

This theory has a both crude and a more sophisticated version. The crude quantity theory of money holds that when the money supply changes by a certain percentage, the price level changes by that same percentage. For example, if the money supply were to rise by 10 percent, the price level would rise by 10 percent. Similarly, if M were to double, then P would double. Using the same figures we have assigned to the equation of exchange, let's see what happens if M and P double.

$$MV = PQ$$
$$900 \times 9 = 81 \times 100$$
$$1,800 \times 9 = 162 \times 100$$
$$16,200 = 16,200$$

If we double M, then MV doubles, and if we double P, PQ doubles. Since both sides of the equation must be equal, it appears that the crude quantity theory of money works out.

There are only two problems here. We are assuming that V and Q remain constant. Do they? If they do, the crude quantity theory is correct. But what if they don't? For example, what if M, P, and Q all double. For the equation to balance, V would have to drop by 50 percent. Similarly, what if M doubles and V declines by 50 percent? In that case the rise in P would be canceled by the decline in V. If M doubles and MV stays the same, can we expect an automatic doubling of P?

During a period of very tight money in the late 1970s and early 1980s, V rose above 10.

Let's take a closer look at V and then at Q. Since 1950, V has risen fairly steadily from about three to a little more than nine. In other words, individuals and businesses are spending their dollars much more quickly. Alternately, they are making more efficient use of their money balances.

There are several explanations for the rise of V. First, there's inflation. Why hold large money balances when they lose their value over time? Second, why hold idle cash balances when they could be earning interest? Finally, the use of credit cards, especially during the last two decades, has allowed people to carry less cash. As a result, V has more than tripled since the mid-1950s.

Now let's see about Q, the quantity of goods and services produced. During recessions, production and therefore Q will fall. For example, during the 1981–82 recession, Q fell at an annual rate of about 4 percent during the fourth quarter of 1981 and the first quarter of 1982. During recoveries, production picks up, so we go from a declining Q to a rising Q.

Obviously then we cannot consider V or Q to be constants. Therefore, the crude version of the quantity theory is invalid.

The sophisticated version of the quantity theory

Today's modern monetarists, those who believe that changes in M are the key economic variable, have come up with a more sophisticated quantity theory. They assume that any short-term changes in V are either very small or predictable. The situation with Q, however, is another story.

Let's say M rises by 10 percent and V stays the same: MV will rise by 10 percent and PQ will rise by 10 percent. So far, so good. In fact, so far the crude and sophisticated quantity theories are identical, but what happens next is entirely up to the level of production, Q.

If there's considerable unemployment and we increase M, most, if not all, of this increase will be reflected in an increase in production, Q. Money flowing into the economy will lead to increased spending, output, and employment. Would it lead to higher prices as well? Probably not. Although our recent experience during recessions makes us a little more wary of large surges in the money supply, it is not unreasonable to expect most of the rise in M to be reflected in a rise in Q.

As we approach full employment, however, further increases in M will begin to lead, more and more, to increases in P, the price level (see Figure 12–2).[2] And it is there that the sophisticated quantity theory becomes oper-

---

[2] Do you recognize our old friend, the aggregage supply curve, which we drew in Chapter 10, Figures 10–10 and 10–11?

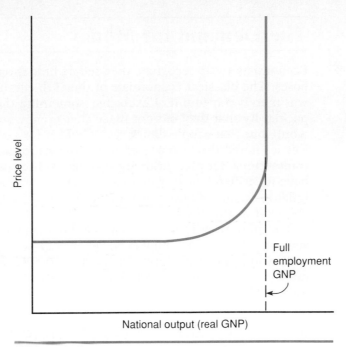

Price level

National output (real GNP)

Full
employment
GNP

Figure 12–2

Sophisticated quantity theory in brief

ative. We therefore can make two statements that summarize the sophisticated quantity theory:

1. If we are well below full employment, an increase in M will lead mainly to an increase in Q.
2. If we arc close to full employment, an increase in M will lead mainly to an increase in P.

That's the sophisticated quantity theory of money. Please don't confuse it with the crude quantity theory, and don't confuse either with the equation of exchange.

What is the sophisticated quantity theory supposed to do? Like most other theories, it makes a prediction. In its least rigorous version it says that changes in the rate of growth of M lead to similar changes in the rate of growth of PQ. If M is increasing slowly, PQ will increase slowly while rapid growth in M leads to rapid growth in PQ. Although no precise mathematical relationship is claimed (as under the crude quantity theory), the monetarists say that changes in M lead to predictable changes in PQ.

We've very deftly sidestepped the whole question of whether V is stable in the shortrun. The monetarists tell us it is, and the validity of the modern or sophisticated quantity theory depends on the short-run stability of V.

Before we can be more definite about the short-run stability of velocity, we need to examine the demand for money, which we shall do in the next section. But as luck would have it, we will still not be ready. We'll need to talk about the supply of money as well, which we shall do in the next chapter. Then will we finally be able to deal with the question of the short-run stability of V? Yes, we will do so in Chapter 14. I know you can hardly wait!

The Demand for Money

Economists today recognize that people hold money for a variety of purposes. The classical economists of the 19th century believed that money was merely a medium of exchange, something that burned a hole in your pocket. By that they did not mean that money was hot (in any sense of the word), but that people didn't really hold it for very long. John Maynard Keynes noted that people had three reasons for holding money: to make transactions, for precautionary reasons, and to speculate. Today economists have identified four factors that influence the three Keynesian motives for holding money: (1) the price level, (2) income, (3) the interest rate, and (4) credit availability.

The amount of money that people hold is called money balances. It consists of currency, checking deposits, checklike deposits held at financial institutions, and traveler's checks. After the Keynesian motives for holding money are discussed, we shall look at the influences that shape the demand for holding money.

The Keynesian Motives for Holding Money

John Maynard Keynes said that people have three motives for holding money. Instead of holding their assets in other forms—stocks, bonds, real estate, commodities—everyone opts to hold at least some of his assets in the form of currency or demand deposits. First we'll look at the transactions motive.

Transactions motive

Individuals have day-to-day purchases for which they pay in cash or by check. You make your rent or mortgage payment by check, your car payment, as well as your monthly bills and your major purchases. Cash is needed for groceries, gasoline, most restaurant meals, the movies, and nearly every other small purchase. Businesses too need to keep substantial checking accounts to pay their bills and to meet their payrolls. Individuals and businesses then both need to hold a certain amount of money for regular expenses. Keynes called this the transactions motive for holding money.

Precautionary motive

Next we have the precautionary motive. People will keep money on hand just in case some unforeseen emergency arises. They do not actually expect to spend this money, but they want to be ready if the need ever arises.

One good example dates back to the 1950s and earlier when women did not have to share the expenses when they went out on dates. Most of my students claim that this situation has not changed and that men still pay. At any rate, back in the 1950s, women used to carry a $10 bill on all their dates—just in case. They called it "mad money," which they would use for cab fare if their date went beyond the limits prescribed by the social mores of those times.

Speculative motive

Finally, there is the speculative motive for holding money. When interest rates are very low—as they were during the Great Depression when Keynes was writing—you don't stand to lose very much by holding your assets in the form of money. Alternately, by tying up your assets in the form of bonds, you actually stand to lose money should interest rates rise since you'd be locked into very low rates. In effect, the speculative demand for money is based on the belief that better opportunities for investment will come along, and that, in particular, interest rates will rise.

Four Influences on the Demand for Money

The amount of money we hold is influenced by four factors: (1) the price level; (2) income; (3) interest rates; and (4) credit availability. Changes in these factors change how much money we hold.

(1) The Price Level As prices rise you need more money to take care of your day-to-day transactions. As a young man during those prosperous years before World War I, I didn't need to carry very much money around. After all, those were the days, my friend. The days of nickel beer and nickel hot-dogs. And believe it or not, two kids could see a movie for a nickel.

In the mid-1950s there was a very popular musical starring Sammy Davis, Jr. called *The Most Happy Fella*. One of its songs, "Standin' on the Corner," had this couplet:

> Saturday and I'm so broke
> Couldn't buy a girl a nickel Coke.

Today it would cost a family of four over $30 to take in a neighborhood movie and a meal at MacDonalds, not to mention the slightly higher priced cuisine at Roy Rogers. Thus, as the price level goes up, so too does the demand for money balances. Nobody leaves home with just a nickel.

Today we must pay a substantial penalty for holding our assets in the form of money. In fact, there are two closely related penalties. First, there's inflation. If the inflation rate is 10 percent, then $100 held for a year will be worth only about $90. That is, $100 will buy what around $90 bought one year ago.

During times of inflation, then, we don't want to hold more than we need to in currency or checking deposits. In other words, we want to get some kind of return on our money, or in some other way to protect its purchasing power.

By holding our assets in the form of money, we would not only be forego-ing interest, but our money would be losing its purchasing power from month to month. Therefore, in times of high interest rates and inflation (the two generally go together), people prefer to hold as little as possible of their assets in the form of money.

We really need to distinguish between two contradictory influences on money balances with respect to the price level. As the price level rises, peo-ple *need* to hold higher money balances to carry out their day-to-day transactions. But as the price level rises (i.e., with inflation), the purchasing power of the dollar declines, so the longer you hold money, the less that money is worth.

A distinction between short run and long run would be helpful. Assume a constant inflation rate of 10 percent so that the price level rises by exactly 10 percent every year. The cost of living would double every seven years.[3] So you would need to carry double the money balance in 1999 that you did in 1992 to handle exactly the same transactions.

On the other hand, with a 10 percent rate of inflation, the longer you hold assets in the form of money, the less that money will buy. Even though there is an inflation penalty for holding money for relatively long pe-riods of time, you will surely keep enough on hand to take care of your day-to-day transactions. And if you compared your money balance in 1992 with

---

[3] Any number that increases by 10 percent a year will double in seven years. This is an application of the rule of 70: Any number that increases by 1 percent a year doubles in 70 years. You can check this out on your calculator or by consulting a book of compound in-terest tables.

that of 1999, you'd find that in 1999 you would be holding about double what you held in 1992, all other things remaining the same.

What we are left with is this conclusion. Even though people tend to cut down on their money balances during periods of inflation, as the price level rises, people will hold larger money balances.

(2) Income Poor people seldom carry around much money. Check it out. Go over to the first raggedy person you see and ask him to change a $50—or a $5. The more you make, the more you spend, and the more you spend, the more money you need to hold as cash or in your checking account. Even if you use a credit card, you still have to pay your bill at the end of the month. Therefore, as income rises, so too does the demand for money balances.

(3) The Interest Rate So far we've had two positive relationships: the quantity of money demanded rose with the level of prices and income. Are you ready for a negative relationship? All right, then. The quantity of money demanded goes down as interest rates rise.

Until recently you did not receive interest for holding money. Cash that you keep in your wallet or under your mattress still pays no interest, and until the late 1970s, neither did checking deposits. Still, even today, nearly all checking deposits pay only 5 to 5½ percent interest and some don't pay any interest whatsoever. The alternative to holding your assets in the form of money is to hold them in the form of bonds, money market funds, time deposits, and other interest-bearing securities. As interest rates rise, these assets become more attractive than money balances. Thus, there is a negative relationship between interest rates and money balances.

(4) Credit Availability If you can get credit, you don't need to hold so much money. Thirty years ago most Americans paid cash for their smaller purchases and used checks, for big-ticket items. The only form of consumer credit readily available was from retail merchants and manufacturers. During the last three decades there has been a veritable explosion in consumer credit in the form of credit cards and bank loans. Over this period then increasing credit availability has been exerting a downward pressure on the demand for money.

We can now make four generalizations:

People tend to hold less money as interest rates rise, inflation rises, incomes fall, and credit availability rises.

1. As interest rates rise, people tend to hold less money.
2. As the rate of inflation rises, people tend to hold less money.
3. As the level of income rises, people tend to hold more money.
4. People tend to hold less money as credit availability increases.

The Demand Schedule for Money

For purposes of analysis, we shall use the Keynesian motives for holding money discussed earlier to derive the demand schedule for money. This schedule, in turn, when brought together with the money supply schedule in the next section, will enable us to derive the interest rate. Right now we'll be combining the transactions, precautionary and speculative demands for money.

How much money individuals and business firms need to hold for their transactions really depends on the size of GNP or total spending. The more we spend, the more we need to hold at any given time. The transactions demand for money is somewhat responsive to interest rate changes. Corporate comptrollers used to leave relatively large balances in their checking accounts in the 1950s when interest rates were very low and checking accounts paid zero interest. Today those funds might be held in the form of seven-day certificates of deposit or other very short-term, very liquid assets to take advantage of the relatively high interest rates. Individuals too, because of today's higher interest rates as well as the widespread use of credit cards, carry much smaller money balances than they would have back in the 1950s.

The precautionary demand for money is least responsive to interest rate changes because people have a specific purpose for holding these funds. However, even these funds would be at least partially converted into other assets at extremely high interest rates.

The speculative demand for money is, as we would expect, the most responsive to interest rate changes. The people who are holding these funds would obviously hold a lot more at low interest rates than they would at higher rates.

The Liquidity Trap

When John Maynard Keynes carried his speculative motive for holding money to its logical conclusion, he determined that at very low interest rates people would not lend out their money, would not put it in the bank, would not buy bonds with it, but would simply hold it. That's right—they'd sit on it, hoard it, but not spend it and not make it available to anyone else.

Why should they, reasoned Keynes. When the interest rate declines to, say, 2 percent, why risk your money for such a low rate of return? And why tie it up at such a low interest rate when perhaps within a few months the interest rate will rise? *Then* sink it into interest-bearing assets, not now. This reasoning is reflected by the horizontal section of the Keynesian money demand curve (which he called a liquidity preference curve) shown in Figure 12–4.

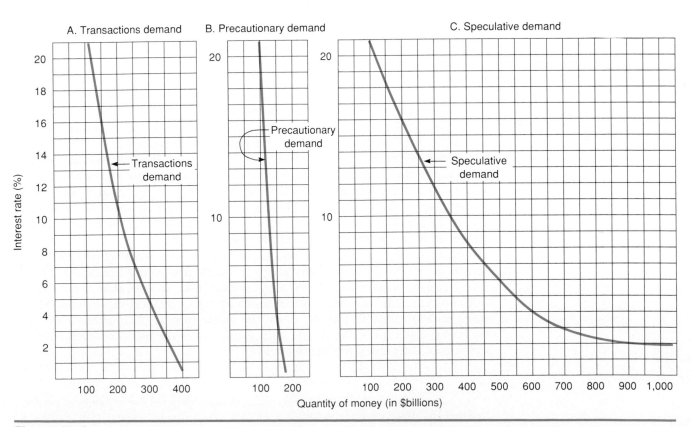

Figure 12–3

Using the data from Figure 12-3, we can derive the total demand schedule for money, shown in Figure 12-4. This demand curve is the sum of the three demand curves shown in Figure 12-4—the transactions, precautionary, and speculative demands for money. In the next section we combine this curve with the money supply curve to determine the interest rate.

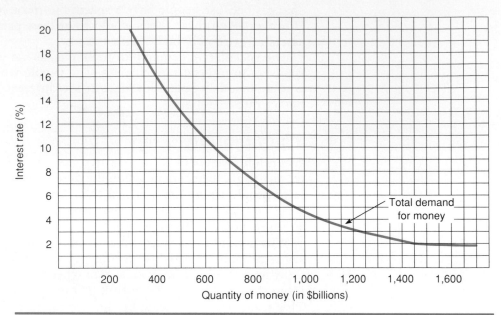

Figure 12–4
Total Demand for Money

Determination of the Interest Rate

The interest rate is determined by the demand for and the supply of money.

In Figure 12-4, we assumed various interest rates and determined that as the interest rate declined, the amount of money that the public wished to hold went up. But what determines the interest rate? If we think of the interest rate as the price of money, then the interest rate, like the price of anything else, is set by the forces of supply and demand.[4]

The supply of money is controlled by the Federal Reserve.[5] At any given time supply is fixed, so we'll represent it as a vertical line at 800 in Figure 12-5. Taking the demand curve from Figure 12-4, we find that it crosses the money supply curve in Figure 12-5 at an interest rate of about 7.2 percent. It's as simple as that. Find the point at which the demand curve and supply curve cross and you've got the interest rate.

Of course both our demand and supply curves are hypothetical, so the interest rate we've found is hypothetical as well. If you find this at all discouraging, maybe you'll take some solace from the fact that there isn't only one interest rate; there are literally scores of interest rates. One of the most widely followed interest rates, the prime rate, is charged by banks to their best customers. We'll now shift gears and make our transition from the subject of money to that of banking.

---

[4] The last section of Chapter 3 provides a cogent explanation of the workings of supply and demand to set the interest rate.

[5] We'll go over how the Federal Reserve sets the money supply in Chapter 13.

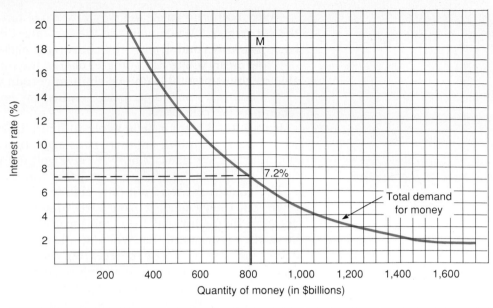

Figure 12–5
Total Demand for Money and Supply of Money

demand
deposits
mutual money market
pool of money

Banking

There are some 15,000 commercial banks in the United States. These are defined as banks that hold demand deposits, but other banks—mutual savings banks, savings and loan associations, credit unions, and mutual money market funds—also issue checking accounts. The distinction between commercial banks and other savings institutions is becoming blurred.

We'll talk about the origins of banking before we discuss how banking is conducted today in the United States. The first modern banks were run by goldsmiths back in the Middle Ages. We'll see that these fellows not only invented banking, but paper money as well.

The Goldsmiths

The origins of banking

In medieval times about the only secure place for your money was in the safes of the goldsmiths, so practically anybody who was anybody kept his money with the local goldsmith. These gentlemen would give receipts that possibly looked a little like hatchecks you get at some of the fancier restaurants. If you left 10 gold coins with the smith, he wrote 10 on your receipt. If you happened to be rich, it was very important to be able to count past 10.

Although no one is quite sure who was the first to accept paper money—that is, goldsmith's receipts—it might well have happened this way.

A knight was having his castle completely redone—new wallpaper, new bearskin rugs, new dungeon, new drawbridge—the works! When the job was finally completed, the contractor handed him a bill for 32 gold pieces.

The knight told the contractor "Wait right here. I'll hitch up the team and take the ox cart into town. I'll get 32 gold coins from the goldsmith. I shouldn't be gone more than three days."

"Why bother to go all the way into town for the 32 gold coins?" asked the contractor. "When you give them to me, I'll have to ride all the way back into town and deposit the coins right back in the goldsmith's safe."

"You mean you're not going to charge me for the job?" The knight, while able to count past 10, came up short in certain other areas.

"Of course I want to get paid," replied the contractor. "Just give me your receipt for 32 gold coins."

It took the knight a little while to figure this out, but after the contractor went over it with him another six or eight times, he was finally able to summarize their transaction: "If I give you my receipt, we each save a trip to the goldsmith." And with that, paper money began to circulate.

The goldsmiths were not only able to count higher than anyone else in town, but they generally had a little more upstairs as well. Some of them began to figure out that they could really start to mint money, so to speak. First, they recognized that when people *did* come in to retrieve their gold coins, they did not insist on receiving the identical coins they had left. Second, they noticed that more and more people were not bothering to come in at all to get their money since they were paying their debts with the receipts. And so, the goldsmiths were struck with this evil thought:—Why not lend out some of these gold coins just sitting here in the safe?

Moment at which modern banking was born

This was the moment modern banking was born. As long as the total number of receipts circulating was equal to the number of gold coins in the safe, we did not have a banking system, but when the number of receipts exceeded the number of coins in the safe, a banking system was created. For example, if a goldsmith had 1,000 coins in his safe and receipts for 1,000 coins circulating, he wasn't a banker. What if he knew that not all his depositors would ever come to him at the same time for their money and he decided to lend out just 10 gold coins? He would then still have receipts for 1,000 coins circulating, but he'd have only 990 coins in his safe.

The "paper money' issued by the goldsmith is no longer fully backed by gold, but there's really nothing to worry about because not everyone will show up at the same time for their gold. In the meanwhile, the goldsmith is collecting interest on the 10 gold pieces he has lent out.

"But why stop there?" asks the goldsmith. "Why not lend out 100 gold coins, or even 500?" And so he does. With 500 coins lent out, he still has 500 in his safe to cover the 1,000 receipts in circulation. And what are the chances that half his depositors will suddenly turn up demanding their coins?

Now we have 500 coins backing up 1,000 receipts, or a reserve ratio of 50 percent. As long as there are no panics, 50 percent is certainly a very prudent ratio. As their ratio declines (from 100 to 50 percent), let's see what happened to the money supply, the gold coins and goldsmith's receipts in the hands of the public (Figure 12–6).

Initially we had 1,000 coins in the safe (or bank) and 1,000 receipts circulating. The reserve ratio was 100 percent (1,000 coins backing 1,000 receipts). Now we have 500 coins in the safe and 500 circulating, along with the 1,000 receipts in the hands of the public. Our reserve ratio is 50 percent (500 coins backing 1,000 receipts). And our money supply? It's grown to 1,500—1,000 receipts and 500 coins in circulation. Thus, as the reserve ratio declines, the money supply rises.

Let's go a step further and have the goldsmith lend out an additional 250 gold coins. See if you can figure out the reserve ratio and the size of the money supply.

Since there are now 250 coins backing 1,000 receipts, the reserve ratio is 25 percent. Meanwhile the money supply has grown from 1,500 to 1,750, because in addition to the 1,000 receipts, we have 750 coins in the hands of the public.

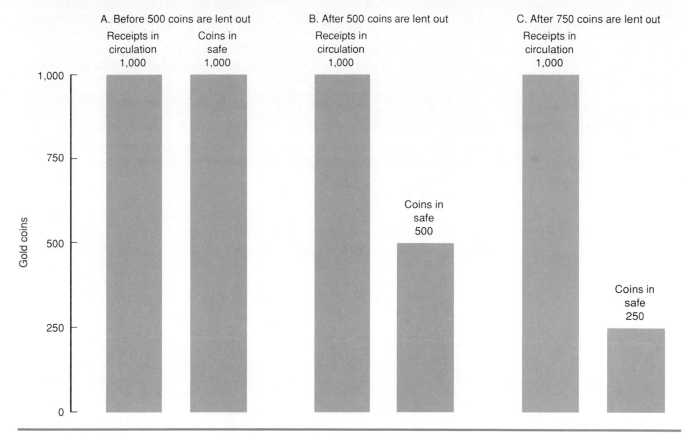

A. Before 500 coins are lent out

Receipts in circulation 1,000   Coins in safe 1,000

B. After 500 coins are lent out

Receipts in circulation 1,000   Coins in safe 500

C. After 750 coins are lent out

Receipts in circulation 1,000   Coins in safe 250

Gold coins

Figure 12–6

If the goldsmith were to continue lending out gold coins, he would end up with none in his safe. His reserve ratio would sink to zero, and the money supply would be 2,000 (1,000 receipts and 1,000 coins).

Since the goldsmith is such a clever fellow, he has noticed that his receipts circulate as easily as gold coins. And so, long before he has lent out all his coins, which he really needs as reserves (or backing for his receipts), he begins to make loans in the form of his receipts. For example, suppose you need to borrow 10 gold coins. The goldsmith merely writes up a receipt for 10 gold coins and off you go with your money.

What is to prevent the goldsmith from merely writing up receipts every time someone wants to borrow? We call this printing money. For example, with his original 1,000 gold coins tucked away in his safe, the goldsmith prints up 2,000 receipts. How much would the reserve ratio be and what would be the size of the money supply?

Since there would be 1,000 coins backing up 2,000 receipts, the reserve ratio is 50 percent. The money supply consists of the 2,000 receipts in the hands of the public. Suppose the goldsmith lent out another 2,000 (units) in the form of receipts. The reserve ratio would be 25 percent (1,000 coins backing 4,000 receipts) and the money supply would be the 4,000 receipts.

If the goldsmith so chose, he could even print up 10,000 receipts, which would bring about a reserve ratio of 10 percent (1,000 coins backing 10,000 receipts) and a money supply of 10,000 receipts. Or he could even lend out 100,000, bringing the reserve ratio down to 1 percent (1,000 coins backing up 100,000 receipts) and a money supply of 100,000 receipts.

The system worked as long as the goldsmiths did not get too greedy.

The system worked as long as the goldsmiths did not get too greedy and as long as the depositors maintained their confidence in their goldsmith's ability to redeem his receipts in gold coins. But, from time to time, individual goldsmiths just went too far in lending out money, whether in the form of gold coins or receipts. When depositors began to notice so many receipts in circulation, they asked themselves if the goldsmith could possibly have enough coins in his safe to redeem all those receipts. And when they thought he might not, they rushed into town to withdraw their gold coins before everyone else tried to.

If too many people reached the same conclusion, a panic ensued and the goldsmith could not possibly meet the demands of his depositors. In effect, then, he went bankrupt, and those left holding his receipts found them worthless. Of course, that was all before the days of the Federal Deposit Insurance Corporation (FDIC), so there was no one to turn to.

Modern Banking

Like the early goldsmiths, today's bankers don't keep 100 percent reserve backing for their deposits. If a bank kept all its deposits in its vault, it would lose money from the day it opened. The whole idea of banking is to borrow cheap and lend dear. The more you lend, the more profits you make.

Banks like to keep about 2 percent of their deposits in the form of vault cash. As long as their depositors maintain confidence in the banks—or at least in the FDIC—there is really no need to keep more than 2 percent on reserve.

Unhappily for the banks, however, they are generally required to keep a lot more than 2 percent of their deposits on reserve. All the nation's 15,000 commercial banks, as well as the 18,000 credit unions, 3,000 savings and loan associations, and 400 savings banks, now have to keep up to 12 percent of their checking deposits and up to 3 percent of their savings deposits on reserve. (See Table 13–1 in the next chapter.)

Banking today is not all that different from the banking conducted by the goldsmiths back in the Middle Ages. Of course today's bankers all have the Federal Reserve looking over their shoulders, not to mention the state banking authorities and the FDIC. Why all this regulation? Basically because people want to know that their money is safe.

The Federal Deposit Insurance Corporation

After the massive bank failures of the 1930s, Congress set up the FDIC, another case of closing the barn door after the horses had run off. This organization taxes its members $\frac{1}{12}$ of 1 percent of their deposits in exchange for insuring all member bank deposits of up to $100,000. The amount insured has progressively been raised, the last time in 1980, when the ceiling was raised from $40,000.

The whole idea of the FDIC

The whole idea of the FDIC is to avert bank panics by assuring the public that the federal government stands behind their bank, ready to pay off depositors if their bank should fail. The very fact that the government is ready to do this has apparently provided enough confidence in the banking system to avoid any situation that could lead to widespread panic.

Until 1977 when Franklin National, then the nation's 20th largest commercial bank, went under, the FDIC had never had to pay out more than $100 million a year to depositors. Since then, however, things have grown a lot worse, particularly with large savings banks, many of which are in the New York area.

The FDIC prefers takeovers to payoffs.

The FDIC would rather have another bank take over an ailing institution than be forced to pay off its depositors. Often, to encourage such takeovers, the FDIC will actually give the cooperatiang bank up to several hundred million dollars to take certain white elephants off its hands.

The FDIC has reluctantly acquired certain assets from failed banks it has had some trouble disposing of. It has held 960 acres of almond groves (in the form of the U.S. National Bank of San Diego), a $40,000 Koran (Moslem bible), courtesy of the Northern Bank of Cleveland, and even part ownership in *The Happy Hooker* (a film acquired in the Franklin National debacle).[6]

All told, federal government institutions insure over $3 trillion in risks. Everything from crops and crime to overseas investments and stockbroker bankruptcies is covered. All these programs underlie the old business adage, without risk there can be no gain. Some critics feel, however, that the federal government is taking the risks and private individuals are making all the gains.

Will the FDIC run out of money? *yes*

Is the FDIC in any danger of running out of money? Although it has over $18 billion on hand, a few more Franklin Nationals or First Chicagos[7] could wipe out this money in no time flat. However, the Federal Reserve, the Treasury, and all the financial resources of the U.S. government are committed to the preservation of this institution.

Over 99 percent of all banks are members of the FDIC. If you want to make sure that yours is, first check to see if there's a sign in the window attesting to this fact. If there isn't, ask inside, and if the answer is no, then very calmly walk up to the teller and withdraw all your money.

Less familiar than the FDIC is the Federal Savings and Loan Insurance Corporation (FSLIC), which, as its name indicates, insures the shares, or deposits, of savings and loan associations.[8] Nearly all credit union deposits as well are insured. This means that your money is safe and that we will probably never have a repetition of what happened back in 1930s when there were runs on the banks, culminating in the Great Depression.

Branch Banking and Bank Chartering

Branch Banking versus Unit Banking

Banking is legally defined as accepting deposits. Branch banking, therefore, would be the acceptance of deposits at more than one location. Since interstate banking is not (yet) legal, branch banking rules are set by the state in which a bank is located. Bank of America, for example, is subject to California banking law, while Citibank and Chase Manhattan are regulated by New York banking law.

law mean bank anywhere in state,

There are three types of branch banking that have evolved under various state laws. First there is unrestricted branch banking, under which a bank may open branches throughout the state. Bank of America, Crocker National Bank, and Wells Fargo have branches all over California.

Three types of branch banking:
(1) Unrestricted branching
(2) Limited branching
(3) Unit banking
(no-branches)

A second variation is restricted, or limited, branch banking. For example, a bank may be allowed to open branches only in contiguous communities. What is permissible varies from state to state.

Finally, there is unit banking. State law forbids any branching whatsoever. A bank that opens an office that receives deposits at a particular location cannot open any other branches. This obviously restricts the size of banks in those states. In fact, banks in unit banking states are, on the aver-

---

[6] See Shirley Hobbs Scheibla, "Call in the Reserves?" *Barron's*, March 8, 1982.

[7] First Chicago, once one of the nation's 15 largest banks, was bailed out in 1986.

[8] The FSLIC did run out of money in 1987, but Congress passed a law providing $10.8 billion. As of mid-1988, it became apparent that at least an additional $25 billion would soon be needed.

age, about one fifth the size of banks in states that permit unrestricted branching.

Right now two out of five states, nearly all in the East and Far West, have unlimited branching. Another two out of five states, mainly in the Midwest and the South, allow limited branching. And finally, the remaining states, mostly in the Midwest, permit only unit banking.

State and Nationally Chartered Banks

Most banks have state charters.

large bank N.

To operate a bank, you must get a charter. More than two thirds of the nation's banks have state charters; the rest have national charters. National charters are issued by the Comptroller of the Currency and are generally harder to obtain than state charters. The second are issued by each of the 50 states.

To get a bank charter you need to demonstrate three things: (1) that your community needs a bank or an additional bank; (2) that you have enough capital to start a bank; and (3) that you are of good character.

Most large banks are nationally chartered. Often the word *national* will appear in their names, for example, First National City Bank or Mellon National Bank. Incidentally, all nationally chartered banks must join the Federal Reserve. State banks may join, but few have been doing so and many have left because of the high reserve requirements.

To summarize, all nationally chartered banks must join the Federal Reserve System. All Federal Reserve member banks must join the FDIC. Only a small percentage of the state-chartered banks are members of the Federal Reserve. Nearly all banks are members of the FDIC.

The Creation and Destruction of Money

The Creation of Money

Banks create money by making loans.

Money consists of checking deposits and currency in the hands of the public. To create money, banks must increase either currency held by the public or checking deposits. The way the banks do this is by making loans.

A businessman will walk into Bank of America and request a loan for $10,000. Later that day he calls the bank to find out if his loan is granted. Since he already has a checking account at Bank of America, the bank merely adds $10,000 to his balance. In return he signs a form promising to pay back the loan with interest on a specified date. That's it. Money has been created. Checking deposits have just increased by $10,000.

If, for some reason, the businessman had asked to be paid in cash, the public would have held $10,000 more in currency. And the bank? The $10,000 it gave away was merely inventory; it was not counted as part of our money supply.

The point is that the bank just created $10,000. Whether demand deposits or currency held by the public rose by that amount, our money supply rose by $10,000.

The Destruction of Money

He who creates can usually destroy as well. That's what happens when the businessman pays back his loan. He'll probably write a check on his account for $10,000 plus the interest that he owes and when the bank deducts that amount from his account, down goes the money supply. Or, if he pays back the loan in cash, again—down goes the money supply. In this case the currency leaves the hands of the public (literally) and goes into the bank's inventory. The bank will stamp the loan agreement form "paid" and the transaction is completed.

The creation and destruction of money is a major function of banking. The basic way this is done is through loans. The most important commercial bank loans are commercial and industrial loans, although consumer loans have grown considerably in importance since World War II.

Money is destroyed when a loan is repaid to the bank.

Limits to Deposit Creation

Since most bank loans involve giving the borrower an additional deposit in his checking account, it would appear that banks could create all the money they wanted by doing this. All you need is a simple bookkeeping operation. A $20,000 loan means you increase that customer's account by $20,000—on paper or by an entry into a computer.

Remember the goldsmith who kept writing receipts until there were 1,000 gold coins in his safe backing 100,000 receipts? Why can't bankers keep issuing loans by increasing the checking accounts of their customers?

The first limit would be prudence. Most banks would try to keep about 2 percent of their demand deposits on reserve in the form of vault cash. Just in case some of their depositors came in to cash checks, there would be enough money on hand to pay them. Thus, if left to their own devices, bankers would expand their loans only up to the point at which they had just 2 percent cash reserves, or a reserve ratio of 2 percent. Of course, most bankers would more prudently reserve ratios of 3 or 4 percent.

But no banker has that choice. The Federal Reserve sets legal requirements to which the banks must adhere, and as we have already mentioned, these limits are substantially higher than those that might be set by the most prudent of bankers.

workbook for Chapter 12
multiple choice Question =

Workbook for Chapter 12

Name _____

Date _____

Multiple-Choice Questions

Circle the letter that corresponds to the best answer.

1. Each of the following except ___d___ is a job of the money supply.

a. medium of exchange   **b.** store of value   **c.** standard of value   **d.** receipt for gold

2. Using the same choices as in question 1, which is the most important job of money?

3. The basic alternative to money in the United States would be

a. gold   **b.** barter   **c.** stealing   **d.** the underground economy

4. Barter involves

a. money   **b.** specialization   **c.** a double coincidence of wants   **d.** demand deposits

5. Which one of the following is not part of our money supply?

a. dollar bills   **b.** demand deposits   **c.** traveler's checks   **d.** gold

6. Which statement is true?

a. M1 is larger than M2.   **b.** M1 + M2 = M3.   **c.** M2 + large-denomination time deposits = M3.   **d.** M1 × M2 = M3.

7. Which statement is true?

a. Checks are not money.   **b.** A small part of our money supply is silver certificates.   **c.** Most of our money supply is in the form of currency.   **d.** None of these statements is true.

8. The dollar is based on _____ currency.

a. British   **b.** French   **c.** Dutch   **d.** Spanish

9. Which is not in M2?

a. currency   **b.** demand deposits   **c.** small-denomination time deposits   **d.** large-denomination time deposits

10. Which statement is true?

a. Credit cards are a form of money.   **b.** M1 is closer to the size of M2 than M2 is to the size of M3.   **c.** M2 is about four times the size of M1.   **d.** M3 is about $2 trillion.

11. MV = PQ _(equation) must balance_

a. all the time   **b.** most of the time   **c.** some of the time   **d.** never

12. The output of our economy is represented by the letter _____ in the equation of exchange.

a. M   **b.** V   **c.** P   **d.** Q

13. If MV rises, PQ

a. must rise   **b.** may rise   **c.** must stay the same   **d.** must fall

14. The crude quantity theory of money states that if MV rises by 20 percent, PQ will

a. fall by 20 percent   **b.** fall   **c.** stay the same   **d.** rise   **e.** rise by 20 percent.

15. The modern monetarists believe that

a. V is very unstable   **b.** V never changes   **c.** any changes in V are either very small or predictable   **d.** if M rises, V will fall by the same percentage

16. As we approach full employment, what will probably happen?

a. V will fall   **b.** Q will fall   **c.** Q will rise   **d.** P will rise   **e.** P will fall

17. John Maynard Keynes identified three motives for holding money. Which one listed below did Keynes not identify?

a. transactions   **b.** precautionary   **c.** psychological   **d.** speculative

18. As the price level rises, the transactions demand for money

a. rises   **b.** falls   **c.** remains about the same

As the

19. As the interest rate rises, the quantity of money demanded

a. rises   **b.** falls   **c.** remains about the same

20. People tend to hold more money as

a. incomes rise and credit availability rises

b. incomes fall and credit availability falls

c. incomes rise and credit availability falls

d. incomes fall and credit availability rises

21. The distinction between commercial banks and other banks is

a. very clear   **b.** becoming blurred   **c.** nonexistent

d. none of these

22. Banking began in

a. biblical times   **b.** medieval times   **c.** the 19th century   **d.** the 20th century

23. What led to the bankruptcy of many goldsmiths was that they

a. had a reserve ratio that was too high   **b.** had a reserve ratio that was too low   **c.** lent out gold coins instead of receipts   **d.** lent out receipts instead of gold coins

24. Bankers would like to hold a reserve ratio of about

a. 2 percent   **b.** 10 percent   **c.** 50 percent   **d.** 100 percent

25. Which statement is true?

a. Most financial institutions are commercial banks.

b. There are currently less than 1,000 commercial banks in the United States.   **c.** Nearly all banks today are regulated by both the Federal Reserve and the FDIC.   **d.** About half the banks in the United States are members of the FDIC.

26. Which statement is false?

a. About 99 percent of all banks are members of the FDIC.   **b.** If the FDIC runs out of money, the federal government will supply it with more funds.

c. The FDIC would rather have another bank take over an ailing institution than be forced to pay off its depositors.   **d.** None of these statements is false.

27. Which statement is true?

a. Most states allow only unit banking.   **b.** Most states allow unlimited branching.   **c.** Most banks have national charters.   **d.** None of these statements is true.

28. To get a bank charter you need to demonstrate each of the following except

a. that your community needs a bank or an additional bank   **b.** that you have sufficient banking experience   **c.** that you have enough capital to start a bank   **d.** that you are of good character

29. Money is created when someone

a. takes out a bank loan   **b.** pays back a bank loan

c. spends money   **d.** saves money

30. Bank deposit creation is limited by

a. reserve requirements   **b.** the interest rate

c. whether a bank is nationally or state chartered

d. whether a bank is in a large city or a rural area

Fill-In Questions

1. The most important job of money is as <handwriting>medium exchange.</handwriting> The other two jobs of money are <handwriting>Store of value</handwriting> and Standard of value.

The job money performs the most poorly is as _____.

2. The alternative to money would be _____.

To do this, you would need a _____

_____.

3. The three main components of our money supply are (1) _____, (2) _____, and (3) _____.

4. The U.S. dollar is based on the _____.

5. The basic function of credit cards is _____

_____.

6. To get from M2 to M3 we add _____.

7. M2 is about _____ times the size of M1.

8. Another name for checking deposits is _____. How did they get this name? _____

_____.

9. The equation of exchange is _____ = _____.

10. The crude quantity theory of money is _____

_____.

11. The sophisticated quantity theory of money is ___

_____.

12. The interest rate is set by *Supply* and *demand*

_____.

13. The total demand for money is the sum of the
(1) _____ demand, (2) the _____ demand, and the
(3) _____ demand for money.

14. The four main influences on the amount of
money that people tend to hold are (1) *Interest rise*
(2) *inflation* (3) *income fall*, and (4) *Credit availabty rise*

15. John Maynard Keynes identified the following
three motives to explain why people hold money:
(1) *Transation*, (2) *precautionary*, and (3) *speculative*.

16. People tend to hold more money as *Interest* and
inflation rises; they tend to hold less money as
income and *credit availabty* rises.

17. People hold more money for their *Transative*
motive than for the other two motives.

18. According to Keyne's liquidity trap, at very low

interest rates people would _____.

19. The world's first bankers were the _____.

20. Modern banking was born when the first bankers
noticed two things: (1) *they didnt retrieve Identical coins*
and (2) *paying debt in reciept*
didn't come in and get coin

21. The world's first paper money was in the form of

_____.

22. If a goldsmith had 100 gold coins sitting in his
safe and lent out 50 of them, this would imply a reserve ratio of _____ percent.

23. The bankruptcy of the goldsmiths who lent out
part of the gold they were safekeeping was caused by

_____.

24. Most bankers today would like to hold a reserve
of about *28* percent.

25. Banks are very heavily regulated. The main reason for this is that _____.

26. The FDIC insures all bank deposits of up to
$_____ in member banks.

27. The FDIC raises its funds by _____.

28. Right now the FDIC has about $_____ in re-
serve in case of future bank failures.

29. Rather than pay off depositors of a failed bank,
the FDIC would prefer that _____.

30. About _____ percent of the states allow only unit
banking.

31. About _____ percent of all banks have state
charters.

32. The main way that banks create money is by

_____; the main way that money is destroyed is

when _____.

Problems

1. If M were 600 and V were 10, how much would
PQ be?

2. According to the crude quantity theory of money,
if M were to increase by 10 percent, what would happen to V, P, and Q?

3. If M were 800, P were 20, and Q were 400, how
much would V be?

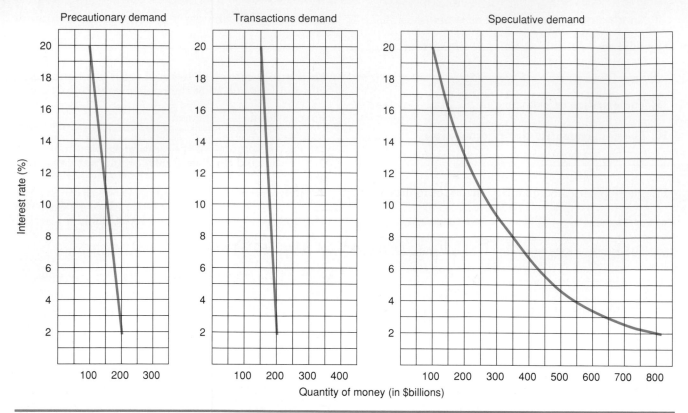

Figure 1

4. Given the information in Figure 1, use Figure 2 to draw a graph of the total demand curve for money.

5. If M were 600, how much would the interest rate be?

6. If M2 were 2,500, small-denomination time deposits were 250, and large-denomination time deposits were 300, how much would M3 be?

7. *a.* A goldsmith has 1,000 gold coins in his safe and 1,000 receipts circulating. How much are his outstanding loans and what is his reserve ratio?
b. The goldsmith then lends out 100 of the coins. What is his reserve ratio?

8. A goldsmith has 100 gold coins in his safe. If there are 500 receipts in circulation, how much is his reserve ratio?

9. *a.* A banker lends a businesswoman $100,000. How does this affect the money supply?
b. The businesswoman pays back the loan. How does this affect the money supply?

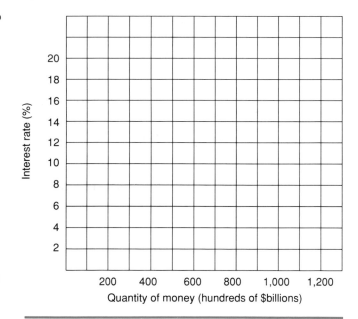

Figure 2

Chapter

13

The Federal Reserve and Monetary Policy

In the first part of the chapter we'll examine the organization and management of the Federal Reserve System (the Fed), especially how it uses open-market operations, changes in the discount rate, and changes in reserve requirements to control the rate of growth of the money supply.

The goals of monetary policy are price stability, relatively full employment, and a satisfactory rate of economic growth. If you go back to the first page of Chapter 11, you'll see that the goals of fiscal and monetary policy are identical. The melodies are the same, but the lyrics are quite different. Fiscal policy is the manipulation of the federal budget while monetary policy controls the rate of growth of the money supply.

Chapter Objectives

The main topics of this chapter are:
- The organization of the Federal Reserve System.
- The deposit expansion multiplier.
- The tools of monetary policy.
- The Fed's effectiveness in fighting inflation and recession.)
- The Banking Act of 1980.

The Federal Reserve System

Unlike most other industrial nations, the United States was without a central bank until 1913.[1] While the Bank of England and the Bank of France acted as the central banking authority, we were left defenseless when financial panics set in. Every few years in the 1880s, 1890s, and early 1900s, financial crises developed and eventually receded until, finally, we had the Panic of 1907.

---

[1] There had been a First United States Bank (1791–1811) and a Second United States Bank (1816–36), but the charters of both had been allowed to lapse, mainly for political reasons.

During this panic people rushed to their banks to take out their money, and business was severely disrupted. The public demanded that the government take steps to prevent this from ever happening again. After six years of intermittent debate, Congress finally passed the Federal Reserve Act of 1913. One of the hopes of its framers was that the 12 Federal Reserve district banks would, at times of crisis, act as a "lender of last resort." In other words, if the bankers were caught with their pants down, someone stood ready to give them a little time to get their affairs back in order.

The Federal Reserve District Banks

The 12 Federal Reserve district banks

There are 12 Federal Reserve District Banks, one in each of the nation's Federal Reserve districts. These are shown in the map in Figure 13–1. Each of these banks prints currency to accommodate the business needs of its district. For example, all the currency issued by the Boston Federal Reserve District Bank in the First District has an *A* on the face side of the bill about an inch and a half from the left side. Currency issued by the Second Federal Reserve District Bank in New York has a *B* while the Philadelphia Bank in the Third District has a *C*.

Each of the Federal Reserve District Banks is owned by the several hundred member banks in that district. A commercial bank becomes a member

Figure 13–1
The Federal Reserve System

by buying stock in the Federal Reserve District Bank. However, effective control is really exercised by the Federal Reserve Board of Governors in Washington.

The Board of Governors

The 7 members of the Federal Reserve Board

This group of seven members is nominated by the president, subject to confirmation by the Senate. Each is appointed for one 14-year term and is ineligible to serve a second term. The terms are staggered so that vacancies occur every two years. That way, in every four-year term, a president appoints two members to the Board of Governors.

The chairman of the board, who generally exercises considerable influence, serves a four-year term, which is part of his 14-year tenure as a member of the board. He is also appointed by the president and may serve more than one term as chairman.

Independence of the Board of Governors

Should the Board of Governors be controlled by or answerable to anyone else?

Does the president "control" the Board of Governors and its chairman? The answer is, "generally, no." First, unless there is a vacancy caused by death or resignation, the president would have to serve two terms to appoint four members to the Board.[2] Second, once someone is appointed to the Board, there is no reason to expect that person to do the president's bidding.

The president does get to appoint a chairman sometime during his term. However, Jimmy Carter had to deal with Arthur Burns (Richard Nixon's appointee) for the first part of his term, and Ronald Reagan did not always see eye-to-eye with Jimmy Carter's appointee, Paul Volcker. There have been proposals that the president be allowed to appoint his own chairman at the beginning of his term so that monetary and fiscal policy can be coordinated, but no action has been taken thus far.

Once a Board member or chairman is confirmed by the Senate, he or she[3] is not answerable to the president or Congress. Although the chairman is legally required to make an annual report to Congress, he is free to stand before that body and tell them, "We have completely defied your wishes. You wanted us to increase the money supply and we lowered it. You wanted interest rates to drop and they've gone up. That is our report."

Of course things are a lot more cordial between the Fed and Congress and between the Fed and the president, but the bottom line remains that the Federal Reserve is an independent agency. There are those who feel that for a group of unelected officials, the members of the Board have too much power. When interest rates soar or inflation rages out of control, these rascals cannot be turned out of office by an angry electorate. About all we can do is hope that over time, better people will be appointed to the Board.

Others feel that the hard unpopular monetary policy decisions must be made by those who are insulated from the wrath of the voters. Tight money is hardly a popular policy, but when the Federal Reserve decides to follow this policy because they think it will help control inflation, why should they be inhibited by fears of political reprisal?

---

[2] Because of a slew of resignations, President Reagan was able to appoint all seven members in his first seven years in office. Interestingly, two of those who resigned did so because the president would not promise them the chairmanship.

[3] Nancy Teeters, appointed by President Carter, and Margaret Seeger, appointed by President Reagan, both economists, are the only women to have served.

Of course the members of the Board of Governors are not immune to the reactions of their fellow citizens, but it is obvious that their independence permits them to follow unpopular policies if they feel that doing so is in the best economic interest of the nation. Attempts have been made in recent years to make the Federal Reserve Board more responsive to the wishes of Congress and the administration, but none has been successful.

Legal Reserve Requirements

The most important job of the Federal Reserve

The Federal Reserve has various jobs, the most important of which is to control our money supply. When it was set up in 1913, the framers of the Federal Reserve Act envisaged the Fed as a "lender of last resort." Obviously the record of widespread bank failures in the early 1930s is a sad commentary on how well the Fed was able to do that job.

Before we consider how the Fed works today, we will look at the focal point of the Federal Reserve's control of our money supply—legal reserve requirements. Every financial institution in the country is legally required to hold a certain percentage of its deposits on reserve, either in the form of deposits at its Federal Reserve District bank or in its own vaults. Since neither Federal Reserve deposits nor vault cash pays interest, no one is very happy about holding 12 percent of most demand deposits on reserve (see Table 13-1).

Table 13–1
Legal Reserve Requirements, May 1987*

Checking accounts:	
$0–$40.5 million*	3 percent
Over $40.5 million	12
Time deposits:	
By original maturity	
Less than 18 months	3 percent
18 months or more	0

* Effective December 29, 1983, this amount was raised from $26.3 million to $28.9 million; on January 1, 1985, to $29.8 million; effective December 31, 1985, to $31.7 million; effective December 30, 1986, the amount was increased to $36.7 million; and effective December 29, 1987, the amount was increased to $40.5 million.
Source: *Federal Reserve Bulletin*, April 1988, p. A9.

The passage of the Monetary Control Act of 1980 (which will be discussed in detail toward the end of this chapter) called for uniform reserve requirements for all financial institutions—commercial banks, savings banks, savings and loan associations, money market mutual funds, and credit unions. Until 1987, when the uniform reserve requirements were fully phased in, only Federal Reserve member banks, about 5,000 in number, were subject to relatively high reserve requirements. The other 30,000 or so of the nation's financial institutions were subject to much lower requirements.

You'll also notice in Table 13-1 that the reserve requirements for time deposits are much lower than for checking accounts. This is so because the first tend to be left in banks for relatively longer periods of time while those that will be held on deposit for more than 18 months have no reserve requirement at all.

Primary and Secondary Reserves

What are the three main aims of bankers?

Bankers are, if nothing else, prudent. Their main aims, other than making high profits, are to protect their depositors and to maintain liquidity. Liquidity is the ability to quickly convert assets into cash without loss.

Even without legal reserve requirements, bankers would have kept some cash on reserve to meet the day-to-day needs of their depositors as well as to meet any unforeseen large withdrawals. The cash that banks *do* keep on hand, together with their deposits at the Federal Reserve District banks, are sometimes called primary reserves. In addition, every bank holds secondary reserves, mainly in the form of very short-term U.S. government securities.

Treasury bills, notes, certificates, and bonds (that will mature in less than a year) are generally considered a bank's secondary reserves. These can quickly be converted to cash without loss if a bank suddenly needs money, whether because of increased withdrawals or perhaps a shortage of primary reserves. Generally, in the case of a shortage of primary reserves, a bank will borrow on a daily basis from other banks in the federal funds market. Another source of short-term funds is the Federal Reserve district bank's discount window.

Deposit Expansion

How Deposit Expansion Works

To see how deposit expansion works, we'll assume a 10 percent reserve ratio because that's an easy number with which to work. Suppose someone comes into a bank and deposits $100,000.

We know that banks don't like to have any idle reserves because they don't earn any interest on them. So what does the bank do with the $100,000? It lends out as much as it can.

With a 10 percent reserve requirement, the bank can lend out $90,000. To keep matters simple, we'll assume the $90,000 was lent to a single company. The bank added $90,000 to the company's checking account by making an entry in its computer.

Normally the bank would need an additional $9,000 in reserves to cover the new $90,000 demand deposit. But why did the company borrow $90,000? Obviously it was needed for certain business expanses; no one pays interest on borrowed money just to sit on it.

Again, keeping things simple, suppose this company wrote a check for $90,000 to pay for additional inventory. The company receiving the check deposits it in its bank and again, the process is repeated. The bank keeps the required 10 percent ($9,000) on reserve and lends out the remaining $81,000. This money is spent and eventually deposited in a third bank, which keeps 10 percent ($8,100) on reserve, and lends out $72,900.

We could go on and on. Indeed, we have in Table 13–2. Were we to continue the process with an infinite number of banks, we would eventually end up with $1 million in deposits and $100,000 in reserves.

The Deposit Expansion Multiplier

Remember the multiplier in Chapter 8? Now we'll look at the deposit expansion multiplier, which is based on the same principle and nearly the same formula.

Table 13–2
Hypothetical Deposit Expansion with
10 Percent Reserve Requirement

Deposits	Reserves
$ 100,000.00	$ 10,000.00
90,000.00	9,000.00
81,000.00	8,100.00
72,900.00	7,290.00
65,610.00	6,561.00
59,049.00	5,904.90
53,541.00	5,354.10
48,186.90	4,818.69
43,368.21	4,336.82
39,031.39	3,903.14
35,128.25	3,512.83
31,615.43	3,161.54
28,453.89	2,845.39
25,608.50	2,560.85
23,047.65	2,304.76
20,742.89	2,074.29
18,668.60	1,866.86
16,812.00	1,681.20
15,130.80	1,513.08
13,617.72	1,361.77
—	—
—	—
—	—
$1,000,000.00	$100,000.00

Any new money injected into the banking system will have a multiplied effect on the money supply. How large this multiplied effect will be depends on the size of the multiplier. In general, when the reserve ratio is low, the multiplier will be high and vice versa.

The formula for the deposit expansion multiplier is:

Deposit expansion multiplier $= \dfrac{1}{\text{Reserve ratio}}$

$$\frac{1}{\text{Reserve ratio}}$$

If the reserve ratio is .10, to find the multiplier we substitute and solve:

$$\frac{1}{\text{Reserve ratio}} = \frac{1}{.10} = 10$$

Remember, how many dimes are in a dollar?

If the reserve ratio is .25, find the deposit expansion multiplier. Do it right here.

Using the formula, we get:

$$\frac{1}{\text{Reserve ratio}} = \frac{1}{.25} = 4$$

How many times does .25 go into 1? How many times does a quarter go into a dollar?

Check Clearing

If you have a checking account at your local bank, at the end of each month you receive a statement listing all your deposits and withdrawals. The withdrawals are more numerous than the deposits because every time you write a check, that money is withdrawn from your account. Together with your statement, your bank encloses a pile of checks you wrote that month.

Did you ever wonder how, if you wrote a check, it ended up with your statement at the end of the month? No? Well, I'm going to tell you anyway. The whole process is called check clearing, and it is a service provided by the Federal Reserve System.

In 1976 we had a series of birthday parties for the nation. You might remember that America was 200 years old that year. I was visiting some friends out in San Francisco at the time and one of them, Bob, sold me a beat-up old bugle, which actually *looked* like it might have dated back to the American Revolution.

This bugle has come in quite handy in my 8 A.M. classes. At the time I bought it, though, the big question was how I would pay for it. I didn't have $50 in cash I could spare. But what was really good about Bob was that he took out-of-state checks.

I gave Bob my check for $50. It was written on Manufacturers Hanover back in Brooklyn. Bob deposited it in his account at Bank of America. From there it went to Bank of America's main office in San Francisco, which, in turn, sent it on to the San Francisco Federal Reserve District Bank. Bank of America's reserves were raised by $50 (the amount of the check). Doing this was a simple bookkeeping operation.

The check was sent to the New York Federal Reserve District Bank, which deducted $50 from the reserves of Manufacturers Hanover. The check then went to Manufacturers Hanover's main office on Park Avenue in Manhattan and then to my branch out on Flatbush Avenue in Brooklyn. The $50 was then deducted from my account and at the end of the month, the canceled check was mailed to me with my statement.

All of these transactions are shown pictorially in the diagram below. As you can see, the check I gave Bob in San Francisco was sent back to me by my Brooklyn bank with my statement at the end of the month.

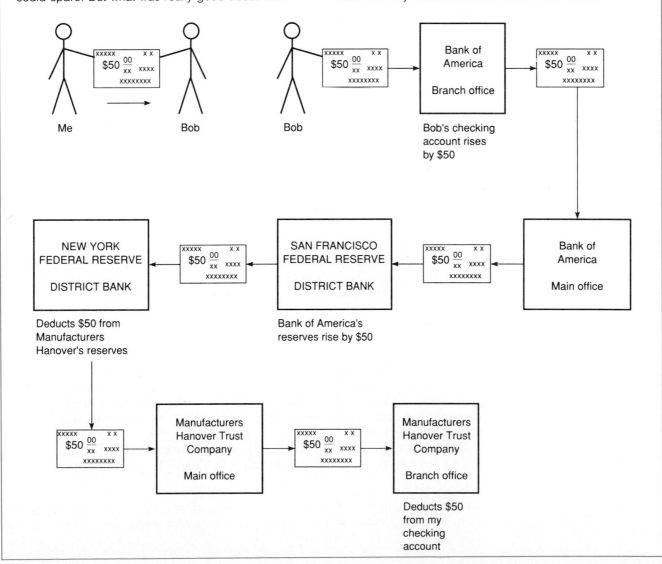

Three Modifications of the Deposit Expansion Multiplier

Not every dollar of deposit expansion will actually be redeposited again and lent out repeatedly. Some people may choose to hold or spend some of their money as currency. For example, an individual receiving a $300 check may deposit $200 and receive $100 back as cash.

This cash leakage tends to cut down on the deposit expansion multiplier because not all the money lent out is redeposited. For example, if $90,000 is lent out but only $81,000 is redeposited, this would have the same effect on the multiplier as a 10 percent increase in the reserve ratio.

It is also possible, although not very likely in times of inflation, for banks to carry excess reserves. To the degree that they do, however, this cuts down on the deposit expansion multiplier. Why? Because it, in effect, raises the reserve ratio. For example, if the reserve ratio rose from .20 to .25 because banks were carrying a 5 percent excess reserve, the multiplier would fall from 5 ($\frac{1}{2} = 5$) to 4 ($\frac{1}{25} = 4$).

Currency leakages do take place, especially during times of recession and low interest rates. During such times it is quite possible for banks to carry excess reserves. One might also keep in mind that during recessions banks might carry excess reserves because of a scarcity of creditworthy borrowers.

Finally there are leakages of dollars to foreign countries caused mainly by our foreign trade imbalance. Since our imports far exceed our exports, there is a large drain of dollars to foreigners. Some of these dollars return to the United States in the form of various investments (particularly in U.S. government securities, corporate securities, and real estate), but there is a definite net outflow of dollars, which, in turn, depresses still further the deposit expansion multiplier.

Where does all this leave us? It leaves us with the conclusion that the deposit expansion multiplier is, in reality, quite a bit lower than it would be if we calculated it solely based on the reserve ratio. In other words, if the reserve ratio tells us it's 10, perhaps it's only 6.

The Tools of Monetary Policy

The goals of monetary policy were outlined at the beginning of the chapter. To attain these goals, the Fed regulates the rate of growth of the nation's money supply. This effort focuses on the reserves held by financial institutions. The most important policy tool used by the Fed to control reserves, and indirectly, the money supply, is open-market operations.

How Open-Market Operations Work

What are open-market operations?

Open-market operations are buying and selling of U.S. government securities in the open market. What are U.S. government securities? They are Treasury bills, notes, certificates, and bonds. The Fed does not market new securities.[4] That's the Treasury's job. Rather, the Fed buys and sells securities that have already been marketed by the Treasury, some of which might be several years old.

The total value of all outstanding U.S. government securities is approaching $3 trillion. If this number is familiar, it should be; it's our national debt.

---

[4] The Fed is legally limited to buying no more than $5 billion in newly issued government securities a year, which is less than 1 percent of what the Treasury issues.

Many students are under the misconception that the Federal Reserve sells newly issued securities for the Treasury, but all it does is buy and sell chunks of the national debt.

What open-market operations consists of then, is the buying and selling of chunks of the national debt. The Fed does this by dealing with government bond houses, which are private bond dealers. If the Fed wants to buy, say, $100 million worth of Treasury notes that will mature within the next three months, it places an order with a few of these bond houses, which then buy up the securities for the Fed. When the Fed wants to sell securities, again they go to the government bond houses and have them do the actual selling.

How the Fed increases the money supply

When the Fed wants to increase the money supply, it goes into the open market and buys U.S. government securities. You might ask, "What if people don't want to sell"? Remember the line from *The Godfather*, "I'll make you an offer you can't refuse"? Well, that's exactly what the Fed does. It tells the government bond houses, "Buy us 30,000 Treasury bills no matter what the price."

If the Fed goes on a buying spree in the open market, it will quickly drive up the prices of U.S. government securities. One by-product of all this buying is that it will push down interest rates. Let's see why.

Suppose a bond was issued by the Treasury with a face value of $1,000 and an interest rate of 8 percent. This means the bond costs the initial buyer $1,000 and pays $80 a year interest. The price of the bond will fluctuate considerably over its life, but when it matures the Treasury must pay the owner $1,000, its face value. And every year the Treasury must pay the owner $80 interest.

Using the formula

$$\text{Interest rate} = \frac{\text{Interest paid}}{\text{Price of bond}}$$

We can observe that a $1,000 bond paying $80 interest pays an interest rate of 8 percent:

$$\frac{\$80}{\$1,000} = 8 \text{ percent}$$

We had been talking about the Fed going into the open market and buying government securities. Suppose the Fed bought enough securities to bid up their price to $1,200. Remember that these securities still pay $80 a year interest. Let's calculate their new interest rate:

$$\text{Interest rate} = \frac{\text{Interest paid}}{\text{Price of bond}} = \frac{\$80}{\$1,200} = 6\frac{2}{3} \text{ percent}$$

As we predicted, when the Fed goes into the open market to buy securities, it bids up the price of securities and lowers their interest rates. In the process, as we shall soon see, this also expands the money supply.

How the Fed contracts the money supply

When the Fed wants to contract the money supply, or at least slow down its rate of expansion, it goes into the open market and sells securities. In the process, it lowers bond prices and raises interest rates.

When selling securities, the Fed also uses the "Godfather principle." Again, it makes an offer that can't be refused, in this case, an offer to sell securities at low enough prices to get rid of a certain amount.

If the Fed bids bond prices down to $800, we use the same formula to find that the interest rate has risen to 10 percent.

$$\text{Interest rate} = \frac{\text{Interest paid}}{\text{Price of bond}} = \frac{\$80}{\$800} = \frac{1}{10} = 10 \text{ percent}$$

When the Fed sells securities on the open market to expand the money supply, bond prices fall and interest rates rise. Falling bond prices and rising interest rates generally accompany a tightening of the money supply.

We should add that although the Fed deals only with U.S. government securities, interest rates and bond prices move together in a broad range. When the Fed depresses the prices of U.S. government securities, all government and corporate bond prices tend to fall. And when the Fed pushes up the interest on U.S. government securities, all interest rates tend to rise.

Let's try another interest rate problem. What would be the interest rate on a bond that pays $100 a year in interest and is currently selling for $800? Work it out right here.

$$\text{Solution:} \quad \text{Interest rate} = \frac{\text{Interest paid}}{\text{Price of bond}} = \frac{\$100}{\$800} = 12.5 \text{ percent}$$

The Federal Open-Market Committee

Open-market operations are conducted by the Federal Open Market Committee (FOMC), which consists of 12 people. Eight are permanent members—the seven members of the Board of Governors and the president of the New York Federal Reserve District Bank. He is a permanent member because nearly all open-market purchases are made in the New York federal securities market. The other four members of the FOMC are presidents of each of the other 11 Federal Reserve District Banks; they serve on a rotating basis. Incidentally, when Paul Volcker, who had been serving as president of the New York Federal Reserve Bank, was appointed chairman of the Board of Governors by President Carter in 1979, he continued to serve on the FOMC, along with Anthony Solomon, the new president of the New York Bank.

How the open market operations are conducted

The FOMC meets about once every three weeks to decide what policy to follow. This is not to say that every three weeks the committee changes directions from buy to sell to buy again.

To fight recessions, the FOMC buys securities.

Assume the FOMC decides to ease credit a bit, perhaps because of the threat of a recession. They might decide to buy $100 million of securities on the open market. The New York Bank, as agent of the Federal Reserve, places an order with several government bond houses. The bonds are paid for by checks written on various Federal Reserve District Banks. Each of the government bond houses deposits the checks in its own commercial banks. From there the checks are sent to the New York Federal Reserve District Bank, which adds the amount of the checks to the banks' reserves.

Say, for example, the Fed gives a $10 million check to bond house number one, which deposits it in its account at Bankers Trust. From there the check is sent a few blocks away to the New York Federal Reserve District Bank, which adds $10 million to the reserves of Bankers Trust.

What does Bankers Trust do with $10 million of reserves? Assuming it now has excess reserves of $10 million, it will lend most of it out. Up goes the money supply! As we noted toward the end of the previous chapter, banks seldom keep excess reserves because they don't earn interest. Thus, we have a multiple expansion of deposits.

The process works the same way if the government bond houses are not the ultimate sellers of the securities. Usually those sellers are individuals, corporations, or banks. If an individual sells a $10,000 bond to the government bond house, which, in turn, sells it to the Fed, the government bond house is only the middleman. When the Fed pays the government bond house, this money will be turned over to the person who sold the bond. When he deposits his check at his local bank, say the National State Bank of New Jersey, the check will still be sent to the New York Federal Reserve District Bank. Ten thousand dollars will be added to the reserves of the National State Bank, which is now free to lend it out.

When banks lend out money, the money supply increases. When the Fed buys $100 million of securities, they are making $100 million worth of reserves available to the banking system. Most of this money will be lent out, and through the deposit expansion multiplier, it will create a multiplied deposit amount. For example, if the reserve ratio were 10 percent, the multiplier would be 10 (multiplier = 1/reserve ratio = $\frac{1}{10}$ = 10). However, allowing for currency leakages and bank holdings of some excess reserves, we'll say that the multiplier is actually only six. A $100 million open-market purchase will lead to about a $600 million expansion of deposits (and therefore a $600 million expansion of the money supply).

To fight inflation, the FOMC sells securities.

During periods of inflation, when the FOMC decides to sell securities, we have exactly the opposite set of events. If the FOMC were to give the government bond houses $100 million worth of securities with orders to sell them at whatever the market will bring, we can easily trace the steps.

Customers will be found and they will pay by check. For example, a corporation with an account at Fulton National Bank in Atlanta might buy $50,000 worth of securities. When its check reaches the Atlanta Federal Reserve District Bank, $50,000 is deducted from the reserves of Fulton National Bank. Similar reserve deductions occur around the country. Soon reserves for the entire banking system are reduced by $100 million.

That's just the first step. The banks will probably be short reserves since they carry little, if any, excess. Where do they get the money? They can borrow from their Federal Reserve District Bank's discount windows, but this will only tide them over temporarily, and it's something they're reluctant to do. They can go into the federal funds market, which is an overnight market in which banks borrow from each other on a day-to-day basis if they are short of reserves. But since most banks are short because of FOMC sales, this source of funds has become more stringent.

Utimately the banks will have to curb their loans, which is what the FOMC wanted all along. Initially, then, we would expect that $100 million less reserves will mean $100 million less in loans. But *had* those loans been made, with a multiplier of six, there would have been some $600 million worth of loans and the money supply would have been $600 million higher.

We're saying that if reserves are reduced by $100 million, this will, with a multiplier of six, ultimately reduce the money supply by $600 million. Or, put slightly differently, when reserves are reduced, the money supply will end up being lower than it would otherwise have been.

Are you ready to apply your knowledge of the monetary multiplier to determine the potential effect of the sale of some securities on the open market? Suppose the Fed buys $200 million of securites and the reserve ratio is 12 percent? By how much could our money supply increase?

Solution: $$\frac{\text{Excess}}{\text{reserves}} \times \frac{\text{Monetary}}{\text{multiplier}} = \frac{\text{Potential expansion of}}{\text{the money supply}}$$

$200 million $\times$ $^1\!/_{12}$ = $200 million $\times$ 8.3 = $1,660,000,000.[5]

Discount Rate Changes

The discount rate is the interest rate paid by member banks when they borrow at the Federal Reserve District Bank. The main reason why today's banks borrow is that they are having trouble maintaining their required reserves. In general, however, by resorting to the discount window, member banks are calling attention to their difficulties, perhaps inviting closer audits when they are visited by their Federal Reserve inspectors. Also, there is always the chance of being turned down for these loans.

How discounting works

The original intent of the Federal Reserve Act of 1913 was to have the district banks lend money to member banks to take care of seasonal business needs. In the busy period before Christmas, firms would borrow money from their banks, which would, in turn, borrow from the Federal Reserve District Banks. Borrowing then was really note discounting. You technically borrowed $1,000, but if the interest rate was 8 percent, the interest—$80 for a one-year loan—was deducted in advance. All you got was $920; you paid back $1,000.

This was called discounting. When the commercial banks took these IOUs or commercial paper to the Federal Reserve District Bank, they would borrow money to cover these loans. This was called rediscounting.

Today, banks no longer rediscount their commercial paper. Instead they borrow directly from the Federal Reserve, and call the interest they pay the discount rate. Although each of the 12 district banks sets its own discount rate, they agree virtually all the time—perhaps with an occasional prod from the Board of Governors—to charge the same rate.

Open-market operations are the day-to-day and most important policy weapon of the Fed. After selling securities in the open market and still not getting the banks to cut back enough on their loans, the Fed will raise the discount rate. Because, however, member banks don't borrow very heavily from the district banks, raising the discount rate is more of a symbolic gesture. Although discount rate changes do occasionally have some impact on the financial markets,[6] more often than not these changes merely reflect the Fed's desire to keep the discount rate in line with other interest rates.

---

[5] Because we rounded after one decimal, we got 8.3. If you rounded after four decimals, you would have gotten 8.3333, which would have given you a deposit expansion of $1,666,660,000.

[6] An unexpected rise in the discount rate sometimes causes about a 20-point drop in the Dow Jones Index of stock prices and a similar decline in the prices of bonds. Unexpected declines in the discount rate sometimes cause these markets to rally.

Changing Reserve Requirements

The Fed's ultimate weapon

A changing of reserve requirements is really the ultimate weapon of the Federal Reserve System. Like nuclear weapons, which are rarely if ever used, it's still nice to know that the mechanism is there.

The Federal Reserve Board has the power to change reserve requirements within legal limits, but in practice they do this only once every few years. The limits for checkable deposits are between 8 and 14 percent.[7] Before the Board takes this drastic step, it usually issues numerous warnings.

The discount rate will be raised by the district banks, often in a unison engineered by the Board of Governors. The FOMC will be actively selling securities; credit will be getting tighter; the chairman will be publicly warning the banks that they are advancing too many loans. This is called moral suasion, and like other appeals to morality, it rarely achieves the desired results (unless the Fed has been following President Teddy Roosevelt's advice: "Speak softly, but carry a big stick"). If this still doesn't do the job—if the banks are still advancing too many loans and if the money supply is still growing too rapidly—the Fed reaches for its biggest stick and raises reserve requirements. The last time this happened, in October 1980, the resulting credit crunch sent the prime rate of interest soaring above 20 percent as the economy plunged into the worst recession since the Great Depression.

Why does Fed rarely change reserve requirements?

The reason that this weapon is so rarely used is because it is simply too powerful. For example, if the Federal Reserve Board raised the reserve requirement on demand deposits by just one half of 1 percent, the nation's banks and thrift institutions would have to come up with over $5 billion in reserves.

Reserve requirements then are raised reluctantly by the Board of Governors, and only after all else fails. On the downside, however, when the economy is gripped by recession, the Fed is less reluctant to turn to its ultimate weapon; but even then, reserve requirement changes are a last resort.

Summary: the Tools of Monetary Policy

What are the three things the Fed can do to fight a recession? List them right here.

1. lower discount rate

2. buy securities on an open market

3. lower the reserve requirement

The answers are: (1) lower the discount rate, (2) buy securities on the open market, and, ultimately, if these two don't do the job, (3) lower reserve requirements.

What are the three things the Fed can do to fight inflation? List them here.

1. raise the discount rate
2. sell security on a open market

---

[7] If five members of the Board deem it desirable, the maximum can be raised to 18 percent, and if conditions are extraordinary, any rate whatsoever may be set.

3. raise the reserves on requirement

2.

3.

The answers are: (1) raise the discount rate, (2) sell securities on the open market, and, ultimately, if these two don't do the job, (3) raise reserve requirements.

b

The Fed's Effectiveness in Fighting Inflation and Recession

The Fed is more effective in fighting inflation than recession.

Cut off the supply of money putting the brakes on inflation

recession, you try to pump-up the Money Supply-1

Federal Reserve policy in fighting inflation and recession has been likened to pulling and then pushing on a string. Like pulling on a string, when the Fed fights inflation, it gets results—provided, of course, it pulls hard enough.

Fighting a recession is another matter. Like pushing on a string, no matter how hard the Fed works, it might not get anywhere.

First we'll consider fighting inflation. Assume all three basic policy tools have been used: securities have been sold on the open market, the discount rate has been raised, and ultimately, reserve requirements have been raised. The results are that bond prices have plunged, interest rates have soared, and money supply growth has been stopped dead in its tracks. Banks find it impossible to increase their loan portfolios. There's a credit crunch and there's credit rationing. Old customers can still borrow, but their credit lines are slashed. My own line of credit, for example, was cut by Citibank during the 1980 credit crunch from $3,500 to $500. New customers are nearly all turned away.

During times like these, the rate of inflation has got to decline. It's hard to raise prices when no one is buying anything. No one can buy because no one has any money. Of course, the Fed is somewhat reluctant to tighten up that much or to tighten up too long because such a policy generally brings on recessions.

The Fed has a far harder time dealing with a recession. Again, assume that the standard tools have been used: securities have been purchased on the open market, the discount rate has been lowered, and reserve requirements have been lowered. All this creates excess reserves for the banks. But now the $64 question. What do they *do* with these reserves?

Do they lend them out? Fine. To whom should they lend them? To a businessman who needs a loan to keep going? To a firm that can't meet its next payroll without a loan? To an individual who has just lost her job and can't meet her car payments?

Never lend money to anyone who needs it.

All these examples bring to mind the first law of banking. Never lend money to anyone who needs it. If you ever want a bank loan, you've got to convince the loan officer that you don't really need the money. I don't mean to make the banks sound quite this bad, but from their point of view, they simply can't afford to take the risks inherent in these loans. A banker's first concern must be: "Will the bank be paid back"?

During recessions, businesses that might have been good credit risks during prosperity have become poor risks. Individuals too lose creditworthiness during recessions, particularly if they've just been laid off. And so the very segment of the economic community most in need of help during recessions is least likely to be accommodated.

Meanwhile, even many of the top credit-rated corporations are not coming in to borrow much money. During recessions the companies to whom the banks will still lend money are not borrowing. Why? Because business isn't so great for them either. Would you borrow to buy more equipment—even at low interest rates—if your equipment was one-third idle? Would you expand your factory if sales were down 20 percent—even if the interest rate fell to 4 percent?

In fact, in October 1982, the economy's capacity utilization rate had fallen to just 68.4 percent—an all-time low since this figure was first compiled in 1948.[8] The Fed had by then loosened credit, but it wasn't until sales finally picked up in early 1983 that investments finally began to rise appreciably.

The Depository Institutions Deregulation and Monetary Control Act of 1980 *Called the bank act*

We have waited until now to deal with this important law. It is clearly the most important piece of banking legislation passed since the 1930s.

The 1970s and 1980s will be marked by economic historians as two decades of swift and significant change in American banking. During this period the distinction between commercial banks and thrift institutions—savings banks, savings and loan associations, and credit unions—has become blurred to the point at which it's hard to tell what is a bank and what isn't.

What is a bank and what isn't?

Until 1980 there was a clear line of demarcation between commercial and thrift institutions. Banks (meaning commercial banks) could issue checking deposits; savings banks, savings and loan associations, and credit unions could not. The only problem was that more and more of the thrifts were doing just that. The way they got around the law was to call those checking deposits something else—negotiable order of withdrawal accounts (or NOW accounts). Thus, technically, people who had deposits at these thrift institutions were not writing checks; they were writing negotiable orders of withdrawal.

While commercial banks were prohibited by Federal Reserve regulation from paying any interest on checking deposits, the thrifts were paying their depositors about 5 percent interest on their NOW accounts. Since these were technically savings accounts rather than checking accounts, it was OK to pay interest. Therefore, the thrifts had it both ways: They were able to give their depositors checking accounts and were able to pay interest on them—which gave them a considerable competitive advantage against commercial banks.

The commercial banks complained to the Fed and to anyone else who would listen, but to little avail. Finally Congress took matters into its own hands and passed the Depository Institutions Deregulation and Monetary Control Act of 1980.

It had three key provisions.

The three key provisions of the Banking Act of 1980

1. All depository institutions were now subject to the Fed's legal reserve requirements. Before this act, only those commercial banks that were

---

[8] The capacity utilization rate is the percentage of the nation's plant and equipment that is being used. In the full-employment and full-production section of Chapter 2, we indicated that a capacity utilization rate of 85 to 90 percent would employ virtually all our usable plant and equipment.

Who Prints our Currency?

The U.S. Treasury prints it, right? Wrong! Our currency is printed by the 12 Federal Reserve District banks. Check it out. Pull a dollar out of your wallet and look at it. What does it say right near the top, about a half inch above George Washington's picture? That's right—"Federal Reserve Note." Then, to the left of Washington's picture is a letter. If you live anywhere near New York, chances are this letter will be a "B." You'll note that the circle around the letter will say "Federal Reserve Bank of New York, New York." There is a "2" printed above and below the "B," which stands for Second Federal Reserve District.

Try another dollar—or a 5, 10, 20, or whatever else you happen to have. Got any L's? That would be the 12th Federal Reserve District Bank in San Francisco. How about A's? That's the First Federal Reserve District Bank in Boston. How about E's—Richmond, in the Fifth District.

If you thought the Treasury issues our currency, they used to (and the Secretary of the Treasury still signs every bill). The last thing they issued, until the mid-1960s, was $1 and $5 silver certificates. These certificates are now out of circulation, snapped up by collectors. The Treasury still issues our pennies, nickels, dimes, quarters, half dollars, and metal (no longer silver) dollars, but, as you might have suspected, that's just the small change of our money supply.

And what about the backing for the dollar? Look on the back of the bill just above the big "ONE." What's the backing for our currency? That's right—"In God We Trust." Actually, there is backing for our currency—the government's word, as well as its general acceptability.

---

members of the Federal Reserve—about one third of all commercial banks were members—were subject to these requirements. The other commercial banks and thrift institutions were subject to state reserve requirements, which were substantially lower.

2. All depository institutions were now legally authorized to issue checking deposits. Furthermore, they could be interest bearing. Until then commercial banks had been forbidden to pay interest on checking accounts while the thrift instituions claimed to be paying interest on savings accounts.

3. All depository institutions would now enjoy all the advantages that only Federal Reserve member banks formerly enjoyed—including check clearing[9] and borrowing from the Fed (discounting).[10]

Remember that the main job of the Federal Reserve is to control the money supply. By bringing all depository institutions—especially the nonmember commercial banks and the savings banks that had NOW accounts—under control of the Fed, the Monetary Control Act made the Fed's job a lot easier.

The number of financial institutions is shrinking quickly.

Another important consequence of this law is that by the end of the 1980s, intense competition will reduce the 40,000 plus financial institutions to about half that number. Should the prohibition against interstate banking be lifted, combined with further advances in electronic banking, there will be still greater consolidation, with perhaps just 60 or 80 giant financial institutions doing most of the business. "Virtually all observers agree that the

---

[9] Check clearing is the mysterious process by which all the checks you wrote last month are mailed to you by your bank at the end of the month. If *you're* not clear on how this gets done, you'd better check back to the box titled "Check Clearing" earlier in this chapter. The Federal Reserve System processes or clears billions of checks each year.

[10] "Reserves of nonmember depository institutions may be held at a correspondent depository institution holding required reserves at a Federal Reserve Bank, a Federal Home Loan Bank, or the National Credit Union Administration Central Liquidity Facility, if such reserves are passed through to a Federal Reserve Bank. The Board may, by regulation or order that is applicable to all depository institutions, permit them to maintain all or a portion of their required reserves in the form of vault cash." See *The Federal Reserve Bulletin*, June 1980, p. 446.

ability of the new financial system to generate credit and meet credit demands will be enhanced, because the system will consist of big, nationwide, all-purpose institutions."[11]

Fiscal and Monetary Policies Should Mesh

It should be apparent that there is little coordination in the making of fiscal and monetary policies. Indeed, there is little fiscal policy as such, but rather a series of compromises within Congress and between Congress and the president. Further, given the independence of the Federal Reserve Board, different groups of people are responsible for monetary and fiscal policy.

Because of the need to make these policies mesh rather than work at cross purposes as they sometimes have, we should consider ways to unifying monetary and fiscal policy. One step in this direction would be to allow each newly elected president to appoint a new chairman of the Board.

Furthermore, it is quite frustrating for Americans to fix the responsibility and the blame for policy failures. In times of high rates of unemployment, inflation, and interest, it seems as if Congress, the president, and the Federal Reserve Board all invoke the immortal words of the late Freddie Prinz: "Is not my job."[12]

---

[11] *Business Week*, November 17, 1980, p. 139.

[12] Freddie Prinz was the star of a TV show, "Chico and the Man," about 10 years ago. If we could elect a former actor as president, it seems appropriate that those responsible for fiscal and monetary policy all seem to be reading from another actor's script.

control money supply - monetary policy - Federal reserve.

Workbook for Chapter 13

Name _____

Date _____

Multiple-Choice Questions

Circle the letter that corresponds to the best answer.

1. Fiscal and monetary policy have the
a. same means and ends   **b.** different means and ends   **c.** same means and different ends
d. different means and the same ends

2. Which statement is true?
a. The United States has always had a central bank.
b. The United States has never had a central bank.
c. The United States had a central bank until 1913.   **d.** The United States has had a central bank since 1913.

3. The most important Federal Reserve policy weapon is
a. changing reserve requirements   **b.** changing the discount rate   **c.** moral suasion   **d.** open-market operations

4. To restrict monetary growth, the Federal Reserve will
a. raise the discount rate and sell securities   **b.** raise the discount rate and buy securities   **c.** lower the discount rate and sell securities   **d.** lower the discount rate and buy securities

5. Monetary policy is conducted by
a. the president only   **b.** Congress only   **c.** the president and Congress   **d.** the Federal Reserve

6. Which statement about the Federal Reserve's Board of Governors is true?
a. They serve seven-year terms.   **b.** There are 14 members.   **c.** Every president appoints his own board.   **d.** The members serve at the pleasure of the president, who can force their resignations at any time.   **e.** None of these statements is true.

7. Control of the Federal Reserve System is vested in
a. the president   **b.** Congress   **c.** the Board of Governors   **d.** the district banks

8. Basically the Board of Governors is
a. independent   **b.** dependent on the president and Congress   **c.** powerless   **d.** on a par with the district banks

9. Legal reserve requirements are changed
a. very often   **b.** on rare occasions
c. never   **d.** none of these

10. Which of these is a secondary reserve?
a. Treasury bills   **b.** gold   **c.** vault cash
d. deposits at the Federal Reserve district bank

11. The larger the reserve requirement, the
a. smaller the deposit expansion multiplier
b. larger the deposit expansion multiplier
c. less the impact of an increase in reserves

12. Each of the following is a leakage from the deposit expansion multiplier except
a. cash   **b.** the foreign trade imbalance   **c.** excess reserves   **d.** all are leakages

13. Check clearing is done by
a. the bank where a check is deposited   **b.** the bank on which a check is written   **c.** the Federal Reserve System   **d.** the Comptroller of the Currency

14. Open-market operations are
a. the buying and selling of U.S. government securities by the Fed   **b.** borrowing by banks from the Fed   **c.** the selling of U.S. government securities by the U.S. Treasury   **d.** raising or lowering reserve requirements by the Fed

15. When the Fed wants to increase the money supply it

a. raises the discount rate   **b.** raises reserve requirements   **c.** sells securities   **d.** buys securities

16. To buy securities the Fed offers

a. a low price and drives up interest rates   **b.** a low price and drives down interest rates   **c.** a high price and drives up interest rates   **d.** a high price and drives down interest rates

17. All open-market operations are carried out for the Fed by

a. private government bond dealers   **b.** the U.S. Treasury   **c.** large Wall Street brokerage houses   **d.** none of the above

18. The original intent of the Federal Reserve Act was to have the district banks lend money to

a. individual borrowers, particularly business firms   **b.** member banks to take care of seasonal needs   **c.** the U.S. Treasury   **d.** none of the above

19. Which statement is true?

a. The Fed is more effective at fighting inflation than recession.   **b.** The Fed is more effective at fighting recession than fighting inflation.   **c.** The Fed is effective at fighting both recession and inflation.   **d.** The Fed is effective at fighting neither inflation nor recession.

20. The Depository Institutions Deregulation and Monetary Control Act of 1980 had two key provisions, one of which was

a. uniform reserve requirements for all financial institutions   **b.** zero reserve requirements for all time deposits   **c.** that no interest may be paid on checking deposits   **d.** that vault cash would no longer count toward reserves

21. The main job of the Fed is to

a. control the rate of growth of the money supply   **b.** to manage the national debt   **c.** provide low-interest loans to all financial institutions   **d.** none of the above

22. One of the main results of the Depository Institutions Deregulation and Monetary Control Act of 1980 may be to

a. lessen the number of financial institutions in the United States   **b.** increase the number of financial institutions in the United States   **c.** discourage the formation of big, nationwide, all-purpose financial institutions   **d.** make it easier for the member banks to borrow money from the Federal Reserve district banks

Fill-In Questions

1. The Federal Reserve System was established in

_____.

2. There are _____ Federal Reserve districts.

3. The members of the Board of Governors are appointed by _____, subject to comfirmation by the

_____.

4. Control of the Federal Reserve is held by

_____.

5. Currently, nearly all checking deposits are subject to a legal reserve requirement of _____ percent.

6. The reason that time deposits are subject to a much lower reserve requirement is because _____

_____.

7. All reserves pay an interest rate of _____ percent.

8. Primary reserves are held in the form of _____ and _____; secondary reserves are held in the form of _____.

9. The process by which a check you write is deposited in another bank, goes through the Federal Reserve System, and is sent back to your own bank is known as _____.

10. The three goals of monetary policy are (1)

_____; (2) _____; and (3) _____.

11. Open-market operations are the _____

_____.

12. If the Fed wants to increase the money supply it

will follow these two steps: (1) _____ and

(2) _____; and if these do not prove sufficient

it may _____.

13. If the Fed wanted to decrease the money supply it

would go into the open market and _____; this

would also _____ interest rates.

14. Open-market policy is conducted by the _____,
which is part of the Fed.

15. The main reason why banks borrow from the Fed

is because they _____.

16. The discount rate is _____.

17. There are _____ members of the Federal Open-

Market Committee; they are the _____

_____.

18. The Federal Reserve Board of Governors will

_____ only as a last resort.

19. Is has been much easier for the Fed to fight

_____ than _____.

20. Until 1980, there was a clear line of demarcation
between commercial banks and the thrifts: commer-

cial banks could _____ while the thrifts could not.

21. A NOW account is a _____.

22. Under the Depository Institutions Deregulation
and Monetary Control Act, all depository institutions

are now subject to the Fed's _____; at the same
time all depository institutions are now legally au-

thorized to issue_____.

23. The degree of coordination between fiscal and

monetary policy today is _____.

24. Our paper currency is issued by _____.

25. Our currency is backed by _____.

26. The part of our money supply issued by the

Treasury is _____.

Problems

1. If you ran a bank with demand deposits of $20
million, you would need to hold reserves of how
much?

2. If you ran a bank with demand deposits of $400
million, you would need to hold reserves of a little
less than how much (assuming you don't remember
the cutoff point).

3. If there were a 15 percent reserve requirement,
how much would the deposit multiplier be?

4. Using your answer from the previous problem, if
the Federal Reserve increased bank reserves by $100
million, by how much would the money supply rise?

5. How much is the interest rate on a bond that has
a face value of $1,000, a selling price of $1,200, and
pays $120 interest?

*Lynne +
shelia*

The Great Money Debate:
The Keynesians versus
the Monetarists

The Keynesian and monetarist schools of economic thought
have been spoiling for a fight since way back in Chapter 10.
After keeping them apart all this time, we've decided to let
them fight it out once and for all. After a preliminary bout
following the chapter objectives, we'll bring you the main
event, a scheduled four rounder for the economic title of the
world. (Actually the title is split several ways, but why go into
that now?)

Chapter Objectives

These four topics will be debated:
- The stability of V.
- The transmission mechanism.
- Monetary policy.
- A question of timing.

Preliminary Debate

As we've frequently noted, the only thing on which economists seem to
agree is that they disagree on just about everything. The two groups of economists who disagree with each other the most are the monetarists and the
Keynesians. We're going to take up three major areas of disagreement, each
of which happens to be related to money.

First there's the question of how stable V, the velocity of money, happens
to be. Then, there's the transmission mechanism, which is the mechanism
by which changes in the demand for and the supply of money affect aggregate demand. Finally, we'll look at the effectiveness of monetary and fiscal
policy.

The time has finally arrived to let the Keynesians and the monetarists
fight it out. This chapter has been given over to them for that purpose.
We'll step back and let them go at it, only occasionally intervening to sepa-

rate them in the clinches and ring the bell at the end of each round. You'll decide who won the bout.

Round One: How Stable Is V?

Velocity and Changes in the Money Supply

The Keynesians believe that changes in the level of the money supply affect the level of aggregate demand through the interest rate. An increase in the money supply lowers the interest rate, raising investment, and consequently, aggregate demand. Similarly, a decrease in the money supply raises the interest rate, lowering investment and aggregate demand.

Monetarists: Money burns holes in people's pockets.

The monetarists see a more direct link between the money supply and the level of GNP than the Keynesians. When the money supply is increased it creates excess money balances held by individuals. This money burns a hole—so to speak—in their pockets, so they spend it. Poof! Up goes aggregate demand or GNP.

A decrease in the money supply, say the monetarists, has the exact opposite effect. Consumers and business firms find themselves short of funds. They would like to carry certain money balances, but find themselves carrying less. What do they do? They cut back on spending, and down goes aggregate demand.

There is, in this reasoning, an implicit assumption about V, or velocity, which you may or may not recall, is part of the equation of exchange we discussed in Chapter 12: $MV = PQ$ (M is the money supply; V, the velocity of circulation, or the number of times each dollar in our money supply is spent during the year; P is the price level, or the average price of all goods and services sold during the year; and Q is the quantity of transactions, or the number of things sold during the year, or simply output).

Monetarists: V must be constant.

If a rise in M raises PQ (or GNP), V must be constant. This, the monetarists maintain, is true in the short run, which might be for a year or two.

If velocity were a perfect constant—that is, a number that stayed exactly the same—changes in M would lead to precisely predictable changes in PQ or GNP. The application of monetary policy would become an exact science, something even the most ardent supporters of the Federal Reserve Board would not dare to hope for. Imagine the power of monetary policy if we knew that a 3 percent rise in the money supply, M, would lead to exactly a 3 percent rise in GNP (PQ). Unfortunately, V will not hold still for us; so the monetarists say V is relatively stable in the short run. And that's the next best thing.

How Stable Is Velocity in the Short Run?

Keynes: V is not stable.

The Keynesians and the monetarists clash sharply with respect to the short-run stability of V. In a word, the monetarists say that V is stable and the Keynesians say it isn't. Perhaps more significant, the monetarists claim that in the short run V is predictable while the Keynesians say it isn't.

The Keynesians maintain that V is sensitive to interest rate changes. When interest rates rise, people will be more likely to hold more interest-bearing assets and less money. Conversely, when interest rates decline, people tend to increase their money holdings. This responsiveness of money balances to interest rate changes is Keynes's speculative demand for money.

Now if interest rates rise and people hold less money, they will have to make more efficient use of their money balances to meet their day-to-day transactions needs—V will rise. And if interest rates fall, people tend to hold more money, some of which will lie idly, thus pushing down V.

Keynesians: A change in M may lead to a change in V in the opposite direction.

The Keynesian view of how changes in M affect V is diametrically opposed to the monetarist position. The last, of course, hold that in the short run V will be constant, but the Keynesians say that a change in M may lead to a change in V in the opposite direction.

The Keynesians maintain that a decline in the money supply pushes up interest rates. Consequently, people buy more bonds (whose prices have fallen). This churns the money supply, increasing velocity.

Conversely, if the money supply rises, interest rates fall, bond prices rise, and people sell some of the bonds they are holding.[1] They end up holding more cash, thereby decreasing velocity.

Therefore, the Keynesians conclude that velocity varies inversely with changes in the money supply. Consequently, an expansionary monetary policy may be partially or fully negated by a decline in velocity. On the other hand, contractionary monetary policy may be similarly canceled by a rising velocity. Although changes in the money supply and velocity are inversely related, the Keynesians know of no way of measuring the magnitude of the changes in velocity caused by changes in the money supply.

It follows then that there is no way, according to the Keynesians, of predicting how changes in the money supply will affect the price level.

Monetarists: Have identified three determinants of V in the short run.

The monetarists, however, dispute the Keynesians' claim that velocity is unstable in the short run. What determines velocity in the short run? The monetarists have identified three determinants: (1) the frequency with which people are paid; (2) people's inflationary expectations; and (3) the level of real interest rates.

The first determinant changes only very gradually. Employers, as a group, do not suddenly change from paying their employees once a week to once a month, or vice versa.

Inflationary expectations too do not suddenly arise, nor do they suddenly subside. It takes years for an inflation to gather momentum and for the public's perception of that inflation to take hold. Similarly, when inflation begins to subside, it will take a few years for inflationary expectations to subside as well.

Finally, we have real interest rates. These are the rates of return that bondholders receive after inflation. Suppose you receive 12 percent interest on a bond when there is currently a 5 percent inflation rate. We would say that the 12 percent interest rate is only the nominal rate, and that after the 5 percent rate of inflation is deducted, you are left with a real rate of interest of only 7 percent. Again, the monetarists believe that while nominal interest rates will rise and fall with the inflation rate, real interest rates remain relatively stable, at least in the short run.

Thus, the monetarists contend, since the three determinants of velocity are each stable in the short run, then velocity must be stable in the short run as well.

Whether or not the monetarists have made a convincing case about the short-run stability of V, they have left themselves an escape hatch: V does not *have* to be stable in the short run for the sophisticated quantity theory to hold up. It just has to be predictable in the short run. Is it?

Again, the Keynesians just say no! They point to the experience of the 1930s and 1940s when V did indeed fluctuate widely, plunging from 4 in 1929 to 3 in 1932, and after fluctuating widely through the rest of the dec-

---

[1] In the "How Open-Market Operations Work" section of the last chapter, we showed that bond prices and interest are inversely related.

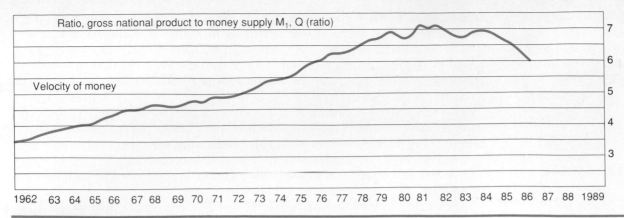

Figure 14–1
The Velocity of Money Circulation,
1962–86

Source: U.S. Department of Commerce, *Business Conditions Digest*, March 1987, p. 31.

ade, dropping to 2 during World War II. The monetarists prefer to look at the postwar period, particularly the 1960s and 1970s (see Figure 14–1). "Aha!" reply the Keynesians, "Then why not look at the 1980s as well?" During this decade, V certainly did have its ups and downs.

The stability of V is in the eye of the beholder.

So the stability of V is certainly in the eye of the beholder. But we make a few generalizations. During wars and recessions, V is prone to decline as people tend to hold onto their money. In the mid-1980s, we may account for V's decline by the change in how the Fed counts our money supply. Until then, only currency and demand deposits at commercial banks were counted. But suddenly the Fed was also including checklike deposits at the thrift institutions. We can show the effect of this change algebraically: GNP is total spending. So is MV (the money supply multiplied by the number of times per year each dollar is spent). Therefore, MV = GNP.

Now divide both sides of this equation by M.

MV = GNP

$$V = \frac{GNP}{M}$$

$$MV/M = GNP/M$$

$$V = GNP/M$$

What happens to the value or size of V if M gets larger? It goes down.

Quite possibly then, the reason V declined in 1985 and 1986 was because of the change in the definition of M. We could conclude then that except for times of war and recession, V has changed very little from one year to the next.

There has been a historical upward trend in V, which the monetarists readily acknowledge. This has been due to the expanded use of credit and credit cards, both of which the monetarists would remind us, are fully predictable. Because people rely more on credit, they make better or more efficient use of their money balances, thereby pushing up V.

Is V stable?

Is V predictable? The monetarists make an excellent case for the "normal years" of the last three-and-a-half decades. But during the "abnormal years" of depression and World War II, V has been neither stable nor predictable. So we may conclude that as long as our economy behaves normally, V is predictable (if not completely stable) in the short run and that the sophisticated quantity theory does hold up.

Round Two: The Transmission Mechanism

Introduction

Before championship bouts we are usually treated to exhaustive analyses of the strategies and tactics of the two opponents. We'll do just that in this section. Then we'll bring you, in the next three sections, the Keynesian view, the monetarist view, and, finally, a comparision of the Keynesian and monetarist transmission mechanisms. The Keynesian position: an increase in the money supply depresses the interest rate. Given a certain MEI (marginal efficiency of investment) schedule, investment becomes more attractive and therefore increases. This, in turn, pushes up aggregate demand, and, as we approach full employment, prices will rise as well.

The monetarist position: a large increase in the money supply creates an imbalance in the money balances held by the public. People are holding more money than they wish to. What do they do? They spend this surplus on stocks and bonds, real estate, money market funds, and consumer durables. This, in turn, pushes up the prices of these assets. Finally, interest rates rise as lenders demand an inflation premium to compensate them for being repaid in inflated dollars.

Effects of a money supply increase: Keynesian and monetarist views

We can now sum up the effects of a money supply increase as seen by the Keynesians and the monetarists, respectively:

$$\text{Keynesians: } M \uparrow \longrightarrow \text{Interest rates} \downarrow \longrightarrow \text{Prices} \uparrow$$

$$\text{Monetarists: } M \uparrow \longrightarrow \text{Prices} \uparrow \longrightarrow \text{Interest rates} \uparrow$$

The monetarists and the Keynesians both believe that large increases in the money supply will lead to rising prices. But they differ with respect to how interest rates and the level of investment is affected. The monetarists expect that rising prices will push up interest rates[2] and consequently that investment will fall. The Keynesians, on the other hand, look for an opposite sequence of events. A large increase in the money supply will push down interest rates and raise the level of investment.

When the Federal Reserve increases the money supply, what effect does this have on the level of interest rates, investment, and GNP? That depends on who answers this question.

The Keynesian View

Keynesians: A rise in M will lead to a decline in the interest rate.

A rise in the money supply will lead to a decline in the interest rate. At this lower interest rate, people will want to hold more money. Why? Number one: the opportunity cost of holding money (the interest rate) has gone down. Number two: at a lower interest rate the price of bonds has gone up. Why buy bonds now? Why not wait until bond prices come back down?

We'll go over the entire process—what an increase in the money supply does to interest rates, the level of investment, and the level of GNP, step-by-step, using the graph in Figure 14–2. Step 1 is shown in Figure 14–2A. The demand for money, D_1, is relatively flat. An increase of $100 billion in the money supply (from M_1 to M_2), leads to a decline of only 1 percent in the interest rate (from 10 percent to 9 percent).

---

[2] This is in the long run. In the short run, they concede that interest rates may fall when the money supply goes up.

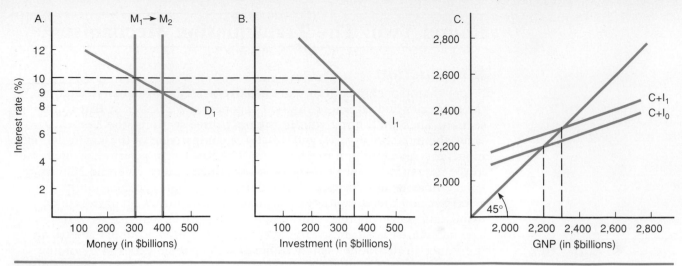

Figure 14-2

Step 2. In Figure 14-2B, what effect does this 1 percent decline in the interest rate have on the level of investment in the Keynesian system? It will raise investment, but not by very much. Why? Because business firms are much more responsive to change in the expected profit rate (or the marginal efficiency of investment) than they are in interest rate changes.

In Figure 14-2B we see a relatively steep investment demand curve, I_1, which means that investment will not rise very much in response to a decline in the interest rate. Here, a 1 percent interest rate decline leads to a rise in investment of just $50 billion.

Step 3. Before we began this whole process, equilibrium GNP stood at 2,200. Now we have a $50 billion increase in investment. By how much will this raise GNP? That depends entirely on the size of the multiplier. Here we'll assume a multiplier of 2, so a $50 billion increase in investment leads to a $100 billion increase in GNP. This last move is shown in Figure 14-2C.

Let's review the three steps of the Keynesian transmission mechanism. In this particular case, when the Fed raises the money supply by $100 billion, the interest rate falls by just 1 percent. This, in turn, leads to an increase in the level of investment of just $50 billion. Finally, with a multiplier of 2, the $50 billion rise in investment leads to a $100 billion rise in GNP. Perhaps $100 billion seems like a big increase, but it is relatively small when compared to the increase that takes place under the monetarist transmission mechanism.

The Monetarist View

Monetarists: A rise in M leads to a rise in spending.

Changes in the money supply, according to the monetarists, cause people to change their spending behavior. When the money supply rises sharply, people find themselves holding more money than they wish to. So what do they do? They spend it.

I don't mean that they rush out to the shopping mall and buy up everything in sight. Rather, they add to their portfolios of assets. They might put the money into stocks and bonds, money market funds, real estate, or perhaps gold, a new car, or a video system.

People are constantly shifting their holdings among the various assets in their portfolios. If real estate becomes relatively attractive, they will shift into that from stocks and bonds and money market funds. If bond prices should fall (i.e., interest rates rise), people will put more money into bonds.

When the money supply is rising quickly, people will be pouring their excess cash balances into these various portfolio holdings, which, in turn, will drive up the prices of these holdings. This explains the heading for this section—the transmission mechanism. As the money supply grows, this increase is transmitted by individual wealth holders into price increases. Put more succinctly by the monetarists, because money burns holes in peoples' pockets, they will spend it, thereby driving up prices.

Let's turn to Figure 14–3A.

Step 1. When the Fed increases the money supply by $100 billion, from M_1 to M_2, this leads to a substantial decline in the interest rate—from 10 percent to 8 percent. Why? Because when people get their hands on this money, they *buy* things with it. Bonds are among the things they buy. When the demand for anything goes up, given a fixed supply, its price is driven up. Since bond prices and the interest rate are inversely related, as bond prices go up interest rates fall.

Why does the interest rate come down so much? Because the demand for money, D_2, is relatively steep, according to the monetarists. Why? Because people have one basic reason to hold money—for transactions purposes. They will hold just enough money to handle their day-to-day personal and business needs, regardless of the interest rate. Thus, people would not alter their money balances very much in response to even substantial interest rate changes.

Step 2. In Figure 14–3B, a 2 percent decline in the interest rate (from 10 percent to 8 percent) leads to a very big increase in investment, from $300 billion to $500 billion. Why so big? Because the investment demand curve, I_2, is relatively flat. In other words, according to the monetarists, investment is very responsive to interest rate changes.

Step 3. This $200 billion investment increase gives rise to a $400 billion increase in GNP, assuming, once again, a multiplier of 2.

Let's review the steps. An increase of $100 billion in the money supply leads to a 2 percent decline in the interest rate, which, in turn, leads to a $200 billion increase in the level of investment. Assuming a multiplier of 2, GNP will then rise by $400 billion.

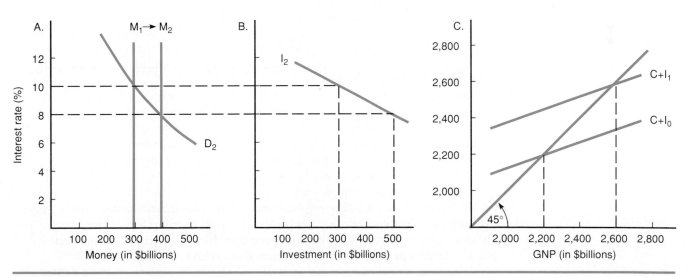

Figure 14–3

Comparison of Keynesian and Monetarist Transmission Mechanisms

The monetarists believe an increase in M will lead to a much greater increase in GNP than the Keynesians do.

When the money supply rises by $100 billion, why does the monetarist analysis lead to a four times larger GNP increase than that of the Keynesian analysis ($400 billion to $100 billion)?

There are two reasons. First, look at the slopes of the money demand curves, D_1 (in Figure 14-2A) and D_2 (in Figure 14-3A). Notice that D_2 is much steeper than D_1. In other words, the demand for money is much less responsive to the interest rate under monetarist analysis. The Keynesians believe that people will want to hold a lot more money as the interest rate declines.

The second basic difference has to do with the responsiveness of the demand for investment funds to interest rate changes. The monetarists believe that investment demand is very responsive to interest rate changes while the Keynesians feel that it is not.

These two very basic differences lead to very different conclusions. The Keynesians feel that an increase in the money supply will not lead to a substantial increase in investment; the monetarists think it will. As we shall see later in this chapter, the Keynesians do not believe monetary policy can have very substantial impact on our economy while the monetarists believe changes in the rate of growth of the money supply have a powerful economic effect.

Who Is Right?

We are going to conclude that as in most economic disputes, both sides make some reasonable points. In this section we will explain what assumptions and disagreements cause the Keynesians and the monetarists to reach such different conclusions about the outcome of the transmission mechanism, but we leave it to you to decide which school is right. Good luck!

We shall take up three basic disputes in turn: (1) the effect of an increase in the money supply on GNP; (2) the stability of velocity; and (3) the stability of the private sector.

Three basic disputes

Conflict number 1: the effects of an increase in the money supply on GNP.

The Keynesians and monetarists are at loggerheads about the long-run consequences of a large-scale increase in the money supply when the economy is operating at less than full employment. The Keynesians maintain that interest rates will be reduced, investment encouraged to some degree, and consequently there will be a moderate rise in output and employment. The monetarists, on the other hand, predict that in the long run a large increase in the money supply will raise inflationary expectations. These will drive up prices, which will, in turn, push up interest rates, discourage investment, and drive down output and employment.

Thus, the Keynesians think that a large increase in the money supply will have a stimulating effect on output and employment while the monetarists believe it will have the opposite effect.

Conflict number 2: how stable is velocity?

In Round 1 of this chapter, we reached this conclusion: in normal years (nondepression and nonwar years) V is at least predictable, if not stable, in the short run. Basically then, we have upheld the monetarist position.

Conflict number 3: the stability of the private sector.

The third bone of contention between the monetarists and the Keynesians has to do with the stability of the nongovernmental sector of the economy. The Keynesians think the private sector is inherently unstable because the expected profit rate, the marginal efficiency of investment, is subject to huge shifts. When these occur, investment will rise or fall substantially, dragging along aggregate demand.

The opposite view is held by the monetarists, who maintain that the business sector is inherently stable at full employment. Any economic instability is caused by the stop-and-go monetary policy of the Fed. If the Fed would merely follow their monetary rule—a steady annual monetary growth rate of 3 percent—the inherent stability of the private economy would correct any deviation from the full-employment norm.

Round 3: Monetary Policy

The common wisdom with respect to the proper monetary policy for the Fed to pursue has long been very simple and explicit. During recessions, stimulate the economy by speeding up the rate of growth of the money supply; during inflations, cool down the economy by slowing down that rate of growth. In this section we'll examine the policy prescription of the Keynesians, who subscribe to the common wisdom, and that of the monetarists, who do not.

Fighting Recessions

Raise rate of growth of M

The Keynesians During recessions the Keynesians would advise the Fed to raise the rate of growth of the money supply. Will this bring us out of the recession? No. Will it be of any help whatsoever? Maybe yes and maybe no. Like chicken soup, the Keynesians tell us, raising the rate of growth of the money supply will certainly not *hurt* us. What would be much better would be to cut taxes, and to raise government spending would be better still, but we're talking here only about monetary policy (not fiscal policy).

Increasing the rate of monetary growth would push down interest rates unless, of course, they are already at around 2 percent. In that case we would already be in the liquidity trap. Raising the money supply any farther would be of no help whatsoever.

But assuming that the recession were not all that bad and that interest rates were well above the 2 percent level, an increase in monetary growth would lower interest rates, thereby encouraging both business firms and individuals to borrow. But, as the Keynesians never tire of pointing out, the marginal efficiency of investment is much more important than the interest rate in determining the level of investment. Again, assuming that we're not in a very deep recession when the marginal efficiency of investment might be negative for most businesses, a decline in the interest rate relative to the marginal efficiency of investment would push up investment to some degree.

Don't change the rate of growth of M.

The Monetarists Suppose we are in the midst of a severe recession. What should the Fed do? Should it increase the rate of growth of the money supply, drive down interest rates, and make more money available for business investment, as the Keynesians suggest? The monetarists agree that such monetary stimulus could quickly get us out of the recession.

"But why bother?" they ask. The economy will get out of the recession all by itself, albeit at a somewhat slower pace. If you were sick and your family doctor made one of those rare home visits, suppose you asked your doctor for some medication to make you better. "You don't need any medication," replies the doctor. "You're going to get better all by yourself." You may start to wonder what doctors are *for*, if not to write prescriptions.

Similarly, the monetarists tell us that the Fed doesn't really have to do anything since our economy will get better by itself. They go on to warn us that if the Fed were to increase the money supply too quickly or let it grow at too rapid a pace for too long, the result would be inflation. That's why, like nature, it's always better to let things take their course.

Fighting Inflations

Slow rate of growth of M

The Keynesians The Keynesians place much greater faith in the Fed's ability to slow down an inflation than to bring us out of a recession. In a word, by slamming on the monetary brakes, the Fed can send interest rates through the roof, making investment unprofitable even at high marginal efficiencies of investment.

The Fed can easily bring the economy to a grinding halt, something it has done most recently in 1980 and 1981. The back-to-back recessions we experienced in those years helped wring most of the inflation out of our economy.

A tight money policy is known in economists' circles as "pulling on a string," and is generally considered effective, if not always desirable—certainly not if it is overdone and causes a recession. Easy money is known as "pushing on a string," a policy that most Keynesians believe is much less effective in ending recessions than tight money is in ending inflations.

Follow monetary rule

The Monetarists Interestingly, the monetarists agree with the Keynesians that tight money is a surefire way to halt inflation. "But what then?" they ask. If the Fed steps off the brake too soon, we have another round of inflation. If it doesn't, we have a really bad recession. Thus, once more we're faced with their only policy prescription—the monetary rule.

Round Four: A Question of Timing

The Lags

Timing, in economic policy as in most other areas, is of utmost importance. The effectiveness of both monetary and fiscal policy depends greatly on timing. Unfortunately, both of these policies are subject to three lags—the recognition, decision, and impact lags.

Suppose our economy enters a recession and the government provides a counteracting stimulus. What if this stimulus does not have full impact until recovery has set in? The end result of this well-intentioned government policy will be to destabilize the economy by making the recovery and subsequent prosperity far too exuberant. Similarly, if the government were to try to damp down an inflation, but the effects of its policy were not felt until the economy had already entered a recession, the policy would end up making the recession that much worse.

The recognition, decision, and impact lags

The recognition lag is the time it takes for the policymakers to realize that a business cycle turning point has been passed, or that either inflation or unemployment has become a particular problem. The decision lag is the time it takes for policymakers to decide what to do and to take action. And finally, the impact lag is the time it takes for the policy action to have a substantial effect. The whole process may last anywhere from about nine months to over three years.

Fiscal Policy Lags

First, the president and Congress must recognize that there is a problem.

The three lags under fiscal policy are not well defined. First, the recognition lag would be the time it takes the president and a majority of both houses of Congress to recognize that something is broken and needs fixing—either an inflation or a recession. You would be amazed at how long this can take. Back in August of 1981 we ended a recession, but in the spring of the following year President Reagan could still not bring himself to admit that we were actually in a recession (which, incidentally, proved to be the worst downturn since the Great Depression).

Congress, which at the time was divided between a Republican Senate and a Democratic House, also took some time to recognize the problem. This state of affairs was similar to that of 1967; inflation was beginning to get out of hand, but first the president and then Congress was reluctant to recognize the obvious.

Next, they must decide what to do about it.

Once the president *and* Congress do recognize that something needs to be done about the economy, they must decide what should be done. After investigating the problem with his advisers, the president may make a fiscal policy recommendation to Congress. This recommendation, among others, is studied by appropriate subcommittees and committees, hearings are held, expert witnesses called, votes taken. Eventually bills may be passed by both houses, reconciled by a joint House-Senate committee, repassed by both houses, and sent to the president for his signature. This process usually takes several months. Finally, if the president likes the bill, he signs it. (If he doesn't, Congress may override his veto, but usually doesn't.)

Finally, it will take time for their action to have an impact.

All this delay is part of the decision lag. We still have the impact lag. If a spending bill, say a highway reconstruction measure, has been passed for the purpose of stimulating an economy that is mired in recession, it may be another year before the bulk of the appropriated funds is actually spent and has made a substantial economic impact. By then, of course, we may already have begun our recovery from the recession.

Monetary Policy Lags

Recognition lag is usually shorter for monetary than for fiscal policy.

One would expect monetary policy time lags to be somewhat shorter than fiscal policy time lags. The Board of Governors, which always has at least three or four professional economists among its membership, continually monitors the economy. Further, because the Board has only seven members, with the chairman playing the dominant role, a consensus with respect to policy changes is reached far more easily than it is under our political method of conducting fiscal policy. While the legislative wrangling among the members of both houses of Congress, between the two houses, and between the president and Congress may take several months, consensus among the seven members of the Fed is reached relatively quickly.

How long is the impact lag time before monetary policy changes have a substantial effect? Economists estimate this time as anywhere from nine months to about three years. Further, there is some agreement that a tight money policy will slow down an inflation more quickly than will an easy money policy hasten a recovery. Still, there is no general agreement about whether monetary or fiscal policy is faster—or more effective.

While the goals of both monetary and fiscal policy are identical—low unemployment and stable prices—the effects of each are felt in different economic sectors. Fiscal policy is generally directed toward the consumer sector (tax cuts) or the government sector (spending programs). Monetary policy, however, has its strongest impact on the investment sector. In a word, tight money discourages investment while a rapidly growing money supply has the opposite effect. The only question, then, is how long it takes before the investment sector feels the impact of monetary policy changes.

Corporate investment does not fall off precipitously when the interest rate rises, nor does it shoot up when the interest rate falls. Although investment in plant and equipment becomes more attractive when the interest rate declines, as a rule large corporations take months, and sometimes years, to formulate investment plans. Therefore, transitory changes in the availability of investment funds or the rate of interest do not have a substantial impact on the level of investment in the short run. However, over a two- or three-year period, it's another story.

Thus, when we talk about the impact lag for monetary policy, we have to discuss that lag in terms of years rather than months. This is not to say that monetary policy changes have no impact for years, but rather that the substantial impact of these changes may not be felt for two or three years.

During a period of inflation, the proper monetary policy for the Fed to pursue would be to slow down or even halt the growth of the money supply. But what if, by the time this was done and had any impact, the economy had already entered a recession? Clearly it would make that recession even worse.

During a period of recession, what would be the proper monetary policy? Speed up the rate of growth of the money supply. But suppose that by the time this policy had any impact, the recovery had begun? Oh no! Now this monetary expansion will fuel the next round of inflation.

To sum up, because of the recognition, decision, and impact lags, monetary policy is too slow to have its intended effect. By the time the monetary brakes are applied to halt an inflation, the economy may have already entered a recession; and when an expansionary monetary policy is pursued to bring the economy out of a recession, recovery has already set in. In a word, because of the time lags, monetary policy may actually be destabilizing. The Fed surely did not intend to have that effect, but the road to economic instability is often paved with good intentions.

The time lag in monetary policy invites a good-news bad-news scenario. The good news is that there's a time lag. *That's* the *good* news? What's the *bad* news? It's a variable time lag. How variable? Monetarists believe it may be as short as six months or as long as two years.

Therefore, even if the Fed could take the time lag into account when it decides to slow the monetary growth rate to fight an inflation, how long a lag should it allow for? Six months? A year? A year and a half? Two years?

Fiscal versus Monetary Policy: A Summing Up

Keynesians: Fiscal policy is more powerful than monetary policy

The Keynesians argue that fiscal policy is a much more powerful and reliable macropolicy tool than monetary policy. Why? Because fiscal policy, particularly increasing government spending during a recession, has a direct and substantial effect on GNP whereas monetary policy is relatively weak and uncertain in effect.

When the government spends more money, G rises, and has a multiplied effect on GNP. It happens one two three: (1) G rises; (2) it has a multiplier effect on GNP; and (3) GNP rises. That's fiscal policy—short and sweet.

But monetary policy, say the Keynesians, involves a longer and less variable sequence. Let's look at the effects of an expansion in the money supply. The Fed buys securities on the open market, creating more bank reserves. Will the banks lend out all these reserves? Only if they want to and are able to. Will there be a sufficient number of creditworthy borrowers who will want to borrow money during a recession to build new plant and equipment and expand their inventories?

If this money *is* lent out, the money supply will expand, but keep in mind the Keynesian assumptions of a relatively flat monetary demand curve and a relatively steep investment demand curve. A substantial increase in the money supply will lead to a relatively small decline in the interest rate. This, in turn, will lead to a small increase in investment, and eventually, a small increase in GNP.

Monetarists: Monetary policy is more powerful than fiscal policy

Unlike the Keynesians, the monetarists believe that changes in monetary policy have a short, direct, and powerful effect on GNP. An increase in M will, assuming a stable or predictable V, have a direct and predictable effect on PQ (which is GNP). The monetarists, like the classical economists before them, believe that the private economy tends to operate near, or at, full employment. Therefore, any large increase in M will be translated into increases in P.[3]

Where does all this leave us? Who won the fight? I think you would agree that both the monetarists and the Keynesians got in some good licks. But who won? That's a good question. I don't know. Who do you think won?

---

[3] If we are near or at full employment, Q can't be increased very much; the only give would be in P. Since PQ must rise in proportion to the increase in M, the rise in PQ will be all, or nearly all, in P.

All quest. 05

Workbook for Chapter 14

Name _____

Date _____

Multiple-Choice Questions

Circle the letter that corresponds to the best answer.

1. The two groups of economists who disagree with each other more than anyone else are the

a. supply-siders and Keynesians   **b.** supply-siders and monetarists   **c.** monetarists and Keynesians

2. The Keynesians believe that change in the level of the money supply affects _____ through the interest rate.

a. velocity   **b.** the level of aggregate supply   **c.** the level of aggregate demand   **d.** the price level

3. One of the basic disagreements between the Keynesians and the monetarists is with regard to the

a. stability of V   **b.** rate of growth of M   **c.** level of prices   **d.** importance of real GNP versus nominal GNP

4. Which statement is true?

a. Both the Keynesians and the monetarists believe that V is sensitive to interest rate changes.

b. Neither the Keynesians nor the monetarists believes that V is sensitive to interest rate changes.

c. The Keynesians believe that V is sensitive to interest rate changes while the monetarists do not.

d. The monetarists believe that V is sensitive to interest rate changes while the Keynesians do not.

5. The Keynesians say that change in M will lead to

a. no changes in V   **b.** proportionate changes in V

c. changes in V in the same direction   **d.** changes in V in the opposite direction

6. The Keynesians say that a decline in the money supply

a. pushes down interest rates and causes people to buy more bonds   **b.** pushes down interest rates and causes people to buy less bonds   **c.** pushes up interest rates and causes people to buy more bonds

d. pushes up interest rates and causes people to buy less bonds

7. Each of the following has been identified by the monetarists as a determinant of velocity in the short run except

a. people's inflationary expectations   **b.** the frequency with which people are paid   **c.** changes in the level of output   **d.** the level of real interest rates

8. Is V predictable in the short run?

a. The monetarists say yes and the Keynesians say no.   **b.** The Keynesians say yes and the monetarists say no.   **c.** The Keynesians and the monetarists both say yes.   **d.** The Keynesians and the monetarists both say no.

9. Which statement is true about the Keynesian and monetarist transmission mechanisms when the money supply is increased?

a. Under both aggregate demand will rise.   **b.** Under both aggregate demand will decline.   **c.** Under the Keynesian mechanism aggregate demand will rise, but under the monetarist mechanism it will fall.

d. Under the monetarist mechanism aggregate demand will rise, but under the Keynesian mechanism it will fall.

10. According to the monetarists, when the money supply rises

a. interest rates rise   **b.** inflation declines

c. people spend less on assets   **d.** people spend more on assets

11. An increase in M of $100 billion will lead to

a. the same increase in GNP under the Keynesians as under the monetarists   **b.** a larger increase in GNP under the Keynesians than under the monetarists

c. a larger increase in GNP under the monetarists than under the Keynesians   **d.** none of the above

12. The Keynesians and the monetarists have three basic disputes that are connected with the transmission mechanism. They include each of the following except

a. the effect of an increase in the money supply on GNP   **b.** the stability of interest rates   **c.** the stability of V   **d.** the stability of the private sector

13. The Keynesians believe that monetary policy is

a. more effective in fighting inflations than recessions
b. more effective in fighting recessions and inflations
c. effective in fighting both inflations and recessions
d. effective in fighting neither inflations nor recessions

14. The monetarists say that if we are in a recession, the Fed should

a. increase the rate of growth of M   **b.** decrease the rate of growth at M   **c.** do nothing

15. Which statement is true?

a. the monetarists agree with the Keynesians that easy money is a good way to fight inflation.
b. The monetarists disagree with the Keynesians contention that easy money is a good way to fight inflation.   **c.** The monetarists agree with the Keynesians' contention that tight money is a good way to fight inflation.   **d.** the monetarists disagree with the Keynesians' contention that tight money is a good way to fight inflation.

16. Each of the following is a policy lag except the _____ lag.

a. psychological   **b.** impact   **c.** recognition
d. decision

17. The lags under fiscal policy are _____ the lags under monetary policy.

a. more clearly defined than   **b.** as well defined as
c. less defined than

18. Monetary policy lags may last

a. up to six months   **b.** up to one year   **c.** from six months to two years   **d.** from one year to four years

19. Which statement is true?

a. The Keynesians and the monetarists agree that fiscal policy is more effective than monetary policy.

b. The Keynesians and the monetarists agree than monetary policy is more effective than fiscal policy.
c. The Keynesians believe more in fiscal policy and the monetarists in monetary policy.   **d.** The Keynesians believe more in monetary policy and the monetarists in fiscal policy.

20. The Keynesians assume a _____ monetary demand curve and a _____ investment demand curve.

a. relatively flat, relatively flat   **b.** relatively steep, relatively steep   **c.** relatively steep, relatively flat
d. relatively flat, relatively steep

21. The monetarists believe that monetary policy has a _____ effect on GNP.

a. direct and powerful   **b.** direct but not powerful
c. indirect and powerful   **d.** indirect and weak

Fill-In Questions

1. The monetarists see a _____ between the money supply and the level of GNP.

2. If V were a perfect constant, a change in M would lead to a _____

3. The Keynesians believe that changes in the level of the money supply affect the level of aggregate demand through the _____

4. The best course of action for the Fed, say the monetarists, would be to have the money supply grow at _____.

5. The monetarists say that V is _____ and the Keynesians say that V is _____

6. If interest rates rise, according to the Keynesians, people hold less money and will have to _____

7. Compared to the monetarist position, the Keynesians view of how changes in M affect V is _____.

8. The Keynesians maintain that an increase in M _____ interest rates.

9. The Keynesians say that V varies _____ with M.

10. The monetarists have identified three determinants of V in the short run: (1) _pay period frequency_; (2) _people inflationary expectations_, and (3) _level of real interest rate_.

11. You can most easily predict V in _____ years; it is harder to predict in _____ years.

12. According to the monetarists, a large increase in the money supply created an _____. In response, people _____.

13. Both the Keynesians and the monetarists believe that a large increase in M will lead to _____.

14. The monetarists expect rising prices to push up

_____ .

15. The effect of a large increase in the money supply on the level of investment, say the Keynesians, will

be _____.

16. The long-run consequences of a large-scale increase in the money supply when the economy is operating at less than full employment will lead to

_____

according to the Keynesians; it will lead to

_____

according to the monetarists.

17. The three basic disputes between the Keynesians and the monetarists with respect to the transmission mechanism are (1) _effect_ _lay people_, (2) _inflation expectation_, and (3) _level of real interest rate_.

18. The Keynesians say that if we are in a recession, the Fed should _____, while the monetarists say the Fed should _____.

19. The Keynesians place much greater faith in the Fed's ability to fight _inflation_ than to fight _recession_.

20. The three policy lags are the (1) _recog_ lag, (2) the _____ lag, and (3) the _____ lag. _recognition, decision, impact_

21. The monetarists believe the monetary policy lags last between _six mos_ and _two years_.

22. The Keynesians argue that _fiscal_ policy is a much more powerful and reliable macropolicy tool than _monetary_ policy.

23. Unlike the Keynesians, the monetarists believe that changes in the monetary policy have a _short_, _direct_, and _powerful_ effect on GNP.

Twentieth-Century Economic Theory

An economist is someone good with numbers who didn't have the personality to become an accountant.

—Anonymous

Economists are not easy to follow when they talk about familiar, day-to-day events like the unemployment rate changes and the rising consumer price index. When they talk theory, however, even their fellow economists have difficulty understanding, let alone agreeing with, what they are saying to each other. I'll repeat the saying that if you took all the world's economists and laid them out in a line, head-to-foot, head-to-foot, they still would not reach a conclusion.

John Maynard Keynes put all of this into perspective much more elegantly:

> The ideas of economists and political philosophers, both when they are right and when they are wrong, are more powerful than is commonly understood. Indeed, the world is ruled by little else. Practical men, who believe themselves to be quite exempt from any intellectual influences, are usually slaves of some defunct economist.

What conclusion will you reach at the end of this chapter? If you're like my fellow economists, you will choose one school of economic thought to defend while attacking each of the others. Hopefully you'll take each economic theory with a grain of salt, ferreting out what you can't accept while appreciating the cogency of the arguments that have been advanced.

Chapter Objectives

No attempt is being made to do more than outline some of the underlying ideas of each of the five main schools of this century.

After you've read this chapter you will have a better understanding of the basics of:

- Classical economics.
- Keynesian economics.
- The monetarist school.
- Supply-side economics.
- The rational expectations theory.

Classical Economics

There were very bad recessions, even depressions, in the 1830s, 1870s, and 1890s, but we always did eventually recover. If the government tried to get us out of a recession, said the classicals, it only made things worse.

Recessions cure themselves.

The classical school of economics was mainstream economics from roughly 1775 to 1930. Adam Smith's *The Wealth of Nations*, which was a plea for laissez-faire (no government interference), was virtually the economics bible through most of this period. The classicals believed that our economy was self-regulating. Recessions would cure themselves, and there was a built-in mechanism that was always pushing the economy toward full employment.

Say's Law

As we saw at the beginning of Chapter 10, the centerpiece of the classical system was Say's Law: Supply creates its own demand. Everything that is produced gets sold. Why? Because people work so that they can spend.

Savings will be invested.

What if people save some of their incomes? No problem, said the classicals, because that savings will be invested. With that, they pointed to Figure 15-1, which shows a graph of savings and investment. The two are equal at an interest rate of 10 percent.

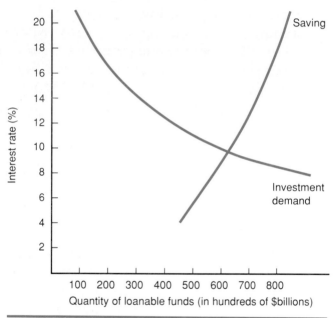

Figure 15–1

Interest rate mechanism

What if the amount of money people wanted to save at 10 percent interest were greater than the amount businesspeople wanted to invest? Still no problem, said the classicals. The interest rate would fall automatically. People would be inclined to save less at lower interest rates and businesspeople would be inclined to invest more. Eventually the interest rate would fall far enough and savings and investment would be equal.

Flexible wages and prices

The classicals also assumed flexible wage rates and prices. If there happened to be a temporary recession and business firms could not sell their entire inventories, they would simply lower their prices until their inventories were depleted. Similarly, if some workers were unemployed, they would offer to work for lower wage and would find new jobs.

Quantity theory of money

Another basic classical tenet was the quantity theory of money, which we discussed in Chapter 12. Stated in its crudest version, when the money supply changes by a certain percentage, the price level changes by that same percentage. Thus, when the money supply is increased by 5 percent, the price level rises by 5 percent.

Resorting once again to the equation of exchange (whose components are defined in that section of Chapter 12):

$$MV = PQ$$

V and Q are constant.

If M rose by 5 percent and P rose by 5 percent, that would mean that V and Q remained constant. We held a full-scale debate between the Keynesians and the monetarists about the stability of V at the beginning of the last chapter and concluded that V is stable during nonrecession and peacetime years. And Q? Well, Q, the output of goods and services, rises during nonrecession years and falls during recession years.

Where does all this leave us with the quantity theory? In its crude version, which the classicals espoused, we could hardly expect V *and* Q to stay constant from year to year. So much, then, for the crude quantity theory.

Finally, we'll take a closer look at the classical contention that recessions are temporary phenomena, which, with the help of Say's Law, the interest rate mechanism, and flexible wages and prices, cure themselves. This leads to the basic classical macroeconomic policy when there is a recession: do nothing!

Government can't cure recessions.

If the government attempted to cure a recession by spending more money or cutting taxes, these measures would not get us out of the recession. Why not? Because the recession would cure itself. Government intervention could not help and it might even hurt.

What about monetary policy? If there were a recession, the standard monetary policy would be to increase the rate of growth of the money supply. What would this accomplish? Ask the Classicals. Since the recession would be curing itself, output, Q, would go up automatically. Since V would be stable, a rise in M would simply be translated into a rise in P, so the attempt to cure the recession by means of monetary policy would only cause inflation.

The classical school dominated economic thought until the time of the Great Depression. If recessions cured themselves automatically, asked John Maynard Keynes in the 1930s, why was the entire world economy dragging along from year to year in unending depression? And if the economy wasn't curing itself, said Keynes, government intervention was in order.

Keynesian Economics

John Maynard Keynes wrote his landmark work, *The General Theory of Employment, Interest, and Money,* during the depths of the Great Depression. While Herbert Hoover (perhaps the last political leader to uphold the theories of classical economics) was telling everyone who would listen that recovery was just around the corner, things were going from bad to worse. As the unemployment rate mounted, production plummeted, and soup kitchens proliferated, more and more Americans demanded that the federal government do something. When Franklin Roosevelt defeated Hoover by a landslide in 1932, he had a mandate for the government to do whatever was necessary to bring about recovery.

Keynes: The problem with recessions is inadequate aggregate demand.

Keynes provided a blueprint. The problem, he said, was inadequate aggregate demand. People were just not buying enough goods and services to employ the entire labor force. In fact, aggregate demand was so low that only the government could spend enough money to provide a sufficient boost.

Keynes defined aggregate demand as consumer spending, investment spending, and government spending (plus net exports, which at that time were negligible). Consumption was a function of disposable income. When disposable income was low, said Keynes, consumption was low. This was the problem we were having during the Great Depression.

Investment, which was largely a function of the marginal efficiency of investment, or the expected profit rate, was also very low during the depression. So we could not hope that an upturn in investment would lead us out of the depression. The only hope was for the government to spend enough money to raise aggregate demand sufficiently to get people back to work.

Cure for recession: government spending

What type of spending was necessary? Any kind, said Keynes. Quantity was much more relevant than quality. Even if the government employed some people to dig holes, said Keynes, and others to fill up those holes, we would still be able to spend our way out of the depression.

Where would the government get the money? There were two choices: print it or borrow it. If we printed it, wouldn't that cause inflation? Keynes thought this unlikely; during the depression we had been experiencing *deflation*, or falling prices. Who would even think of raising prices when he was having trouble finding customers?

In a campaign speech in Brooklyn in the fall of 1932, Roosevelt castigated Hoover for not balancing his budget.

What about budget deficits? Nothing improper about these, said Keynes. Although the common wisdom of the times was that the government must balance its budget, there was absolutely nothing wrong with deficits during recessions and depressions. We needed to prime the pump by sucking up the idle savings that businesses were not borrowing and using those funds to get the economy moving again.

Once government spending was underway, people would finally have some money in their pockets. And what would they do with that money? You guessed it—they'd spend it. This money would then end up in other people's pockets, and they, in turn, would spend it once again.

That money would continue to be respent again and again, putting more and more people back to work. In the process, the deficit would melt away. The government could cut back on its spending programs while tax receipts swelled, so we could view the budget deficits as a temporary expedient to get the economy off dead center.

But what of the classical automatic mechanism that ensured that the economy always moved toward full employment? In the long run, Keynes conceded, maybe it really *did* work. But in the long run, noted Keynes, "we'll all be dead."

Why invest in new plant and equipment when most of your capacity is idle?

Why didn't the classical mechanism work in the short run? Keynes observed that interest rates fell to about 2 percent during the depression, but business firms still were not borrowing all that much to build new plant and equipment. After all, who in his right mind would invest in new plant and equipment when his factory was operating at only 30 or 40 percent of capacity. Besides, said Keynes, at an interest rate of 2 percent, many people would not be willing to lend out their savings. Why tie them up at such a low interest rate? Why not just sit on this money until interest rates rose again?

So much for the interest rate mechanism. With respect to downwardly flexible wages and prices, there were institutional barriers. Labor unions would oppose lowered wage rates while highly concentrated industries would tend to prefer output decreases to price cuts during recessions.

If M rises, what if people don't spend additional money, but just hold it?

Keynes also raised some objections to the quantity theory of money. Most significantly, he asked what would happen to the money that would be printed if the government *did* increase the money supply. The classicals had assumed it would be spent, thus pushing up the price level. This could happen, conceded Keynes, but during a bad recession, perhaps people would just hold their money, waiting for interest rates to rise before they lent it out. Wouldn't they spend it, as the classicals suggested?

Poor people would. But if they were poor, what would they be doing with money in the first place? If the money supply were increased during a bad recession, said Keynes, that money would simply be held as idle cash balances by relatively well-to-do people. Nothing would happen to the money until the economy was well on its way toward recovery, interest rates rose, and more investment opportunities became available.

By the mid-1930s, the classical school of economics had lost most of its adherents. Not everyone became a Keynesian. Conservative economists in particular could never fully reconcile themselves to the vastly increased economic role that the Keynesians awarded to the federal government. In fact, the remaining economic schools to be considered here—the monetarists, the supply-siders, and the rational expectationists—would all rail against the evils of big government.

Is Keynesian economics valid just during recessions?

But big government was here to stay. Although the massive spending programs of Franklin Roosevelt's New Deal did not get us out of the depression, the much bigger defense spending during World War II certainly did. There was no question that Keynes had been right, but since the war we had been plagued not just by periodic recessions, but by almost unending inflation. There was growing feeling not just among professional economists, but among the populace as well, that perhaps Keynesian economics was just recession and depression economics, that it could not satisfactorily deal with curbing inflation.

Keynesian economics may have reached its high point in 1964 when personal income tax rates were cut by about 20 percent. This tax cut, combined with accelerating military spending during our escalating involvement in the Vietnam War, brought about a rapid rate of economic growth in the mid-to-late 1960s; but this growth was accompanied by increasing inflation, which reached double-digit proportions in the early 1970s. By the time President Richard Nixon proclaimed "I am a Keynesian," this school of economics had already been receiving a lot of bad press. In the 1970s, being a Keynesian was out; to be in you had to be a monetarist.

The Monetarist School

The Importance of the Rate of Monetary Growth

Monetarist obsession: rate of growth of M

Monetarism begins and ends with one obsession—the rate of growth of the money supply. Most of our major economic problems, especially inflation and recessions, are due to the Federal Reserve's mismanagement of our rate of monetary growth.

Milton Friedman, an economist who did exhaustive studies of the relationship between the rate of growth of the money supply and the rate of increase in prices, reached a couple of not surprising conclusions. First, we have never had a serious inflation that was not accompanied by rapid monetary growth. Second, when the money supply has grown slowly, we have had no inflation.

In a study of the monetary history of the United States for a period of nearly a century after the Civil War, Friedman and his longtime collaborator Anna Jacobson Schwartz, reached this conclusion: "Changes in the behavior of the money stock have been closely associated with changes in economic activity, money income, and prices."[1] Once again, the answer to all important economic questions is: the rate of growth of the money supply.

Building on the quantity theory of money, the monetarists agreed with the classicals that when the money supply grew, the price level rose, albeit not at exactly the same rate. But they refuted Keynes's argument that if the money supply were raised during a recession, people might just hold onto these added funds. Like the classicals, the monetarists assumed that to get it is to spend it—not necessarily on consumer goods, but on stocks, bonds, real estate, and other noncash assets.

If people *did* spend this additional money, the prices of what they bought would be bid up. In other words, the monetarists were saying that the quantity theory basically held true.

So far so good. Now for recessions. What causes them? When the Federal Reserve increases the money supply at less than the rate needed by business—say anything less than 3 percent a year—we're headed for trouble. Sometimes, in fact, the Fed does not let it grow at all, and may even cause it to shrink slightly.

By and large the monetarists' analysis has been borne out by the facts. Without a steady increase in the money supply of at least 3 percent a year, there is a high likelihood of a recession.

The Basic Propositions of Monetarism

(1) The Key to Stable Economic Growth Is a Constant Rate of Increase in the Money Supply Has our economic history been one of stable growth? No inflation? No recessions? Since World War II alone we've had at least four waves of inflation and eight recessions.

The monetarists place almost the entire blame on the Federal Reserve Board of Governors. If only they had been increasing the money supply by a steady 3 percent a year, we could have avoided most of this instability.

Let's trace the monetarist reasoning by analyzing the Fed's actions over the course of a business cycle. As a recession sets in, the Fed increases the rate of growth of the money supply. This stimulates output in the short run, helping to pull the economy out of the recession. In the long run, however, this expanded money supply causes inflation. So what does the Fed do? It slams on the monetary brakes, slowing the rate of growth in the money supply. This brings on a recession. And what does the Fed do in response? It increases the rate of monetary growth.

"Is this stop-go stop-go monetary policy any way to run an economy?" ask the monetarists. This type of policy inspires about as much confidence as the student driver approaching a red light. First he hits the brakes about 100 yards from the corner. Then, overcompensating for his error, he hits the accelerator much too hard. When the car shoots forward, he hits the brakes again, bringing the car to a dead stop about 50 yards from the corner. Again he repeats the whole process.

In the first half of the 1940s the Fed helped finance the huge increase in the national debt (incurred by World War II) by pumping up the money supply by tens of billions of dollars. The 1950s, however, were a time of tight money, marked, incidentally, by three recessions.

Again, in the late 1960s, an accelerating rate of monetary growth was accompanied by a rising rate of inflation, which, in the early 1970s, reached double-digit proportions. In 1973, the Federal Reserve Board put on the

---

[1] Milton Friedman and Anna Jacobson Schwartz, *A Monetary History of the United States, 1867–1960* (Princeton, N.J.: Princeton University Press, 1971), p. 676.

Monetarists modified crude quantity theory.

Monetarists' analysis borne out by the facts

The Fed is blamed for our economic instability

brakes and we went into the worst recession we had suffered since World War II. In 1975, the Fed eased up and we recovered. Then, in late 1979, the brakes were applied. The prime rate of interest soared over 20 percent and in January 1980, we went into a sharp six-month recession. What happened next? You guessed it. The Fed eased up again. Interest rates came down again and economic recovery set in. But in 1981, the Fed, alarmed at the rising inflation rate, stepped on the monetary brakes once again and we entered still another recession in August of 1981. The prime once again soared over 20 percent. This recession proved even deeper than that of 1973–75. In the summer of 1982, the Fed saw no course but to ease up once again on the brakes and, sure enough, by November of that year the recession had ended.

(2) Expansionary Monetary Policy Will Only Temporarily Depress Interest Rates

In the short run, when the Fed increases the rate of monetary growth, interest rates decline. If the interest rate is the price of money, it follows that if the money supply is increased and there is no change in the demand for money, its price, the interest rate, will decline.

In long run, a rise in M pushes up inflation and interest rates.

The monetarists tell us that in the long run, an increase in monetary growth will not lower interest rates; the increased money supply causes inflation. Lenders demand higher interest rates to compensate them for being repaid in inflated dollars.

Let's say, for example, that there's no inflation and that the interest rate is 5 percent. This is the real rate of interest. If the rate of inflation then rises to 8 percent, that means that if it cost you $10,000 to live last year, your cost of living is now $10,800. If lenders can anticipate the rate of inflation, they will insist that they be paid not just for the real interest rate of 5 percent, but also for the anticipated inflation of 8 percent. This raises the interest rate from 5 percent to a nominal rate of 13 percent.

What happens when the Federal Reserve allows the money supply to grow quickly is that interest rates are kept down for a while until lenders realize that the rate of inflation (caused by faster monetary growth) is rising. They will then demand higher interest rates. Thus, a higher rate of monetary growth will, in the short run, keep interest rates low, but in the long run, it will lead to higher interest rates.

(3) Expansionary Monetary Policy Will Only Temporarily Reduce the Unemployment Rate

The first two basic propositions partially explain the third. First, when monetary growth speeds up, output is expanded, but in the long run, only prices will rise. Since rising output would lower the unemployment rate, in the short run unemployment is reduced. But in the long run, an increase in the rate of monetary growth will raise prices, not output, so the unemployment rate will go back up. We'll come back to why this happens.

The second basic proposition states that expansionary monetary policy only temporarily depresses interest rates. In the short run, more money means lower interest rates. These lower interest rates encourage more investment and, consequently, less unemployment.

But in the long run the added money in circulation causes inflation, which, in turn, raises interest rates. As interest rates rise, investment declines and the unemployment rate goes back up.

The monetarists have explained the temporary reduction in the unemployment rate more directly. As labor union members begin to anticipate inflation, they will demand higher wage rates. New labor contract settlements will reflect the higher cost of living, but these higher wage settlements will price some workers out of the market, thus raising the unemployment rate.

(4) Expansionary Fiscal Policy Will Only Temporarily Raise Output and Employment Here we have another conflict—this time a basic one—between the monetarists and the Keynesians. The last believe that fiscal policy, particularly heavy government spending, will pull us out of a recession. But how is this spending going to be financed? By borrowing. The Treasury goes into the market for loanable funds and borrows $50 billion, $100 billion, $150 billion, or even $200 billion.

Crowding-out effect

The monetarists point out that such huge government borrowing comes directly into conflict with that of business firms and consumers. Not only will it be harder for these groups to borrow, but interest rates will be driven up. This is called the crowding-out effect, and represents, according to the monetarists, a substitution of public for private spending. All we're really doing is spending more on government goods and services and less on consumer and investment goods and services. Aggregate demand is not increased.

How well would a budget surplus restrain inflation? Not very, say the monetarists. The Treasury would not be borrowing now, but repaying part of the national debt, which would tend to push down interest rates and make borrowing easier. Private borrowing would replace public borrowing. The hoped for restraint would not materialize since private borrowers would now be spending these borrowed funds on goods and services. In effect then we would still have the same level of spending.

The Monetary Rule

Increase the money supply at a constant rate.

The policy prescription of the monetarists is simply to increase the money supply at a constant rate. When there is a recession, this steady infusion of money will pick up the economy. When there is inflation, a steady rate of monetary growth will slow it down.

You might ask why the money supply should be increased at all during inflation. There are two answers. First, the monetarists would tell you that if we didn't increase the money supply at all, we would be going back to the old, failed, discretionary monetary policies of the past—the start-and-stop, start-and-stop policies that only made the business cycle worse. Second, over the long run, the economy *does* need a steady infusion of money to enable economic growth.

The monetarists' steady monetary growth prescription is analogous to the feeding policy of the American army. Every day, in every part of the world, at every meal, the soldiers walk along the chow line and receive, in addition to the main course and dessert, two pieces of white bread, two pats of butter, and one pint of whole milk. The main course is also dished out in equal portions. The food servers do not dole out portions whose size varies with that of the eater. They look from the serving pan to the eater's tray, slopping out serving spoonfuls of whatever it is that the army decided to cook that day.

So we have 6 foot 6 inch 300-pound people getting the same sized portions as those of 5 foot 6 inch 130-pound people. My theory is that the army wants everyone to be the same size—a theory that seems to be borne out by the single uniform size that is issued. If everyone eats the same portion, presumably, they will all end up this same size.

Perhaps the monetarists got the idea of increasing the money supply by a constant percentage by observing army chow lines. They believe that our economic health will be relatively good—if not always excellent—if we have a steady diet of money. No starts and stops, no extreme ups and downs, and, to complete the analogy, no very fat years and no very lean years.

The Decline of Monetarism

Interestingly, when the Fed really began to pay attention to what the monetarists were saying, this may have led to the ultimate decline of the monetarists. In October of 1979, Federal Reserve Chairman Paul Volcker announced a major policy shift. No longer would the Fed focus only on keeping interest rates on an even keel. From now on the Fed would set monetary growth targets and stick to them.

This new policy was followed for most of the next three years. The double-digit inflation that prevailed in 1979 and 1980 was finally brought under control by late 1982—but not until we had gone through a period of sky-high interest rates, very high unemployment, and two recessions.

Even though the Fed had finally followed the advice of the monetarists— at least to a large degree—and even though the nagging inflation of the last 13 or 14 years had finally been wrung out of the economy, people began to look elsewhere for their economic gurus. They looked to the White House, which had become a stronghold of the latest school of economics, the supply-side school.

Supply-Side Economics

Cut tax rates, government spending, and government regulation.

Supply-side economics came into vogue in the early 1980s when Ronald Reagan assumed the presidency. Supply-siders felt very strongly that the economic role of the federal government had grown much too large and that high tax rates and onerous government rules and regulations were hurting the incentives of individuals and business firms to produce goods and services. President Reagan suggested a simple solution: get the government off the backs of the American people. How? By cutting taxes and reducing government spending and regulation.

Raise aggregate supply.

The objective of supply-side economics then is to raise aggregate supply, the total amount of goods and services we produce. The problem, said the supply-siders, was that high tax rates were hurting the incentive to work and to invest. All we needed to do was cut tax rates and voilà! Up goes production.

Many of the undesirable side effects of high marginal tax rates are explained by the work effect, the savings and investment effect, and the elimination of productive market exchanges, which we shall take up in turn.

The Work Effect

Work-leisure decisions

People are often confronted with work-leisure decisions. Should I put in that extra couple of hours of overtime? Should I take on that second job? Should I keep my store open longer hours? If you answer yes to any of these, you'll have to give the government a pretty big slice of that extra income. At some point you may well conclude, "I'd have to be nuts to take on any extra work; I'll only be working for the government."

At what point do you start working for the government? When it takes 20 cents out of each dollar of extra income (a marginal tax rate of 20 percent)? When it takes 30 cents? Or 40 cents? Each of us makes his or her own decision about the cutoff point. If you are a wage earner, you will have to pay Social Security tax, federal income tax, and possibly some state income tax. Back in 1980, before the passage of the Kemp-Roth tax cut and the tax cuts that came under the Tax Reform Act of 1986, people earning over $30,000 a year often had marginal tax rates of over 50 percent.[2] If you paid more than half your overtime earnings in taxes, would *you* consider yourself working for the government?

Facing high marginal tax rates, many people refuse to work more than a certain number of hours of overtime, second jobs, or other forms of extra work. Instead, they opt for more leisure time. In a word, high marginal tax rates rob people not only of some potential income, but of the incentive to work longer hours. People working shorter hours obviously produce less so that total output is lower than it might have been with lower marginal tax rates. This, and the saving-investment argument, considered next, are the two key points made by supply-siders for lower marginal tax rates.

The Saving and Investment Effect

The supply-side economists really make two arguments against high marginal tax rates. First, when people save money, they earn interest on their savings. But a high marginal tax rate on interest income will provide a disincentive to save, or at least to make savings available for investment purposes.

Similarly, money borrowed for investment purposes—new plant and equipment and inventory—will hopefully lead to greater profits. But if those profits are subject to a high marginal tax rate, once again there is a disincentive to invest.[3]

If people are discouraged from working, total output will be reduced. And if they are discouraged from saving and investing, the economy will be stagnant. Supply-side economists point to the economic stagnation of the late 1970s and early 1980s as proof of the basic propositions of their theory. On the other hand, the economic record, particularly with respect to savings, investment, and economic growth during the Reagan years, has been nothing to write home about either.

The Elimination of Productive Market Exchanges

Most people have jobs at which they are good: an accountant, a carpenter, an automobile mechanic, and a gourmet chef are all relatively good at their professions. That's probably why they chose that line of work to begin with—and all that on-the-job training didn't hurt either.

When you need your taxes prepared—especially if you stand to save several thousand dollars—you go to an accountant. When you need your transmission fixed, unless you're a skilled mechanic, you'd certainly be better off going to someone who is. In fact, one of the main reasons our standard of living is so high is because a large proportion of our labor force is composed of individuals with specialized skills.

What happens when your roof must be reshingled? Do you hire a roofer or do you do it yourself? Do you do it yourself because it's cheaper?

Well, maybe it's cheaper and maybe it isn't. Suppose you can reshingle your roof in 100 hours and a roofer can do the job in 60 hours. If the roofer charges you $12 an hour (in addition to materials), it would cost you $720. How many hours would you have to work to earn $720? Suppose your cler-

---

[2] Under Kemp-Roth, personal income taxes were slashed 23 percent from 1981–84. The top marginal tax rate was cut from 70 percent to 50 percent. Personal income tax rates were cut further under the Tax Reform Act of 1986 to marginal rates of 33, 28, and 15 percent.

[3] Under the Tax Reform Act of 1986, the basic corporate income tax rate was reduced from 46 percent to 34 percent.

ical job paid $9 an hour and you were in the 40 percent marginal tax bracket. You would take home only $5.40 an hour (that is, 60 percent of $9).

Do you hire the roofer or do it yourself? If you do it yourself, it will take you 100 hours. If you hire the roofer, you must pay him $720. How many hours would you have to work to bring home $720? Figure it out: $720/$5.40 = 133⅓ hours. I think even *I* would rather spend 100 hours on my roof than 133⅓ hours in front of a class. And I'm afraid of heights!

There is a serious misallocation of labor when the productive market exchange—your clerical work for your roofer's labor—is eliminated; but because of the high marginal tax rate, it pays for you to work less at your regular job (at which you are presumably good) and more at household tasks (at which you are not so good). When you add up all the productive market exchanges short circuited by high marginal tax rates, you may well be talking about hundreds of billions of dollars in misallocated resources.

High tax rates discourage productive market exchanges.

The Laffer Curve

Policy prescription: cut taxes!

Supply-side economists have one basic policy prescription: cut tax rates! This will raise output. There *is* one slight problem. Won't federal tax revenue fall precipitously? Some supply-side economists feel this would not be an altogether bad idea. After all, the more the federal government takes in, the more it spends. All the Democrats did, they argued, was "tax, tax, tax, spend, spend, spend." But Arthur Laffer, an orthodox supply-side economics professor, said it isn't necessarily true that a tax rate cut will lead to a fall in tax revenue. *Au contraire* (that's French for just the opposite).

The Laffer curve

Imagine that we're at point A on the Laffer Curve drawn in Figure 15–2. We cut the marginal tax rate from 50 percent to 40 percent and, lo and be-

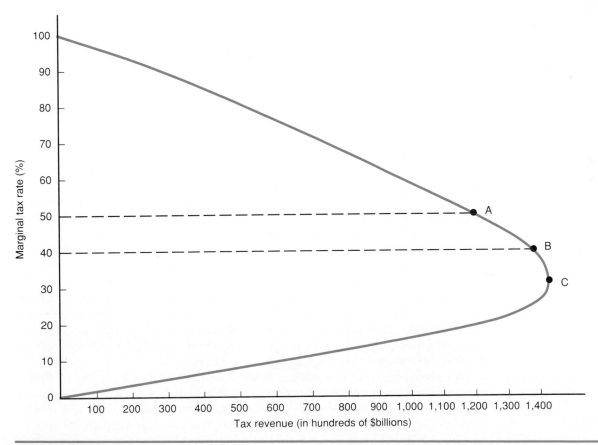

Figure 15–2
The Laffer Curve

hold, tax revenue rises from $1,200 billion to nearly $1,400 billion. Is that sophistry? (That's Greek for pulling a fast one.)

Let's see how this works by looking at the case of a specific individual. Suppose this person pays $50,000 on an income of $100,000. If this person's tax rate were lowered to 40 percent, he would pay $40,000. Right? Wrong say the supply-siders! He would now have an incentive to work harder. How much harder? Hard enough, say, to earn $130,000 by working every available hour of overtime or taking on a second job.

How much is 40 percent of $130,000? It comes out to exactly $52,000. How much did the government collect from him before the tax cut? Only $50,000. So by cutting tax rates, say the supply-siders, the government will end up collecting more revenue.

Is this true? If we go back to the Laffer Curve, apparently it is—at least at very high tax rates. But when we cut tax rates in 1981 and 1982, tax revenue actually declined. Of course, there was a recession going on.

What if we were at, say, point C on the Laffer Curve and we cut tax rates? What would happen to federal tax revenue? Obviously it would decline.

The only problem then is to figure out where we are on the Laffer Curve, or what the parameters of the curve itself are, before we start cutting taxes. There really *is* a Laffer Curve out there. The trouble is we don't know exactly where, so when we try to use it as a policy tool, it's kind of like playing an economic version of pin the tail on the donkey. When you play a game blindfolded, you run the risk of looking a lot like the six-year-old kids who miss the donkey completely. And this game is for somewhat higher stakes.

During the last two years of the Reagan administration, it had become apparent that supply-side economics, like the administration, was an idea whose time had gone. Although inflation had been brought under control and interest rates had declined as well (largely because of the efforts of the Federal Reserve), the supply-side policies had not yielded the rapid rate of economic growth that the public had been led to expect.

Conservative economists, many of whom had never been entirely comfortable with supply-side economics, had yet another banner to rally round. This one was called rational expectations.

Rational Expectations Theory

Most economists agree on two sets of policies.

Whatever else you have learned about economic policy, you have certainly learned that economists don't all agree on what policies we should follow. Nevertheless, with certain notable exceptions, most economists today would more or less agree on two sets of policies. To fight inflation, you want to lower the rate of growth of the money supply and reduce federal government budget deficits. And to fight recessions, you want to do the opposite: increase the rate of growth of the money supply and increase the size of the deficits. Although there are some economists who would admit to only partial acquiescence to these policies, there has been a greater consensus for these stated policies than for any others.

You probably never saw *Monty Python and the Holy Grail*, but in that movie, there was a group of knights who distinguished themselves solely by saying "Nuh." No matter what questions they were asked, they would always answer, "Nuh." Assuming that "Nuh" was Middle English for nay or no, those knights were the rational expectations theorists, or the new classical economists of their day.

Like the "old" classical economists, today's rational expectationists say no to any form of government economic intervention. Such intervention, no matter how well intentioned would do a lot more harm than good. In fact, they maintain that antiinflationary and antirecessionary policy, at best, would have no affect whatsoever. More likely, said the new classical economists, these policies would end up making things worse.

The three assumptions of rational expectations theory

Rational expectations theory is based on three assumptions: (1) that individuals and business firms learn through experience to instantaneously anticipate the consequences of changes in monetary and fiscal policy; (2) that they act instantaneously to protect their economic interests; and (3) that all resource and product markets are purely competitive.

Now we'll translate. Imagine that the Federal Reserve decided to sharply increase the rate of growth of the money supply. Why would the Fed do this? To stimulate output and raise employment.

The scenario, according to the Fed would be as follows: (1) the money supply rises; (2) business firms order more plant and equipment and more inventory; (3) more jobs are created and output rises; (4) wages do not rise right away, but prices do; (5) since prices rise and wages stay the same, profits rise; (6) eventually wages catch up to prices, profits go back down, and the expansion comes to an end.

This may have happened in the old days, say the rational expectations theorists, but surely people have learned something from all this experience. Everybody knows that when the Fed sharply increases the monetary growth rate, inflation will result. Business firms, of course, will raise prices. But what about labor? Anticipating the expected inflation, wage earners will demand wage increases *now*. No more playing catch-up after the cost of living has already risen.

If wage rates are increased along with prices, do profits increase? No! If profits are not rising, there goes the main reason for increasing output and hiring more people—which, of course, was why the rate of monetary growth was raised in the first place.

Let's return to the rational expectations theorists' three assumptions. The first one is plausible enough—that through experience, we learn to anticipate the consequences of changes in monetary and fiscal policy. So, if a sharp increase in the rate of growth in the money supply always leads to inflation, eventually we will all learn to recognize this pattern.

It would follow from the next two assumptions that the intended results of macroeconomic policy shifts will be completely frustrated. Why? If you knew that prices would be increasing, would you be willing to sit back and passively accept a decline in your standard of living? Wouldn't you demand a higher wage rate to keep pace with rising prices? The rational expectations theorists say that people can always be expected to promote their personal economic interests and that furthermore, in a purely competitive market, they are free to do so.

In a purely competitive labor market, workers are free to leave one employer for another who offers higher wages. In a purely competitive products market, all firms are subject to the law of supply and demand, and will automatically pass along any wage increases in the form of higher prices.

Most macroeconomic policy changes are predictable.

Most macroeconomic policy changes are, say the rational expectations theorists, very predictable. When there's inflation, there are extended debates in Congress, demands for cuts in government spending and tax increases, and a slowdown in the rate of monetary growth. Both Congress and the Federal Reserve generally telegraph policy moves, often months in advance. The point is that when these moves are made, no one is surprised. And because they're anticipated by the public, the intended effects of these policy changes are canceled out by the actions taken by individuals and business firms to protect their economic interests. In the case of policies aimed at raising output and employment, all we get for our efforts is more inflation.

What should the government do?

What should the government do? It should do, say the rational expectations theorists, as little as possible. Like the classical economists, they believe that the more the government tries to be an economic stabilizing force, the more it will destabilize the economy.

Basically then the federal government should figure out the right policies to follow and stick to them. What *are* the right policies? Funny you should ask. As you might expect, they've taken up the conservative economists' agenda: (1) steady monetary growth of 3 to 4 percent a year (the monetarists' monetary rule) and (2) a balanced budget (favored by the classical economists, among others).

Criticism of the rational expectations school

Like every other school of economics, the rational expectations school has certainly had its share of criticism. In fact, only a small minority of economists today would consider themselves new classical economists, mainly because this group just goes too far in ascribing rationality to both the general population and themselves.

Is it reasonable to expect individuals and business firms to accurately predict the consequences of macroeconomic policy changes when economists themselves come up with widely varying predictions, most of which are wrong? Since economists place so little faith in each other's rationality, would it be rational to expect them to ascribe a greater prescience to the general population than they give themselves?

In a world of constant change, is it possible for people to accurately predict the economic consequences of policy changes? Indeed, when a constantly changing cast of policymakers, each with his or her own economic agendas, seems to be calling for entirely new economic approaches every few years, it's awfully hard to tell the players without a scorecard—it's even harder to predict the final score.

A second criticism of the rational expectations school is that our economic markets are not purely competitive; some are not competitive at all. Labor unions are not an economist's idea of purely competitive labor market institutions. Nor would industries such as automobiles, petroleum, cigarettes, and breakfast cereals, each of which has just a handful of firms doing most of the producing, be considered very competitive.

Finally, critics raise the question of the rigidities imposed by contracts. The labor union with the two- or three-year contract cannot reopen bargaining with employers when greater inflation is anticipated because of a suddenly expansionary monetary policy. Nor can business firms that have long-term contracts with customers decide to charge higher prices because they perceive more inflation in the future.

Does all this mean that we should summarily dismiss the rational expectations school because it is so vulnerable to criticism? Most economists would probably concede that this school is correct in calling their attention to the importance of expectations in affecting the outcome of macroeconomic policy changes. In recent years then, economists have become more aware that to the degree that policy changes are predictable, people will certainly act to protect their economic interests. Since to some degree they will succeed, in doing so, they will partially counteract the effect of the government's macroeconomic policy.

In other words, rational expectations theory has a certain validity, as do each of the other theories we discussed. The question we're left with is how valid is each theory relative to each of the others?

Conclusion

What policies *should* we follow?

What policies *should* we follow? Classical economists subscribed to Thomas Jefferson's dictum that "The government that governs best, governs least." Since recessions will cure themselves, said the classicals, the government should adhere to a laissez-faire policy, allowing the private economic system to function without interference.

The Keynesians stress fiscal policy. During recessions, run federal budget deficits; during inflations, run surpluses. Monetary policy? The latter-day Keynesians conceded that an expansionary monetary policy would be helpful, but Keynesian economics has always stressed the primacy of fiscal policy.

The supply-side school, sometimes considered the flipside of the Keynesian school, stressed the importance of tax rate cuts to give people greater work incentive. Although they basically believed in balanced budgets, temporary deficits were justified as unfortunate by-products of the tax rate cuts.

The monetarists wanted rules—a 3 to 4 percent rate of monetary growth and balanced budgets. Why? Because we simply did not know enough about the workings of our economy to successfully practice discretionary macroeconomic policy.

Finally, we have the new classical economists, who believe that macroeconomic stabilization policy is self-defeating because people not only anticipate government actions, but protect their own economic interests so that the intended effects of the government policy is immediately and fully canceled out.

Where does all of this leave us? It leaves us just about where we started at the beginning of this chapter: about the only thing economists can agree on is that they disagree.

Don't dispair. We'll try to tie things together in the next and last chapter on macroeconomics. We'll attempt to draw on the collective wisdom of the five schools of economics to attain the oft-stated goals of stable prices, high employment, and a satisfactory rate of economic growth.

Despite the fact that he (Labor Secretary John Dunlop) is an economist, basically I have great confidence in him.

—George Meany

Workbook for Chapter 15

Name _____

Date _____

Multiple-Choice Questions

Circle the letter that corresponds to the best answer.

1. Say's Law states that
a. Supply creates its own demand   **b.** demand creates its own supply   **c.** demand will always exceed supply   **d.** supply will always exceed demand

2. The Bible of classical economics was written by
a. John Maynard Keynes   **b.** Milton Friedman
c. Karl Max   **d.** Adam Smith

3. According to the classical economists, if the quantity of money that people wanted to save was greater than the amount that people wanted to invest
a. there would be a recession   **b.** there would be inflation   **c.** the interest rate would fall.   **d.** the interest rate would rise

4. The classical economists believed that
a. both wages and prices were flexible downward
b. neither wages nor prices were flexible downward
c. wages, but not prices, were flexible downward
d. prices, but not wages, were flexible downward

5. The classicals believed that recessions were
a. impossible   **b.** potential depressions
c. temporary   **d.** hard to end without government intervention

6. The problem during recessions, said John Maynard Keynes, was
a. inadequate aggregate supply   **b.** inadequate aggregate demand   **c.** too much inflation   **d.** too much government intervention

7. According to Keynes, _____ was necessary to get us out of a depression.
a. investment spending   **b.** consumer spending
c. foreign spending   **d.** any kind of spending

8. Keynes felt that budget deficits were
a. to be avoided at all costs   **b.** bad during recessions   **c.** good during recessions   **d.** good all the time

9. The key to investment spending, said Keynes, was
a. the interest rate   **b.** the expected profit rate
c. foreign spending   **d.** government spending

10. Classical economics lost most of its popularity in
a. the 1920s   **b.** the 1930s   **c.** the 1960s   **d.** the 1980s

11. Big government was ushered in in the
a. 1920s   **b.** 1930s   **c.** 1960s   **d.** 1980s

12. To the monetarists, the most important thing was
a. the rate of growth of the money supply
b. balancing the federal budget   **c.** raising the federal government's tax base   **d.** giving the Federal Reserve free reign

13. During a recession, if the money supply were increased
a. The Keynesians and the monetarists agree that people would probably just hold onto these funds
b. The Keynesians and the monetarists agree that people would spend this money on assets of one kind or another   **c.** The Keynesians believe that people would probably just hold on to these funds while the monetarists believe that people would spend this money on assets of one kind or another.

14. Which of the following is a basic proposition of monetarism?
a. The key to stable economic growth is a constant rate of increase in the money supply.

b. Expansionary monetary policy will permanently depress the interest rates.   **c.** Expansionary monetary policy will permanently reduce the unemployment rate.   **d.** Expansionary fiscal policy will permanently raise output and employment.

15. The monetary rule states that
a. the federal budget must be balanced every year
b. the money supply must increase at the same rate as the price level   **c.** the money supply must remain a constant from year to year   **d.** the money supply must be increased at a constant rate

16. The monetarists critized
a. the stop-and-go policies of the Federal Reserve
b. the ineffectiveness of monetary policy at fighting inflation   **c.** the importance given to money by the Keynesians   **d.** the Fed for keeping a heavy foot on the monetary brake and allowing the money supply to rise by only 3 percent a year

17. Supply-sides felt that
a. the federal government played too large an economic role   **b.** the federal government played too small an economic role   **c.** tax rates were too low
d. the federal government was not spending enough to meet the needs of the poor

18. According to the supply-siders, each of the following resulted from high marginal tax rates except
a. the work effect   **b.** the savings-investment effect   **c.** the elimination of productive market exchanges   **d.** lagging demand for imported goods and services

19. Each of the following is associated with supply-side economics except
a. Ronald Reagan   **b.** Arthur Laffer   **c.** Milton Friedman   **d.** Kemp-Roth

20. According to the Laffer Curve, when very high marginal tax rates are lowered, tax revenue will
a. decline considerably   **b.** decline slightly   **c.** stay the same   **d.** increase

21. The rational expectations theorists said that anti-inflationary policy will
a. generally work   **b.** definitely do more harm than good   **c.** either do no good or do harm

22. According to the rational expectations theorists, everyone learns that when the Fed sharply increases monetary growth
a. inflation will result and people must move to protect themselves   **b.** a recession will result and people must move to protect themselves   **c.** people will continue to make the same mistakes over and over again

23. Most macroeconomic policy changes, say the rational expectations theorists, are
a. very hard to predict   **b.** very easy to predict
c. slow, that is, they take place over a period of many years   **d.** irrational

24. The advice the rational expectations theorists give the federal government is to
a. change macropolicy often   **b.** figure out the right policies to follow and stick to them   **c.** figure out what the public is expecting and then do the opposite

25. Which school would advocate government spending to end a recession?
a. classical   **b.** Keynesian   **c.** monetarist
d. supply-side   **e.** rational expectations

26. Which school would consider cutting tax rates as the cure for all our economic ills?
a. classical   **b.** Keynesian   **c.** monetarist
d. supply-side   **e.** rational expectations

Fill-In Questions

1. Say's Law states that _____.

2. According to the classical economists, if there is a recession, the government should _____.

3. The classicals, applying Say's Law, believed that all our income would be _____; all our production would be _____; and all our savings would be ____.

4. The classicals said that if the amount of money people wanted to save was greater than the amount business people wanted to invest, _____.

5. The classical school dominated economic thought until _____.

6. John Maynard Keynes defined aggregate demand as _____ plus _____ plus _____.

7. According to Keynes, the most important determinant of the level of investment was the _____.

8. According to Keynes, the main institutional barriers to downward wage and price flexibility were (1) _____ and (2) _____.

9. The main success of Keynesian economics in the 1960s was _____.

10. John Maynard Keynes said that during recessions and depressions the main problem was _____ _____.

11. To solve that problem, Keynes suggested _____ _____.

12. Monetarism begins and ends with one obsession: _____.

13. Milton Friedman concluded that we have never had a serious inflation that was not accompanied by _____.

14. The monetarists believed that if the money supply were raised during a recession, people would _____ _____.

15. According to the monetarists, recessions are caused by _____.

16. The key to stable economic growth, according to the monetarists, is _____.

17. The record of the Fed, say the monetarists, is analagous to _____.

18. The monetary rules states that _____.

19. The monetarists say that expansionary monetary policy will _____ depress interest rates and the unemployment rate. They further say that expansionary monetary policy will _____ raise output and employment.

20. Supply-side economics came into vogue in _____.

21. The objective of supply-side economics is to _____ _____; the problem, said the supply-siders, was that _____ were hurting the incentive to work and invest.

22. The way to get people to work more, say the supply-siders, is to _____.

23. According to the Laffer Curve, when marginal tax rates are very high, if they are reduced, the result will be _____ federal tax revenue.

24. The three assumptions on which rational expectations theory are based are: (1) _____, (2) _____, and (3) _____.

25. Most macroeconomic policy changes are, say the rational expectations theorists, _____.

26. The rational expectations theorists have taken up two key items on the conservative economists' agenda: (1) _____ _____, and (2) _____.

27. The main criticism leveled at the rational expectations theorists is that _____.

Problem

1. Suppose you are in the 50 percent tax bracket, that is, you pay 50 percent of the last $10,000 you earned in taxes. If this tax bracket were lowered to 30 percent on all your earnings over, say $30,000 (you currently earn, say, $40,000), show how the government could end up collecting more taxes from you.

A Guide to Macropolicy

The three main goals of macropolicy are stable prices, high employment, and a satisfactory rate of economic growth. All economists agree to these goals; they disagree about the means of achieving them.

This will necessarily be a very short chapter because virtually nothing I can say about macropolicy will not offend at least one school of economists. What I will propose here, while not particularly daring or innovative, will give the reader some sense of overall macropolicy, its potential, and its limitations.

Chapter Objectives

In this chapter we shall consider:
- Conventional monetary and fiscal policies to fight recessions and inflations.
- Incomes policies.
- How to attain a satisfactory rate of economic growth.

Fighting Recessions

Conventional Fiscal Policy

Run deficits to fight recessions.

We'll begin with the simplest of fiscal policy measures drawn from Chapter 11; then we'll get a bit more fancy. The most conventional fiscal policy to fight a recession is to run a budget deficit. Indeed, given the automatic stabilizers as well as our tax laws, deficits are virtually inevitable during recessions.

The question then is how big the deficits should be. Assuming that the deficit rises about $30 billion for each point the unemployment rate rises and that a 5 percent unemployment rate represents full employment, at a 6 percent unemployment rate, we should run a deficit of about $30 billion. How much should the deficit be when the unemployment rate is 7 percent? You have it—$60 billion. This is our famous full-employment balanced budget.

Conventional Monetary Policy

Speed up M growth to fight recessions.

Were we to enter a recession, the conventional monetary policy would be to speed up the rate of growth of the money supply (see the last part of Chapter 13). Here we need to be careful: if we sped it up too much, we would have to worry about an inflation and possibly rising interest rates, which, in time, would kill off any recovery. Surely there would be no justification for as much as a 10 percent rate of monetary growth over any extended period of time.

Two Policy Dilemmas

Suppose we are running a budget deficit of $90 billion and the annual rate of monetary growth is 8 percent. What could go wrong?

The huge budget deficits are financed by massive borrowings by the Treasury. As the economy begins to recover, business and consumer borrowing picks up as well. What does all this loan demand do to interest rates? It drives them up. And when interest rates, which were high even during the recession, rise still higher in the early stages of recovery, what happens next? The recovery collapses.

Thus, a budget deficit, designed to stimulate the economy, necessitates massive Treasury borrowing, driving up interest rates and ultimately choking off recovery.

Let's see about rapid monetary growth. It stimulates recovery, making funds available to business firms and consumers. Interest rates may decline. So far so good. But when we increase the money supply this rapidly, we also court inflation, and with inflation, people will demand more interest for their savings. And so, with inflation and higher interest rates, it won't be long before the recovery will sputter to a stop.

Fighting Inflation

Conventional Fiscal Policy

To fight inflation, reduce deficit.

One thing we would want to do immediately is reduce the size of the federal budget deficit—if we happen to be running one. It would be too much of a shock to try to reduce it by more than $40 or $50 billion in one year, but in the face of persistent inflation, we would need to reduce the deficit year by year and ultimately run budget surpluses.

Conventional Monetary Policy

To fight inflation, slow rate of M growth.

The obvious policy move here would be to slow down the rate of growth of the money supply. Indeed, if inflation were beginning to rage out of control, not only would the Fed have to stop the money supply from growing, but it would have to cause it to contract slightly.

Fighting Inflationary Recessions: Two More Policy Dilemmas

Some people think of inflations and recessions as two separate problems. They once were. However, beginning with the recession in 1957–58, the price level has risen during every recession. To add insult to injury, during the three most recent recessions, 1973–75, 1980, and 1981–82, inflation was of double-digit proportions.

Let's review conventional fiscal policy to fight recessions and inflation. To fight recessions, we run budget deficits; to fight inflation, we run surpluses. Very well then, what do we do to fight an inflationary recession? That's one dilemma.

We'll go on to the second dilemma. What is the conventional monetary policy to fight a recession? Speed up the rate of monetary growth. And to fight an inflation? Slow it down.

Here's the $64 question. How do we fight an inflation *and* a recession simultaneously using conventional fiscal and monetary policy? The answer: we can't.

Don't give up; there *is* hope.

One approach would be to try a combination of tight money to fight the inflation and a budget deficit to provide the economic stimulus needed to fight the recession. We kind of stumbled onto this combination during the recession of 1981–82, but it wasn't until the Fed eased up on the tight money part that the economy finally began to recover. By then, much of the inflation had been wrung from the economy.

The above suggests a second approach. First deal with the inflation, then cure the recession. In the early 1950s, we suffered from a surge of inflation brought on by the Korean War. Over the course of just eight years, we had three recessions. By the end of the third recession, the consumer price index was virtually stable. Then, through almost the entire decade of the 1960s, we had a recession-free expansion.

Conventional policies are not ideal for fighting inflationary recessions.

Conventional monetary and fiscal policy tools are sufficient to deal with simple recessions and inflations, but inflationary recessions pose additional problems. They cannot be cured by conventional macropolicy without a great deal of suffering, particularly by those who lose their jobs.

Incomes Policies: An Alternate Approach

In addition to conventional monetary and fiscal policies, we shall consider two more ways of fighting inflation: wage and price controls, and tax-based incomes policies. Neither is particularly popular with the economics profession.

Wage and Price Controls

During World War II and again in 1971, wage and price controls were imposed by the federal government. The argument for such controls is that they force a legal end to inflation by making wage and price increases illegal.

Two main arguments against controls

There are two main arguments against such controls. First, they interfere with the price mechanism (i.e., the law of supply and demand). Without question, this is the case. Because we are substituting a bureaucratic control system for an extremely complex and well-functioning private decision-making system, we would have to be desperate indeed to impose such a system.

A second objection to wage and price controls is that once they are removed, there will be a surge in wages and prices to make up for lost time. Indeed, this is exactly what happened both after World War II and in the early 1970s, after the controls were removed.

Tax-Based Incomes Policies

These policies involve the carrot and stick approach: the carrot is a tax cut and the stick a tax increase. If a corporation raises prices or grants wage increases beyond a certain predetermined percentage, say, 4 percent, its corporate income tax rate is raised by a certain percentage. Similarly, if it holds wage and price increases below a certain percentage, its taxes could be lowered.

Would this work? Some skeptics point to the large bureaucracy that would be needed to keep watch over such a system. Of course, if only rewards for good behavior were handed out, the corporations could be counted on to give the good news to the IRS at the end of the tax year.

Attaining a Satisfactory Rate of Economic Growth

Historical U.S. growth rate: 3.5 percent

Historically we have grown at a rate of about 3½ percent a year. Most people would call that a satisfactory growth rate because it enabled the United States to become the world's leading economic power. Surely a rate of, say, 4 percent year after year would satisfy nearly everyone.

In recent years, particularly since the early 1970s, our growth rate has been lagging. Two factors that have held down the growth rate have been a low rate of investment (which, in turn, is largely due to a low savings rate), and a low rate of productivity increase.

In recent years Americans have been saving less than 5 percent of their incomes compared to a rate of about 25 percent in Japan. Furthermore, the federal government has been running huge budget deficits, which more than absorb all the personal savings we have been able to generate. Additionally, we as a nation have been on an international buying spree, racking up huge trade deficits. Fortunately, foreigners have been recycling most of those dollars by buying up not only huge chunks of our national debt, but also tens of billions of dollars in corporate bonds and stocks each year. Thus, it is essentially foreign saving that has enabled our businesses to continue investing in new plant and equipment.

Productivity is defined as output per unit of input. Labor productivity is measured by output per hour worked. Productivity is what makes our economy go. From 1963–73, our productivity rose by nearly one third. Between 1977–87, it rose by only about 9 percent.

Two problems: lagging productivity and lagging investment

The problems of lagging productivity and lagging investment are intertwined. The less plant and equipment backing each worker, the lower our productivity will be. The lower our rate of productivity increase, the less plant and equipment will be produced (along with less consumer goods).

One way of channeling more income into saving would be to make interest income tax free. Such a proposal would be objected to on the grounds that it was a giveaway to the rich, who derive a major portion of their incomes from interest. We'll overlook the fact that much of rich people's interest income is derived from tax-free state and municipal bonds, and address ourselves to the general objection that tax-free interest income would merely be a boon to the rich. Fine, let's limit tax-free interest to the first $5,000 of interest income.

Another possibility would be a national sales tax such as a value-added tax, which is used in several European countries. At each stage of the production process, a uniform tax of, say, 2 percent is charged. Not only would such a tax discourage consumption and encourage saving, but it would drastically reduce the federal budget deficit.

One criticism of such a tax is that it would be regressive. While that is certainly true, its regressiveness could be greatly reduced by exempting food, most rents, and other goods and services purchased by the poor.

Conclusion

Where does all of this leave us? Clearly the economics profession does not have all the answers. But we do occasionally come up with some interesting questions and we're very good at providing cogent explanations about why our predictions almost always seem to go awry.

Now we're ready to go on to the second half of the principles of economics—microeconomics. And as they like to say over at the stadium, it's a brand new ball game.

Workbook for Chapter 16

Name _____

Date _____

Multiple-Choice Questions

Circle the letter that corresponds to the best answer.

1. The conventional fiscal policy to fight a recession would be to
a. increase the rate of monetary growth   **b.** decrease the rate of monetary growth   **c.** run budget deficits   **d.** run budget surpluses

2. The conventional monetary policy to fight inflations would be to
a. increase the rate of monetary growth   **b.** decrease the rate of monetary growth   **c.** run budget deficits   **d.** run budget surpluses

3. One problem or dilemma we might face in fighting a recession is that
a. we might end up with budget surpluses
b. output might rise too quickly   **c.** interest rates might fall   **d.** interest rates might rise

4. During recessions we want
a. budget deficits and faster monetary growth
b. budget deficits and slower monetary growth
c. budget surpluses and faster monetary growth
d. budget surpluses and slower monetary growth

5. During inflations we want
a. budget deficits and faster monetary growth
b. budget deficits and slower monetary growth
c. budget surpluses and faster monetary growth
d. budget surpluses and slower monetary growth

6. Which statement is true?
a. In recent years inflation and recession have become separate problems.   **b.** In recent years inflation and recession have become related problems.   **c.** Inflation and recession have never been related problems.   **d.** Inflation and recession have always been related problems.

7. Each of the following could be used to fight inflation except
a. tax-based incomes policies   **b.** wage and price controls   **c.** budget surpluses   **d.** budget deficits

8. Historically, we have had an annual growth rate of about
a. 2 percent, which we have exceeded over the last 15 years   **b.** 2 percent, which exceeds the rate we have had over the last 15 years   **c.** 3½ percent, which we have exceeded over the last 15 years   **d.** 3½ percent, which exceeds the rate we have had over the last 15 years

9. In recent years
a. our saving rate and our productivity growth have both been lagging   **b.** neither our saving rate nor our rate of productivity growth has been lagging
c. our saving rate has been lagging, but our rate of productivity growth has not   **d.** our productivity rate of growth has been lagging, but our saving rate has not

Fill-In Questions

1. The three main goals of macropolicy are
(1) _____, (2) _____, and (3) _____.

2. The conventional fiscal policy to fight a recession is to _____ while the conventional monetary policy is to _____.

3. The conventional fiscal policy to fight an inflation is to _____ while the conventional monetary policy is to _____.

4. One problem with both expansionary monetary and fiscal policies used to fight recessions is that they could lead to _____.

5. The dilemma of fighting an inflationary recession with conventional fiscal policy would be _____

_____.

6. The dilemma of fighting an inflationary recession with conventional monetary policy would be _____

_____.

7. Two incomes policies used to fight inflation are

(1) _____; and (2) _____.

8. Two factors that have held down the rate of

growth have been_____

and _____.

9. Two possible ways of increasing our savings rate

would be _____

and _____.

Demand

You would do well to reread Chapter 3 before you begin the present chapter. In that chapter we defined demand as "the schedule of quantities of a good or service that people will purchase at different prices." That will be our starting point.

Chapter Objectives
In this chapter, you will find out everything you always wanted to know about:
- Individual and market demand.
- Changes in demand.
- The elasticity of demand.
- Marginal and total utility.
- Consumer surplus.

Demand Defined

Demand is the schedule of quantities that people purchase at different prices.

Let's look at the demand for sirloin steak. At $1 a pound, it would create traffic jams as people rushed to the supermarket, but at $2 a pound, sirloin steak would be somewhat less of a bargain. At $3 a pound, it would lose many of its previous buyers to chicken, chuck steak, and other substitutes.

Law of demand

As the price of an item goes up, the quantity demanded falls, and as the price comes down, the quantity demanded rises. This inverse relationship may be stated as the Law of Demand. *When the price of a good is lowered, more of it is demanded; when it is raised, less is demanded.*

Individual Demand and Market Demand
The law of demand holds for both individuals and markets. Individual demand is the schedule of quantities that a person would purchase at different prices. Market demand is the schedule of quantities that everyone in the market would buy at different prices.

First, in Table 17–1, we'll show four examples of individual demand. Then we'll add them up to total market demand. We've added straight across. For example, at a price of $30, the quantity demanded on an individual basis is 0, 1, 2, and 1. Adding them together, we get total or market

| | Quantity Demanded by | | | | |
Price	Richard	Gerald	Jimmy	Ronald	Total
$30	0	1	2	1	4
25	2	1	3	3	9
20	3	2	5	4	14
15	3	3	6	6	18
10	4	5	7	7	23
5	5	6	7	8	26

demand of 4. Similarly, by adding all the individual quantities demanded at a price of $25, we get 2 plus 1 plus 3 plus 3 equals 9. And so forth.

What is the market?

There is one interesting question about market demand: What is the market? The market is where people buy and sell. Generally there is a prevailing price in a particular market. Take gasoline. In New York City the price of regular gas in May 1988 at most gas stations varied between 85 cents and 95 cents. But just across the bay in New Jersey, most stations charged between 75 cents and 80 cents.

New York City and New Jersey were two separate markets for gasoline. People in New York would not go to New Jersey to save 10 cents a gallon because the trip would not only have been inconvenient, it would have cost them a $3 toll.

The market for gasoline is very local because the money you'd save by driving to the next market would be more than canceled by the money it would cost you to go there. Another local market would be grocery shopping. Again, you wouldn't drive to the other side of your city or perhaps three towns down the highway just to save a dollar or two.

The market for automobiles is a regional one. If you lived in Boston and could save a couple of hundred dollars by going to a dealer in Portland or Providence, you probably would, but you wouldn't go from Chicago to San Francisco to save two hundred dollars on a car.

On a very local basis then, prices for most goods will not vary very much, but as the area covered grows larger, so do price variations. If people are willing to travel to get a bargain, the market will be much larger.

The market for some goods and services may be national or even international. A company that was shopping for a sophisticated computer system would look all over the world for the right system at the right price. And a person who needed a brain surgeon or a heart transplant would not go to his local doctor and ask him to operate in his office.

Changes in Demand

The definition of demand is our point of departure, so to speak, when we take up changes in demand. Once again, demand is the schedule of quantities that people purchase at different prices. A change in demand is a change in, or a departure from, this schedule.

Using the market demand schedule in Table 17-1, let's say that the product in question becomes much more desirable, perhaps because it suddenly is discovered to be worth votes in presidential elections. The people listed in Table 17-1 just might be somewhat interested in this discovery and might well decide that they are willing to pay even more for each unit.

An increase in demand

This takes us from Table 17-1 to Table 17-2, and it involves an increase in market demand. At each price, buyers are willing to buy more. That is,

Table 17–2
Hypothetical Market Demand
Schedule Illustrating an Increase
in Demand

Price	(1) Quantity Demanded	(2) Quantity Demanded
$30	4	5
25	9	11
20	14	18
15	18	28
10	23	38
5	26	50

by definition, there is an increase in demand. It is important to emphasize that an increase in demand is an *increase in the quantity people are willing to purchase at all prices.*

It would be helpful to illustrate this increase by means of a graph. This is done in Figure 17-1. Notice that the second demand curve, D_2, representing the increase in demand, is to the right of D_1. You should also note that at each price the quantity demanded in D_2 is greater than the quantity demanded in D_1.

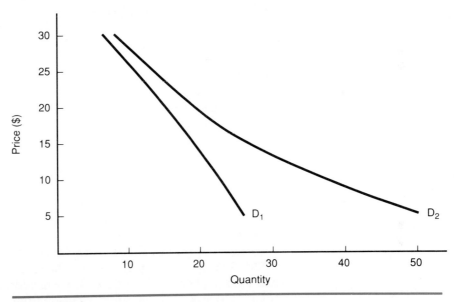

Figure 17–1

Now we're ready for a decrease in demand, also illustrated in Figure 17-1. You should be able to guess what the decrease would be. After all, there are only two curves on the graph and if going from D_1 to D_2 is an increase, ... That's right! Going from D_2 to D_1 is a decrease.

A decrease in demand means that *people are willing to buy less at each price.* In Figure 17-1, D_1 lies entirely to the left of D_2. If the curves were to cross, we would have neither an increase nor a decrease in demand; rather, we would have only a change in demand.

Figure 17-2 illustrates a change in demand, whether we go from D_1 to D_2 or from D_2 to D_1. My students often dispute this point. In Figure 17-2, they argue, when price is over $5, if we go from D_1 to D_2, this represents an increase in demand since people are willing to purchase more. And, they add,

A decrease in demand

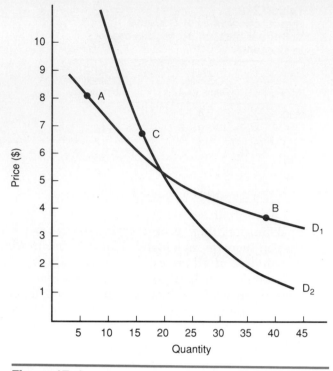

Figure 17–2

when we go from D_1 to D_2 at prices below $5, there is a decrease in demand.

Although I argue cogently and with considerable skill, many students remain convinced that there is an increase in demand from D_1 to D_2 above $5, and a decrease from D_1 to D_2 below $5. So what can I do? I'll give you the same arguments I gave them and if you insist that above $5 there's an increase in demand and below there's a decrease—then you should live and be well.

Let's give it another try. If we go back to Table 17-2, we see that for every price the quantity demanded in the second column is greater than in the first. At $30, the quantity demanded in column 2 is 5 compared with 4 in column 1. At $25, column 2 has a quantity of 11 compared with one of 9 for column 1.

In Figure 17-1, we see that D_2 is entirely to the right of D_1. At each price, $30, $25, $20, $15, $10, and $5, the quantity demanded is greater for D_2 than for D_1. If D_1 and D_2 crossed, we could not say that for every price the quantity demanded was greater for D_2 than for D_1.

We must consider demand curves in their entireties, not just by fragments. Fifth Avenue and Broadway cross at 23rd Street. Above 23rd Street, Broadway is west of Fifth Avenue and below 23rd Street it is east. Just as we cannot make the statement that Broadway is west of Fifth, so we cannot say that one demand curve is greater than another if they cross.

Look back at Figure 17-2. If we go from point A to Point B, does that represent a change in demand? Going back once more to our definition of demand—the schedule of quantities that people will purchase at different prices—when we go from A to B, has there been any change in the demand schedule? If both A and B are on that schedule, there has been no change in demand.

On the graph, we can easily see that both A and B are on the same demand curve. For a change in demand to have taken place, you have to move off the demand curve. If you moved from point A on D_1 to point C on D_2, that would be a change in demand.

If the move from A to B is not a change in demand, what is it? It's simply a change in quantity demanded in response to a price change. Price fell and quantity demanded rose. Incidentally, a favorite exam question is: If price falls and in response quantity demanded rises, does this represent a change in demand. Please—answer no!

Here are some problems to see if you're following what I've been talking about. They are each based on Figure 17–3. There are four possible answers: (a) a change in quantity demanded, (b) a change in demand, (c) an increase in demand, and (d) a decrease in demand.

1. When we move from E to F, it is _____ .

2. A move from F to G is _____ .

3. A move from G to H is _____ .

4. A move from H to I is _____ .

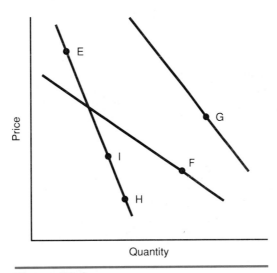

Figure 17–3

Now we'll go over each of the answers. A move from E to F is a change in demand because these points are on different demand curves that cross; neither is a higher demand curve because they cross. A higher demand would mean that people would buy more at every price. When two curves cross, they don't fulfill this condition.

From F to G is an increase in demand since the demand curve on which G is situated is to the right of F's demand curve. Note that there is an increase in demand because people are willing to buy more at all prices on G's demand curve.

From G to H is a decrease in demand for the same reason. On H's demand curve people would be willing to buy *less* for every price than on G's curve.

From H to I is a change in the quantity demanded. As long as we remain on the curve, there's no change in demand.

We need to talk about an ordering or ranking of changes. We had four choices in these problems. The least significant change is a change in quantity demanded since we stay on the same curve. It's simply no big deal.

When we move off the curve, now *that's* something! If we move off the curve, where do we go? Presumably to some other curve. Which one? A higher one? A lower one? If we move to another demand curve that crosses the original curve, all we can say is that there's been a change in demand.

But if we move to a curve that is entirely to the right of the first curve, we clearly have an increase in demand. To say we have an increase in demand is a much stronger statement that to merely say there's been a change in demand. Similarly, a decrease in demand is an equally strong statement.

The strongest thing we can say is that there has been an increase or a decrease in demand. The next strongest statement is that there has been a change in demand. The least powerful thing we can say is that there is a change in quantity demanded. As we move from point to point, we try to make the strongest possible statement.

Go back to the second problem. When we go from F to G, there has been not merely a change in demand, but an *increase* in demand. And in the third problem, when we go from G to H, why should we settle for a change in demand when we have a *decrease* in demand?

Now we'll try another set of problems using the same four possible answers. These are based on Figure 17-4.

5. A move from J to K is _____ .

6. A move from K to L is _____ .

7. A move from L to M is _____ .

8. A move from M to N is _____ .

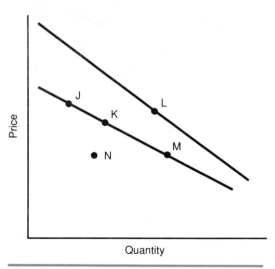

Figure 17-4

From J to K is clearly a change in the quantity demanded since we stay on the same demand curve. From K to L is an increase in demand since L's demand curve is entirely to the right of K's curve. Similarly, from L to M is a decrease in demand since M's curve is entirely to the left of L's.

Some students have questioned whether the curves would cross if they were extended. Obviously they would, but there are a couple of reasons why we can't extend the lines. First, how do we know that they would continue as straight lines? Perhaps if we had additional demand data, we'd find that they don't cross after all. Second, we have plotted these curves over some relevant price range. They're not plotted at extremely low or extremely high prices because no seller would be interested in charging such prices. So we must confine ourselves to the relevant price ranges within which the demand curves are drawn.

The move from M to N is a difficult one. Since we leave M's demand curve, it's not a change in quantity demanded. Because N lies to the left of M's curve, it couldn't possibly lie on a demand curve to the right of M's curve. But—and once again we have the $64 question—is N on a curve to the left of the demand curve on which M is situated?

Think about possible demand curves. If N is on a demand curve that is parallel to M's curve, clearly there would be a decrease in demand. But what if N were on a demand curve that intersected M's curve? What would we have then? A *change* in demand!

These possibilities are illustrated in Figure 17–5. First we have D_2, which is roughly parallel to D_1 on which M lies. D_3 and D_4 both cross D_1. Since we don't know on which of an infinite number of possible demand curves N is situated, we cannot assume that there is a decrease in demand when we go from M to N. The most we can say is that there is a change in demand.

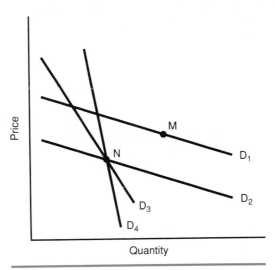

Figure 17–5

What Causes Changes in Demand?

Normal goods

Inferior goods

Changes in Income When your income goes up, you can afford to buy more goods and services. Suppose that the incomes of most Americans rise. That means a greater demand for cars, new homes, furniture, steaks, and motel rooms. Conversely, if incomes declined, as they do during recessions, there would be a smaller demand for most goods and services.

Most goods are normal goods. The demand for these goods varies directly with income: when income goes up, the demand for these goods goes up (see shift from D_1 to D_2 in Figure 17–1). When incomes decline, the demand for these goods declines as well (we go from D_2 to D_1).

However, certain goods are inferior goods because the demand for them varies inversely with income. For example, as income declines, the demand for potatoes, spaghetti, rice, and intercity bus rides increases. Why? Because these are the types of goods and services that are purchased by poorer people, and if income declines people are poorer. As incomes rise, the demand for these inferior goods declines because people can now afford more meat, cheese, and other relatively expensive foods, and they'll take planes rather than ride in buses.

Changes in the Prices of Related Goods and Services Suppose the tuna fish suddenly discovered a way to evade tuna fishermen, the supply of tuna fish drastically declined, and the price of tuna fish shot up to $2 a can. What do you think would soon happen to the price of salmon, chicken, and other close substitute goods? Obviously they would be driven up.

Let's see why this happens. First, the supply of tuna goes down and its price goes up. Most shoppers would say to themselves, "Two dollars a can! I've had tuna fish sandwiches for lunch every day of my life, but I'm not going to pay two dollars!" And so the former tuna fish buyers end up buying salmon and chicken. What has happened to the demand for salmon and chicken? It has gone up. And when the demand for something goes up, what happens to its price? Clearly it too goes up.

Substitute goods

Now we can generalize. The prices of substitute goods are directly related. If the price of one good goes up, people will increase their purchase of close substitutes, driving their prices up. Conversely, if the price of one good comes down, people will decrease their purchases of close substitutes, driving *their* prices down.

Complementary goods

There is another set of goods and services, complementary goods, whose prices are inversely related. That is, when the price of one goes down the price of the other goes up, or vice versa.

Suppose the price of videotape rentals falls from $2 a day to $1 a day. Many people would rush out to buy VCRs, driving up their prices. On the other hand, what would happen if gasoline went up to $5 a gallon? People would drive a lot less. This would lower the demand for tires, pushing down their prices.

Changes in Tastes and Preferences Imagine if the American Cancer Society and the Surgeon General mounted a heavy TV campaign with rock stars, professional athletes, movie actors and actresses, and other celebrities. The message: stop smoking. Imagine what a successful campaign would do to cigarette sales.

Sometimes tastes and preferences change by themselves over time. Over the last two decades Americans have opted for smaller cars, less fattening foods, and growing numbers of people have become more fashion conscious, buying only designer clothing and accessories. No one of my generation would have ever guessed that children would one day demand "fashionable" sneakers at $50 and $60 a pair.

Changes in Price Expectations If people expect the price of a product to rise, they rush out to stock up immediately, before its price does go up. On the other hand, if price is expected to fall, they will tend to hold off on their purchases.

When it appears that a war will break out, people will stock up on canned food, appliances, and anything else they think may be hard to buy in the coming months. On the other hand, when prices seem inordinately high, as the Manhattan coop and condominium market did in early 1985, potential buyers will hold out for lower prices. Incidentally, the prices of coops and condominiums did come down considerably in 1985 and 1986, partly because buyers expected a decline and waited for it to happen.

The Elasticity of Demand

Elasticity of demand measures the change in quantity in response to a change in price. When price goes up, we know that quantity demanded declines. But by how much? Elasticity provides us with a way of measuring this response.

We'll start with this problem. A business firm, which had been charging $10, was selling 100 kitchen chairs. It runs a sale, charging $8. People recognize this great bargain and sales go up to 140 chairs. If P_1 is the initial price charged and P_2 is the sale price, Q_1 the initial quantity sold and Q_2 the quantity sold during the sale, we can use this formula.

Elasticity formula

$$\text{Elasticity} = \frac{\dfrac{Q_2 - Q_1}{\dfrac{(Q_1 + Q_2)}{2}}}{\dfrac{P_2 - P_1}{\dfrac{(P_1 + P_2)}{2}}}$$

This formula looks a lot more complicated than it is. It simply calls for finding the percentage change in quantity and the percentage change in price, and then dividing the first by the last. Go ahead and substitute into the formula in the space below and then solve.

Solution:
$$\frac{\dfrac{140 - 100}{\dfrac{(100 + 140)}{2}}}{\dfrac{8 - 10}{\dfrac{(10 + 8)}{2}}} = \frac{\dfrac{40}{\dfrac{(240)}{2}}}{\dfrac{-2}{\dfrac{(18)}{2}}} = \frac{\dfrac{40}{120}}{\dfrac{-2}{9}} = \frac{33.33\%}{-22.22\%} = -1.5^{[1]}$$

Our elasticity comes to -1.5, but by convention, we ignore the sign, which by the way, will always be negative for elasticity of demand. In this case our answer is 1.5.

Most students initially have some difficulty calculating elasticity, so we'll work out a few more problems. When you become confident that you can do this type of problem, you may skip the remaining problems and begin the next section.

Problem: Price is raised from $40 to $41 and quantity sold declines from 15 to 12. Solve in the space below.

---

[1] If you're at all uncomfortable figuring out percentages, reread the section on the average tax rate near the beginning of Chapter 6.

Solution: $P_1 = \$40$; $P_2 = \$41$; $Q_1 = 15$; and $Q_2 = 12$.

$$\frac{\dfrac{Q_2 - Q_1}{(Q_1 + Q_2)}}{\dfrac{P_2 - P_1}{(P_1 + P_2)}} = \frac{\dfrac{12 - 15}{(15 + 12)}}{\dfrac{41 - 40}{(40 + 41)}} = \frac{\dfrac{-3}{\frac{27}{2}}}{\dfrac{1}{\frac{81}{2}}} = \frac{\dfrac{-3}{13.5}}{\dfrac{1}{40.5}} = \frac{-22.22\%}{2.47\%} = 8.996 \text{ or } 9$$

Problem: Price is lowered from \$5 to \$4 and quantity demanded rises from 80 to 82.

Solution: $P_1 = \$5$; $P_2 = \$4$; $Q_1 = 80$; and $Q_2 = 82$.

$$\frac{\dfrac{82 - 80}{(80 + 82)}}{\dfrac{4 - 5}{(5 + 4)}} = \frac{\dfrac{2}{(162)}}{\dfrac{-1}{(9)}} = \frac{\dfrac{2}{81}}{\dfrac{-1}{4.5}} = \frac{2.47\%}{22.22\%} = .11$$

Problem: Price is raised from \$30 to \$33 and quantity demanded falls from 100 to 90.

Solution: $$\frac{\dfrac{90 - 100}{(100 + 90)}}{\dfrac{33 - 30}{(30 + 33)}} = \frac{\dfrac{-10}{(190)}}{\dfrac{3}{(63)}} = \frac{\dfrac{-10}{95}}{\dfrac{3}{31.5}} = \frac{-10.53\%}{9.52\%} = 1.11$$

Why We Don't Use a Simpler Elasticity Formula?

Since elasticity is the percentage that quantity sold changes in response to a change in price, wouldn't it be a lot easier to use the formula percentage change in quantity divided by percentage change in price? There are economists who do use this formula. Let's try it for this problem. Price drops from $10 to $9 and quantity demanded rises from 100 to 120.

Using the formula:

$$\frac{\text{Percentage change in quantity}}{\text{Percentage change in price}}$$

we get: $\frac{20\%}{10\%} = 2$. So far, so good. What if we look at the same price range, but reverse the direction so that price rises from $9 to $10 and quantity demanded falls from 120 to 100. Here our percentage change in quantity divided by percentage change in price would be:

$$\frac{16\frac{2}{3}\%}{11\frac{1}{9}\%} = 1.5$$

That's quite a discrepancy for the range of the demand schedule between $9 and $10. When price is lowered from $10 to $9, elasticity = 2, but when it is raised from $9 to $10, elasticity is only 1.5. Therefore, the same formula, measuring elasticity over the same range of the demand curve, yields two very different answers.

Let's try the more complex formula on the same data. Go ahead and do it in the space above, first trying the price decrease and then the price increase.

Solution: (when price declines from $10 to $9)

$$\frac{\dfrac{120 - 100}{\dfrac{(100 + 120)}{2}}}{\dfrac{9 - 10}{\dfrac{(10 + 9)}{2}}} = \frac{\dfrac{20}{\dfrac{(220)}{2}}}{\dfrac{-1}{\dfrac{(19)}{2}}} = \frac{\dfrac{20}{110}}{\dfrac{-1}{9.5}} = \frac{18.18\%}{10.53\%} = 1.726$$

(when price rises from $9 to $10)

$$\frac{\dfrac{100 - 120}{\dfrac{(120 + 100)}{2}}}{\dfrac{10 - 9}{\dfrac{(9 + 10)}{2}}} = \frac{\dfrac{-20}{\dfrac{(220)}{2}}}{\dfrac{1}{\dfrac{(19)}{2}}} = \frac{\dfrac{-20}{110}}{\dfrac{1}{9.5}} = \frac{18.18\%}{10.53\%} = 1.726$$

Elasticity

The Meaning of Elasticity

What does all this mean? First, we say that when elasticity is greater than one, demand is elastic. Remember that elasticity is the percentage change in quantity brought about by a price change. In essence, it is percentage change in quantity divided by percentage change in price. Thus, for elasticity to be greater than one, percentage change in quantity must be greater than percentage change in price. A price change of a certain percentage causes quantity to change by a larger percentage. When this happens, we say that demand is elastic.

When demand is elastic the quantity demanded is responsive to price changes

We mean that the quantity demanded is responsive to price changes. When demand is elastic, it kind of stretches as price changes. And when demand is not very elastic, it does not stretch much.

Inelastic demand is defined as having an elasticity of less than one; anything from 0 to .99 would be inelastic. We can make somewhat finer distinctions. An elasticity of .1 or .2 would be very inelastic while one of .8 or .9 would be slightly inelastic. Similarly, an elasticity of 1.5 or 2 would be slightly elastic. And one of 8 or 10 would be very elastic.

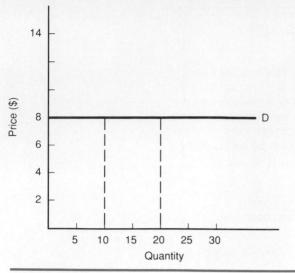

Figure 17–6

The border between elastic and inelastic is one. We call that unit elastic. Thus, if elasticity is less than one, it is inelastic. If it is exactly one, it is unit elastic. If elasticity is more than one, it is elastic.

Now we'll deal with perfect elasticity and perfect inelasticity. In Figure 17-6 we have a perfectly elastic demand curve. It is horizontal. Go ahead and calculate its elasticity from a quantity of 10 to one of 20. Note that price remains fixed at $8.

Solution:

$$\frac{\dfrac{20-10}{\dfrac{(10+20)}{2}}}{\dfrac{8-8}{\dfrac{(8+8)}{2}}} = \frac{\dfrac{10}{\dfrac{(30)}{2}}}{\dfrac{0}{\dfrac{16}{2}}} = \frac{\dfrac{10}{15}}{\dfrac{0}{8}} = \frac{66\frac{2}{3}\%}{0\%} = \infty$$

How big is infinity? Big. Very, very big. How elastic is the demand curve in Figure 17-6? Very, very elastic. Infinitely elastic, or as we say here, perfectly elastic.

Now we'll move on to perfect inelasticity. If perfect elasticity is ∞, how large is perfect inelasticity? −∞? Nope. Go back to what I said about the range of inelasticity—anything from 0 to .99. The lowest we can go is 0. That's perfect inelasticity.

Using the data in Figure 17-7, calculate the elasticity of that vertical demand curve. Quantity stays put at 15 but price varies. Let's say the price has fallen from 20 to 10. Calculate the elasticity. Again, use the formula, substitute, and solve.

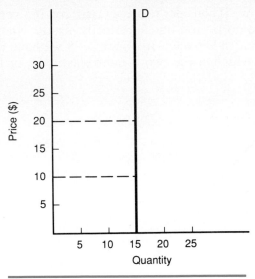

Figure 17–7

Solution: $\dfrac{\dfrac{15 - 15}{(15 + 15)}}{\dfrac{10 - 20}{(20 + 10)}} = \dfrac{\dfrac{0}{15}}{\dfrac{-10}{(30)}} = \dfrac{0}{\dfrac{-10}{15}} = \dfrac{0\%}{-66\frac{2}{3}\%} = 0$

How many times does 66⅔ percent go into 0? None. You can't divide *any* number into 0. Therefore, our elasticity is 0. The elasticity of a perfectly inelastic line is 0.

Approaching Perfect Elasticity and Perfect Inelasticity Arithmetically

If you had trouble dividing 0 into 66⅔, try answering this series of questions:

How many times does 100 go into 100? _____ .
How many times does 10 go into 100? _____ .
How many times does 1 go into 100? _____ .
How many times does .1 go into 100? _____ .
How many times does .01 go into 100? _____ .
How many times does 0 go into 100? _____ .

If somehow you haven't gotten the right answers, they are: 1; 10; 100; 1000; 10,000; and finally, infinity, or ∞.

Now we'll do a corresponding set of questions for perfect inelasticity. Again we'll use 100.

How many times does 100 go into 100? _____ .
How many times does 100 go into 10? _____ .
How many times does 100 go into 1? _____ .
How many times does 100 go into .1? _____ .
How many times does 100 go into .01? _____ .
How many times does 100 go into 0? _____ .

The right answers are: 1; .1; .01; .001; .0001; and finally, 0.

Next we'll consider relative elasticity. If a vertical line is perfectly inelastic and a horizontal line is perfectly elastic, what about lines that are somewhat in between? In Figure 17-8 we have two such lines. The question here is, which of the two is more elastic, D_1 or D_2?

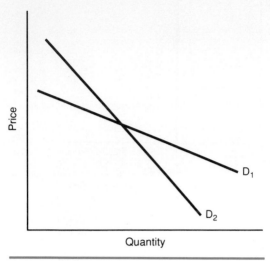

Figure 17-8

D_1 is more elastic because it is closer to being horizontal. Remember, the more horizontal, the more elastic the demand curve, and the more vertical the curve, the more inelastic it is.

Finally, we'll calculate the elasticity of a straight line. Surprisingly, it is not constant. Using Figure 17-9, let's calculate the elasticity at three points.

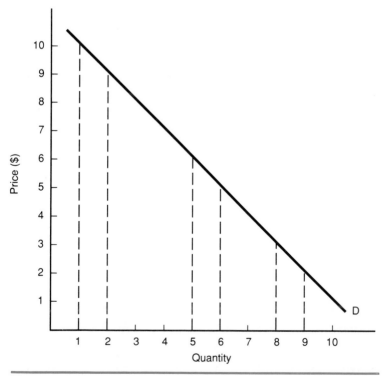

Figure 17-9

First, do the calculations when price falls from $10 to $9 and quantity rises from 1 to 2.

Solution:

$$\frac{\dfrac{2-1}{(1+2)}}{\dfrac{9-10}{(10+9)}} \;=\; \frac{\dfrac{1}{(3)}}{\dfrac{-1}{(19)}} \;=\; \frac{\dfrac{1}{1.5}}{\dfrac{-1}{9.5}} \;=\; \frac{66.67\%}{-10.53\%} \;=\; 6.33$$

An elasticity of 5.33 is fairly high. Next we'll calculate the elasticity when price falls from $6 to $5 and the quantity demanded rises from 5 to 6.

Solution:

$$\frac{\dfrac{6-5}{(5+6)}}{\dfrac{5-6}{(6+5)}} \;=\; \frac{\dfrac{1}{(11)}}{\dfrac{-1}{(11)}} \;=\; \frac{\dfrac{1}{5.5}}{\dfrac{-1}{5.5}} \;=\; 1$$

What we have here is unit elasticity, when a price change causes quantity demanded to change by the same percentage. Notice that in Figure 17–9 this occurs at the middle of the demand curve.

Now let's calculate the elasticity when price falls from $3 to $2 and quantity demanded rises from 8 to 9.

Solution:

$$\frac{\frac{9-8}{(8+9)}}{\frac{2-3}{(3+2)}} = \frac{\frac{1}{(17)}}{\frac{-1}{(5)}} = \frac{\frac{1}{8.5}}{\frac{-1}{2.5}} = \frac{11.76\%}{40\%} = .29$$

The answer, .29, is rather inelastic. When we compare the three elasticities we have calculated, this time moving to Figure 17–10, we reach this conclusion: a straight line demand curve that moves downward to the right is very elastic at the top and progressively less elastic as we move down the curve. As we approach the bottom it becomes more and more inelastic.

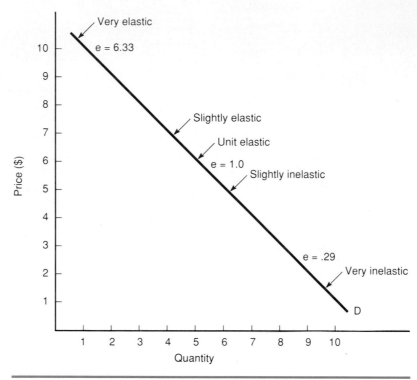

Figure 17–10

Elasticity and Total Revenue

Another aspect of elasticity has to do with a firm's total revenue. We want to see what effect elasticity has on total revenue when we raise or lower price.

First we'll go over total revenue or total sales. A firm will charge a particular price for some good or service and it will be able to sell a certain quantity at that price. If the price were $7 and the quantity sold were 4, total revenue would be $28 ($7 × 4). That's all there is to it. If price were $12 and quantity sold 6, total revenue = $72.

Suppose price were raised from $10 to $12 and quantity demanded fell from 20 to 12. Let's try a three-part question: (1) calculate elasticity; (2) state whether demand is elastic, unit elastic, or inelastic; and (3) calculate total revenue where price is $10 and $12.

Solution:

$$\frac{\dfrac{12-20}{\dfrac{(20+12)}{2}}}{\dfrac{12-10}{\dfrac{(10+12)}{2}}} = \frac{\dfrac{-8}{\dfrac{(32)}{2}}}{\dfrac{2}{\dfrac{(22)}{2}}} = \frac{\dfrac{-8}{16}}{\dfrac{2}{11}} = \frac{-50\%}{18.18\%} = 2.75$$

Demand is elastic.

Price	Quantity Demanded	Total Revenue
$10	20	$200
12	12	144

If demand is elastic, a price increase will lead to a fall in total revenue.

We see then that *when demand is elastic, if we were to raise price, total revenue would fall.* This would make another good exam question. "If price rises and demand is elastic, total revenue will *(a)* rise, *(b)* fall, or *(c)* remain the same?"

What do most students do when their instructor goes over this problem and tells them it might make a good exam question? They write down what appears in italic type in the previous paragraph. Then, on the exam, if they happen to remember that rule—there will be about 20 such rules to be memorized—they'll get it right. After the test, the rule is forgotten along with 99 percent of the other material that was memorized.

In this course you can figure out a lot of the answers to exam questions right on the spot. Take the exam question I quoted: "If price rises and demand is elastic, total revenue will *(a)* rise, *(b)* fall, or *(c)* remain the same?" To figure this out, make up a problem like the one we just did. The key here is that you want demand to be elastic. That means percentage change in quantity is greater than percentage change in price.

To derive our next rule, we'll use the same problem we've just solved (when elasticity was found to be 2.75). Try this question. "If price declines and demand is elastic, total revenue will *(a)* rise, *(b)* fall, or *(c)* remain the same?" In that problem, when price dropped from $12 to $10, what happened to total revenue?

Since total revenue rose from $144 to $200, we can state our second rule. *When demand is elastic, if we were to lower price, total revenue would rise.*

Now we're ready for the third and fourth rules. What happens to total revenue when demand is inelastic and price is raised? You can make up your own problem, or, if you'd like, you can use the data from our straight line graph in Figure 17-9. When price was raised from $2 to $3, quantity demanded declined from 9 to 8. How much then is total revenue at a price of $2 and at a price of $3?

If demand is inelastic, a price increase will lead to an increase in total revenue.

At a price of $2 it is $18 ($2 × 9); at a price of $3 it is $24 ($3 × 8). We now have our third rule. *When demand is inelastic, if we were to raise price, total revenue would rise.*

Can you guess the fourth rule? Using the same data but reversing the process (i.e., lowering price), we would find: *When demand is inelastic and price is lowered, total revenue will fall.* (Price goes from $3 to $2 and total revenue falls from $24 to $18.)

As a businessman facing an inelastic demand curve, you would never lower your price because your total revenue would decline. You would be selling *more* units and getting *less* revenue. If someone offered to buy 8 units from you for $24, would you agree to sell 9 units for $18? Think about it. What would happen to your total revenue? What would happen to your total cost? Obviously your total revenue would decline from $24 to $18. And your total cost? Surely it would cost you more to produce 9 units than 8 units. If your total revenue goes down when you lower your price and your total cost goes up, it would hardly make sense to do this.

Determinants of the Degree of Elasticity of Demand

The demand for certain goods and services is relatively elastic while that for others is relatively inelastic. Take heart medicine, for example. Suppose this medicine keeps you alive and its price doubles. Would you cut back on your purchases? Your demand curve would probably look like the one in Figure 17–11.

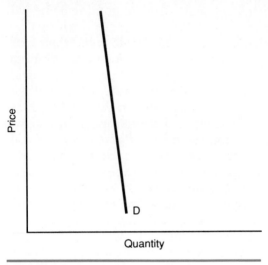

Figure 17–11

What about relatively elastic demand? Take steak, for example. When its price goes too high we substitute chicken, fish, and other meats. The demand curve for steak might look something like the one in Figure 17–12.

Figure 17–12

What makes demand elastic or inelastic? By far the most important influence is the availability of substitutes. Steak has a lot of reasonably close substitutes. If its price gets too high, people will substitute other cuts of meat, fish, and fowl. A relatively small percentage increase in price leads to a large percentage decline in quantity demanded.

In the case of heart medicine, demand is quite inelastic; there are no close substitutes. If price rises, quantity sold will not fall very much.

There are other influences on the degree of elasticity in addition to the availability of substitutes. If the product is a necessity, its demand will tend to be more inelastic than if it is a luxury. When the price of a movie ticket goes up a dollar, you might stay home and watch television, but if the price of gasoline goes up, say by 50 percent, you'll still buy it because you need it.

Another factor affecting elasticity is the product's cost relative to the buyer's income. Once, after I had just purchased a spool of thread, my friend told me that I could have gotten it for 2 cents less in another store several miles away. Thread is not exactly a big-ticket item. But if you're earning $20,000 a year and you're interested in a $7,000 car, a price change of just 3 or 4 percent will determine whether you buy that car.

Finally, the number of uses a product has affects the elasticity of its demand. The more uses, the higher the elasticity. Salt, for example, has two main uses: to season food and to make your sidewalk less slippery when it snows. At $30 a pound, salt will still be purchased by most people to season food, but only when the price gets down to around 20 cents a pound will it be used on the sidewalks.

Advertising

What is the purpose of advertising? Everyone knows that it's supposed to get the consumer to buy more of a product. Some industries such as tobacco, toothpaste, and liquor spend very heavily on advertising. In terms of what we've already discussed, we'll talk about how advertising affects demand.

In a nutshell, advertisers try to make demand for their products greater, but at the same time less elastic. They want to push their firm's demand curve over to the right; but they also want to make it steeper or more vertical.

First, an increase in demand. In Figure 17–13, because of massive advertising, people are willing to buy more of the product at *all* prices. If D_1 is

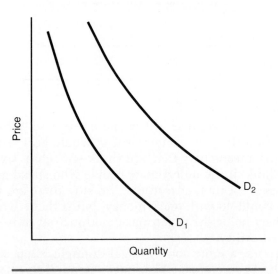

Figure 17–13

demand before advertising, D_2 would be demand after a successful advertising campaign.

A second way in which advertising can influence a product's demand curve is by making it more inelastic. This is often done by means of brand identification.

There are two very similar products that have been extremely well advertised—Bayer aspirin and St. Joseph's aspirin for children. The fact that both are familiar product names alone attests to their popularity. If you go into the drugstore and see Squibb, Johnson & Johnson, and Bayer aspirin, which do you buy? Do you buy Bayer even if it's more expensive?

It happens that aspirin is aspirin. What they've got in the Squibb and Johnson & Johnson bottles is identical to what Bayer puts in their bottles. But Bayer has convinced a lot of people that somehow their aspirin is better, so people are willing to pay more for it. Bayer's advertising has been able to make their demand curve more inelastic. This company could raise their price and still not lose many sales. That is the essence of inelastic demand.

Advertising attempts to change the way we *think* about a product. It tries to make us think a product is more useful, more desirable, or more of a necessity. Ideally an ad will make us feel that we *must* have that product. To the degree that advertising is successful, the demand curve is made steeper and is pushed farther to the right (from D_1 to D_2) in Figure 17–14.

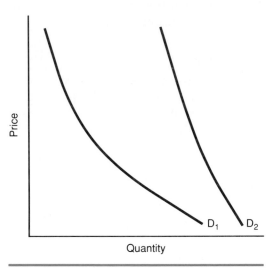

Figure 17–14

Utility

What Is Utility?

Utility is measured by how much you are willing to pay for something.

People often confuse utility and usefulness. Why did he buy the thing? It has no utility. In economics that would be a self-contradicting statement. Utility means only that you think enough of something to buy it.

Think of the unfortunate people who spend good money to get whipped, spanked, beaten, or tortured. I'm sure there are many more pleasant things one could do with one's money, but if that's what someone wants, obviously he or she is getting something out of it. What they're getting is called utility.

To use a more conventional example, suppose you were ravenously hungry and came upon a hamburger stand. If the attendant told you he had just one hamburger left—you're hungry enough to put away four—and told you that you'd have to pay $3 for it, would you do it?

If you did, that hamburger would have given you at least $3 worth of utility. What if you had refused to pay $3, but when he lowered the price to $2.75, you bought it? Then that hamburger's utility would have been $2.75.

Marginal Utility

You were still hungry and soon came upon a second hamburger stand. You said to yourself as you approached, "I'd be willing to spend $2 on a second hamburger." Why not $2.75? Because you're not as hungry as you were before you wolfed down that $2.75 hamburger.

Suppose you do spend $2 on a second hamburger and would be willing to pay just $1 for a third. Notice how the utility derived from consuming that third hamburger is much less than what the second one was worth.

If you managed to find someone who would let you have that third hamburger for no more than a dollar, what then? You'd try to get a fourth hamburger for a quarter. Why only a quarter? Because you're still feeling a little piggy and besides, we need you to still be a little hungry so we can illustrate a couple of things.

We're going to sum things up in Table 17–3. That's your demand schedule for hamburgers when you're ravenously hungry.

Table 17–3
Hypothetical Demand Schedule for Hamburgers

Price	Quantity Demanded
$2.75	1
2.00	2
1.00	3
.25	4

Once we know your demand schedule, we can derive your marginal utility and total utility schedules as well. Now we'll toss in a couple of new terms. *Marginal utility is the additional utility derived from consuming one more unit of some good or service.* Notice how your marginal utility declined as you gobbled each hamburger? The first had a utility of $2.75, but the second was worth only $2 to you, the third was worth just $1, and the fourth a mere 25 cents.

Marginal utility

Total Utility

Total utility is the utility you derive from consuming a certain number of units of a good or service. To get total utility, just add up the marginal utilities of all the units purchased. We've done that in Table 17–4.

Table 17–4
Hypothetical Utility Schedules

Units Purchased	Marginal Utility	Total Utility
1	$2.75	$2.75
2	2.00	4.75
3	1.00	5.75
4	.25	6.00

We've now come to *the law of diminishing marginal utility*. As we consume more and more of a good or service, we like it less and less. That might be OK for an exam answer, but we have to be a bit more elegant here, so we'll restate the law as follows. *As we consume increasing amounts of a good or service, we derive diminishing utility or satisfaction from each additional unit consumed.*

Think about it. How many movies would you want to go to in a day? In a week? How many plane trips to Europe? How many times do you want to take this economics course?

If you had a million dollars, how would you spend it? You'd really have to like hamburgers to spend it all on Big Macs. Chances are, if you don't weigh 800 pounds, you'd spend some of your money on nonfood items, which brings us to the question of maximizing utility.

Maximizing Utility

How much we buy of any good or service depends on its price and on our marginal utility schedule. Go back to the hamburger example. We can see in Table 17–3 how many hamburgers we'd buy at each price. Unlike that example, however, there's only one price. No one will ever offer us that first hamburger at $2.75, the second at $2, the third at $1, and the fourth at a quarter. For every good or service at any given time, there's just one price.

What we do then with our limited incomes is try to spend our money on what will give us the most satisfaction or utility. Keep in mind that as we consume more and more of any good or service, according to the law of diminishing marginal utility, its marginal utility declines. How much do we buy? We keep buying more and more until our marginal utility declines to the level of the price.

Since we buy a good or service up to the point at which its marginal utility is equal to its price, we could form this simple equation:

$$\frac{\text{Marginal utility}}{\text{Price}} = 1$$

For example, if the price of hamburgers were 25 cents, we'd buy four hamburgers. The marginal utility of the fourth hamburger would be 25 cents. So

$$\frac{\text{Marginal utility}}{\text{Price}} = \frac{25¢}{25¢} = 1$$

If we buy hamburgers up to the point where $\dfrac{\text{MU of hamburgers}}{\text{P of hamburgers}} = 1$, we would do the same with everything else we buy. How many records or cassettes do we buy? We keep buying them until their MU falls to the level of their price. If there are 93 different records we like equally, do we buy them all, even if we have the money? Maybe we buy two or three. The first one we buy is worth more to us than the price if we go ahead and buy a second one; and that second one is worth more than the price if we buy a third record. If we stop at three, the third record is worth the price, but a fourth would not be.

We keep buying records until their MU declines to the price level. In fact, the same thing can be said about everything we buy. To generalize,

$$\frac{MU_1}{P_1} = \frac{MU_2}{P_2} = \frac{MU_3}{P_3} = \frac{MU_n}{P_n}$$

We have been making an implicit assumption throughout our discussion of utility: that we are getting bargains on each unit we purchase until the last one. The MU of that last one is just equal to price, but the MU of the earlier units purchased is greater than price. It is on this assumption that the last topic of this chapter—this is some long chapter—consumer surplus, is based.

Consumer Surplus

Definition of consumer surplus

Consumer surplus is the difference between what you pay for some good or service and what you would have been willing to pay. I used to live in a very classy neighborhood. In fact, this neighborhood was so classy that none of the supermarkets bothered to stay open on Sunday. There was one tiny grocery store that was open all the time, and I'd make a point of never shopping there because the place was an unbelievable rip-off.

As fate would have it, a friend who was visiting wanted meatballs and spaghetti. I warned her that the only place to buy it was at that store. She went there and came back with an eight-ounce can. "How much?" I asked.

"Don't ask," she replied.

Later I saw the price on the can. It was $3.99.

Why did I go into that whole story and what does it have to do with consumer surplus? First of all, was my friend ripped off? The answer, surprisingly, is no! Forget about their being open on Sunday, the convenience, and all the rest. The bottom line is, my friend bought that can of meatballs and spaghetti. If it wasn't worth at least $3.99 to her, she wouldn't have bought it.

When you're really thirsty, wouldn't you be willing to pay $3 for a bottle of beer? Luckily you don't have to, unless of course, you live in my old neighborhood, you have no beer in the house, and it's a Sunday. Usually, when you buy something, you actually would have been willing to pay even more.

In the previous section, we said that a person keeps buying more and more of a good or service until that person's marginal utility falls to the price level. Therefore, each unit purchased except the last one was a bargain because MU was greater than price. This must be observed in Figure 17–15, where we once again use the hamburger problem.

If the price of hamburgers were a quarter, four would be purchased and the consumer surplus would be the triangular-shaped area above the price line in Figure 17–15. The total consumer surplus would be based on the difference between what you paid for each hamburger (25 cents) and what you would have been willing to pay. You would have been willing to pay $2.75 for the first one, so your consumer surplus on the first hamburger is $2.50. You would have been willing to pay $2.00 for the second, so on that one your consumer surplus is $1.75. Similarly, on the third hamburger your consumer surplus is $1.00 − .25 = .75. On the fourth hamburger, since MU = price (25 cents = 25 cents), there is no consumer surplus. Your total consumer surplus would be: $2.50 + $1.75 + $.75 = $5.00. Looked at another way, your total utility derived from the four hamburgers is $6 and if you pay 25 cents for each four hamburgers, $6 − $1 = a consumer surplus of $5.

The next time you go shopping, don't complain about being ripped off. No one ever paid more than he or she was willing to pay; no one ever bought anything whose price exceeded its utility; and anyone who ever bought several units of the same product at a fixed price enjoyed a consumer surplus.

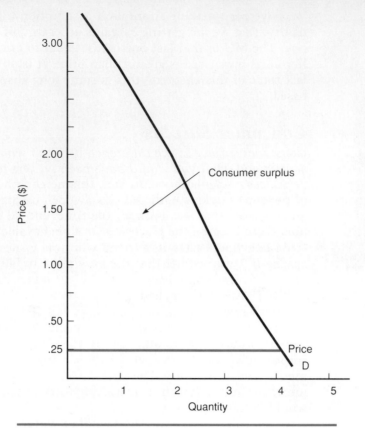

Figure 17–15

Workbook for Chapter 17

Name _____

Date _____

Self-Review Examination

Questions 1–9: Answer true or false.

_____ 1. An increase in demand is illustrated graphically by a shift upward and to the right by the demand curve.

_____ 2. If price falls, and in response quantity demanded rises, this represents an increase in demand.

_____ 3. A perfectly elastic demand curve has an elasticity of zero.

_____ 4. When demand is elastic and price is raised, total revenue will fall.

_____ 5. When demand is inelastic and price is lowered, total revenue will rise.

_____ 6. Utility is measured by a product's usefulness.

_____ 7. As increasing amounts of a product are consumed, marginal utility will decline.

_____ 8. If you were to purchase five beers at $1 each, you would enjoy a consumer surplus.

_____ 9. Elasticity of demand is found by dividing the percentage change in price by the percentage change in quantity.

10. Define marginal utility.

11. Explain the law of diminishing marginal utility.

12. What is a consumer surplus?

13. How do we measure a person's utility for any good or service that she buys?

14. State the formula used for calculating elasticity of demand.

15. Suppose demand is very, very elastic. What would happen if you *(a)* raised your price? *(b)* lowered your price?

16. What is meant by unit elasticity?

Multiple-Choice Questions

Circle the letter that corresponds to the best answer.

1. If demand is inelastic and price is raised, total revenue will

a. rise **b.** fall **c.** stay the same **d.** possibly rise and possibly fall.

2. If demand is elastic and price is lowered, total revenue will

a. rise **b.** fall **c.** stay the same **d.** possibly rise and possibly fall.

3. A product's utility to a buyer is measured by

a. its usefulness **b.** its price **c.** how much the buyer is willing to pay for it **d.** none of the above

4. Demand is elastic when

a. percentage change in price is greater than percentage change in quantity **b.** percentage change in quantity is greater than percentage change in price

c. the demand curve is vertical **d.** price increases raise total revenue

5. In Figure 1, consumer surplus is bounded by (price is OA)

a. OBD **b.** OACD **c.** ABC **d.** none of these

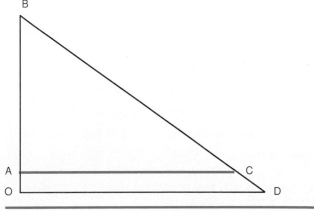

Figure 1

6. When you buy three units of a particular good or service

a. you will have no consumer surplus   **b.** you will have a consumer surplus   **c.** there is no way of knowing whether you have a consumer surplus

7. Each of the following may lead to a change in the demand for product A except

a. a change in the price of product A   **b.** a change in people's taste for product A   **c.** a change in people's incomes   **d.** a change in the price of product B (a substitute for product A)

8. The retail market for gasoline is

a. local   **b.** regional   **c.** national
d. international

9. Suppose the price of a service falls and people buy more of that service. What has happened is that

a. quantity changed   **b.** demand changed
c. demand increased   **d.** demand decreased

10. The most important determinant of the degree of elasticity of demand is

a. whether the item is a big-ticket item   **b.** whether the item is a luxury or not   **c.** how many uses the product has   **d.** the availability of substitutes

11. The advertiser wants to push her product's demand curve

a. to the right and make it more elastic   **b.** to the right and make it less elastic   **c.** to the left and make it more elastic   **d.** to the left and make it less elastic

12. As you purchase more and more of any good or service your

a. total utility and marginal utility both decline
b. total utility and marginal utility both rise
c. total utility rises and your marginal utility declines   **d.** total utility declines and your marginal utility rises

13. A person will buy more and more of a good or service until

a. marginal utility is greater than price   **b.** price is greater than marginal utility   **c.** price is equal to marginal utility

14. Which statement is true about the graph in Figure 2?

a. Demand is perfectly elastic.   **b.** Demand is perfectly inelastic.   **c.** Demand is more elastic at point X than at point Y.   **d.** Demand is more elastic at point Y than at point X.

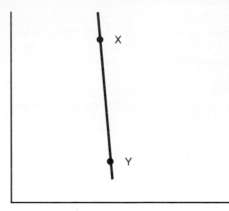

Figure 2

15. As income rises, the demand for inferior goods

a. rises   **b.** falls   **c.** stays about the same
d. cannot be determined

16. A person would be maximizing her total utility when

a. she had a consumer surplus   **b.** her marginal utility was zero   **c.** her marginal utility was equal to her total utility   **d.** she had no consumer surplus

For questions 17–22, use choices A–D (the same choice may be used more than once) and Figures 3 and 4 below.

a. change in quantity demanded   **b.** change in demand   **c.** increase in demand   **d.** decrease in demand

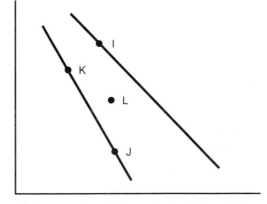

Figure 3

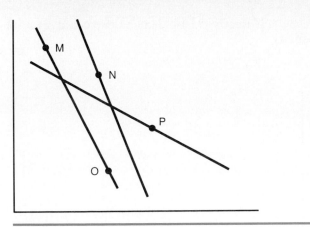

Figure 4

_____ **17.** A move from I to J

_____ **18.** A move from J to K

_____ **19.** A move from K to L

_____ **20.** A move from M to N

_____ **21.** A move from N to O

_____ **22.** A move from O to P

Problems

1. Suppose your demand schedule for cans of beer is shown in Table 1. Your total utility from three cans of beer would be _____. Your marginal utility from the third can of beer would be _____. If price were $1.50, how much would your consumer surplus be? _____

Table 1

Price	Quantity Demanded
$3.00	1
2.00	2
1.50	3

2. If price were increased from $40 to $42 and quantity demanded fell from 50 to 45, calculate elasticity, state whether demand is elastic, unit elastic, or inelastic, and find how much total revenue was when price was $40 and $42.

3. If price were lowered from $50 to $43 and quantity demanded rose from 15 to 16, calculate elasticity, state whether demand is elastic, unit elastic, or inelastic, and find how much total revenue was when price was $50 and $43.

4. Draw a demand curve, D_1. Then draw a second demand curve, D_2, that is more elastic.

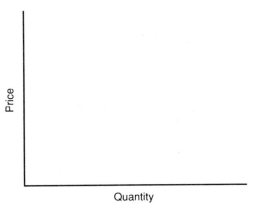

5. Draw a demand curve, D_1. Then draw a second demand curve, D_2, that illustrates an increase in demand.

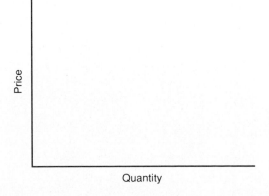

6. Draw a demand curve, D_1. Then draw a second demand curve, D_2, that is less elastic.

8. Draw a perfectly elastic demand curve and state its elasticity.

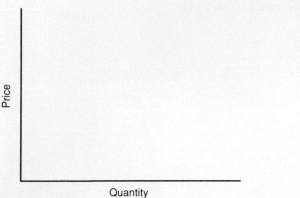

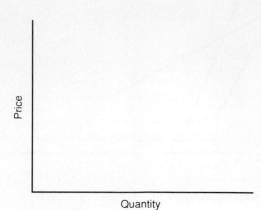

7. Draw a demand curve, D_1. Then draw a second demand curve, D_2, that illustrates a decrease in demand.

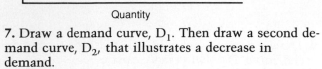

Supply

The analysis used in the first third or so of this chapter will closely follow the material we've worked on in the previous chapter. But when we reach the section on costs, we will begin to cover virgin territory. In fact, you might well proceed through the entire analysis of costs with your virtue intact. That would be too bad—you'd be missing a lot of fun. But probably you've heard *that* one in all your courses.

Chapter Objectives

The main topics that will be covered are:

- Individual and market supply.
- Changes in supply.
- Elasticity of supply.
- Fixed, variable, total, and marginal cost.
- The short and long run.
- The shutdown decision.
- Price floors and ceilings.

Supply Defined

Definition of supply

Supply is a schedule of quantities that people would be willing to sell at various prices. As prices rise, they would be willing to sell more. Thus, we have a positive or direct relationship between price and quantity: as price rises, quantity supplied rises; as price falls, quantity supplied falls.

You may ask *why* quantity supplied rises as price rises. Let me answer by asking you a question. Can you type? I mean, can you type at all? Even using the two-finger method with four mistakes on each line? Most people can type at least that well.

What happens when your professor wants a term paper typed? "I don't own a typewriter." "My typewriter is broken." "I don't know how to type." "I have a broken hand—tomorrow I'll bring in the cast."

But if the professor insists on a typed term paper, somehow everyone eventually comes up with one. Some students pay people to type them. Some students even pay people to *write* them. If the going rate were $2 and you were a terrible typist, you might well go out and hire a typist.

What if suddenly millions of term papers were assigned and because of the unprecedented demand for typists, the price was bid up to $20 a page. Would *you* pay someone $20 a page to do what you could do yourself? Why stop there? Twenty dollars a page! Why not set *yourself* up in business as a typist?

Let's analyze what has happened. At very low prices, many students are willing to hire typists, but at very high prices, they'd not only do their own typing, but they'd hire themselves out as typists. This helps explain why, at very high prices, the quantity supplied will be high.

Try this one on for size. Over the last 20 or 30 years, doctors have become very reluctant to make house calls. "You broke your leg, have a 108-degree fever, and you're hallucinating? You must be if you think I make house calls. Why don't you hop right over to the office and we'll have a look at you?" How do you get this joker to make a house call? Do what you'd do when you want a ringside table at a club: grease the guy's palm. Tell your doctor there's an extra fifty in it for him if he can make it over to your place before your mortician. Now there's one fella who *does* make house calls.

Individual Supply and Market Supply

Definition of market supply

Market supply is the sum of the supplies of all the firms in a given market. Back in the late 1950s, the supply of automobiles in the U.S. market was completely dominated by the big three—General Motors, Ford, and Chrysler. American Motors, Volkswagon, and a handful of mainly European firms sold a combined total of some 10 percent of the cars in the United States.

Market supply today includes each of the firms mentioned, but several Japanese companies have made tremendous inroads so that foreign-made cars comprise one third of all the sales in the American market. When we talk about individual supply, we mean the quantity supplied at different prices by each firm. Market supply is the sum of the quantities supplied at different prices by the firms in the industry.

Changes in Supply

In the last chapter we presented a series of problems dealing with changes in demand. In this section we're going to present a similar group of problems, this time dealing with changes in supply. The first set is based on Figure 18-1. You have four choices.

a. A change in quantity supplied.

b. A change in supply.

c. An increase in supply.

d. A decrease in supply.

    A move from E to F _____

    A move from F to G _____

    A move from G to H _____

    A move from H to I _____

When we go from E to F, there is merely a change in the quantity supplied since we never leave the supply curve.

The move from F to G is an increase in supply. Why an increase? Because we are going to a higher supply curve; G is situated on a supply curve that provides greater quantities at *all* prices than the one on which F is located.

The move from G to H is a change in supply. Although we leave G's supply curve—that's the change—because H is located on a supply curve that crosses G's, we cannot say that this is either an increase *or* a decrease in supply.

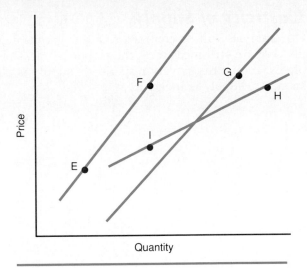

Figure 18–1

Finally we have the move from H to I, which is similar to the move from E to F. It is also a change in the quantity supplied.

Now we'll do another set of problems using Figure 18-2.

A move from J to K _____
A move from K to L _____
A move from L to M _____
A move from M to N _____

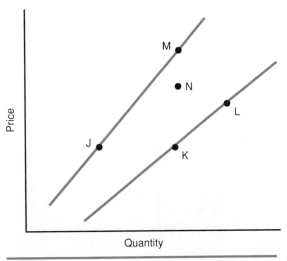

Figure 18–2

The move from J to K is an increase in supply because we have moved to a higher supply curve (at *every* price more is offered for sale).

When we go from K to L we stay on the same supply curve, so it is just a change in the quantity supplied.

The move from L to M is the opposite of that from J to K, so it is a decrease in supply.

Finally, the move from M to N is a change in supply. Since we don't know the shape of the supply curve on which N is situated, we don't know whether or not it crosses the one on which M is located. Thus, the most definitive thing we can say is that there has been a change in supply.

Elasticity of Supply

Our analysis will be confined to a few graphs depicting the elasticity of supply. We are still measuring the responsiveness of quantity to changes in prices. If quantity is very responsive, supply is elastic; if it is not very responsive, supply is inelastic.

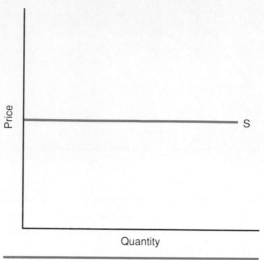

Figure 18–3

Figure 18-3 shows a perfectly elastic supply curve, which is exactly the same as a perfectly elastic demand curve. Similarly, Figure 18-4 shows a perfectly inelastic supply curve, which would be identical to a perfectly inelastic demand curve.

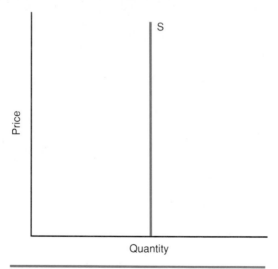

Figure 18–4

Supply tends to be inelastic during very short periods of time. In the United States right after World War II, it was nearly impossible to get a car at *any* price. It took time to reconvert from tank, jeep, and plane production to turn out those shiny new Hudsons, Studebakers, Kaiser-Fraisers, Nashes, and Packards. Even if you were willing to part with a big one—that's right, a thousand bucks—you still had to put your name on a waiting list a year long. After a few years, supply became more elastic as more firms entered the industry and existing firms increased their output.

Finally, we'll look at relative elasticity of supply in Figure 18-5. Which curve is more elastic? You should recognize S_2 as the more elastic since it is flatter and quantity supplied would be fairly responsive to price changes.

Figure 18–5

Costs

In a business firm, costs are half the picture. The other half is sales. The equation that every businessperson knows better than anything else in the world is:

$$\text{Sales} - \text{Costs} = \text{Profits}$$

If you write it vertically

$$
\begin{array}{r}
\text{Sales} \\
- \text{ Costs} \\
\hline
\text{Profits}
\end{array}
$$

you can quickly grasp what is meant by looking at "the bottom line."

We are going to analyze costs in two ways. First, we'll divide them into fixed and variable costs. A little later, we'll divide them into costs in the short and long run.

Fixed Costs

Definition of fixed cost

Fixed costs stay the same no matter how much output changes. Examples are rent, insurance premiums, salaries of employees under guaranteed contracts, interest payments, and most of depreciation allowances on plant and equipment. Even when the firm's output is zero, these same fixed costs are incurred.

Variable Costs

Definition of variable cost

Variable costs vary with output. When output rises, variable costs rise; when output falls, variable costs fall. What are examples of variable costs? The most important would be wages, particularly the wages of production workers. If you cut back on output, some of these people would be laid off. If you reduced output to zero, none of them would be paid.

Another variable cost is fuel. When you raise or lower output, you vary your fuel bill. The same is true with raw materials, for example, steel, glass, and rubber in automobile production.

Total Cost

Definition of total cost

Total cost is the sum of fixed cost and variable cost. The data in Table 18-1 illustrate that relationship. Notice that as output rises, fixed cost stays the same and variable cost rises. Notice also how the increase in total cost

Table 18–1
Hypothetical Cost Schedule for a Business Firm

Output	Fixed Cost	Variable Cost	Total Cost
0	$1,000	—	$1,000
1	1,000	$ 500	1,500
2	1,000	900	1,900
3	1,000	1,300	2,300
4	1,000	1,800	2,800
5	1,000	2,400	3,400
6	1,000	3,200	4,200

is due to the increase in variable cost. These relationships may also be observed in Figure 18-6, which is based on Table 18-1.

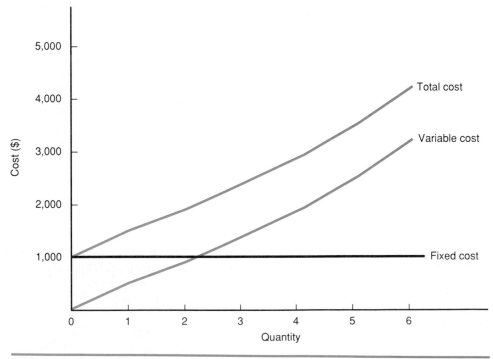

Figure 18–6

Marginal Cost

Definition of marginal cost

Marginal cost is the cost of producing one additional unit of output. If we look back at Table 18-1, we can calculate the marginal cost of producing one unit of output. It is $500. That is because the total cost of producing one unit of output is $1,500 and the total cost of producing zero units of output is $1,000 (we still have fixed costs of $1,000 even at zero output). The additional cost of producing that first unit is $500.

Now figure out the marginal cost of the 2d, 3d, 4th, 5th, and 6th units of output. Write them down and then check your answers against these. The marginal cost of the 2d unit is $400 ($1,900 − $1,500); the 3d unit is also $400 ($2,300 − 1,900); the 4th unit is $500 (2,800 − 2,300); the 5th is $600 (3,400 − 2,800); and the 6th is $800 (4,200 − 3,400).

Table 18–2
Hypothetical Cost Schedule for a Firm

Output	Fixed Cost	Variable Cost	Total Cost	Marginal Cost
0	$500	—		
1		$ 200		
2		300		
3		450		
4		650		
5		950		
6		1,500		

Here's another problem to work out. Fill in the column for total cost and marginal cost in Table 18-2. Try to do this in ink so you won't be able to sell back this book. If everyone does this, we'll double sales. After you've done this problem, you can check your answers against those in Table 18-3.

Table 18–3
Hypothetical Cost Schedule for a Firm

Output	Fixed Cost	Variable Cost	Total Cost	Marginal Cost
0	$500	—	$ 500	—
1		$ 200	700	$200
2		300	800	100
3		450	950	150
4		650	1,150	200
5		950	1,450	300
6		1,500	2,000	550

The Short Run

Definition of short run

The short run is the length of time it takes all fixed costs to become variable costs. As long as there are any fixed costs, we are in the short run. How long is the short run? In some businesses, only a couple of minutes.

When I was growing up in New York during the years immediately following the Civil War, there was a guy who would make an announcement on the subway train as it went over the Manhattan Bridge. Then he'd open his raincoat; he had hundreds of ballpoint pens hanging in rows from the lining of the coat. He was selling pens. He would tell us that he had a short-term lease, which was true. It took the train about five minutes to go over the bridge and his lease was up. That was the length of his short run.

Most firms have considerably longer short runs. A steel firm might need a couple of years to pay off such fixed costs as interest and rent. Even a grocery store would need several months to find someone to sublet the store and to discharge its other obligations.

The Long Run

The long run is the time at which all costs become variable costs. Although we've defined it, the long run never exists except in theory. Why not? Because you'll never have a situation in which all your costs are variable. It would mean no rent, no interest, insurance, depreciation, and no guaranteed salaries. That would indeed be a hard way to do business.

Toward the end of the short run, as one and then another of your fixed costs begin to run out, you have to decide if you're going to stay in business. If you are, when your lease is up, you sign a new one. When a machine wears out, you replace it. And so forth.

You never really reach the long run. Like Moses, you can see the mountains of Canaan from afar, but you never get to set foot in the promised land. On any given day, you can gaze out beyond your short run and your long run, but as you proceed through the short run, you have to make decisions that will push your long run farther and farther into the future.

The Shutdown Decision

Firm has two options in short run

A firm has two options in the short run: it can operate or shut down. If it operates it will produce the output that will yield the highest possible profits; if it is losing money, it will operate at that output at which losses are minimized.

If the firm shuts down, its output is zero. Shutting down does not mean zero total costs. The firm must still meet its fixed costs. Look at Table 18–1 again. At an output of zero, fixed costs, and therefore total costs, are $1,000.

Why can't the firm go out of business in the short run? Because it still has fixed costs. These obligations must be discharged. Any plant, equipment, inventory, and raw materials must also be sold off. All of this takes time. How long? In some types of businesses, such as retail food, garment manufacturing, TV production, and most service industries, it would be a matter of two or three months. But in heavy industry, such as iron and steel, nonferrous metals, automobiles, oil refining, and other types of manufacturing, it might take a couple of years.

We'll work out some problems involving the shutdown decision. If a firm has fixed costs of $5 million, variable costs of $6 million, and prospective sales of $7 million, what does it do in the short run? It has two choices: (1) to operate or (2) to shut down.

If you owned this firm, what would you do? No matter what you do, you'll lose money. If you operate, your total cost will be $11 million ($5 million fixed cost plus $6 million variable cost). Sales − costs = profits, so $7 million − $11 million = −4 million. That's not too good.

How much will you lose if you shut down? You will still have to pay out $5 million in fixed costs. Your variable cost will be zero. How much will your sales be? Zero. If you shut down, you produce nothing. If you shut down, your fixed and total costs are the same—$5 million. Since sales are zero, you lose $5 million by shutting down.

What do you do? Shut down and lose $5 million, or operate and lose $4 million? Remember, in the short run, these are your only options. What you do is operate. It's a lot better to lose $4 million than to lose $5 million. How can you go on month after month and possibly year after year losing so much money? You can't. In the long run you have the added option of going out of business.

Here's another problem. What does this firm do in the short run if its fixed costs are $10 million, its variable costs are $9 million, and its prospective sales are $8 million? Will the firm operate or shut down? Back up your answer with numbers after you've figured out the right option.

If the firm shuts down it will lose its $10 million in fixed costs. If it operates it will have sales of $8 million and total costs of $19 million ($10 million fixed plus $9 million variable). If it operates the firm will lose $11 million (sales of $8 million minus costs of $19 million). And so the firm will shut down since it's obviously better to lose $10 million than $11 million.

This whole discussion of losing money may seem depressing and perhaps beside the point. Why go into business in the first place if you're going to lose money? Remember, however, that most businesses fail. Many others, at one time or another, lose money. Although we will continually stress the fact that businesspersons are always striving to maximize their profits, when faced with losses they strive just as hard to minimize those losses. Perhaps they try even harder because their very economic survival is at stake. During the recession years of 1980 and 1981, Chrysler, and Ford were struggling to hold their losses to $1 billion.

We'll try one more problem. What does a firm do in the short run with prospective sales of $10 million, variable costs of $12 million, and fixed costs of $8 million?

If the firm shuts down it will lose its $8 million in fixed costs. If it operates it will lose $10 million (sales of $10 million minus total costs of $20 million).

When a firm will operate in short run

We are now ready for another rule. When does a firm operate in the short run? *A firm will operate in the short run when prospective sales exceed variable costs.* Go back to the first problem. Prospective sales were $7 million and variable costs were $6 million. By operating it added $7 million in sales and had to pay out only an additional $6 million in costs. By operating, it cut its losses by $1 million.

When a firm will shut down in the short run

A firm will shut down when variable costs exceed prospective sales. Check back on problems 2 and 3. In the second problem, when variable costs are $9 million and prospective sales are $8 million, it saves $1 million by shutting down. In the third problem, variable costs are $12 million and prospective sales $10 million, so $2 million is saved by shutting down.

The long-run choices are a lot easier: (1) stay in business or (2) go out of business. If a firm has prospective sales of $4 million, fixed costs of $3 million, and variable costs of $2 million, what does it do in the long run?

This firm will go out of business because in the long run it will be losing money. Prospective sales of $4 million − total costs of $5 million ($3 million fixed + $2 million variable) = −$1 million profit.

What would you do in the long run if your prospective sales were $8 million, fixed costs were $4 million, and variable costs were $3 million?

You would stay in business because you would make a profit of $1 million (sales of $8 million minus costs of $7 million).

Appendix

Price Floors and Price Ceilings

What is a price floor?

It is very easy to get price floors and price ceilings mixed up. A price floor does one job: it keeps prices from falling below a certain level. Unfortunately, a price floor is located high up on a graph, well above the point of which you might expect a floor to be.

What is a price ceiling?

Price ceilings keep prices from rising higher than a certain level. They too turn up in an unexpected place on the graph—down much farther than one would expect a ceiling to be.

Figure 18-7 illustrates a price floor. Equilibrium price would normally be $10, but a price floor of $15 has been established. At $15, businesses are not normally able to sell everything they offer for sale. Quantity supplied is much larger than quantity demanded. Why? At the equilibrium price of $10, sellers are willing to sell less while buyers are willing to buy more.

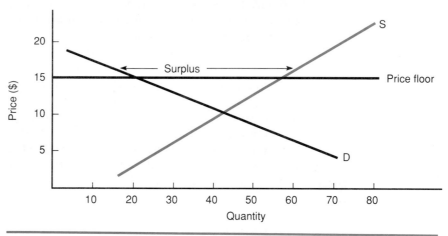

Figure 18–7

Floors and surpluses

At a price of $15 there is a surplus of 35 units. The government would have created this price floor and surplus to keep the price at a predetermined level. This has been the case for certain agricultural commodities, most notably wheat and corn. It was hoped that these relatively high prices would encourage family farms to stay in business. That the bulk of farm price support payments has gone to huge corporate farms has not discouraged Congress from allocating billions of dollars a year toward this end.

The way the government keeps price floors in effect is by buying up the surpluses. In the case of Figure 18-7, the Department of Agriculture would have to buy 35 units.

Price ceilings are the mirror image of price floors. An example appears in Figure 18-8.

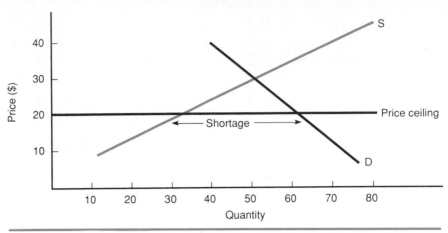

Figure 18–8

Price ceilings are set by the government as a form of price control. "No matter what," the government tells business firms, "don't charge more than this amount."

Ceilings and shortages

A ceiling prevents prices from rising. The last time we had widespread price ceilings was during World War II. Because ceilings cause shortages, a rations system was worked out to enable everyone to obtain their "fair share" of such commodities as butter, meat, and sugar.

In Figure 18-8, when a ceiling of $20 is established, there is a shortage of 30 units. Had price been allowed to stay at the equilibrium level of $30, there would have been no shortage. However, at this lower price, business firms will sell 20 units less than at equilibrium and consumers will demand 10 units more. This explains the shortage.

One way the market deals with a shortage is to create what is known as a black market. Products subject to the price ceiling are sold illegally to those willing to pay considerably more. During World War II, there was an extensive black market.

The confusion over the location on the graph of price floors and ceilings may be overcome by considering what the government is doing by establishing them. A price floor keeps price artificially high. Normally price would fall to the equilibrium level. Think of a floor holding price above equilibrium; therefore, a price floor would be located above equilibrium price.

By the same token, a price ceiling is intended to keep price *below* equilibrium. If not for that ceiling, price would rise. Therefore, a price ceiling must be located below equilibrium to keep price from rising to that level.

Keep in mind then that the normal tendency of prices is to move toward the equilibrium level. A price ceiling will prevent prices from rising to that level while a price floor will prevent prices from falling to equilibrium.

Tax Incidence

A tax lowers supply and raises price.

A tax on a good or service will raise its price. In terms of supply, such a tax, in effect, lowers supply. This is so because at every price, sellers will be offering less for sale. Supply is defined as the quantities people sell at different prices, so the supply curve will be shifted to the left.

As a result of the tax, people are willing to sell less at every price. That is a decrease in supply.

A decrease in supply, as we see in Figure 18-9, has two effects. The first is to raise price and the second is to lower the quantity sold.

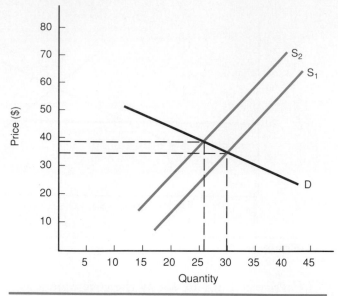

Figure 18-9

Who bears the burden of a tax? Most people would say the consumer does. After all, doesn't the seller merely act as the agent for the government and collect the tax? Or, put slightly differently, doesn't the seller just pass on the tax to the consumer?

Actually, it really depends on the relative elasticities of supply and demand. In Figure 18-9, we have a relatively elastic demand and a relatively inelastic supply. A tax of $10 is borne mainly by the sellers because price rises by only about $3 (from $35, the original equilibrium price, to the new

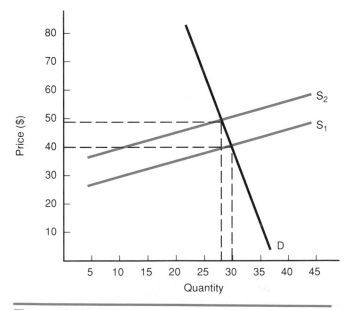

Figure 18-10

equilibrium price of $38). Sellers, who had been getting $35, now get only $28 ($38 minus $10, which they pay the government).

In Figure 18-10, we have the opposite situation. Here demand is relatively inelastic and supply, relatively elastic. Now it is the buyer who bears most of the tax burden. Equilibrium price rises from $40 to about $48, so the buyer must pay $8 more; but the seller, who collects $48 and returns $10 to the government, gets to keep $38. That means he's out only $2 to the buyer's $8.

Workbook for Chapter 18

Multiple-Choice Questions

Circle the letter that corresponds to the best answer.

1. As price rises

a. supply rises   **b.** supply falls   **c.** quantity supplied rises   **d.** quantity supplied falls

2. A perfectly elastic supply curve is

a. a horizontal line   **b.** a vertical line   **c.** neither a horizontal nor a vertical line

3. Over time the supply of a particular good or service tends to

a. become more elastic   **b.** become less elastic

c. stay about the same

4. Total cost is the sum of

a. marginal cost and fixed cost   **b.** marginal cost and variable cost   **c.** variable cost and fixed cost

5. In the short run

a. all costs are fixed costs   **b.** all costs are variable costs   **c.** some costs are fixed costs   **d.** all costs are marginal costs

6. In the short run the firm has two options:

a. stay in business or go out of business   **b.** stay in business or shut down   **c.** operate or go out of business   **d.** operate or shut down

For questions 7–12, use choices **a**, **b**, **c**, and **d**, and Figures 1 and 2. Each choice may be used more than once.

a. change in quantity supply   **b.** change in supply   **c.** increase in supply   **d.** decrease in supply

7. A move from E to F is a(n) _____ .

8. A move from F to G is a(n) _____ .

9. A move from G to H is a(n) _____ .

10. A move from I to J is a(n) _____ .

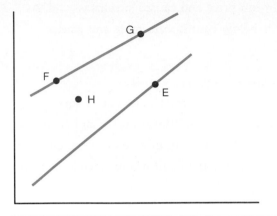

Figure 1

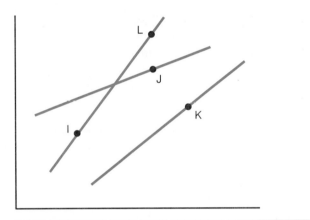

Figure 2

11. A move from J to K is a(n) _____ .

12. A move from K to L is a(n) _____ .

13. Which statement is true?

a. A firm will operate in the short run when prospective sales exceed fixed costs.   **b.** A firm will operate in the short run when prospective sales exceed variable costs.   **c.** A firm will shut down when total cost exceeds prospective sales.   **d.** None of these statements is true.

14. Which statement is true?

a. A price floor is above equilibrium price and causes surpluses.   **b.** A price floor is above equilibrium price and causes shortages.   **c.** A price floor is below equilibrium price and causes surpluses.   **d.** A price floor is below equilibrium price and causes shortages.

15. Price ceilings keep market price

a. above the equilibrium price and creates surpluses   **b.** above the equilibrium price and create shortages   **c.** below the equilibrium price and create surpluses   **d.** below the equilibrium price and create shortages

16. A tax will

a. lower price and raise supply   **b.** lower price and lower supply   **c.** raise price and lower supply
d. raise price and raise supply

17. When demand is relatively inelastic and supply is relatively elastic, the burden of a tax will be borne

a. mainly by sellers   **b.** mainly by buyers
c. equally between sellers and buyers
d. it is impossible to determine the relative burdens of the tax

Fill-In Questions

1. Supply is defined as _____

_____ .

2. Over time, the elasticity of supply for a particular good or service tends to become _____ .

3. Variable costs change with _____ .

4. Total cost is the sum of _____ and

_____ .

5. Marginal cost is the _____ .

6. At zero units of output, total cost is equal

to _____ .

7. The short run is the length of time it takes all fixed costs to become _____ .

8. In the short run the firm has two options: (1)

_____ or (2) _____ .

9. A firm will operate in the short run as long as

_____ are greater than _____ ;
a firm will operate in the long run as long as

_____ are greater than _____ .

10. Shortages are associated with price

_____ ; surpluses are associated with price

_____ .

11. When there are price ceilings _____
tend to develop.

12. A decrease in supply _____ price and

_____ the quantity sold.

13. A tax on a service that has a relatively elastic demand and a relatively inelastic supply will be borne

mainly by the _____ .

Problems

1. In the space below, draw a perfectly elastic supply curve.

P

Q

2. Draw a perfectly inelastic supply curve.

P

Q

3. Draw a supply curve, S_1. Then draw a more elastic supply curve, S_2.

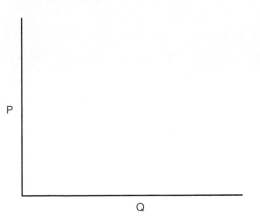

4. Draw a supply curve, S_1, and a second supply curve, S_2, that represents an increase in supply.

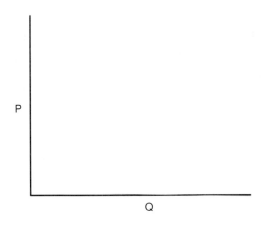

5. Fill in Table 1.

Table 1

Output	Fixed Cost	Variable Cost	Total Cost	Marginal Cost
0	$800	—		
1		$100		
2		150		
3		200		
4		270		
5		360		

6. If a firm's prospective sales are $5 billion, its fixed costs are $3 billion, and its variable costs are $1.5 billion, what does it do in the *(a)* short run? *(b)* long run?

7. If a firm's prospective sales are $20 million, its fixed costs are $12 million, and its variable costs are $22 million, what does it do in the *(a)* short run? *(b)* long run?

8. Given the information in Figure 3, *(a)* Is $12 a price ceiling or a price floor? *(b)* Is there a shortage or a surplus? *(c)* How much is it?

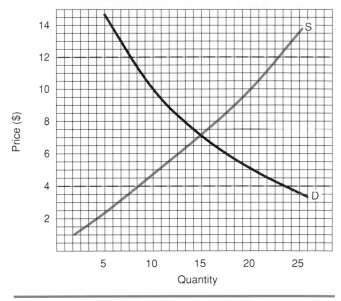

Figure 3

9. Given the information in Figure 4, *(a)* Is $16 a price ceiling or a price floor? *(b)* Is there a shortage or a surplus? *(c)* How much is it?

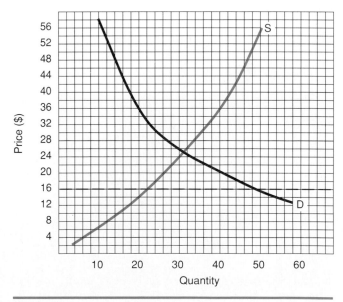

Figure 4

Supply in the Short Run and the Long Run

In this chapter you will learn how to calculate the average fixed cost, the average variable cost, and the average total cost. These three, along with the marginal cost, are then plotted on a graph. After the concept of marginal revenue is introduced, the demand and marginal revenue curves are graphed. Marginal analysis is then used to calculate the firm's total profit at its maximum. Using these concepts we derive the firm's short-run and long-run supply curves. In the final sections the long-run planning envelope curve and the market supply are discussed.

Chapter Objectives

After reading this chapter, you will be familiar with:

- Average fixed cost, average variable cost, and average total cost.
- Profit maximization and loss minimization.
- Derivation of the firm's supply curve.
- The long-run planning envelope curve.
- The market supply.

Average Cost

In this section we'll find average fixed cost, average variable cost, and average total cost. To get each we do simple division, dividing by output.

Average Fixed Cost

Average fixed cost is fixed cost divided by output. It gets progressively smaller as output rises because we are dividing a larger and larger number into one that stays the same. If fixed cost were $1,000, how much would average fixed cost be at one unit of output?

$$\text{AFC} = \frac{\text{Fixed cost}}{\text{Output}}$$

$$\text{Average fixed cost} = \frac{\text{Fixed cost}}{\text{Output}} = \frac{1,000}{1} = 1,000$$

Now figure out AFC at 2 units of output. Just plug the numbers into the formula.

$$\text{AFC} = \frac{\text{Fixed cost}}{\text{Output}} = \frac{1,000}{2} = 500$$

Calculate AFC for 3, 4, 5, and 6 units of output to the nearest dollar in the space below.

Solutions:

$$\text{AFC} = \frac{\text{Fixed cost}}{\text{Output}} \quad \frac{1,000}{3} = 333. \frac{1,000}{4} = 250. \frac{1,000}{5} = 200.$$

$$\frac{1,000}{6} = 167.$$

Average Variable Cost

Average variable cost is variable cost divided by output. Unlike fixed cost, variable cost rises with output. What about AVC? Usually it declines for a while as output increases. Eventually, however, AVC will level off and begin to rise.

In Table 19–1, we have a variable cost schedule. I've worked out the AVC for 1 and 2 units of output. I'd like you to work out the rest and fill in the table.

$$\text{AVC} = \frac{\text{Variable cost}}{\text{Output}}$$

$$\text{Average variable cost} = \frac{\text{Variable cost}}{\text{Output}} = \frac{500}{1} = 500$$

$$\frac{800}{2} = 400$$

Table 19-1
Hypothetical Cost Schedule

Output	Variable Cost	Total Cost	Average Fixed Cost	Average Variable Cost	Average Total Cost
1	$ 500	$1,500			
2	800	1,800			
3	1,000	2,000			
4	1,300	2,300			
5	1,700	2,700			
6	2,400	3,400			

Average Total Cost

Average total cost is total cost divided by output. Like AVC, ATC also declines with output for a while, but it eventually levels off and then begins to rise. We'll see that ATC lags slightly behind AVC, leveling off when AVC begins to rise and not rising after AVC is well on the way up.

We'll use Table 19-1 repeatedly. I'll work out ATC for the first two outputs and you work out the rest.

$$\text{ATC} = \frac{\text{Total cost}}{\text{Output}}$$

$$\text{ATC} = \frac{\text{Total cost}}{\text{Output}} \quad \frac{1,500}{1} = 1,500$$

$$\frac{1,800}{2} = 900$$

You'll find everything worked out in Table 19-1. I'd like you to note that AFC and AVC add up to the ATC at each output. You can use this as a check on your work. If they don't add up, you've made a mistake.[1]

We'll work out one more table and then move on to a graph. Table 19-2 has all the numbers you'll need to calcualte AFC, AVC, and ATC. Also fill in the marginal cost, which we worked on in the last chapter. Please fill in Table 19-3, then check your work using Table 19-4. Assume that fixed cost is $500.

---

[1] Incidentally, AFC and AVC don't add up to ATC when the output is 3. Actually this slight discrepancy is due to rounding: 333⅓ + 333⅓ = 666⅔. We rounded 333⅓ down to 333 and 666⅔ up to 667, so if the sum of AFC and AVC doesn't add exactly to what ATC is, it is probably due to rounding.

Table 19–2
Hypothetical Cost Schedule

Output	Variable Cost	Total Cost	Average Fixed Cost	Average Variable Cost	Average Total Cost
1	$ 500	$1,500	$1,000	$500	$1,500
2	800	1,800	500	400	900
3	1,000	2,000	333	333	667
4	1,300	2,300	250	325	575
5	1,700	2,700	200	340	540
6	2,400	3,400	167	400	567

Table 19–3
Hypothetical Cost Schedule

Output	Variable Cost	Total Cost	AFC	AVC	ATC	Marginal Cost
1	$ 200					
2	300					
3	444					
4	650					
5	900					
6	1,300					
7	2,000					

Table 19–4
Hypothetical Cost Schedule

Output	Variable Cost	Total Cost	AFC	AVC	ATC	Marginal Cost
1	$ 200	$ 700	$500	$200	$700	$200
2	300	800	250	150	400	100
3	444	944	167	148	315	144
4	650	1,150	125	163	288	206
5	900	1,400	100	180	280	250
6	1,300	1,800	83	217	300	400
7	2,000	2,500	71	285	357	700

The Graphing of the AFC, AVC, ATC, and MC Curves

Much of the procedure in microeconomics involves three steps: filling in a table, drawing a graph based on that table, and doing an analysis of the graph. We're ready for the second step.

When you draw a graph, you should plan it first. Label both axes. Figure out how high you'll need to go. Then figure out your scale. Will each box on your graph paper represent $5, $10, or $20? But before you can draw a proper graph, you'll need graph paper.

Your output will be from 1 to 7. What will be the highest point on your graph? AFC starts at $500 and goes down. AVC only goes up to $286. Both ATC and MC have highs of 700, so the vertical axis should go up to $700.

The AFC curve is plotted out in Figure 19-1. Using the same setup, I'd like you to draw a graph of the AVC, ATC, and MC curves, which are also shown in Figure 19-1. If you've drawn them correctly, they'll come out like those in Figure 19-1.

Plan your graph before you draw it.

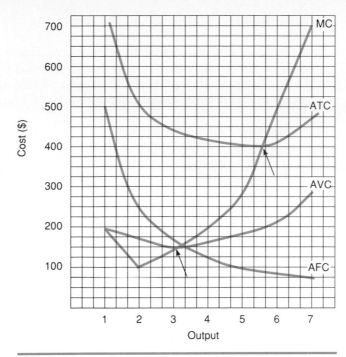

Figure 19–1

There are a few things of interest in Figure 19–1. First notice that AFC declines continually as output rises. The most important thing, though, is the shape of the AVC and ATC curve. Both are U shaped and both are intersected by the MC curve at their minimum points. When students begin to draw graphs, they connect all the points with straight lines, often using rulers. For starters, don't use a ruler to connect the points. You're drawing curves, not a series of straight lines that meet each other at odd little angles.

Why does the MC curve pass through the AVC and ATC curves at their minimum points?

Why does the MC curve pass through the AVC and ATC curves at their minimum points? I'll explain why indirectly, but the basic reason is that each marginal value changes the average value.

We'll digress for a moment by discussing grades on exams. Suppose you took three exams and got 80, 70, and 60. Your average would be 70. What if, on the next exam you got a 66? What would your average be? It would be $276/4 = 69$.

Suppose on the next exam you got a 67? Now what would your average be? It would be $343/5 = 68.6$.

If you got a 68 on the next exam, what would happen to your average? $411/6 = 68.5$.

If your next exam mark were exactly 68.5? $479.5/7 = 68.5$. No change.

If on the next exam you got a 69, what would your average be? $548.5/8 = 68.56$.

All of this is meant to show you how the marginal score affects the average score. Notice that as long as the marginal score is below the average score, the latter is declining, but when the marginal score is 68.5, it is just equal to the average score. And the average score is neither rising nor falling; it is at its minimum point.

Similarly, when MC intersects AVC and ATC, it does so at *their* minimum points. As long as MC is below AVC, AVC must be falling. Once MC cuts through the AVC curve, the last begins to rise. The same is true of the relationship between MC and ATC.

Incidentally, when you draw the curve, if you start with the MC curve, it will be much easier to draw in the AVC and ATC curves.

We'll try another problem. First fill in Table 19-5. A completed table appears in Table 19-6. Assume here that fixed cost is $400.

Table 19–5
Hypothetical Cost Schedule

Output	Variable Cost	Total Cost	AFC	AVC	ATC	Marginal Cost
1	$100					
2	150					
3	210					
4	300					
5	430					
6	600					
7	819					

Hopefully your table matched Table 19-6. Now we're ready for the graph. We'll use only three of the curves in the analysis that comes a little later in the chapter—the AVC, ATC, and MC. The AFC curve doesn't serve any analytic purpose, so from here on in we won't draw it.

Table 19–6
Hypothetical Cost Schedule

Output	Variable Cost	Total Cost	AFC	AVC	ATC	Marginal Cost
1	$100	$ 500	$400	$100	$500	$100
2	150	550	200	75	275	50
3	210	610	133	70	203	60
4	300	700	100	75	175	90
5	430	830	80	86	166	130
6	600	1,000	67	100	167	170
7	819	1,219	57	117	174	219

Compare your graph with the one in Figure 19-2. How did your minimum points come out on the AVC and ATC curves? If you drew your curves in the order I suggested—MC first, then AVC and ATC—your MC should have intersected both the AVC and ATC curves at their minimum points.

Before we move on to the even more spectacular analysis toward the end of the chapter, we'll do a bit of preliminary analysis. Read off the minimum points of the AVC and ATC curves. At what outputs do they occur? Write down these two points: the output at which the minimum point of the AVC occurs and how much AVC is at that point. Then do the same for the minimum point on the ATC curve.

Your answers should be somewhere within these ranges. For AVC your output should be somewhere between 3.1 and 3.3 when AVC is between $67 and $69. Where do we get these numbers? If you were careful when you drew your graph—otherwise use mine—at an output of 3, AVC is $70. MC is still a bit below AVC at 60. What happens as output goes beyond 3 is that MC continues to rise while AVC declines slightly.

For ATC your output should be somewhere between 5.6 and 5.9. ATC is between $165 and $165.90. Notice that the MC curve intersects the ATC

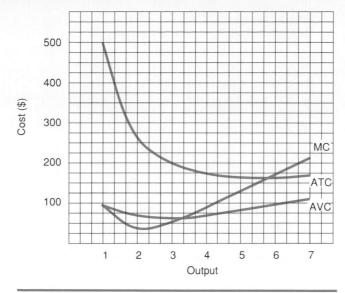

Figure 19–2

curve between outputs of 5 and 6, closer to 6. Notice that at an output of 5 ATC is $166 and at an output of 6 it is $167, but since the MC curve cuts the ATC curve at its minimum point, ATC must be *less* than $166.

Revenue and Profit

Total Revenue and Marginal Revenue

With just one more piece in place, we'll be ready to do some pretty heavy analysis. That piece is marginal revenue. Marginal revenue parallels marginal cost in its use as an analytic tool. It also has a parallel definition.

Definition of marginal revenue

Marginal revenue is the additional revenue for selling one more unit of output. To calculate MR, we need total revenue, which we covered during our discussion of elasticity in Chapter 17. Total revenue is price times output. Marginal revenue is the increase in total revenue when output goes up by 1 unit.

We'll be making an assumption for the next couple of chapters that a seller can sell as much output as he or she wants at the market price. Thus, if the market price is $5, we can easily calculate the total revenue and marginal revenue. I'd like you to do just that by filling in Table 19–7. Then you can check your work by looking at Table 19–8.

Table 19–7
Hypothetical Revenue Schedule

Output	Price	Total Revenue	Marginal Revenue
1	$5		
2	5		
3	5		
4	5		
5	5		
6	5		

Table 19–8
Hypothetical Revenue Schedule

Output	Price	Total Revenue	Marginal Revenue
1	$5	$ 5	$5
2	5	10	5
3	5	15	5
4	5	20	5
5	5	25	5
6	5	30	5

Now we're ready to draw the graph of the demand and marginal revenue curves. The demand curve for this firm is the output, which runs from 1 to 6, at a price of $5. And the marginal revenue curve is the output, from 1 to 6, at whatever the marginal revenue happens to be. Go ahead and draw a graph of the firm's demand and MR curves on graph paper.

Now check your work against that in Figure 19–3. You should have drawn just one line, perfectly elastic, which serves as the firm's demand and MR curves. When price is constant so is MR, and MR and demand are identical.

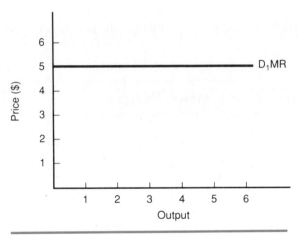

Figure 19–3

Try another one. If price is $8 and output ranges from 1 to 6, draw a table of output, price, total revenue, and marginal revenue in the space below Table 19–7. Then draw a graph of the demand and marginal revenue curves.

How did you do? Better this time? Do your table and graph check out with mine? (See Table 19–9 and Figure 19–4.) See, there's really nothing to

Table 19–9
Hypothetical Revenue Schedule

Output	Price	Total Revenue	Marginal Revenue
1	$8	$ 8	$8
2	8	16	8
3	8	24	8
4	8	32	8
5	8	40	8
6	8	48	8

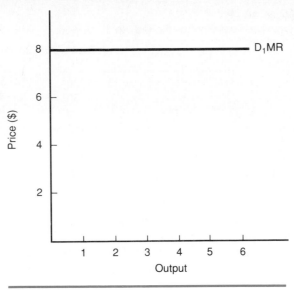

Figure 19–4

it. In this and the next chapter, the demand and marginal revenue curves will be one and the same and will be perfectly straight horizontal lines.

Profit Maximization and Loss Minimization

We're finally ready to do some marginal analysis, which is the basis of much of microeconomic decision making. The big decision we'll be making here is choosing the output at which the business firm should produce. If we choose correctly, profits will be maximized (or losses minimized).

We'll decide on output two ways. First we'll use the data in Table 19–10. Just subtract total cost from total revenue. Do this for each unit of output. Put your answers in the column labeled Total Profits.

Table 19–10
Hypothetical Revenue, Cost, and
Profit Schedule

Output	Price	Total Revenue	Marginal Revenue	Total Cost	ATC	Marginal Cost	Total Profits
1	$200	$ 200	$200	$ 500	$500	$100	
2	200	400	200	550	275	50	
3	200	600	200	610	203	60	
4	200	800	200	700	175	90	
5	200	1,000	200	830	166	130	
6	200	1,200	200	1,000	167	170	
7	200	1,400	200	1,205	176	219	

It would appear from Table 19–10 (I've done a separate profits table, Table 19–11) that profits are maximized at an output of 6, with 7 a close second. But we're missing something if we're trying to pinpoint exactly where we maximize our profits. The maximum profit point may well be between two numbers. In fact, we'll soon see that it is between outputs of 6 and 7, and somewhat closer to 7. How? By doing marginal anlaysis.

Profit maximization point:
MC = MR

In a nutshell, *profits are maximized when marginal cost is equal to marginal revenue*. We're going to draw a graph. Then we'll see how much output is when profits are maximized, after which we'll see how much prof-

Table 19–11
Hypothetical Profits Schedule

Output	Total Profits
1	− $300
2	− 150
3	− 10
4	100
5	170
6	200
7	195

its are at that output. I guarantee that they'll be more than the $200 they are at an output of 6.

The graph we'll draw will need just three curves: MC, MR, and ATC. Remember that the demand curve and the marginal revenue curve are identical, but be sure to label that curve properly.

Your graph should have come out something like Figure 19–5. Marginal cost and marginal revenue are equal at an output of about 6.7. If your output is something like 6.6 or 6.75, that's close enough—in fact, maybe you're closer to the truth than I am. Occasionally that happens.

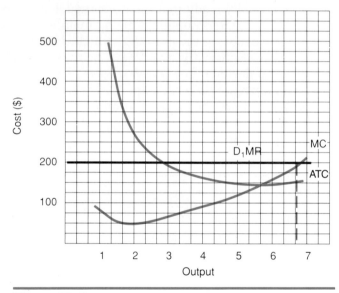

Figure 19–5

Let's see how much profits are at 6.7. To calculate profits we subtract total cost from total revenue. Total revenue is easy to figure because we already know price. Total revenue = price × output: $200 × 6.7 = $1,340. How much is total cost? To find out, we need to know ATC. At an output of 6.7, it looks like about $170. We know that total cost is $167 at an output of 6 and $176 at an output of 7, so judging from how we have drawn the curve, $170 seems about right. To get total cost we multiply ATC by output: $170 × 6.7 = $1,139.00. Since profits = total revenue − total cost: $1,340 − 1,139 = $201.

Let's try another problem. First we can approximate total profits in Table 19–12. Write in the total profits figures (total revenue minus total cost). Then we'll use marginal analysis.

Table 19–12
Hypothetical Revenue, Cost, and
Profit Schedule

Output	Price	Total Revenue	Marginal Revenue	Total Cost	ATC	Marginal Cost	Total Profits
1	$450	$450	$450	$1,500	$1,500	$500	
2	450	900	450	1,800	900	300	
3	450	1,350	450	2,000	667	200	
4	450	1,800	450	2,300	575	300	
5	450	2,250	450	2,700	540	400	
6	450	2,700	450	3,400	580	700	

As you will have calculated (and as I have in Table 19–13), total profits appear to be maximized at an output of 5. That is, total losses are minimized here. You may have noticed that MC is still below MR. We have not maximized our profits—or minimized our losses—until MC rises to meet MR.

Table 19–13
Hypothetical Profits Schedule

Output	Total Profits
1	− $1,050
2	− 900
3	− 650
4	− 500
5	− 450
6	− 700

Let's plot our graph and see when we minimize our losses. We'll need three curves: the demand/marginal revenue curve, the MC curve, and the ATC curve.

According to Table 19–13, we minimize our losses at an output of 5, when total losses = $450. Do we do any better with marginal analysis? First, we find our best output, which comes to about 5.25 in Figure 19–6 (anything between 5.2 and 5.3 is acceptable). Now we calculate total losses at output 5.25.

$$
\begin{aligned}
\text{Total profit} &= \text{Total revenue} - \text{Total cost} \\
&= (\text{Price} - \text{ATC})\,\text{Output} \\
&= (\$450 - 530)\,5.25 \\
&= (-\$80)\,5.25 \\
&= -\$420
\end{aligned}
$$

It looks as though we can cut our losses to $420 by producing at an output of 5.25 instead of at 5. Notice also that I've shortened the total profit formula somewhat since both price and ATC must be multiplied by output. Finally, please remember that we can use the same formula to find total losses, which are negative total profits.

Producing exactly where MC equals MR enables us to maximize total profit (or minimize total losses). Let's see why. MR is the additional revenue from selling one more unit of output. MC is the additional cost from producing one more unit of output. Thus, by producing and selling more, we're adding to our costs and to our revenues.

How far should we go? As long as we're adding more to our revenue than to our costs, our total profit is rising. For example, if MC is 10 and MR is

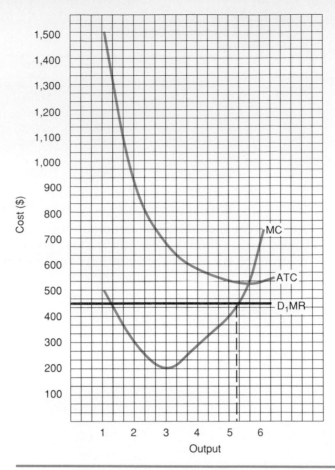

Figure 19–6

18, by producing and selling that unit our total profits have gone up by 8. Suppose the MC of the next unit is 13 and the MR is 18. By producing *that* unit our total profit goes up by 5. Now if, on producing still another unit, MC goes to 17 while MR is 18, it still pays to expand because we're adding one more dollar to our profits. If MC of the next unit is 24 and MR is 18, we won't produce that unit, but theoretically if we could produce a small part of it, we would because *then* we would be maximizing our profits.

The Short-Run and Long-Run Supply Curves

Derivation of Firm's Short-Run Supply Curve

This section is basically a proof of why the individual firm has a certain supply curve. We'll draw on several concepts developed in this and the previous chapter. When we finish we'll have four more rules that the firm always follows. Now we'll show you how those rules are derived. You now have the analytic equipment to follow the proof.

We'll start by citing the profit maximization rule. *A business firm will always choose that output where MC = MR.* Since maximizing profits is the main—some economists say the only—objective of the business firm, we'll accept this without proof.

A firm will always produce where MC = MR.

Let's get back to those problems from the last chapter dealing with prospective sales, fixed cost, and variable cost. We derived a rule with respect to prospective sales and variable costs. *A firm will operate if sales are greater than variable costs; a firm will shut down if variable costs are greater than sales.*

A business firm, at any point in time, will have a certain set of cost curves: AVC, ATC, and MC. Those curves are determined mainly by the firm's capital stock—its plant and equipment. Over time these curves can change, but at any given time they're fixed. What concerns us here is the MC curve. We can assume it doesn't change.

What about MR? That changes with price. There are an infinite number of possible prices. Since the firm will always operate where MC equals MR, there are an infinite number of possible prices and therefore an infinite number of MR's, but only one MC curve. It follows then that we could slide along the MC curve so that no matter what the MR, MC would equal MR.

Let's go over these points. MC must equal MR. MC stays the same. MR can change—to any value. Whenever price changes, we have a new MR line, but the MC curve remains the same. The MC will equal MR, but at some other point on the MC curve.

This can be illustrated. In Figure 19–7, we'll start with MC = MR at an output of 9. MR = $43. At an output of 8, MC = MR = $28. At an output of 7, MC = MR = $19. And so forth down the MC curve.

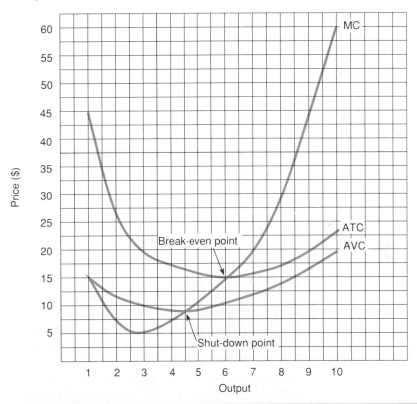

Figure 19–7

When we get below an output of about 6.1, we run into a problem. We're losing money. In the long run, no firm will stay in business if it's losing money, so for every output above 6.1 we can just move along the MC curve and, in effect, we will be moving along the firm's long-run supply curve.

At outputs below 6.1, the firm is losing money because ATC is above price. Remember that price and MR are the same. Below output 6.1, MC is less than ATC; and since the firm will produce where MC = MR, it should be obvious that below output 6.1, MR is less than ATC. In other words, the firm would be receiving less for each unit sold than the cost of producing that unit.

This is consistent with what we concluded toward the end of the last chapter when we said that in the long run, a firm would go out of business if total cost were greater than sales. It would be exactly the same thing to say that a firm would go out of business if ATC was greater than price (or MR). Why? Because if we divided total cost by output, we'd get ATC. If we divided sales by output, we'd get price.[2] In other words, if we'd go out of business if total cost were greater than sales, we'd also go out of business if ATC were greater than price.

Now, on to the firm's short-run supply curve. If we were to continue our way down the firm's MC curve below an output of 6.1, we'd find that at an output of 6, MC = MR = $14. At an output of 5, MC = MR = $10. But we see in Figure 19–7 that at an output of about 4.5, the MC curve passes through the AVC curve, signifying the minimum point of the AVC. That means that any price (and MR) below that point, say, about $8.40, would mean that price would be below AVC.

We know from the previous chapter that if variable cost exceeds sales, the firm will not operate in the short run. Now we have AVC exceeding price, and this amounts to the same thing as variable cost exceeding sales.

If we were to divide variable cost by output, we'd get AVC. If we were to divide sales by output, we'd get price. Again, we see that when AVC is greater than price, it is the same as saying that variable cost is greater than sales. And the firm does not operate; it shuts down.

The firm's short-run supply curve

Thus, the firm's short-run supply curve does not go below the point at which MC is lower than AVC. In this case, the short-run supply curve does not go below an output of 4.5. We call this the shutdown point. *The firm's short-run supply curve begins at the shutdown point and moves all the way up the firm's MC curve as far as it goes.* It does *not* stop at the point at which the MC curve intersects the ATC curve. The short-run supply curve runs all the way up the firm's MC curve.

The firm's long-run supply curve

The firm's long-run supply curve also runs up the MC curve, beginning at the point at which the MC curve intersects the ATC curve. That is called the break-even point. In this case it is at an output of 6.1. So *a firm's long-run supply curve begins at the break-even point and runs all the way up the MC curve.*

Now let's identify the firm's shutdown and break-even points. In other words, how much is AVC at the shutdown point and how much is ATC at the break-even point?

To help answer these questions as accurately as possible, we'll use Table 19–14, on which Figure 19–6 is based. The shutdown point is at an output of 4.5. At this output, AVC is at a minimum. From the table we see that at an output of 4, AVC is $8.50 and at an output of 5, it is $8.80. Do *not* assume that $8.50 is a minimum point. That minimum occurs at an output of 4.5 and is, say, $8.40. The same is true at the break-even point. It lies at an output of 6.1, and not, as some casual observers might have it, at 6. At an output of 6, MC is below ATC. In Table 19–14, MC = $14 and ATC is $14.67. ATC hits its minimum at an output of 6.1 and is perhaps $14.65.

Shutdown and break-even points

These points—the break-even and shutdown points—become important when we determine the lowest prices acceptable to the firm in the long run and in the short run. *In the short run, if price is below the shutdown point, the firm will cease operations, and in the long run it will go out of business if price is below the break-even point.*

---

[2] Sales = Price × Output. Sales/Output = Price.

Table 19–14
Hypothetical Schedule of Revenues and Costs*

Output	Variable Cost	AVC	Total Cost	ATC	Marginal Cost
1	$ 15	$15	$ 45	$45	$15
2	22	11	52	26	7
3	27	9	57	19	5
4	34	8.50	64	16	7
5	44	8.80	74	14.80	10
6	58	9.67	88	14.67	14
7	77	11	107	15.29	19
8	105	13.33	135	16.88	28
9	148	16.23	178	19.78	43
10	210	21	240	24	62

* Fixed cost = $30.

In this problem, the shutdown point is at $8.40, so if the price is less than $8.40, the firm will shut down in the short run. In the long run, if the price is less than $14.65, the firm will go out of business.

Here then are our four rules. In the short run: (1) if price is below the shutdown point, the firm will shut down; (2) if price is above the shutdown point, the firm will operate. In the long run: (3) if price is below the break-even point, the firm will go out of business; (4) if price is above the break-even point, the firm will stay in business.

The Long-Run Planning Envelope Curve

We have been making an implicit assumption about the business firm. We've assumed that it has been operating with a plant of given size. What's wrong with assuming that? Nothing, unless the firm alters the size of its plant.

What is a plant?

What is a plant? It's a factory, office, store, or any combination of factories, offices, or stores. The plant used by Procter & Gamble consists of hundreds of factories and offices. The plant of A&P consists of hundreds of stores, factories, and offices, and the plant of Kone's ice cream parlor on Kings Highway in Brooklyn consists of that one store, and, some would say, of the Kone "boys," who must now be in their 60s.

What happens to the supply of a firm when its plant size is altered? If the plant becomes larger, the firm's ATC and MC curves shift to the right. The firm's MC curve, which is its supply curve—above the shutdown point in the short run and the break-even point in the long run—shifts to the right. This means that supply is increased.

If a firm were to build a larger factory, it might be able to lower its costs. For example, in Figure 19–8, ATC_2 reflects lower costs for outputs greater than 135 than does ATC_1. And ATC_3 reflects lower costs than ATC_2 for outputs of over 220.

How much would it cost to produce at ATC_1's break-even point? How much would it cost to produce at the break-even points of ATC_2 and ATC_3?

Notice that we have declining costs: $39 at the break-even point of ATC_1, $34 at that of ATC_2, $30 at that of ATC_3, and $26 at that of ATC_4. Why are costs declining? For a variety of reasons, which could be lumped under the heading of economies of scale (which is covered in Chapter 2). These economies include quantity discounts by making massive purchases from trade suppliers and the three economies noted in Adam Smith's discussion of mass production in a pin factory in Chapter 2. These are specializa-

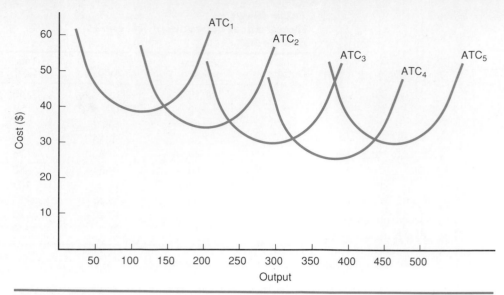

Figure 19–8

tion at a particular job, the use of specialized machinery, and the time saved by not having workers go from job to job.

Just as a firm may realize economies of scale as output rises, a certain point is reached when ATCs begin to rise. It is here that diseconomies of scale (also discussed toward the end of Chapter 2) set in. Basically, the firm grows so large that management becomes inefficient. One hand does not know what the other is doing. Divisions of a corporation begin to work at cross-purposes.

When a firm grows, it increases its plant.

Thus, as the firm grows in size and output, it increases its plant. ATC will fall through a certain range of output, but eventually it will begin to rise. This is seen in Figure 19–8. Costs decline from ATC$_1$ to ATC$_2$ to ATC$_3$ to ATC$_4$. After ATC$_4$, they begin to rise.

In the short run a firm is stuck with a certain size plant. If output were 175 and the firm were operating with ATC$_1$, there would be nothing it could do about it in the short run. But in the long run it would expand so it could operate a plant that would be better suited to producing at 175. That plant would be signified by ATC$_2$. If it were producing in plant ATC$_5$ with an output of 500, if output should decline to 275 and that decline was perceived as a permanent decline, the firm would contract its plant size to ATC$_3$.

These changes in the size of plant are long-run changes; they take time. New factories, offices, and stores would have to be constructed. Old ones would have to be sold or sublet. In the long run a firm could be virtually any size, provided of course, it had the requisite financing to expand.

We can say there are an infinite number of plant sizes. Theoretically then Figure 19–9 could consist of an infinite number of ATC curves, one for each size plant.

Now we come to the firm's long-run planning envelope curve. If the firm were to stay with one size plant over the long run, its long-run supply curve would simply run along the MC curve above the break-even point, as it does in Figure 19–7. If the firm were to consider many different plant sizes, we would need to take this fact into account.

We do this by means of the long-run planning envelope curve, shown in Figure 19–9. Here we have combined the break-even points of several different sized plants, represented by their ATCs. The long-run planning envelope

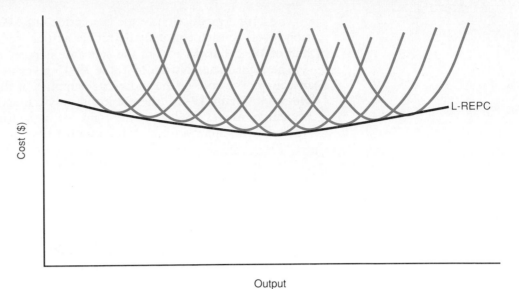

Figure 19–9

curve, which is tangent to these curves, is also U shaped. It reaches a low point at the break-even point of the lowest ATC curve. This point represents the lowest possible cost at which the product can be produced. A firm will produce at that output and with a plant of that size only if that is the output at which it would maximize its profits.

The Market Supply

We have looked at the industry through the eyes of the individual entrepreneur, but what actually happens in a given market is determined by the actions of all business firms. In this concluding section we shall consider how market supply is determined.

Definition of market supply

In a word, *market supply is the sum of the supply schedules of all the individual firms in the industry.* In Table 19–15, we have a simplified supply schedule for the American automobile industry (excluding exports).

Table 19–15
Hypothetical Supply of American Cars
(in thousands)

Price	GM	Ford	Quantity Supplied by Chrysler	American	Volks-wagen	Total
9,000	5,311	2,356	1,245	256	279	9,447
8,000	4,617	1,984	991	188	196	7,976
7,000	4,002	1,584	796	134	136	6,616
6,000	3,623	1,216	601	104	104	5,648
5,000	3,190	996	483	90	91	4,858

There are two main simplifications in this supply schedule. Obviously Volkswagen Beetles, Ford Mavericks, Oldsmobiles, Pacers, as well as the whole range of Chryslers, Chevys, and Buicks vary greatly in price, so we'll assume that each of these five American car manufacturers produces an identical car. A second simplification is that these companies would actually be willing to sell *any* car at relatively low prices.

The actual production levels (at a price of $7,000) and the relative production levels of each company do reflect actual production figures for the first half of 1982, but the rest of the schedule is purely hypothetical.

The right-hand column of Table 19-15 gives us the market supply. It is, of course, the sum of the individual supplies of the five companies; and, as we see in Figure 19-10, the market supply curve, like each individual supply curve, moves upward to the right. At higher and higher prices, the market will supply an increasing number of cars.

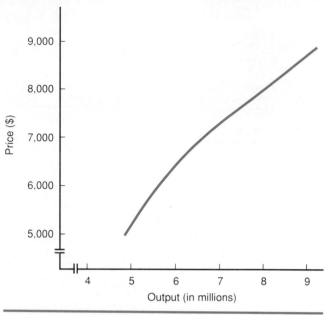

Figure 19-10

Note: We don't go down to 0 on the price scale; we don't go down to 0 on the output scale. Since we don't need those figures, why put them in the graph?

Why quantity supply rises with price

There are two reasons for this. As we have illustrated, as price rises, each of the existing firms will produce and sell more cars, but at high enough prices, other firms—both domestic and foreign—will be attracted to the industry. Why does the quantity supplied rise as price goes up? Because existing firms will raise their outputs and new firms will be attracted to the industry.

We will carry this analysis still further in the next chapter. We will soon see that the ease with which firms may enter the industry is a key characteristic of perfect competition.

Workbook for Chapter 19

Name _____

Date _____

Self-Review Examination

Questions 1–9: Answer true or false.

_____ 1. When marginal cost is less than average variable cost, average variable cost is rising.

_____ 2. As output rises, average fixed cost declines.

_____ 3. When output is zero, total cost is zero.

_____ 4. Average fixed cost plus average variable cost equals average total cost.

_____ 5. Average total cost is always greater than average variable cost, but as output rises, the difference between them narrows.

_____ 6. The marginal cost curve always intersects the average total cost curve at the latter's minimum point.

_____ 7. Marginal revenue is the additional revenue for selling one more unit of output.

_____ 8. A firm will always produce at an output at which marginal revenue is greater than marginal cost.

_____ 9. The firm's short-run supply curve runs up the marginal cost curve from the shutdown point to the break-even point.

10. Define market supply.

11. Define marginal cost.

12. Define marginal revenue.

13. At an output of three, if fixed cost is 100 and variable cost is 180, how much is average fixed cost, average variable cost, and average total cost?

14. Prove whether this statement is true or false. As output rises, average fixed cost rises.

15. Profits are always maximized when _____ equals _____ .

Multiple-Choice Questions

Circle the letter that corresponds to the best answer.

1. The lowest point on the average variable cost curve is

a. always when it is crossed by the marginal cost curve   b. sometimes when it is crossed by the marginal cost curve   c. never when it is crossed by the marginal cost curve

2. A firm will always produce at that output at which

a. marginal cost = marginal revenue   b. it minimizes its costs   c. it operates at peak efficiency   d. it maximizes its total revenue

3. Total revenue divided by output equals

a. marginal cost   b. average total cost   c. price   d. average variable cost   e. none of the above

4. As output is increased, eventually

a. average total cost will rise because the increase in average variable cost will be larger than the decline in average fixed cost   b. average fixed cost will exceed average variable cost   c. average total cost will rise as long as marginal cost is rising   d. marginal cost will rise because average fixed cost is declining

5. The lowest point on a firm's short-run supply curve is at the

a. break-even point   b. shutdown point   c. most profitable output point   d. lowest point on the marginal cost curve

6. As output increases, eventually

a. economies of scale become larger than diseconomies of scale   b. diseconomies of scale become larger than economies of scale   c. economies of scale and diseconomies of scale both increase   d. economies of scale and diseconomies of scale both decrease

7. When marginal cost is rising, but marginal cost is less than average total cost, we are definitely below the

a. shutdown point   **b.** break-even point

c. maximum profit point

8. The marginal cost curve intersects the average variable cost curve at the

a. shutdown point   **b.** break-even point

c. maximum profit point

9. In Figure 1, if you wanted to produce an output of 100, in the long run you would choose a plant whose size was represented by

a. ATC_1 **b.** ATC_2 **c.** ATC_3

d. ATC_4 **e.** ATC_5

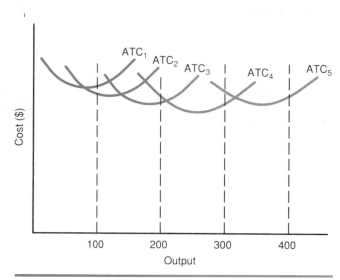

Figure 1

10. In Figure 1, if you wanted to produce an output of 200, in the long run you would choose a plant whose size was represented by

a. ATC_1 **b.** ATC_2 **c.** ATC_3

d. ATC_4 **e.** ATC_5

11. The firm's long-run supply curve runs along its _____ curve.

a. ATC   **b.** AVC   **c.** MC   **d.** MR

12. The MC curve intersects the AVC and ATC curves at their minimum points

a. none of the time   **b.** some of the time   **c.** most of the time   **d.** all of the time

13. Which statement is true?

a. AFC declines with output.   **b.** ATC declines with

output.   **c.** AFC – AVC = ATC.   **d.** Output divided by fixed cost = AFC.

14. AVC reaches a minimum at

a. the same output as ATC   **b.** a lower output than ATC   **c.** a higher output than ATC

15. In general, a firm's

a. total cost rises as output rises up to a certain point, and then begins to decline   **b.** marginal cost rises as output rises up to a certain point, and then begins to decline   **c.** average cost declines as output rises up to a certain point and then begins to rise.

16. If AVC is declining

a. marginal cost must be less than AVC   **b.** marginal cost must be greater than ATC   **c.** AVC must be greater than AFC   **d.** ATC must be declining

Problems

1. Fill in Table 1. Assume a fixed cost of $50.

Table 1

Output	Variable Cost	AFC	AVC	ATC	MC
1	$20	_____	_____	_____	_____
2	35	_____	_____	_____	_____
3	55	_____	_____	_____	_____
4	80	_____	_____	_____	_____

2. When the output is zero, total cost is always equal to _____ .

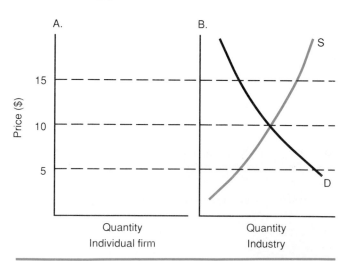

Figure 2

3. Given the industry supply and demand shown in Figure 2B, use Figure 2A to draw the perfect competitor's demand, marginal revenue, average total cost, and marginal cost curve for its long-run situation.

4. Please label the firm's break-even point, shutdown point, short-run, and long-run supply curves in Figure 3.

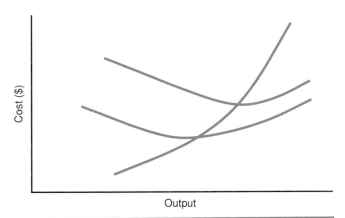

Figure 3

5. Use Figure 4 to sketch a firm's average fixed cost curve and explain why it has that shape.

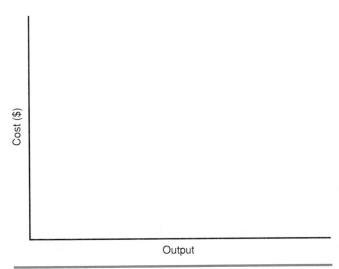

Figure 4

6. As price rises, what happens to the quantity supplied in a market? What are the two reasons for this?

7. This problem should be done in three steps. First: Fill in Table 2. Assume that fixed cost is $100 and price is $64.

Table 2

Output	Variable Cost	Total Cost	Average Variable Cost	Average Total Cost	Marginal Cost
1	$ 30	____	____	____	____
2	50	____	____	____	____
3	80	____	____	____	____
4	125	____	____	____	____
5	190	____	____	____	____
6	280	____	____	____	____

Next: use the graph paper (Figure 5) to draw a graph of the firm's demand, marginal revenue, average variable cost, average total cost, and marginal cost curves. Be sure you label the graph correctly. On the graph, indicate the break-even and shutdown points and the firm's short-run and long-run supply curves. Third: Calculate total profit in the space below, then answer questions *a* through *d*.

a. The minimum price the firm would accept in the short-run would be $_____ . **b.** The minimum price the firm would accept in the long-run would be $_____ . **c.** The output at which the firm would maximize profits would be _____. **d.** Complete Table 3.

Table 3

If the price were	What would the firm do in the Long run?	Short run?	How much would output be in the short run?
$90	____	____	____
40	____	____	____
20	____	____	____

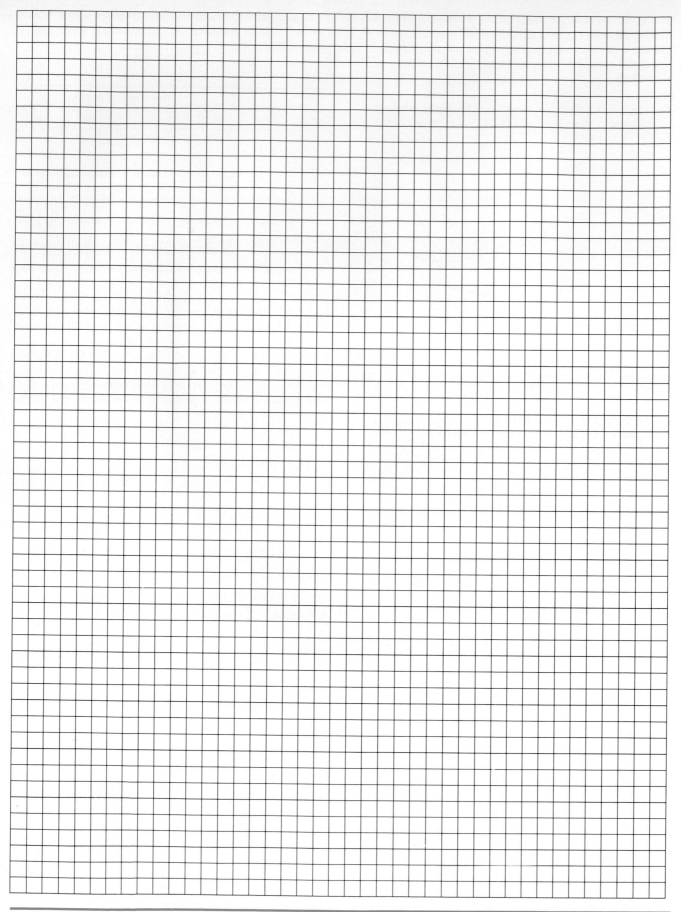

Figure 5

Perfect Competition

Perfect competition, as economists fondly point out, is an ideal state of affairs, which, unfortunately, does not exist in any industry. Why bother then with a nonexistent form of competition? The reason is kind of like the Judeo-Christian tradition. We're all sinners, but we still need to know right from wrong.

Perfect competition attains the ideal of always being right. It is held up as the example of what we should strive to approach, even if we can never hope to attain its state of grace. But who knows—maybe we'll get lucky.

For our purposes, perfect competition will be considered an unattainable standard by which the other forms of competition—monopoly, monopolistic competition, and oligopoly—will be judged. Thus, even though it doesn't exist, perfect competition has its uses.

Chapter Objectives

In this chapter you will be introduced to these terms and concepts:

- The characteristics of perfect competition.
- The perfect competitor's demand curve.
- The short run and the long run.
- Economic and accounting profits.
- Decreasing, constant, and increasing cost industries.

Definition of Perfect Competition

Under perfect competition there are so many firms that no one firm has any influence over price. What is influence? If any action taken by the firm has any effect on price, that's influence. If a firm, by withholding half its output from the market, were able to push up price, that would be influence. If a firm doubled its output and forced down price, that too would be influence. Even if a firm left the industry, which would make price go up, *that* would be influence on price.

The industry under perfect competition includes many firms. How many? So many that no one firm has any influence on price. How many would *that* be? There's no exact answer, but we can agree on some numbers. Would a million firms be many? Obviously yes. Would 80,000? Definitely. Ten thousand? Yes. Would three be many? No! Ten? No! Seventeen? No.

There's no clear dividing line. Not too many students seem happy with more than 17 but less than 10,000. If you want my guess—and its only an arbitrary number—I'd say that perhaps 200 firms would constitute many. But that's just *my* guess and in macroeconomics, there's no one "correct" answer to this question of how many is many.

The perfect competitor is a price taker rather than a price maker. Price is set by the industrywide supply and demand; the perfect competitor can take it or leave it.

Another part of the definition of perfect competition has to do with the product. *For perfect competition to take place, all the firms in the industry must sell an identical product.* That is, those who buy the product cannot distinguish between what one seller and another sells. So, in the buyer's mind, the product is identical. The buyer has no reason to prefer one seller to another.

Definition of perfect competition

Now we can define perfect competition. *A perfectly competitive industry has many firms selling an identical product.* How many is many? So many that no one firm can influence price. What is identical? A product that is identical in the minds of buyers so that they have no reason to prefer one seller to another.

Agriculture, particularly wheat growing, has been held up as an example of perfect or near-perfect competition. The rise of the giant corporate farm has made this example somewhat obsolete, but we haven't been able to come up with any other examples of perfect competition.

The Perfect Competitor's Demand Curve

Horizontal demand curve

The perfect competitor faces a horizontal or perfectly elastic demand curve (see Figure 20–1.) As we noted in the last chapter, a firm with a perfectly elastic demand curve has an identical MR curve. This is significant because

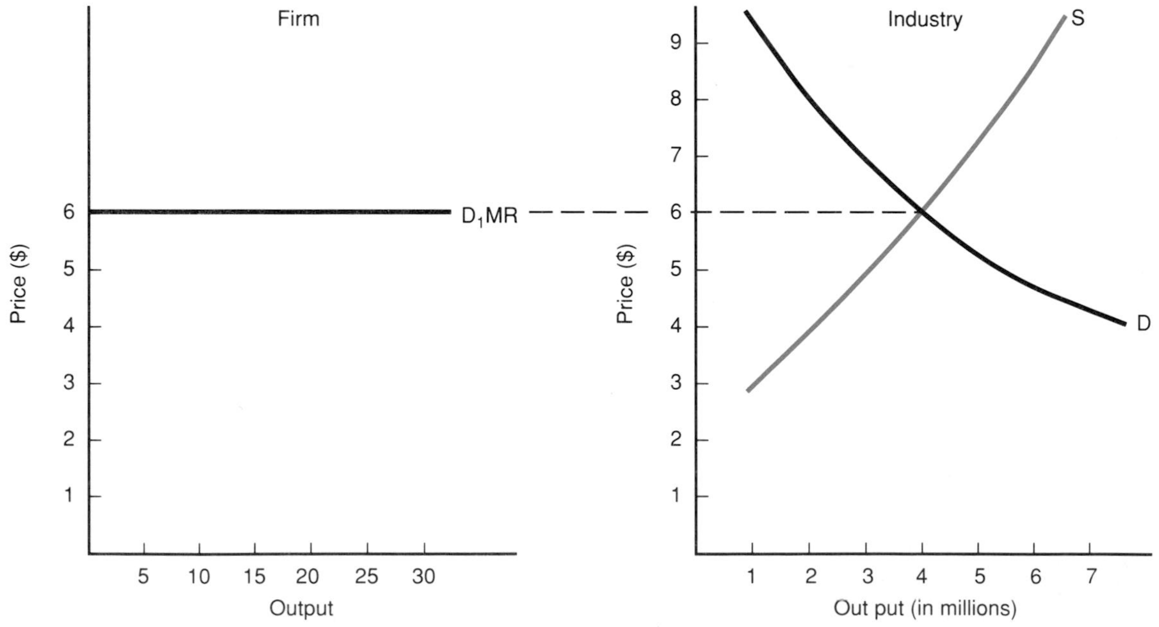

Figure 20–1

Identical Products Are in the Minds of the Buyers

Are all hamburgers identical? Is the Whopper identical to the Big Mac? Are Wendy's hamburgers identical to those of White Castle? Maybe *you* can differentiate among these choices, but what if every buyer in the market considered them identical? They *would* be identical.

This identity takes place in the minds of the buyers. If all cars—Toyotas, Fords, Volkswagons, Plymouths, and Cadillacs—are the same, they're the same. If all buyers are indifferent about whether they're offered station wagons, stretch limos, or subcompacts, all cars are identical. A car is a car. Remember: the customer is always right.

the firm can sell as much as it wants at the market price. It's not necessary to lower price to sell more.

What determines the market price? Supply and demand. In Figure 20–1, we have a supply curve and a demand curve. Where they cross is the point of market price.

In our graph the market price is $6. The firm can sell all it wants at that price. What would happen if it should raise its price one penny to $6.01? It would lose all its sales to its many competitors who would still be charging $6, so the firm would never raise its price above market price.

Would a firm ever lower its price below market price, say to $5.99. Why do that? To get sales away from its competitors? There is no need to do this because the perfect competitor can sell as much as he or she desires at the market price. There is no point in charging less.

Why is the demand curve flat instead of curving downward to the right?

If the firm's demand curve is derived from the intersection of the industry demand and supply curves, why is it flat? Why isn't it sloping downward to the right like the industry supply curve? Actually it is. I know it doesn't look that way, but it really is.

Look at the scale of industry output in Figure 20–1; it's in the millions. The output scale of the individual firm goes up to 30. When the industry demand curve slopes downward to the right, it does so over millions of units of output. For example, as the price falls from $6 to $5, output goes from 4 million to 5.5 million. In fact, it takes a price change of just $1 to bring about a change in the quantity demanded of 1.5 million units.

On the left side of Figure 20–1, we can consider output changes between 0 and 30 units. It would take a far greater change in output to change price, even by one cent. That's why the demand curve of the individual firm is seen as flat; and that's why the firm is too small to have any effect on price.

Theoretically, the firm's demand curve slopes ever so slightly downward to the right. But we can't see that slope, so we draw the curve perfectly horizontal and consider it perfectly elastic.

Characteristics of Perfect Competition

We've already discussed the two most important characteristics—really requirements—of perfect competition: many firms and an identical product. Two additional characteristics are perfect mobility and perfect knowledge.

Firms must be free to move wherever there's an opportunity for profits. Land, labor, and capital will move where they can secure the highest possible return. An entrepreneur will give up his or her business and work for someone else if the wage offered is higher than the firm's profit.

There are usually certain barriers to entry in various markets that inhibit mobility. Licenses, long-term contracts, government franchises, patents, and control over vital resources are some of these barriers. Under perfect competition, there would be perfect mobility and none of these barriers could exist. As in an open game of poker, anyone with a sufficient stake is welcome to play. In fact, hundreds of firms are entering or leaving each year. There are no significant barriers to entry, with the possible exception of money.[1]

Perfect knowledge or information is another characteristic. Everyone knows about every possible economic opportunity. One example would be the market for audiologists in New York; everyone knows every job that exists and every opening when it occurs. In fact, if one person leaves one job for another, several other people become involved in a game of musical chairs as each fills the next vacated position. The audiologist from New York Eye and Ear who fills the position at Brooklyn Jewish Hospital leaves a position vacant at New York Eye and Ear. His or her position is taken by someone from Long Island College Hospital, which now leaves *that* position open. And so forth.

The Short-Run

Short run: profit or loss

Long run: break-even

In the short run the perfect competitor may make a profit or lose money. In the long run, as we'll see, the perfect competitor just breaks even.

Figure 20-2 shows one example of a perfect competitor in the short run. Is the firm making a profit or is it losing money? How do you know?

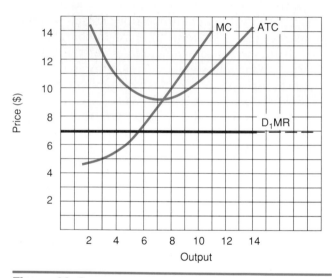

Figure 20-2

You can always tell by looking at the demand curve and the ATC curve. If the demand curve is above the ATC curve at any point, the firm will make a profit. If the demand curve is always below the ATC curve, the firm will lose money.

In this case the firm is losing money. How much? You should be able to figure that out for yourself. Go ahead. You'll find the solution in Figure 20-3.

---

[1] To go into any business these days you not only need to lay out several thousand dollars for rent, inventory, equipment, advertising, and possibly salaries, but you also need money on which to live for at least six months.

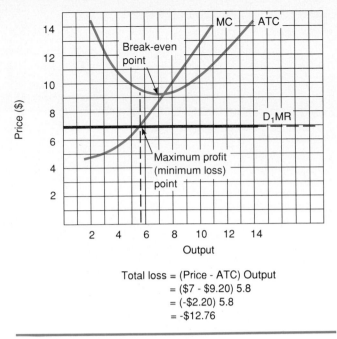

Total loss = (Price - ATC) Output
= ($7 - $9.20) 5.8
= (-$2.20) 5.8
= -$12.76

Figure 20-3

Here's another problem. In this case, is the firm also losing money or is it making a profit? Just check out the demand and ATC curve. How much is the profit or loss? Figure it out; you have the tools. The problem is Figure 20-4; the solution is Figure 20-5.

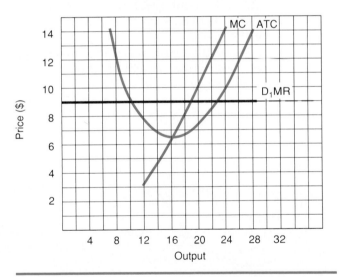

Figure 20-4

Now we go from the firm to the industry. Price is set by the industry supply and demand. Let's see how the graphs of the industry and firm line up. First we'll use the firm's demand/MR, ATC, and MC curves from Figure 20-2 (and 20-3), which have been reproduced on the left side of Figure 20-6. On the right side we have put in industry supply and demand.

The important thing to notice is that price is the same for the firm and the industry. The price is set by industry supply and demand. It then be-

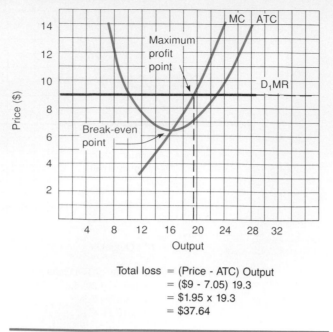

Total loss = (Price - ATC) Output
= ($9 - 7.05) 19.3
= $1.95 x 19.3
= $37.64

Figure 20-5

comes the demand/MR curve for the firm, which can sell as much as it wants at that price. Also notice that the amount the firm does choose to sell is determined by the intersection of the firm's MC curve with its demand/MR curve.

We've done the same thing in Figure 20-7, the left side of which is taken from Figure 20-4 (and 20-5), where the firm is making a profit. Again, notice that the price set in the industry market is identical to the price taken by the firm.

In the short run a firm will either make a profit or take a loss. There is a remote possibility that it will just break even, but that possibility is about the same as that of tossing a coin, which instead of landing on its head or tail, lands on its side or edge. It's not something you can count on having happen with too much regularity.

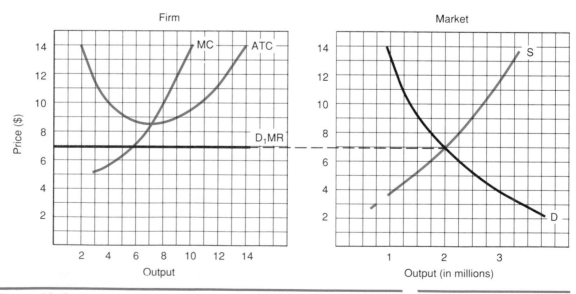

Figure 20-6

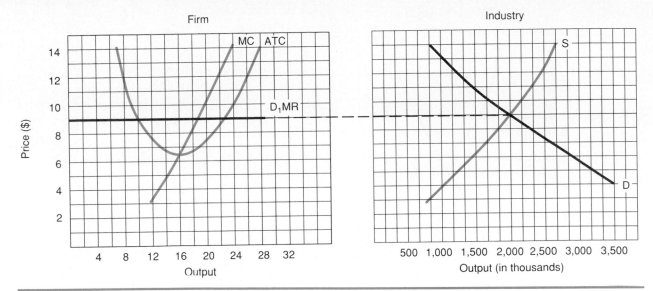

Figure 20-7

The Long Run

Long run: firms may enter or leave industry

In the long run there is time for firms to enter or leave the industry. This factor ensures that in the long run the firm will make zero profits. What was an unlikely outcome for the firm in the short run—zero profits—becomes an absolute certainty in the long run.

Remember that in the long run no firm will accept losses. It will simply close up shop and go out of business. Given the situation in Figure 20-2 (and 20-3 and 20-6), where the individual firm is losing money, it will leave the industry. But as we said at the beginning of the chapter, one firm cannot influence price, so if one firm leaves the industry, market price will not be affected.

If one firm is losing money, presumably others are too; given the extent of the short-run losses this individual firm is suffering, the chances are other firms too are ready to go out of business. When enough firms go out of business, the industry supply curve shifts downward to the left. This shifts price upward (in Figure 20-8) from $7 to $9.

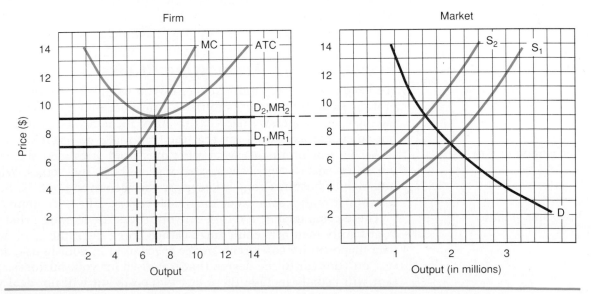

Figure 20-8

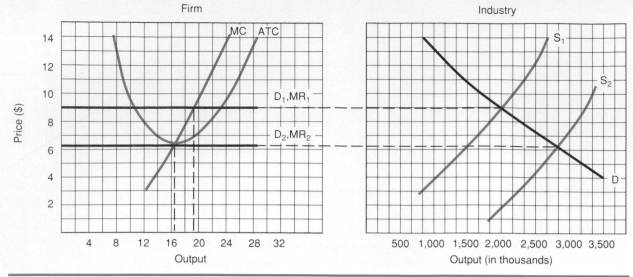

Figure 20–9

There is a secondary effect on the firms that remain in the industry. Each will expand output slightly to the right. On the left side of Figure 20–8, we see that the firm's output rises from 5.8 to 7.

Figure 20–9 is based on Figure 20–7. It shows the long-run effect of a short-run profit. If one firm is making a profit, we can assume that others are too. New firms will spring up and entrepreneurs will enter the industry to get their share of the profits. As more and more firms enter the industry, market supply increases, pushing the supply curve to the right (on the right side of Figure 20–9). As market supply rises, market price comes down until it reaches $6.40.

Here, once again, industry price and the price taken by the individual firm are equal. The output for the individual firm has been reduced slightly, but more significant, the new firms that have entered the industry increased market supply. This, in turn, reduced the price to $6.40, and profits for the individual firm are now zero. Along with this, as we can see on the left side of Figure 20–9, output has fallen from 19.3 to 16.4.

The left side of Figure 20–8 and the left side of Figure 20–9 are identical. Notice that the ATC and the demand/MR curves are tangent (just touching). At that point of tangency, MC = MR, so that is where the firm produces. ATC = price at that point, so profit is zero.

Economic and Accounting Profits

We keep saying that profits are zero. Who would stay in business with no profits? Actually there *are* profits. A firm's accountant might tell the businessman or businesswoman that the firm made $55,000 (in the long run), but an economist would say that the firm made no profit whatsoever.

Accounting profits

Accounting profits are what's left over from sales after the firm has paid out all its costs—rent, wages, cost of goods sold, fuel, taxes. What the businessman or businesswoman keeps are the accounting profits. But the economist makes some additional deductions, called "economic costs."

Economic profits

These costs include a return on your investment, wages that you and your family members could have earned doing the same work for another firm (opportunity cost), rent on the space used in your house, and wear and tear on your car to the degree that it is used for your business. Your accountant will usually include these last two costs but will not deal with the first two.

Suppose you've invested $100,000 of your own money in your business. You could have earned $15,000 in interest had you lent these funds to another business of comparable risk. If you and your spouse, working 12 hours a day for your business, had worked for another firm the two of you would have earned $40,000. The economist will subtract these $55,000 in economic costs from your $55,000 accounting profits. And poof—your economics profits are zero.

Why, you ask, should economic costs be subtracted from accounting profits? Because they represent alternatives that you have foregone to have your own business. You *could* have earned $15,000 interest on your $100,000 by investing it elsewhere and you and your spouse *could* have earned $40,000 working for someone else. The cost of not availing yourselves of these opportunities—your opportunity cost—is $55,000. Being in business for yourselves cost you $55,000.

Why stay in business if your economic profit is zero? Because you *are* still making accounting profits. And you wouldn't do any better if you invested your money elsewhere and worked for someone else; you'd be in exactly the same economic situation. And, of course, by having your own business, you're your own boss.

When economic profits become negative—particularly if these losses are substantial and appear permanent—many people would close their businesses and go to work for another company. That way they would be able to earn $55,000 a year ($15,000 in interest and $40,000 in wages).

On the other hand, when, in the short run, there are economic profits, more people are attracted to the industry. Market supply goes up as more firms are formed by people who perceive that they could do better working for themselves than for other people. Eventually, in the long run, economic profits in the industry fall to zero. At that point, no one else enters the industry.

Efficiency

Efficiency defined

In economics we have some rather peculiar definitions. We define *efficient* as cheap. When a firm is an efficient producer, it produces its product at a relatively low cost. A firm operates at peak efficiency when it produces its product at the lowest possible cost. That would be at the minimum point of its ATC curve.

For the perfect competitor in the long run, the most profitable output is at the minimum point of its ATC curve. Check it out on the left side of Figures 20-8 and 20-9. At any other output the firm would lose money; just to stay in business, it must operate at peak efficiency.

This is the hallmark of perfect competition. The firm, not through any virtues of its owners but because of the degree of competition in the marketplace, is forced to operate at peak efficiency. As we'll see in the next three chapters, the other forms of competition do not force peak efficiency.

This is very good for the consumer. He or she can buy at cost. That's right, price is equal to ATC. Remember—no economic profit. And consumers have the firm's competitors to thank for such a low price. Competition will keep businessmen and businesswomen honest—that is, if there's enough competition.

Decreasing, Constant, and Increasing Cost Industries

The long-run planning envelope curve, pictured in Figure 19-9 in the last chapter, really makes two statements. For virtually every industry, a firm would be able to lower its ATC if it could expand up to a certain point. If it were to expand beyond that point, ATC would rise.

This gives us two concepts: decreasing costs and increasing costs. In a decreasing cost industry, firms could expand and lower their costs while in an increasing cost industry, any expansion would lead to rising costs. There's also a third possibility: a constant cost industry, where ATC does not change as output rises.

Factor costs—wages, rent, and interest—are by far the most important determinants of whether costs are falling, constant, or increasing. Usually factor costs will eventually rise, which would ultimately make every industry an increasing cost industry. As more and more land, particularly in a given locality, is used by the expanding industry, rent will be bid up. And as more labor and capital are used by the industry, wages and interest rates will be bid up as well.

All industries then are really increasing cost industries, but the range of output within which they happen to operate is often one of decreasing or constant costs.

Decreasing Costs and the Breakdown of Perfect Competition

If a firm continually expands to take advantage of decreasing costs, its output will keep increasing. At some point it will become so large that it will have some discernible influence over price in the industry. At that point, by definition, the industry will cease being perfectly competitive.

If we were to take our original firm—the one presented in Figure 20-1—with an original output of 20 or 30 units, how much would it have to expand to end perfect competition? If industry output were 4 million, as shown in Figure 20-1, if any firm in that industry produced, say, 80,000 units (1 percent of output), perhaps that would be enough. If not 80,000, then 100,000 or 150,000. At some point, every economist would agree (some observers say all economists *never* agree) that the firm is too big for perfect competition to exist.

Workbook for Chapter 20

Name _____

Date _____

Multiple-Choice Questions

Circle the letter that corresponds to the best answer.

1. Perfect competition is
a. the prevalent form of competition in the United States   **b.** the only form of competition in the United States   **c.** found occasionally   **d.** probably impossible to find

2. Under prefect competition
a. many firms have some influence over price   **b.** a few firms have influence over price   **c.** no firms have any influence over price

3. Under perfect competition there are
a. many firms producing an identical product   **b.** a few firms producing an identical product   **c.** many firms producing a differentiated product   **d.** a few firms producing a differentiated product

4. The perfect competitor is a
a. price maker rather than a price taker   **b.** price taker rather than a price maker   **c.** price taker and a price maker   **d.** neither a price maker nor a price taker

5. The determination of whether two products are identical
a. is done by market research   **b.** takes place in the minds of the buyers   **c.** is done by the government
d. is done by the sellers

6. The perfect competitor's demand curve is
a. always horizontal   **b.** always vertical
c. sometimes horizontal   **d.** sometimes vertical

7. Which statement is true about the perfect competitor?
a. She may charge a little below market price to get more customers.   **b.** She may charge a little above market price to imply that her product is superior.
c. She will always charge the market price.
d. None is true.

8. Each of the following is a characteristic of perfect competition except
a. many firms   **b.** identical products   **c.** perfect mobility   **d.** varying prices charged by different firms

9. In the short run the perfect competitor will probably
a. make a profit or break even   **b.** take a loss or break even   **c.** make a profit or take a loss

10. In the long run the perfect competitor will probably
a. make a profit   **b.** break even   **c.** take a loss

11. Under perfect competition _____ profits are always zero in the long run.
a. accounting   **b.** economic   **c.** both economic and accounting   **d.** neither accounting nor cconomic

Use the choices below to answer questions 12 and 13.
a. in the long run making a profit   **b.** in the long run breaking even   **c.** in the long run taking a loss   **d.** in the short run making a profit   **e.** in the short run breaking even   **f.** in the short run taking a loss

12. Figure 1 shows the perfect competitor

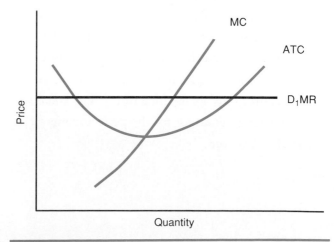

Figure 1

13. Figure 2 shows the perfect competitor

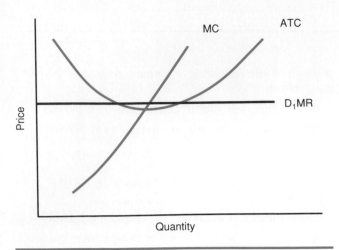

Figure 2

14. The perfect competitor's demand and marginal revenue curves are
a. identical only in the long run   **b.** identical only in the short run   **c.** never identical   **d.** always identical

15. Decreasing, constant, and increasing costs refer to
a. accounting costs   **b.** economic costs
c. marginal costs   **d.** average total costs

16. Which statement is true?
a. Accounting profits are greater than economic profits.   **b.** Economic profits are greater than accounting profits.   **c.** Accounting profits are equal to economic profits.

17. The most efficient output
a. is always equal to the most profitable output for the perfect competitor   **b.** is never equal to the most profitable output for the perfect competitor
c. is equal to the most profitable output for the perfect competitor only in the long run   **d.** is equal to the most profitable output for the perfect competitor only in the short run

Fill-In Questions

1. Under perfect competition there are so many firms that no one firm has any influence over

_____ .

2. Under perfect competition all sellers sell an

_____ product.

3. The determination that a product is identical takes place in _____ .

4. The perfect competitor's demand curve is a

_____ ; the marginal revenue curve is a

_____ .

5. A perfect competitor would never charge more than market price because _____ ; the perfect competitor would never charge less than market price because _____ .

6. In a perfectly competition industry, price is set by

_____ and _____ .

7. The four main characteristics of perfect competition are (1) _____ , (2) _____ , (3)

_____ , and (4) _____ .

8. In the short run the perfect competitor may make

a _____ or take a _____ ; in the long run

the perfect competitor will _____ .

9. In a perfectly competitive industry, if firms are

making profits, _____ , which will result in zero profits in the long run; if there are losses

in the short run, _____ resulting in zero profits (and losses) in the long run.

10. In the long run economic profits are _____ .

11. The perfect competitor operates at the _____ point of her average total cost curve in the long run.

12. In a decreasing cost industry a firm that is a perfect competitor cannot keep growing because

ultimately it will _____ .

Problems

1. Given the information in Figure 3, how much are total profits (or losses)? Is the firm in the short or long run?

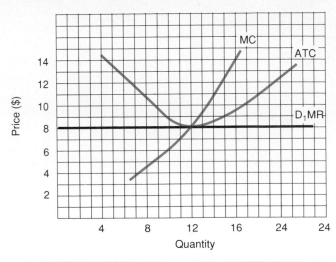

Figure 4

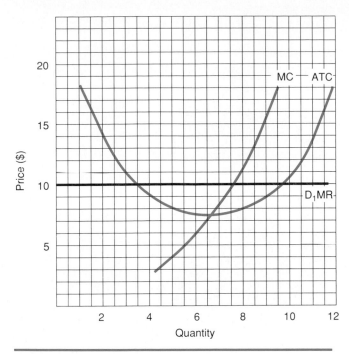

Figure 3

2. Given the information in Figure 4, how much are total profits (or losses)? Is the firm in the short or long run?

3. How much is the most efficient output *(a)* in Figure 3? *(b)* in Figure 4?

4. Given the information that follows, how much are *(a)* accounting profits? *(b)* economic profits? Sales: $400,000; total costs: $250,000; return you could have earned by investing your money elsewhere: $15,000; wages you and your family members could have earned doing the same work for another firm: $40,000; rent on space used in your house: $5,000; wcar and tear on your car: $1,000.

Monopoly

When you were a kid, did you ever play the game of Monopoly? The whole idea was to control strips of properties, such as Broadway and Park Place. There are some people who get to play Monopoly even after they've grown up—and they get to keep all the money. In this and the next three chapters, we'll see how this game is played by the big boys.

Chapter Objectives

We'll look at these topics:

■ The graph of the monopolist.
■ How the monopolist's profits are calculated.
■ Economies of scale and natural monopoly.
■ What makes bigness bad.

Monopoly Defined

What are *close* substitutes?

A monopoly is a firm that produces all the output in an industry. There's nobody else selling anything like what the monopolist is producing. In other words, there are no close substitutes.

Examples of monopoly include DeBeers diamonds, the local gas and electric companies, and until recently, AT&T. During the years after World War II, IBM, Xerox, and Alcoa (Aluminum Company of America), also had monopolies.

One might ask how close substitutes would need to be to disqualify firms from being monopolies. Surely a Cadillac Seville is a reasonably close substitute for a Lincoln Continental. Further, there are many close substitutes for a Xerox photocopying machine, but there are no close substitutes for diamonds, gas, electricity, and telephone calls.

We should also distinguish between local and national monopolies. Someone may be the only doctor in the vicinity and have a local monopoly, but there are over 500,000 doctors in the United States. A hardware store, grocery, drugstore, or cleaners may have a monopoly in its neighborhood, but within a few miles each has several competitors.

The Graph of the Monopolist

Monopoly is the first of three types of imperfect competition. Monopolistic competition and oligopoly follow in the next two chapters. The distinguishing characteristic of imperfect competition is that the firm's demand curve is no longer a perfectly elastic horizontal line; now it curves downward to the right. This means that the imperfect competitor will have to lower price in order to sell more.

Table 21–1
Hypothetical Demand and Cost Schedule for a Monopoly

Output	Price	Total Revenue	Marginal Revenue	Total Cost	ATC	MC
1	$15			$20		
2	14			30		
3	13			36		
4	12			42		
5	11			50		
6	10			63		
7	9			84		

Using the data in Table 21-1, we'll draw our four standard curves: demand, marginal revenue, marginal cost, and average total cost. First, fill in Table 21-1 and check your figures with those in Table 21-2. Please observe that the demand and marginal revenue schedules no longer coincide. After you've completed Table 21-1, use these figures to draw a graph of these curves in Figure 21-1.

A common mistake in Table 21-1 is to use some number, in this case 20, for MC at one unit of output. We'll go over exactly what MC is; then we'll see why there's no way of finding MC at one unit of output.

Definition of marginal cost

MC is the additional cost of producing one more unit of output. Remember that as output rises, fixed cost stays the same and variable cost rises. So far so good. The only problem is we don't know how much fixed cost is at one unit of output; nor do we know how much variable cost is at one unit of output. The MC of the first unit of output would be total cost at output one minus total cost at output zero. How much is total cost at output zero? It's fixed cost. But we don't know fixed cost, so we can't figure out MC at output one. For the remaining outputs, we *can* figure out MC because we know how much total cost rises.

Table 21–2
Hypothetical Demand and Cost Schedule for a Monopoly

Output	Price	Total Revenue	Marginal Revenue	Total Cost	ATC	MC
1	$15	$15	$15	$20	$20	—
2	14	28	13	30	15	$10
3	13	39	11	36	12	6
4	12	48	9	42	10.50	6
5	11	55	7	50	10	8
6	10	60	5	63	10.50	13
7	9	63	3	84	12	21

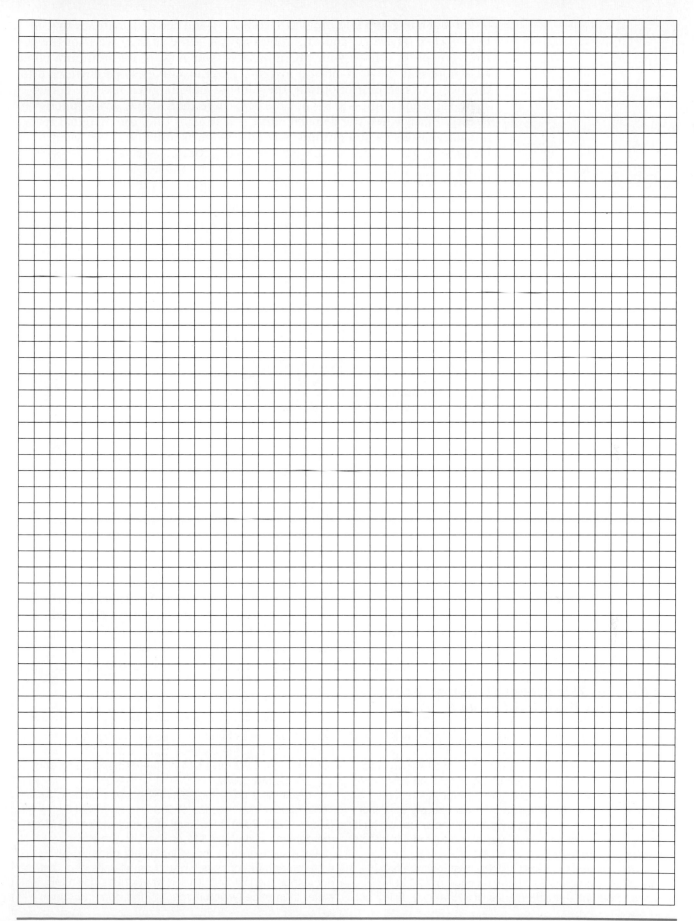

Figure 21–1

Look at the graph you drew in Figure 21-1 and see if it matches that in Figure 21-2. The ATC and MC curves are the same as they were for the perfect competitor. I hope your MC intersects your ATC at its minimum point. Also note that the demand and marginal revenue curves slope downward to the right. At one unit of output, the demand and marginal revenue curves share the same point—$15—but the MR curve then slopes down much faster. In fact, when the demand curve is a straight line, the marginal revenue curve is also a straight line that falls twice as quickly. If you want to know why, take a look at the accompanying box.

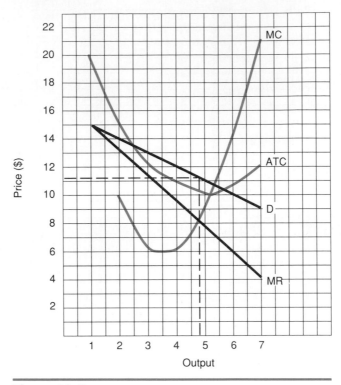

Figure 21-2

When the demand curve falls $1 to $14 at 2 units of output, the MR curve falls $2 to $13. At 3 units of output, when the demand curve falls $1 to $13, the MR curve falls $2 to $11.

Why the MR Curve Declines Faster Than the Demand Curve

In Table 21-2, when the output is one, price is $15, and MR for the first unit sold is also $15, but to sell two units of output, the seller must lower price to $14. Two units at $14 = $28 (total revenue). Notice that the seller can't charge $15 for the first unit and $14 for the second. That's because the seller has to post one price. (If the seller manages to charge more than one price, we have price discrimination, which we'll talk about in the middle of the next chapter.)

When price is lowered to $14, total revenue is $28. Marginal revenue is $13 (total revenue of $28 at two units of output − total revenue of $15 at one unit of out-

put). At two units of output, since we charge a price of $14, the point on the demand curve is $14. So at two units of output, we have $14 on the demand curve and $13 on the MR curve.

To sell three units, the seller must lower price to $13. That yields a total revenue of $39 and an MR of $11 ($39 − $28). So at three units of output, we're at $13 on the demand curve and $11 on the MR curve.

Let's summarize. If the seller lowers price to sell more output, the price is lowered on all units of output, not just on the last one. This is what drives down MR faster than price (which is read off the demand curve).

Calculating the Monopolist's Profit

At what output does the monopolist produce?

Now we'll get down to business. At what output does the monopolist produce? In Table 21-2, it appears to be at an output of four, where total profit would be $6 (total revenue of $48 − total cost of $42). But marginal analysis gives us a more accurate answer—and a more profitable one as well.

Go ahead and perform the marginal analysis to determine the most profitable output. I'll tell you your first step. Go back to the graph and find the point at which your marginal cost curve crosses your marginal revenue curve. That's your output. Do your calculations right here.

According to the graph, MC = MR at about 4.7 units of output. Using the formula

$$\text{Total profit} = (\text{Price} - \text{ATC}) \times \text{Output}$$
$$= (\$11.35 - \$10.05) \times 4.7$$
$$= \$1.30 \times 4.7$$
$$= \$6.11$$

we substitute and solve.

Now that we've found the point at which the monopolist produces, let's figure out the most efficient output. Find that point on your graph. How much is output? You should get approximately 5.4. That's where ATC is at its minimum. How does this compare with the monopolist's output?

Output, using the formula: Total profit = (Price − ATC) × Output. We substitute and solve:

$$\text{Total profit} = (\text{Price} - \text{ATC}) \times \text{Output}$$
$$= (\$11.35 - \$10.05) \times 4.7$$
$$= \$6.11$$

We have a conflict here that didn't exist under perfect competition. The perfect competitor produced at the most profitable output, which in the long run always happened to be the most efficient output. But we see that the monopolist does not produce where output is at its most efficient level (the minimum point of the ATC curve). Remember, *every firm will produce at its most profitable output, where MC = MR*. If that does not happen to be at the most efficient output, if, for example, that firm is a bakery—get ready for a terrible pun—that's the way the cookie crumbles.

Every firm produces where MC = MR.

Let's compare the price of the monopolist with that of the perfect competitor. In the very long run, the perfect competitor would charge $9.90, the minimum point of its ATC curve, and the monopolist's price is $11.35. Finally, we'll compare output. The perfect competitor would produce at an output of 5.4, which is where ATC is at its minimum, but the monopolist's output is 4.7.

To summarize, the monopolist makes a profit whereas in the long run the perfect competitor makes zero profit. The monopolist operates at less than peak efficiency while the perfect competitor operates at peak efficiency

How to Read a Graph

Let's go over some of the points we've already covered. First, refer to the graph below. How much is the output of this monopolist? Write down your answer. Next question. How much is price? Again, write down your answer. Finally, how much is total profits? Work it out.

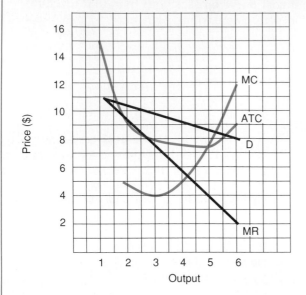

We'll go over each of these questions in turn. First, *our output is always determined by the intersection of the MC and MR curves.* That occurs at an output of about 4.25.

How much is price? First, price is read off the demand curve. Remember that. Where on the demand curve—at what output? At the maximum profit output we just found—4.25. How much is price at that output? It appears to be about $8.75.

Next we calculate total profits.

$$\text{Total profits} = (\text{Price} - \text{ATC}) \times \text{Output}$$
$$= (\$8.75 - \$7.20)\ 4.25$$
$$= \$1.55 \times 4.25$$
$$= \$6.59$$

You might have noticed that once we find output (where MC = MR), everything else lines up. Price is located on the demand curve above the output of 4.25. ATC is on the ATC curve, also above an output of 4.25. When we find total profits, we plug price, ATC, and output into our formula.

(the lowest point on the ATC curve). Finally, the perfect competitor charges a lower price and produces a larger output than the monopolist.[1]

This last point bears some explanation. The monopolist operates on a much larger scale than the individual perfect competitor. But the sum of output under perfect competition would be larger than it would be under monopoly.

I haven't bothered to distinguish between the short run and the long run mainly because the monopolist has no rivals. With perfect comeptition, the fact that the firms entered the industry (attracted by profits) or left the industry (driven out of business by losses) made the short run different from the long run. Under monopoly, even larger profits wouldn't attract rival firms; otherwise it would no longer be a monopoly. If a monopoly were losing money, in the long run it too would go out of business.

How could a monopolist lose money?

How could a monopoly lose money, you might ask. What if, given both the demand for its product and its ATC schedule, no matter what the output, the firm lost money?

I once started a mail-order business. I had invented a fantastic liquid diet. Interested? OK, here's what I did. Just drink these liquids—low-fat skim milk (Carnation has cans of 0.25 percent fat), Alba 77 shakes, clear soup, plain yogurt (liquid or frozen), grapefruit, watermelon, fruit pops, fruit juice, vegetable juice (and a daily vitamin pill)—and you'll lose about a pound a day. It also helps to run 25–30 miles a week.

---

[1] In theory, the perfect competitor produces 5.4 units and the monopolist 4.7. But since the perfect competitor is a tiny firm, we can't really compare its output with that of the monopolist, who produces the industry's entirc output. Thus, when we say the perfect competitor would produce an output of 5.4, we must realize that the firm would no longer be a perfect competitor. Do you follow this? If you don't, don't worry. This is only a footnote.

I had what I thought was a great slogan: "What have you got to lose?" But I needed to advertise, rent a post office box, and print up my diet. I charged $2. What happened? What do you *think* happened? I spent about $350 and got 20 or 30 orders. If you happen to want to go into the diet business, I'll sell you *my* business—cheap.

So I was a monopolist, but I lost money. You can be a monopolist too. Start an autograph club. For just $1 people can send for your signature; no one else can do that. The only problem is that nobody else would want to do that. But you'd be a monopolist. That is, you'd be one until you got sick and tired of losing money.

Review of the Monopolist's Economic Analysis

We're throwing a lot of new stuff at you, so let's step back for a few minutes and review the monopolist's table and graph. Microeconomics is based largely on the three-step problems you've come to know and love: (1) filling in the table, (2) drawing the graph, and (3) doing the analysis.

You may begin by filling in Table 21–3 and then seeing if it corresponds to the data in Table 21–4.

Table 21–3

Output	Price	Total Revenue	Marginal Revenue	Total Cost	ATC	MC	Profit
1	$20	————	————	$30	————	————	————
2	19	————	————	40	————	————	————
3	18	————	————	48	————	————	————
4	17	————	————	57	————	————	————
5	16	————	————	70	————	————	————
6	15	————	————	93	————	————	————

Table 21–4

Output	Price	Total Revenue	Marginal Revenue	Total Cost	ATC	MC	Profit
1	$20	20	20	$20	20	—	0
2	19	38	18	30	15	10	8
3	18	54	16	36	12	6	18
4	17	68	14	45	11.25	9	23
5	16	80	12	58	11.60	13	22
6	15	90	10	78	13	20	12

Next comes the graph. Draw in the demand, marginal revenue, marginal cost, and average total cost curve in Figure 21–3. Then check your work with that in Figure 21–4.

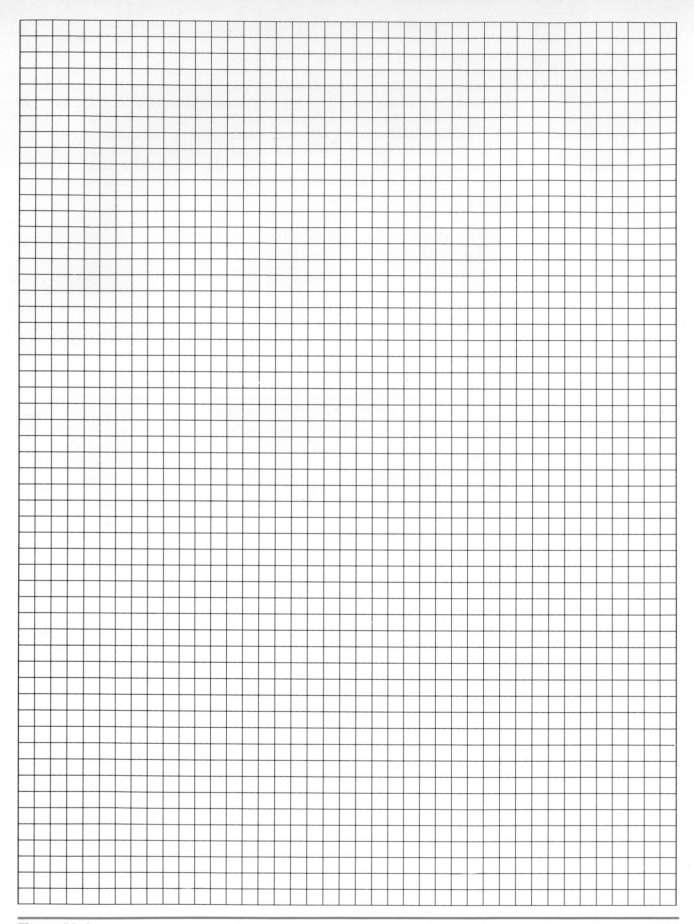

Figure 21-3

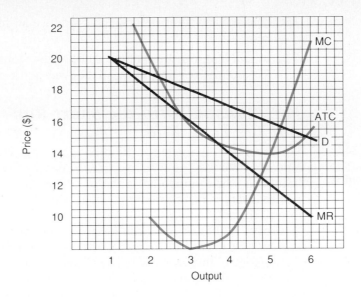

Are you ready to do some analysis? Ready or not, we need to find the monopolist's total profit. Do that right here. Then check your work with the calculations that follow.

Output looks like about 4.85. Before calculating total profit, let's glance at the profit column of Table 21–4. At an output of 4 there's a profit of $10, so what we'll be looking for at an output of 4.85 is a profit that is slightly over $10.

First we'll calculate total revenue, which is price × output. At an output of 4.85, price is $16.15. Not *about* $16.15, but *exactly* $16.15. Why all this certainty? Because the demand curve is a straight line. At an output of 4, it is $17; at an output of 5, it is $16. At an output of 4.85, it is exactly $16.15.

Total revenue = price ($16.15) × output (4.85) = $78.33.

Total cost = ATC × output. We know our output is 4.85, but we'll need to estimate ATC. It appears to be about $11.25, give or take a few cents.

Total cost = ATC ($11.25) × output (4.85) = $54.56.

Finally, we have total revenue ($78.33) − total cost ($54.56) = total profit ($23.77).

There's a shortcut if you're interested. Subtract ATC from price and multiply by output: ($16.15 − $11.25 = $4.90 × 4.85 = $23.77).

We're not going to let you off the hook just yet. Try these three questions.

1. At what output would the firm produce most efficiently?
2. At what output would the perfect competitor produce in the long run?
3. What price would the perfect competitor charge in the long run?

Here are the answers.

1. The output at which the firm would produce most efficiently would be about 4.55, which is the minimum point of the ATC curve.

2. The perfect competitor would produce at an output of 4.85 in the long run.

3. In the long run the perfect competitor would charge a price of about $11.00 (the minimum or break-even point of the ATC curve).

The Monopolist in the Short Run and the Long Run

There is no distinction between the short run and the long run for the monopolist.

No distinction is made for the monopolist between the short and long run. Why not? Because no other firms will enter or leave the industry since, by definition, the monopolist is the only firm.

If the firm is losing money, is it in the short run or the long run? What do *you* think?

It must be in the short run because no firm will stay in business and lose money. Not even the Chicago Cubs. For years the Wrigley family (Wrigley's chewing gum) lost money on the Cubs. It was an expensive hobby. Eventually it became too expensive even for the Wrigleys, who evidently decided that they could double their pleasure *and* their fun by selling the team.

If the firm is making a profit, is it in the long run or the short run? Can you tell? Think about it.

If the firm were in the short run, would this monopolist stay in business? Yes! And so, it would go on and on making a profit. In the long run then, it would be making a profit. Therefore, there is no way of distinguishing between the long and the short run if the firm is making a profit.

Let's sum things up. If the firm is making a profit, for analytic purposes, it doesn't matter if it's in the short or the long run. If the firm is losing money, it must be in the short run; in the long run it will go out of business.

Barriers to Entry

We'll consider, in turn, three barriers to entry: (1) control over an essential resource, (2) economies of scale, and (3) legal barriers to entry.

Basic resources are land, labor, and capital.

Control over an Essential Resource We tend to think of resources as natural resources—oil, coal, iron ore, arable land—but in economics the basic resources are land, labor, and capital. The Metropolitan Opera has a near monopoly because it has most of the world's opera stars (labor) under contract.

Until the early 1960s, the National Football League (NFL) had a monopoly, but this was challenged by the American Football League. The NFL had virtually all the established star football players under contract, so the AFL went after college stars. In 1964, when the New York Jets signed Joe Namath, that action broke the back of the NFL's monopoly.

DeBeers Diamond Company in South Africa controls most of the world's diamond production simply because it owns the diamond mines in South Africa, where most of the world's diamonds are mined.

The Standard Oil Company controlled the oil industry in the 1880s and later because it owned over 90 percent of the nation's oil fields and refineries. At that time the American Tobacco Company happened to control 90 percent of U.S. tobacco production.[2]

---

[2] In 1911, the Supreme Court broke up these monopolies. (See the second section of Chapter 24.)

Economies of Scale Typically, heavy industry—iron and steel, copper, aluminum, and automobiles—has high setup costs. But once your plant and equipment are set up, by increasing your output you can take advantage of economies of scale.

General Motors, Ford, and Chrysler were able to realize these economies much more than American Motors and Volkswagon of America, both of which are relatively small.[3] So we are really talking about two things: having the wherewithal to set up, and having enough demand so that your product sells enough to realize economies of scale.

Imagine how difficult it would be to set up a rival phone network or even a rival electric company in a large city. What protects monopolies from potential rivals is that they're selling enough units to have a relatively low ATC (see Figure 21–5). If you were to enter the industry, how could you hope to have the capital to set yourself up so that you could compete effectively?

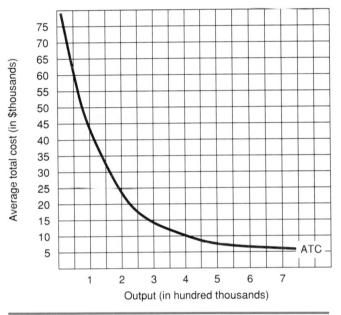

Figure 21–5
Hypothetical Production Costs for Cars

Figure 21-5 illustrates the problem of economies of scale faced by the small producer of cars. At relatively low levels of production, say, 100,000–200,000 cars, the firm will not be able to take advantage of the economies of mass production that are available to rival firms. According to this illustration, ATC continues to decline appreciably through an output of at least 700,000.

Legal Barriers These include licensing, franchises, and patents. The whole idea is for the government to allow just one firm or a group of individuals to do business.

---

[3] American Motors has been absorbed by Chrysler, and Volkswagon has stopped producing cars in the United States.

Licensing prevents just anybody from driving a taxi, cutting hair, peddling on the street, practicing medicine, or burying bodies. Often the licensing procedure is designed to hold down the numbers of people going into a certain field and thereby keeping prices in that field high.

Patents are granted to investors so that they have a chance to get rich before someone else uses their idea. They have 17 years to get their act together. In some cases, perhaps most notably U.S. Shoe Machinery Company, a firm buys up patents and uses them to prevent competition.

The most important legal barrier is the government franchise. By giving out a number of franchises—to local radio stations, for example—the government does not introduce a significant barrier. However, cable TV in many localities is another story. There have been scandals in various towns and cities across the nation—most notably, Wisconsin, Pennsylvania, and New York. Anxious cable companies have quite blatantly offered bribes to local officials, usually in the form of large blocs of company stock, to secure cable franchises.[4]

The most important form of local franchise is the public utility—your gas and electric companies. Only one to a locality. The local government grants the franchise and, like it or not, the company's got you. Monopolies don't have to worry about giving poor service at outrageous prices. Where else can you go?

Limits to Monopoly Power

Limits to the three barriers to entry

First, we'll consider limits to the three barriers to entry. We saw how the National Football League lost its monopoly when it lost its control over an essential resource—star football players. Similarly, ALCOA, which at one time controlled nearly all the world's known bauxite (aluminum ore) reserves, lost its monopoly when other reserves were discovered.[5]

Economies of scale and high capital requirements are a significant barrier to entry, but in recent years Volkswagon of America, and very soon Datsun and Toyota, will have joined the parade of American automobile producers. Of course, each of these producers was set up by its friendly giant company back home.

Finally, even legal barriers have been overcome. Rival phone companies have gone to court to win the right to plug into the AT&T network while providing a competing and generally lower priced long distance service. In general, however, government franchises are there for a reason: it makes economic sense to have only one firm in a given locality, so it may well be a barrier we don't want to overcome.

The ultimate limit of monopoly power may come from the government or from the market itself. If a firm gets too big or too bad, the federal government may decide to trim that firm's sails. We'll take that up in the antitrust section of Chapter 24.

How the market limits monopoly power

Let's consider how the market limits monopoly power, basically through the development of substitutes. Take Kleenex for example. To this day, some people call tissues Kleenexes. In the late 1940s, Kleenex was the only paper tissue on the market, so tissues and Kleenexes, could quite properly

---

[4] The most celebrated case involved John Zaccaro, husband of Geraldine Ferraro, the Democratic party's 1984 vice presidential nominee, who was accused of demanding a $1 million bribe to secure a cable contract for a company that had aspired to wire the borough of Queens in New York City. Zaccaro was acquitted.

[5] The Alcoa case is discussed in the second section of Chapter 24.

be considered synonymous. But over the years, scores of competitors have sprung up and today, the market share of Kleenex is very small indeed.

Another interesting case is that of Xerox. Having invented the first "dry" photocopy machine, Xerox had the market all to itself during the late 1950s and early 1960s. Shortly thereafter, IBM, Savin, Sharp, Pitney-Bowes, Multilith-Addressograph, and a multitude of other firms began marketing their own photocopy machines. Nonetheless, to this day, chances are when someone needs a photocopy, he or she will ask you to "xerox" it, which is a lot easier than asking you to "multilith-addressograph" it.

Economies of Scale and Natural Monopoly

The two justifications for monopoly

There are really only two justifications for monopoly: economies of scale and natural monopoly. Economies of scale justify bigness because only a firm with a large output can produce near the minimum point of its ATC curve. When the firm's output is so large that it is almost equal to the output of the entire industry, this state of monopoly is justified by calling it efficient. Of course, we have just seen that the firm is not operating at the minimum point of its ATC curve (see Figure 21–1), but that's another story.

Natural monopoly is closely related to economies of scale. There are those who think that a natural monopoly occurs when someone gains complete control of the wheat germ supply or of the entire crop of Florida oranges. Close but no cigar. Cigar? No, even Cuban cigars are not a natural monopoly.

Examples of natural monopolies

Examples of natural monopolies are the local gas and electric companies, the phone company, and local cable TV companies. Why are these natural monopolies? Because they can provide cheaper service as monopolies than could several competing firms. Let's see why.

In Figure 21–6, there is one electric company that serves an entire suburban town. Pictured here is one street in that town, its houses lined up properly just as they might be anywhere else in suburbia. Every house on the block uses the same company. After all, what choice do they have?

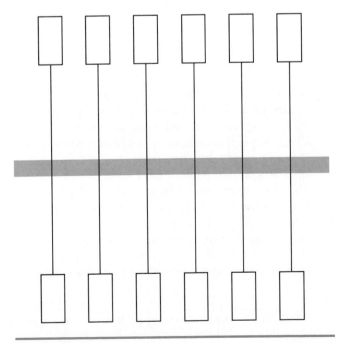

Figure 21–6

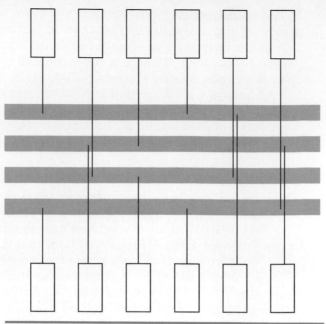

Figure 21-7

Figure 21-7 shows four competing electric companies on an identical street of an identical town somewhere else in suburbia. Notice that there are four power lines running along the street. In this town, there's freedom of choice; you can hook up with any of these four companies.

There's only one problem with this arrangement. It's much more expensive. You see, each company, assuming customers are evenly distributed, does only one quarter of the business that would be done by a company that had a monopoly. While it must construct the same system of power lines, it realizes only one quarter the output. Its costs are much higher than that of the monopoly.[6]

From society's viewpoint, these higher costs reflect a great waste of resources. Why construct four parallel power lines when one will do as nicely? And one might add parenthetically, why dig up the street four times rather than once to lay and repair the cables?

This is the case for natural monopoly. It's cheaper, it's more efficient, and it's more convenient. The bottom line is that our bills are much lower.

Another case for natural monopoly can be made for local telephone service. Imagine if we had four, six, or eight competing phone companies. Placing a call would be like playing Russian roulette. Imagine your surprise if you actually got through?

It would not be very easy to conduct business. "Let's see now, I call this client on the orange phone, my lawyer on the gray phone, and my accountant on the yellow phone." And what if the president needs to reach his opposite number in the Kremlin in a hurry and can't remember: "Was it the red phone for the Kremlin and the green phone for MacDonalds—or was it the other way around?" You can imagine the puzzlement in Moscow from getting an order for two Big Macs and a large order of fries.

Imagine if we had six or eight competing local phone companies.

---

[6] Technically these are average fixed costs. They're four times as high as that of the electric company that has a monopoly. For example, if it cost $4 million to lay cable through a town, and if 40,000 families lived in the town, the monopoly would have an AFC of $1,000 ($4,000,000/40,000). The four competing companies would each have AFCs of $4,000 per family ($4,000,000/10,000).

Why is Bigness Bad?

From what we've seen so far, monopoly certainly isn't *all* bad. At times only a monopolist can fully take advantage of economies of scale; and in certain instances, particularly with respect to local public utilities, there are natural monopolies. In the case of such innovative firms as Xerox, Kleenex, and IBM, monopolies once existed simply because these were the first companies to enter their fields.

Why then do so many people dislike monopolies? For one thing, monopolies tend to be inefficient. As illustrated in Figure 21-1, a monopoly does not produce at the minimum point of its ATC curve. Furthermore, by always restricting output to some point to the left of that minimum, the monopoly is preventing resources from being allocated in the most efficient manner. Land, labor, and capital that would have otherwise flowed into the monopolized industry are kept out and will eventually find their way into other industries where they will not be as efficiently used.

Politically, big business has always been extremely powerful, especially when several large firms have joined together in common cause. The power of the oil-auto-construction lobby has been awesome in the post-World War II period. This group managed to get an oil depletion allowance through Congress that reduced the income taxes of oil firms by 27 percent (no other industry got this tax break). To stimulate housing, there were Federal Housing Administration mortgages plus, of course, the interest deduction on the personal federal income tax. To get to these houses and from city to city, Congress appropriated the funds to build a national highway network (through the Highway Trust Fund). One of the legacies of these policies has been our utter dependence on gasoline and the consequent energy crises of 1973 and 1979.

We've seen then that economic power is easily transformed into political power, and that political power is used to enhance economic power. A large corporation rarely hesitates to use its vast power to get what it wants. The law firms of many legislators do business with large corporations. Others sit on the boards of banks, insurance companies, and other firms, which do business with the nation's largest corporations. Although corporate campaign contributions are illegal, corporate (voluntary) political action committees (PACs) have contributed hundreds of millions of dollars to congressional and presidential campaign coffers, not to mention additional tens of millions in personal contributions by corporate officials and major stockholders.

Often large firms, most notably defense contractors, do sizable business with the government. It is the standard career path for the higher-ranking military officers to step into the top job slots with defense contracting firms upon their retirement from the military. To paraphrase the legendary words of General Douglas MacArthur, old soldiers never die, they just get jobs with Lockheed, General Dynamics, Pratt and Whitney, Boeing, McDonell Douglas, and the rest of the defense establishment. In the words of another old general, Dwight D. Eisenhower, "Beware of the military-industrial complex."

What we have are the people who used to buy the weapons systems going to work as salesmen for the firms with which they used to do business. And with whom do they now do business? With their old subordinates, who have finally been able to move up to the higher ranks now that these slots have been vacated by their superiors. These people are so used to taking orders, it usually isn't hard for them to continue accommodating themselves to their erstwhile superiors. Further, there is the added consideration of what they'll do when *they* retire from the military. At the present time

Big business has always had great political power.

Economic power is easily converted into political power.

"Beware of the Military-Industrial Complex."

some 2,000 high-ranking military officers have found second careers with defense contracting firms.

What are the consequences of this system, which accounts for well over half of all federal government purchases? Most obvious is the huge amount of waste, the multibillion dollar cost overruns, the weapons that simply do not work. The tragic 1980 hostage rescue attempt that was aborted in the Iranian desert when three of eight helicopters malfunctioned symbolizes the shoddiness of the armanent industry—not to mention the $500 screwdrivers and toilet seats that this industry has been known to sell to the government.

In the long run, of still greater consequence is the arms race we have been engaged in over the last four decades. Not only have trillions of dollars gone down this rathole, but the entire world has been forced to live under the nuclear gun. At any time, either because of some miscalculation or perhaps even some intentional act, we may all perish under a huge mushroom cloud. But this balance of terror is good for business, and the business of the American people, as Calvin Coolidge used to say, is business.

Bigness may be bad for the economy but our society is prepared to take only limited action against it and only when a large company breaks the rules. Our main set of rules is our antitrust laws, which are discuussed in Chapter 24.

Two Policy Alternatives

We have accepted certain instances of monopoly—mainly local public utility companies. These companies are natural monopolies and provide the public with better and more cheaply priced service than it would get from most competing firms. How can we prevent these public utilities from taking advantage of their power and charging outrageous prices? There are two ways: (1) government regulation, and (2) government ownership.

Government Regulation We will use Figure 21-1 as our point of departure to illustrate the effect of government regulation. Suppose Figure 21-1 represents the market situation of the Rochester Electric Company, which is now regulated by the New York State Public Service Commission.

The commission would have two objectives: a lower price for electricity consumers and a higher output of electricity than we see in Figure 21-1. To accomplish both ends, the commission would set the price of electricity at $10.20, which is lower than the current market price of $11.35. How much would output now be? How about total profits?

Notice that price is equal to ATC, so using the formula for total profits we get:

$$(\text{Price} - \text{ATC}) \times \text{Output}$$
$$(\$10.20 - \$10.20) \times 5.75$$
$$0 \times 5.75$$
$$0$$

All this is illustrated in Figure 21-8. Consumers now pay a lower price and receive more electricity than they would have under unregulated monopoly. But this is not a perfect solution because even the regulated natural monopoly does not produce at the minimum point of its ATC curve.

Two ways to prevent public utilities from charging outrageous prices.

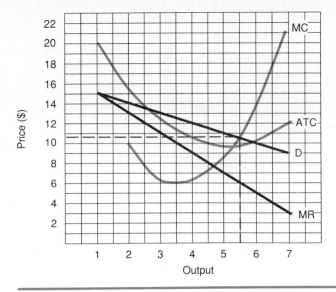

Figure 21-8

Government Ownership The second option for a natural monopoly is government ownership. The post office, the Tennessee Valley Authority, the New York State Power Authority, the New Jersey Transit System, and the Metropolitan Transit Authority of Boston are all examples.

Are these inefficient government boondoggles whose jobs could be better done by private enterprise? Consider the origins of the New Jersey public transportation system. When the private bus lines were unable to operate, even with massive public subsidies, the state of New Jersey reluctantly took them over.

The case of the Tennessee Valley Authority (TVA) is even stranger. TVA uses itself as a yardstick with which to measure the costs of power provided by privately owned utilities. The latter complain about "unfair" government competition and they do have a point because TVA sometimes provides electricity at half the cost of that incurred by privately owned companies.

This is rather interesting when one considers the origins of TVA. Much of rural Tennessee, Arkansass, Alabama, as well as parts of other states near the Tennessee Valley, were not provided with electricity by private power companies as late as the early 1930s because they were not deemed worthy customers. They were too poor, they lived too far apart, and it was simply not economically feasible to run transmission cables into this part of the country. So TVA, without competing with private companies, went into this area and provided it with electricity at half the going rate.

The general thrust of public policy in the area of natural monopoly is to let private enterprise do the job but to closely regulate prices. Only as a last resort, when private enterprise is unwilling or unable to do the job, does the government take on the job itself.

Conclusion

Is monopoly good, bad, or indifferent? One fair conclusion would be that natural monopoly is good, if only its power were not abused. But monopolies based on other factors—I refrain from calling them "unnatural monopolies"—must be looked on with suspicion. They may be up to no good, and as we shall see in Chapter 24, they may be illegal.

Workbook for Chapter 21

Name _____

Date _____

Multiple-Choice Questions

Circle the letter that corresponds to the best answer.

1. Which statement is true?
a. All monopolists' products have close substitutes.
b. Most firms in the United States are monopolies.
c. There are no monopolies in the United States.
d. A monopoly is a firm that produces all the output in an industry.   **e.** None of these is true.

2. The monopolist is
a. an imperfect competitor and has a horizontal demand curve   **b.** an imperfect competitor and has a downward sloping demand curve   **c.** is a perfect competitor and has a horizontal demand curve
d. is a perfect competitor and has a downward sloping demand curve

3. A downward sloping demand curve means that
a. you have to lower your price to sell more
b. demand falls as output rises   **c.** demand rises as output rises   **d.** total revenue declines as price is lowered

4. The monopolist's demand and marginal revenue curves
a. are exactly the same   **b.** are completely different
c. coincide only at one unit of output   **d.** cross

5. The monopolist produces
a. where MC = MR   **b.** at the minimum point of ATC   **c.** at maximum output   **d.** when price is highest

6. If a monopolist has a straight-line demand curve, its marginal revenue curve
a. will be the same as the demand curve   **b.** will fall twice as quickly as the demand curve   **c.** will lie below the demand curve at all points   **d.** will cross the demand curve

7. Which statement is true?
a. The monopolist and the perfect competitor both produce where MC = MR.   **b.** Neither the monopolist nor the perfect competitor produce where MC = MR.   **c.** The monopolist, but not the perfect competitor, produces where MC = MR.   **d.** The perfect competitor, but not the monopolist, produces where MC = MR.

8. Which statement is true about economic profit in the long run?
a. The monopolist and perfect competitor make one.
b. Neither the monopolist nor the perfect competitor make one.   **c.** Only the perfect competitor makes one.   **d.** Only the monopolist makes one.

9. Which statement is true?
a. The monopolist cannot lose money.   **b.** The monopolist always operates a large firm.   **c.** The monopolist will not lose money in the short run.
d. The monopolist will not lose money in the long run.

10. Price is always read off the _____ curve.
a. MC   **b.** MR   **c.** ATC   **d.** demand

11. The most efficient output is found
a. where MC and MR cross   **b.** at the bottom of the ATC curve   **c.** when the demand and MR curves are equal   **d.** where the ATC and demand curves cross

12. When the monopolist is losing money
a. we are in the short run   **b.** we are in the long run   **c.** it is impossible to tell if we are in the short or the long run   **d.** we have to go back and check our work because monopolists don't lose money

13. The basis for monopoly in the automobile industry would most likely be

a. control over an essential resource   **b.** economies of scale   **c.** legal barriers

14. Which statement is true?

a. It is impossible for monopolies to exist in the United States.   **b.** Once a monopoly is set up, it is impossible to dislodge it.   **c.** Monopolies can be overcome only by market forces.   **d.** Monopolies can be overcome only by the government.   **e.** None of these statements is true.

15. Which of the following is a natural monopoly?

a. the National Football League   **b.** a local phone company   **c.** DeBeers Diamond Company   **d.** IBM

16. Which statement is true?

a. Big business has a great deal of economic power but very little political power.   **b.** Big business has a great deal of political power but very little economic power.   **c.** Big business has a great deal of economic and political power.   **d.** Big business has neither very much political nor economic power.

17. An example of government ownership of a monopoly would be

a. the Tennessee Valley Authority   **b.** The New York State Public Service Commission   **c.** AT&T   **d.** General Motors

Fill-In Questions

1. A monopoly is a firm that produces _____ _____ .

2. A monopoly is a firm that has _____ substitutes.

3. The demand curve of an imperfect competitor slopes _____ .

4. The monopolist always produces at that output at which _____ ; is equal to _____ .

5. If a firm's demand curve is a straight line sloping downward to the right, its marginal revenue curve will be a _____

_____ .

6. In the long run the perfect competitor makes _____ profit; in the long run the monopolist makes _____ profit.

7. The three barriers to entering a monopolized industry are: (1) _____ ,

(2) _____ ,

and (3) _____ .

8. There are really only two justifications for monopoly: (1) _____

and (2) _____ .

9. Local gas and electric companies, the phone company, and local cable TV companies are all examples

of _____ monopolies.

10. The main economic criticism of monopolies and

big business in general is that they are _____ .

11. Economic power is easily translated into _____

_____ .

12. One group of firms that does a lot of business

with the government is _____ .

13. President Eisenhower warned us to "Beware of

the _____ .

14. There are two ways to prevent public utilities

from taking advantage of their power: (1) _____

_____ and (2) _____ .

Problems

1. *(a)* Fill in Table 1. *(b)* Draw a graph of the firm's demand, marginal revenue, marginal cost, and average total cost curves (use Figure 1).
(c) Calculate the firm's total profit.

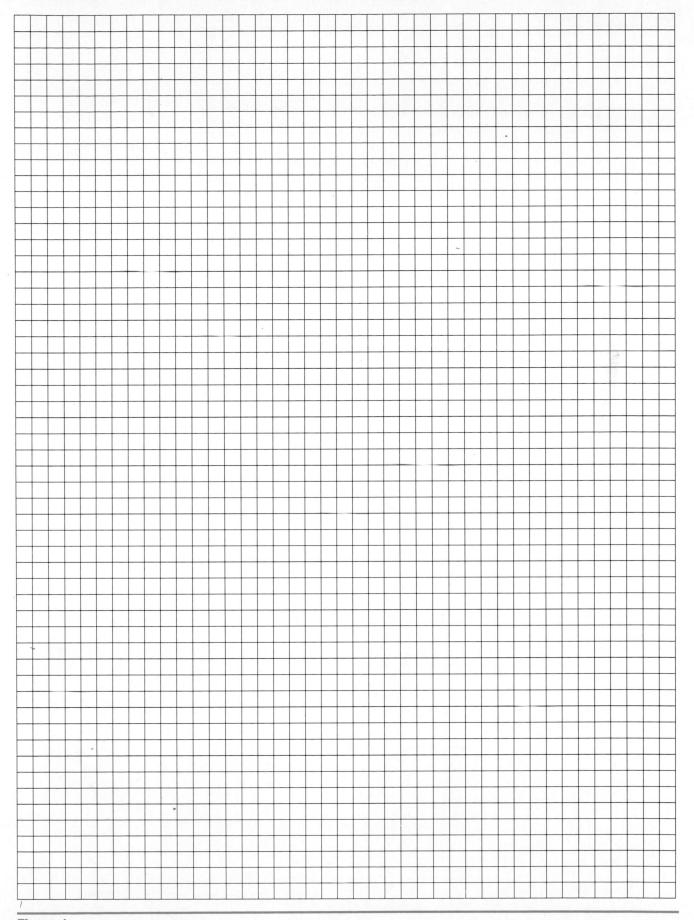

Figure 1

Table 1

Output	Price	Total Revenue	Marginal Revenue	Total Cost	ATC	MC	Profit
1	$18	————	————	$25	————	————	————
2	17	————	————	35	————	————	————
3	16	————	————	40	————	————	————
4	15	————	————	46	————	————	————
5	14	————	————	55	————	————	————
6	13	————	————	69	————	————	————
7	12	————	————	91	————	————	————

2. Using the data from problem 1, please answer these questions:
(a) If the firm operated at optimum efficiency, how much would its output be?
(b) If the firm were a perfect competitor, how much would its price be in the long run?

3. Using Figure 2, calculate the firm's total profit.

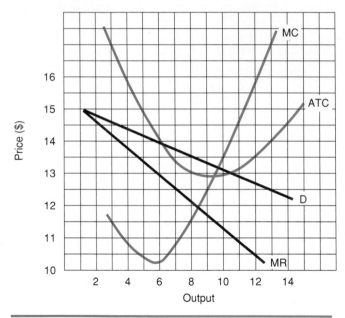

Figure 2

Monopolistic Competition

Over 99 percent of the 20 million business firms in the United States are monopolistic competitors—so the least we can do is give them a chapter all to themselves.

Chapter Objectives

By the time you have completed this chapter you will be familiar with:

- The monopolistic competitor in the short and long run.
- Product differentiation.
- Price discrimination.
- The characteristics of monopolistic competition.

Monopolistic Competition Defined

Definition of monopolistic competition

A monopolistically competitive industry has many firms selling a differentiated product. How many is many? So many that no one firm has any influence over price.

Now we encounter a differentiated product for the first time. Notice that the definition of monopolistic competition differs from that of perfect competition only in that now we have a differentiated product. You'll remember that under perfect competition, all the sellers sold an identical product.

The difference between identical and differentiated

Why did we say the product was identical? Because none of the buyers differentiated among all the products. Each product was considered the same; number 2 wheat is number 2 wheat. A large grade A egg is a large grade A egg.

If the buyer doesn't differentiate among the various products sold, the products are identical. If he or she does differentiate, the product is then differentiated. But who determines whether the product is differentiated or identical? The buyer—that's who.

The Monopolistic Competitor in the Short Run

Make a profit or take a loss in short run

Like the perfect competitor, the monopolistic competitor can make a profit or take a loss in the short run, but in the long run the firm will break even. The reason the monopolitic competitor makes zero economic profits in the long run is the same as that under perfect competition.

In the long run, if firms are losing money, many will leave the industry, lowering industry supply and raising market price. And if, in the long run, firms are realizing substantial profits, new firms will be attracted to the industry, raising supply and lowering market price. But we're getting ahead of ourselves since we're only beginning the short run.

Figure 22–1 shows a monopolistic competitor in the short run. Notice how its demand and MR curves slope downward, like that of the monopolist. Theoretically, we may opt for a somewhat more elastic demand curve for the monopolistic competitor than for the monopolist because the latter faces the entire demand curve for the industry. The monopolistic competitor as only one firm in a crowded industry must have a very elastic demand curve because there are many close substitutes for the firm's product. In fact, no one can get too far out of line with respect to price because buyers are always ready to purchase substitutes from a rival firm.

Very elastic demand curve

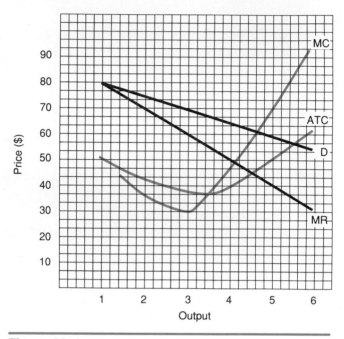

Figure 22–1

Getting back to Figure 22–1, how much is the firm's output? How much is its price? How much profit does it make?

First the output. When MC = MR, output is 4.2. We find that at an output of 4.2, the price, which we read off the demand curve, is $64 and ATC at that output is $41. Total profit = (price − ATC) output = ($64 − $41) 4.1 = ($23) 4.1 = $94.30.

Now we're ready for Figure 22–2, which also shows the monopolistic competitor in the short run. How much are output and price? What about total profits?

At an output of 3.75, MC = MR. At that output, price (read from the demand curve) is $17.40 and ATC is $20. Total profit = (price − ATC) × output = ($17.40 − $20) 3.75 = $2.60 × 3.75 = −$9.75. In other words, the firm suffered a loss of $9.75.

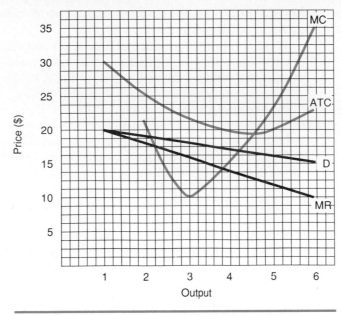

Figure 22-2

The Monopolistic Competitor in the Long Run

Zero economic profits in the long run

As I said earlier, in the long-run the monopolistic competitor makes zero economic profits. If there are short-run profits, more firms will enter the industry, driving down market price and profits. If there are losses, some firms will leave the industry, pushing up market price and reducing losses.

Figure 22-3 is a model of the monopolistic competitor in the long run. Notice how the point at which the MC and MR curves cross is directly be-

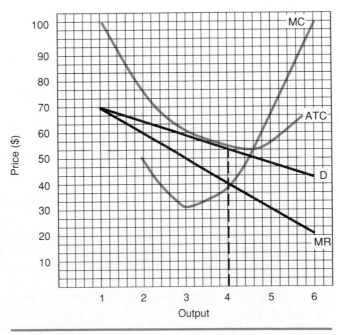

Figure 22-3

low the price. Output is four and price is $55. Notice also that price is equal to ATC at that output.

Were the firm to produce at any other output, what would happen to its profits? I'm sure you figured out that they would be losses. At any other output the demand curve lies below the ATC curve, so price is less than ATC.

Notice that the price in Figure 22-3 is higher than the minimum point of the ATC curve. This means that in the long run price is higher under monopolistic competition than it is under perfect competition.

What about output? Again, since the monopolistic competitor produces to the left of the minimum point of its ATC curve, output is lower than it is under perfect competition.

Who is more efficient—the perfect competitor or the monopolistic competitor?

Finally, we have efficiency. Who is more efficient—the monopolistic competitor or the perfect competitor? There is one test for efficiency: What is your ATC? Since the perfect competitor produces at the minimum point of its ATC curve and the monopolistic competitor does not, clearly the perfect competitor is more efficient.

To sum up, both the monopolistic competitor and the perfect competitor make zero economic profits in the long run. The monopolistic competitor charges a higher price and has a lower output than the perfect competitor. And the perfect competitor is a more efficient producer than the monopolistic competitor.

Product Differentiation

The crucial factor: product differentiation

Product differentiation is crucial to monopolistic competition. In fact, product differentiation is really what stands between perfect competition and the real world. People differentiate among many similar products.

What makes one good or service different from another? We need only for the buyer to believe it's different because product differentiation takes place in the buyer's mind. What's the difference between a Buick Electra and Chrysler Imperial—besides $8,000? There is absolutely no difference between these two cars *if* the buyer sees no difference. Suppose someone is given the choice and says, "I don't care—they're both the same to me." To this buyer, the cars are identical. One is longer, maybe; one has nicer upholstery.

In the real world, however, buyers generally do differentiate. "I like the refreshing taste of Kools." "I'm a man, so I smoke Chesterfields, even though they're killing my throat." "I'm a modern woman (in contradistinction to an ancient woman), so I smoke Virginia Slims." "I'm a modern man, so I smoke Virginia Slims." Huh?

We're always differentiating.

We're always differentiating, and it doesn't have to be based on taste, smell, size, or even any physical differences among the products. Two record shops might carry the same poor excuse that passes for music these days—it can only be played loud, so those young people suffering from hearing loss can still pick up some of the sounds. Both shops charge exactly the same prices. Both shops are conveniently located. But one is always crowded and the other is always empty.

Why? Ambience Perhaps one place lets you play a record before you buy it. Perhaps one place will make special orders for you. Perhaps the sales clerks and owner are nice helpful people while in the other store, they're all grouches.

Now we're dealing with a differentiated product. The records are the same. The prices are the same. But one store's got ambience up to here and the other has to send out for it. The buyer prefers Mr. Nice Guy's store over the grouch's store, so we have a differentiated product.

When sellers try to get buyers to differentiate between their products and those of competitors, the sellers do so based on not just physical differences between their product and those of the competitors. Also used are convenience, ambience, reputation of the seller, and appeals to your vanity, unconscious fears and desires, as well as snob appeal.

The Typical Monopolistic Competitor

Nearly all business firms in the United States are monopolistic competitors. They are monopolistic rather than perfect competitors. They are monopolistic rather than perfect competitors because, in the mind of the buyer, their products are differentiated from one another. The monopolistic element is the uniqueness of each seller.

The monopolistic competitor tries to set his or her product apart from the competition.

Each monopolistic competitor attempts to set his or her firm apart from the competition. A major way of doing this is by advertising. As we saw in Chapter 17, when this is done successfully the demand curve faced by the monopolistic competitor becomes more vertical or inelastic. Buyers are willing to pay more for this product because they believe it's wonderful. Or they'll undergo acts of great physical endurance: "I'd walk a mile for a Camel."

Typical monopolistic competitors are beauty parlors and barbershops, grocery stores, drugstores, restaurants and fast-food emporiums, gas stations, dry cleaners and laundries, (small) accounting and law firms, doctors, dentists, electricians, plumbers, and all the other small businesses you'd see along any Main Street, USA. Each has many competitors and each produces a differentiated product.

Think of all the 7-Elevens, diners, coffee shops, greasy spoons, the beauty parlors and barbershops, the mom 'n pop groceries and the general stores, the bars, the hamburger joints, and the millions of other tiny retail stores where people spend time eating, drinking, getting groomed, or picking up a couple of everyday household items. There's one thing most of them dispense and you won't find it on the menu. And that's local gossip. People stop by in the morning with last night's news and later that afternoon they come to pick up that day's latest scoop. If you lived in a small town, where would *you* rather do business?

You eat in one luncheonette rather than any of the others because the counterman talks to you while you're having lunch or the waitress keeps your coffee cup filled. You prefer one grocery because they'll take your order over the phone. You'd rather shop in a particular drugstore because it has a much more cheerful atmosphere than all the other drugstores in town.

Why do business at one store rather than at its competitors?

Ambience, cleanliness, personal attention, convenience of location, easy credit, free delivery service, and good service in general are all reasons why buyers might shop at one store rather than at its competitors. Thus, product differentiation does not necessarily mean there are any physical differences among the products. They might all be the same, but how they're sold may make all the difference.

On the other hand, there are, of course, some very real product differences that are physical. Different cigarettes, beer, cigars, ice cream, and hamburgers *do* taste differently and *are* different in physical composition. Buyers often differentiate based on very real physical differences among products. But that differentiation takes place only in the buyer's mind and it may or may not be based on real physical differences.

Price Discrimination

Price discrimination sounds like a terrible thing, something that violates our basic constitutional rights. Sometimes it is bad and other times it's not bad at all. In fact, price discrimination is often a disguised subsidy to the poor.

Price discrimination occurs when a seller charges two or more prices for the same good or service. Doctors often charge rich patients 10 times as much for the same service as poor patients. Airlines allow riders under 16 years of age to fly at half-fare ("youthfare").

The most notorious example of price discrimination was probably that of A&P during the 1940s. A&P had three grades of canned goods: A, B, and C. Grade A was presumably of the highest quality, B was fairly good, and C was—well, C was edible. My mother told me that she always bought grade A, even though it was the most expensive. Nothing but the best for our family.

Our family was friendly with another family in the neighborhood. The husband, a man in his early 50s, found out he had stomach cancer. "Aha!" exclaimed my mother, "Mrs. S. always bought grade C!"

A few years later the Federal Trade Commission (FTC) prohibited A&P from selling grades A, B, and C. The FTC didn't do that because of Mr. S.'s stomach cancer but because there was absolutely no difference among the grades.

Why had A&P concocted this elaborate subterfuge? Because it was worth tens of millions of dollars in profits! Take a can of green peas that had a demand schedule like the one in Table 22–1.

Table 22–1
Hypothetical Demand Schedule for Canned Peas

Price	Quantity Demanded	Total Revenue
$.50	100	$50
.40	140	56
.30	170	51

To keep things simple, suppose A&P had a constant ATC of 20 cents a can. How much should they charge? To figure this out, add a total cost column to Table 22–1 and then a total profits column. Now figure out the total profits at prices of 50 cents, 40 cents, and 30 cents, respectvely.

In Table 22–2, these calculations are all worked out. If A&P could charge only one price, it would be 50 cents; total profit would be $30. Now let's see how much profit would be if they are able to charge three different prices.

Table 22–2
Hypothetical Demand Schedule for Canned Peas

Price	Total Revenue	Total Cost	Total Profit
$.50	$50	$20	$30
.40	56	28	28
.30	51	34	17

At 50 cents, they would be able to sell 100 cans. These are sold to the people who won't buy anything if it isn't grade A. Then there are those who would like to buy grade A but just can't afford it. These people buy 40 cans of grade B. Finally, we have the poor, who can afford only grade C; they buy 30 cans.

All this is worked out in Table 22–3. Total revenue now is $75 for the 170 cans sold, and total cost of 170 cans remains $34. This gives A&P a total profit of $41.

Table 22–3
Hypothetical Demand Schedule for
Canned Peas, by Grades

Grade	Price	Quantity Demanded	Total Revenue	Total Cost	Total Profit
A	$.50	100	$50	$20	$30
B	.40	40	16	8	8
C	.30	30	9	6	3
			$75	$34	$41

Why is total profit so much greater under price discrimination ($41) than it is under a single price ($30)?[1] Because the seller is able to capture some or all of the consumer's surplus (consumer's surplus was covered at the end of Chapter 17). People are willing to buy only 100 cans at 50 cents, 40 more at 40 cents, and another 30 at 30 cents. But the people who buy only grade A will buy *all* their cans of green peas at that price while those buying grade B will buy all their peas at 40 cents and grade C buyers will buy all their peas at 30 cents. By keeping its markets separate, A&P had been able to make much larger profits than by charging a single price.

To practice price discrimination, you need to be able to (1) distinguish between at least two sets of buyers, and (2) prevent one set of buyers from reselling the product to another set.

The firm that practices price discrimination needs to be able to distinguish between two or more separate groups of buyers. The doctor clearly does this when he or she sizes up the patient's ability to pay, so when you go to the doctor, wear your most ragged clothes, ask if food stamps are accepted, and be sure to say you're a college student.

In addition to distinguishing among separate groups of buyers, the price discriminator must be able to prevent buyers from reselling the product (i.e., stop those who buy at a low price from selling to those who would otherwise buy at a higher price).[2] If the 15-and-a-half year old buys an airline ticket at half-fare and resells it to someone 35 years old, the airline loses money. Most 15-and-a-half year olds don't have too much money, so that's a way of filling an otherwise empty seat, but when the 35 year old flies half-fare and would have been willing to pay full fare, the airline loses money. In the case of A&P, there was no problem preventing the grade C customers from reselling their food to the grade A customers because these people voluntarily separated themselves into these markets.

Is the Monopolistic Competitor Inefficient?

It appears from our analysis of the long-run position of the monopolistic competitor in Figure 22–3 that the firm does not produce at the minimum point of its ATC curve. Economists criticize monopolistic competition as wasteful on two counts: too many firms in the industry and overdifferentiation.

Are there too many firms in monopolistically competitive industries?

Are there too many beauty parlors? Not if you want to get your hair done on Friday or Saturday afternoon. Too many gas stations? Not when there are gas lines. Too many Chinese restaurants? Not on Sundays. Are there too

---

[1] Total profit would be $30 at 50 cents; it would be $28 at 40 cents; it would be $17 at 30 cents.

[2] Remember when you had passed your 12th birthday and could no longer get into the movies at the children's price? Did you ever get a younger-looking kid to buy your ticket for you and try to pass yourself off as under 12 to the ticket taker? What? You still do it?

many grocery stores and too many real estate offices? Only when they're not busy. But most business firms, which apparently carry excess capacity during certain times of the day or the week, are set up to handle peak loads, so there aren't necessarily too many monopolistic competitors.

With respect to the second criticism, is there really overdifferentiation? Perhaps there don't seem to be substantial differences among grocery stores, drugstores, luncheonettes, cleaning stores, and ice cream parlors, but consider the alternative. Consider the drab monotony of the stores in much of Eastern Europe, including the Soviet Union. Maybe this lack of differentiation, this standardization, enables the sellers to cut costs somewhat. But is it worth it?

What are you really buying when you go to a fancy restaurant? Surely not just a meal. Undoubtedly you'll order something on a somewhat higher culinary plane than a Big Mac, large fries, and a Coke, but is that meal worth $80? It is when it is served by a waiter with a phony French accent, there are flowers on your table, a nice linen tablecloth, candlelight, soft music, a solicitous maitre d', and the restaurant is a restored 18th-century carriage house.

Is monopolistic competition wasteful and inefficient?

Monopolistic competition, with its attendant product differentiation, may be viewed as wasteful and inefficient and a case can easily be made that it is. Think of all the money spent on advertising, packaging, marketing, sales promotion, as well as interiors, facades, and window displays. All these expenses add perhaps 10 or 20 percent to the prices of most things we buy, so we may well ask, is it worth it? You decide.

I'll bet you're saying to yourself, "There he goes again, copping out and passing the buck." And you're right. You see, the buck stops with you because it's *your* buck and it's *your* decision about how to spend it.

Do you want to spend it on advertising, ambience, service, and convenience, or are you basically a no-frills person? Do you usually buy no-frills brands in the supermarket, fly coach rather than first class, drive an "economy car," and consider dinner in a fast-food emporium "eating out"? If you have answered yes to each of these questions, you are indeed a no-frills person who knows the value of a dollar.

Can you imagine a no-frills world?

On the other hand, if you answered no to all of the above, you are clearly a person of refined taste, high style—a very au courant person (that's french for "up to date"). Whether we like it or not, product differentiation is the way monopolistic competitors compete. And whether we're aware of it or not, our entire environment is flavored by product differentiation. Imagine that next December every commercial display is done with no-frills products. Christmas done in black and white boxes, jars, and cans. Imagine what our supermarkets would look like in black and white. And imagine what people would look like if they all wore the same styles and colors. In a word, product differentiation adds flavor, texture, and variety to our lives. Whether we want to pay the price is a matter of individual taste.

Finally, we will consider the nature of competition. Monopolistic competitors *do* compete with respect to price, but they compete still more vigorously with respect to ambience, service, and the rest of the intangibles that go along with attracting customers. It is in this arena that American business does engage in lively innovative competition. The next time you're walking along a shopping street, take note of how the storekeepers try to entice you with their window displays. To the degree that they're successful, they have gotten you to differentiate their product from all the others. That is what monopolistic competition is all about.

Workbook for Chapter 22

Name _____

Date _____

Multiple-Choice Questions

Circle the letter that corresponds to the best answer.

1. Monopolistic competition differs from perfect competition only with respect to
a. the number of firms in the industry **b.** product differentiation **c.** barriers to entry **d.** economies of scale

2. Figure 1 shows a monopolistic competitor
a. in the short run breaking even **b.** in the short run taking a loss **c.** in the short run making a profit **d.** in the long run breaking even **e.** in the long run taking a loss **f.** in the long run making a profit

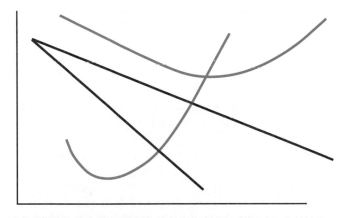

Figure 1

3. In the long run the monopolistic competitor is
a. more efficient than the perfect competitor
b. less efficient than the perfect competitor **c.** as efficient as the perfect competitor

4. In the short run the monopolistic competitor will be
a. definitely making a profit **b.** definitely taking a loss **c.** definitely breaking even **d.** either taking a loss or making a profit

5. In the long run the monopolistic competitor will be
a. making a profit **b.** taking a loss **c.** breaking even

6. The demand curve of a monopolistic competitor is
a. identical to that of the perfect competitor
b. identical to that of the monopolist **c.** unlike either the perfect competitor's demand curve or the monopolist's demand curve

7. For product differentiation to take place
a. there must be physical differences among the products **b.** there may be physical differences among the products **c.** there may not be physical differences among the products

8. Which statement is true?
a. When you decide which doctor to go to, your only concern is the quality of the medical service you will receive. **b.** People differentiate among goods and services not only based on physical differences, but also ambience, convenience, and service.
c. Monopolistic competitors are usually large firms.
d. None of these statements is true.

9. Which of the following would not be a monopolistic competitor?
a. Joe's barbershop **b.** a mom 'n pop grocery store
c. a storefront lawyer **d.** a restaurant **e.** all are monopolistic competitors

10. Which statement is true about price discrimination?
a. It generally hurts the poor. **b.** It is inherently evil. **c.** It involves charging at least two separate prices for the same good or service. **d.** It generally involves deceiving the consumer.

11. Each of the following is an example of price discrimination except
a. airline youth fares   **b.** higher priced movie tickets after 5 P.M. and on weekends   **c.** doctors charging more to patients who need lab tests   **d.** A&P's old grades A, B, and C

12. In the long run in monopolistic competition
a. most firms make a profit   **b.** the absence of entry barriers ensure that there are no profits
c. economies of scale ensure that there are no profits
d. most firms lose money

13. Which statement is true?
a. Most firms in the United States are monopolistic competitors.   **b.** Most firms in the United States are perfect competitors.   **c.** Most consumers would prefer lower prices and less product differentiation.
d. None of these statements is true.

Fill-In Questions

1. A monopolistically competitive industry has
_____ firms producing a _____ product.

2. The most crucial feature of monopolistic competition is _____.

3. The monopolistic competitor gets people to buy his or her product by providing better (1) _____, (2) _____, and (3) _____.

4. A monopolistic competitor makes a profit only in the _____.

5. The monopolistic competitor's demand curve slopes _____.

6. Price discrimination occurs when a seller charges _____ for the same good or service.

7. The reason A&P sold grades A, B, and C of the same product was to _____.

8. The firm that practices price discrimination needs to be able to distinguish _____;
the seller also has to be able to prevent _____.

9. In the long run, the monopolistic competitor
_____ produces at the minimum point of his or her ATC.

Problems

1. Given the information in Figure 2, how much profit does this monopolistic competitor make?

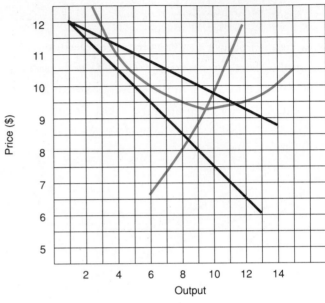

Figure 2

2. Is the firm in Figure 2 operating in the short run or the long run? How do you know?

3. Draw a graph of a monopolistic competitor in the long run in Figure 3.

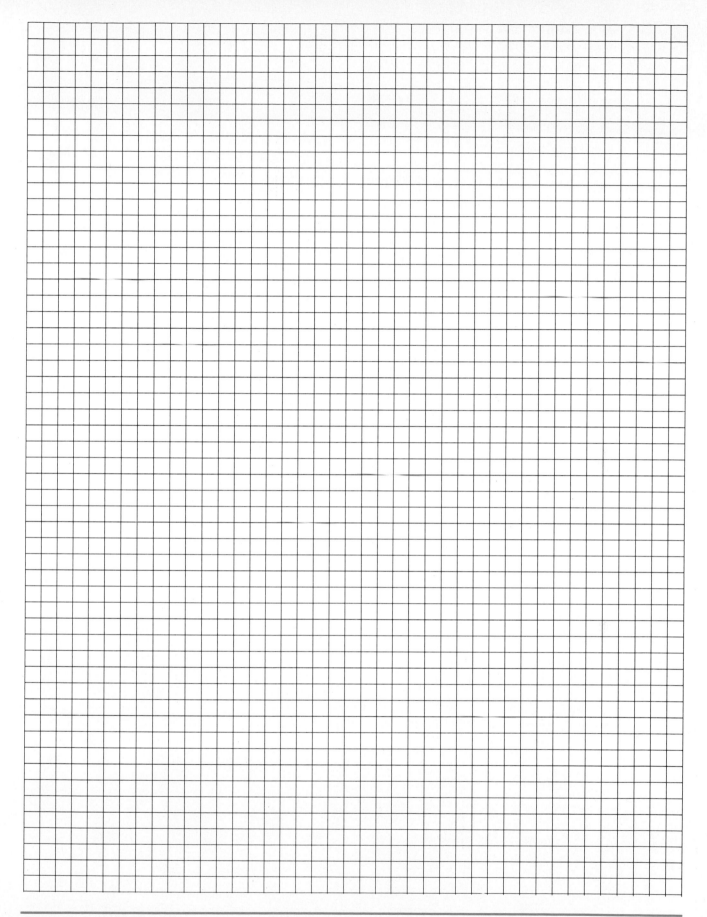

Figure 3

Oligopoly

The prefix *oli*, contrary to popular opinion, does not stand for Colonel Oliver North. It means "few." An oligarchy is a government that is controlled by only a few rulers. An oligopoly is an industry that is controlled by only a few firms.

Chapter Objectives

In this chapter we'll cover these topics:
- Concentration ratios.
- The competitive spectrum.
- The kinked demand curve.
- Administered prices.

Oligopoly Defined

Definition of oligopoly

An oligopoly is an industry with just a few sellers. How few? So few that at least one firm is large enough to influence price.

Oligopoly is the prevalent type of competition in the United States as well as in most of the noncommunist industrial West. Table 23–1 lists some of the more important American industries that are oligopolies. In terms of production, the vast majority of our GNP is accounted for by firms in oligopolized industries.

Is product identical or differentiated?

Is the product identical or differentiated? It doesn't matter. In the case of the steel, copper, and aluminum industries, the product happens to be identical, but in most other cases the product is differentiated.

The crucial factor under oligopoly is the small number of firms in the industry. Because there are so few firms, every competitor must think continually about the actions of his rivals, since what each does could make or break him. Thus there is a kind of interdependence among oligopolists.

In 1954 Charles Wilson, then secretary of defense in President Eisenhower's cabinet and formerly the president of General Motors, made this statement: "What's good for General Motors is good for the country." Although this seemingly innocuous statement offended many people, Wilson was merely pointing out the economic importance of his former employer.

Big business is oligopoly.

General Motors has been our largest or second largest industrial company for more than five decades, producing over half of all American-made cars. The company typified American business. When we talk about big business in the United States, we're talking about oligopolies such as GM, Ford, Ex-

Table 23–1
Concentration Ratios in Selected
Industries

Product	Largest Firms	Concentration Ratio
Tennis balls	General Tire, Spalding, Dunlop	100
Automobiles	General Motors, Ford, Chrysler, Volkswagon	99
Disposable diapers	Procter & Gamble, Kimberly-Clark, Curity, Romar Tissue Mills	99
Telephone service	AT&T, General Telephone and Electronics, United Telecommunications, Continental Telephone	98
Razor blades	Gillette, Warner-Lambert, Sunbeam, Philip Morris	98
Sanitary napkins	Tampax, Esmark, Kimberly-Clark, Johnson & Johnson	98
Cameras and film	Eastman Kodak, Polaroid, Bell & Howell, Berkey Photo	98
Chewing gum	Wm. Wrigley, Warner-Lambert, Squibb, Philip Morris	97
Electric razors	Norelco, Remington, Warner-Lambert, Sunbeam	96
Telephones	Western Electric, General Telephone, United Telecommunications, Continental Telephone	95
Breakfast cereals	Kellogg, General Mills, General Foods, Quaker Oats	91
Canned soup	Campbell, Heinz	90
Photocopiers	Xerox, Minnesota Mining & Manufacturing (3M), SCM, Addresso-Multigraph	90
Computers	IBM, Honeywell, Sperry-Rand, Burroughs	89
Cigarettes	Philip Morris, American Brands, Brown & Williamson, R. J. Reynolds	88
Detergents	Procter & Gamble, Lever Bros., Colgate-Palmolive	86
Portable typewriters	SCM, Royal, Brother, Olivetti	86
Office typewriters	IBM, Royal, SCM, Olivetti	85
Tires and tubes	Goodyear, Firestone, Uniroyal, B. F. Goodrich	85

xon, Mobil, IBM, Xerox, Boeing, and all the other industrial giants that have become household names.

Because the graph of the oligopolist is similar to that of the monopolist, we will analyze it in exactly the same manner with respect to price, output, profit, and efficiency. Price is higher than the minimum point of the ATC curve and output is somewhat to the left of this point. And so, just like the monopolist, the oligopolist has a higher price and a lower output than the perfect competitor.

The oligopolist, like the monopolist and unlike the perfect competitor, makes a profit. With respect to efficiency, since the oligopolist does not produce at the minimum point of its ATC, it is not as efficient as the perfect competitor.

We're going to consider a whole range of oligopolistic models, from close collusion to cutthroat competition. Each type, theoretically, has its own graph, but we'll only do the graphs of the two extreme cases. First, however, we'll look at concentration ratios, which measure the degree of oligopoly in various industries.

Concentration Ratios

What is a concentration ratio?

Economists use concentration ratios as a quantitative measure of oligopoly. *The total percentage share of industry sales by the four leading firms is the industry concentration ratio.* It is plain that industries with high ratios are very oligopolistic.

How much should the concentration ratio be for an industry whose four largest firms produced, respectively, 10, 8, 7, and 5 percent of the industry's output? Work it out right here.

Just add them together to get 30.

The concentration ratios in Table 23-1 range from 85 in office typewriters and tires and tubes to 99 in automobiles and disposable diapers and 100 in tennis balls. In the last two industries, the entire output is produced by no more than four firms.

Two key shortcomings of concentration ratios should be noted. First, they don't include imports. For example, in the auto industry, foreign cars account for about one third of the American market.

Second, the concentration ratios tell us nothing about the competitive structure of the rest of the industry. Are the remaining firms all relatively large, as in the cigarette industry, which has a total of just 13 firms, or are they small, as in the aircraft and engine parts industry, which totals about 190 firms? This distinction is important because when the remaining firms are large, they are not as easily dominated by the top four as are dozens of relatively small firms.

The Competitive Spectrum

In this section we shall consider the possible degrees of competition from cartels and outright collusion down through cutthroat competition. These possibilities are shown later in Figure 23-3.

Cartels With so few firms in our basic industries, there is a strong temptation for the leading firms to band together to restrict output and consequently increase prices and profits. An extreme case is a cartel, where the firms behave as a monopoly in a manner similar to that of the Organization of Petroleum Exporting Countries in the world oil market.

A cartel is an extreme case of oligopoly.

Given a certain market demand for a good or service over which the oligopolies exercise little control, firms that openly collude can control industry supply, and to a large degree, market price. For example, by withholding part or most of supply, the colluding firms can bid the market price way up. This was done by OPEC in 1973 when the price of oil quadrupled (see Figure 23-1).

If the cartel is able to operate successfully, securing the full support of all its members (who don't try to undercut the cartel price to sell some extra output under the table), its situation will approximate that of a monopoly. Just like a monopoly, which faces the entire market demand curve, the cartel will control the entire industry supply. OPEC, which controlled most of the world's oil exports, was able to take advantage of a relatively inelastic demand for oil by withholding supply in late 1973 and early 1974, thereby quadrupling world oil prices.

In the next chapter we'll talk about the formation of trusts or cartels in the late 19th century in many basic American industries, most notably oil,

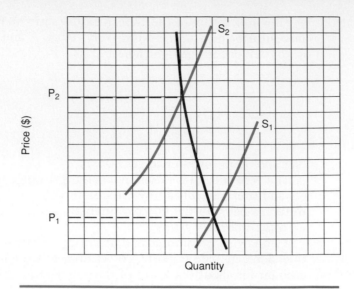

Figure 23–1

which led to the Sherman and Clayton Acts, outlawing such behavior. Today the only cartels we need to worry about are those that exist outside our borders.

A cartel operates like the Mafia.

Outright Collusion Slightly less extreme than a cartel would be a territorial division of the market among the firms in the industry. This would be a division similar to that of the Mafia, if indeed there really is such an organization. An oligopolistic division of the market might go something like this. All prostitution, dope, loan-sharking, and gambling in New England is run by Angelo (The Fence); New York is run by Frankie (Big Frank); Philly and Atlantic City by Vinnie (Little Vin); the Midwest by Mike (The Banker); Florida by Joey (Three Fingers); the Gulf Coast by Carlo (The Professor); the mountain states by Guido (Dog Ears); and the West Coast by Anthony (Fat Tony).

Nobody messes with someone else's territory. That arrangement will continue until there is a new power alignment within the family or a new firm tries to enter the industry.

This cozy arrangement would give each operation a regional monopoly. On a national basis, each operation's market situation is depicted by Figure 23-2.

You may have noticed that this graph is identical to that of a monopoly. Although the firm may have only 15 or 20 percent of the market, its pricing behavior is that of the monopolist and the results are similar. Compared to the perfect competitor, the colluding oligopolist charges a higher price (not one equal to the minimum point of the ATC), has a higher ATC (and is therefore less efficient), restricts output (i.e., operates to the left of the minimum point of the ATC), and finally, unlike the perfect competitor, the oligopolist makes a profit.

These are extreme cases but they would be impossible, even during the last few years of less than stringent enforcement of the antitrust laws. Now, as we move to somewhat less extreme cases of collusion, we begin to enter the realm of reality. This brings us to the celebrated electric machinery conspiracy case.

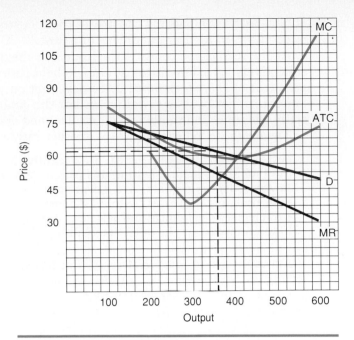

Figure 23–2
The Colluding Oligopolist

Covert Collusion: The Electric Machinery Conspiracy Case In the late 1950s, officials of General Electric, Westinghouse, Allis-Chalmers, and other leading electrical firms met periodically at various hotels and motels around the country. These secret meetings were set up to fix the prices of electric transformers, turbines, and other electrical equipment. Although government contracts were awarded based on the lowest sealed bid, the conspirators rigged the bidding so that even the lowest bid would be extremely profitable. In fact, the firms took turns making low bids. The public too was bilked out of hundreds of millions of dollars in higher prices.

Finally, in 1961, seven high-ranking company officials were found guilty by the Supreme Court of illegal price-fixing and market-sharing agreements. They were given fines, which their companies took care of, and short jail sentences, during which time their salaries were paid. Upon release from jail, each was given back his old job. Talk about tying yellow ribbons round the old oak tree!

As a footnote to this story, some 11 years later two of the companies involved in the 1961 case, General Electric and Westinghouse, were charged with fixing prices on turbine generators. Oh well, nobody's perfect.

Was this case the tip of the iceberg or an unfortuante aberration, a group of unethical executives who gave big business a black eye? There have been other cases. Some of the executives of Marcor Paper Company (now a division of Mobil Oil), which made containers, and a few other container manufactuers also received short jail sentences for illegal price setting, but these cases are few and far between. Surely there is not any overwhelming evidence that big business is any more corrupt than any other sector of American life, although that is a somewhat underwhelming testimonial.

Price Leadership Short of meeting in hotel rooms to secretly set prices, do oligopolists conspire in less overt fashion? Until the 1930s, U.S. Steel exercised open price leadership in the steel industry. One day U.S. Steel would post a price for a particular type of steel and the next day Bethlehem, Re-

A case of price fixing.

Other cases of collusion

Playing follow the leader

public, Armco, Inland and the rest of the industry would post an identical price, down to the last hundredth of a cent.

At the turn of the century, the leaders of the major steel firms actually collectively agreed on prices at dinners held periodically by Judge Gary, president of U.S. Steel. Since those days, not only has it become much more difficult to get away with collusion, but the quality of the dinners—especially the hotel and motel food—has declined drastically.

The cigarette industry provided another instance of price leadership.

> Between 1923 and 1941, virtual price identity prevailed continuously among the "standard" brands. During this period there were eight list price changes. Reynolds led six of them, five upward and one downward, and was followed each time, in most cases, within 24 hours of its announcement. The other two changes were downward revisions during 1933 led by American and followed promptly by the other standard brand venders.[1]

The prime rate set by big banks

Another form of price leadership that has sprung up in recent years is the setting of the prime rate of interest by the nation's leading banks. That rate might stay the same for several months, when suddenly one of the top 10 banks raises its prime by a quarter of a percent and within 24 hours, the rest of the nation's 15,000 banks raise theirs a quarter of a percent. What is interesting here is that rarely do the same banks change the rate two times in a row, but in virtually every instance the other 14,999 banks play follow the leader. Bankers and other oligopolists engaging in price leadership would have us believe that they are "locked in competition" and that the forces of supply and demand dictate the same price to everyone. But this explanation strains credulity since no two firms—and certainly not 15,000—face exactly the same demand schedules or have the same cost schedules.

A community of interest

Conclusion Perhaps there is no collusion at all, or at least not very much. But there is surely a certain community of interest, a community that may go well beyond the confines of specific industries. In the box that follows this idea is explored, using the New York banks as an example. This could be repeated for the Texas oil interests, the Michigan automobile industry, the Silicon Valley computer establishment in California, and the high-technology complex along Route 128 in the Boston suburbs.

Whatever the degree of collusion, it would be hard for firms in oligopolized industries to ignore each other's actions and anticipated reactions with respect to price and output. In the next section we'll investigate the situation of oligopoly with no collusion. This is at the other end of the spectrum from the point at which we began when we discussed cartels.

When is collusion most likely to succeed?

When is collusion most likely to succeed? Mainly when there are few firms in the industry and when there are high barriers to entry. Basically, it's much easier to keep secrets—when you're violating the antitrust laws, you have to keep secrets—when there aren't too many people to deal with. In a farfetched example, the American Communist party back in the 1950s was considered a group of people conspiring to advocate the violent overthrow of the American government. It turned out that several thousand of their somewhat under 20,000 card-carrying members were actually FBI agents or paid informers. Some conspiracy!

Conspiracies need to be kept very small. When entry barriers, particularly capital requirements, are high enough, you don't have to worry about new firms entering the industry, and presumably, being taken into the conspiracy.

---

[1] F. M. Scherer, *Industrial Pricing: Theory and Evidence* (Skokie, Ill.: Rand McNally, 1970), p. 38.

The Old Boy Network at Six Big Banks

Directors of supposedly competing banks are meeting with each other continually—on the boards of other companies.

> *People of the same trade seldom meet together, even for merriment and diversion, but the conversation ends in a conspiracy against the public, or in some contrivance to raise prices.*
>
> —Adam Smith
> *The Wealth of Nations*

Under the Clayton Antitrust Act, it is illegal for a person to sit on the boards of two competing firms, since this would tend to lessen competition. But there is a way around this prohibition; it is called the "indirect interlock," by which members of the boards of competing firms serve together on the boards of companies in non-related industries.

It turns out that the directors of New York's six leading banks—Bankers Trust, Chase Manhattan, Chemical, Citibank, Manufacturers Hanover, and Morgan—hold hundreds of other directorships. Many of these directorships are in the top industrial, retail, and nonbank financial corporations. On some of these boards there are directors from three or four of the six banks. General Electric's board includes directors from no less than five of the six.

Although it could be argued that boards of directors have little power and that interlocking directorships are really irrelevant, this situation is at least evidence of the trend toward economic concentration. As recent statistics show, there has been a steady increase in the share of business done by the biggest industrial, retail, and financial corporations. On the indirectly interlocked directorates of these firms sit many men who know each other, share certain economic and political views, and yet are often connected with supposedly competing businesses. Are these men really competing, or is competition merely a facade behind which they pursue their common business interests?

The pattern that emerges in the banking industry shows a coincidence of interest among a relatively small group of men. Each bank shares at least five boards with representatives of every other bank. Morgan and Citibank are represented together on 12 corporate boards, Morgan and Manufacturers on 10, and Manufacturers and Citibank on 9. There are even some bank directors who sit together on more than one board outside the banking industry.

When we look at individual corporations, the results are equally clear. There are 14 large corporations whose directors also sit on the boards of three of the New York banks. Interestingly, five of these companies (American Express, Fidelity Union Bancorp, National Life, New York Life, and Royal Globe) are financial institutions, which are presumably in competition with commercial banks.

The collapse of Penn Central in 1970 provides a good example of possible abuses of power through bank interlocks. Thomas Perkins served on the boards of both Morgan and Penn Central; Stuart Saunders, board chairman of Penn Central, served on Chase's board. It so happened that, shortly before it became publicly known that Penn Central was nearly bankrupt, Morgan and Chase sold off much of their holdings in Penn Central.

Of course, membership on boards is not the only meeting ground for industrial competitors. Country clubs, dining clubs, trade associations, professional societies, and other social institutions provide ample opportunity for collusion. Nevertheless, there seems to be a growing community of interest among the Big Six New York banks. When each extends a line of credit to Exxon, where directors of four of the banks serve on the board, there is a common bond among the banks. This bond is cemented by similar shared loans to other companies on whose boards sit representatives from these same banks.

There has got to be a great temptation to cooperate, to not rock the boat. Although it violates no antitrust statute, this arrangement could undermine competition. Unfortunately, there are probably no legal remedies because the indirect interlock is more a symptom of economic concentration than a conspiracy to create it.

One might also wonder how a director divides his loyalties between AT&T and Chase or Citibank. Are these roles of simultaneous creditor and debtor so inconsistent as to be, perhaps, schizophrenic? Or is this apparent dichotomy overcome by a stronger loyalty—to the small group of men who hold most of the country's economic power?

Bankers and Bedfellows

Listed below are those companies with at least three directors who also sit on the boards of the six largest New York banks.

Company	Banks Represented on the Board
American Express	Chase, Chemical, Manufacturers
Bell Labs	Chase, Citibank, Morgan
DuPont	Chemical, Citibank, Morgan
Fidelity Union Bancorp	Chase, Chemical, Manufacturers
Ford	Bankers Trust, Citibank, Morgan
General Foods	Bankers Trust, Chase, Chemical
General Motors	Chase, Citibank, Morgan
International Paper	Bankers Trust, Chase, Chemical
Johns-Manville	Bankers Trust, Manufacturers, Morgan
Mutual Life (of N.Y.)	Bankers Trust, Chemical, Citibank
New York Life	Chemical, Manufacturers, Morgan
Phelps-Dodge	Citibank, Manufacturers, Morgan
Royal Globe Insurance	Bankers Trust, Citibank, Manufacturers
Sears	Chemical, Citibank, Manufacturers
AT&T	Chase, Chemical, Citibank, Manufacturers
Exxon	Chase, Chemical, Citibank, Morgan
IBM	Bankers Trust, Chemical, Citibank, Morgan
U.S. Steel	Chase, Citibank, Manufacturers, Morgan
General Electric	Chase, Chemical, Citibank, Manufacturers, Morgan

Source: Reprinted from Stephen L. Slavin, "The Old Boy Network at Six Big Banks," *Business and Society Review* 23 (Fall 1977), p. 62.

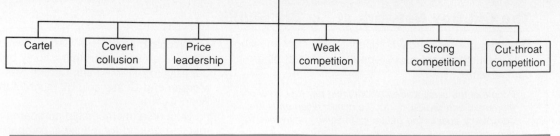

Figure 23-3

Let's take another look at the chart in Figure 23-3. At one end we have the cartel, something that no longer operates within the American economy although it may be found in world markets (most notably in the oil market). At the opposite end of the spectrum we have the cutthroat competitor, the firm that will stop at nothing to beat out its rivals. Industrial espionage and sabotage, underselling, disparaging of rival products, and other unfair competitive practices are the trademarks of such firms. We'll be considering the case of the cutthroat oligopolist for the rest of this chapter.

Near the middle are the mildly competing oligopolists and the occasionally cooperating oligopolists. Sometimes their leaders are called corporate statesmen.

Where on this spectrum is American industry?

Where on this spectrum is American industry? Where do we place the industries listed in Table 23-1? Near the middle? Toward the cutthroat end of the spectrum? Or toward the cartel end?

The answer is that there *is* no answer. You won't pin me down on that one. There are two reasons why there is no answer to this question.

First, there is no one place where American industry is located because different industries have different competitive situations. In a word, some oligopolized industries are more competitive than others, so to say that *all* industries are located at a certain point on the spectrum—regardless of where—has got to be wrong.

Second there is widespread disagreement about the degree of competition in any given industry. Take banking, for example.

If one were to judge the degree of competitiveness among banks by all the newspaper advertising they do to attract depositors and to get people to take out car loans and mortgages, it would appear that this is a very competitive industry. But one would reach a very different conclusion by observing that when one or two major banks change their prime rate of interest,[2] within a day or so all the other major banks, not to mention the rest of the banks around the country, join in playing follow the leader.

Oligopoly without Collusion: The Kinked Demand Curve

Cutthroat competition: an extreme case

Now we deal with the extreme case of oligopolists who are cutthroat competitors, firms that do not exchange so much as a knowing wink. Each is out to maximize its profits. These oligopolists are ready to issue the same order that Lawrence of Arabia issued. (See the next box.)

Before changing price, a firm will try to gauge its competitors' reactions.

The uniqueness of this situation leads us to the phenomenon of the kinked demand curve, pictured in Figure 23-4. For the first time in this course, we have a demand curve that is not a straight line.

---

[2] Bankers would tell us that they're not oligopolists to begin with, and that in any event, their concentration ratio was no more than about 15. On the other hand, there is no question that the 20 largest banks in the country do over one third of all the banking business.

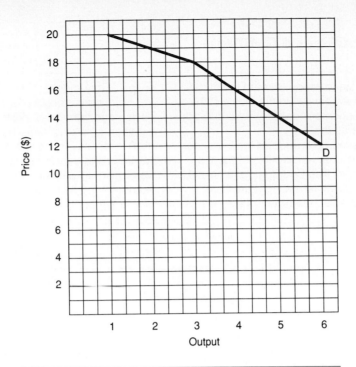

Figure 23–4

Why does the demand curve of the fiercely competing oligopolist have a kink? The answer is that it is based on the oligopolist's assumption about his or her rivals' behavior in response to his own actions. There are three possible things the oligopolist can do: raise price, lower price, or not change price.

Suppose the price has been the same for a fairly long period of time. The oligopolist thinks about raising price. If I raise my price, what will my competitors do? Who knows? What would *I* do if one of my rivals raised his or her price? If I did nothing, I would get some of my rival's customers, so I wouldn't change my price.

Even though I hate to admit it, my competitors are as smart as I am, so if *my* response to a rival's price increase is to keep my price the same and get some of my rival's customers, surely my rivals would respond in the same way to *my* price increase. Therefore, I don't raise my price.

What about lowering my price and stealing some of my competitors' customers? Now I ask myself, how would *I* react? I'd immediately lower my price in response to a move by one of my competitors. And my competitors would lower their prices in response to my lowering mine. So I won't lower my price.

If I don't lower my price (because my competitors would follow) and if I don't raise my price (because my competitors won't follow), what *do* I do? Nothing. I leave my price where it is.

What makes sense for me also makes sense for my competitors. None of them will raise or lower price. We all keep price where it is, and that happens to be where the kink is in the demand curve.

This explains why price does not change often under very competitive oligopoly. You're afraid to make a move for fear of what your rivals might or might not do. Underlying that fear is the memory of price wars touched off by one firm lowering its price. So it's better to leave well enough alone.

Let's examine the kinked demand curve a little more closely. It's really two demand curves in one, the left segment being relatively elastic (or horizontal) and the right less elastic (more vertical).

If I raise my price, they won't raise theirs.

If I lower my price, they lower theirs.

Lawrence of Arabia and Cutthroat Competition

Cutthroat competitors stand ready to issue the same order that Lawrence of Arabia did in the movie of the same name (it won a bunch of Academy Awards back in 1963). Which order was that?

His forces were arrayed on the top of a hill overlooking the smoldering ruins of an Arab village that had been burned by the Turks. The bedraggled remnants of the Turkish army were slowly retreating. Lawrence raised his sword and shouted his order: "Take no pris-oners!" They didn't.

The cutthroat oligopolist gives no quarter and expects none from his or her competitors. They don't drink together, sit on the same boards together, and they won't even stay in the same room together. They don't socialize and they're not even on speaking terms. If they were baseball pitchers, they'd throw at each other's heads. If they had knives, presumably they'd cut each other's throats. In short, they really compete.

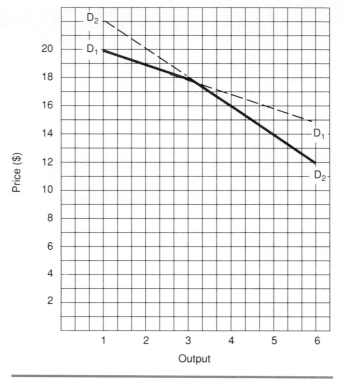

Figure 23–5

In Figure 23-5, both segments of the demand curve have been extended. This was done to set up the next step, the MR curves of Figure 23-6. Before we can figure out the oligopolist's actual MR curve, we'll have to see how each of the MR curves in Figure 23-6 is drawn.

First, look at MR_1, which corresponds to D_1. Notice that it is equal to D_1 at one unit of output and that it slopes downward to the right, falling twice as quickly as D_1. These two characteristics of straight line demand and MR curves always hold true. *If a demand curve is a straight line, its MR curve will also be a straight line that will coincide with it at one unit of output and decline twice as quickly.* (By convention, we refer to demand and MR curves as curves, even if they should happen to be straight lines.)

Let's take a look at MR_2, which corresponds to D_2. Notice how D_2 and MR_2 are equal at one unit of output, and how MR_2 slopes downward to the right, falling twice as quickly as D_2. Using this information we're ready to draw a graph for an oligopolist. First I'll do one. Then you'll do a couple.

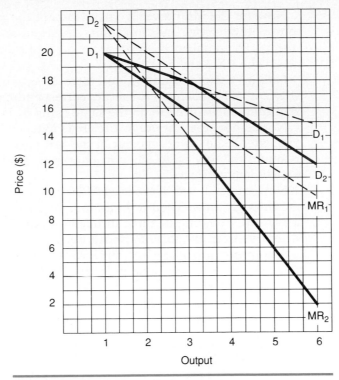

Figure 23-6

First, we'll go over the demand curve in Figure 23-7, which is the now familiar kinked curve. The price and output are always at the kink, so in this instance price is $18 and output three.

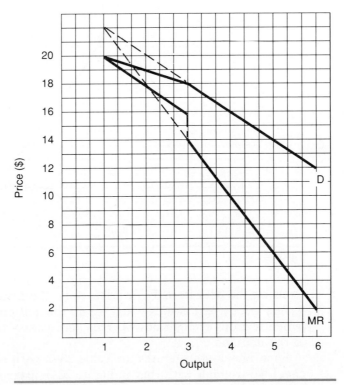

Figure 23-7

Now for the MR curve. We have each of the points. We can connect the points between one and three units of output and also four to six units of output. The problem is, what do we do about drawing the MR curve between the third and fourth units?

Let's go back for a minute to Figure 23-6, when we drew two MR curves, MR$_1$ and MR$_2$. Each curve met its corresponding demand curve at one unit of output, so we need to do the same thing in Figure 23-7.

Notice how the MR curve already is extended to one unit of output. Now let's extend the lower segment of the MR curve running from outputs four to six all the way up to one unit of output. Notice how it is equal to the extended demand curve in Figure 23-7.

Now we're all set. The actual MR curve is the heavy line from outputs one through three. Then it drops straight down and continues along the heavy line from output three through output six. The key is to extend the MR curve from the third to fourth unit.

Don't make this mistake.

A common mistake is to connect the one to three segment with the four to six segment, as I've done in Figure 23-8. You have to drop straight down at three units of output and then extend the MR curve from three to four at the same slope or angle at which it has been running from four to six. Let's see what you can do.

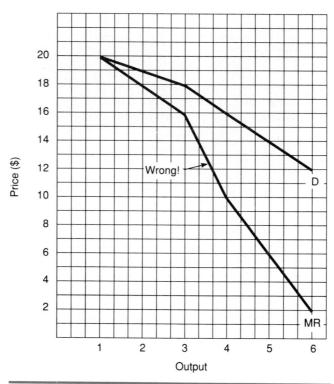

Figure 23-8

Using the data from Table 23-2, draw the firm's demand and MR curves. A very tricky part comes when we do the MR curve at its discontinuity (when it drops straight down). This part always lies directly below the kink in the demand curve.

First, check your figures for Table 23-2 with mine in Table 23-3. Then check your graph with that in Figure 23-9 (page 444). How much is output? How much is price?

Table 23-2
Hypothetical Demand Schedule for
Competing Oligopolist

Output	Price	Total Revenue	Marginal Revenue
1	$50	_____	_____
2	49	_____	_____
3	48	_____	_____
4	47	_____	_____
5	44	_____	_____
6	41	_____	_____
7	38	_____	_____

Table 23-3

Output	Price	Total Revenue	Marginal Revenue
1	$50	$ 50	$50
2	49	98	48
3	48	144	46
4	47	188	44
5	44	220	32
6	41	246	26
7	38	266	20

The firm operates where the kink is.

The output is at the kink in the demand curve, which occurs at four units of output. At that output, price is $47. The key in the graph, of course, is the discontinuity of the MR curve, which is directly below the kink. By extending the lower segment of the MR curve (which runs from seven to five units of output) up to four units of output, all you need to do is extend the dotted line connecting the two MR segments.

At this point we're ready to add the ATC and MC curves, draw a graph, and do some analysis. I'd like you to (1) fill in Table 23-4; (2) draw a graph

Table 23-4
Hypothetical Demand and Cost
Schedule for a Competitive
Oligopolist

Output	Price	Total Revenue	Marginal Revenue	Total Cost	ATC	Marginal Cost
1	$30	_____	_____	$ 40	_____	_____
2	29	_____	_____	60	_____	_____
3	28	_____	_____	75	_____	_____
4	27	_____	_____	96	_____	_____
5	24	_____	_____	125	_____	_____
6	21	_____	_____	162	_____	_____
7	18	_____	_____	210	_____	_____

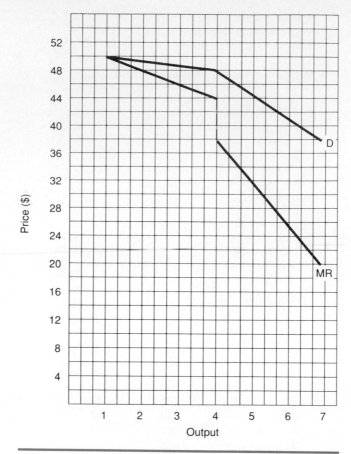

Figure 23-9

of the firm's demand, MR, MC, and ATC curves; and (3) find the firm's output, price, and total profit.

First check your figures with those of Table 23-5. Next, check your graph with the one shown in Figure 23-10. Finally, how much are output, price, and total profit?

Table 23-5

Output	Price	Total Revenue	Marginal Revenue	Total Cost	ATC	Marginal Cost
1	$30	$ 30	$30	$ 40	$40	—
2	29	58	28	60	30	$20
3	28	84	26	75	25	15
4	27	108	24	96	24	21
5	24	120	12	125	25	29
6	21	126	6	162	27	37
7	18	126	0	210	30	48

Output, which is directly under the kink, is four. Price, which is at the kink, is $27. Remember that price is *always* read off the demand curve. And now, total profit.

$$\text{Total profit} = (\text{Price} - \text{ATC}) \times \text{Output}$$
$$= (\$27 - \$24)\ 4$$
$$= \$3 \times 4$$
$$= \$12.$$

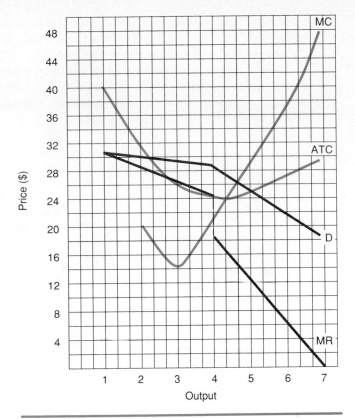

Figure 23–10

In passing, let us note that the oligopolist does not produce at the minimum point of the firm's ATC curve, so we do not have peak efficiency even though there is considerable competition. Price tends to stay at $27. This is the main reason why, under competition, oligopolists' prices tend to be "sticky." We call such sticky prices administered prices, which are the topic of the last section of this chapter.

Administered Prices

Definition of administered prices

Administered prices are prices set by large corporations for relatively long periods of time, without responding to the normal market forces, mainly changes in demand. For example, during the Great Depression, although demand fell substantially, many firms, most notably the railroads, did not lower their prices.

We already saw how, under the constraints of fierce competition, the oligopolist is reluctant to raise or lower price. Prices are said to be sticky.

If we take the firm's MC curve as its supply curve, we will see that the oligopolist operates within a fairly wide range of possible MRs before it is necessary to change price. Look back at Figure 23-9. Because of the discontinuity of the MR curve (the vertical broken line), the firm would charge the same price at the same output no matter how much MC varied within the range of $38 to $44. In Figure 23-10, MC could vary between $18 and $24 and still equal MR.

Administered prices occur only under oligopoly

Administered prices are peculiar to oligopoly. Perfect competitors and monopolistic competitors would be too small to dictate price. Monopolists would change their output and price in response to changes in demand to maximize their profits. But under competitive oligopoly, the firms would rarely shift output or price because they would continue to maximize profit as long as MC was within the range of MR.

Thus, administered prices can occur only under oligopoly, and are most likely under very competitive oligopoly. But oligopoly is the dominant type of competition in the American economy, though many would question just *how* competitive our oligopolies are.

Workbook for Chapter 23

Name _____

Date _____

Multiple-Choice Questions

Circle the letter that corresponds to the best answer.

1. Which statement is true?

a. All oligopolized industries have only a few firms.

b. Most oligopolized industries have only a few firms.

c. Some oligopolized industries have only a few firms.

2. The auto industry has a concentration ratio of over _____ percent.

a. 10   **b.** 30   **c.** 50   **d.** 70   **e.** 90

3. Which statement is closest to the truth?

a. The six big New York banks engage in cutthroat competition.   **b.** The six big New York banks are perfect competitors.   **c.** There is some evidence of possible conflict of interest when people sit on the boards of banks and large industrial corporations and have financial ties to the banks.   **d.** Those who sit on the boards of large New York banks simultaneously sit together on the boards of other large corporations but have little in common.

4. Price is

a. always read off the demand curve   **b.** sometimes read off the demand curve   **c.** always read off the marginal revenue curve   **d.** sometimes read off the marginal revenue curve

5. Compared to the perfect competitor in the long run, the cutthroat oligopolist has a

a. lower price and lower profits   **b.** higher price and higher profits   **c.** higher price and lower profits   **d.** lower price and higher profits

6. Which statement is true?

a. All firms in oligopolized industries are large.

b. Most firms in the United States are oligopolies.

c. The crucial factor in oligopolized industries is product differentiation.   **d.** Most of our GNP is produced by oligopolies.

7. Which of the following is not an oligopoly?

a. Exxon   **b.** General Motors   **c.** your local phone company   **d.** Xerox

8. Which statement is false about oligopolies?

a. They operate at the minimum point of their ATC curves.   **b.** They charge higher prices than perfect competitors.   **c.** They make profits in the long run.   **d.** They cannot legally form cartels in the United States.

9. Which statement is false?

a. The cigarette and auto industry have high concentration ratios.   **b.** OPEC is a cartel.   **c.** Most oligopolies engage in outright collusion.   **d.** None of these statments is false.

10. The electric machinery case involved

a. a cartel   **b.** covert collusion   **c.** cutthroat competition   **d.** none of the above

11. The least competitive industry is one that has

a. price leadership   **b.** covert collusion   **c.** overt collusion   **d.** a cartel

12. Which statement is true?

a. A person who sits on the board of Chase may also sit on the board of Citibank.   **b.** The people who run our large banks share a community of economic interest.   **c.** People on boards of major banks rarely run into each other.   **d.** Most members of bank boards are involved in conflicts of interest.

13. Which statement is true?

a. Most of American industry is engaged in cutthroat competition.   **b.** Most of American industry does not compete.   **c.** Some oligopolized industries are more competitive than others.   **d.** None of these statements is true.

14. According to the theory of the kinked demand curve, if a firm were to raise its price, its competitors would

a. lower theirs   **b.** raise theirs   **c.** keep theirs the same

15. According to the theory of the kinked demand curve, if a firm were to lower its price, its competitors would

a. lower theirs   **b.** raise theirs   **c.** keep theirs the same

16. The kinked demand curve depicts
a. cutthroat competition   **b.** cartels   **c.** collusive oligopoly   **d.** price leadership

17. The kinked demand curve is associated with
a. sticky prices   **b.** OPEC   **c.** covert collusion
d. none of the above

18. The discontinuity in the oligopolist's marginal revenue curve occurs
a. to the right of the kink   **b.** to the left of the kink   **c.** directly below the kink   **d.** at different places at different times

19. Administered prices are most likely to occur under
a. perfect competition   **d.** monopolistic competition   **c.** monopoly   **d.** oligopoly

Fill-In Questions

1. An oligopoly is an industry with _____.

2. One measure of the degree of competitiveness (or of oligopoly) is called a _____.

3. The oligopolist _____ at the minimum point of his or her ATC curve.

4. The total _____ of industry sales by the four leading firms is the industry concentration ratio.

5. The most important cartel in the world today is _____.

6. An important Supreme Court case involving covert collusion was the _____ case.

7. U.S. Steel and a few cigarette companies were all engaged in _____ to attain their economic ends.

8. Most of the dominant banks in the United States are located in _____.

9. The sign of cutthroat competition on a graph would be the _____.

10. One of the outcomes of the kinked demand curve is _____ prices.

11. Administered prices are set by _____ for _____. without responding to _____.

12. Administered prices are peculiar to _____.

Problems

1. *a.* Fill in Table 1.
b. Use Figure 1 to draw a graph of the demand, marginal revenue, average total cost, and marginal cost curves for this form.

Table 1

Output	Price	Total Revenue	Marginal Revenue	Total Cost	Average Total Cost	Marginal Cost
1	$50	_____	_____	$ 60	_____	_____
2	48	_____	_____	100	_____	_____
3	46	_____	_____	132	_____	_____
4	44	_____	_____	168	_____	_____
5	40	_____	_____	212	_____	_____
6	36	_____	_____	270	_____	_____
7	32	_____	_____	343	_____	_____

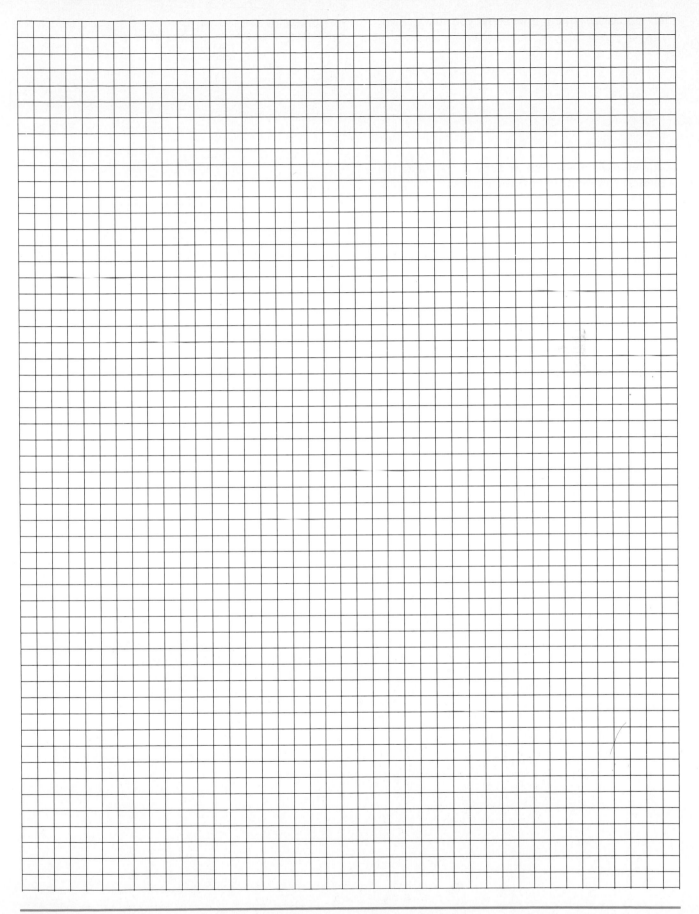

Figure 1

c. Calculate total profit. Show your work right here.

2. Given the information in Table 2, calculate the concentration ratio of this industry. *Show your work.*

Table 2

Firm	Percent of Sales
A	14%
B	4
C	23
D	5
E	2
F	8
G	17
H	10
I	2
J	15
Total	100%

Corporate Mergers
and Antitrust

There has been an unmistakable trend toward bigness in business for the last 125 years. Corporate mergers and takeovers have become so common that anything less than a billion dollar deal is not even considered financial news. Let's see how this trend has developed and how the government has attempted to regulate it.

Chapter Objectives
When you complete this chapter, you will be familiar with each of the following:
- Explanation of antitrust.
- The major antitrust laws.
- Modern antitrust.
- Types of mergers.
- The effectiveness of antitrust.
- The trend toward bigness.

A Historical Perspective on Corporate Concentration

The history of the American economy since the time of the Civil War has been one of growing corporate concentration. Like the tides, this concentration has had its ebbs and its flows.

A high watermark was reached in the early years of this century when J. P. Morgan put together a couple of huge deals with his fellow captains of industry Andrew Carnegie, Edward Harriman, and John D. Rockefeller. Then, in the years before World War I, came the first "trustbusters," Presidents Teddy Roosevelt and William Howard Taft. A new wave of corporate mergers took place in the 1920s, only to be succeeded by the antitrust enforcement policies of Presidents Franklin Roosevelt and Harry Truman in the 1930s and 1940s. Since then there has been a new wave of mergers that has apparently continued for nearly four decades.

During the last century and a quarter, a few hundred huge companies have come to dominate our economy. There have been a few setbacks—the

1911 breakup of the Standard Oil and American Tobacco trusts, and the antitrust enforcement of the 1930s and 1940s—but the trend has been unmistakable.

Antitrust

The Political Background

The common view is that during the 19th century, the federal government rarely intervened in the economy, allowing businesses to go their own way. There were, however, two major forms of intervention, both of which were key issues in the events leading up to the Civil War.

First, at various times the government passed a high protective tariff that generally made certain imports more expensive and greatly aided northern manufacturers. The transcontinental railroad, which completely bypassed the South, was built with a tremendous amount of federal aid. This aid took the form of 10-mile strips of land on alternating sides of the track so that for every mile of track built, the railroad received 10 square miles of land.

Both these policies were benevolent with respect to big business, so few protests were raised about government intervention in that arena. Furthermore, with the election of Abraham Lincoln in 1860, the Republican party would virtually dominate the federal government for the next 70 years. In fact, only two Democrats were even elected president during those years: Woodrow Wilson, who squeaked in after a three-way race with two Republicans, and Grover Cleveland, whose politics were as conservative as that of most Republicans.

This was the political backdrop against which the first antitrust legislation was passed in 1890. The Sherman Act was passed by a Republican Congress and signed by a Republican president. For a law like this to have been passed by "the party of big business," the economic situation had to have been pretty desperate.

What is a trust?

The late 19th century was the era of the "trust." Trusts were cartels that set prices and allocated sales among their member firms. In some cases, most blatantly oil, a single company was formed that controlled most or all production in the industry. The Standard Oil trust, which was carved out of 39 independent oil companies by John D. Rockefeller, controlled 90 percent of all U.S. oil production, refining, and marketing. In 1892, the American Sugar Refining Company was formed by 40 independent sugar companies. Still other trusts were formed in meat packing, leather, whiskey, tobacco, electrical goods, coal, steel, and the railroads.

In his landmark work on those times, Matthew Josephson pictured

> an America in which the citizen was born to drink the milk furnished by the milk Trust, eat the beef on the beef Trust, illuminate his home by grace of the oil Trust, and die and be carried off by the coffin Trust.[1]

Even more grating were the insults hurled at the public by those who ran these huge industrial empires. Probably the most famous was the remark by railroad tycoon Billy Vanderbilt: "The public be damned. I am working for my stockholders."[2]

---

[1] Matthew Josephson, *The Robber Barons* (New York: Harcourt Brace Jovanovich, 1962), p. 358.

[2] Ibid., p. 187.

The Sherman Antitrust Act

In 1890, the Sherman Antitrust Act was passed to curb the trust movement. Senator John Sherman, brother of General William Sherman (of Civil War fame and to this day voted the least popular person in Atlanta), was one of the most powerful politicians of his day. Senator Sherman was so popular that the leaders of his party kept urging him to run for president. Sherman found it necessary to make a statement that latter-day politicians—Hubert Humphrey, Ted Kennedy, Bill Bradley, and Mario Cuomo, to name just a few, would never make—"If nominated I will not run; if elected, I will not serve."

Senator Sherman had mixed feelings about the growing concentration of corporate power and its abuses. After all, he was a leader of the Republicans, the party of big business. He hoped his law would slow down the powerful trend toward monopolization of American industry, but the language of the law was left rather vague.

The key passage

The key passage stated that "every contract, combination in the form of trust or otherwise, in restraint of commerce among the several states, or with foreign nations, is hereby declared illegal." It went on to state that "Every person who shall monopolize, or conspire with any other person or persons to monopolize any part of the trade or commerce of the several states, or with foreign nations shall be guilty of a misdemeanor."

It was left to the courts, most specifically the Supreme Court, to interpret this language. Who were these men? They had been appointed by the Republican presidents who had served since the time of Lincoln, so they were conservative. And they were old. Generally, as people get older, their politics grow more conservative—and these men were conservative to start with.

Addyston Pipe case

The only case of significance to come before the Court during the first 20 years the law was on the books was the Addyston Pipe and Steel Case in 1899. Six cast-iron pipe producers in Ohio and Pennsylvania had set up a bidding ring. Each of the six would take turns making the low bid. This was blatant price fixing and was found a clear violation of the Sherman Act. In a revealing footnote to the case, the six firms found a legal solution to their problem: they merged.

The Standard Oil and American Tobacco cases

Finally, after years of preparation by the Roosevelt and Taft administrations, suits were brought against two of the biggest trusts of the day, the Standard Oil and American Tobacco trusts. Standard Oil was broken into five main companies known today as Exxon, Mobil, Sohio (Standard Oil of Ohio), Amoco, and Chevron, as well as several smaller companies (see the next box). The American Tobacco Company was broken up into three companies: the American Tobacco Company, Liggett & Myers, and P. Lorillard.

Were these trusts broken up because they were big? No! Bigness per se did not offend the Court. The trusts were broken up because they had behaved badly.

What did the Standard Oil trust in particular do that was bad? It forced the railroads, which were then the basic means of shipping oil, to give it rebates or discounts not just on the oil it shipped, but also on the oil shipped by its competitors. Basically it was using its tremendous market power to force its rivals out of business.

The problem with the Supreme Court's interpretation of Sherman was that it did not prohibit monopoly per se, but only certain illegal tactics that had been practiced by Standard Oil and American Tobacco. It was clear that the Court was even more conservative than other Republican branches of government. Still, the breakup of these companies was a very radical measure that indicated how serious the problem of monopolization had become to the rest of the business establishment. In a sense then, their breakup was deemed necessary to preserve the status quo.

The rule of reason

From this decision the Supreme Court formulated its "rule of reason," which set the tone of antitrust enforcement for the next two decades. Bigness itself was no offense as long as that bigness was not used against rival firms.

The rule of reason was applied in the U.S. Steel case of 1920 when the Wilson administration sought the same legal remedy against the steel trust that had been applied nine years earlier against the oil and tobacco trusts.

Mere size is no offense

The Court concluded that the U.S. Steel Corporation, which produced over half the nation's steel, did not violate the Sherman Act just because it was big. "The law does not make mere size an offense," said the Court, provided that the company does not use its power against its competition. And the very existence of competitors disproves the contention that U.S. Steel misused its power.

The Clayton Act

For the first time since before the Civil War, the Democrats were finally in the catbird seat, with Woodrow Wilson occupying the White House and a Democratic majority in both houses of Congress. In 1914, they passed two laws aimed at bolstering the Sherman Act by specifically outlawing all the bad business practices that continued to go unpunished.

The Clayton Act prohibited practices that lessened competition or tended to create a monopoly.

The Clayton Act prohibited five business practices when their effect was to "substantially lessen competition or tended to create a monopoly."

1. Price Discrimination   We took this up in Chapter 22, using airlines charging half-fare to teenagers, doctors charging widely varying rates based on patients' income, and grades A, B, and C, set up by A&P. Generally price discrimination has not been held illegal by the courts.

2. Interlocking Stockholding   This occurs when one firm buys the stock of another. Although it goes on every day, on occasion the courts will find it illegal. In the 1950s, Du Pont, together with Christiana Securities, both controlled by the Du Pont family, were forced to sell the huge bloc of General Motors stock they had accumulated.[3] The question is whether a stock acquisition is deemed to lessen competition.

The Breakup of Standard Oil

In 1911, the Supreme Court ordered the breakup of the Standard Oil Company for violating the Sherman Act. The five largest pieces were Standard Oil of New York, New Jersey, Ohio, Indiana, and California.

Standard Oil of New York evolved into Standard Oil Company of New York into SOCONY-Mobil-Vacuum and, finally, into Mobil Oil, the nation's second largest oil company today.

Standard Oil of New Jersey became ESSO, and about 15 years ago, it became Exxon, which is the largest oil company in the world.

Standard Oil of Ohio (Sohio), Standard Oil of Indiana (Amoco), and Standard Oil of California (Chevron) are still known by their original names.

Additional derivative firms include Continental Oil, recently acquired by Du Pont, Marathon Oil, which was merged with U.S. Steel, and Atlantic Richfield.

The Rockefeller family and Chase Manhattan Bank, while holding large blocs of stock in each of these companies, own too little to exercise control.

---

[3] Du Pont bought about 25 percent of General Motors' stock in 1919. Over the next four decades, GM bought most of its seat-cover fabrics, paints, and glues from Du Pont. In 1957, the Supreme Court found that other firms had been unfairly excluded from selling paint, glues, and fabrics to GM and forced Du Pont to sell its GM stock.

3. Interlocking Directorates   It is expressly forbidden for a person who is a director of one corporation to sit on the board of another corporation that is in the same industry. This would plainly be a conflict of interest, and could easily be detected since corporate boards are widely published. (To some degree, indirect interlocks sidestep this prohibition. See the box in Chapter 23 titled "The Old Boy Network at Six Big Banks.")

4. Tying Contracts   It is illegal to sell one product on condition that another product or products be purchased from the same seller. For example, the law prohibits General Electric from telling a buyer it can purchase GE toasters only if it also purchases GE light bulbs.

5. Exclusive Dealings   It is illegal to say to a retailer that he or she must not carry some rival firm's product line. For example, RCA cannot tell an appliance dealer that if he wants to carry RCA televisions and video recorders he can't also carry SONY and Sharp competing products.

The Clayton Act also expressly exempted labor unions from prosecution under the Sherman Act. This was very significant because, until the 1911 oil and tobacco cases, the prime target of the Sherman Act had been the Hatters Union in Danbury, Connecticut back in 1908. The union was construed by the Court to be a monopoly in restraint of trade and was fined the huge sum of $210,000 (the equivalent of over $3 million in today's dollars).

The Federal Trade Commission Act (1914)

FTC as a watchdog

The Federal Trade Commission (FTC) was set up as a watchdog of the anticompetitive practices outlawed by the Sherman and Clayton Acts. Although empowered to investigate anticompetitive business practices and issue cease-and-desist orders, most of its powers were stripped by the courts by the 1920s. In 1938, the Wheeler-Lea Amendment gave the Federal Trade Commission what has become its most important job—preventing false and deceptive advertising.

Modern Antitrust

Partial Breakdown of the Rule of Reason

Keep in mind that the Supreme Court continued to be dominated, right into the 1940s, by a conservative majority that had been appointed by the almost unbroken string of Republican presidents who served from the Civil War to the Great Depression. To ensure that the Sherman Act was not applied too vigorously, they developed the "rule of reason" doctrine. First applied in the 1911 Standard Oil case, and refined in the 1920 U.S. Steel case, the rule prevailed until the ALCOA case of 1945. Until then, you had to be big *and* bad before the Court would find you guilty under Sherman.

The ALCOA case

The membership of the Supreme Court changed radically during the Roosevelt and Truman administrations, which extended for 20 years. In a landmark 1945 decision, the Court found that the Aluminum Company of America (ALCOA), which held 90 percent of the aluminum market, was an illegal monopoly.

The two arguments that ALCOA presented in its defense were rejected. The first, based directly on the rule of reason, was that although it did have a nominal monopoly on aluminum production, it had not intended to exclude competitors and had not in fact behaved badly. This argument was rejected by the Court, which noted that the absence of competitors was itself proof of monopolizing.

A second argument advanced by ALCOA was to define the relevant market more broadly than just aluminum. Steel, copper, and even recycled aluminum should be included as well, which would reduce ALCOA's market share from 90 percent to about one third. This argument too was rejected by the Court.

Rule of reason eclipsed

This decision appeared to sweep away the last vestiges of the rule of reason, making monopoly per se and not merely monopolization, illegal. This change was underscored by the fact that ALCOA had been big, but hadn't been bad.

The ALCOA case represented the high watermark of antitrust enforcement. Eight years later, in the Du Pont case, the defendant was able to use the relevant market argument that ALCOA had unsuccessfully raised. Du Pont and a licensee had 100 percent of the nation's cellophane market (and 75 percent of the market for transparent wrapping material). But the Court accepted the argument that the relevant market included all "flexible packaging materials," such as aluminum foil and waxed paper, as well as cellophane. Since Du Pont had only 18 percent of the flexible packaging materials market, this would hardly constitute a monopoly.

The 60 Percent Rule

A firm must be big *and* bad

What has apparently evolved from these antitrust decisions is what might be called "the 60 percent rule." Should a firm have a share of at least 60 percent of the relevant market *and* should that firm have behaved badly toward its competitors, it would then be subject to prosecution. However, whether it would be prosecuted would depend on the political and economic outlook of the current administration, and whether it would be found guilty would depend on the outlook of the nine Supreme Court justices.

The Celler-Kefauver Antimerger Act

Soon after World War II, the pace of the merger movement picked up again after a 15-year slowdown caused by the Great Depression and the war. In fact, during the decade following the war, some 2,000 mergers involving large corporations took place. The Celler-Kefauver Act in 1950 was an attempt to slow that pace.

Bethlehem Steel-Youngstown Sheet and Tube case

The act forbade the merger with, or the acquisition of, other companies where the effect "may be substantially to lessen competition, or tend to create a monopoly." Its first test came in the 1958 Bethlehem Steel-Youngstown Sheet and Tube case. The Court agreed with the Justice Department that a merger between the number 2 and the number 6 steel producers would violate the Celler-Kefauver Act. Even mergers that threatened to reduce *potential* competition were prohibited by the courts in subsequent cases. But all the act really seemed to do was slow down the flood tide of mergers that continued right through the 1960s.

The problem that succeeding Justice Departments had to deal with was the *type* of merger that was now taking place—the conglomerate merger. The laws on the books—the Sherman, Clayton, and Celler-Kefauver Acts— were certainly adequate to deal with mergers that lessened actual or potential competition. But none addressed itself to mergers that do not directly threaten competition in any given industry because they occur between firms in two or more different industries.

Three Recent Cases

The government has brought suit against three virtual monopolies: Xerox, AT&T, and IBM. The government won a clear-cut victory in the Xerox suit in 1975, attained a compromise in the AT&T suit in 1982, and unceremoniously aborted the IBM suit in the same year.

Xerox

This case hinged on whether the relevant market was (as Xerox maintained) *all* paper copiers, which would have given the company less than a 50 percent market share by 1973, or just plain paper copiers (as the government maintained), which would have given Xerox close to 100 percent of the market. What's the difference between a plain paper copier and other copiers? Believe me, you would know. "Other" copiers (which are now obsolete) used coated paper that gave off a chemical smell and was rather disgusting to touch.

Xerox, which held the patents on its paper copiers, agreed to license these patents to its competitors. By this time, Japanese competitors were also entering the American market so that Xerox's market share of the plain paper market fell below 50 percent.

AT&T

AT&T was accused of having a monopoly on local phone service (which it could hardly contest) and of making it hard for its long distance competitors (like MCI and Sprint) to use its local phone network. In exchange for giving up its 22 local phone companies, AT&T was not only allowed to keep its long distance service, Bell Labs, and Western Electric, but it was allowed to enter the telecommunications-computer field.

IBM

Originally initiated in 1969, this suit continued for 13 years until the Reagan Justice Department decided to drop it. In 1969, IBM had about 70 percent of the mainframe computer market, which it still held in 1982. But the word processor and minicomputer markets had become very important segments of the overall computer market during this period. Thus, the Justice Department reasoned that the changing computer market had made IBM's continued dominance in mainframes much less relevant.

In the next section we take up three types of mergers—horizontal, vertical, conglomerate—and a fourth type that has become very important in recent years, a sort of diversifying merger.

Types of Mergers

(1) Horizontal Mergers

Conventional mergers

This is the conventional merger. Two firms in the same industry will form one larger company. Usually a larger firm swallows a smaller one. When John D. Rockefeller was running Standard Oil, he swallowed 39 competing firms.

Horizontal integration has become particularly prevalent among the airlines. In recent years, Eastern Airlines has merged with Caribbean-Atlantic, Mohawk with Allegheny, and PanAm with National. There are indications that the oil industry too may be facing a period of horizontal mergers beginning with Occidental petroleum's 1982 takeover of Cities Service.

The legal problem with horizontal mergers is that they appear to violate the Sherman Act. Two competing firms that merge may well lessen competition. The question then is where do the Justice Department and the courts draw the line? If the number 12 firm merges with the number 16 firm, does this lessen competition? The answer depends on the makeup of the administration and the courts at that time, which varies widely from the relatively restrictive Roosevelt administration to the relatively permissive Reagan administration, as well as with the widely varying personnel shifts in the courts.

(2) Vertical Mergers

When firms that have been engaged in different parts of an industrial process or in manufacturing and selling join together, we have a vertical merger. If a TV and stereo maker bought out a retail chain and marketed its TVs and stereos through this new outlet, that would be an example. If an auto company merged with a steel mill, a tire company, or a glass manufacturer, we would have a vertically integrated company.

(3) Conglomerate Mergers

Two companies in unrelated fields

A conglomerate merger occurs between two companies in unrelated industries—telephones and hotels, real estate and auto parts, oil and steel. A conglomerate, the product of such mergers, is a group of unrelated companies under one corporate umbrella.

There was a huge wave of conglomerate mergers in the 1960s, which was the cutting edge of the long-term trend toward corporate concentration. During that decade, about 80 percent of the mergers were of the conglomerate variety. In recent years that figure has fallen to about 50 percent. Firms that were miniscule in the 1950s became corporate giants over the course of 10 or 15 years. In fact, by the late 1950s, conglomeration was not only a short cut to rapid corporate growth, but it was virtually the only available opportunity left for such growth.

The spectacular growth of the larger conglomerates was summarized by Anthony Sampson.

> James Ling of Ling-Temco-Vought built up an obscure defense contractor in 1960 into the fourteenth biggest American industrial company in 1969, including a meat-packing business, an airline, a car-rental firm, and a big manufacturer of jet planes. Charles Bluhdorn . . . set up Gulf & Western in 1956, when it was making car bumpers in Grand Rapids, and then bought up 92 companies, making anything from zinc and sugar to cigars and Paramount films. Thornton bought up a small electronics firm, Litton Industries, for a million dollars and added 103 companies in nine years, with products from ships and calculating machines to textbooks and seismic equipment.[4]

How did they do it? Gulf & Western happened to have a friend at Chase Manhattan, which financed many of its acquisitions. Chase then got the accounts of the acquired firms, and often the cash of these firms was used to make still further acquisitions.

ITT also had a case unto itself that was settled in 1972 when it agreed to sell off some of its component firms.

ITT is really a case unto itself. We tend to think of the firm as just a telephone company, but some of the firms associated with it at one time or another have some very familiar names—Avis, Inc., Sheraton hotels, Hartford Insurance, Levitt Houses (builders of Levittowns in Pennsylvania and on Long Island), and Wonder bread. As the biggest conglomerate, it is an almost self-sufficient company. Its executives at one time could have attended conventions in Sheraton hotels in many different cities, all of which may have been insured by Hartford. They could have used Avis cars and eaten sandwiches dispensed by Canteen machines and made with Wonder bread (also ITT firms).

There are several advantages to conglomerating. In addition to providing ready-made markets for the goods and services produced by various divisions, the very diversity of the company is insurance against economic adversity. A downturn in one industry will not hurt too much because the firm is diversified into many industries. A strike in one component firm or division will shut down only a small part of the entire conglomerate be-

---

[4] Anthony Sampson, *The Sovereign State of ITT* (New York: Fawcett Crest, 1974), p. 152.

cause virtually all unions are organized along industry or craft lines. For example, if the Screen Actors Guild (Ronald Reagan was its first president) went out on strike, Gulf & Western would hardly notice.

There are also tax advantages to conglomerating. If you happen to purchase a firm that lost money, those losses can be subtracted from your profits before you pay taxes. For example, if the conglomerate made $100 million, it would have to pay about $34 million in taxes. But if it picks up a firm that lost, say, $50 million, its income is now $50 million and it would have to pay only about $17 million in corporate income tax.

Most important is the power derived from forming a big company. Roy Ash of Hewlett-Packard became President Nixon's director of Management and Budget. G. William Miller went from the presidency of Textron to Federal Reserve chairman and then secretary of the Treasury under President Carter. Within the corporate world itself, it's much more fun and it's much more ego gratifying to see your company grow from a nothing into a major force in just a few years.

(4)   Recent Mergers

The most recent wave of mergers could hardly qualify as conglomerate mergers. Some of the big ones—Du Pont-Continental Oil and U.S. Steel-Marathon Oil—matched companies in different industries but created relatively diversified companies rather than conglomerates. The ITT's, LTVs, and Gulf & Westerns are relatively unfocused companies whereas the most recent mergers have tended to match companies representing just two industries.

Another distinction has been that the more recent mergers have sometimes been exceedingly big. When ITT took over Hartford Insurance, a $400 million company, there was a tremendous hue and cry. Just a little over a decade later, Du Pont spent $6.8 billion for Continental Oil, and then U.S. Steel parted with some $6.2 billion for Marathon Oil. The Justice Department barely seemed to notice. And when Occidental swallowed Cities Service for $4.2 billion, the Federal Trade Commission registered a mild objection while the Justice Department looked the other way.

These were three of the largest mergers in history.[5] Every other day another merger seems to be announced, but those for less than $1 billion rarely make the first page of the *New York Times* financial section—unless it's a slow day. In the last section of this chapter, we'll have a closer look at the most recent corporate mergers.

How Effective Is Antitrust?

What is it we want antitrust to do? If we want something approximating perfect competition, antitrust has failed miserably. If we would like to prevent further oligopolization of American industry, it has been a qualified success. *How* qualified?

As Al Smith, the governor of New York over 60 years ago, used to say, "Let's look at the record." Since the Sherman Act (1890) and the Clayton Act (1914), we have seen industrial concentration become still greater. When firms in the Fortune 100 merge—Du Pont and Continental Oil, U.S. Steel and Marathon Oil, Occidental and Cities Service—this increases the degree of concentration. Were these mergers to continue at that pace, by the

---

[5] A few acquisitions listed in Table 24-1 set new historical records.

early part of the next century we'd have just a handful of companies doing most of the nation's business.

On the other hand, things could have been a lot worse. Without antitrust, there would have been no legal means with which the government could curb even those mergers that most blatantly stifled competition. Furthermore, many firms hesitate to merge because they are fairly certain that the Justice Department *would* take legal action.

Few of the recent mergers have involved leading firms in any industry. Texaco and Getty Oil came about the closest. Presumably, even the rather permissive Reagan Justice Department would have stepped in to block the merger of, say, General Motors (number 1) and Ford (number 2).

If we were to judge the antitrust record not just on the basis of what has happened, but also on what has not happened, it wouldn't look all that bad. Should it have been better? Some critics point out that antitrust really freezes the status quo. Small firms are sometimes prevented from merging while larger firms are left alone. To allow more competition, the number 9 and 10 firms should be able to merge and the number 1 and 2 firms should not.

This criticism is not completely valid, at least in recent years, because small firms *do* merge. And so do not so small firms.

Other critics argue that antitrust policy is a misguided numbers game. By worrying only about the number of competitors in an industry or the degree of concentration, the Justice Department ignores the role of dynamic competition. The innovator may attain a temporary monopoly—Kleenex, Xerox, IBM—but other entrepreneurs will quickly imitate this product or process if it is successful.

Again, this view has a certain validity; no one would want the government to stifle industrial creativity. However, the whole focus of antitrust policy has been on mergers and not on firms that generate their own growth. Still, the point is well taken that antitrust cannot play it solely by the numbers.

Things could have been a lot worse without antitrust.

Is antitrust a misguided numbers game?

The Trend toward Bigness

One of the refreshing things about economists is that we can all look at exactly the same data and come to widely varying conclusions. My own bias, if it has somehow escaped you, is that American business is steadily becoming more and more concentrated.

Take manufacturing. In 1929, after a decade of considerable consolidation (General Motors alone gobbled up over 100 independent car makers), the 200 largest firms produced less than 40 percent of our manufactured goods. Today they produce over 60 percent.[6]

If you'd care to glance back at Table 23-1 (near the beginning of the last chapter), you'd see still more evidence of corporate concentration. But I've saved my best shot for last—Table 24-1.

Here we have the $2 billion and over mergers that have taken place since 1980. The two largest to date took place in 1984—Chevron with Gulf and Texaco with Getty (if the litigation with Pennzoil is ever settled). These two oil mergers are even larger than the previous three largest mergers in history—Du Pont with Conoco (Continental Oil Company) (1981), U.S.

---

[6] For a study that reaches the opposite conclusions, see William G. Shepherd, "The Causes of Increased Competition in the U.S. Economy, 1939–1980," *Review of Economics and Statistics* (November 1982).

Table 24–1
Two Billion Dollar Mergers,
1980–1986

Acquiring Company	Acquired/Merged Company	Value in $ Millions
1980		
Kraft Inc.	Dart Inc.	$ 2,500
Sun Company	Texas Pacific Oil Co.	2,300
Saudi Arabia	Arabian American Oil Co.	2,000
1981		
Du Pont	Conoco	6,820
Societe Nationale	Texasgulf Inc.	2,742
Elf Aquitaine Seagram & Co.	Du Pont (20 percent)	2,552
Freeport Minerals	McMoran Oil and Gas	2,540
Kuwait Petroleum	Santa Fe International	2,500
Fluor Corp.	St. Joe Minerals	2,340
1982		
U.S. Steel Corp.	Marathon Oil Co.	6,150
Connecticut General	INA Corp.	4,300
Occidental Petroleum	Cities Service	4,202
Norfolk & Western Railway	Southern Railway	2,900
1983		
Santa Fe Industries	Southern Pacific Co.	2,300
1984		
Standard Oil of California (Chevron)	Gulf Corp.	13,300
Texaco	Getty Oil Co.	10,125
Mobil Oil	Superior Oil	5,700
Kiewit-Murdock Investment Corp.	Continental Group	2,750
Beatrice Cos. Inc.	Esmark Inc.	2,710
General Motors	Electronic Data Systems	2,601
Broken Hill Proprietory Co.	Utah International	2,400
1985		
Royal Dutch Shell	Shell Oil Co. (remaining 30.5 percent)	5,670
Philip Morris Cos.	General Foods Corp.	5,628
General Motors	Hughes Aircraft Co.	5,025
R. J. Reynolds Inc.	Nabisco Brands Inc.	4,905
Allied Corp.	Signal Cos. Inc.	4,851
Baxter Travenol Laboratories	American Hospital Supply Corp.	3,703
Nestle SA	Carnation Co.	2,894
Monsanto Co.	G. D. Searle & Co.	2,717
Coastal Corp.	American Natural Resources	2,454
InterNorth Inc.	Houston Natural Gas Corp.	2,260
1986		
Kohlberg, Kravis, Roberts & Co.	Beatrice Cos. Inc.	6,250
General Electric	RCA Corp.	6,142
Kohlberg, Kravis, Roberts & Co.	Safeway Stores Inc.	5,336
Burroughs Corp.	Sperry Corp.	4,432
Campeau Corp.	Allied Stores Corp.	3,608
Capital Cities Communications Inc.	American Broadcasting Co.	3,530
Macy Acquiring Corp.	R. H. Macy & Co.	3,501
U.S. Steel Corp.	Texas Oil & Gas Co.	2,997
Occidental Petroleum	MidCon Corp.	2,686
May Department Stores Co.	Associated Dry Goods Corp.	2,386
1987		
British Petroleum	Standard Oil (remaining 45 percent)	7,565
AV Holdings Corp.	Borg-Warner (90 percent)	4,359
Thompson Co.	Southland Corp.	4,004
Kohlberg, Kravis, Roberts & Co.	Owens-Illinois	3,688
National Amusements	Viacom International	3,299
Unilever NV	Chesebrough-Ponds	3,095
Hoechst AG	Celanese Corp.	2,724
Burlington Holdings	Burlington Industries	2,156
Health Trust Inc.—The Hospital Co.	Hospital Corp. of America	2,100

Source: *Mergers and Aquisitions*, various issues, 1980–1988.

Steel with Marathon Oil (1982), and Occidental Petroleum with Cities Service (1982), each also involving oil companies.[7]

You might notice also that before 1984 there were just four acquisitions of over $4 billion. Then there were three in 1984, five in 1985, four in 1986, and three in 1987. Is this a portent of things to come?

Even if the government were to begin to move against future mergers, it would be years until these cases were actually settled. It would probably be safe to say that the latest wave of mergers, which began in the 1950s, will continue unabated until at least the beginning of the 21st century.

---

[7] The third largest merger in history took place in 1987 when British Petroleum purchased the remaining 45 percent of Standard Oil. The trend toward concentration in this industry has become very clear during the decade of the 1980s.

Workbook for Chapter 24

Name _____

Date _____

Multiple-Choice Questions

Circle the letter that corresponds to the best answer.

1. Which statement is true?
a. Since the Civil War we have a steady expansion of corporate concentration.   **b.** Since the Civil War corporate concentration has become much less pronounced.   **c.** Corporate concentration has remained about the same since the Civil War.   **d.** None of these statements is true.

2. The first "trustbusters" were Presidents
a. Teddy Roosevelt and William Howard Taft
b. Franklin Roosevelt and Harry Truman
c. Dwight D. Eisenhower and John Kennedy
d. Jimmy Carter and Ronald Reagan

3. The first major setback to the consolidation and concentration of business occurred in
a. 1865   **b.** 1900   **c.** 1911   **d.** 1920

4. Which statement is true?
a. The federal government never intervened in our economy until the 1930s.   **b.** Federal government intervention in our economy has grown steadily since the time of the Civil War.   **c.** The federal government has intervened in our economy from time to time throughout our history.   **d.** None of these statements is true.

5. The first antitrust act passed was the _____ Act.
a. Clayton   **b.** FTC   **c.** Celler-Kefauver
d. Sherman

6. John D. Rockefeller was the leader of the _____ trust.
a. oil   **b.** whiskey   **c.** railroad   **d.** tobacco

7. A key passage of the _____ Act stated that "every contract, combination in the form of trust or otherwise, in restraint of commerce among the several states, or with foreign nations, is hereby declared illegal."
a. Clayton   **b.** FTC   **c.** Celler-Kefauver
d. Sherman

8. The trusts won only the _____ case.
a. Addyston Pipe   **b.** steel   **c.** tobacco   **d.** oil

9. In 1911, the Supreme Court decided to
a. allow the trusts to keep functioning as they had in the past   **b.** break up the trusts   **c.** let the trusts off with small fines   **d.** put the leaders of the trusts in jail

10. Until the ALCOA case the Supreme Court generally held that
a. bigness was all right as long as the company wasn't bad   **b.** bigness was all right under any circumstances   **c.** a company could do as it pleased as long as it wasn't big

11. The Supreme Court's "rule of reason" was applied
a. from the time of the Civil War   **b.** from 1911 to 1945   **c.** after 1945   **d.** after 1970

12. The high watermark of antitrust enforcement was marked by the _____ case.
a. ALCOA   **b.** U.S. Steel   **c.** Addyston Pipe
d. IBM

13. The Clayton Act prohibited each of the following except
a. price discrimination   **b.** interlocking stockholding   **c.** interlocking directorates   **d.** trusts

14. The most important job of the Federal Trade Commission today is to
a. prevent false and deceptive advertising   **b.** break up unlawful trusts   **c.** issue cease-and-desist orders when anticompetitive business practices occur
d. promote commerce with foreign nations

15. The rule of reason today is
a. outlawed **b.** partially in force **c.** completely irrelevant

16. Antitrust today could best be summed up by the
a. 90 percent rule **b.** 60 percent rule **c.** rule of reason **d.** one-year rule

17. Labor unions became exempt from antitrust enforcement under the _____ Act.
a. Sherman **b.** Clayton **c.** FTC **d.** Celler-Kefauver

18. The Celler-Kefauver Act was aimed at mergers that
a. may substantially lessen competition or tend to create a monopoly **b.** result in the formation of conglomerates **c.** result in diversifying the products and services produced by a corporation **d.** may help competition but reduce the number of firms in the industry

19. In the 1950s and 1960s the predominant form of merger was the _____ merger.
a. horizontal **b.** vertical **c.** conglomerate **d.** diversifying

20. In recent years the government decided to drop the _____ case.
a. U.S. Steel **b.** AT&T **c.** Xerox **d.** IBM

21. When two firms in the same industry form one larger company this is a _____ merger.
a. horizontal **b.** vertical **c.** conglomerate **d.** diversifying

22. ITT, Ling-Temco-Vought, Textron, and Gulf & Western are all the products of _____ mergers.
a. horizontal **b.** vertical **c.** conglomerate **d.** diversifying

23. Since 1929 the percent of our manufactured output produced by the 200 largest industrial firms has
a. decreased **b.** stayed about the same **c.** increased substantially **d.** doubled

24. Over the last six or eight years, the size of companies acquired in mergers is
a. getting smaller **b.** staying about the same **c.** getting larger

25. Which prediction would seem the most reasonable?
a. The merger movement of the last four decades is definitely over. **b.** The merger movement of the last four decades will probably continue for at least another 10 years. **c.** The merger movement of the last four decades will probably slow down over the next few years. **d.** The merger movement of the last four decades will probably accelerate over the next 10 years.

Fill-In Questions

1. The first "trustbuster" presidents were

_____ and _____.

2. In 1911, the Supreme Court broke up the

_____ and the _____.

3. Most of the federal economic policies of the 19th century were _____ toward big business.

4. In the late 19th century trusts were formed. They were _____; the largest trust was the _____ trust.

5. "Every person who shall monopolize, or conspire with any other person or persons to monopolize any part of the trade or commerce of the several states, or with foreign nations shall be guilty of a misdemeanor," was a key passage of the _____ Act.

6. The first case to be tried under the Sherman Act was the _____ case; the companies were found _____ of _____.

7. In 1911, the Supreme Court broke up the

_____ trust into three component parts:
(1) _____, (2) _____, and
(3) _____.

8. The reason the Supreme Court broke up the trusts in 1911 was because they _____.

9. Bigness was no offense was the underpinning of the _____.

10. A _____ makes the sale of one product only on condition that another product or products be purchased from the same seller: _____ stipulate that a retailer must not carry some rival firm's product line.

11. Expressly forbidding a person who is a director of one corporation to sit on the board of another corporation that is in the same industry is a provision of the _____ Act.

12. The Clayton Act exempted _____ from prosecution under the Sherman Act.

13. ALCOA, which produced about _____ percent of the country's aluminum, maintained in its 1945 case that while it was big, it was not _____ . The Supreme Court found that _____ .

14. _____ used the relevant market argument successfully in its case, just eight years after the ALCOA case.

15. The 60 percent rule states that _____
_____ .

16. The Celler-Kefauver Act forbids the merger with, or the acquisition of, other companies where the effect may be _____
_____ .

17. By the 1950s and 1960s the most prevalent type of merger was the _____ merger.

18. In its case, AT&T was forced to give up its
_____ .

19. The government's reason for dropping the IBM case was that _____ .

20. A vertical merger takes place when two firms that _____ join together, whereas a horizontal merger takes place when two firms that _____ join together.

21. Had there been no antitrust, there probably would have been _____ .

22. The largest mergers have been in the _____ industry.

23. In 1929, the largest 200 firms produced about _____ percent of our manufactured goods; today they produce _____ percent.

24. During the last three years we have averaged _____ mergers or acquisitions per year of over $4 billion.

The Four Types of Competition: A Review

This chapter will summarize some of the high points of Chapters 20–24, especially the graphs. No new material will be introduced. In fact, virtually all the graphs are taken from the earlier chapters.

Chapter Objectives
This chapter provides:
- Perfect competition.
- Monopoly.
- Monopolistic Competition.
- Oligopoly.

Perfect Competition

Definition of perfect competition

A perfectly competitive industry has many firms selling an identical product. How many is many? So many that no one firm can influence price. What is identical? A product that is identical in the minds of buyers so that they have no reason to prefer one seller to another.

The short run

Figure 25-1 shows the perfect competitor in the short run making a loss. Figure 25-2 shows the perfect competitor making a profit in the short run. Neither of these possibilities exists in the long run when the perfect competitor makes zero economic profit.

In the long run, if the firm had been losing money, it may well have left the industry. Enough firms would have left to reduce market supply and raise price high enough to eliminate the economic losses of the firms that remained in the industry. Thus in the long run, the perfect competitor will make zero economic profit.

The long-run

In the long run, if the firm had been making a profit, additional firms would have been attracted to the industry, raising industry supply and reducing market price. Thus, in the long run, profit is reduced to zero. The long-run situation of the perfect competitor is shown in Figure 25-3.

In the long run, the perfect competitor's price is equal to the low point on the firm's ATC curve. Since the firm produces at that output, it operates at peak efficiency. That is, it operates at the minimum point of its ATC curve, which means that it produces at the lowest possible cost.

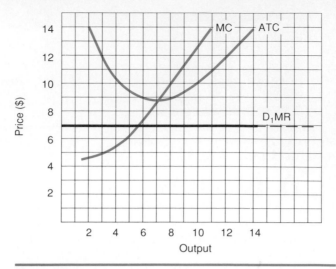

Figure 25–1

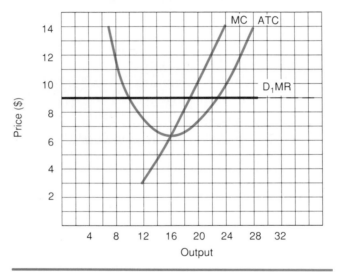

Figure 25–2

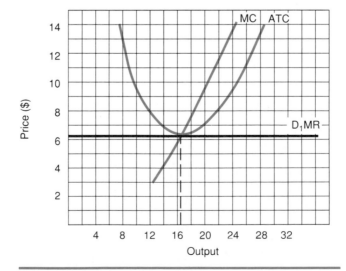

Figure 25–3

Monopoly

Definition of monopoly

A monopoly is a firm that produces all the output in an industry. There's nobody else selling anything like what the monopolist is producing. In other words, there are no close substitutes.

No distinction between short and long run

There is no distinction between the short and long run under monopoly because the monopolist is the only firm in the industry. No firms enter or leave as with perfect competition. The market demand curve *is* the monopolist's demand curve.

Figure 25–4 shows the monoplist's market situation. The firm has a higher price than the perfect competitor because it is higher than the minimum point of the firm's ATC curve. Similarly, output is restricted because the monopolist produces at some point to the left of that minimum ATC point. Finally, the monopolist makes an economic profit in the long run since price (read from the demand curve) is higher than ATC.

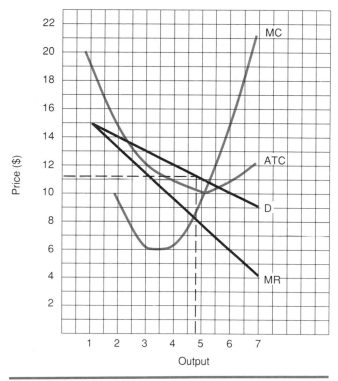

Figure 25–4

Monopolistic Competition

Definition of monopolistic competition

A monopolistically competitive industry has many firms selling a differentiated product. How many is many? So many that no one firm has any influence over price.

If the buyer doesn't differentiate among the various products sold, the product is identical. If a buyer does differentiate, the product is differentiated. Who determines whether the product is differentiated or identical? The buyer.

The short run

Like the perfect competitor, the monopolistic competitor can make a profit or take a loss in the short run, but in the long run, the firm will break even. The reason the monopolistic competitor makes zero economic profits in the long run is the same as that under perfect competition.

In the long run, if firms are losing money many will leave the industry, lowering industry supply and raising market price. If, in the long run, firms are realizing substantial profits, new firms will be attracted to the industry, raising supply and lowering market price.

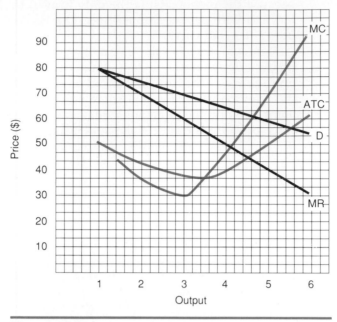

Figure 25–5

The monopolistic competitor is shown making a short-run profit in Figure 25–5 and taking a short-run loss in Figure 25–6. Finally, Figure 25–7 shows the long-run situation of the monopolitic competitor when economic profit is zero.

Under monopolistic competition, the firm's price is higher than the mini-

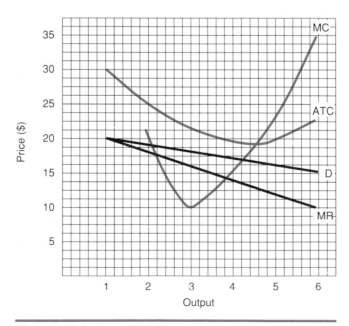

Figure 25–6

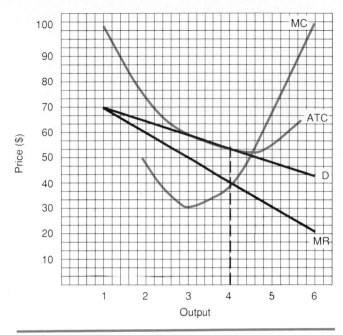

Figure 25–7

mum point of its ATC curve and output is restricted to a point to the left of the minimum ATC. The firm does not produce at peak efficiency because ATC is not at its minimum, and again, there are zero economic profits.

Oligopoly

Definition of oligopoly

An oligopoly is an industry with just a few sellers. How few? So few that at least one firm is large enough to influence price.

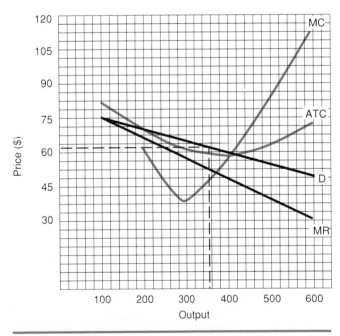

Figure 25–8
The Colluding Oligopolist

In Figure 25-8 we have the noncompeting oligopolist and in Figure 25-9, the competing oligopolist. Both charge prices that are higher than the minimum point of their ATC curves, both restrict output to a point to the left of the minimum ATC, neither operates at peak efficiency, and both make an economic profit.

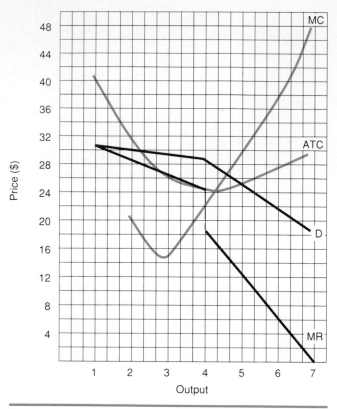

Figure 25-9

Summary Tables

Let's summarize what we've covered here with respect to number of sellers, type of product, price, output, profit, and efficiency. This is done in Tables 25-1, 25-2, and 25-3.

Table 25-1
The Four Types of Competition:
Number of Sellers and Type of
Product

Type of Competition	Number of Sellers	Type of Product
Perfect competition	Many	Identical
Monopoly	One	—
Monopolistic competition	Many	Differentiated
Oligopoly	Few	Either identical or differentiated

Table 25–2
The Four Types of Competition:
Price and Output

Type of Competition	Price	Output
Perfect competition	At minimum ATC	At minimum point of ATC
Monopoly	Higher than minimum ATC	Restricted (to left of minimum ATC)
Monopolistic competitor	Higher than minimum ATC	Restricted (to left of minimum ATC)
Oligopolist	Higher than minimum ATC	Restricted (to left of minimum ATC)

Table 25–3
The Four Types of Competition:
Profit and Efficiency

Type of Competition	Profit	Efficiency
Perfect competition	Zero economic profit	Peak efficiency
Monopoly	Makes an economic profit	Less than peak efficiency
Monopolistic competition	Zero economic profit	Less than peak efficiency
Oligopolist	Makes an economic profit	Less than peak efficiency

Multiple-Choice Questions

Write in the letter that corresponds to the best answer, using choice **a**, **b**, **c**, or **d**.

a. perfect competiton   **b.** monopoly   **c.** monopolistic competition   **d.** oligopoly

1. A firm in an industry with many sellers selling a differentiated product would be a(n) _____ .

2. A firm that faces the entire demand curve of an industry would be a(n) _____ .

3. In the long run only a(n) _____ operates at the minimum point of its ATC curve.

4. The crucial factor in _____ is the low number of sellers.

5. The crucial factor in _____ is product differentiation.

6. Under _____ and _____ there are no profits in the long run.

7. A firm with many sellers and an identical product is a(n) _____ .

8. The kinked demand curve takes place under competitive _____ .

Fill-In Questions

1. How many firms is many? So many that _____

_____ .

2. A product is identical in the _____ .

3. In the long run, if firms are losing money, _____

_____ . In the long run, if firms are

making a profit, _____ .

4. In the long run, the perfect competitor's price is

equal to the _____ on the firm's ATC

curve. Therefore, the firm is operating at _____ efficiency.

5. A monopolist's product has no _____ .

6. The monopolist's price is _____ than the perfect competitor's; in the long run the monopolist's

profit is _____ than the perfect competitor's.

7. A monopolistically competitive industry has

_____ firms selling a _____ product.

8. Product differentiation takes place in the _____

_____ .

9. In the long run, the monopolistic competitor's

price is _____ the minimum point on its ATC.

10. An oligopoly is in an industry with _____

_____ .

11. Only the _____ in the _____ produces at the minimum point of its ATC.

Problems

Use Figure 1 on the next page to do these problems.

1. Draw the graph of the demand, marginal revenue, marginal cost, and average total cost curves of the perfect competitor in the *(a)* short run making a profit; *(b)* short run taking a loss; *(c)* long run.

2. Draw the graph of the monopolist.

3. Draw the graph of the monopolistic competitor in the *(a)* short run making a profit; *(b)* short run taking a loss; *(c)* long run.

4. Draw the graph of the *(a)* colluding oligopolist; *(b)* competitive oligopolist.

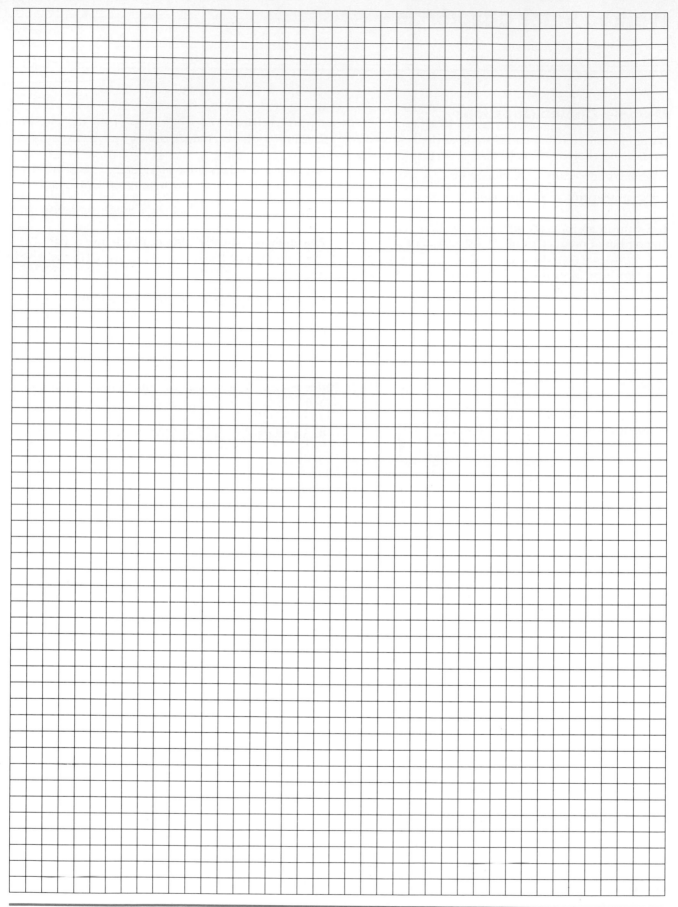

Figure 1

Demand in the Factor Market

In Chapter 2, we talked about the factors of production, or resources. In this chapter, we'll have a lot to say about how their prices are determined.

Right now we'll look at demand in the factor market. We'll develop the concept of marginal revenue product, on which demand is based. This will set up the next two chapters, when we'll deal specifically with the determination of wages, rent, interest, and profits.

The main thing we'll do in this chapter is use the concept of marginal revenue product to determine how many units of a factor will be hired by perfect and imperfect competitors. As we shall see, the law of demand and supply plays a central role.

Chapter Objectives

The main concepts we'll cover are:

- Derived demand.
- Productivity.
- Marginal revenue product.
- Changes in resource demand.
- The substitution and output effects.
- Optimum resource mix for the firm.

Derived Demand

In previous chapters we dealt with demand for goods and services. The demand for these goods and services is sometimes called final demand. Examples of final demand would be the demand for cars, TVs, haircuts, medical services, or gasoline.

What is derived demand derived from?

Now we'll look at derived demand, which is the demand for resources. There are four resources: land, labor, capital, and entrepreneurial ability. The demand for those resources is derived from the demand for the final products. For example, the demand for land on which to grow corn is derived from the demand for corn, and the demand for labor with which to produce cars is derived from the demand for cars.

A change in the demand for the final product brings about a change in derived demand. The Arab oil embargo and the quadrupling of oil prices in 1973 led to a decline in the demand for large cars. This caused massive layoffs in Detroit, so a decline in the demand for the final product, cars, led to a decline in the derived demand, auto workers. Simultaneous with the falling demand for American cars, the Russian wheat crop failed and the Soviet Union made massive purchases of American wheat. This, in turn, drove up the demand for farm labor and farmland in the United States.

Productivity

In addition to the demand for the final product, two other factors influence the demand for the productive resources (land, labor, capital, and entrepreneurial ability). First, we'll consider the productivity of the resource and then the relative prices of substitutable resources.

Productivity defined

Productivity is output per unit of input. We've introduced two new words. Productivity itself is really measured by what is produced. "I had a productive night," my friend confided over a plate of lo mein in an all-night Chinese restaurant after a party. "Productive?" I asked. "Sure," he said, "I got 16 phone numbers." That's productive! Especially since he's 84 years old.

What about units of input? Inputs measure the four resources—land, labor, capital, and entrepreneurial ability. Thus a unit of input might be an hour of labor, an acre of land, or an automobile assembly line.

Let's put these together. Productivity is output per unit of input. If John produces 8 microchips per hour and Sally produces 16, Sally is twice as productive as John. If 30 bushels of wheat are harvested from acre one and 10 bushels from acre two, acre one is three times as productive as acre two.

The more productive a resource is, the more it will be in demand. Obviously acre one is in much greater demand than acre two. This would be reflected in both their prices and their rents. Similarly, Sally can obtain much higher wages than John since she is so much more productive.

Prices of Substitute Resources

There are usually many different ways of producing a given good or service. We could use various combinations of resources. The Chinese, for example, don't have many capital goods available, so when they build a factory, they use a very labor-intensive method of construction. Thousands of workers will dig the hole for the foundation, carting off the dirt in wicker baskets. In America, where we have a great deal of capital equipment, we use a capital-intensive method of production. Bulldozers and other earth-moving equipment get the job done with much less labor.

Every country uses the cheapest production method.

In each country, the cheapest production method is used. China happens to be a labor-intensive country because capital is relatively expensive. In the United States, we use a capital-intensive method because labor is relatively expensive.

Figure it out. Do you type each individual resumé when you're looking for a job, or do you get a few hundred photocopied or offset for 5 cents a piece? If the wage rate were just 7 or 8 cents an hour—as it still is in some of the poorer countries of the world—you'd be typing your resumes.

When wages rise, many companies seek to substitute machinery for relatively expensive labor. By automating, they will be able to lower their costs of production. If land became more expensive, farmers would work each acre much more intensively, substituting labor and capital for relatively more expensive land.

Marginal Revenue Product

The demand for resources is derived mainly from the demand for the final product. Resource productivity and the relative prices of other resources that can be substituted also help determine price. Now we're ready to see how a firm decides how much of a resource to purchase.

How much of a resource is purchased depends on three things.

How much of a resource a firm will purchase depends on three things: (1) the price of that resource, (2) the productivity of that resource, and (3) the selling price of the final product that the resource helps to produce. We'll do a few numerical examples to help us find out how much land, labor, and capital will be purchased by a firm. Along the way, we'll introduce three new terms: *marginal physical product, marginal revenue product,* and *marginal revenue product schedule.* The last is the firm's demand schedule for a given resource.

In Table 26–1, we have an output schedule for a firm that is using up to 10 units of labor. What I'd like you to do is to fill in the third column, marginal physical product, remembering to do it in ink so we can sell a lot of new books. Just treat marginal physical product like marginal cost and marginal revenue. Marginal physical product is simply the additional output produced by one more unit of input (in this case, one more unit of labor).

Table 26–1
Hypothetical Output of Labor Hired by a Firm

Units of Labor	Output	Marginal Physical Product
1	15	
2	29	
3	41	
4	51	
5	58	
6	62	
7	63	
8	63	
9	62	
10	60	

Hopefully your marginal physical product schedule checks out with mine in Table 26–2. Notice that the marginal physical product was zero with the 8th worker and negative with the 9th and 10th workers. The 8th worker added nothing to output while the 9th and 10th actually were in the way. No business firm would hire more than seven workers under these circumstances, even if the wage rate were a penny an hour.

Table 26–2
Hypothetical Output of Labor Hired by a Firm

Units of Labor	Output	Marginal Physical Product
1	15	15
2	29	14
3	41	12
4	51	10
5	58	7
6	62	4
7	63	1
8	63	0
9	62	−1
10	60	−2

In Table 26-3, we've added a column—product price. Why is it always the same no matter how large output is? Because in this case we're dealing with a perfect competitor. Later in the chapter we'll have an imperfect competitor. If a monopolist, monopolistic competitor, or oligopolist wants to sell more, he or she must lower price.

Table 26–3
Hypothetical Marginal Revenue Product Schedule

(1) Units of Land	(2) Output	(3) Marginal Physical Product	(4) Price	(5) Total Revenue	(6) Marginal Revenue Product
1	20		$10		
2	38		10		
3	53		10		
4	65		10		
5	73		10		
6	78		10		
7	80		10		
8	80		10		
9	79		—		

Go ahead and fill in the third column of Table 26-3. That should be old hat to you by this time. Now for the fifth column, total revenue. Try your luck on that one.

Let's check your methodology. Did you multiply output (column 2) by price (column 4)? If you did, you definitely got total revenue (column 5) completely right because it's pretty hard to multiply a number by 10 and get the wrong answer.

Oh yes, I almost forgot! How do we find marginal revenue product? First, **Definition of MRP** we'll define it. *MRP is the additonal revenue obtained by selling the output produced by one more unit of a resource.* To find MRP, just take the difference in total revenue between units of land. We'll start with the first unit of land; it produces a total revenue of $20. Since zero or no units of land produces no revenue, the MRP of the first unit of land is $20. How about the second unit of land? Just take the total revenue produced by two units of land and subtract the total revenue produced by one unit of land. And so forth. After you've done all that, check your results with those in Table 26-4.

Table 26-4
Hypothetical Marginal Revenue Product Schedule

(1) Units of Land	(2) Output	(3) Marginal Physical Product	(4) Price	(5) Total Revenue	(6) Marginal Revenue Product*
1	20	20	$10	$200	$200
2	38	18	10	380	180
3	53	15	10	530	150
4	65	12	10	650	120
5	73	8	10	730	80
6	78	5	10	780	50
7	80	2	10	800	20
8	80	0	10	800	0
9	79	-1	—	790	-10

* There's a much easier way of finding the marginal revenue product. Just multiply the marginal physical product by the price. This works for the perfect competitor; unfortunately, it doesn't for the imperfect competitor. To avoid confusion, as well as to ensure that we get the right answers when we find the MRP for the imperfect competitor, let's stick with our method of using total revenue to find the MRP.

Let's do some marginal analysis.

Now we're ready to do some marginal analysis. How many units of land would you hire if you needed to pay $200 rent per unit? Think about it. How much is that land worth to you? The answer lies in the MRP schedule, which is the firm's demand schedule for land.

OK, time's up. You'd hire just one unit of land because only that first unit is worth $200. Sorry if you missed that one, but don't despair. We'll give you another chance. How many units of land would you hire if the rent were $150? Go back to the MRP schedule. What do you say? Three units? Did you say three units? If you did, then you may proceed to the next plateau.

Careful now. How many units of land would you hire if its price were $90? Assume the land is indivisible. That means you can't subdivide it. OK, what's your answer? Four units? Five units? Sorry, only one guess to a customer. The answer is—four units. Why not five? Because the fifth unit of land is worth only $80 according to your own MRP schedule. Would you shell out $90 for something that is worth only $80 to you? I hope you wouldn't.

Let's work out one more MRP schedule. Fill in Table 26-5 and check your work with the figures in Table 26-6.

Table 26-5
Hypothetical MRP Schedule

(1) Units of Labor	(2) Output	(3) Marginal Physical Product	(4) Price	(5) Total Revenue	(6) Marginal Revenue Product
1	18		$12		
2	34		12		
3	48		12		
4	59		12		
5	68		12		
6	74		12		
7	77		12		
8	78		12		

Table 26–6
Hypothetical MRP Schedule

(1) Units of Labor	(2) Output	(3) Marginal Physical Product	(4) Price	(5) Total Revenue	(6) Marginal Revenue Product
1	18	18	$12	$216	$216
2	34	16	12	408	192
3	48	14	12	576	168
4	59	11	12	708	132
5	68	9	12	816	108
6	74	6	12	888	72
7	77	3	12	924	36
8	78	1	12	936	12

One last question. Is the firm whose MRP schedule is shown in Table 26–6 a perfect competitor or an imperfect competitor? The envelope, please. The answer is, the firm is a perfect competitor. How do we know? We know because the firm can sell its entire output at the same price—$12.

Graphing the MRP

In Figure 26–1, I've drawn a graph of the MRP schedule shown in Table 26-4. This curve represents the firm's demand curve for labor. As you would expect, it slopes downward to the right. Now I'd like you to draw a graph of the MRP schedule shown in Table 26-5. Draw it in the space provided in Figure 26-2. Then see if it matches my graph in Figure 26-3.

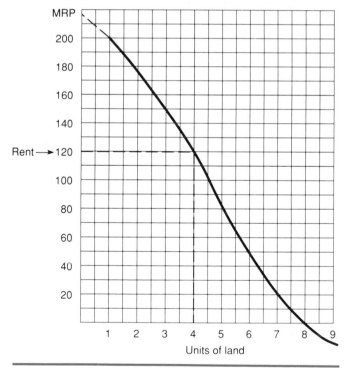

Figure 26–1

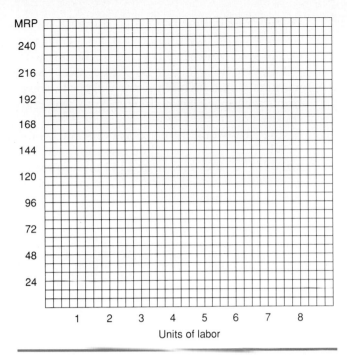

Figure 26–2

Let's do some graphical analysis.

Are you ready for a little graphical analysis? In Figure 26-1, I've assumed a rent of $120. How many units of land are hired? You'd have to be blind to answer anything other than four. How much rent is collected (total rent)? Obviously it would be $480 (4 × $120).

Notice that there is what we call the producer's surplus in the triangular area at the top of Figure 26-1. This is the difference between how much this land is worth to the firm and how much it actually had to pay in rent. How much it actually paid in rent is shown in the rectangle below the triangle.

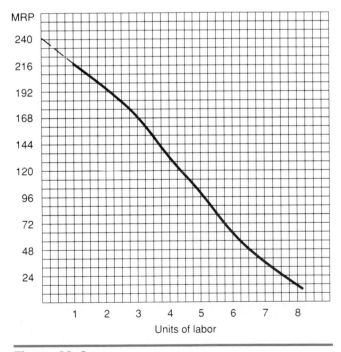

Figure 26–3

Producer's surplus parallels consumer's surplus (how much consumers would have been willing to pay for a final product minus how much they had to pay), which we covered in the last part of Chapter 17.

Now we'll use Figure 26-3 to answer two more questions. How many workers would be hired if the wage rate were $72 and how much would the firm's wages be? If you draw in your wage rate line, both answers will be staring you in the face.

The firm would hire six workers and would have a wage bill of $432.

While we're hot, we'll do one more set. How many workers would be hired if the wage rate were $144 (assuming that workers are indivisible) and how much would the firm's wage bill come to?

Three workers would be hired and the firm would pay a total of $432 in wages.

The MRP of the Imperfect Competitor

How do we distinguish between the perfect competitor and the imperfect competitor?

How do we distinguish between the perfect competitor and the imperfect competitor? Suppose we compared the demand curve of the perfect competitor with those of the monopolist, the monopolistic competitor, and the oligopolist. While the perfect competitor has a horizontal demand curve, the demand curves of the others slope downward to the right. A horizontal demand curve reflects the fact that the firm can sell its entire output at a constant price. A downward sloping demand curve means that the firm must continually lower its price to sell more and more output.

We're concerned here with how a downward sloping demand curve for the final product affects the demand for resources. In Table 26-7, we have the same outputs and marginal physical products as in Table 26-6, but instead of holding price constant we've lowered it as output increases. This reflects the downward sloping demand curve of the imperfect competitor.

Table 26–7
Hypothetical MRP Schedule

(1) Unit of Labor	(2) Output	(3) Marginal Physical Product	(4) Price	(5) Total Revenue	(6) Marginal Revenue Product
1	18	18	$12		
2	34	16	11		
3	48	14	10		
4	59	11	9		
5	68	9	8		
6	74	6	7		
7	77	3	6		
8	78	1	5		

Fill in the total revenue and MRP columns of Table 26-7 and then check your work with the data in Table 26-8. AFter that, draw an MRP curve in Figure 26-4 and see if it matches the curve shown in Figure 26-5.

How many workers would the firm hire if the wage rate were $150 and how much would the wage bill come to?

At a wage rate of $150, two workers would be hired, so the firm's wage bill would be $300.

Table 26-8
Hypothetical MRP Schedule

(1) Unit of Labor	(2) Output	(3) Marginal Physical Product	(4) Price	(5) Total Revenue	(6) Marginal Revenue Product
1	18	18	$12	$216	$216
2	34	16	11	374	158
3	48	14	10	480	106
4	59	11	9	531	51
5	68	9	8	544	13
6	74	6	7	518	−26
7	77	3	6	462	−56
8	78	1	5	390	−72

If the wage rate were $51, how many workers would be hired and how much would the firm's wage bill be?

At a $51 wage rate, four workers would be hired and the firm would pay $204 in wages.

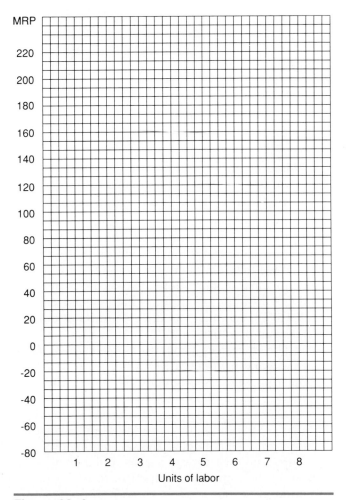

Figure 26-4

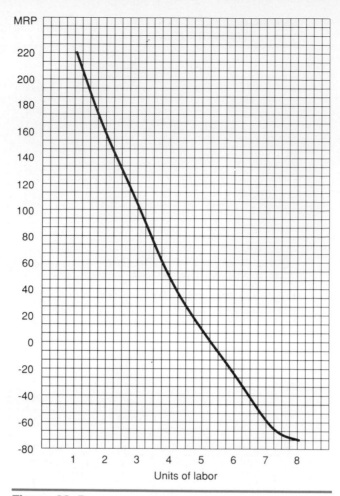

Figure 26-5

The MRP curve for the perfect competitor is flatter than that of the imperfect competitor.

You may have noticed that the MRP curve of the perfect competitor (shown in Figure 26-3) is much flatter (or more elastic) than the MRP curve of the imperfect competitor (shown in Figure 26-5). Why? Because the imperfect competitor must lower price to sell additional output.

If we take a numerical example from Tables 26-6 and 26-8, this will become clear. Using Table 26-6 of the perfect competitor, 1 unit of labor produces 18 units of output, which is sold at $12, yielding total revenue of $216. Two workers produce 34 units of output sold at $12 each for a total revenue of $408.

The imperfect competitor (Table 26-8) has somewhat different data. The first worker produces 18 units sold at $12 each for a total revenue of $216; but two workers, producing 34 units, which are sold at just $11, produce a total revenue of only $374.

Why then do two workers under perfect competition produce a product that is sold for $408 while the same two workers under imperfect competition produce a product that is sold for only $374? The answer is that the perfect competitor can sell as much as he or she wants at a constant price while the imperfect competitor must lower his or her price to sell additional units of output.

Since the MRP schedule is derived from the total revenue schedule, it follows that since the total revenue of the imperfect competitor rises more slowly than that of the perfect competitor, the imperfect competitor's MRP schedule will decline more rapidly.

You may have noticed that the MRP curve of the perfect competitor (shown in Figure 26–3) is a lot flatter (or more elastic) than that of the imperfect competitor (shown in Figure 26–5). To make this comparison easier, I've put the two curves together in Figure 26–6.

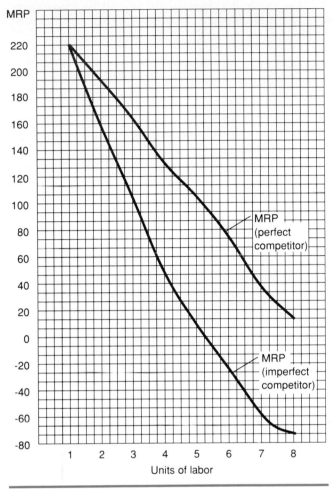

Figure 26–6

Why should the MRP curve of the imperfect competitor decline so much more rapidly than that of the perfect competitor? For the same reason that the MRP schedule in Table 26–8 declines much more rapidly than that shown in Table 26–6. The reason is that the imperfect competitor must lower price to sell additional units of output while the perfect competitor can sell all its output at the same price.

Changes in Resource Demand

Changes in Resource Demand versus Changes in Quantity of Resource Demanded

The firm's MRP curve is its demand curve for a resource.

A firm's demand for a factor of production or resource is depicted by the firm's MRP curve. So far we've been looking at shifts along that curve. For instance, when rent declines, the firm will lease more units of land. This shift would be a downward movement along the MRP curve for land. Similarly, a rise in the wage rate would result in a decline in the number of workers hired. We would slide up the firm's MRP curve for labor.

Now we're ready—or at least I am—to discuss shifts in the MRP curve (rather than shifts along the curves). A shift from MRP_1 to MRP_2 in Figure 26-7 represents an increase in the demand for capital. How would a decrease in the demand for capital be represented? Obviously by a shift from MRP_1 to MRP_2.

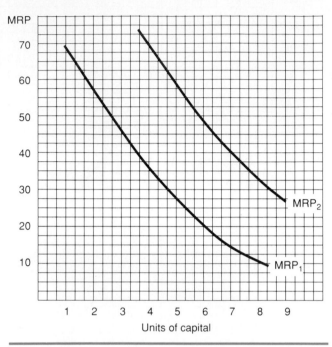

Figure 26–7

The Four Reasons for Changes in Resource Demand

There are four things that cause shifts in the MRP curve: (1) changes in the demand for the final product; (2) productivity changes; (3) changes in the prices of other resources; and (4) changes in the quantities of other resources.

Changes in the Demand for the Final Product This is by far the most important influence on the demand for a factor of production. A firm that had no sales would have no demand for land, labor, capital, or entrepreneurial ability. Looking at things more optimistically, let's suppose that the demand for the final product shown in Table 26-4 were to rise so much its price was driven from $10 to $20. What would happen to the firm's MRP curve?

Would the MRP schedule in Table 26-4 be raised or lowered (i.e., will the firm's demand for land be raised or lowered)? There's only one way to find that out. Turn back to Table 26-4, change price from $10 to $20, and recalculate the MRP schedule. Once you've done the necessary calculations, check your work with that in Table 26-9.

Next, I'd like you to superimpose the new MRP curve on Figure 26-1. Label it MRP_2. How does it look? If you did it correctly, it should look like MRP_2 in Figure 26-8. Which would lead you to the inescapable conclusion that a rise in the demand for the final product leads to a rise in the demand for the factors of production. You can therefore derive that a fall in the demand for the final product will lead to a fall in the demand for the factors of production.

Table 26–9
Hypothetical MRP Schedule

(1) Units of Labor	(2) Output	(3) Marginal Physical Product	(4) Price	(5) Total Revenue	(6) Marginal Revenue Product
1	20	20	$20	$ 400	$400
2	38	18	20	760	360
3	53	15	20	1,060	300
4	65	12	20	1,300	240
5	73	8	20	1,460	160
6	78	5	20	1,560	100
7	80	2	20	1,600	40
8	80	0	20	1,600	0
9	79	−1	20	1,580	−20

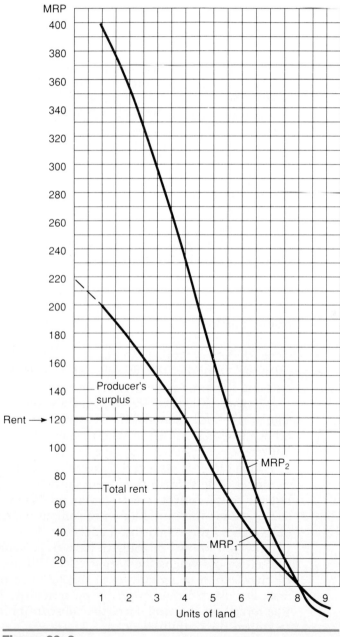

Figure 26–8

Productivity Changes Productivity is output per unit of input. If output per unit of input is doubled, what would happen to productivity? Check it out. This time, use the data in Table 26–6. Double the marginal physical product and multiply each by price.

What happened to your MRP? It doubled at each price. Right?

What raises productivity?

Now we'll ask what raises productivity? Nearly all of it comes from two sources—better capital and better trained and educated labor. The computerization of the American industrial and service sectors has been the main factor responsible for the productivity increases of the last 25 years. Not only have we introduced more and better computer systems, but much of our labor force, particularly those in office jobs, has acquired the necessary skills to use them.

Changes in the Prices of Other Resources There are four factors of production. Sometimes one factor may be used as a substitute for another. When land is scarce, as it is in Bangladesh, labor is substituted for land. Each acre of land is cultivated much more intensively than in the United States. When a new machine replaces several workers, we are substituting capital for labor.

The substitution effect

a. *Substitute Factors* If the price of a factor of production, say labor, goes up, business firms tend to substitute capital or land for some of their now more expensive workers. This is the *substitution effect.* Similarly, a decline in the wage rate would lead to a substitution of labor for capital and land. We're assuming, of course, that the price of capital and land hasn't changed (or even if it has, it hasn't risen as much as the wage rate).

The output effect

There's also an *output effect,* which works in the opposite direction. When the price of any resource rises, this raises the cost of production, which in turn, lowers the supply of the final product. When supply falls, price rises, consequently reducing output. In other words, according to the output effect, if the cost of a factor of production rises, output will decline, thereby reducing the employment of all factors of production. Conversely, a decline in the cost of a factor will raise output, thereby raising the use of all factors of production.

What we're left with is this: (1) The substitution effect: If the price of a resource is raised, other resources will be substituted for it. If the price of a resource is lowered, it will be substituted for other resources. (2) The output effect: If the price of a resource raises, output of the final product will decline, thereby lowering the employment of all resources. Conversely, if the price of a resource falls, output of the final product will rise, thereby increasing the employment of all resources.

Two contradictory effects

What we have then are two contradictory effects. When the price of a resource rises, for example, the substitution effect dictates that more of the other resources will be used, thus increasing their employment. But the output effect pushes their employment down.

Which effect is stronger?

Which effect is stronger? Take the case of the introduction of computers in offices. The substitution effect pushed down the employment of labor, but the output effect pushed it way up. White-collar employment has risen sharply since the introduction of computers, so clearly the output effect has outweighted the substitution effect.

Now you *know* I'm going to have to present a case where the substitution effect outweighs the output effect. I'll use the example of the mechanization of agriculture in the South in the late 1940s when output rose, but over three quarters of the agricultural labor force in the deep South was forced off the land. Here the substitution effect (of capital for labor) swamped the output effect.

Sometimes then the substitution effect is stronger than the output effect while at other times the opposite holds true. Thus, if you were asked if automation raises or lowers the employment of labor, you could sound very well informed when you explained that it would raise employment if the output effect were stronger and lower it if the substitution effect predominated.

Complementary factors of production

b. *Complementary Factors* Although resources are usually substitutable at least to some degree, they also usually work well together. In fact, you need at least some labor to produce virtually every good or service, and productivity may be greatly enhanced by land, capital, and entrepreneurial ability.

We say that two factors are complements in production if an increase in the use of one requires an increase in the use of the other. If a bicycle messenger service purchased 100 new bicycles, it would need to hire 100 messengers to ride them; or if 100 new messengers were hired, the firm would need to purchase 100 bicycles.

To carry our example further, suppose the price of bicycles rose considerably. What would happen to the firm's demand for bicycles (or capital)?

You said it would go down, right? What would happen to the firm's demand for riders (labor)? It too would go down.

What if instead the wage rate for bicycle riders rose sharply? What would happen to the firm's demand for bicycle riders and for bicycles? It would fall.

Now we can generalize. When the price of a resource rises, the demand for a complementary resource will fall; when the price of a resource falls, the demand for a complementary resource rises.

Changes in the Quantities of Other Resources If we go back to one of the eternal questions of economics, why are workers in one country more productive than those in another country, the answer is that they have more land, capital, and entrepreneurial ability with which to work.

Why are workers in one country more productive than those in another country?

As we've already noted, the farmer in Bangladesh has a lot less land with which to work than the American farmer, and the Chinese construction worker has a lot less capital backing him than his American counterpart. It would follow that an increase in land would greatly raise the productivity of the farmer in Bangladesh while the Chinese construction worker's productivity would soar if he were given heavy construction equipment.

We can conclude then that an addition of complementary resources would raise the MRP of any given resource while a decrease in complementary resources would have the opposite effect.

Optimum Resource Mix for the Firm

So far, we have been deciding how much of a resource should be hired by a firm. We hire more and more labor until the MRP of the last worker hired is equal to the going wage rate. Similarly, we hire land until the MRP of the last unit of land hired is equal to the going rent. Finally, more and more capital is hired until the last unit of capital hired is equal to the interest rate.

We can generalize by saying that the firm will use increasing amounts of a resource until the MRP of that resource is equal to its price. We'd hire workers until the MRP of labor equals the price of labor (or the wage rate). Suppose we divide both sides of the equation by the price of labor.

(1) MRP of labor = Price of labor

(2) $\dfrac{\text{MRP of labor}}{\text{Price of labor}} = \dfrac{\text{Price of labor}}{\text{Price of labor}}$

This may be simplified to:

(3) $\dfrac{\text{MRP of labor}}{\text{Price of labor}} = 1$

(3) $\dfrac{\text{MRP of labor}}{\text{Price of labor}} = 1$

Now let's do the same thing with land.

(1) MRP of land = Price of land

(2) $\dfrac{\text{MRP of land}}{\text{Price of land}} = \dfrac{\text{Price of land}}{\text{Price of land}}$

(3) $\dfrac{\text{MRP of land}}{\text{Price of land}} = 1$

(3) $\dfrac{\text{MRP of land}}{\text{Price of land}} = 1$

And for capital:

(1) MRP of capital = Price of capital

(2) $\dfrac{\text{MRP of capital}}{\text{Price of capital}} = \dfrac{\text{Price of capital}}{\text{Price of capital}}$

(3) $\dfrac{\text{MRP of capital}}{\text{Price of capital}} = 1$

(3) $\dfrac{\text{MRP of capital}}{\text{Price of capital}} = 1$

Next, we may combine the three equations into one.

$\dfrac{\text{MRP of labor}}{\text{Price of labor}} =$
$\dfrac{\text{MRP of land}}{\text{Price of land}} =$
$\dfrac{\text{MRP of capital}}{\text{Price of capital}} = 1$

$$\dfrac{\text{MRP of labor}}{\text{Price of labor}} = \dfrac{\text{MRP of land}}{\text{Price of land}} = \dfrac{\text{MRP of capital}}{\text{Price of capital}} = 1$$

After all, things equal to the same thing (in this case 1) are equal to each other.

The reason I've dragged you through all of this (except to show off my algebra) is to reinforce the conclusion we reached a few minutes ago. *A firm will keep hiring more and more of a resource up to the point at which its MRP is equal to its price.* This great truth enables us to do another set of problems. You may have slept through everything up to this point, and still get this right.

Given the data in Table 26–10 how many units of land, labor, and capital would you hire? It's easy. Just reread the underlined statement in the previous paragraph.

The answers? Do we have the envelope? Ah yes. We would hire three units of land, four units of labor, and five units of capital.

Now we'll take up in turn each of the four resources, beginning with labor, in the next chapter. The questions we will answer are why the wage rates are what they are, and why rent, interest, and profit are what *they* are.

Table 26–10
Hypothetical MRP Schedules for a Firm

Units of Land	MRP of Land	Units of Capital	MRP of Capital	Units of Labor	MRP of Labor
1	$12	1	$15	1	$30
2	10	2	13	2	26
3	8	3	10	3	21
4	6	4	7	4	15
5	4	5	3	5	8
6	2	6	0	6	1
Rent = $8		Interest = $3		Wage rate = $15	

Workbook for Chapter 26

Multiple-Choice Questions

Circle the letter that corresponds to the best answer.

1. Derived demand is the demand for
a. final goods and services   **b.** resources   **c.** both final goods and services and resources   **d.** neither final goods and services nor resources

2. When the demand for wheat rises, the demand for farm labor
a. rises   **b.** falls   **c.** may rise or fall

3. The demand for resources is based on
a. the demand for the final product   **b.** the productivity of that resource   **c.** both the demand for the final product and the productivity of the resource
d. neither the demand for the final product nor the productivity of the resource

4. Which statement is true?
a. Resources and final products are both measured by units of input.   **b.** Resources and final products are both measured by units of output.   **c.** Resources are measured by units of input and final demand is measured by units of output.   **d.** Resources are measured by units of output and final products are measured by units of input.

5. Which statement is true?
a. Productivity is output per unit of input.
b. Productivity is input per unit of output.
c. Productivity is neither of the above.

6. Relative to the Chinese economy, ours is
a. more capital intensive   **b.** more labor intensive   **c.** more labor intensive and more capital intensive   **d.** less labor intensive and less capital intensive

7. The added output for which one additional input of labor is responsible is its

a. marginal revenue product   **b.** marginal physical product   **c.** average revenue product   **d.** average physical product

8. A rise in the wage rate would lead to a movement
a. down the MRP curve and a rise in the number of workers hired   **b.** down the MRP curve and a decline in the number of workers hired   **c.** up the MRP curve and a decline in the number of workers hired   **d.** up the MRP curve and a rise in the number of workers hired

9. The firm's demand schedule for a resource is its _____ schedule.
a. MPP   **b.** MRP   **c.** total revenue   **d.** output

10. The MRP curve for the perfect competitor is _____ the MRP curve for the imperfect competitor.
a. identical to   **b.** steeper than   **c.** flatter than

11. The triangular area above the rent line and below the MRP line in Figure 1 is called the _____ .
a. total rent   **b.** consumer's surplus   **c.** producer's surplus   **d.** none of the above

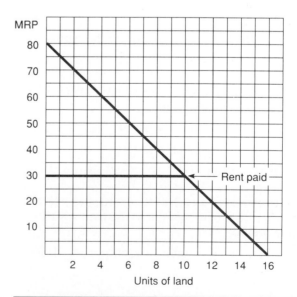

Figure 1

12. In Figure 1, total rent would be

a. $300 b. $500 c. $800 d. unknown

13. An increase in the demand for capital would be reflected in a movement to the

a. left of the firm's MPP curve b. left of the firm's MRP curve c. right of the firm's MPP curve

d. right of the firm's MRP curve

14. The firm will hire workers until the wage rate and the _____ of the last worker hired are equal.

a.   marginal physical product b. MRP

c. output

15. A firm will operate at that point where _____ is equal to one.

a. the marginal physical product of capital/price of capital b. the MRP of capital/price of capital

c. the price of capital/marginal physical product of capital d. the price of capital/MRP of capital

16. A firm will keep hiring more and more of a resource up to the point at which its MRP is equal to

a. one b. its MPP c. its price d. its output

17. If the MRP of the last worker hired is lower than the wage rate, the firm has

a. hired too many workers b. hired too few workers c. hired the right number of workers

18. If the wage rate were higher than the MRP of the last worker hired

a. the firm might be able to profitably hire at least one more worker b. the firm already had already hired too many workers c. there is no way of knowing if the firm had too few or too many workers

19. The most important influence on a firm's demand for a factor of production is

a. the quantities of other resources b. the prices of other resources c. its productivity d. the demand for the final product

20. If the price that a perfect competitor received for his or her final product doubled, the firm's MRP schedule would

a. rise b. fall c. double at each price d. stay about the same

21. The most effective way to increase the productivity of labor would be to

a. increase capital b. increase labor c. lower capital d. shift workers from white-collar work to blue-collar work

22. Capital and labor are _____ factors of production.

a. substitute b. complementary c. both complementary and substitute d. neither complementary nor substitute

23. Automation will raise the level of employment if the

a. output effect is equal to the substitution effect

b. output effect is greater than the substitution effect c. substitution effect is greater than the output effect

24. A firm will try to be in each of these situations except

a. MRP of capital = price of capital b. MRP of land/price of land = 1 c. 1 − price of labor = MRP of labor d. MRP of land/price of land = MRP of labor/price of labor

Fill-In Questions

1. Derived demand is the demand for _____ .

2. A firm will use increasing amounts of a resource until the _____ of that resource is equal to its _____ .

3. Productivity is defined as _____ per unit of _____ .

4. If Melissa produces twice as much per hour as Adam, we would say that she is _____ as productive as he is.

5. Our economy is relatively _____ intensive while the Chinese economy is relatively _____ intensive.

6. If farmland became five times as expensive, farmers would use much more _____ and _____ per acre.

7. When the productivity of a resource rises, its

_____ and its _____ also rise.

8. When the price of a substitute resource declines, the price of a resource will _____ .

9. The MRP of the fourth unit of output = the

_____ less the _____ .

10. The MRP is the additional _____ obtained

by _____ .

11. The producer's surplus of rented land is the difference between how much this land is _____

and how much _____ .

12. The optimum resource mix for a firm would be

denoted by this equation: _____ /_____ =

_____/_____ = _____/_____ = 1.

13. A firm will keep hiring more and more of a resource up to the point at which its _____ is

equal to its _____ .

14. The MRP curve of the perfect competitor declines

_____ than that of the imperfect competitor.

15. A firm will keep leasing additional units of land

until the MRP of that land is equal to the _____.

16. An increase in the productivity of labor will

_____ the MRP of labor.

17. The four reasons for changes in resource demand

are: (1) _____, (2) _____,

(3) _____, and (4) _____.

18. If the price of labor goes up and a firm replaces some workers with more machines, this is the

_____ effect; when the price of a resource declines, and consequently the level of production rises,

this is the _____ effect.

19. If labor and capital are complementary resources, if the price of labor goes up, the employment of capital

ital _____ .

Problems

1. *a.* Fill in Table 1. *b.* Using the data in Table 1, use Figure 2 to draw a graph of the firm's MRP curve. *c.* Is the firm a perfect or an imperfect competitor? *d.* If the wage rate were $60, how many workers would be hired? How much would the total wage bill come to? *e.* If the wage rate were $35, how many workers would be hired? How much would the total wage bill come to?

Table 1
Hypothetical MRP Schedule

(1) Units of Labor	(2) Output	(3) Marginal Physical Product	(4) Price	(5) Total Revenue	(6) Marginal Revenue Product
1	15	___	$6	___	___
2	28	___	6	___	___
3	40	___	6	___	___
4	50	___	6	___	___
5	57	___	6	___	___
6	62	___	6	___	___
7	64	___	6	___	___
8	65	___	6	___	___

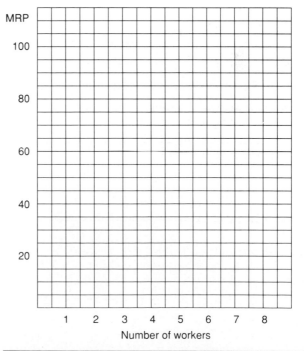

Figure 2

2. *a.* Fill in Table 2. *b.* Using the data in Table 2, draw a graph of the firm's MRP curve in Figure 3. Is the firm a perfect or an imperfect competitor? *d.* If the wage rate were $250, how many workers would be hired? How much would the total wage bill come to? *e.* If the wage rate were $99, how many workers would be hired? How much would the total wage bill come to?

3. Given the data in Table 3, how many units of land, labor, and capital would you hire?

Table 2
Hypothetical MRP Schedule

(1) Units of Labor	(2) Output	(3) Marginal Physical Product	(4) Price	(5) Total Revenue	(6) Marginal Revenue Product
1	22	___	$20	___	___
2	43	___	19	___	___
3	63	___	18	___	___
4	81	___	17	___	___
5	96	___	16	___	___
6	109	___	15	___	___
7	119	___	14	___	___
8	127	___	13	___	___

Table 3

Units of Land	MRP of Land	Units of Capital	MRP of Capital	Units of Labor	MRP of Labor
1	$20	1	$35	1	$31
2	17	2	33	2	24
3	13	3	27	3	16
4	8	4	20	4	9
5	2	5	12	5	5
6	1	6	4	6	2
Rent = $8		Interest = $27		Wage rate = $24	

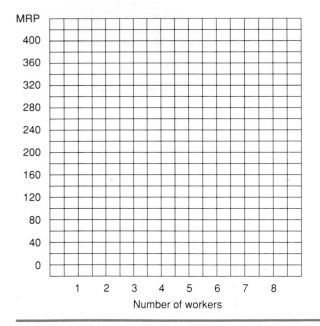

MRP

Number of workers

Figure 3

Labor pates (handwritten)

Unions, Labor Markets, and Wage Rates

In Chapters 17–25, we saw that the price of every final product—cars, gasoline, sugar, steak, shoes—is determined by two things, supply and demand. This held true whether the firm was a perfect competitor, monopolistic competitor, or oligopolist.

In Chapter 26, we talked quite a bit about the demand for labor and the other factors of production. Now we'll deal specifically with how wage rates are set. First we'll look at how labor unions affect the supply of labor. Then we'll examine the overall supply of labor. Finally, after a brief discussion of the demand for labor, we'll put it all together and reach a conclusion that will startle no one: every wage rate is determined by supply and demand.

Chapter Objectives

These are the high points of this chapter:

- A short history of the labor movement.
- Labor legislation.
- The economic power of unions and employers.
- The strike.
- The supply of labor.
- The demand for labor.
- High wage rates and economic rent.
- Real wages and productivity.
- The minimum wage dispute.

In the United States, as well as in most other countries, there is a wide disparity in income. There are people like Fernando Valenzuela, John Elway, Magic Johnson, Michael Jackson, and Johnny Carson, the presidents of major corporations, as well as heart surgeons, and even the writers of best-selling economics textbooks, who make hundreds of thousands and even millions of dollars a year. And, of course, there are the rest of us, who barely scrape by on $100,000 a year or even less.

We're going to try to answer the question of why people earn such widely varying incomes. There are several reasons for this disparity but the bottom line remains the same. You guessed it—supply and demand.

A Short History of the American Labor Movement

The Early Years

Labor unions were considered subversive until the 1940s.

Labor unions are a traditional American institution, rivaling motherhood and apple pie as objects of national affection. This, of course, was not always so. Until the 1940s, most Americans had an unfavorable opinion of unions. In the popular mind, they were subversive organizations set up to obtain exorbitant wage increases and possibly to overthrow the American economic system. And union leaders were regarded as racketeers, communists, or political bosses.

Some of these views were not wide of the mark, and to this day, labor unions and their leaders do not always put the national good before their more immediate goals. But most Americans have come to accept unions as part of the national scene, not very different from other U.S. institutions.

The AF of L in 1886 rang in the modern era of unions.

Although the trade union movement in the United States is some two centuries old, most labor historians consider the modern era to have begun with the founding of the original American Federation of Labor in 1886, or with its predecessor, the Knights of Labor, which rose to prominence in the mid-1880s. Within the ranks of these organizations there was an almost continual struggle between those who sought specific gains—better wages, hours, and working conditions—and those who advocated more far-reaching reforms—a universal eight-hour day, elimination of the wage system, and the establishment of producers' cooperatives to replace private enterprise.

Terence Powderly, who in 1879 attained the office of Grand Master Workman of the Knights of Labor, held the view that wage increases of just a few cents an hour were entirely inadequate since the workers were entitled to the full price of their labor. But the strike, which Powderly termed a "relic of barbarism," was not the proper means of securing these gains. The Knights would use reason, persuasion, and, if necessary, arbitration. You can guess how far this got them.

Fortunately or unfortunately, depending on your viewpoint, many of the member unions of the Knights went out on strike in the early 1880s. Often they won. Their biggest victory was in 1885, when Jay Gould's Wabash Railroad gave in. Ironically, the ranks of the Knights of Labor, whose leadership opposed the strike, rose in 1886 from only 100,000 to some 700,000 members.

The Haymarket affair

But what goes up, at least sometimes, must come down. The Haymarket affair took place in 1886. At a rally sponsored by various labor organizers in Chicago's Haymarket Square, a terrible tragedy occurred. It had been raining and the leaders were getting ready to end the rally when a bomb was thrown into a group of policemen, eight of whom were killed. The organizers of the rally were blamed, quickly tried, and four were hung. Later, considerable evidence was brought forth to show that the six who were hung were innocent and that no union members had been involved in the killings. But public opinion had already turned against the Knights.

By the late 1880s, the American Federation of Labor, or the AF of L (AFL), as it became known, had become the predominant labor organization. Sam-

Bread-and-butter unionism

uel Gompers, who served as its president until his death in 1924, stressed the importance of "bread-and-butter unionism." Why the AF of L succeeded where the Knights had failed is explained largely by their opposing philosophies as well as by the changing conditions of the American economy.

The wage relationship was here to stay.

The emergence of the large corporation, which replaced the small workshop, meant that the wage relationship was here to stay. Forget about small producers' cooperatives and start worrying about securing enough bargaining strength to obtain better wages, hours, and working conditions. An individual worker has little bargaining power against a huge corporation, but thousands of workers, banded together in craft unions—the iron workers, cigar makers, carpenters—did have a certain amount of leverage. They could, if they didn't get what they wanted, withhold their labor. In other words, they could go out on strike.

This might not sound all that radical, but during the first three decades of the 20th century, unions were seen by most Americans as subversive, foreign, and, in some cases, downright evil. Employers fought them tooth and nail. Union members were blacklisted, those suspected of having union sympathies were fired, court orders were obtained prohibiting strikes as well as milder forms of union activity, and sometimes private detectives, labor goons, and sympathetic local police were used to violently put down strikes.

Key Labor Legislation

The Wagner Act

National Labor Relations Act (Wagner Act) (1935) This and the Taft-Hartley Act are, by far, the two most important pieces of labor legislation. The Wagner Act committed the federal government not only to promoting collective bargaining, but to actually supporting union organizing. Twelve years later the Taft-Hartley Act was put forth as a measure that would redress this imbalance by protecting "employers' rights."

Prohibition of unfair labor practices

The Wagner Act prohibited employers from engaging in such "unfair labor practices" as (1) coercion or interference with employees who are organizing or bargaining; (2) refusal to bargain in good faith with a union legally representing employees; and (3) in general, penalizing employees for union activity.

It set up a three-member (now a five-member) board to protect workers in organizing unions and to administer representation elections (i.e., to determine which union will represent the workers of a company). If 30 percent of the employees in an entire company, or just one unit of that company, decide to be represented by a union, they petition the National Labor Relations Board to conduct an election. If the union gets a majority of votes, it then represents *all* the employees of that company or unit, even those who are not members of the union.

Put force of government behind collective bargaining

This law put the force of the federal government behind collective bargaining, at the same time lending unions a certain legitimacy. It established unions as an American institution. In addition, the Wagner Act provided the necessary machinery to ensure that large corporations would allow unions to organize and would bargain in good faith.

During World War II, it was considered unpatriotic to strike, but 1946 set a record for strikes, a record that still stands. The late 1940s were a time of inflation and prosperity, and labor used the strike weapon to get what it considered its fare share of the economic pie. Partially in response to these disturbances, the Republicans captured control of Congress for the first time in 14 years. They felt they had a mandate not only to redress the imbalance between the power of labor and management, but as many observers noted, "to put labor in its place."

Taft-Hartley Act (1947) This act has three main provisions: (1) it has an 80-day "cooling-off" period; (2) it allows the states to ban the union shop; and (3) it severely limits the closed shop.

Strikes that "imperil the national health or safety" may be halted by court order at the request of the president, who determines just which strikes imperil our health and safety. If a settlement is not reached during the 80 days allowed, the union may resume the strike.

The most controversial part of the law is Section 14–b, which allows the states to enact "right-to-work" laws, which prohibit union shop contracts. (About 20 states—mainly in the South—have laws that prohibit contracts that require union membership as a condition of employment.)

The law severely limited the extent of the closed shop (closed to non-union members). However, unions have sometimes gotten around this prohibition by calling a closed shop a union shop (see the box that follows).

Taft-Hartley also prohibits jurisdictional disputes and secondary boycotts. The first occur when two unions, each vying to organize a company, picket that company, which has no dispute with either union. A secondary boycott is directed against a company not party to a strike, such as a trade supplier or a customer or retail outlet.

The 80-day cooling-off period puts the union at a strategic disadvantage. For 80 days, the company can stockpile inventory, making it easier for them to weather a strike and perhaps less likely to be willing to reach a settlement. On the other hand, by committing itself to ensuring labor peace, not to mention to protecting the nation's health and safety, the administration is more likely to put pressure on both parties to settle their dispute.

At every Democratic presidential convention (until 1988), delegates representing labor unions got the convention to adopt a platform plank demanding repeal of Section 14–b of the Taft-Hartley Act (which permits states to pass "right-to-work" laws). Even when the Democratic party swept to victory, capturing the presidency and Congress as it did in 1948, 1960, 1964, and 1976, somehow they never got around to Section 14–b.

In the late 1950s, widespread publicity about labor racketeering and corruption, highlighted by televised congressional committee hearings, created a demand for remedial legislation. The jailing of Teamster President Dave Beck, complaints from union members that their unions were undemocratic and curbed dissent, and widespread instances of conflict of interest (where

---

The Closed Shop, Union Shop, Open Shop, and "Right-to Work" Laws

(1) Closed Shop An employer may hire only union members. The Taft-Hartley Act outlawed this arrangement, but sometimes union hiring halls operate as de facto closed shops. If an employer, generally a construction firm, hires only those sent by the union, we have a closed shop, even though, nominally, it is a union shop.

(2) Union Shop Under a union shop contract, all employees must join the union, usually within 30 days after they are hired. This arrangement effectively increases union membership since many workers would not have joined the union unless they were forced to. A variation of the union shop is the agency shop in which you don't have to join the union, but you must pay dues.

(3) Open Shop No one is forced to join the union, although it does represent all the workers in contract negotiations. Union members often resent nonmembers who "are getting a free ride," since they don't have to pay dues.

(4) Right-to-Work Laws Section 14–b of the Taft-Hartley Act permitted the states to pass laws prohibiting the union shop. Some 20 states have done this, which means that in those states you can work in a shop that is organized without having to join the union. Organized labor has struggled vainly since 1947 to get this controversial section repealed because the "right-to-work" laws it permits have been responsible for lower membership in the states that passed them.

union officials had financial interests in the companies with whom they conducted labor negotiations) led to the Landrum-Griffin Act.

Landrum-Griffin Act

Landrum-Griffin Act (1959) This act had four main provisions: (1) a "bill of rights" for union members; (2) provision of election procedures; (3) limits on takeovers of locals by national unions; and (4) a listing of the financial responsibilities of union officials.

Was this law necessary?

Why was this law necessary? Consider this provision from the "bill of rights": "No member of any organization may be fined, suspended, expelled, or otherwise disciplined except for nonpayment of dues . . . unless such member has been *(a)* served with written specific charges; *(b)* given a reasonable time to prepare his defense, and *(c)* afforded a full and fair hearing."

Why outline election procedures? Because in many unions, the leadership was able to perpetuate itself in office. Why limit takeovers of locals? Because this device was often used to silence opposition. Finally, the main reason to deal with union finances is to cut down on embezzlement of union funds.

The Labor Movement since the New Deal

The atmosphere surrounding labor organizing in the 1930s was poles apart from that of the earlier decades of the century. Where there had been prosperity, there was depression. The government, which had been an enemy, was now an ally. And the national mood had changed. Those who ran corporate America had made a mess of things. Perhaps the unions, which stressed higher pay, better working conditions, and job security, were really on the right track.

Union membership rose spectacularly in the mid-1930s.

Union membership rose spectacularly in the mid-1930s. The major impetus was the Wagner Act, which more than anything else gave unions a

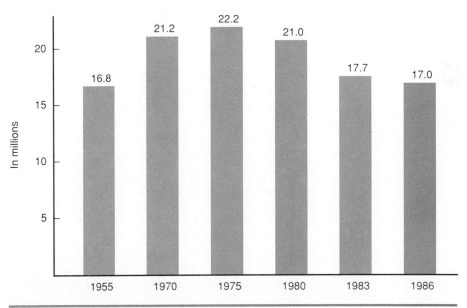

Figure 27–1
Membership in Labor Unions, Selected Years, 1955–1986 (in millions)

Sources: U.S. Dept. of Labor, *Handbook of Labor Statistics; Statistical Abstract of the United States,* 1988, pp. 401–2.

legitimacy and facilitated their organizing workers in the nation's basic industries such as autos, steel, and rubber. During this time a split developed within the AFL, leading to the formation of the Congress of Industrial Organizations (CIO) in 1935. The split was caused by a dispute over whether to organize along craft lines, as the AFL had been doing for 50 years, or along industry lines, as advocated by the leaders of the CIO.

Craft unions

Craft unions are organized along the lines of particular skills, such as air traffic controllers, plumbers, operating engineers, airline pilots, or teachers. These are generally relatively well-paid jobs requiring years of training.

Industrial unions

Industrial unions, such as the United Steel Workers, the United Auto Workers, and the United Mine Workers, are organized along industry lines, without regard to craft. Lumped together in one union are skilled and unskilled workers doing varied types of work. What bonds them together is that they are all work in the same industry.

In some industries, particularly those with unskilled or semiskilled mass-production workers, it makes a lot more sense to organize along industrial rather than craft lines. Unlike plumbers or airline pilots, the people who put together cars can be trained in a couple of hours—and replaced just as quickly. They simply don't have a craft that sets them apart from their co-workers.

The conflict within the AFL over whether to organize along craft or industrial lines led to the great schism of the organization in 1935. Most of the AFL leadership, who headed the craft and building trades unions believed, for example, that machinists, whether employed in autos, steel, or any other industry, should be organized into a machinists' union. But the leaders of the breakaway Congress of Industrial Organizations, the CIO, felt that all the workers in an industry should be organized into industrywide unions regardless of craft.

In the mid-to-late 1930s there was a tremendous spurt of labor organizing by the CIO in steel, autos, rubber, oil, and other areas of heavy industry. The AFL also began organizing along industrial lines during this period. These were the golden days of union organizing.

AFL-CIO merger

One of the unintended effects of the Taft-Hartley Act was to spark efforts to reunite the AFL and the CIO. The main obstacle to the merger was no longer the philosophical one of whether organization should be carried out along craft or industrial lines. That issue had been settled by the late 1930s when the AFL began to organize its own industrial unions.

The problem that still had to be resolved was jurisdictional. Unions belonging to the AFL and the CIO had been organizing workers in the same fields, often competing with each other. The member unions involved entered into "no-raiding" agreements and even appointed umpires to resolve any cases the unions could not settle between themselves. The way was then cleared for the merger, which took place in 1955.

Union membership peaked in the early 1970s (see Figure 27–1). From the mid-1950s through the mid-1970s, nearly one out of every four American workers was in a union; today only one out of seven workers is a union member. What has happened is that we have shifted from a manufacturing to a service economy; it's much harder to organize computer programmers, word processors, financial analysts, and insurance adjusters than factory workers.

One of the factors, then, affecting union membership is the decline of manfacturing employment, particularly in the nation's industrial heartland. In a sense, the auto and steel industry are in a long-term decline that began during the 1973–75 recession and intensified during the recession of 1981–82. This decline has been largely offset by the rapid unionization of public employees during the 1960s, particularly on the state and local levels.

However, the rapid rise in the public employment rolls of the 1960s and 1970s has apparently halted.

The South continues to be the least unionized section of the country. Long the target of AFL-CIO organizers, this region has remained a tough nut to crack. "Right-to-work" laws, strong local conservatism, and antiunion feeling, as well as the economic power of the local firms, has kept labor organizing at low ebb.

The Economic Power of Labor Unions

Are labor unions too powerful?

Are labor unions too powerful? When a powerful union like the United States Steel Workers shuts down not just steel, but depresses several related industries, as it did for 116 days in 1959, is this something we can afford to tolerate? Or when the Teamsters, the International Longshoremen, or any other union's members walk off their jobs because they disapprove of certain business decisions, why must the rest of us suffer? Don't unions have too much political power, having at their disposal millions of dollars as well as tens of thousands of campaign workers? Finally, aren't unions really forcing up prices and causing inflation?

Many people accuse unions of being monopolies. Indeed, they were prosecuted under the Sherman Antitrust Act during the first two decades of the century. In a sense, of course, unions *are* monopolies. For example, the painters', plumbers', carpenters', longshoremens', and teamsters' trades are nearly 100 percent unionized. Aren't those monopolies?

We define a monopoly as the seller of a good or service for which there are no close substitutes. Of course, labor is not really a good or service, but rather a factor of production that helps produce that good or service. But if we brush aside that technicality, then for all intents and purposes, unions are sometimes monopolies.

Unions have two ways of asserting power.

Unions have two basic ways of exerting power. One way is to take in as members virtually everyone who works in a particular craft or industry. This is the method of inclusion and it could give the union a monopoly. Examples are the United Steel Workers, the United Auto Workers, and the Teamsters.

A second way of exerting power, which is quite common in the building trades, is the principle of exclusion. You don't take in just anyone. There are tests, you might need experience, and, believe it or not, it probably wouldn't hurt to know someone—preferably a close relative like a father or an uncle who happens to be an influential member of the union. By keeping people out, you keep the supply of carpenters, plumbers, bricklayers, and electricians down, and amazingly, wages go all the way up.

The principle of exclusion works like a charm. Wages were extremely high in the building trades for most of the 1960s and the nonrecession years of the 1970s. But in recent years things were not so great, perhaps because of a nationwide construction slump caused by high interest rates, and possibly because the high union scale wage rates have priced new building construction out of the market.

Let's see what principles of inclusions and exclusion look like graphically using Figure 27-2. In Figure 27-2A, we have the inclusive union, generally a large industrial union like the United Steel Workers. The union tries to obtain a high standard wage from U.S. Steel, Bethlehem, Republic, and the other companies. But at a high wage rate, the companies will hire fewer workers than they would have at lower wages.

We get the same results from the exclusive union (Figure 27-2B). This time, however, the union has restricted the supply of workers by allowing only certain people into its ranks. We see then that either exclusion or inclusion will lead to higher wages.

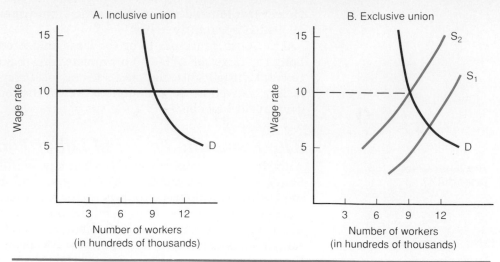

Figure 27-2

Are unions too powerful? Public opinion is divided on this issue but before we even attempt to answer this question, we should look at the other side of the coin. Are large corporations too powerful?

The Economic Power of Large Employers

We've seen that workers who were once powerless to bargain individually with huge corporate employers, have formed unions that themselves have become quite powerful. One is apt to forget that these corporations have remained quite powerful, and some would say—myself included—that this power has become increasingly concentrated because of the rapid pace of corporate mergers (see Chapter 24).

The case of monopsony   Let's consider an extreme case of corporate power, that of monopsony. The seller of a product for which there are no close substitutes is a monopolist. Monopsony is the situation in which there is only a single buyer for a product. The most common example of monopsony is a labor market where there is only a single employer. The Hershey Company in Hershey, Pennsylvania, was once one such example. At one time or another, General Electric in Schenectady, New York, J. P. Stevens in several towns in the South, and the military bases in various towns around the country have completely dominated the local job markets. Sometimes 60 to 80 percent of the jobs in these areas have been provided by a single employer. Technically, a monopsony is a single buyer, but these towns came pretty close. The late Senator Henry (Scoop) Jackson of Washington was long known as the Senator from Boeing because of the huge defense contracts he was able to secure for the Seattle firm. Incidentally, in the mid-1970s, when defense spending was cut, Seattle went into a depression.

Monopsonist faces entire supply curve of labor.   The monopsonist faces the entire supply curve of labor. Since that curve sweeps upward to the right, that is, to induce more people to work more, you have to pay them a higher wage rate, the monopsonist who wants to hire more workers will have to offer a higher wage rate.

The question is really one of relative power. Historically, workers have increased their power relative to large corporations by forming unions, but there is a wide variation in the relative power of corporations and unions in different industries. The International Ladies Garment Workers Union (ILGWU) was relatively weak until the 1930s but became the dominant force in an industry characterized by thousands of tiny manufacturers. This situation changed somewhat during the last two decades, as mergers among these firms left the manufacturers' side dominated by 10 or 12 large corporations.

The Oil and Chemical Workers Union is pitted against Big Oil, which is not just a national power, but an international one as well. Another relatively weak union is the Amalgamated Clothing and Textile Workers Union. But that is only half true. It is weak relative to the textile giants, Burlington Industries and J. P. Stevens, but their situation in the mens' clothing industry is analogous to that of the ILGWU in women's clothing.

Collective Bargaining

The main arena

Collective bargaining is the main arena of the power struggle between labor and management. In general, labor tries to secure substantial increases in wages, fringe benefits, and perhaps better working conditions. Management, of course, offers considerably less. And so they bargain. But backing up their bargaining power are their two ultimate weapons. For labor, it is the strike. For management, it is the ability to take a strike.

The strike and the ability to take a strike

The lockout

Some observers call the lockout management's ultimate weapon. That is like saying that if labor's ultimate weapon is to punch management in the nose, management can beat labor to the punch, so to speak, by punching itself in the nose.

If a strike hurts the company by cutting off production, so too does a lockout. Surely it doesn't make a whole lot of sense to lock out workers who were about to leave anyway.

No, the ultimate weapon of management is the ability to take a strike. To carry our analogy farther, a good fighter must be able to take a punch. Perhaps in other fields the term *glass jaw* or *canvas back* might be laudatory, but not in boxing—and not in collective bargaining. If the union knows that management cannot withstand a strike, it will certainly push much harder for a favorable settlement.

Which firms and industries can best withstand a strike?

The ability to take a strike, of course, varies from firm to firm and industry to industry. Generally manufacturing fares better than services because the first can build up inventories in anticipation of a strike. On the rare occasions when the Taft-Hartley Act is invoked by the president, the companies can add even further to their stockpiles. Meanwhile, as the strike wears on, orders can be filled from this large inventory. Also, delivery times can be stretched out from, say, the normal two months to three or four months. When the strike is over, workers can be put on overtime and extra workers temporarily hired to help build up the depleted inventories and fill any backlog of orders.

Firms in service industries are less able to take a strike than those in manufacturing because they do not have an inventory than can help them cushion the effects of lost production. An airline, an insurance company, a bank, a computer firm, or a real estate company cannot make up lost sales because their competitors will have picked up the slack.

A diversified firm, particularly a large conglomerate, can ride out a strike more easily than the firm that produces a single good or service. Since a strike will affect only one or two divisions, the others will keep operating. Similarly, a large firm has a better chance of surviving a strike than a small firm because it has greater financial resources.

All this brilliant analysis notwithstanding, one can occasionally draw the exact opposite conclusion about negotiating strength varying with the ability to take a strike. It's like the rhetorical question, would you hit a person with glasses? Then, of course, you put on a pair of glasses.

What does this have to do with the ability to take a strike? I'm glad you asked. If you worked for a company that might go under, would you call for a strike? You'd probably win the strike and be out of a job. That's why, in the 1970s and early 1980s, the United Auto Workers who could have easily defeated Chrysler, did not dare call a strike. To carry this a bit farther, if a company like Chrysler is financially weak, you won't ask for much of a wage increase. In fact, during the 1981–82 recession, there were actually unions that negotiated not only no wage increases, but even wage reductions.

Both union and management bargaining teams operate under certain constraints.

Both the union and management bargaining teams operate under certain constraints. This union team cannot go back to its membership without some minimum acceptable package. Often they talk of trying to "sell" a particular agreement to the union's members. Regardless of whether a vote is taken on the proposal (sometimes the union negotiating team has carte blanche to reach a binding settlement), if that settlement is unacceptable to the rank and file, the negotiating team will soon be out of a job.

The management team also operates under certain constraints. The first is money. How much can the company afford? Of course, how much it *says* it can afford and how much it can *actually* afford may be widely divergent figures. Furthermore, the team cannot go beyond what top management is willing to pay or it too will be out of a job.

Furthermore, there is the issue of management prerogatives. These, it is said, are more jealously guarded by management than the virtue of their spouses. If the management team were to agree to allow the union to share in the company's decision making, this would not be received too favorably by the boys upstairs.

Besides power, what about negotiating skills? Although good negotiators come away with better settlements than bad negotiators, the real test of a good negotiator is how to get the best possible package—or from the management standpoint, give away the smallest possible package—*without* precipitating a strike.

Anybody can avoid a strike by reaching a disadvantageous agreement, just as anyone can allow a strike to develop by being intransigent. The trick is to get the best possible deal without a strike. And that takes a good negotiator.

The pressure to reach a settlement

The pressure on both sides to reach a settlement without a strike is considerable. The cost of a strike to management is considerable. For example, General Motors lost $90 million a day in sales during the 67-day strike in 1970, and the striking members of the United Auto Workers did not do too much better, losing an estimated $50–$60 million a day in pay.

I don't mean to give the impression that collective bargaining is solely a test of power. Real issues are presented and discussed. The rising cost of living, worker productivity, as well as other recent settlements, are generally bandied about. For example, during a period of inflation, the union team will be sure to point out if, in terms of actual purchasing power, its members have lost ground over the life of the expiring contract. One might add, parenthetically, that they would be hard put to go back with any wage settlement that did not at least keep pace with the cost of living. Today, about one third of the union contracts now have escalator, or COLA (cost-of-living-adjustment) clauses, which provide protection against inflation during the life of the contract.

COLAs

The issue of productivity increases

Productivity increases are a key issue because they provide the basis for pay increases. If workers produce more, they have a good argument for increased pay; and if more is produced, the company can afford to pay more. Unfortunately, however, productivity—output per labor hour—is not often measured very accurately. A union might argue that productivity is rising 4 percent a year, and management might just as reasonably counter that the figure is only 2 percent. It's practically impossible for one side to convince the other that it has a monopoly on the truth.

Finally, there's the issue of pattern-setting wage increases. For example, after the uniform services (police, fire, and sanitation) negotiations are completed in New York, the city then begins negotiations with the other municipal unions. The bargaining teams for those unions do not want to go back to their members with less than the other guys got. It's as simple as that. During periods of rapid inflation, with the added pressures of keeping up with the rising cost of living, the pattern-setting settlements sometimes tend to be viewed as minimums that must be exceeded. This tends to create still newer pattern setters, which themselves are goals to be surpassed.

Pattern-setting wage increases *(margin note)*

The Collective Bargaining Agreement

The collective bargaining negotiations will end with either an agreement or a strike. (The lockout option, as I pointed out, is really no option at all, and has rarely been used since the 1930s.) Less than 5 percent of the negotiations end in strikes, but as we know, no news is good news, or to put it another way, the media always plays up the bad news.

The collective bargaining agreement is a contract that may run from a page or two up to several hundred pages. The two key provisions are wages and hours and job security and seniority. Other areas often covered include grievance procedures, working conditions, and the role of the union in the day-to-day running of the firm. Also spelled out in the contract are the number of paid holidays, paid sick leave and personal leave days, vacation days, and health benefits.

Focal point of negotiations: amount of wage increase *(margin note)*

The focal point of the negotiations is generally the amount by which wage rates will be increased. In fact, progress reports of the negotiations generally refer to the latest wage offer. Everything else gets lumped together as "other issues."

Job security and seniority *(margin note)*

Job security and seniority are also important contract provisions. Generally the last people hired are the first to be laid off. Seniority is often the most important criterion for promotion as well. This has tended to pit the older, more experienced workers against the younger workers, but the union negotiating team will almost always regard seniority as sacrosanct, especially since older workers tend to dominate most unions.

Union wage scales and seniority provisions are often disliked by company officials because they require that everyone be paid at the same wage rate regardless of individual productivity differences. Furthermore, officials are legally bound to lay off the least senior workers during bad economic times—times when it would make more sense to lay off the least efficient workers. Union officials counter that it would be arbitrary and unfair to use any other criteria but seniority as the basis for wage rates, promotion, and order of layoffs.

Grievance procedure *(margin note)*

Another important provision in many contracts is the grievance procedure, which is spelled out step by step. For example, an assembly line worker whose supervisor yelled at her might first have to go to her shop steward, who talks to the supervisor. If the grievance is not settled at that level, it might go to the chief steward and the head of the department. Beyond that, the contract may specify two or three still higher levels. However, most grievances are settled at the steward-supervisor level.

Other grievances may involve interpretations of the contract—when are you entitled to overtime, who is more qualified for promotion, or whether an employee is eligible for full leave benefits during pregnancy leave.

Mediation versus Arbitration

A mediator is literally a go-between. President Carter forged the Camp David Agreement by running back and forth with proposals and counterproposals by Israel's Menachem Begin and Anwar Sadat of Egypt. A labor mediator tries to speed up the process of negotiations, getting each side to give a little more and take a little less. Often he or she will sit down with each side separately, and then, when an agreement seems possible, will get both sides together for what is, hopefully,

the final bargaining session.

The mediator does not have the power to impose a settlement, but can play a valuable role as an expeditor. The job of an arbitrator is to impose settlements. This takes the decision out of the hands of labor and management, a situation both sides usually want to avoid. Under compulsory arbitration, a labor contract or law actually stipulates that if both parties cannot reach an agreement, an arbitrator will make the decision.

The Strike

The public eye is captured by the most spectacular strikes—the 1981 air traffic controllers' and baseball players' strikes, followed the next year by the National Football League's Players' Association strike.[1] And yet, none of these strikes directly affected more than a few thousand workers, with very little effect on our economy.

> **Very few strikes have disrupted our economy.**

In fact, very few strikes *have* disrupted our economy. Since the passage of the Taft-Hartley Act in 1947, only two have caused major economic disruption: the 1959 steel strike and the one by the United Auto Workers against General Motors in 1970. The worst year was 1946 and that year was an aberration because the unions had been restricted from striking during the war while inflation was pushing up the cost of living. With the exception of 1946, in no year did strikes result in as much as a 1 percent loss in total labor hours worked.

One might ask why unions go on strike when what they are fighting over—the 10 or 15 cents an hour—cannot possibly compensate for the wages lost during the strike. For example, suppose labor and management are 1 percent apart when the strike is called. In one week, the workers will have lost $\frac{1}{50}$ or 2 percent of their annual pay. A strike lasting one month means foregoing 8 percent of your annual pay.

> **Four good reasons for going on strike**

Why go on strike then? I'll give you four good reasons. First, most union members don't make these calculations. Second, sometimes you are not 1 percent apart, but 3 or 4 percent apart. Third, you're hoping that the strike will be settled quickly. I've walked a few picket lines in my day, and the prime topic of conversation is whether or not "they're" meeting.

The fourth reason is a combination of macho and credibility. In New York, many people remember Mike Quill, who, back in the 1950s and 1960s, was president and chief negotiator for the Transit Workers Union (TWU). It seems that every New Year's Eve there were two shows on television—Mike Quill and Guy Lombardo.

Every other New Year's Eve, the city's contract with the Transit Workers Union would expire and negotiations always went down to the wire. Most people in New York got around by public transportation in those days and we never knew if we'd make it home from the parties. Usually they would "stop the clock" during negotiations (which meant that although the contract had expired at midnight, as long as negotiations were proceeding, no strike would be called).

---

[1] The 1987 football strike had even less economic impact, mainly because the NFL was able to field teams manned by strike-breakers (called "scabs"), who jumped at the chance to play professional football.

Finally, about 4 A.M., the mayor would announce that the city had "found" the money to give the TWU most of what they wanted, and a strike would be averted in the nick of time. But a lot of people began to doubt whether Quill would actually have the guts to call a strike. As Quill got older, his Irish brogue got thicker, and by Christmas 1965, the word was out that Quill was ready for a strike. Of course, no one knew for sure because it had become pretty hard to understand what he was saying due to the brogue. John Lindsay, the patrician mayor-elect, would be taking office at 12:01 A.M. on January 1. Robert Wagner, the outgoing mayor, had been unable to reach a settlement with Quill, so he flew to Mexico during the last hours of his term, throwing the whole mess in Lindsay's lap.

Quill and Lindsay sat across the table from each other and it quickly became apparent that Quill was not overly fond of the younger mayor. When the city put forth an offer, Quill turned it down with scorn. "Do you take me for a *schmuck*?"[2] asked Quill, somewhat managing to make himself understood. "You're offering *bubkes*."[3]

Lindsay whispered to an aide, "*Schmuck* I know, but what is *bubkes*?" It didn't really matter because Quill was bound and determined to call a strike. Why? Some people thought he hated Lindsay but there was a better reason. Quill really had to put up or shut up. He was like the boy who cried wolf; if he cried wolf this one last time, no one would believe the transit workers would ever strike.

You have to strike *sometime* to maintain credibility.

You have to strike *some*time to maintain credibility. If management gets the idea that you are afraid to strike, they won't make a decent offer. Why should they? But as I've emphasized, strikes are the exception, not the rule. And so, what it really comes down to in collective bargaining—the incentive to settle—is the threat of a strike. It is that threat rather than its occasional occurrence that provides the motivation necessary to make collective bargaining work.

Have Unions Raised Wages?

Yes—but by how much?

Have unions raised wages? The answer is yes. The only question is, how much? Various studies done in the 1960s and 1970 indicate that unions, among them the Teamsters, electricians, airline pilots, and plumbers, have raised the wages of their members by 10–45 percent.

There has been a tendency for unions to spring up in relatively productive occupations, often in very profitable industries. There is evidence that even without unions, the pay would be better than in the other non-unionized sectors. Perhaps we will see some decline in the pay differentials between unionized and nonunionized work with the decline of the nation's industrial sector.

One field that demonstrates the power of labor oganization is medicine. That's right! And the American Medical Association (AMA), although it would consider a union label beneath contempt, has been amazingly successful in raising the wage rates of doctors—well in excess of $100,000 a year—by restricting their numbers. It works the same as with sheet metal workers, bricklayers, and electricians, but the AMA does it better.

Unions *do* raise wages and they provide a badly needed measure of job security. Until unions were organized, workers were powerless to bargain with huge corporate employers. Now there are many who fear that the power has shifted too far the other way.

---

[2] Fool, idiot (in Yiddish).

[3] Peanuts, an insultingly small amount (in Yiddish).

The Supply of Labor

Noncompeting Groups

Skilled, semiskilled, and un-skilled labor

There are various classes or strata of labor. There is skilled labor, which includes carpenters, plumbers, machinists, computer programmers, printers, schoolteachers, and airline pilots. There is semiskilled labor, such as assembly line workers, file clerks, receptionists, and supermarket checkout clerks. Finally, we have unskilled labor, which would include freight handlers, dishwashers, porters, janitors, and gas station attendants.

There are also professional (who are the amateurs?), managerial, sales, and service occupations. *The Dictionary of Occupational Skills* lists tens of thousands of job classifications, each of which has its own special code. If you happen to collect unemployment insurance benefits, when you go to the state employment office, they'll put a sticker in your booklet listing your code so that your skill is readily identifiable.

In a sense, there are thousands of noncompeting groups. But that doesn't mean there's no overlap, or that people with one skill do not compete for jobs with those who have other skills. In fact, an employer is often faced with the decision about whether to hire a highly paid, skilled worker, or a lower-paid trainee. One might say that in the long run, we are all potential competitors for the same jobs.

Suppose hundreds of thousands of jobs became available to play major league baseball. Perhaps the major leagues expanded to Mars, Venus, and Jupiter. I know I haven't revealed this to too many people, but I still harbor ambitions to have a major league career.[4] And so do a lot of other economics professors. We could start our own teams—the Keynesians, the monetarists, the supply-siders.

Before we carry things too far, let's return to the point I was making. If the opportunities arise in certain fields—professional sports, engineering, accounting, computer programming, medicine—people will go through the necessary training and compete for jobs. If there are really a lot of relatively high-paying jobs, people currently in those fields will eventually be joined by huge numbers of competitors.

We are all competitors in the same employment pool.

In still another sense, we are all competitors in the same employment pool. Certain skills are partially substitutable for other skills. One 100-word-per-minute typist is a perfect substitute for another 100-word-per-minute typist; but an electrician who can type 20 words per minute is only a partial substitute. Similarly, a plumber's assistant is a partial substitute for a plumber, and a file clerk is an even more partial substitute for a plumber's assistant.

In the long run most of us can learn to do many different jobs. In some cases it takes just a few hours, but it takes many years to learn other skills. In the short run, however, we are all partial substitutes for one another. The only question is, how partial?

There *are* noncompeting groups, but these distinctions tend to blur in the long run. To the degree that there is a high degree of labor mobility—the ability to change occupations and/or geographic location—there is less demarcation among the nation's various occupational groups.

---

[4] For those who are skeptical about this, I quote a sentence about me on page 187 of *The Einstein Syndrome: Corporate Anti-Semitism in America Today* (Lanham, Md.: University Press of America, 1982): "He plans to enter the free agent draft this fall and pursue a major league baseball career."

The Theory of the Dual Labor Market

The primary and secondary labor markets

Obviously we are not all in the same labor market, primarily because we are separated by skill, ability, and training. A more radical theory than that of noncompeting groups places the entire labor force into two broad categories: the primary and secondary labor markets.

The primary market has most of the good jobs, which not only pay well, but offer a good chance for advancement. Examples of such jobs include the skilled crafts, management, the professions, and virtually all the other jobs requiring college degrees.

The secondary market consists of all the jobs that are left over. The pay is low and there is little chance for advancement. These include jobs in laundries, hospitals, fast-food chains, and clothing factories. These positions are often filled by minority group members and women.

The rich stay rich and the poor stay poor.

The dual labor market theory is a class theory of employment. The rich stay rich and the poor stay poor. The college degree seems to be a dividing line, a line that is seldom passed by those from poorer economic backgrounds.

One problem with this theory is that it doesn't account for the huge middle level of occupations—nursing, teaching, social work, and noncollege graduate positions in insurance, banking, and retailing. But the theory *does* support the contention that there are noncompeting groups in the labor market. The only question is, how many?

The Backward-Bending Supply Curve

When we talk about the supply of labor, I ask my students if they would be willing to do clerical work for $3 an hour. Nobody wants to. How about $10 an hour? A lot of hands go up. And at $100 an hour, everyone volunteers.

The substitution effect

This demonstrates the substitution effect. As the wage rate rises, people are willing to substitute more work for leisure time because leisure time is becoming more expensive. Imagine if an hour of leisure time cost you $100! Suppose the wage rate were increased to $1,000 an hour. Now an hour of leisure time would cost you $1,000! That's a lot of money to give up for just one hour of TV watching, playing bingo, or hanging around the shopping mall.

Something else is happening as your wage rate keeps getting higher. You're making all this money. You're rich! You're making $1,000 an hour. But if you keep working more and more hours, when are you going to be able to spend your money? When are you going to have time to see your family and friends? And when are you going to have time to sleep?

At some point, as your wage rate continues to rise, you will say to yourself, "I'll want more leisure time for myself, if only so that I'll be able to spend some of my money." Now you're willing to give up some income in exchange for more leisure time. We call that the income effect.

The income effect

Turning to Figure 27–3, we see that as the wage rate rises from very low levels to higher and higher levels, people substitute extra work for leisure time. That's the substitution effect. And that happens up to point J. Beyond point J the curve now begins to move upward to the left as the wage rate continues to rise. That's the income effect.

We call curve S in Figure 27–3 the individual labor supply curve. Perhaps the typical individual will work a maximum of 60 or 70 hours a week. I had a friend called Shreiking Jack. (Never mind how he got that name. Believe me, it fit.) He used to work 108 hours a week.

"Why, Jack, why do you do it?" Jack pointed at his brand new Chevy Impala—remember the cars that had what looked like bow ties on their rear

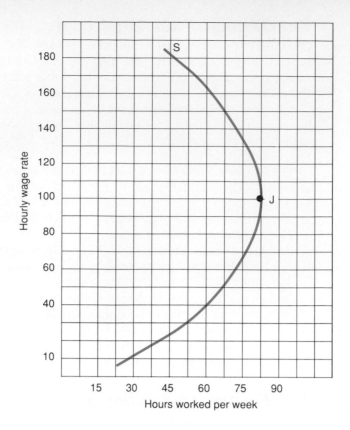

Figure 27–3
Hypothetical Individual Labor Supply Curve

At about $100 an hour, this person would work a maximum of about 82 hours. This is designated by point J.

ends? "With time and a half and double time on both jobs, I paid for that car in three weeks! Of course I had to work 324 hours." Then he shreiked.

We can now generalize our findings in Figure 27–4. Here we have the general supply curve of labor. Why is it general? Because nearly everyone will increase his or her hours of work up to a point as the wage rate rises and then cut back. Of course, people will cut back at different points, some at 30 hours, some at 40, some at 60, or 80, and Shreiking Jack at 108.

At relatively low wage rates, as the wage rate rises, the substitution effect outweighs the income effect, but at some point, the two are just in balance (point J). Finally, as the wage rate is increased still farther, the income effect overcomes the substitution effect.

Although we talk about a general supply curve for labor, in the short run, since there are different types of work (and noncompeting groups to perform each of these jobs), there are many different labor supply curves. For example, the general supply curve for heart surgeons might look like the one in Figure 27–5A, while that of clerical workers looks like the one in Figure 27–5B. If the wage rate for heart surgeons is $145 an hour, we find that we are above point J, and the supply curve has already begun to bend backward. In Figure 27–5B, the wage rate for clerical workers is $6 an hour, so we are well below point J.

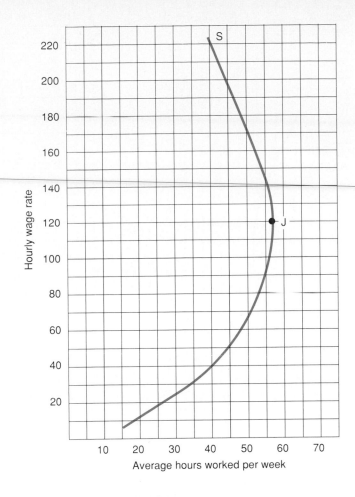

Figure 27–4
Hypothetical General Supply Curve
for Labor

At about $120 an hour, on the average, people would
work a maximum of about 57 hours. This is
designated by point J.

The popular name for the general supply curve among economists is the backward-bending supply curve. This shows that economists are capable, every so often, of fooling around. What's so funny about a backward-bending supply curve? I'm not too sure myself, but it's about the funniest thing we've been able to come up with.

The Demand for Labor

The Marginal Revenue Product Schedule

You may have noticed that I have been trying to impress on you the idea that the wage rate is determined by two factors—supply and demand. We just covered supply. Demand is the firm's MRP schedule for labor. In the more general sense, the demand for a particular type of labor is the sum of all the firm's MRP schedules.

Demand for labor is represented by the MRP
schedule.

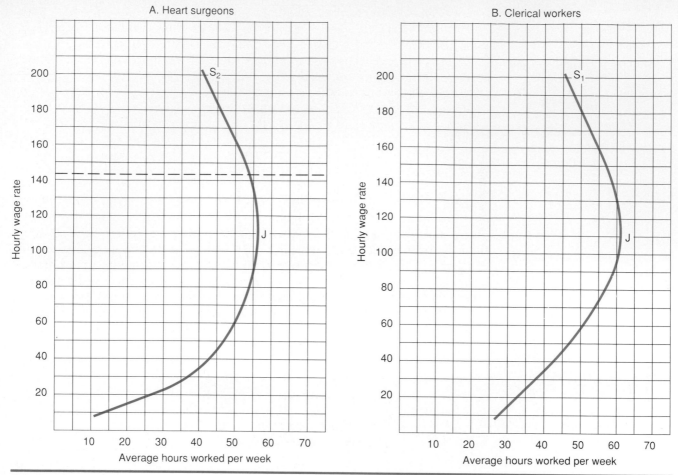

Figure 27–5
Hypothetical General Supply Curve
for Labor—Examples

We may ask what determines the demand for labor, or more specifically, the MRP schedule of each firm. Remember that the demand for each factor of production—land, labor, and capital—is a derived demand. It is derived from the demand for the final product.

Firms hire labor because that labor produces a final product that is then sold. Not all labor is identical. Some people are more productive because they are better trained, more skilled, or have more natural ability.

Obviously workers who are more productive will generally be more in demand and better paid than less productive workers. The more highly skilled machinist and the better basketball player will usually earn more than their less productive colleagues.

Productivity: the role of education

Some people become more productive because of education and training, some because of work experience, and of course, some are just born with greater natural ability. It has often been noted that high school graduates earn considerably more than those who never got past the eighth grade, and that there is also a wide differential between the earnings of high school and college graduates. But perhaps too much is made of these differences, which may be explained not just on the basis of education, but on general ability and connections as well. For example, the average college graduate has a considerably higher IQ than a high school graduate, so you won't raise your IQ by going to college. Furthermore, the college graduate comes from a family with better business connections than the high school graduate.

What I'm getting at is that relatively high productivity cannot be completely explained by education when we compare high school and college graduates. Furthermore, we have many cases where people of widely varying productivity earn the same wages regardless of education or ability. None of these matter in an office or factory where there is a standard wage rate for someone who has put in a certain number of years on the job; everyone gets the same wages no matter how productive. Often labor unions, civil service rules, and institutional custom enforce these standards. In sum, productivity partially explains wages differentials, but it is not the entire story.

Specialized skills

Closely related to worker productivity are specialized skills possessed by some workers, which also influence the demand for labor. Generally the highly skilled worker or the highly trained specialist will earn higher wages than the person with less well-developed skills. Specialists in medicine and dentistry, in law and in engineering, are usually among the best paid practitioners of their professions. This is especially true when their skills are in relatively high demand in relation to their supply.

Finally, some workers are in demand because of a natural ability they possess. Obvious examples abound in show business and professional athletics. A little later we'll consider the special cases of Johnny Carson and Willie Mays.

Nonhomogeneous Jobs

Still another factor determining different wage rates is worker preference with respect to working hours and conditions. Those willing to work longer hours, night shifts, and weekends will usually earn higher wage rates than will those who work the standard Monday-to-Friday nine-to-five workweek; those who work under unsafe conditions earn higher wages as well. Pay differentials are institutionalized, for example, for window washers who work above the 20th floor.

Pay differentials for harder, more unpleasant, less convenient work

The harder, more unpleasant, less convenient work is usually somewhat better paid than the more conventional occupations. Night workers and those who work overtime get pay differentials. The out-of-town salesman is better paid than his home territory counterpart while the sandhog who builds tunnels is given much shorter hours and higher pay than most other construction workers.

Graph of the Demand for Labor

In the previous chapter we saw that the demand curve for labor—the MRP schedule—slopes downward to the right. Similarly, the general demand curve for labor, which encompasses the sum of the demand curves of every firm, also slopes downward to the right. This curve is shown in Figure 27–6.

The Wage Rate: Supply and Demand

Here's what we've all been waiting for. Oh I know, it's a bit anticlimactic, but who needs surprises. It's all there in Figure 27–7.

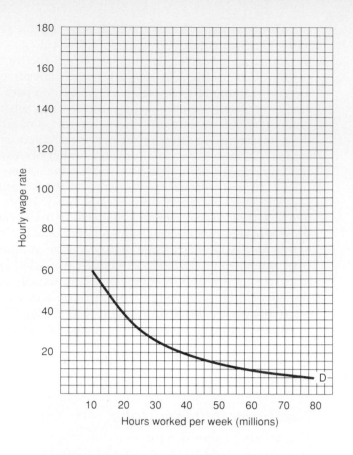

Figure 27–6
**Hypothetical General Demand Curve
for Labor**

We have gone from average hours worked per week
to millions of hours worked per week to reflect the
total labor market with millions of people selling their
labor.

High Wage Rates and Economic Rent

In the early 1950s, when the Giants still played baseball at New York's Polo
Grounds, Willie Mays joined the team as a young rookie and quickly established himself as the most exciting player in the game. Like most ball
players of his generation, Mays came from an economically deprived background and was eventually earning unheard of sums of money.

There was something mysterious about Mays that aroused the curiosity
of his teammates. He would often disappear on summer afternoons when no
games were scheduled, but he never said where he was going. Some of his
friends worried about a 20-year-old country kid and what could happen to
him in the big bad city.

It turns out that on those summer afternoons, Willie Mays, center fielder
for the New York Giants, was playing stickball in the streets of Harlem
with the neighborhoods kids. Why was he doing this? Because he loved
playing ball.

Professional baseball, football, basketball, and other sports give a few
thousand men a chance to make a living playing a boy's game. Although

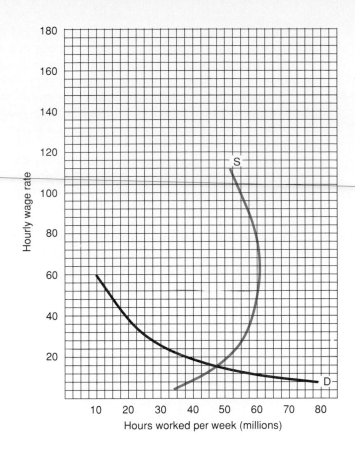

Figure 27–7
Hypothetical General Demand and Supply Curves for Labor

We have gone from average hours worked per week to millions of hours worked per week to reflect the total labor market with millions of people selling their labor.

Economic rent

they negotiate for huge salaries, there are many who, like Willie Mays, would have been willing to play for a lot less. Perhaps it's a chance to prolong one's boyhood for another few years. Perhaps that's what gave Roger Kahn the idea for the title of his story of the 1953 Brooklyn Dodgers, *The Boys of Summer.*

Whenever a person gets paid more than the minimum he or she would have been willing to accept, we call the excess over the minimum economic rent. For example, I might be willing to accept just $20,000 to be an economics professor. Since I am now collecting a salary of $950,000, $930,000 is my economic rent.

To cite the example of another celebrity, Johnny Carson, who collects an even larger salary than Willie Mays, we'll see if he's really worth all that money. Mr. Carson asked me not to disclose his exact earnings, but they are estimated at $6 million a year. I will try to put aside my personal misgivings about a mere show business personality earning even more than I do.

Have you ever gone to a club, maybe to hear a particular singer, or maybe to hear a certain group? While you're waiting, this comic comes out and announces, "On my way over to the club tonight. . . ." Each joke is worse than the last. You look at your friends and ask why you have to pay good money to listen to this clown. Finally, the comic is finished and the crowd claps wildly as he makes his exit. He knows and everybody else knows his act bombed, but the audience is clapping out of sarcasm, out of relief that he's leaving, and in anticipation of the featured act, or maybe some combination of the three.

Why do comedians make so much money?

If you wonder why Johnny Carson—or any of the other half dozen or so stand-up comedians—makes so much money, just take a look at their competition. It's like the guy who ends up in a prison where everyone knows the jokes by number. Finally, he gets up the courage to yell out "66!" No one laughs. "Why?" he asks his cellmate. "It's all in the way you *tell* it." And it's people like Johnny Carson who know how to tell it. The split-second timing, the deadpan expression, the scornful look (at Ed MacMahon)— these are the successful comedian's stock-in-trade. But only a handful are as gifted as Carson.

It all comes back to supply and demand.

We come back again to supply and demand. There may be thousands of would-be comics occasionally getting a gig here and there, but there are perhaps half-a-dozen really good ones. Thus, we have a graph like that in Figure 27–8 in which the wage rate comes to $6 million.

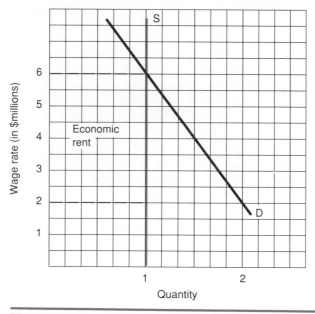

Figure 27–8

Now Johnny Carson could probably scrape by on $2 million a year if he really had to. If that were his secret bottom line—if he were really willing to work for that paltry sum—his economic rent would be some $4 million.

Is Johnny Carson overpaid? It all boils down to supply and demand. Good stand-up comedians, great athletes, cosmetic surgeons, and authors capable of writing best sellers are all in relatively short supply, so if supply is relatively low in relation to demand, the resulting wage rate will be high.

Real Wages and Productivity

When I was a boy growing up in Brooklyn during the Spanish-American War, I got a part-time job selling subscriptions to a local newspaper called the *Kingsway Courier*. The subscription manager, who doubled as the sports editor, told us he was a $12,000-a-year man. Understand that he was trying to impress us because when I was a kid, to earn $12,000 meant selling 60,000 subscriptions.

If you were offered a job today at, say, $100,000, you probably would be inclined to take it. But what if you were locked into that salary for life? Isn't it conceivable that by the time you reached middle age, $100,000 wouldn't buy all that much? What with the cost of living quadrupling since 1967, who knows what will happen to prices over the next 20 or 30 years?

What are real wages?

By real wages, we mean what you can actually buy with your wages. If the rate of inflation were 10 percent a year, you'd need a 10 percent pay raise each year just to be able to maintain the same standard of living. And so we say that a person who earned $10,000 in 1967 would need about $30,000 today to continue living the same lifestyle.

Most of us are not content to just maintain the same standard of living from year to year. We like to see it go up, if not steadily from one year to the next, at least in sizable jumps every four or five years. Why can't we do this by giving everyone pay increases—increases that more than keep pace with inflation?

What can you buy with your earnings?

The key question is, what can you buy with this money? You can't buy more unless we produce more. In a word, the national standard of living cannot rise unless national production rises.

When we talk about the relationship between real wages and production, what is really important is output per labor hour. In other words, how much do people produce in an hour? For real wages to grow, output per labor hour must grow. In fact, this is an almost exactly identical relationship.

Between 1947 and 1978 output per labor hour rose 104 percent. During this period real wages rose 105 percent. Since 1978 things haven't gone so well. Output per labor hour rose only about 2 percent per year between 1978 and 1987. And real wages also rose about 2 percent a year.

Relationship between real wages and output per labor hour

The historical relationship between real wages and output per labor hour is a fact—and you can't argue with a fact. Any efforts to raise real wages must center on raising output per labor hour. It is not enough to raise money wages without raising output; to do that would only cause inflation. Then we'd all be making $100,000 a year, but our living standard would be the same as when we were earning considerably less.

Should There Be a Minimum Wage?

Conservatives: The minimum wage law hurts the very people it is supposed to help.

According to many conservative economists, the minimum wage law hurts the very people it is supposed to help—young workers, the unskilled, and those whose productivity is low. They use marginal revenue product analysis (which we covered in the last chapter) to support their claim that the basic effect of the minimum wage is to cause millions of marginal workers to be unemployed. And they point to the rising teenage unemployment rate as their proof.

There are two ways of presenting this proof. Table 27–1 shows the upward trend in teenage unemployment from the mid-1950s to the early 1980s. The point here is that as the minimum wage level has gone up, so too has the teenage unemployment rate.

In Figure 27–9, we have a hypothetical MRP curve for unskilled labor (i.e., the demand for unskilled labor) and a hypothetical labor supply curve. It is obvious that at $3.35 an hour (the minimum wage in 1982) there was a surplus of unskilled labor. By allowing the wage rate to fall to the equilibrium level, substantially more people would find work.

Table 27–1
The Teenage Unemployment Rate
and the Minimum Wage

Period	Minimum Wage	Overall Unemployment Rate	Teenage Unemployment Rate
1954–55	$ .75	5.0%	11.8%
1963–66	1.25	6.1	15.7
1982	3.35	9.6	30.0

Source: *Economic Report of the President*, 1984.

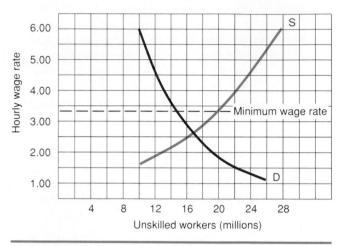

Figure 27–9
Hypothetical Demand and Supply Schedules for Unskilled Labor

According to hypothetical schedules, equilibrium wage rate is $2.75. At minimum wage rate of $3.35, there is a surplus of about 5 million workers. These are people who would be willing to work at $3.35, but can't find jobs. If the minimum wage were lowered or suspended for teenagers, more would be able to find employment. The question is, how many?

Many younger workers are familiar with the catch-22 of job interviews: "Come back when you have some experience." And where are you supposed to get that experience when you can't get that first job? The conservative economists would help younger workers get that experience by suspending the minimum wage. Once they acquire the requisite experience, they would be able to get a job and earn at least the minimum wage.

For those who remember Richard Nixon and the many "irregularities" of his presidency, one of the less publicized "capers" was the one involving Ray Kroc, the guiding spirit of MacDonald's. It seems that MacDonald's, along with scores of other corporations, illegally contributed to Nixon's campaign war chest. In return, the president tried to exempt teenage employment from the minimum wage law. Undoubtedly he was concerned with the high teenage unemployment rate and was anxious to help young people acquire meaningful work experience.

This raises another issue. My students—many of whom staff the fast-food emporiums of America—claim they do the same work as older workers. Were the minimum wage lowered for teenagers, this would just be an excuse to pay them even less. In fact, the whole attack on the minimum wage is suspect on the same grounds.

Who in America can live on $3.35 an hour? And who is worth *less* than $3.35 an hour? Wasn't the idea of minimum wage legislation to help abolish sweatshop wage levels? Would those who would abolish the minimum wage have us return to those conditions?

President Ronald Reagan did not propose abolishing the minimum wage but just lowering it during the summer months for teenagers, from $3.35 an hour to $2.50 an hour. This way, Mr. Reagan reasoned, millions of teenagers would gain valuable work experience. Year after year he sent this proposal to Congress and year after year the Congress ignored it.

Those who would lower or eliminate the minimum wage make two implicit assumptions, which become apparent when we look at Figures 27–10 and 27–11. They assume a very elastic (or flat) MRP (or demand) curve for inexperienced or low-skilled labor, and a very elastic supply of that labor.

To "help" teenagers, President Reagan proposed lowering their minimum wage to $2.50 an hour.

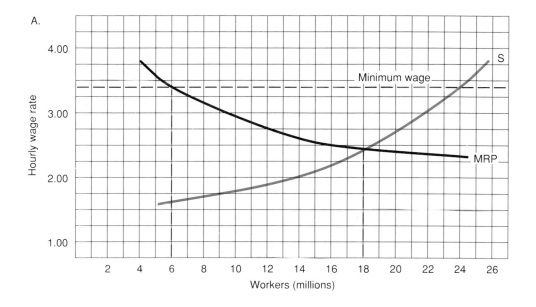

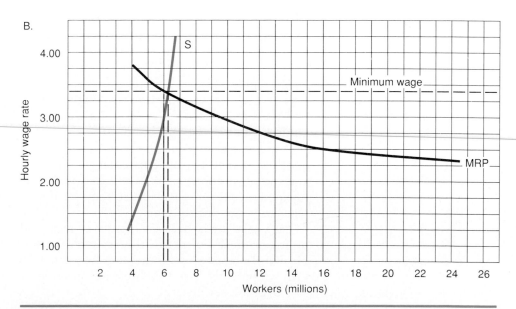

Figure 27–10

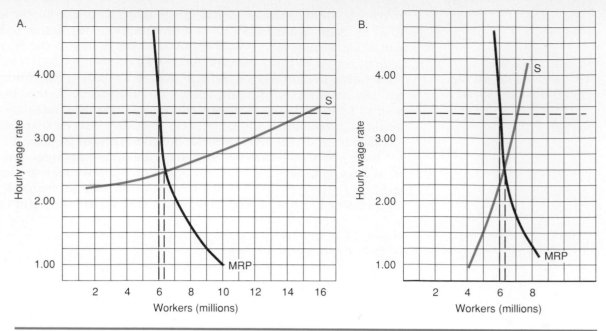

Figure 27–11

That occurs only in Figure 27–10A. As we can see, the elimination of the minimum wage (at $3.35 an hour) allows the wage rate to fall to an equilibrium level of $2.50 an hour. The big news here is the huge jump in employment, from 6 million to 18 million. This shows us graphically (no pun intended) what *could* happen if we abolished the minimum wage. But *will* it happen? It will if both the MRP (or demand) for unskilled labor and the supply of unskilled labor are very elastic.

In Figure 27–10B, we show an elastic demand with an inelastic supply of unskilled labor. When the minimum is eliminated, there is only a small jump in employment. Similarly, in Figure 27–11A (inelastic demand, elastic supply) and Figure 27–11B (inelastic demand, inelastic supply), we show only tiny rises in employment in response to the abolition of the minimum wage.

Let's sum up the prospects of an employment rise if we get rid of the minimum wage. Question number one: Will employment of the unskilled and inexperienced workers rise if we eliminate the minimum wage? Answer: Yes! Check it out. When we drop the minimum wage in Figures 27–10 and 27–11, employment *does* rise. Question number two: How much does it rise? Answer: It rises very little unless both the demand for labor and the supply of labor are very elastic. Are they both very elastic? They could be, but I wouldn't bet on it.

One must also question the validity of the MRP argument. There is no question that teenagers, particularly nonwhite teenagers, are the last hired and the most poorly paid. Is this because they are relatively unskilled and inexperienced? Or is it because they are discriminated against? Are older workers more productive?

Let's take a parallel case. In the average college today a young assistant professor, fresh out of graduate school, is paid less than half the salary of an older full professor, who incidentally, generally has a lighter teaching load. Can we possibly base this huge pay differential on productivity?

Wages are set institutionally.

Wages are set institutionally, with little regard to marginal analysis. Labor unions, corporate bureaucracies, and government agencies all play a role.

Suppose you go to the personnel officer of some large corporation and say you are willing to work for that company at less than the entry-level wage. You'll be laughed right out of the office.

Where does all this leave us? Since wages are set institutionally rather than by marginal analysis, it makes little sense to abolish the minimum wage law. On the other hand, there is some truth to the contention of conservative economists that *some* teenagers are priced out of the labor market by the minimum wage. The only question is, how many?

One might also raise the question of the teenage labor supply. How many unemployed teenagers would, if given the opportunity, work at less than the minimum wage? We don't know. Again, the question is, how many?

The wage rate is set by the law of supply and demand.

If our analysis of how wage rates are set leaves you less than fully satisfied, you still have the economist's one eternal truth: the price of labor, like the price of just about everything else, is set by the law of supply and demand. Now we shall see how well that eternal truth holds up with respect to rent, interest, and profits.

Multiple-Choice Questions

Circle the letter that corresponds to the best answer.

1. Which statement is true about incomes in the United States?
a. Almost everyone earns about the same income.   **b.** Almost everyone is either very rich or very poor.   **c.** There is a wide disparity in income.   **d.** None of these statements is true.

2. Which statement is true about labor unions in the United States?
a. They have always been very popular.   **b.** They did not gain widespread acceptance until the 1940s.   **c.** They have never gained widespread acceptance.   **d.** None of these statements is true.

3. The Knights of Labor
a. were philosophically opposed to strikes, but occasionally engaged in strikes   **b.** were philosophically in favor of strikes, but almost never struck   **c.** were philosophically opposed to strikes and never struck   **d.** were philosophically in favor of strikes and never engaged in strikes

4. The American Federation of Labor became the nation's predominant labor organization in
a. the early 19th century   **b.** the 1880s   **c.** the early 20th century   **d.** the 1940s

5. The AFL has always been basically interested in
a. better wages, hours, and working conditions
b. the formation of small producers' cooperatives
c. the creation of true socialism   **d.** none of the above

6. The act that supported union organizing was the
a. National Labor Relations Act   **b.** Taft-Hartley Act   **c.** Landrum-Griffin Act   **d.** Sherman Antitrust Act

7. Employers' rights were protected in the
a. National Labor Relations Act   **b.** Taft-Hartley Act   **c.** Landrum-Griffin Act   **d.** Sherman Antitrust Act

8. Jurisdictional disputes and secondary boycotts are prohibited under the _____ Act.
a. National Labor Relations   **b.** Taft-Hartley
c. Landrum-Griffin   **d.** Sherman Antitrust

9. Limits on takeovers of locals by national unions and a listing of the financial responsibilities of union officials were provisions of the _____ Act.
a. National Labor Relations   **b.** Taft-Hartley
c. Landrum-Griffin   **d.** Sherman Antitrust

10. Under a _____ shop, an employer may hire only union members.
a. closed   **b.** union   **c.** open

11. Right-to-work laws promote the formation of
a. closed shops   **b.** union shops   **c.** open shops

12. In 1935, the
a. AFL was organizing along industry lines and the CIO was organizing along craft lines   **b.** AFL was organizing along craft lines and the CIO was organizing along industry lines   **c.** AFL and the CIO were both organizing along craft lines   **d.** AFL and the CIO were both organizing along industry lines

13. The AFL and CIO split up in _____ and got back together in _____ .
a. 1915, 1935   **b.** 1935, 1955   **c.** 1955, 1975
d. 1975, 1985

14. The only prolabor name among the following is
_____ .
a. Landrum   **b.** Griffin   **c.** Taft   **d.** Hartley
e. Wagner

15. Which statement is true?

a. No union is a monopoly.   **b.** Some unions are monopolies.   **c.** All unions are monopolies.

16. Which statement is true with respect to the two basic ways unions have of exerting power?

a. Only inclusion leads to higher wages.   **b.** Only exclusion leads to higher wages.   **c.** Both inclusion and exclusion lead to higher wages.   **d.** Neither inclusion nor exclusion lead to higher wages.

17. A monopsony is

a. the seller of a product for which there are no close substitutes   **b.** the buyer of a product for which there are no close substitutes   **c.** both the seller and buyer of a product for which there are no close substitutes   **d.** neither the seller nor buyer of a product for which there are no close substitutes

18. Each of the following companies except _____ was once a monopsony.

a. General Electric   **b.** J. P. Stevens   **c.** the Hershey Company   **d.** AT&T

19. The ultimate weapon that management can use against unions is

a. collective bargaining   **b.** the strike   **c.** the ability to take (or withstand) a strike   **d.** the lockout

20. The firm with the least ability to withstand a strike would be a

a. manufacturing firm   **b.** service firm **c.** diversified firm

21. A collective bargaining negotiation is

a. solely a test of power   **b.** solely a presentation and discussion of real issues   **c.** both a test of power and a presentation and discussion of real issues   **d.** neither a test of power nor a presentation and discussion of real issues

22. Pattern-setting wage increases tend to be viewed as

a. minimums by unions engaged in subsequent bargaining   **b.** maximums by unions engaged in subsequent bargaining   **c.** irrelevant by unions engaged in subsequent bargaining

23. Collective bargaining negotiations _____ end with a strike.

a. always   **b.** usually   **c.** occasionally   **d.** never

24. The two key areas covered by provisions of collective bargaining agreements are

a. wage and hours and job security and seniority **b.** wages and hours and working conditions   **c.** job security and seniority and working conditions

25. The job of a(n) _____ is to impose a settlement.

a. arbitrator   **b.** mediator   **c.** collective bargaining team leader

26. Most strikes

a. cause widespread economic disruption   **b.** cause little economic disruption   **c.** cause no economic disruption

27. Unions have

a. raised wages   **b.** had no effect on wages **c.** lowered wages

28. Which statement is true?

a. Over time the distinctions among noncompeting groups tend to blur.   **b.** Over time the distinctions among noncompeting groups tend to become sharper.   **c.** Over time there is no tendency for the distinctions among noncompeting groups to change.

29. Which statement is true?

a. The primary job market has most of the good jobs.   **b.** The secondary job market has most of the good jobs.   **c.** Neither the primary nor the secondary job market has the best jobs.   **d.** None of these statements is true.

30. According to the theory of the backward-bending labor supply curve

a. first the substitution effect sets in, then the income effect   **b.** first the income effect sets in, then the substitution effect   **c.** the substitution effect and the income effect set in at the same time   **d.** there is neither a substitution effect nor an income effect

31. According to the backward-bending supply curve, as the hourly wage rate increases from 0 to $10,000, the number of hours per week worked by the average person will

a. be constant   **b.** decrease, then increase

c. increase, then decrease   **d.** increase steadily

e. decrease steadily

32. The demand for labor in a particular market is

a. the sum of all the individual labor supply curves

b. the sum of all the firm's MRP curves   **c.** the sum of all the individual labor supply curves and all the firms' MRP curves   **d.** none of these

33. Which statement is true?

a. Differences in wage rates are explained entirely by differences in productivity.   **b.** Differences in wage rates are explained entirely by differences in education and training.   **c.** Differences in wage rates are explained entirely by who you know (rather than what you know).   **d.** None of these statements is true.

34. The possibility of earning economic rent is great if

a. the supply of a factor is very high relative to demand   **b.** the demand for a factor is very high relative to supply   **c.** both demand for a factor and supply of a factor are high   **d.** both demand for a factor and supply of a factor are low

35. If you are earning $20,000 a year today and you were to earn $40,000 a year 10 years from today, your

a. real wages and money wages will both have increased   **b.** real wages and money wages will both have decreased   **c.** real wages will have increased

d. money wages will have increased

36. In general, when output per labor hour increases, real wages

a. rise by about the same percentage   **b.** rise by a larger percentage   **c.** rise by a smaller percentage

d. stay about the same   **e.** fall

37. Conservative economists believe the minimum wage law

a. helps all workers equally   **b.** hurts all workers equally   **c.** hurts teenagers more than other workers   **d.** helps teenagers more than other workers

38. President Reagan advocated

a. lowering the minimum wage for teenagers

b. raising the minimum wage for teenagers

c. exempting teenagers from the minimum wage entirely

39. If the minimum wage were eliminated, the employment of marginal workers would

a. rise a lot   **b.** rise a little   **c.** stay exactly the same   **d.** fall a little   **e.** fall a lot   **f.** fall by an indeterminant amount   **g.** rise by an indeterminant amount

40. There would be a very large increase in employment of low-wage workers if the minimum wage law were abolished and the MRP of workers were

a. very elastic and the supply of workers were very elastic   **b.** very elastic and the supply of workers were very inelastic   **c.** very inelastic and the supply of workers were very elastic   **d.** very inelastic and the supply of workers were very inelastic

41. When the minimum wage is abolished, the wage rate will

a. fall and employment will fall   **b.** fall and employment will rise   **c.** rise and employment will rise

d. rise and employment will fall

Fill-In Questions

1. Until the _____ , most Americans had an unfavorable opinion of labor unions.

2. The predecessor to the AFL was the _____.

3. The main weapon advocated by the AFL to win their demands was the _____ .

4. The Knights of Labor sought to use _____, _____, and if necessary, _____, to win their demands.

5. The two most important pieces of labor legislation were the _____Act and the _____ Act.

6. The Wagner Act prohibited employers from engaging in such "unfair labor practices" as

(1) _____ , (2) _____ , or (3) _____ .

7. The apparatus for conducting union representation elections was set up under the _____ Act.

8. The three main provisions of the Taft-Hartley Act were (1) _____ , (2) _____ , and (3) _____ .

9. Widespread publicity about labor racketeering and corruption led to passage of the _____ Act.

10. The _____ Act put the force of the federal government behind collective bargaining.

11. Jurisdictional disputes and secondary boycotts are prohibited under the _____ Act.

12. Under the _____ shop, an employer may hire only union members.

13. Under the _____ shop, no one is forced to join the union.

14. Industrial unions are organized along _____ lines while craft unions are organized along _____ lines.

15. The biggest spurt in union membership occurred during the decade of the _____ .

16. The conflict within the AFL over whether to organize on a craft or industrial basis led to _____ .

17. The _____ continues to be the least unionized section of the country, mainly because of

(1) _____ , (2) _____ , (3) _____ , and (4) _____ .

18. Unions have two basic ways of exerting power. They are to (1) _____ and (2) _____ .

19. A monopsony is _____ .

20. _____ is the main arena of the power struggle between labor and management.

21. The ultimate weapon for labor is _____ while the ultimate weapon for management is _____ .

22. At collective bargaining sessions, management operates under two main constraints: (1) _____ and (2) _____ .

23. Collective bargaining negotiations will end with either _____ or _____ .

24. The focal point of collective bargaining negotiations is generally _____ .

25. Our worst year for strikes was _____ .

26. The two key accomplishments of labor unions have been to _____ and provide some _____ .

27. The dual labor market consists of a _____ market and a _____ market.

28. The substitution effect (on the backward-bending labor supply curve) takes place when _____ ; the income effect takes place when _____ .

29. At very low wage rates the _____ effect outweighs the _____ effect; at very high wage rates the _____ effect outweighs the _____ effect.

30. The wage rate is always determined by two factors: _____ and _____ .

31. Economic rent is _____ _____ .

32. By real wages, we mean what you can _____ _____ .

33. If we abolished the minimum wage law, employment of low-wage workers would _____ .

34. President Reagan wanted to lower the minimum wage rate for _____ ; he thought this would result in _____ .

35. If the minimum wage were eliminated, wages would definitely _____ for some marginal workers and the employment of marginal workers would definitely _____ .

36. There would be a substantial increase in the employment of marginal workers if the minimum wage were to be abolished only if the MRP for marginal labor were very _____ and the supply of marginal labor were very _____ .

Rent, Interest, and Profit

We're ready to tackle the payments to the remaining three factors of production—land, capital, and entrepreneurial ability. As you might have expected, rent and interest are determined by supply and demand. Profits, however, are determined somewhat differently.

Chapter Objectives

We'll take up each of these topics in turn:
- What is land?
- Economic rent.
- Are prices high because rents are high, or are rents high because prices are high?
- What is capital?
- How is the interest rate determined?
- The net productivity of capital.
- The capitalization of assets.
- The present value of future income.
- How are profits determined?
- Theories of profit.

Rent

What Is Land?

Land is a resource or a factor of production. The owner of land is paid rent for allowing its use in the production process. The amount of rent that is paid for a piece of land is based on the supply of that land and the demand for that land.

This raises four questions: (1) Exactly what *is* land? (2) How does one piece of land differ from another? (3) How is the supply of land derived? (4) How is the demand for land derived?

Exactly What Is Land? Land is land. An acre of land in Lake Forest, Illinois, an affluent Chicago suburb, is a suitable site for building a home. A half acre in downtown Los Angeles could be used for an office building, and 160 acres in Kansas might do well for growing wheat. How land is used depends on its location, its fertility, and whether it possesss any valuable minerals.

Sometimes we confuse land with what is built on it.

Sometimes we confuse land with what is built on it. A plot of land with apartment houses, stores, or office buildings will pay a lot more rent than a plot that lies vacant. But strictly speaking (in economic terms), we pay rent on the land itself. We'll call the payments on buildings and other capital goods a form of interest, which we'll cover in the next part of this chapter.

How Does One Piece of Land Differ from Another? As we've explained, a plot of land may have a few alternative uses. If it is used at all, it will be used by the highest bidder—the one who is willing to pay the most for it. For example, several dairy farms in central New Jersey were bought up by real estate developers over the last two decades. The developers made these farmers offers they could not refuse. In effect, then the land was worth more as housing sites than as farms.

The basic way in which one piece of land differs from another is its location. Only four plots of land can be located at the four corners of the most expensive piece of real estate in the world—Fifth Avenue and 57th Street in Manhattan. Land that is just off this intersection is nearly as expensive. Land near airports, near highway interchanges, in shopping malls, or in the downtown sections of cities is more expensive than less desirably located land.

How Is the Supply of Land Derived? The supply of land is virtually fixed. Aside from the efforts of the Dutch to reclaim small parcels of land from the North Sea, and relatively minor dredging and draining projects around the world, about one quarter of the Earth's surface is land. Until we're ready for interplanetary travel, everything we've got to work with is on the Earth's surface. To go one step further, at any given location there's a fixed amount of land.

Of course, we can make more efficient use of that land. In cities, for example, we build straight up so that thousands of people can work on just one acre. Unfortunately we've been unable to duplicate this feat in the suburbs because of the extensive acreage we've found it necessary to devote to parking lots.

There is a finite amount of land.

Any way we slice it, we still have a finite amount of land. In economics, we say that the supply of land is fixed. We represent the supply of land as a vertical line, such as the one in Figure 28-1. We're lumping all land together in that graph, but technically there are tens of thousands of different supplies of land since each location is different from every other location.

The demand for land is derived from a firm's MRP curve.

How Is the Demand for Land Derived The demand for land, like the demand for labor and capital, is derived from a firm's MRP curve. Since the land will go to the highest bidder, the demand curve in Figure 28-1 represents the MRP schedule of the firm that is willing to pay the most for the land.

Why does the demand curve for land slope downward to the right? You might remember in Chapter 26 that a firm's MRP curve declines with output because its marginal physical product declines with output (due to diminishing returns). In addition, if the firm is an imperfect competitor, to increase its sales it must lower its price, thereby further depressing MRP as output expands.

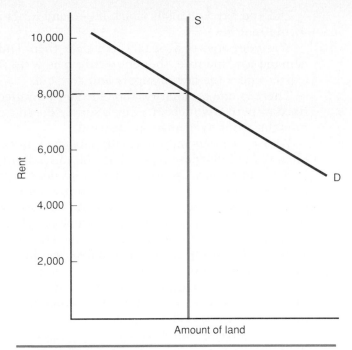

Figure 28–1

How Is Rent Determined?

From what we've been saying in the last 10 chapters and from the big buildup we've gone through in the last section, you do not have to be a great economist to answer the question, how is rent determined? It is determined by the law of supply and demand. In Figure 28-1, we find that rent is $8,000.

Just to make sure we've got this straight, if the demand for land were D_1 in Figure 28-2, how much would the rent be?

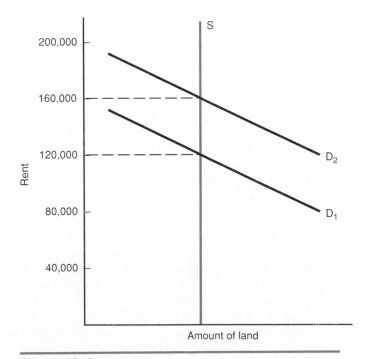

Figure 28–2

Did you say $120,000? Good. If demand for land were D_2, how much would rent be?

Was your answer $160,000? All right then. Did you notice that when the demand for land rose, the rent went up as well? This is exactly what you'd expect under the law of supply and demand.

There is one peculiarity, though. You've noticed that the supply of land is fixed or perfectly inelastic. Since supply doesn't change, changes in price are brought about by changes in demand.

We can use this information to analyze rents charged on three different plots of land. Suppose plot one is 100 miles from the nearest city and is not in demand for any use. How much rent does it pay?

It pays nothing because no one wants to use it. It's what we call marginal land. Suppose someone sets up a store on this land with the permission of the landlord, but pays no rent. Very few people shop in this store because it's out in the middle of nowhere. If the store owner's capital costs were $10,000, the cost of his labor, $20,000, and his sales were $30,000, he would make zero economic profits.

Now we'll move on to plot two, just 30 miles from the center of town. This store also had capital costs of $10,000 and labor costs of $20,000, but its sales were $45,000. Guess how much rent this store would pay?

It would pay $15,000. You see, business is so good at this location that if the rent were anything less than $15,000, the guy who built his store on the marginal or free land way out in the boondocks would have bid $15,000. The location of *this* land, where so many more potential customers pass by, makes plot two worth $15,000 to at least one firm.

Finally, we have plot three, right in the center of town where people pass by in droves. How much rent would this lot pay? It would pay much more than $15,000. If the cost of capital were $10,000, the cost of labor $20,000, and sales were $100,000, how much would this land rent for?

It would rent for $70,000. If it were renting for less, someone would come along and offer the landlord $70,000. The owner of the store on plot one certainly would; and so would the owner of the store on plot two.

Now I'd like you to try this one on for size. Suppose costs remain the same, but sales on plot one rise to $40,000. Would plot one pay any rent? How much?

It would pay $10,000 rent. If sales on plot two rose to $55,000, how much rent would it pay?

It would pay $25,000. If sales on plot three rose to $110,000, how much rent would it pay?

It would pay $80,000. To summarize, location is the basic differentiating factor in the rents of various plots of land, and how much rent is paid is determined by the demand for each piece of land.

Economic Rent

Payment in excess of what people would be willing to accept

In the last chapter we introduced the concept of economic rent, the amount of money certain people are paid beyond what they would be willing to work for. For example, baseball players, like the legendary Willie Mays, would certainly be willing to play for a lot less than they're paid, and perhaps Johnny Carson would take a measly $2 million a year instead of whatever it is that he earns. That surplus is called economic rent.

Economic rent then is the payment above the minimum necessary to attract this resource to the market. Rent paid to landlords (exclusive of any payment for buildings and property improvements) is, by definition, economic rent.

Should landlords be paid anything at all?

We may ask if landlords should indeed be paid any rent at all for their land. After all, land was always there; it certainly wasn't created by the landlords. Whether they expropriated it, inherited it, or even purchased it, the land really belongs to society. A man named Henry George even started a single tax movement about a century ago whose objective was to finance government solely by taxing land rent. George reasoned that since the land did not really belong to the landlords and since the payment of rent did not increase production (because the land is there for the taking), why not tax away this unearned surplus?

Although this tax proposal has been criticized on several counts,[1] it does have considerable merit. A tax on land would raise revenue and such a tax would fall largely on unproductive resource owners.

What Henry George overlooked

But Henry George overlooked an important attribute of rent: as the price for the use of land, it serves as a guidance mechanism, directing the most productive (i.e., highest paying) enterprises to the most desirable (i.e., expensive) land. Because the most desirable locations pay the highest rents, they are inevitably occupied by the highest bidders. If we taxed away these rents, we might conceivably have some effect on the allocation of land. For instance, if I owned a plot of land in midtown San Francisco and all my rent were taxed away, I might just as soon rent it to a candy store as to a fancy boutique.

Are Prices High Because Rents Are High, or Are Rents High Because Prices Are High?

Do certain stores charge high prices *because* they have to pay high rents?

How many times have you gone into a store in a high-rent district and been overwhelmed by their prices? Didn't you say to yourself, "Their prices are high because they have to pay such a high rent?" Fair enough. A store situated in an expensive area has to charge high prices to make enough money to pay its greedy landlord.

We're going to digress for a couple of minutes and a couple of centuries because this same question came up in early 19th-century England. David Ricardo, the great economist, set the record straight: "Corn is not high because a rent is paid, but a rent is paid because corn is high."[2]

The reason the price of corn (and wheat) was high was because there was a great demand for it caused by the Napoleonic Wars. Since the supply of farmland in England was entirely under cultivation (and therefore fixed), a rise in the demand for corn raised the demand (or the MRP) for farmland, thereby driving up rents.

Now back to the present. You've seen that stores in expensive neighborhoods charge high prices and pay high rents. But why do they pay high rents? Because they outbid all the other prospective tenants. Why did they bid so high? Because of the desirable location. Stores located in busy shopping areas pay much higher rents than stores in less busy areas. Why? Because their locations are so desirable that their rents are bid up.

Now we'll look at the same question from the other side. Suppose a store happens to pay a low rent—say a mom 'n pop grocery not far from where you live. How do their prices compare with supermarket prices? They're higher, right? But you'd expect them to be lower, if low rents lead to low prices.

---

[1] It would raise only a small fraction of needed government revenue; landlords sometimes improve the land; and other kinds of income, like rent, are unearned.

[2] David Ricardo, *The Principles of Political Economy and Taxation* (Homewood, Ill.: Richard D. Irwin, 1963), p. 34.

Here's the final word. High rents don't cause high prices. Desirable locations attract many prospective renters who bid up rents because they believe they will get a lot of business. In other words, following Ricardo's analysis, the reason rents are high is because the demand for the final product, and consequently the derived demand, is high.

Interest

What Is Capital?

Capital consists of office buildings, factories, stores, machinery and equipment, computer systems, and other synthetic goods used in the production process. When we invest, we are spending money on new capital. When we build an office park, a shopping mall, an assembly line, or we purchase new office equipment, we are engaged in investment.

Economists feel good when they can think in terms of stocks and flows. We add to our stock of capital by means of a flow of investment. Suppose you have half a glass of water; that's your capital stock. You can fill up that glass by letting tap water flow into it; that's your investment flow. When you've filled your glass, you have doubled your capital stock.

To use a machine example, you've got a capital stock of four machines. You buy two more. That's your investment for the year. Now you've got a capital stock of six machines.

How Is the Interest Rate Determined?

You guessed it! The interest rate is determined by the law of supply and demand. This is shown in Figure 28–3.

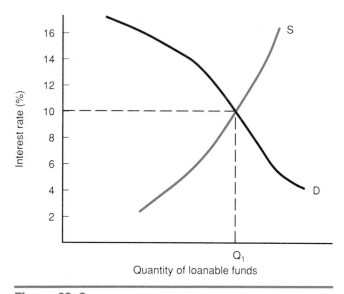

Figure 28–3

The demand for capital is the firm's MRP schedule for capital. As we've seen, MRP curves always slope downward to the right.

The supply of loanable funds, however, unlike the supply of land (which is perfectly inelastic), slopes upward to the right. You may remember that the backward-bending labor supply curve of the previous chapter sloped upward to the right, until at extremely high wage rates, it bent backward.

Why does the supply of loanable funds or savings slope upward to the right? Because the amount of money people save is somewhat responsive to interest rates. The higher the interest paid, the more people will save.

Determination of the Level of Investment

How much investment an individual business firm does depends on its MRP and the current interest rate. We'll suppose the interest rate is 10 percent, as shown in Figure 28–4. At that rate the firm will undertake $40 million worth of investment projects. At lower interest rates, the firm would invest more than $40 million and at higher rates, it would invest less. If the interest rate were 18 percent, how much would be invested? While you're at it, how much would be invested at an interest rate of 4 percent?

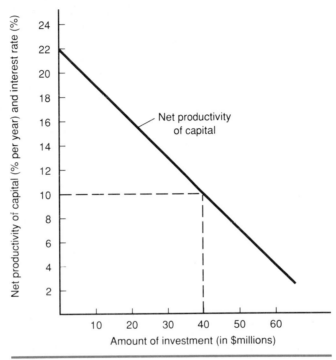

Figure 28–4

At an interest rate of 18 percent, about $13 million would be invested while at 4 percent, investment would be $60 million.

Many firms have a drawer full of investment projects just waiting to be carried out. If they were arranged in order of their profitability, they would be, in effect, the firm's MRP curve. A firm will undertake its most profitable projects first, then its somewhat less profitable ones, and finally, its least profitable ones. But it will be limited by interest rates. The lower the rate of interest, the more investment projects will be undertaken. To see how this works from the viewpoint of the individual firm, we'll work out a numerical problem in the next section.

The lower the interest rate, the more investment projects will be undertaken.

The Net Productivity of Capital

The expected profit rate

To help us figure out whether a certain capital project should be undertaken, economists have developed the concept of net productivity of capital, which translates into the expected profit rate.

Net productivity of capital =
   Dollar value
of net productivity
   Capital cost

To get this figure, which we'll express as a percentage, we'll need to follow two easy steps: (1) Subtract all costs (including an allowance for a normal profit) from sales. This gives us the dollar value of net productivity. (2) Assuming that this value is positive, we divide it by our capital cost to give us our net productivity of capital, which we express as a percentage. To summarize: (1) Sales − costs (including a normal profit) = dollar value of net productivity. (2) Net productivity of capital = dollar value of net productivity/capital cost.

We'll illustrate this with a problem. Find the net productivity of capital if sales = $150,000; labor costs = $30,000; raw materials = $10,000; fuel and maintenance = $5,000; normal profit = $5,000; and capital cost = $80,000.

Figure out the net productivity of capital by following the two steps we've just outlined. Then check with the solution below.

Solution: Sales ($150,000) − costs (including a normal profit) ($30,000 + $10,000 + $5,000, + $5,000 + $80,000 = $130,000) = dollar value of net productivity ($20,000).

$$\frac{\text{Dollar value of net productivity (\$20,000)}}{\text{Capital cost (\$80,000)}} = \text{Net productivity of capital (25 percent)}$$

A 25 percent net productivity of capital looks pretty good. Would you go ahead and invest in this capital good? Yes, you would. Unless. . . . Unless what? What if you needed to borrow the money to invest? Would you *still* go ahead? You would unless the interest rate you had to pay exceeded 25 percent. Of course, that wouldn't be very likely, but it *could* happen. In 1980 and 1981 the prime rate of interest—the rate charged by banks to major corporations—went above 20 percent. That meant that smaller businesses were charged 22, 23, or 24 percent. And some less creditworthy borrowers found themselves paying over 25 percent.

What if you didn't need to borrow? Would you go ahead and invest in the capital good that would yield a 25 percent return? Not if interest rates were above 25 percent. Why not? Because you would get more than a 25 percent return by simply lending out your funds. Why invest in your own business for a 25 percent return when you could do better elsewhere?

Of course it is unusual for interest rates to be anywhere *near* 25 percent. What if your net productivity of capital were 25 percent and the interest rate were 10 percent? Would you invest? Definitely! If the interest rate were 20 percent, would you invest? Yes, you would. We'll say you'd invest right up to the point (or just short of the point) at which the interest rate equals your net productivity of capital.

The Capitalization of Assets

Economists never seem to be able to leave well enough alone. No sooner do they give us a rule to follow—keep investing until your net productivity of capital declines to the level of the interest rate—when they come up with an alternate way of dealing with capital investment. In this case we have the concept of capitalization of assets.

If an asset yields X dollars per year in profits, how much is that asset worth?

This concept enables a business firm to make a decision about whether to purchase a particular piece of machinery, equipment, building, or other capital asset. If a particular asset yields X number of dollars per year in profits, how much is that asset worth? To find out we need to know one more thing—the current interest rate.

Let's set up an illustration. Suppose the going interest rate is 10 percent. If you bought a corporate bond, you'd get a 10 percent return. Why not invest the money in your own business by purchasing a machine? The question is, how much is that machine worth to you?

If the machine yields an annual return of $80, which goes on forever, should you buy it? That depends on two things: (1) it's price, and (2) the going rate of interest. We already know that the going rate of interest is 10 percent.

What if the machine cost you $100. Would you buy it? Think about it. What would your annual rate of return be (as a percentage)?

It would be 80 percent ($80/$100). Would you buy that machine? You'd be crazy not to. An 80 percent return! How much would your rate of return be if you put your money into corporate stocks or bonds? A paltry 10 percent!

What if the machine cost $400? Would you buy it?

You would? All right! That would still be a 20 percent return ($80/$400). OK, are you ready? Up to how much would you be willing to pay for this machine? Figure it out.

Time's up! Your answer, please. Was your answer $800? Then you're right. Why $800? Because $800 would yield a return of 10 percent ($80/$800). You would be willing to pay $800 for the machine, but not a penny more. Why not? Because if you paid more than $800, your rate of return would fall below the 10 percent return you could earn elsewhere.

I know you'd hate to have to go through all those steps every time you think of buying a machine or any other capital good, so I'll tell you what I'm gonna do. I'm gonna give you an easy formula. All you'll have to do is plug in a couple of numbers and you'll have your answer staring you in the face. Are you ready? Then here it comes.

Value of asset =
$$\frac{\text{Annual income from asset}}{\text{Interest rate}}$$

$$\text{Value of asset} = \frac{\text{Annual income from asset}}{\text{Interest rate}}$$

OK, try this one. How much is the value of a building that provides an annual income of $200 when the going interest rate is 8 percent?

Solution: $$\frac{\text{Annual income from asset}}{\text{Interest rate}} = \frac{\$200}{.08} = \$2,500$$

What would happen to the value of an asset if interest rates fell? Figure *that* out.

It would rise. For instance, if the interest rate fell to 4 percent, what would the value of this asset rise to?

Solution: $$\frac{\$200}{.04} = \$5,000$$

If interest rates rise, what would happen to the value of an asset? It would fall.

The reason why this is so is that once you have your money tied up in a particular asset, you no longer have alternative investment opportunities. If those opportunities improve (i.e., the interest rate rises), then you're stuck with a relatively low-yielding asset; it isn't worth as much as it had been. If you tried to sell it, you would get less than you paid for it. You may recall our discussion in Chapter 13 (in the open market operations section) in which we concluded that interest rates and bond prices were inversely related.

If interest rates fall, the value of your asset rises.

On the up side, if interest rates fall, the value of your asset rises. The yield you're getting is better than that of alternative assets. So if you can predict interest rate changes accurately, you stand to make a lot of money. Unfortunately no one has come up with a formula for that. About the best I can do for you is to tell you to buy when interest rates are high and sell when they're low.

The Present Value of Future Income

Economists are fond of saying that a dollar today is worth more than a dollar you will have in the future. Why? Inflation?

A dollar today is worth more than a dollar you will have in the future.

While it's true that most of us have never known anything *but* inflation in our lifetimes, a dollar today would be worth more than a future dollar even if there *were* no inflation. If no inflation were expected in the future, lenders would charge borrowers what we call the real rate of interest.[3]

If you had a dollar today and no inflation were expected over the next year, if you could get 5 percent interest, that would mean one year from now you would have $1.05. On the other side of the coin, so to speak, the person who borrowed the dollar from you today would be willing to pay you $1.05 in one year. Why then is a dollar today worth more than a future dollar? Because it can be lent out and earn interest.

Next question. If a dollar today is worth more than a future dollar, how *much* more is it worth? If the interest rate were 8 percent, how much would $100 today be worth in terms of dollars you will have one year from now?

Your answer? $108 is correct. Naturally we have a formula to figure these things out.

Present value of a dollar received n years from now =
$$\frac{1}{(1 + r)^n}$$

The present value of a dollar received one year from now is $1/1 + r$, when r is the interest rate. Substitute .08 for r (remember that 8 percent is equivalent to the decimal .08) in the formula and see what you get.

Did you get 92.59 cents? (The actual answer is 92.592592592, with the three numbers repeating themselves *ad infinitum*. So a dollar one year from now would be worth only 92.59 cents today.

---

[3] During times of inflation, the expected inflation rate is factored into the interest rates charged to borrowers. You may recall this from the section titled "Anticipated and Unanticipated Inflation" near the end of Chapter 9.

What if the interest rate were 5 percent? How much would a dollar received one year from now be worth today?

Solution: $$\frac{1}{1 + r} = \frac{1}{1.05} = 95.24 \text{ cents}$$

We'll do one more—when the interest rate is 12 percent.

Solution: $$\frac{1}{1 + r} = \frac{1}{1.12} = 89.29 \text{ cents}$$

We can say then that when the interest rate rises, the present value of future dollars will decline; when the interest rate falls, the present value of dollars held in the future will rise.

There is a general formula we can use for the present value of dollars held any number of years into the future.

$$\text{Present value of a dollar received } n \text{ years from now} = \frac{1}{(1 + r)^n}$$

If you're uncomfortable with algebra, don't worry. Once you plug in the numbers for r and n, it's no longer algebra, but just arithmetic.

The letter n is an exponent. It tells us to multiply what's inside the parentheses by itself n times. If the numbers inside the parentheses are $(1 + .12)$ and n is 3, what should we do?

We should multiply $1.12 \times 1.12 \times 1.12$.

Now we'll work out a couple of problems using the formula. If the interest rate is 6 percent and a dollar will be paid to you in two years, what is the present value of that dollar? Work it out to the nearest cent.

Solution: $$\frac{1}{(1 + r)^n} = \frac{1}{(1.06)^2} = \frac{1}{(1.06) \times (1.06)} = \frac{1}{1.1236} = 89 \text{ cents}$$

What is the present value of $1,000 that will be paid to you in three years if the interest rate is 5 percent? Work it out to the nearest cent.

Solution: $$\text{Present value} = \$1000 \times \frac{1}{(1 + r)^n} =$$

$$\$1,000 \times \frac{1}{(1.05)^3} = \$1,000 \times \frac{1}{(1.05)(1.05)(1.05)} =$$

$$\frac{1}{1.157625} \times \$1,000 = \$1,000 \times 86.3838 = \$863.84$$

Profits

How Are Profits Determined?

Profits are considered a residual left after payment of rent, interest, and wages.

Until now we've been saying that the law of supply and demand determines the price of just about everything. Now we're going to have to change our tune. Economists treat profits as a residual left to the entrepreneur after rent, interest, and wages have been paid. We could argue that since these three resource payments are determined by supply and demand, then what's left over, profits, are indirectly determined by supply and demand.

What do *you* think? Does that sound plausible? Should we just leave it at that? Profits are indirectly determined by supply and demand?

Since this section goes on for another few pages, apparently *I'm* not too thrilled with leaving it at that. After all, if profits are the catalytic agent, the prime motivating factor, the ultimate reward for the entrepreneur, surely we can do better than treat them as a mere residual. True, the business firm must pay rent, interest, and wages, and it may keep any remaining profits, but surely profits are a little sexier than that, if I may be so bold.

How Large Are Profits?

What do we know about profits so far? At the beginning of Chapter 2, we talked about their role as an economic incentive under capitalism. The lure of profits is what gets business firms to produce the huge array of goods and services that provide the industrial countries of the world with such high standards of living.

We also know (from the section titled "Economic and Accounting Profits" near the end of Chapter 20) that economists derive profits somewhat differently from the way accountants derive them. Both subtract explicit costs (out-of-pocket or dollar costs, such as wages and salaries, cost of materials, fuel, electricity, rent, insurance, and advertising) from sales. But economists also subtract implicit costs (opportunity costs of additional resources used, such as the wages the owner of the firm and family members could have earned working elsewhere, and interest on money tied up in the firm that could have been earned by investing it elsewhere). Therefore, economic profits are somewhat lower than accounting profits since we are subtracting both explicit and implicit costs from sales.

How large are profits? In 1987, corporate profits before taxes were $305 billion and proprietors' income was $328 billion. Profits then were a total of $633 billion of a national income of $3,636 billion paid to all the factors of production.

Large corporations have no implicit costs, but the majority of the nation's three million corporations are very small businesses with substantial implicit costs.

Keep in mind, though, that these are all accounting profits. Over half the profits of proprietorships and a somewhat smaller share of corporate profits were implicit costs, so economic profits were probably not much more than $350 billion, or a little less than 10 percent of national income.

While we're on the subject, we should mention that wages and salaries (including fringe benefits) came to $2,648 billion in 1987, and that figure does not include implicit wages of at least another $100 billion. The rest of national income is made up of rent and interest, so any way you slice it, wages and salaries come to about 80 percent of national income, profits are close to 10 percent, and rent and interest payments account for the rest.

Theories of Profit

Economic profit is the payment for entrepreneurial ability—whatever *that* is. The entrepreneur is rewarded for recognizing a profit opportunity and taking advantage of it. There are four somewhat overlapping theories of how the entrepreneur earns a profit: (1) as a risktaker; (2) as an innovator; (3) as a monopolist; and (4) as an exploiter of labor. We'll take up each in turn.

The Entrepreneur as a Risk Taker Have you ever played the lottery? Did you ever hit the number? The $5 or $10 that most lottery players spend each week or each month is a very risky "investment." Why do it? Because the payoff is so high. And if you don't play, then you can't even *dream* of winning.

To get people to make risky investments, offer them high rates of return.

The only way we can get people to make risky investments is to offer high rates of return. In general, the riskier the investment, the higher the average rate of return. I mean, would *you* play the lottery if your chance of winning was one in a million and the payoff was 10 percent? Or 100 percent? Or even 1,000 percent?

According to Frank Knight's classic *Risk, Uncertainty, and Profit*, all economic profit is linked with uncertainty. Think of the telephone, television, automobile, and airplane. Who knew for certain that they would work technologically and catch on commercially? Think of the wildcat oil well drillers. These people took risks and made huge fortunes, but a lot of other people took risks and failed. As many rich Texans have long been fond of saying, money is just a way of keeping score.

Frank Knight saw profit as the reward for riskbearing. And those profits, while relatively uncertain and unstable, are also much higher than the normal profits earned by the owners of mainstream business enterprises.

Distinction between invention and innovation

The Entrepreneur as an Innovator We need to distinguish between invention and innovation. An invention is a new idea, a new product, or a new way of producing things. An innovation is the act of putting the invention to practical use. Sometimes the inventor comes up with something that is commercially feasible, but for one reason or another—usually a shortage of capital—he or she does not market it. The Wright brothers, for example, never made a penny from commercial air flight, although Alexander Graham Bell, of all people, tried to steal their ideas.

Schumpeter's theory of innovation

Joseph Schumpeter, one of the foremost business cycle theorists, stressed the preeminence of innovation as the basis for economic advance.

> Whenever a new production function has been set up successfully and the trade beholds the new thing done and its major problems solved, it becomes much easier for other people to do the same thing and even to improve upon it. In fact, they are driven to copying it if they can, and some people will do so forthwith. It should be observed that it becomes easier to do the same thing, but also to do similar things in similar lines—either subsidiary or competitive ones—while certain innovations, such as the steam engine, directly affect a wide variety of industries. . . . Innovations do not remain isolated events, and are not evenly distributed in time, but . . . on the contrary they tend to cluster, to come about in bunches, simply because some, and then most, firms follow in the wake of successful innovation.[4]

Schumpeter went on to say that "risk bearing is no part of the entrepreneurial function."[5] That's done by the capitalist who puts up the money. If the entrepreneur himself put up the money, then he bears the risk of losing it as a capitalist, not as an entrepreneur. Finally, Schumpeter notes that in a purely competitive economy profit "is the premium put upon successful innovation in capitalist society and is temporary by nature: it will vanish in the subsequent process of competition and adaption."[6]

---

[4] Joseph A. Schumpeter, *Business Cycles* (New York: McGraw-Hill, 1964), p. 75.

[5] Ibid., p. 79.

[6] Ibid., pp. 79–80.

If we distinguish then between the capitalist and the entrepreneur, the reward for entrepreneurship would be profits due to innovation. The capitalist's return would be interest, not profits. How high the capitalist's interest rate was would depend on the risk.

So far we've depicted the entrepreneur as a risk taker and an innovator. No more Mr. Nice Guy. From here on in, we'll see the entrepreneur cast in the role of economic villain.

The Entrepreneur as a Monopolist Do the monopolist and the oligopolist, for that matter, make a profit? They sure do! We devoted Chapters 21 and 23 to these firms and we concluded that they were able to make profits because of a shortage of competition. If this shortage of competitors is due to hard work, foresight, and innovation, one could hardly complain about the evils of big business.

Still, we need to make a distinction between "natural scarcities" and "contrived scarcities." A firm that develops a technology before anyone else (like IBM or Xerox) or one that possesses a unique location, like the owner of land at a busy intersection, is the beneficiary of a natural scarcity and consequently earns monopoly profits.

Then there are the other guys, who have created or are able to take advantage of a contrived scarcity. The controllers of patents and those who have cornered the market or own a vital resource (the National Football League, DeBeers Diamonds) will almost always restrict output so they can earn monopoly profits. These are the economic bad guys because they are holding output below the levels at which the public wishes to purchase.

The Entrepreneur as an Exploiter of Labor Karl Marx based his theory of profits on the supposition that the capitalist exploited the worker. To illustrate this relationship, we'll take a simple numerical example. Suppose a worker needs to work 12 hours a day to have enough money to buy food. But suppose he could produce this food in just six hours working for the capitalist. The reason he can produce so much food is because he uses the capitalist's machinery.

The worker produces enough food for two people in 12 hours. The capitalist gives him just enough wages to buy one day's food and he keeps the other day's food for himself. Thus, a capitalist's role is to exploit his employees. Not bad work if you can get it.

Marx calls the expropriation of the proceeds of six hours of labor time "surplus value." The capitalist uses this to buy more capital. Then he will be able to exploit even more workers.

Capital then comes from the surplus value that has been stolen from the worker, and that surplus value represents the capitalist's profit.

Conclusion

What does all of this add up to? Which theory of profits is the correct one? Well, you know my style by now. I ask you what you think, I let you sweat for a while, and then, finally, I reveal the truth to you. I'll give you some time to go back over each of the four theories of profit. Imagine that we're playing a couple of minutes of music while the clock is ticking away. OK— time's up! What's your answer?

Whichever answer you chose is right because there is a lot of truth in each of the four theories—even the Marxist theory. After all, 1 billion Chinese and close to 300 million Russians can't all be completely wrong! It's undeniable that monopolists *do* make profits. And surely there are plenty of profits earned by innovators and risk takers.

What we may conclude then, is that everybody's right. And that nobody has a monopoly on the truth.

Workbook for Chapter 28

Name _____

Date _____

Multiple-Choice Questions

Circle the letter that corresponds to the best answer.

1. Which statement is true?
a. All land has the same economic value.   **b.** The most important factor affecting rent is location.
c. The economic value of a plot of land is determined exclusively by the raw materials it contains.
d. None of these is true.

2. The supply of land (is)
a. fixed   **b.** varies from time to time   **c.** rises with demand   **d.** higher in urban areas than in rural areas

3. Land is most efficiently used in
a. cities   **b.** suburban areas   **c.** rural areas

4. The rent on a particular piece of land is based on
a. the supply of land   **b.** the buildings located on that land   **c.** the MRP schedule of the highest bidder   **d.** the MRP schedule of the lowest bidder

5. When the demand for a plot of land rises
a. its supply will fall   **b.** its supply will rise   **c.** its price will fall   **d.** its price will rise

6. The supply of land is
a. perfectly elastic   **b.** perfectly inelastic
c. relatively elastic   **d.** variable in elasticity

7. Rent on marginal land is
a. very high   **b.** above zero   **c.** zero   **d.** negative

8. Economic rent is paid
a. only to landlords   **b.** to resources that would be made available for lower payments   **c.** illegally
d. only in socialist economies

9. Henry George advocated each of the following except that
a. all land should be free   **b.** all rents should be taxed away   **c.** the government should raise all its tax revenue from a single tax on land   **d.** since land

did not really belong to the landlords, rent was an unearned surplus

10. Each of the following is a valued criticism of Henry George's ideas except that
a. a tax on land would raise only a small fraction of needed government revenue   **b.** landlords sometimes improve the land   **c.** other kinds of income, like rent, are unearned   **d.** a tax on land would result in a decrease in the supply of land

11. Which statement is true?
a. Prices are high because rents are high.   **b.** Rents are high because prices are high.   **c.** David Ricardo believed that high rents would drive English farmers out of business.   **d.** None of these statements is true.

12. Each of the following is an example of investment except
a. the purchase of a new machine   **b.** the purchase of corporate stock   **c.** the purchase of a new computer system   **d.** the building of an office park

13. Which statement is true?
a. Capital is a stock and investment is a flow.   **b.** Investment is a stock and capital is a flow.   **c.** Capital and investment are both stocks.   **d.** Capital and investment are both flows.

14. As interest rates rise
a. more investment will be undertaken   **b.** less investment will be undertaken   **c.** there is no change in the level of investment

15. The net productivity of capital is found by
a. adding capital cost to dollar value of net productivity   **b.** subtracting capital cost from dollar value of net productivity   **c.** multiplying capital cost by dollar value of net productivity   **d.** dividing dollar

value of net productivity by capital cost   **e.** dividing capital cost by dollar value of net productivity

16. A firm will not carry out an investment project if the net productivity of capital is
a. greater than the interest rate   **b.** equal to the interest rate   **c.** smaller than the interest rate

17. In general, when your net productivity of capital is 25 percent you
a. will not invest   **b.** will invest   **c.** will be indifferent about whether you invest since you will exactly break even

18. Whether you purchase a new machine or a new building depends on
a. only its price   **b.** only the going rate of interest   **c.** both its price and the going rate of interest   **d.** neither its price nor the going rate of interest

19. The value of an asset is equal to
a. the annual income from the asset plus the interest rate   **b.** the annual income from the asset times the interest rate   **c.** the annual income from the asset divided by the interest rate   **d.** the interest rate divided by the annual income from the asset

20. If there were no inflation, a dollar today would be worth
a. exactly the same as a dollar received in the future   **b.** more than a dollar received in the future   **c.** less than a dollar received in the future

21. Which statement is true?
a. Profits are determined by supply and demand.
b. Profits are solely a reward for risk taking and innovation.   **c.** Profits are derived solely from the exploitation of workers.   **d.** None of these statements is true.

22. Which statement is true?
a. Profits are about one quarter of GNP.   **b.** Profits are about 1 percent of GNP.   **c.** Accounting profits are larger than economic profits.   **d.** None of these statements is true.

23. Which economist believes that all profits are linked with uncertainty and risk?
a. Frank Knight   **b.** Joseph Schumpeter   **c.** Karl Marx   **d.** John Maynard Keynes

24. Who made this statement? "Innovations do not remain isolated events, and are not evenly distributed in time, but . . . on the contrary they tend to cluster, to come about in bunches, simply because some, and then most, firms follow in the wake of successful innovation."
a. Frank Knight   **b.** Joseph Schumpeter   **c.** Karl Marx   **d.** John Maynard Keynes

Fill-In Questions

1. The amount of rent paid for a piece of land is based on the _____ and the _____ .

2. In economic terms, we pay rent only on _____ .

3. Plots of land are differentiated mainly with respect to _____ .

4. The amount of land in the world is virtually _____ .

5. In a demand and supply graph for land, supply is represented by a _____ line.

6. The demand for land is derived from _____ .

7. The rent paid is $_____ on marginal land.

8. Economic rent is the amount of money that _____ .

9. The main thing Henry George advocated was a _____ .

10. An important attribute of rent overlooked by Henry George was its role as a _____ , directing the most productive enterprises to the _____ .

11. Rent is high because _____ .

12. We can add to our stock of _____ by means of a flow of _____ .

13. The interest rate is determined by the law of _____ and _____ .

14. The demand for capital is the firm's _____ schedule for capital.

15. The supply of loanable funds slopes upward to _____ .

16. The amount of investment undertaken by an individual business firm depends on its MRP and the _____ .

17. To derive the net productivity of capital we subtract _____ from _____ to get the dollar value of net productivity and then divide that figure by our _____ .

18. A firm will keep carrying out additional investment projects as long as its _____ is higher than the _____ .

19. The value of an asset is found by dividing the _____ by the _____ .

20. If interest rates rise, the value of an asset will _____ .

21. If the interest rate were 7 percent, $100 today would be worth $____ in dollars you will have one year from now.

22. If interest rates fall, the present value of future dollars will _____ .

23. Economists treat profits as a _____ left to the entrepreneur after _____ , _____ , and _____ have been paid.

24. Economic profits are somewhat lower than accounting profits because we are subtracting both _____ and _____ costs from sales.

25. In 1986, total profits (corporate before-taxes profits and proprietors' income) totaled $_____ billion.

26. Profits are about _____ percent of national income.

27. The four somewhat overlapping theories of how the entrepreneur is able to earn a profit are:

(1) _____ , (2) _____ ,

(3) _____ , and (4) _____ .

28. In general, the riskier the investment, the _____ the profit rate.

29. Joseph Schumpeter said that profits were a reward for _____ : Frank Knight said that profits were a reward for _____ .

30. A firm that develops a new technology is the beneficiary of a _____ scarcity, while a firm that controls a patent is the beneficiary of a _____ scarcity.

31. According to Karl Marx, surplus value is created when the capitalist _____ .

Problems

1. Given the information in Figure 1, how much would the firm invest if the interest rate were: *(a)* 15 percent *(b)* 10 percent *(c)* 5 percent?

2. Find the net productivity of capital if sales = $200,000; labor costs = $50,000; raw materials = $20,000; advertising = $5,000; fuel and maintenance = $5,000; normal profit = $25,000; and capital cost = $75,000.

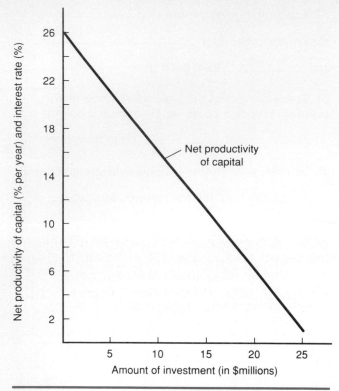

Figure 1

3. How much is the value of a machine that provides an annual income of $500 when the going rate of interest is 7 percent?

4. How much is the value of a shopping mall that provides an annual income of $20 million when the going interest rate is 9 percent?

5. If the interest rate were 10 percent and a dollar will be paid to you in three years, what is the present value of that dollar (to the nearest 10th of a cent)?

6. What is the present value of $10,000 that will be paid to you in four years if the interest rate is 8 percent? Work it out to the nearest cent.

International Trade and Finance

Trillions of dollars worth of business in international trade is conducted every year. Certain trading nations—Japan, the United Kingdom, Hong Kong, Korea, and Taiwan among them—draw their economic lifeblood from foreign trade while others, such as the United States, West Germany, the Soviet Union, and China, are relatively self-sufficient. Yet, even we have become increasingly dependent on imported TVs, VCRs, compact cars, oil, and other consumer goods.

How this trade is conducted is the subject of the first half of this final chapter; how it is financed is the subject of the second half. In fact, trade is only one part of international finance, which encompasses foreign investment, exchange rates, and other international transactions. The one thread that runs throughout international trade and finance is specialization and exchange. If all the nations of the world were self-sufficient, there would be no international trade and little need for international finance. But if that were to happen, the world would have a much lower standard of living.

Chapter Objectives

These are the topics we'll cover:
- Specialization and trade.
- Domestic exchange equations.
- Absolute advantage and comparative advantage.
- The arguments for protection.
- Financing international trade.
- Exchange rate systems.
- Freely floating exchange rates.

International Trade

In recent years there has been a growing consensus in the United States that we need more protection against the import of foreign goods. As American markets have been flooded with Japanese cars, Korean VCRs, Brazilian steel,

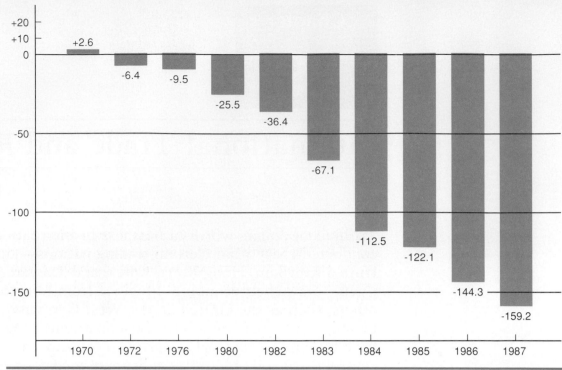

Figure 29-1
U.S. Balance of Trade, Selected
Years, 1970–1987

Source: *The Economic Report of the President*, 1988,
p. 364.

**Alarming trend in our
balance of trade**

Canadian lumber, and Hong Kong textiles, we have seen an alarming trend in our balance of trade. As shown in Figure 29-1, we went from a positive balance of $2.6 billion in 1970 to a negative balance of $159.2 billion in 1987.

What caused this dramatic turnaround and what can we do to reverse this trend? Should we restrict this flood of imports or should we listen to the reasoning of the economics profession, which is nearly unanimous in arguing for free trade?

Specialization and Trade

**Specialization is the basis
for international trade.**

The basis for international trade is specialization. Different nations specialize in the production of those goods and services for which their resources are best suited. Such an allocation of the world's resources lends itself to the efficient production of goods and services. If you check back with our definition of economics, given in Chapter 2—the allocation of the scarce means of production toward the satisfaction of human wants—you'll see that international specialization and trade conform to that definition.

If we go from individual specialization and trade to national and international specialization and trade, we'll see that each induces an efficient allocation of resources.

An individual who attempts to be entirely self-sufficient would have to make his own nails, grow his own food, spin his own cloth, sew his own clothes, make his own tools, *ad infinitum*. It would be much easier and a lot cheaper to work at one particular job or specialty, and use one's earnings to buy those nails, food, clothes, and so on.

On a national basis that's exactly what we do—we specialize and trade. But it would be impossible to do this unless there were a big enough market

It pays for nations to specialize, just as it pays for individuals.

in which to buy and sell the goods and services we produce. Of course, the United States has long been the world's largest national market.

What makes sense individually, also makes sense internationally. Thus, just as it pays for individuals to specialize and trade, it also pays for nations to do so.

Adam Smith recognized the advantages of foreign trade more than two centuries ago when he wrote:

> If a foreign country can supply us with a commodity cheaper than we ourselves can make it, better buy it of them with some part of the produce of our own industry, employed in a way in which we have some advantage. The general industry of the country . . . will not thereby be diminished, . . . but only left to find out the way in which it can be employed with the greatest advantage.[1]

Suppose there were just two products in the world—photocopy machines and VCRs. The United States as well as every other industrialized country has the necessary resources and technology to produce both. The production possibilities curve in Figure 29-2A shows a hypothetical range of various combinations of outputs of photocopiers and VCRs.

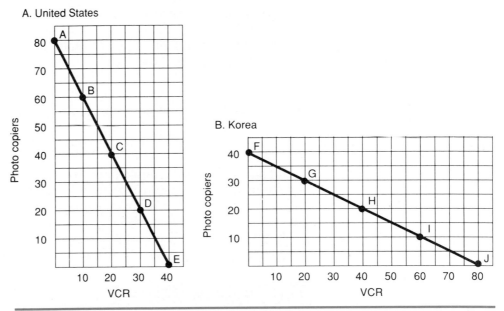

Figure 29-2

You may recall from the discussion of the production possibilities curve in Chapter 2 that a couple of assumptions are made: (1) a nation is using all its resources to produce just two products; and (2) it is using the best available technology. You may further recall that if a nation is operating on its production possibilities curve, it is operating at full capacity and full employment.[2]

You may also have noticed that the production possibilities curves in Figure 29-2 are straight lines rather than the rounded (concave to the origin)

---

[1] Adam Smith, *The Wealth of Nations*, vol. 1, ed. Edwin Cannan (London: University Paperbacks by Methuen, 1961), pp. 478-79.

[2] What I am hinting at in a not very subtle way is that if you don't recall these things, it would be a very good idea to reread the production possibility curve section of Chapter 2.

curves of Chapter 2. This reflects constant opportunity costs; in Chapter 2 we showed increasing opportunity costs.[3]

Just glancing at Figure 29-2 you will notice that the United States is better at making photocopiers and Korea is better at making VCRs. Before we conclude that the United States should specialize in photocopy machines and Korea in VCRs, let's consider what would happen if each nation produced both products and they didn't trade.

Domestic Exchange Equations

If we examine a few points along the United States' production possibilities curve (Figure 29-2A), we will find various combinations of photocopiers and VCRs that we could produce. At point A, with all of its resources devoted to photocopier production, the U.S. output is 80 copiers. At point B we make 60 copiers and 10 VCRs. At C it's 40 copiers and 20 VCRs, at D it's 20 copiers and 30 VCRs, and finally, at E we make 40 VCRs.

From this information we can derive this equation:

Domestic exchange equation for U.S.

$$2 \text{ photocopiers} = 1 \text{ VCR}$$

In other words, the opportunity cost of producing one more VCR is two photocopiers. Or, alternatively, the cost of producing two more copiers would be one VCR.

Let's turn now to Figure 29-2B, which depicts the production possibility curve of South Korea. At point F, that country would make 40 photocopy machines. At G, production would total 30 photocopiers and 20 VCRs. Thus, the opportunity cost of 20 additional VCRs would be 10 copiers. Obviously then the Korean domestic exchange equation is:

Domestic exchange equation for Korea

$$1 \text{ photocopier} = 2 \text{ VCRs}$$

A comparison of the American and South Korean domestic exchange equations tells us that the Koreans are twice as efficient at VCR production than they are at making photocopy machines; Americans have the exact opposite situation. Again, instinct would tell us that it would make economic sense for Korea to devote all its resources to VCR production and to trade those for American photocopiers, in whose production we would specialize.

The Terms of Trade

Korea will trade their VCRs for our photocopiers and we will trade our copiers for their VCRs.

We're finally ready to set up trading between South Korea and the United States. We know that Korea will trade their VCRs for our photocopiers. What we don't know are the terms of trade. Specifically, how many VCRs will Korea be willing to trade for each copier? Or, alternatively, how many copiers will the United States be willing to trade for each VCR?

To help answer these questions, we will make a couple of simple observations. Let's look at the American domestic exchange equation again:

$$2 \text{ photocopiers} = 1 \text{ VCR}$$

Surely the United States would be unwilling to trade more than two photocopiers for one VCR. But what if Korea offered *more* than one VCR for

---

[3] In the real world, every industry eventually faces increasing opportunity costs. But here we use constant opportunity costs because straight lines lend themselves much better than curved lines to our analysis.

two copiers? This would be a better deal for the United States than trying to produce VCRs by itself. Let's see why.

By devoting a fixed amount of resources it could produce either two copiers or one VCR. If it devoted those resources to producing two copiers and trading them for *more* than one VCR, the United States would be better off than it would have been using those resources to produce just one VCR.

The same logic applies to South Korea, whose domestic exchange equation is:

$$2 \text{ VCRs} = 1 \text{ photocopier}$$

Obviously Korea would be unwilling to trade two VCRs for *less* than one photocopier. If Korea could trade two VCRs and get more than one photocopier in exchange, it would be better off concentrating on VCR production and trading some of it for copiers.

Two general observations We can now make two general observations.

1. No nation will engage in trade with another nation unless it will gain by that trade.
2. The terms of trade will fall somewhere between the domestic exchange equations of the two trading nations.

The first observation is virtually a truism, but the second might require further elaboration. We'll state the two domestic exchange equations sequentially and then derive the terms of trade.

$$\begin{array}{ll} \text{United States} & 2 \text{ photocopiers} = 1 \text{ VCR} \\ \text{Korea} & 1 \text{ photocopier} = 2 \text{ VCRs} \end{array}$$

Looking at these two equations, we ask ourselves if the United States and Korea can do business. The United States is willing to trade two photocopiers for more than one VCR; the Koreans are willing to trade two VCRs for more than one copier. Can a trade be worked out to the satisfaction of both parties? Go ahead and try to work out such an exchange. How many copiers for how many VCRs?

Use trial and error. Would the United States accept 1½ VCRs for 2 copiers? Yes! Would Korea give up 1½ VCRs for 2 copiers? Yes! That's one possibility for what we call their terms of trade.

Here's another. Would the United States accept 2½ VCRs for 2 copiers? Obviously. Would the Koreans give up 2½ VCRs for 2 copiers? Yes. There's another possibility. In fact, we could easily demonstrate a large number of possible terms of trade.

What *are* the terms of trade between the United States and Korea? At this point you may well ask what *are* the terms of trade? The best we can do is say that they will definitely be between the two domestic exchange equations. But where? That depends on the forces of supply and demand in the world market. Let's suppose that VCRs are selling for $200 and that copiers are also selling for $200. What do you think the terms of trade for these two products would be?

I hope you said one copier for one VCR. Would these terms of trade satisfy both the United States and Korea? The answer is definitely yes.

Over the last two centuries, economists have insisted that when two countries trade, both gain from the trade. Now we'll prove it. In Figure 29–3, we have reproduced the production possibilities curves of the United States and South Korea from Figure 29–2. And we've added trade possibilities curves. The last tell us that these countries are trading copiers for VCRs on a one-for-one basis.

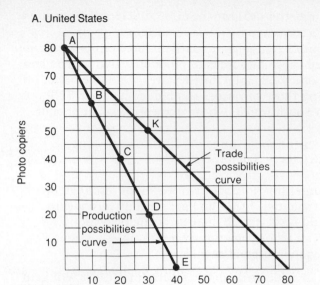

A. United States

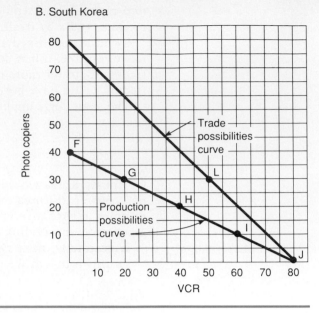

B. South Korea

Figure 29–3

Both countries end up with more copiers *and* more VCRs.

In effect, through international trade, both countries end up with more copiers *and* more VCRs. Suppose the United States had been operating at point C of its production possibilities curve (before discovering the benefits of international trade). At C, we would have produced 40 copiers and 20 VCRs. But if we concentrated our resources on copier production (i.e., produced 80 copiers) and traded some copiers for VCRs, we would go to point K of our trade possibilities curve. At K, we would have 50 copiers and 30 VCRs. What we've done then is to produce 80 copiers and trade 30 of them for 30 VCRs.

It can easily be demonstrated that South Korea experiences similar gains from trade. Start at point H on its production possibilities curve and figure how much better off Korea is at point L of its trade possibilities curve. Do your calculations in this space.

Korea produces 80 VCRs and sells 30 of them to the United States in exchange for 30 copiers. It now has 50 VCRs and 30 copiers. At point H, it had only 40 VCRs and 20 copiers. Its gain is 10 VCRs and 10 copiers.

Absolute Advantage and Comparative Advantage

In the trade example we have used, you may have easily inferred that South Korea made VCRs more efficiently (that is, at a lower cost per unit) than the United States does and that the United States is more efficient than Korea in photocopier production.

This may well be the case, but we don't have cost figures. If it *did* cost the United States the same to make a copier as it cost Korea to make a VCR, clearly we're better at making copiers and they're better at making VCRs.

Absolute Advantage Let's make the assumption that the United States *does* make copiers for exactly the same production costs as does Korea for its VCRs. Expressed somewhat differently, it takes the United States an expenditure of the same resources to produce a copier as it does Korea to make a VCR. Suppose it cost Korea $200 to make a VCR; it would follow that it would cost the United States $200 to make a copier.

Now try this one on for size. If the United States attempted to produce its own VCRs, how much would it cost to make them? If you're not sure, glance at Figure 29-3A. With the same amount of resources, we produce 80 copiers (point A) or 40 VCRs (point E), so it cost us twice as much to make a VCR as a copier, Or $400.

The bottom line is that Americans can buy Korean VCRs at half the price that American manufacturers would charge. Thus, the Koreans have an *absolute advantage* in making VCRs. They're better than we are at making VCRs, so we would do well to take advantage of their low prices while we concentrate on making things we're good at making.

In this problem we are particularly good at making copiers. In fact, we are so good that we enjoy an absolute advantage over Korea. And so, just as we find it advantageous to buy their VCRs, they buy American copiers rather than produce their own.

With absolute advantage it is perfectly clear (a phrase favored by ex-President Richard Nixon) that each country sells what it produces most efficiently and buys what it produces least efficiently. What about countries that do not enjoy an absolute advantage in producing anything? If your country can't make anything for less than other countries, what can it sell? In the next section, we'll find out.

Comparative Advantage In the previous problem South Korea was better at making VCRs than copiers. How much better? A glance back at Figure 29-3 would show us that South Korea could turn out twice as many VCRs as copiers, using the same resources.

How about the United States? Using the same resources, the United States could turn out twice as many copiers as VCRs.

We also found that there was a basis for trade because both countries stood to gain. Now let's go a step farther and ask if there would be any basis for trade if Korea were more efficient than the United States at making both VCRs *and* copiers? What do you think? No? Guess again.

Imagine that there are only two countries in the world—the United States and South Korea—and there are only two goods they produce, VCRs and copiers. To keep things simple, we'll assume that the only resource used to make these goods is labor. We know it takes Korea twice as much labor to produce a copier as a VCR.

Suppose it takes 10 hours to make a VCR in Korea and 20 hours to make a copier. Using the same analysis for the United States, suppose it takes 30 hours to make a copier and 60 to make a VCR. This data is summarized in Table 29-1.

Table 29-1
Hours of Labor Required to Produce Copiers and VCRs in the United States and South Korea

	Copiers	VCRs
United States	30	60
South Korea	20	10

Koreans have an absolute advantage at making VCRs.

We have an absolute advantage at making copiers.

Table 29-2 shows how many VCRs and copiers the United States and Korea can make in 600 hours of labor time. Since the United States can make one copier in 30 hours, in 600 hours it can make 20 copiers. Similarly, the United States can make 10 VCRs in 600 hours because it takes 60 hours to make one.

Table 29–2
Copiers and VCRs Produced by the
United States and South Korea Using
600 Hours of Labor

United States	20 copiers or 10 VCRs
South Korea	30 copiers or 60 VCRs

What if we used 300 hours of labor to build copiers and 300 to build VCRs? In that case we would have 10 copiers and 5 VCRs. Similarly, Korea would produce 15 copiers and 30 VCRs. Together then the United States and Korea could turn out 25 copiers and 35 VCRs without trading. This is shown in Table 29-3.

Table 29–3
Copiers and VCRs Produced by the
United States and South Korea Using
600 Hours of Labor

United States	10 copiers and 5 VCRs
South Korea	15 copiers and 30 VCRs
Total	25 copiers and 35 VCRs

Each country devotes 300 hours to VCR and copier production, respectively.

Are you wondering what all this is leading up to? It's all leading up to Table 29-4, which will demonstrate how a shift in VCR and copier production will lead to an increased output of both VCRs and copiers. That's right! You're going to try to figure out which country should raise VCR production and which should increase its production of copiers. Use Table 29-3 as your starting point.

Table 29–4
Copiers and VCRs Produced by the
United States and South Korea Using
600 Hours of Labor

United States	20 copiers and 0 VCRs
South Korea	9 copiers and 42 VCRs
Total	29 copiers and 42 VCRs

The United States devotes 600 hours to copier production; South Korea devotes 180 hours to copier production and 420 to VCR production.

If you answered correctly, you may have reasoned that because Korea is relatively efficient at making VCRs, it will raise its VCR output while reducing its output of copiers. The United States will do the opposite. If that's what you figured, you figured right.

In Table 29-4 we have the United States shift all 600 hours of labor into copier production so that we produce 20 copiers. Korea, on the other hand, shifts 120 hours of its labor from copiers to VCRs. Thus, in 420 hours it turns out 42 VCRs; in 180 hours it makes 9 copiers.

When we add up the total output of copiers and VCRs in Table 29-4, we find that we have exceeded our outputs in Table 29-3. There is a gain of 4 copiers (from 25 to 29) and 7 VCRs (from 35 to 42).

If Korea and the United States are the only two countries in the world and copiers and VCRs their only products, then we are ready to trade. The trade will be American copiers for Korean VCRs. As we did in the previous problem, let's have a one-for-one exchange.

A one-for-one trade would end up leaving both countries better off than they had been before they specialized. Let's say that Korea trades 8 VCRs for 8 copiers. Korea would now have 34 VCRs and 17 copiers while the United States would end up with 8 VCRs and 12 copiers (see Table 29-5).

Table 29-5
Copiers and VCRs Owned by the
United States and Korea after United
States trades 8 copiers for 8 VCRs

Unites States	(20 − 8) 12 copiers and (0 + 8)	8 VCRs
South Korea	(9 + 8) 17 copiers and (42 − 8)	34 VCRs

How does this compare with what each country would have had before specialization. For this comparison, look back at Table 29-3. Korea would have a net gain of two copiers and four VCRs while the United States would have three more VCRs and two more copiers. These gains are summarized in Table 29-6.

Table 29-6
U.S. and Korean Gains from Trade

United States	(12 − 10) 2 copiers and (8 − 5)	3 VCRs
South Korea	(17 − 15) 2 copiers and (34 − 30)	4 VCRs

This is what is meant by a trade that helped both parties. We see that even though one nation is better at producing both products, it still pays for each nation to specialize in the production of the product it is relatively good at making and trading for the product the other is relatively good at making.

Let's go back once again to the concept of opportunity cost. What is the opportunity cost for the United States of producing one VCR? In other words, to raise VCR output by one unit, what do you give up? You give up two copiers. What is the opportunity cost of producing one VCR in Korea? You guessed it: one half of one copier.

Now we'll consider the opportunity cost of producing copiers. In the United States it's one-half of one VCR; in Korea it's two VCRs. In other words, the opportunity cost of producing VCRs is lower in Korea. How about the opportunity cost of producing copiers? It's lower in the United States.

The principle of comparative advantage

We're finally ready for the principle of comparative advantage, which is what this section is all about. Are you ready? OK, here it comes. The principle of comparative advantage states that *total output is greatest when each product is made by that country which has the lowest opportunity cost*. In our case, copiers should be made in the United States and VCRs in Korea. This is so because the United States has a comparative advantage in copiers while Korea has one in VCRs. This is true even though Korea can make both copiers *and* VCRs at a lower cost than the United States.

The Arguments for Protection

Four main arguments for protection

Four main arguments have been made for protection. Each seems plausible and strikes a responsive chord in the minds of the American public. But under closer examination all four are essentially pleas by special interest groups for protection against more efficient competitors.

We'll first consider the argument that certain industries, while not as efficient as their foreign competitors, are essential to the defense of the country. The next three arguments are related, especially the last two. Each uses the premise that industries based in foreign countries are not competing fairly with their American counterparts.

The infant industry argument is addressed to American consumers who would be seduced into buying foreign goods by their temporarily lower prices. The low-wage and the employment arguments are addressed to the workers who would be hurt by foreign competition. Interestingly, the owners of American companies who would stand to gain the most from protection are conspicuously silent about the benefits they would receive from protection.

(1) The National Security Argument

Originally this argument may have been advanced by American watchmakers, who warned us not to get dependent on Swiss watchmakers, because in the event of war, we would need Swiss expertise to make the timing devices for explosives. During long, drawn-out wars like World War II, we were able to develop synthetics, most notably rubber, to replace the supplies of raw materials that were cut off. And the Germans were able to convert coal into oil. It would appear then that the Swiss watch argument may have been somewhat overstated.

If we were involved in a limited war, it is conceivable that our oil supplies from the Mideast might be cut off (although no American president would stand by passively), but we would probably be able to replace these imports by producing more oil ourselves. And if there were a third world war, we would certainly not have to worry about a cutoff of needed war material because the war would last only a few minutes.

If the national security argument were applied only to limited or local wars, rather than to worldwide wars, it is possible that we would indeed need to maintain certain defense related industries. A justification that the United States should make its own aircraft, ordinance (bombs and artillery shells), and nuclear submarines might well be valid on a national security basis. But these industries have done extremely well in international markets and are hardly in need of protection.

(2) The Infant Industry Argument

In the late 18th century American manufacturers clamored for protection against "unfair" British competition. British manufacturers were "dumping" their products on our shores. By pricing their goods below cost, the British would be able to drive the infant American manufacturers out of business. Once their American competition was out of the way, the British companies would then jack up their prices.

Are American industries *still* infant industries?

Whatever validity this reasoning had has long since vanished. American manufacturers are no longer produced by infant industries being swamped by foreign giants. About the best that could be said is that some of our infant industries never matured while others went well beyond the point of maturity and actually attained senility. Perhaps a senile industry argument might be more applicable to such stalwarts as steel, textiles, clothing, and automobiles.

(3) The Low-Wage Argument

Competing against countries that pay "coolie wages"

The reasoning here can be best summed up by this question: How can American workers compete with foreigners who are paid "coolie wages"?

There are certain goods and services that are very labor intensive (i.e., labor constitutes most or nearly all of the resource costs). Clothing manufacturing, domestic work, rice cultivation, most kinds of assembly line work, as well as repetitive clerical work are examples. There is no reason for American firms to compete with foreign firms to provide these goods and services. If we look at our national experience over the last 150 years, Americans have always left the least desirable, most labor-intensive, low-paying work to immigrants. It was the Irish who did the domestic work, built the railroads and canals, and did much of the rest of the back-breaking work of the mid-19th century. Then, in sequence, the Germans, Chinese, Italians, Poles, other Eastern Europeans, Jews, and more recently, the Vietnamese and Koreans have been accorded the lowest place on the economic totem pole. And of course, a special place near the bottom has long been reserved for blacks and hispanics not because they were recent immigrants, but simply because they were systematically excluded from the economic mainstreams due to discrimination.

Those were the rules of the game and by and large they served us well. Gradually they began to change in the early 1970s as a growing number of relatively cheap foreign imports began to dominate the American market.

What happened? What brought about these changes? First, Japan and West Germany, which had been rebuilding their industrial plants from scratch since World War II, had finally attained parity with the American industrial plant. At the same time their workers were being paid, on the average, less than half the wages of American workers. But in the 1970s, the wages of both German and Japanese workers rose very sharply relative to those of American workers (the average German worker earned more than the average American worker by 1980). Yet, throughout the 1970s our trade balances with both these countries continued to deteriorate.

Why *are* some countries high-wage countries, while others are low-wage countries?

Why *are* certain workers paid higher wage rates than others? Why *are* some countries high-wage countries while others are low-wage countries? In general, high-wage workers produce more than low-wage workers. The main reason workers in high-wage countries produce more is because they have more capital with which to work than workers in low-wage countries.

And so, the reason labor was paid more in the United States than anywhere else in the world during the three decades following World War II was because we had more capital (plant and equipment) per worker than any other country. But as other countries succeeded in rebuilding and adding to their capital, our advantage began to disappear.

A new group of industrializing nations, among them South Korea, Taiwan, Hong Kong, Singapore, and Brazil, is challenging the older industrial powers. By combining capital with low wage rates they are able to undersell even Japan. Although, over time, the wage rates in these emerging industrial nations will rise to reflect the growing productivity of their workers, they *do* have a clear competitive edge over higher-wage nations.

The question then is how to deal with low-wage competition. The answer is to deal with it the way we always have. We have always imported labor-intensive goods—sugar, handmade rugs, wood carvings, even Chinese back scratchers—because they were cheap. And we always let immigrants do the most back-breaking, low-paying, thankless labor. By specializing in the production of goods and services in which we excel, we can use the proceeds to buy the goods and services produced by people who are forced to work for low wages.

(4) The Employment Argument

Hasn't the flood of imports thrown millions of Americans out of work? The answer is, yes—but.

First we'll deal with the yes. There is no denying that hundreds of thousands of workers in each of these industries—autos, steel, textiles, clothing, petroleum—has lost their jobs due to foreign competition. If we had restricted our imports of these goods by means of tariffs or quotas, there is no question but that most of these workers would not have lost their jobs.

If we restrict our imports our exports will decline.

Unfortunately the governments of our foreign competitors would reciprocate by restricting our exports. Furthermore, the way a nation pays for its imports is by selling its exports.[4] By curbing our imports, we will be depriving other nations of the earnings they need to buy our exports. In a word then, if we restrict our imports, our exports will go down as well.

Even such unabashed free traders as President Reagan's Council of Economic Advisors conceded that 25,000 to 30,000 jobs may be lost for each additional billion dollars of imports. They then go on to say, "Protection may save jobs in import-competing industries, but this is likely to be matched by the less visible loss of jobs elsewhere in the economy."[5]

Thus, the jobs we save in steel, autos, textiles, clothing, and petroleum will be lost in our traditional export industries, machinery, office equipment, aircraft, chemicals, and agricultural products. From an economic standpoint, this would involve a considerable loss because we would be shifting production from our relatively efficient export industries to our relatively inefficient import industries. Is that any way to run an economy?

What about the workers who lose their jobs because of imports?

Still, you may ask about the human cost. What happens to the workers who are thrown out of work by foreign competition? Should their employers help them or should the government? And what can be done to help them?

Ideally these displaced workers should be retrained and possibly relocated to work in our relatively efficient industries. Those who cannot be retrained or cannot move should be given some form of work, if only to keep them off the welfare rolls.

Who should help these displaced workers readjust? In a sense their employers are responsible because these people were loyal and productive employees for perhaps 20 or 30 years. Unfortunately, however, the companies who should bear most of the responsibility for helping their employees are hardly in a position to do so. After all, they wouldn't be laying off workers if business were good to begin with.

That leaves the party of last resort—the federal government. What does the federal government do for workers who are displaced by foreign competition? Not very much. These workers receive extended unemployment benefits, are eligible for job retraining, and may receive some moving expenses. But the bottom line is that a middle-aged worker who loses her $15 an hour job will probably not find another one that pays close to that, and government programs will not begin to compensate for this loss.

Does this mean we should keep out foreign goods that displace so many workers? No, not at all. We need better government programs to get these people into well-paying, productive jobs.

---

[4] The United States, Argentina, Brazil, Mexico, Poland, and several other countries have discovered another way of paying for imports. Together they have borrowed hundreds of billions of dollars a year to finance this spending binge. In the second part of this chapter we'll take a closer look at this borrowing.

[5] See *The Economic Report of the President* (February 1986), pp. 107–8.

Tariffs or Quotas

Politically, it is very hard to resist the pleas of millions of Americans who have been losing their jobs because of imports. Furthermore, some very powerful industries have been hurt by imports, most notably autos. Surely General Motors, Ford, and Chrysler are not without influence in the halls of Congress.

Although economists are loathe to be in such a situation, suppose it came down to choosing between the two main forms of protection—tariffs or import quotas. Which would be better? Or more accurately, which is the lesser of two evils? Perhaps an apt analogy would be to pick the good guy of the 20th century and have Hitler and Stalin as the only nominees.

A tariff is a tax on imports.

A tariff is a tax on imports. Throughout most of our history until World War I, the tariff was our main source of federal revenue. The United States, which has lower tariffs than most other countries, charges less than 10 percent of the value of most imports.

A quota places a limit on the import of certain goods.

A quota is a limit on the import of certain goods. Sometimes this is a legal limit as in the case of textiles and sugar and sometimes a "voluntary" limit as was the case with cars from Japan. In the early and mid-1980s, the Japanese limited their export of cars to the United States to under 2.5 million a year, but only because of the threat of more stringent legal limits in the form of higher tariffs.

A third interference with free trade is export subsidies. Although several countries, most notably Japan and Korea, do subsidize their export industries, this is a relatively minor expedient in the United States. The effect of export subsidies, of course, is to make these products cheaper, an effect many Americans complain, that gives foreign competitors an "unfair advantage."

Both tariffs and quotas raise the price that consumers in the importing country must pay. However, there are three important differences in the effects of tariffs and quotas.

First, the federal government receives the proceeds of a tariff. Under import quotas there *are* no tax revenues.

Second, a tariff affects all foreign sellers equally, but import quotas are directed against particular sellers on an arbitrary basis. For example, in 1986, various Japanese car manufacturers had widely varying quotas, but the import of South Korean Hyundais was unrestricted.

A third difference involves relative efficiency. Efficient foreign producers will be able to pay a uniform tariff that less efficient producers will not be able to meet. But arbitrary import quotas may allow relatively inefficient foreign producers to send us their goods while keeping out those of their more efficient competitors. What this all comes down to is somewhat higher prices for the American consumer because less efficient producers will charge higher prices than more efficient producers.

Tariffs are better than quotas, but free trade is best.

In sum then, tariffs are better than quotas, but free trade is best. In the long run it is the American consumer who must pay for trade restrictions in the form of higher prices.

Conclusion

The case for free trade is one of the cornerstones of economics. Economics is all about the efficient allocation of scarce resources, so there is no reason why this efficient allocation should not be applied beyond national boundaries. A baseball team that has more pitchers than it knows what to do with, but needs a good-hitting shortstop, will trade that extra pitcher or two for the shortstop. It will trade with a team that had an extra shortstop but needed more pitching. This would help both teams.

Petition of the Candlemakers to Shut out the Sun

The case of protection against "unfair" competition was extended to its absurd conclusion by Frederic Bastiat, a mid-19th-century French economist who wrote an imagined petition to the Chamber of Deputies. Parts of that petition follow.*

We are suffering from the intolerable competition of a foreign rival, placed, it would seem, in a condition so far superior to ours for the production of light, that he absolutely inundates our national market with it at a price fabulously reduced. The moment he shows himself, our trade leaves us—all consumers apply to him, and a branch of native industry, having countless ramifications, is all at once rendered completely stagnant. This rival . . . is all other than the Sun.

What we pray for is, that it may please you to pass a law ordering the shutting up of all windows, skylights, dormerwindows, outside and inside shutters, curtains, blinds, bull's eyes; in a word, of all openings, holes, chinks, clefts, and fissures, by or through which the light of the sun has been in use to enter houses. . . .

* Frederic Bastiat, *Economic Sophisms* (Edinburgh: Oliver and Boyd, Tweeddale Court, 1873), pp. 49–53.

International trade helps every country; we all have higher living standards because of it. To the degree that we can remove the tariffs, import quotas, and other impediments to free trade, we all will be better off.

It has been estimated that lower-priced imports kept the rate of inflation one or two points below what it would otherwise have been in the mid-1980s. This is still another important reason for not restricting imports.

None of this is to deny that there are problems. The millions of workers who are losing their jobs due to foreign competition cannot be expected to cheerfully make personal sacrifices in the interest of the greater national economic well-being. Nor will the American people stand by patiently awaiting the readjustment or deindustrialization of our economy to conform to the new world economic order. In the long run we may all be better off if there is worldwide free trade. But as John Maynard Keynes once noted, "In the long run we'll all be dead."

The economics profession nearly unanimously backs free trade.

While the economics profession is nearly unanimous in advocating free trade, there is nearly complete disagreement over what to do about our huge trade deficit. Among the proposals advanced have been: (1) further devaluation of the dollar (discussed in the second part of this chapter) to make American goods relatively cheap in comparison to foreign goods; (2) a national value-added tax (or national sales tax) to discourage consumption; (3) faster economic growth for our trade partners so they will buy more from us; (4) higher productivity growth to make American goods relatively inexpensive; and (5) related measures such as higher investment in plant and equipment, emulation of Japanese management techniques, and more spending on research and development—all to enhance productivity.

It goes well beyond the scope of this book to analyze these proposals, but whatever we eventually do to bring down the trade deficit will take years to accomplish. In the meanwhile foreigners will continue to accumulate American dollars and that alone will have a profound impact on international finance, which constitutes the second half of this chapter.

International Finance

Think of international trade and finance as an extension of our nation's economic activities beyond our borders. Instead of buying microchips from a firm in California, we buy them from a firm in Japan. Instead of selling Cadillacs in Miami, we sell them in Rio de Janeiro. And rather than building a factory in Chicago, we build it in Hong Kong.

The whys and wherefores of international trade were discussed in the first half of this chapter; now we'll see how that trade is financed. Ideally, our exports pay for our imports, but since the mid-1970s, we have had a rapidly growing negative balance of trade. That is, our imports have grown much faster than our exports.

The balance of trade is part of the balance of payments.

The balance of trade is only part of the big picture of international finance. That picture includes not only imports and exports of goods, but of services as well. Also included are investment income, transfers of funds abroad, and capital inflows and outflows. The whole shooting match is called the balance of payments, which we'll take up after we look at the mechanics of how trade is financed. Toward the end of the chapter—and this is some long chapter—we'll talk about international exchange rate systems, including the gold standard.

Financing International Trade

When an American importer buys $2 million worth of wine from a french merchant, how does he or she pay? In dollars? In francs? In gold? Gold is used only by governments, and then only on very rare occasions, to settle international transactions. Dollars, although sometimes acceptable as an international currency, are not as useful to the French wine merchant as francs. After all, the merchant will have to pay his employees and suppliers in francs.

There's no problem exchanging dollars for francs in either the United States or France. Many banks in New York have plenty of francs on hand and virtually every other bank in the country can get francs (as well as yen, marks, pounds, and other foreign currencies) within a day or two. In Paris and every other French city, dollars are readily available from banks. Since on any given day, actually at any given minute, there is a market exchange rate of francs for dollars, all you need to do is find the right teller and within minutes you can exchange your dollars for francs or francs for dollars.

Financing international trade is part of the economic flow of money and credit that crosses international boundaries every day. For the rest of this chapter we'll see where these funds are going, and in particular, how the United States is involved. We'll begin with our balance of payments, which provides an accounting of our international financial transactions.

The Balance of Payments

Often people confuse our balance of payments with our balance of trade. Actually the balance of trade is a major part of the balance of payments. The entire flow of U.S. dollars and foreign currencies into and out of the country constitutes our balance of payments while our trade balance is just the difference between our imports and our exports.

Until the mid-1970s we generally had a positive balance of trade, that is, the value of our exports was greater than that of our imports. All this changed drastically due to the quadrupling of oil prices in late 1973, as well as several other factors we'll be enumerating toward the end of this chapter. But an unmistakable trend, which had been going on for decades, foreshadowed the negative trade balances we have been experiencing for these last 15 years.

The balance of payments has two parts—the current account and the capital account.

The balance of payments consists of two parts. First there is the current account, which summarizes all the goods and services produced during the current year that we buy from or sell to foreigners. The second part is the capital account, which records the long-term transactions that we conduct with foreigners. The total of the current and capital accounts will always be zero, that is, our balance of payments never has a deficit or surplus. When we look at these accounts in more detail, the picture should become a lot clearer.

In Table 29-7, we have the U.S. balance of payments in 1987. The great villain of the piece is our huge trade services deficit of about $159 billion.

Table 29–7
U.S. Balance of Payments, 1987
(in $ billions)

Current account

U.S. merchandise exports	+250.8
U.S. merchandise imports	−410.0
Balance of trade	−159.2
U.S. export of services	+169.2
U.S. import of services	−157.2
Balance of services	+12.1
Net unilateral transfers abroad . . .	−13.5
Balance on current account	−160.7

Capital account

Capital inflows to the U.S.	+202.6
Capital outflows to the U.S.	−63.8
Balance on capital account	+138.8
Statistical discrepancy	+21.9
Total	0

Source: *Survey of Current Business*, March 1988.

The next item, services, is comprised mainly of income from investments abroad, tourist spending, and financial services. Since the turn of the century, the U.S. has had a substantial net investment income because Americans had invested much more abroad than foreigners had invested in the United States. Because of our huge trade deficits in recent years, however, foreigners have been left holding hundreds of billions of dollars, most of which they have invested in the U.S. The return on this investment has been growing very rapidly.

Finally, we have net transfers, which include foreign aid, military spending abroad, remittances to relatives living abroad, and pensions paid to Americans living abroad. Since the United States does not receive foreign aid, there are no foreign troops stationed here, and there are few personal remittances or pensions paid to U.S. residents from abroad, net transfers will continue to be a negative figure into the foreseeable future.

When we add up the numbers that go into our current account, it is easy to see why this figure is negative and why our current account deficit has been growing in recent years. But what international finance takes away with one hand, it pays back with the other. Thus, by definition, our current account deficit is balanced by our capital account surplus.

What have foreigners done with all the dollars they have earned from trading with us, as well as from their other current account dealings with us? Nearly all this money has been reinvested in the United States in the form of corporate stocks and bonds, U.S. Treasury bills, notes, and bonds, as well as real estate and direct investment in plant and equipment.

Until the early 1980s Americans were investing much more in foreign countries than foreigners were investing in the United States. But as our balance of trade worsened, it was inevitable that the flow of capital would be reversed. There are some relatively minor items included in the capital account, most notably the statistical discrepancy. Now $22 billion is a

Our current account deficit is balanced by our capital account surplus.

pretty big discrepancy. This was money that flowed into the United States, but was never recorded.[6]

Technically, the balance of payments has no deficits or surpluses.

Technically, there are no balance of payments deficits or surpluses because the current account deficit, by definition, will be balanced by a capital account surplus. In 1987, we ran $161 billion current deficit, which was matched by a $139 billion capital account surplus plus the $22 billion statistical discrepancy.

Was this a mere coincidence? Not at all! We've been running current account deficits for years and these have always been matched, dollar-for-dollar, by capital account surpluses plus statistical discrepancies that, until the mid-1970s, were rarely over $2 billion.

The way it works is that we buy much more from foreigners than they buy from us. In effect, they lend or give us the money to make up the difference between our imports and our exports. Add to that the fact that we "import" more services than we "export", and we are left with the question, where do we get the funds to finance our voracious appetite for all things foreign?

It would not be accurate to say that we so much borrow from foreigners to finance our current account deficits as that we sell them pieces of the American rock, so to speak. Those pieces consist mainly of corporate stock and real estate, but there are also tens of billions of dollars they *do* lend us each year in the form of purchases of corporate and government bonds and other debt instruments.

We go deeper and deeper into debt each year.

While technically we don't run balance-of-payments deficits, we *do* go deeper and deeper into hock each year. Should this last much longer, most of the country will be owned by foreign investors, so it is hard to refrain from calling the huge shortfalls in our balance of payments account "deficits."

Exchange Rate Systems

The basis for international finance is the exchange of well over 100 national currencies. Until the 1930s, the world's currencies were based on gold. Since then we have evolved into a relatively free-floating exchange rate system. Under this system, exchange rates are determined largely by the forces of supply and demand. In other words, how many yen, marks, francs, or pounds you can get for your dollars is determined largely by the impersonal forces of the market.

Three distinct periods

There are three fairly distinct periods that we'll consider. First, the period before 1934, when most of the world was on the gold standard. Second, we'll look at the period from 1934 to 1973, when international finance was based on fixed exchange rates. Finally, we shall review the period from 1973 to the present, when we have had relatively freely floating exchange rates.

Exactly what *is* the gold standard?

There has been a lot of talk in recent years about a return to the gold standard, but it's not going to happen. Exactly what *is* the gold standard, what are its advantages, and what are its disadvantages? Funny you should ask.

---

[6] Statistical discrepancy is just another way of saying, "Something's just not adding up." This very issue came up once in a course taught by the late Oscar Morgenstern, the mathematical economist.

Sometime during the 1930s, Austria exported 10,000 horses to Czechoslovakia, but the Czechs had no record of having imported 10,000 horses. "Did the horses disappear into thin air when they crossed the border?" asked Morgenstern. No, he concluded. The 10,000 horses were swallowed by a statistical discrepancy.

A nation is on the gold standard when it defines its currency in terms of gold. Until 1933, the U.S. dollar was worth 1/23 of an ounce of gold. In other words, you could buy an ounce of gold from the Treasury for $23 or sell them an ounce for $23. In 1933, just before we went off the gold standard (along with the rest of the world), we raised the price of gold to $35 an ounce, which meant that a dollar was defined as worth 1/35 of an ounce of gold.

To be on the gold standard a nation must maintain a fixed ratio between its gold stock and its money supply. That way, when the gold stock rises, so too does the money supply. Should gold leave the country, the money supply declines.

That brings us to the third and last requirement of the gold standard. There must be no barriers to the free flow of gold into and out of the country.

When we put all these things together, we have the gold standard. The nation's money supply, which is based on gold, is tied to the money supply of every other nation on the gold standard. It is the closest we have ever come to an international currency. This system worked quite well until World War I, when most of the belligerents temporarily went off the gold standard because many of their citizens were hoarding gold and trying to ship it off to neutral nations.

How the gold standard works

Ideally, here is how the gold standard works. When Country A exports as much as it imports from Country B, no gold is transferred. But when Country A imports more than its exports, it has to ship the difference, in gold, to the trading partners with whom it has trade deficits.

Suppose the United States had to ship one million ounces of gold to other countries. This would lower our gold stock, and consequently our money supply. When our money supply declined, so would our price level. This would make our goods cheaper relative to foreign goods. Our imports would decline and our exports would rise because foreigners would find American imports cheaper than their own goods.

A self-correcting mechanism

What we had then was a self-correcting mechanism. A negative balance of trade caused an outflow of gold, a lower money supply, lower prices, and ultimately, less imports and more exports. And so, under the gold standard, negative trade balances eliminated themselves.

After World War I, those nations who had left the gold standard returned to the fold, but some nations' currencies were overvalued (relative to their price in gold) while others were undervalued. Adjustments were difficult because the nations whose currency was overvalued would have faced a gold drain, and consequently, lower prices and lower wages. But wages and prices are rarely flexible downward.

An alternative was to devalue, that is, lower the price of your money in relation to gold. For example, a 10 percent devaluation would mean that instead of getting 10 pounds for an ounce of gold, you now get 11. As the Great Depression spread, one nation after another devalued and within a few years virtually everyone was off the gold standard.

Evaluation of the gold standard.

Let's step back for a moment and evaluate the gold standard. It *did* work for a long time, automatically eliminating trade surpluses and deficits. And it *did* stimulate international trade by removing the uncertainty of fluctuating exchange rates.

But then there's the downside. First, it will work only when the gold supply increases as quickly as the world's need for money. By the early 20th century, this was no longer the case. Second, it will work only if participating nations are willing to accept the periodic inflation and unemployment that accompany the elimination of trade imbalances. In today's world, political leaders must pay far more attention to their domestic constituencies than to their trading partners.

With the breakdown of the gold standard in the 1930s, protectionism returned as one nation after another erected higher and higher tariff barriers. Devaluation followed devaluation until the entire structure of international trade and finance was near complete collapse. Then came World War II—and with it, a great revival of economic activity. While the war was still raging, the Bretton Woods conference was called to set up a system of international finance that would lend some stability to how exchange rates were set.

The Gold Exchange Standard, 1944–73

Fixed exchange rates

The Bretton Woods (New Hampshire) conference set up the International Monetary Fund (IMF) to supervise a system of fixed exchange rates, all of which were based on the dollar, which in turn, was based on gold. The dollar was defined as it had been for the last 10 years as being worth $\frac{1}{35}$ of an ounce of gold, so gold was $35 an ounce, and dollars were convertible into gold at that price.

Other currencies were convertible into dollars at fixed prices so that indirectly these currencies were convertible into gold. But this was short of a gold standard because the money supplies of these nations were not tied to gold, and no longer would trade deficits or surpluses automatically eliminate themselves. If a nation ran consistent trade deficits it could devalue its currency relative to the dollar. If that devaluation were not more than 10 percent it could be done without the IMF's permission (larger cuts required permission).

The new system functioned well for the next 25 years after World War II. That the United States ran almost continual balance-of-payment deficits during the 1950s and 1960s eventually led to an international financial crisis in 1971, but until that year these deficits contributed to international liquidity. This is because U.S. dollars as well as gold were held as a reserve for international payments by virtually every country in the world but the United States.

Why were U.S. dollars so acceptable?

Why were U.S. dollars so acceptable? First, the United States held the largest stock of gold in the world and stood ready to sell that gold at $35 an ounce to the central banks of every nation. Second, the American economy was by far the largest and strongest in the world.

By the late 1960s, as our gold stock dwindled and as foreign governments found themselves with increasing stocks of dollars, these nations began to ask some embarrassing questions. If the United States continued to run balance-of-payments deficits, would we be able to redeem the dollars they were holding for gold at $35 an ounce? Would the United States be forced to devaluate the dollar, thus making their dollar holdings less valuable?

Sure enough, in 1971 President Richard Nixon announced that the United States would no longer redeem dollars for gold. With one fell swoop, out the window went the Bretton Woods agreement to maintain fixed exchange rates. The dollar would now float, and with it, every other currency as well. Now the forces of demand and supply would determine exchange rates.

Why did U.S. balance of payments deteriorate in the 1950s and 1960s?

Let's step back for a minute and ask just why the U.S. balance-of-payments deteriorated so badly during the 1950s and 1960s. There were several reasons, but there is one that is easily overlooked and is really the most important. You see, our positive balance of payments and, in particular, our huge trade surpluses in the late 1940s were only a temporary situation brought about by World War II. Of all the major belligerents, only the United States escaped unscathed from the vast war damage. The industrial machines of Germany and Japan, not to mention England, France, Italy, and the rest of Europe, were reduced to rubble.

Renewed foreign
competition

Thus, our industrial goods had virtually no competition in the world's markets until well into the 1950s when the postwar recovery finally took hold. By then, the best our competitors could do was to narrow our leads in some areas and provide products we didn't bother to manufacture, most notably small cars. By the early 1950s, our huge trade surpluses began to narrow.

Military and foreign-aid
spending

A second reason for our growing payments deficits was our huge military and foreign-aid spending. American soldiers stationed abroad required the expenditure of billions of dollars a year,[7] as did the military and economic aid we provided to our foreign friends and allies.

Increasing private
investment abroad

A third factor was the rapidly increasing U.S. private investment abroad, which went from an annual rate of just $2 billion in the early 1950s to $8 billion in the late 1960s.

Inflation

Then there was inflation, particularly in the late 1960s and through the 1970s and early 1980s. Because our inflation rate was higher than that of most of our trading partners, some American goods were priced out of both foreign and domestic markets.

Oil price shocks

Just two more to go. First the oil price shock of 1973, when oil prices quadrupled, and the subsequent shock of 1979, when oil prices again rose sharply. This put our balance of trade into the negative column and has helped keep it there.

The productivity factor

Finally, we have the productivity factor. Believe it or not, not only does the United States produce more goods and services than any other country in the world (Japan, number two, produces less than half as much), but American workers remain the world's most productive among the larger nations. The only problem is that we have been losing our productivity lead. That, combined with Americans' prodigious appetite for consumer goods—both American and foreign—and their refusal to save, has added considerably to our mounting trade deficits.

To return to 1971, when our payments deficits finally forced us to abandon the gold exchange standard—and forced the rest of the world off as well—the IMF needed to set up a new system fast and that system was, in computer terminology, a default system.

Back to the law of supply
and demand

We were back to the old system that economists fondly refer to as the law of supply and demand. How does it apply to foreign exchange? The same way it applied to everything else.

In Figure 29–4, we have the supply and demand curves for German marks. According to these curves you can get 5 marks for a dollar or 1 mark for 20 cents—and vice versa.

Who sets this exchange rate? Basically the forces of supply and demand. The question then is, where did the supply and demand for marks come from?

The demand curve for marks represents the desire by Americans to exchange their dollars for marks. Why do they want marks? To buy German goods and services, stocks, bonds, real estate, and other assets.

Likewise, the supply curve of marks represents the desire of German citizens to purchase American goods, services, and financial assets.

Now we get to the beauty of the law of supply and demand. The point at which the two curves cross tells us the exchange rate of marks and dollars. In Figure 29–4, we have a rate of 5 marks for 1 dollar.

---

[7] Each of our major military bases abroad employs thousands of local workers and buys millions of dollars worth of locally produced food stuffs. In addition, service personnel stationed abroad spend billions of dollars each year on travel and entertainment.

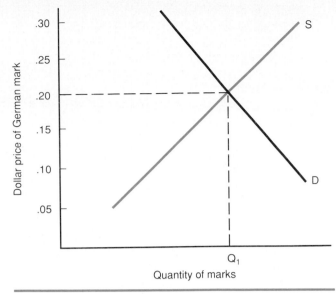

Figure 29–4

Not completely freely floating exchange rates

If we had completely freely floating exchange rates (i.e., no government
interference), the market forces of supply and demand would set the exchange rates. To a large degree this is what happens, but governments do
intervene, although usually for just a limited time. In other words, government intervention may temporarily influence exchange rates, but under the
current system, in the long run, exchange rates are set by the forces of supply and demand.

Several factors influence the exchange rates between countries. (Let's continue using the United States and West Germany as examples.) The most
important is the relative price levels of the two countries. If American goods
are relatively cheap compared to German goods, there will be a relatively
low demand for marks and a relatively high supply of marks. In other
words, everyone—Germans and Americans—wants dollars to buy American
goods.

A second factor is the relative growth rates of the American and German
economies. Whichever is growing faster generates a greater demand for imports. If the American economy is growing faster, it will raise the demand
for marks (to be used to buy imported goods from Germany) while decreasing the supply of marks (the Germans will hold more marks and fewer
dollars because they are not buying many American goods).

The third and final factor is the relative level of interest rates in both
countries. If the interest rates are higher in Germany than in the United
States, American investors will want to take advantage of those higher rates
by buying German securities. They will sell their dollars for marks, driving
up the price of marks. In effect then, the demand for marks will rise and
their supply will decline.

How Do Freely Floating (Flexible)
Exchange Rates Work?

Until 1973, most countries had fixed exchange rates because they feared
that flexible rates would fluctuate wildly. Has that happened since 1973?
While there certainly have been some ups and downs, most notably with

So far, so good

the dollar over the last 10 or 12 years, we can still say, so far, so good.

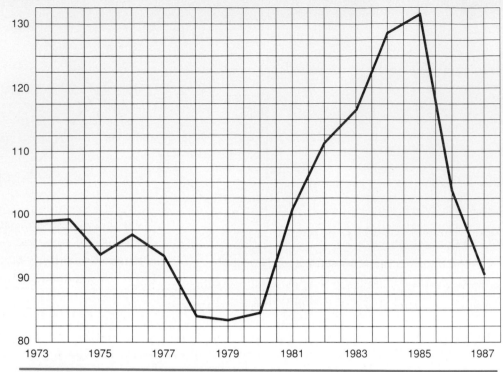

Figure 29–5
The Fluctuation of the Dollar against the World's Other Major Currencies, 1973–1987*

* March 1973 = 100.

Source: *The Economic Report of the President, 1988,* p. 371.

The dollar declined by well over 20 percent relative to other major currencies during the late 1970s, but this trend was completely reversed in the early 1980s. Between 1980 and 1983 its value rose by about 50 percent. But in the mid-1980s another major decline set in (see Figure 29–5). International trade and finance have adjusted extremely well to these ups and downs while government intervention has not been a major factor. Barring a major international financial crisis—such as a chain of loan defaults by Third World countries or the refusal of foreign investors to extend further credit to the U.S. government and to American corporations—we will continue to have freely floating exchange rates. While far from perfect, it may be the best system we have known.

Workbook for Chapter 29

Name _____

Date _____

Multiple-Choice Questions

Circle the letter that corresponds to the best answer.

1. Our balance of trade

a. has always been positive   **b.** turned negative in the mid-1970s   **c.** turned negative in the mid-1980s   **d.** has always been negative

2. Which makes the most sense economically?

a. individual self-sufficiency   **b.** national self-sufficiency   **c.** national specialization   **d.** none of these

3. If the United States were to devote all its resources to producing washing machines, it could turn out 50 billion a year; if it devoted all its resources to producing cars, it could turn out 10 billion a year. Our domestic exchange equation is

a. 5 cars = 1 washing machine   **b.** 5 washing machines = 1 car   **c.** 1/5 of a washing machine = 1 car   **d.** 1/2 of a car = 1 washing machine

4. If the United States were to trade its cars for another country's washing machines, it would not trade one car unless it received at least _____ washing machines.

a. one   **b.** more than one   **c.** five   **d.** more than five

5. Which statement is false?

a. No nation will engage in trade with another nation unless it will gain by that trade.   **b.** The terms of trade will fall somewhere between the domestic exchange equations of the two trading nations.

c. Most economists advocate free trade.

d. None of these statements is false.

6. If Hong Kong can make TVs more efficiently than France, it enjoys

a. a comparative advantage   **b.** an absolute advantage   **c.** no advantage

7. Under the principle of comparative advantage, total output is greatest when each product is made by that country which

a. enjoys an absolute advantage   **b.** has the lowest opportunity cost   **c.** has the lowest wage rates   **d.** has the lowest degree of specialization

8. The least applicable argument for protection of American industry against foreign competition would be the _____ argument.

a. national security   **b.** infant industry   **c.** low-wage   **d.** employment

9. Imports would be lowered by

a. tariffs only   **b.** import quotas only   **c.** both tariffs and import quotas   **d.** neither tariffs nor import quotas

10. Of these three choices—tariffs, quotas, and free trade—economists like _____ the most and _____ the least.

a. tariffs, quotas   **b.** tariffs, free trade   **c.** free trade, tariffs   **d.** free trade, quotas   **e.** quotas, free trade   **f.** quotas, tariffs

11. Trade restrictions cause

a. higher prices   **b.** economic inefficiency   **c.** both higher prices and economic inefficiency   **d.** neither higher prices nor economic inefficiency

12. When country X imports goods from country Y

a. only country X benefits   **b.** only country Y benefits   **c.** both country X and country Y benefit   **d.** neither country X nor country Y benefit

13. Which statement is true?

a. International trade is part of international finance.

b. International finance is part of international trade.   **c.** International trade and international finance are identical.

14. An American importer of Italian shoes would pay in

a. dollars   **b.** gold   **c.** lira

15. The total of our current and capital accounts

a. will always be zero   **b.** will always be negative
c. will always be positive   **d.** may be positive or
negative

16. In recent years we bought _____ from foreigners than they bought from us and we invested
_____ in foreign countries than foreigners invested
in the United States.

a. more, more   **b.** less, less   **c.** less, more
d. more, less

17. Today international finance is based on

a. the gold standard   **b.** a relatively free-floating exchange rate system   **c.** fixed rates of exchange

18. The international gold standard worked well until

a. World War I   **b.** 1940   **c.** 1968   **d.** 1975

19. If we were on an international gold standard

a. inflations would be eliminated   **b.** recessions
would be eliminated   **c.** trade deficits and surpluses
would be eliminated   **d.** no nation would ever have
to devaluate its currency

20. Which of the following is false?

a. The gold standard will work only when the gold
supply increases as quickly as the world's need for
money.   **b.** The gold standard will work only if all
nations agreed to devalue their currencies simultaneously.   **c.** The gold standard will work only if
participating nations are willing to accept periodic inflation.   **d.** The gold standard will work only if
participating nations are willing to accept periodic
unemployment.

21. The gold exchange standard was in effect from
a. 1900 to 1934   **b.** 1934 to 1973   **c.** 1955 to
1980   **d.** 1973 to the present

22. The United States first began running balance-of-
payments deficits in the
a. 1940s   **b.** 1950s   **c.** 1960s   **d.** 1970s   **e.** 1980s

23. Today currency exchange rates are set by
a. the International Monetary Fund   **b.** the U.S.
Treasury   **c.** bilateral agreements between trading
nations   **d.** supply and demand

24. The most important influence on the exchange
rates between two countries is

a. the relative price levels of the two countries

b. the relative growth rates of the two countries

c. the relative level of interest rates in both countries

d. the relative wage rates of both countries

25. Devaluation would tend to

a. make the devaluating country's goods cheaper

b. make the devaluating country's goods more expensive   **c.** have no effect on the value of the
devaluating country's goods

Fill-In Questions

1. The basis for international trade is _____.

Use Figures 1 and 2 to answer Questions 2 through 6.

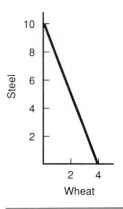

Figure 1
Brazil

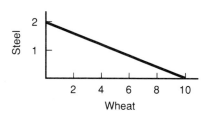

Figure 2
Argentina

2. Brazil is better at producing _____ than at pro-

ducing _____. Argentina is better at producing

_____ than at producing _____.

3. The domestic equation of exchange for Brazil is _____. The domestic equation of exchange for Argentina is _____.

4. If Argentina and Brazil traded, Argentina would trade _____ for _____, while Brazil would trade _____ for _____.

5. Brazil would be willing to trade one ton of steel for more than _____ ton of wheat. Argentina would be willing to trade five tons of wheat for more than _____ ton of steel.

6. State the terms of trade in steel and wheat.
a. One ton of steel will be exchanged for more than _____ and less than _____ tons of wheat.
b. One ton of wheat will be exchanged for more than _____ and less than _____ tons of steel.

7. If one country is better at growing wheat than another country, it enjoys a(n) _____ advantage in wheat production.

8. The principle of comparative advantage states that total output is greatest when each product is made by that country which has the _____.

9. Four main arguments have been made for trade protection: (1) the _____ argument, (2) the _____ argument, (3) the _____ argument, and (4) the _____ argument.

10. Although economists dislike both, they would prefer tariffs to _____.

11. A tariff is a tax on _____; a quota is a limit on _____.

12. If it costs three times as much to make a car in Nigeria as in Mexico and it cost twice as much to grow wheat in Mexico as in Nigeria, we say that Mexico enjoys an absolute advantage in the production of _____ and Nigeria enjoys an absolute advantage in the production of _____.

13. The entire flow of U.S. dollars and foreign currencies into and out of the country constitutes our _____.

14. Nearly all the dollars that foreigners have earned from trading with the United States have been _____ in the form of _____.

15. The two parts of the balance of payments are the _____ account and the _____ account.

16. The basis for international finance is the exchange of _____.

17. A nation is on the gold standard when it _____.

18. To be on the gold standard a nation must maintain a fixed ratio between its gold stock and _____.

19. Under the gold standard, if country J imports more than it exports, it has to ship _____ to the trading partners with whom it has trade deficits. This would depress country J's _____ and its price level would _____.

20. Under the gold standard, if country K's price level declined, its imports would _____ and its exports would _____.

21. If a country's gold supply were dwindling under the gold standard, an alternative to lower prices and wages would be to _____.

22. The gold standard had two main drawbacks: (1) _____ and (2) _____.

23. The Bretton Woods conference set up the _____ to supervise a system of _____ exchange rates.

24. For the 25 years following World War II, dollars functioned well as reserves for two reasons: (1) _____ and (2) _____.

25. The three reasons for the deterioration of our balance of payments in the 1950s and 1960s were:

(1) _____ ,

(2) _____ ,

and (3) _____ .

26. Today exchange rates are set by _____ and

_____ .

27. The three factors that influence the exchange

rates between countries are (1) _____

_____ ,

(2) _____ ,

and (3) _____

_____ .

Glossary

Ability-to-Pay Principle The amount of taxes that people pay should be based on their ability to pay (i.e., their incomes).

Absolute Advantage The ability of a country to produce a good at a lower cost than its trading partners.

Accelerator Principle If sales or consumption is rising at a constant rate, gross investment will stay the same; if sales rise at a decreasing rate, both gross investment and GNP will fall.

Accounting Profit Sales minus explicit cost. Implicit costs are not considered.

Aggregate Demand The sum of all expenditures for goods and services.

Aggregate Supply The nation's total output of goods and services.

Antitrust Laws These laws, including the Sherman and Clayton Acts, attempted to enforce competition and to control the corporate merger movement.

Arbitration An arbitrator imposes a settlement on labor and management if they cannot reach a collective bargaining agreement.

Automatic Stabilizers Programs such as unemployment insurance benefits and taxes that are already on the books to help alleviate recessions and hold down the rate of inflation.

Autonomous Consumption The minimum amount that people will spend on the necessities of life.

Average Fixed Cost Fixed cost divided by output.

Average Propensity to Consume The percentage of disposable income that is spent; consumption divided by disposable income.

Average Propensity to Save The percentage of disposable income that is saved; saving divided by disposable income.

Average Tax Rate The percentage of taxable income that is paid in taxes; taxes paid divided by taxable income.

Average Total Cost Total cost divided by output; represented by ATC.

Average Variable Cost Variable cost divided by output; represented by AVC.

Backward-Bending Labor Supply Curve As the wage rate rises, more and more people are willing to work longer and longer hours up to a point. Then, they will substitute more leisure time for higher earnings.

Balance of Payments The entire flow of U.S. dollars and foreign currencies into and out of the country.

Balance of Trade The difference between the value of our imports and our exports.

Balanced Budget When federal tax receipts equal federal government spending.

Benefits-Received Principle The amount of taxes people pay should be based on the benefits they receive from the government.

Bonds (See government bonds or corporate bonds.)

Break-Even Point The low point on the firm's average total cost curve. If the price is below this point, the firm will go out of business in the long run.

Budget Deficit When federal tax receipts are less than federal government spending.

Budget Surplus When federal tax receipts are greater than federal government spending.

Business Cycle Increases and decreases in the level of business activity that occur at irregular intervals and last for varying lengths of time. _What actually has occurred_

CPI (See consumer price index.)

Capital All means of production created by people, mainly plant and equipment.

Cartel A group of firms behaving like a monopoly.

Circular Flow Model Goods and services flow from business firms to households in exchange for consumer expenditures while resources flow from households to business firms in exchange for resource payments.

Classical Economics Laissez-faire economics. Our economy, if left free from government interference, tends toward full employment. The prevalent school of economics from about 1800 to 1930.

Closed Shop An employer may hire only union members; outlawed under the Taft-Hartley Act.

Collective Bargaining Negotiations between union and management to obtain agreement on wages, working conditions, and other issues.

Comparative Advantage Total output is greatest when each product is made by the country that has the lowest opportunity cost.

Competition Rivalry among business firms for resources and customers.

Concentration Ratio The percentage share of industry sales by the four leading firms.

Conglomerate Merger Merger between two companies in unrelated industries.

Consumer Price Index The most important measure of inflation. This tells us the percentage rise in the price level since the base year, which is set at 100; represented by CPI.

Consumer Surplus The difference between what you pay for some good or service and what you would have been willing to pay.

Consumption The expenditure by individuals on durable goods, nondurable goods, and services; represented by C.

Consumption Function As income rises, consumption rises, but not as quickly.

Corporate Bonds This is a debt of the corporation. Bondholders have loaned money to the company and are its creditors.

Corporate Stock Share in a corporation. The stockholders own the corporation.

Corporation A business firm that is a legal person. Its chief advantage is that each owner's liability is limited to the amount of money he or she invested in the company.

Cost-Push Inflation Rising costs of doing business push up prices.

Creeping Inflation A relatively low rate of inflation; under 4 percent in the United States in recent years.

Crowding-Out Effect Large federal budget deficits are financed by Treasury borrowing, which in turn, crowds private borrowers out of financial markets and drives up interest rates.

Cyclical Unemployment When people are out of work because the economy is operating below the full-employment level. It rises sharply during recessions.

Deflation A general decline in the price level.

Deflationary Gap Occurs when equilibrium GNP is less than full-employment GNP.

Demand A schedule of quantities of a good or service that people will buy at different prices; represented by D.

Demand, Law of When the price of a good is lowered, more of it is demanded; when the price is raised, less is demanded.

Depository Institutions Deregulation and Monetary Control Act of 1980 All depository institutions now subject to the Federal Reserve's legal reserve requirements and all depository institutions may issue checking deposits.

Depression A deep and prolonged business downturn, the last of which occurred in the 1930s.

Derived Demand Demand for resources derived from the demand for the final product.

Diminishing Returns, the Law of If units of a resource are added to a fixed proportion of other resources, eventually marginal output will decline.

Direct Tax Tax on a particular person. Most important are federal personal income tax and payroll (Social Security) tax.

Discount Rate The interest rate charged by the Federal Reserve to depository institutions.

Disequilibrium When aggregate demand does not equal aggregate supply.

Disposable Income After-tax income. Term applies to individuals and to the nation.

Economic Growth An outward shift of the production possibilities frontier brought about by an increase in available resources and/or a technological improvement.

Economic Problem When we have limited resources available to fulfill society's relatively limitless wants.

Economic Profit Sales minus explicit costs and implicit costs.

Economic Rent The excess payment to a resource above what it would be necessary to pay to secure its use.

Elasticity of Demand Measures the change in quantity demanded in response to a change in price.

Entrepreneurial Ability Ability to recognize a business opportunity and successfully set up a business firm to take advantage of it.

Equation of Exchange Shows the relationship among four variables: M (the money supply), V (velocity of circulation), P (the price level), and Q (the quantity of goods and services produced). MV = PQ.

Equilibrium When aggregate demand equals aggregate supply.

Equilibrium Point Point at which quantity demanded equals quantity supplied; where demand and supply curves cross.

Exchange Rates The price of foreign currency, for example, how many dollars we must give up in exchange for marks, yen, and pounds.

Excise Tax A sales tax levied on a particular good or service, for example, gasoline and cigarette taxes.

Expected Rate of Profit Expected profits divided by money invested.

FDIC (See Federal Deposit Insurance Corporation.)

Federal Deposit Insurance Corporation Insures bank deposits up to $100,000.

Federal Reserve System Central bank of the United States, whose main job is to control our rate of monetary growth.

Fiscal Policy The manipulation of the federal budget to attain price stability, relatively full employment, and a satisfactory rate of economic growth.

Fiscal Year Budget year. U.S. federal budget fiscal year begins on October 1.

Fixed Costs These stay the same no matter how much output changes.

Frictional Unemployment Refers to people who are between jobs or just entering or reentering the labor market.

Full Employment When all a society's resources are being used with maximum efficiency.

Full-Employment GNP That level of spending (or aggregate demand) that will result in full employment.

GNP (See gross national product.)

Government Bonds Long-term debt of the federal government.

Gross Investment Total investment in plant, equipment, and inventory by a company. Also, plant, equipment, inventory, and residential housing investment by nation.

Gross National Product The nation's expenditure on all the goods and services produced during the year at market prices; represented by GNP.

Horizontal Merger Conventional merger between two firms in the same industry.

Hyperinflation Runaway inflation; in the United States, double-digit inflation.

Incomes Policy Wage controls, price controls, and tax incentives used to try to control inflation.

Increasing Costs, the Law of As the output of one good expands, the opportunity cost of producing additional units of this good increases.

Indirect Tax Tax on a thing rather than on a particular person, for example, sales tax.

Induced Consumption Spending that is induced by changes in the level of income.

Inflation A general rise in the price level.

Inflationary Gap Occurs when equilibrium GNP is greater than full-employment GNP.

Interest Rate Interest paid divided by amount borrowed.

Interlocking Directorates When one person serves on the boards of at least two competing firms.

Investment The purchase or building of any new plant, equipment, residential housing, or the accumulation of inventory; represented by I.

Keynesian Economics As formulated by John Maynard Keynes, this school believed the private economy was inherently unstable and that government intervention was necessary to prevent recessions from becoming depressions.

Labor The work and time for which employees are paid.

Labor Force The total number of employed and unemployed people.

Laffer Curve Shows that at very high tax rates, very few people will work and pay taxes so that government revenue will rise as tax rates are lowered.

Laissez-Faire The philosophy that the private economy should function without any government interference.

Liquidity Trap At very low interest rates, said John Maynard Keynes, people will not lend out their money or put it in the bank, but will simply hold it.

Long Run When all costs become variable costs and firms can enter or leave the industry.

M The money supply—currency, checking deposits, and checklike deposits (identical to M1).

M1 Currency, checking deposits, and checklike deposits.

M2 M1 plus savings deposits, small-denomination time deposits, and money market mutual funds.

M3 M2 plus large-denomination time deposits.

Malthusian Theory of Population Population tends to grow in a geometric progression (1, 2, 4, 8, 16) while food production tends to grow in an arithmetic progression (1, 2, 3, 4, 5).

Marginal Cost The cost of producing one additional unit of output; represented by MC.

Marginal Propensity to Consume Change in consumption divided by change in income; represented by MPC.

Marginal Propensity to Save Change in saving divided by change in income; represented by MPS.

Marginal Revenue The revenue derived from selling one additional unit of output; represented by MR.

Marginal Revenue Product The demand for a resource, based on that resource's marginal output and the price at which it is sold; represented by MRP.

Marginal Tax Rate Additional taxes paid divided by taxable income.

Marginal Utility The additional utility derived from consuming one more unit of some good or service.

Maximum Profit Point A firm will always produce at this point; marginal cost equals marginal revenue.

Measure of Economic Welfare A measure developed by James Tobin and William Nordhaus that modifies GNP by excluding "economic bads" and "regrettable necessities" and adding household, unreported, and illegal production.

Mediation A third party acting as a go-between for labor and management during collective bargaining.

Minimum Wage The legal minimum that may be paid for one hour of labor. For most of the 1980s that minimum was $3.35.

Monetarism A school of economics that places paramount importance on money as the key determinant of the level of prices, income, and employment.

Monetary Policy Control of the rate of monetary growth by the Board of Governors of the Federal Reserve.

Money Main job is to be a medium of exchange; also serves as a standard of value and a store of value.

Money Supply Currency, checking deposits, and checklike deposits (M or M1). *liquid Money*

Monopolistic Competition *(bonds are not part)* An industry that has many firms producing a differentiated product.

Monopoly A firm that produces all the output in an industry. The good or service produced has no close substitutes.

Multiplier Any change in spending (C, I, or G) will set off a chain reaction leading to a multiplied change in GNP. Equation is $\frac{1}{1 - MPC}$.

NNP (See net national product.)

National Debt (See public debt.)

National Income Net national product minus indirect business taxes.

Natural Monopoly An industry in which a single firm can provide cheaper service than could several competing firms.

Net Investment Gross investment minus depreciation equals net investment.

Net National Product Gross national product minus depreciation equals net national product.

Net Productivity of Capital The expected annual profit rate.

Nominal Interest Rate The real interest rate plus the inflation rate.

Noncompeting Groups Various strata of labor do not compete for jobs, for example, doctors and secretaries, skilled and unskilled workers.

Oligopoly An industry with just a few firms.

Open-Market Operations The purchase or sale of Treasury securities by the Federal Reserve; main monetary policy weapon.

Open Shop When no one is forced to join union, although it does represent all the workers in contract negotiations.

Opportunity Cost The foregone value of what you gave up when you made a choice.

Output Effect When the price of any resource rises, this raises the cost of production, which, in turn, lowers the supply of the final product; when supply falls, price rises, consequently reducing output.

P The price level, or the average price of all goods and services produced during the current year.

Paradox of Thrift If everyone tries to save more, they all will end up saving less.

Partnership A business firm owned by two or more people.

Payroll Tax (See Social Security tax.)

Per Capita Real GNP Real GNP divided by population.

Perfect Competition An industry with so many firms that no one firm has any influence over price, and firms produce an identical product.

Permanent Income Hypothesis Formulated by Milton Friedman, it states that the strongest influence on consumption is one's estimated lifetime income.

Personal Income Income received by household, including both earned income and transfer payments.

Price Ceiling Government-imposed maximum legal price.

Price Discrimination Occurs when a seller charges two or more prices for the same good or service.

Price Floor Government-imposed minimum price (used almost entirely to keep up agricultural commodity prices).

Price Leadership One firm, often the dominant firm in an oligopolistic industry, raises or lowers price, and the other firms quickly match the new price.

Price System Mechanism that allocates resources, goods, and services based on supply and demand.
law of Supply + demand

Production Any good or service for which people are willing to pay.

Production Possibilities Frontier A curve representing a hypothetical model of a two-product economy operating at full employment.

Productivity Output per unit of input; efficiency with which resources are used.

Progressive Tax Places greater burden on those with best ability to pay and little or no burden on the poor (e.g., federal personal income tax).

Proprietorship A business firm owned by just one person.

Public Debt The amount of federal securities outstanding, which represents what the federal government owes (the accumulation of federal deficits minus surpluses over the last two centuries).

Q Output or number of goods and services produced during the current year.

Quantity Theory of Money Crude version: Changes in the money supply cause proportional changes in the price level. Sophisticated version: If we are well below full employment, an increase in M will lead to an increase in output. If we are close to full employment, an increase in M will lead mainly to an increase in P.

Rational Expectations Theory This is based on three assumptions: (1) that individuals and business firms learn, through experience, to instantaneously anticipate the consequences of changes in monetary and fiscal policy; (2) that they act instantaneously to protect their economic interests; and (3) that all resource and product markets are purely competitive.

Real GNP GNP corrected for inflation; actual production.

Real Interest Rate Nominal interest rate minus inflation rate.

Recession A decline in real GNP for two consecutive quarters.

Regressive Tax Falls more heavily on the poor than on the rich; for example, Social Security tax.

Required Reserve Ratio Percentage of deposits that must be held as vault cash and reserve deposits by all depository institutions.

Required Reserves Minimum vault cash or reserves; held at the Federal Reserve District Bank.

Right-to-Work Laws Under the Taft-Hartley Act, states are permitted to pass these laws, which prohibit the union shop (union membership cannot be made a condition of securing employment).

Rule of Reason Mere size is no offense. Market conduct rather than market share should determine if antitrust laws have been violated.

Saving Function As income rises, saving rises, but not as quickly.

Say's Law Supply creates its own demand.

Short Run The length of time it takes all fixed costs to become variable costs.

Shutdown Point The low point on the firm's average variable cost curve. If price is below the shutdown point, the firm will shut down in the short run.

Social Security Tax A tax that is paid equally by employee and employer, based on employee's wages. Most of proceeds used to pay Social Security retirement and Medicare benefits. _Employee + employer pay_

Specialization Division of productive activities so that no one is self-sufficient.

Stock (See corporate stock.)

Strike When a collective bargaining agreement cannot be reached, a union calls for a work stoppage to last until an agreement is reached.

Structural Unemployment When people are out of work for a couple of years or longer.

Substitution Effect If the price of a resource, say, labor, goes up, business firms tend to substitute capital or land for some of their now expensive workers.

Supply A schedule of quantities that people will sell at different prices; represented by S.

Supply-Side Economics Main tenets: economic role of federal government is too large and high tax rates and government regulations hurt the incentives of individuals and business firms to produce goods and services.

Terms of Trade The ratio of exchange between an imported good and an exported good.

Transfer Payment Payment by one branch of government to another or to an individual. Largest transfer payment is Social Security. _– Government spending_

Transmission Mechanism The series of changes brought about by a change in monetary policy that ultimately changes the level of GNP.

Unemployment Rate Number of unemployed divided by the labor force.

Union Shop All employees must join the union, usually within 30 days after they are hired.

Utility The satisfaction you derive from a good or service that you purchase. How much utility you derive is measured by how much you would be willing to pay.

Variable Costs These vary with output. When output rises, variable costs rise; when output declines, variable costs fall.

Velocity The number of times per year each dollar in the money supply is spent; represented by V.

Vertical Merger The joining together of two firms engaged in different parts of an industrial process, or the joining of a manufacturer and retailer.

Index